Bricolage, Care and Information

TECHNOLOGY, WORK AND GLOBALIZATION

The Technology, Work and Globalization series was developed to provide policy makers, workers, managers, academics and students with a deeper understanding of the complex interlinks and influences between technological developments, including information and communication technologies, work organizations and patterns of globalization. The mission of the series is to disseminate rich knowledge based on deep research about relevant issues surrounding the globalization of work that is spawned by technology.

Also in the series:

GLOBAL SOURCING OF BUSINESS AND IT SERVICES
Leslie P. Willcocks and Mary C. Lacity

ICT AND INNOVATION IN THE PUBLIC SECTOR
Francesco Contini and Giovan Francesco Lanzara

EXPLORING VIRTUALITY WITHIN AND BEYOND ORGANIZATIONS
Niki Panteli and Mike Chaisson

KNOWLEDGE PROCESSES IN GLOBALLY DISTRIBUTED CONTEXTS
Julia Kotlarsky, Ilan Oshri and Paul C. van Fenema

GLOBAL CHALLENGES FOR IDENTITY POLICIES
Edgar Whitley and Ian Hosein

E-GOVERNANCE FOR DEVELOPMENT
Shirin Madon

OFFSHORE OUTSOURCING OF IT WORK
Mary C. Lacity and Joseph W. Rottman

OUTSOURCING GLOBAL SERVICES
Ilan Oshri, Julia Kotlarsky and Leslie P. Willcocks

BRICOLAGE, CARE AND INFORMATION
Chrisanthi Avgerou, Giovan Francesco Lanzara and Leslie P. Willcocks

Bricolage, Care and Information

Claudio Ciborra's Legacy in Information Systems Research

Chrisanthi Avgerou, Giovan Francesco Lanzara and Leslie P. Willcocks

palgrave
macmillan

First published 2009 by
PALGRAVE MACMILLAN

Palgrave Macmillan in the UK is an imprint of Macmillan Publishers Limited, registered in England, company number 785998, of Houndmills, Basingstoke, Hampshire RG21 6XS.

Palgrave Macmillan in the US is a division of St Martin's Press LLC, 175 Fifth Avenue, New York, NY 10010.

Palgrave Macmillan is the global academic imprint of the above companies and has companies and representatives throughout the world.

Palgrave® and Macmillan® are registered trademarks in the United States, the United Kingdom, Europe and other countries.

ISBN-13: 978–0–230–22073–7 hardback
ISBN-10: 0–230–22073–8 hardback

This book is printed on paper suitable for recycling and made from fully managed and sustained forest sources. Logging, pulping and manufacturing processes are expected to conform to the environmental regulations of the country of origin.

A catalogue record for this book is available from the British Library.

A catalog record for this book is available from the Library of Congress.

10 9 8 7 6 5 4 3 2 1
18 17 16 15 14 13 12 11 10 09

Printed and bound in Great Britain by
CPI Antony Rowe, Chippenham and Eastbourne

Contents

Illustrations

Tables

Figures

Preface

Claudio Ciborra was one of the most innovative thinkers in the field of information systems. He was one of the first scholars who introduced institutional economics in the study of IS; he elaborated new concepts, such as 'the platform organization'; and he contributed to the development of a new perspective altogether to the study of information systems through Heideggerian phenomenology. His untimely death left this work scattered in journals, edited books, conference proceedings, and some still unpublished.

This book contains some of the most seminal work of Claudio Ciborra and work of other authors who were inspired by this work and built on it. It is composed of three parts:

The introduction, by Giovan Frencesco Lanzara, takes the reader through the unfolding of Ciborra's thought and elaborates on the main themes of his work, namely socio-technical systems, institutional economics of information systems, IT and organizational learning, and finally his phenomenological analyses of information systems.

The first part of the book contains 11 of Claudio Ciborra's publications, selected by the editors to convey best the development of his work; it includes articles on all the thematic categories identified at the introduction, though the largest category is on his phenomenological work, which, we believe, was his most significant contribution.

The second part contains eight articles by other authors whose research was founded on Ciborra's ideas[1]:

In *Knowledge: Climbing the Learning Ladder TO A 'Phenomenological' View* Andrea Resca points out that questions of epistemology have been a constant preoccupation in Ciborra's work, from his writings on transaction costs to his phenomenological analyses. He thus traces the thread that connects his analyses of knowledge and rationality in economic and administrative behaviour, of knowledge, learning and organizational strategy, and of improvisation and situated action.

In *Hospitality, Improvisation and Gestell: A Phenomenology of Mobile Information,* Martin Brigham and Lucas Introna provide a clear presentation of these three concepts and demonstrate the way they can enhance our understanding of IS and organizational change by using them to examine changes that occurred in the practice of a fire brigade in the UK when they started using mobile data systems.

In *The Hospitality Metaphor AS A Theoretical Lens to Understand the Process of ICT Adoption* Saccol and Reinhard discuss 'hospitality' as a new approach for ICT adoption that departs from positivist models. They trace the philosophical origins of this metaphor and its emergence in the IS field mainly through Ciborra's work and they apply it to gain insights on a case study of a Brazilian Bank that equipped its employees with mobile technology.

Amany Elbanna's paper *The Validity of the Improvisation Argument in the Implementation of Rigid Technology: The Case of ERP Systems* draws on Ciborra's work on improvisation and drift. She examines whether these concepts are relevant and valid for ERP projects, which are generally understood as rigid and therefore in need of careful planning. She combines Ciborra's ideas with an Actor Network Theory (ANT) analysis to argue that improvisation, bricolage and drift are constituent processes of highly structured projects of rigid technology.

Edgar Whitley and Mary Darking, in *Object Lessons and Invisible Technologies* examine the nature of technology artefacts – a longstanding theme in IS research – by contrasting ideas stemming from recent research in the ANT perspective and Ciborra's phenomenology. They use a European Union project that aims at developing a new technological infrastructure to demonstrate the explanatory capacity of these perspectives and emphasize the significance of the concept of *Gestell* that Ciborra drew from Heidegger.

Petter Nielsen and Margunn Aanestad in *Control Devolution as Information Infrastructure Design Strategy: A Case Study of a Content Service Platform for Mobile Phones in Norway* draw on Ciborra's critical writings on control in IS development and the development of ICT infrastructures. They focus on the control versus autonomy choices made in the process of the development of an infrastructure for mobile content by two Norwegian operators. They argue for 'control devolution' as a successful strategy that should be followed by the industry in order to address risks in infrastructure projects and maintain innovative capacity.

Antonio Cordella's article *Transaction Costs and Information Systems: Does it Add Up?* builds on Ciborra's work on transaction costs economics, which was among the earliest efforts to sensitize the IS field on the way ICT affects information aspects of economic exchange. Following this path of thought Cordella discusses the effects of ICT in terms of the interdependences of the factors contributing to transaction costs.

Finally, Ian Angell and Fernando Ilharco, in Chapter 19, *Dispositioning it All: Towards a Theory for Thriving without Models*, builds on Heidegger's ideas in Being and Time and Clausewitz's On War, and introduces the notion of disposition as an appropriate notion for understanding and coping in a world entangled in information and communication technologies.

Note

1. Chapters 12–18, as well as their description in this Preface, were first published in the *Journal of Information Technology*, 21(3), 2006, in a special issue: 'Claudio Ciborra and the IS field: legacy and development', edited by Chrisanthi Avgerou, Ole Hanseth and Leslie Willcocks. We are grateful to Palgrave Macmillan for giving us permission to reproduce these articles, some with minor modifications, in this book.

Acknowledgements of Permission to Reprint

Grateful acknowledgement is made to the following sources for permission to reprint material in this book:

The Mind Or The Heart? It Depends on (The Definition of) the Situation – Claudio Ciborra (2006) *Journal of Information Technology* **21**(3): 129–139.

Reprinted with permission from Palgrave Macmillan.

Imbrication of Representations: Risk and Digital Technologies – Claudio Ciborra (2006) *Journal of Management Studies* **43**(6): 1339–1356.

Reprinted with permission from Wiley-Blackwell.

Interpreting e-government and Development: Efficiency, Transparency or Governance at a Distance? – Claudio Ciborra (2005) *Information Technology and People* **18**(3): 260–279.

Reprinted with permission from Emerald Group Publishing Limited.

From Tool to Gestell: Agendas for Managing the Information Infrastructure – Claudio Ciborra and Ole Hanseth (1998) *Information Technology and People* **11**(4): 305–327.

Reprinted with permission from Emerald Group Publishing Limited.

The Platform Organization: Recombining Strategies, Structures, and Surprises – Claudio Ciborra (1996) *Organization Science* **7**(2): 103–118.

Reprinted with permission from the Institute for Operations Research and the Management Sciences (INFORMS).

Formative Contexts and Information Technology: Understanding the Dynamics of Innovation in Organizations – Claudio Ciborra and Giovan Francesco Lanzara (1994) *Accounting, Management & Information Technology* **4**(2): 61–86.

Reprinted with permission from Elsevier.

Organizational Learning and Core Capabilities Development: The Role of IT – Raphael Andreu and Claudio Ciborra (1996) *Journal of Strategic Information Systems* **5**: 111–127.

Reprinted with permission from Elsevier.

From Thinking to Tinkering: The Grassroots of Strategic Information Systems – Claudio Ciborra (1992) *The Information Society* **8**: 297–309.

Reprinted by permission of Taylor and Francis Ltd.

Reframing the Role of Computers in Organizations: The Transactions Costs Approach – Claudio Ciborra (1987) *Office, Technology and People* **3**: 17–38.

Reprinted with permission from Emerald Group Publishing Limited.

Markets, Bureaucracies and Groups in the Information Society: An Institutional Appraisal of the Impacts of Information technology – Claudio Ciborra (1983) *Information Economics and Policy* **1**(2): 145–160.
Reprinted with permission from Elsevier.

Knowledge: Climbing the Learning Ladder to a 'Phenomenological' View – Andrea Resca (2006) *Journal of Information Technology* **21**(3): 203–210.
Reprinted with permission from Palgrave Macmillan.

Hospitality, Improvisation and *Gestell*: A Phenomenology of Mobile Information – Martin Brigham and Lucas D. Introna (2006) *Journal of Information Technology* **21**(3): 140–153.
Reprinted with permission from Palgrave Macmillan.

The Hospitality Metaphor as a Theoretical Lens to Understand the Process of ICT Adoption – Amarolinda Zanela Saccol (2006) *Journal of Information Technology* **21**(3): 154–164.
Reprinted with permission from Palgrave Macmillan.

The Validity of the Improvisation Argument in the Implementation of Rigid Technology: The Case of ERP Systems – Amany Elbanna (2006) *Journal of Information Technology* **21**(3): 165–175.
Reprinted with permission from Palgrave Macmillan.

Object Lessons and Invisible Technologies – Edgar A. Whitley and Mary Darking (2006) *Journal of Information Technology* **21**(3): 176–184.
Reprinted with permission from Palgrave Macmillan.

Control Devolution as Information Infrastructure Design Strategy: A Case Study of a Content Service Platform for Mobile Phones in Norway – Petter Nielsen, Margunn Aanestad (2006) *Journal of Information Technology* **21**(3): 15–194.
Reprinted with permission from Palgrave Macmillan.

Transaction Costs and Information Systems: Does IT Add Up? – Antonio Cordella (2006) *Journal of Information Technology* **21**(3): 195–202.
Reprinted with permission from Palgrave Macmillan.

Notes on Contributors

Margunn Aanestad, Ph.D., is an Associate Professor in the Department of Informatics, University of Oslo. She has worked within health care and telecommunications before commencing her Ph.D. study of surgical telemedicine. Her research has been published in Journal of Computer Supported Collaborative Work, Methods of Information in Medicine, Journal of Telemedicine and Telecare, Electronic Journal of Information Systems in Developing Countries, European Journal of Innovation Management, Journal of IT for Development, and MIS Quarterly. Her research interests are broadly related to information infrastructures, particularly within the public sector, in both developed and developing countries.

Ian O. Angell has been a Professor of Information Systems at the London School of Economics since 1986, having also previously taught Computer Science at Royal Holloway College and University College London. He holds a Ph.D. in Algebraic Number Theory from the University of London (1971). His research work concentrates on the global consequences of Information and Communication Technology (ICT); strategic information systems; computers and risk (opportunities and hazards); the limits of computation; the future of work; and on organizational and national policies for ICT. He is well-known on the international lecture circuit as a 'futurologist.'

Rafael Andreu (Ph.D., MIT 1978), is a Professor of Strategic Management and Information Systems at IESE Business School. His main areas of interest are in organizational learning for capability development, and a learning-based view of the management profession.

Chrisanthi Avgerou is a Professor of Information Systems at the London School of Economics and Political Science. Her main interests concern the relationship of ICT to organizational change and the role of ICT in socio-economic development. She is chairperson of the IFIP Technical Committee 9 on Social Implications of Information Technology and she chaired the IFIP WG 9.4 group on computers in developing countries from 1996 till 2003. Among her recent publications are *Information Systems and Global Diversity,* and *The Social Study of Information and Communication Technology: Innovation, Actors, and Contexts,* both published by Oxford University Press.

Martin Brigham is a Lecturer in the Department of Organisation, Work and Technology, Lancaster University Management School, Lancaster University, UK. His research draws on organization and management studies, modern European philosophy and science and technology studies. His research interests focus on the relationship between information technology and organizational change, the discourse of environmentalism and sustainability, and the globalization of management practice. He is a member of the Centre for the Study of Technology and Organisation at Lancaster University. He was previously at the University of Warwick, UK.

Claudio U. Ciborra graduated in Electronic Engineering from the Politecnico di Milano, Italy, before pursuing studies in management, economics and organization theory at the University of California, Los Angeles and Harvard University. He held teaching positions at a number of Italian universities and was Visiting Professor in many European and American universities. He was Professor of Information Systems, Convenor of the Department of Information Systems, and PwC Risk Management Professor at the Centre for Analysis of Risk and Regulation at the London School of Economics and Political Science. He carried out extensive research in the fields of new technologies, organizational design, learning, knowledge and change.

Antonio Cordella is a Lecturer in Information Systems at the London School of Economics and Political Science. His research interests cover the areas of e-government, economic theories of information systems, and the social studies of information systems.

Mary Darking is a Lecturer in Social Policy in the School of Applied Social Science at the University of Brighton. She has an MSc and PhD from the LSE both in Information Systems. Whilst at the LSE Mary was a teaching assistant to Claudio Ciborra for three years on a Masters level course entitled Interpretations of Information Systems. Mary's PhD research looked at the organizational and pedagogical implications of integrating e-learning technologies into higher education. Her current research interests include the governance of large-scale infrastructures and the policy implications of cross sector partnerships. Her recent publications consider the role of FLOSS communities and technologies in initiatives designed to promote sustainable economic development through supporting small and medium sized enterprise.

Amany R. Elbanna is a Lecturer in Information Systems at the Loughborough University's Business School. She holds Ph.D in Information Systems from The London School of Economics. Her research interests include IS innovation and the interaction between technology and organizations, IS project management, and Agile software development.

Ole Hanseth, PhD, is Professor in the Department of Informatics, University of Oslo. His research focuses mainly on the interplay between social and technical issues in the development and use of large-scale networking applications. He is also Visiting Professor at London School of Economics, Department of Information Systems.

Fernando Ilharco is Assistant Professor of the Catholic University of Portugal, Lisbon, where he is Director of the PhD in Communication Sciences Programme. He holds a PhD by the London School of Economics and Political Science, Department of Information Systems, 2002, and an MBA by the Business School of the Catholic University of Portugal (1993). Since his PhD, Ilharco has been publishing regularly in academic journals and books. He worked with a team of consultants oriented by Professor Michael Porter, in Lisbon, between 1993 and 1996. For ten years he kept a regular column on societal issues on *Público*, a leading Portuguese reference newspaper. His areas of interest are (i) ICT and Society and (ii) Leadership and Organisational Theory – both informed by phenomenological lenses.

Lucas D. Introna is Professor of Organisation, Technology and Ethics at Lancaster University Management School, Lancaster University, UK. His research focuses on power, virtual organizing, privacy and embodiment, and draws on recent advances in continental philosophy and ethics, phenomenology and the social construction of information technology. He is co-editor of *Ethics and Information Technology* and an associate editor of *Management Information Systems Quarterly*. He is also a founding member of the *International Society for Ethics and Information Technology*. He was previously at the London School of Economics and Political Science, UK.

Giovan Francesco Lanzara is Professor of Organization Theory at the University of Bologna, Italy and Visiting Professor at the London School of Economics and Political Science (Information Systems and Innovation Group, Department of Management). His main research interests are in the areas of organizational learning and design, ICT-based innovation, and in the evolutionary dynamics of social and political institutions. More recently he did research on the relationships between knowing and organizing. He is the author of several articles published in major international journals and currently co-authoring and co-editing a book on "ICT and Innovation in the Public Sector" for Palgrave MacMillan.

Petter Nielsen, Ph.D., is a Researcher at Telenor Research & Innovation and associated professor at Dept. of Informatics, University of Oslo, Norway. His research circles around the construction, evolution and adoption of large scale and heterogeneous information infrastructures. Empirically he focuses on mobile services and the development of the Mobile Internet in developed as well as emerging markets. His research has been published in the Scandinavian Journal of Information Systems, Journal of Information Technology, Journal of Information Systems in Developing Countries, and Journal of IT for Development.

Nicolau Reinhard is Professor of Management at the School of Economics, Administration and Accounting of the University of São Paulo, Brazil. His research interests and publications are related to the management of the IT function, IT in developing countries, the use of IT in Public Administration and Information Systems Implementation. Prof. Reinhard has a degree in Engineering, a PhD in Management, and, besides his academic career, has held executive and consulting positions in IT management in private and public organizations.

Andrea Resca is Doctoral Candidate at the Luiss "Guido Carli" University, Rome, Centre of Research on Information Systems (Ce.R.S.I). After his undergraduate studies at the University of Bologna (School of Political Science) under the supervision of Claudio Ciborra, moved to South Korea where he obtained a Master of Arts in Korean Studies (Area Studies). Once in Italy again, he joined Claudio

Ciborra at the "Libera Università di Lingue e Comunicazione – IULM", Milan, as Senior Research Fellow researching e-government until 2005. His publications range from the Organisation Theory discipline to Information Systems discipline including e-government and e-participation as his current research domains.

Amarolinda Zanela Saccol is a Lecturer and Researcher of Management and Information Systems at the University of Vale do Rio dos Sinos (UNISINOS) – Brazil. She has a Ph.D. in Business Administration from the University of São Paulo School of Economics, Business Administration and Accounting (FEA/USP). Her research interests include the development, adoption and management of ICT and implications for work and organizations.

Edgar A. Whitley is a Reader in Information Systems in the Information Systems and Innovation Group of the Department of Management at the London School of Economics and Political Science. He has a BSc (Econ) and a PhD in Information Systems both from the LSE. Edgar is the co–editor for the journal *Information Technology & People* and an associate editor for the journal *MIS Quarterly*. Together with Antonio Cordella and Jannis Kallinikos, Edgar organized the special issue of the European Journal of Information Systems (EJIS) celebrating Claudio's life and work (volume 14(5), 2005). Edgar is the research coordinator of the LSE Identity Project and represented the project at the Science and Technology Select Committee review of the Scheme. Edgar has written extensively about the Identity Cards Programme for both academic and trade audiences and is a frequent media commentator on the Scheme.

Leslie P. Willcocks is a professor at the London School of Economics and Political Sciences and is recognized internationally for his work in the Information Systems field. He is co-author of 29 books and over 150 refereed publications and is a visiting professor at three other universities as well as editor of the Journal of Information Technology. His major research interests include outsourcing, IT management, large scale complex projects, e.g. CRM, ERP, organizational change and IT measurement. He is also engaged in looking at technology in globalization and the strategic use of IT, IT leadership, IT enabled organizational change as well as business process outsourcing and offshoring, organizational behaviour, social theory and philosophy for information systems, and public sector IT policy.

Introduction
Information Systems and the Quest for Meaning – An Account of Claudio Ciborra's Intellectual Journey

Giovan Francesco Lanzara

In the Methodological Appendix of *The Labyrinths of Information* – one of his last works – Claudio Ciborra ponders about his method of inquiry and his personal way of doing research – what he refers to as his 'chosen road'. He writes:

> I had never reflected systematically about the process by which (my) papers were generated (...) until I reread, for the nth time, the introduction to Heidegger's Being and Time (1962), specifically his definition of phenomenology. This definition (or rather my interpretation of it) at last helped me to make explicit the way that I understand how I proceed. (Ciborra 2002: 173)

In reflecting about his method he then continues:

> To be sure, I have crafted such method in a dilettante fashion, along the way so to speak (...) I could only find the limits of current models and interpretations, and the roots of alternative ones, by reading between the lines of the stylized explanations; and peering into their wrinkles and especially into the interstices between practice, ongoing interpretations, and what was left out, or explained away by referring to the obvious background that both business practitioners and researchers were supposed to share.... My understanding of Heidegger's phenomenological method helped me to specify, and somewhat systematize, what I was (and am) doing. (Ciborra 2002: 173–175)

I will take my first steps from these reflections to now begin to tell the story of a highly original and intense intellectual adventure. The story can be told in many different ways, but Ciborra's words – so it seems to me – point to the essence of it: his lifelong research work in the information systems discipline has been a story of discovery and unveiling of deeper layers of reality, in a recurrent effort at seeing and going beyond the limitations of current methods and theories and at breaking the veil of appearances that surround phenomena. From the early steps to the very end of his research career and life, Ciborra's search was a relentless quest for meaning or, as he finally came to name it, *aletheia* – the Greek word for 'truth' (in the sense of revelation). His encounter with Heidegger's phenomenology happened indeed as a moment of revelation, a crucial step that led him to explore new paths to understand information systems, and at the same time generated a reflective insight and new self-awareness as a researcher and committed intellectual. The true sense of his work was finally revealed to him, and to us. The researcher has an unveiling role: his goal is to break the veils of appearances and open up a path to *aletheia*.

For sure, Claudio Ciborra pursued multiple paths in the course of his research career, and often, typical of his restless character, different paths at the same time. He was not only a tireless explorer and a natural inquirer, but also a raider and an inseminator of new ideas, relentlessly travelling back and forth through many areas of knowledge and expertise – engineering, computer science, economics, psychology, organization and management studies, philosophy, jumping felicitously from the more technical disciplines to the humanities, with a passionate interest in literature, music, painting and architecture. Since the mid-seventies he witnessed a 30-year long history of information systems research and, along with other scholars and practitioners, contributed to shaping its contours and development in significant and controversial ways – which will be fully assessed and appreciated only with the passing of time. In spite of the many and diverse theoretical ideas he investigated, the basic unity and coherence of Ciborra's work is to be found in the constancy of his method and aims, less in the specific content of the theories developed and applied. He had a peculiar, unique way of practicing research, akin to the modes of artistic creation, in which aesthetic feeling and playfulness went hand in hand with powerful argumentative rhetoric and rigorous analytical reasoning. His idiosyncratic research activities often had the character of *bricolage*, tinkering as he always was with a range of possibilities and combinations. Still, the object of his inquiries was always one and the same: the place and meaning of ICT in human life.

The idea that technology should be designed and used for improving human conditions both at work and in the dealings of everyday life had been present in Ciborra's work since the beginning of his research career. His recurring questions were: What is ICT and how does it affect human beings? How can we understand information as a phenomenon? He engaged with these questions so radically and profoundly that at one stage his search for ICT merged with a quest for the meaning of human life itself. However, the answers he tried to give changed over time. A sequence of phases and significant shifts can be traced in the development of Ciborra's ideas on information systems. He moved from electronic engineering to the socio-technical approach, then to transaction costs theory, to organizational learning, and ultimately he landed onto the final shores of phenomenology. In his wanderings he always strived to take a step beyond the current ways of thinking, challenging the received wisdom of the discipline. Yet, a remarkable aspect of his inquiry is that the shift to new ways of looking at the matter never erased or obliterated the previous ways, but rather filled the gaps and faced the questions left unanswered with the previous theory by capturing novel features of the object and enriching its understanding.

Tracking the shifts and twists of Ciborra's intellectual development and research work is an opportunity to throw light on the making of the Information Systems domain itself, or at least of an important aspect of it, namely its transformation from a basically technical, applied science ruled by mathematical models, to an interdisciplinary domain characterized by multiple contributing theories and methods of inquiry, where interpretive sensibility plays a role comparable to formal modelling. Thanks to Ciborra's work, information systems research mingled with the human and social sciences, and gained a reflective dimension that greatly enriched it as a scientific and practical domain.

Beyond machines and engineering: socio-technics and participative system design

In the mid or late seventies, when Claudio Ciborra, a fresh graduate in Electronic Engineering at the Politecnico of Milan, appeared on the scene, IS was struggling to establish itself as a fully academic discipline in opposition to Computer Science and Electronic Engineering. However, in the process of formation the imprint and influence of computer scientists, software programmers and engineers was still great. Although a few researchers were timidly raising the issue of how to connect the new software artefacts to the working conditions in the firm and called for more empirical and theoretical attention to the nature of work and the social implications of the technology, the dominant paradigm was still solidly rooted in the engineering and applied sciences. Applied calculus was the theoretical core and automation was the buzzword. Computer science, or informatics, was defined as a formal science based on mathematics and logics. In order to legitimate itself as an institutionalized research field IS needed to be grounded in sound theory, and in the search for theory critical problems were the conceptualization of information systems as socio-technical objects and the development of effective methods for system design and implementation in real contexts of use.[1]

The divide between the technical and the social was part and parcel of the emerging information systems discipline, but technical knowledge was still a dominant aspect of it. System development was regarded as a self-contained domain, driven by strictly technical design requirements and structured according to formal methodologies (DeMarco, 1979; Jackson, 1983; Yourdon, 1982). Software engineers and system developers would infuse their technical knowledge into software programs, functionalities and applications, which would be subsequently delivered to end users as black-boxed products (Dijkstra, 1976). This view admits only one rationale – the best (technical) way to design and operate a system – and users should conform or comply to it in their behaviour. Problems other than technical were not 'seen' in an approach of this kind, they were simply 'non-existing', or, when they occurred, they were made sense of by attributing them either to inadequate design methods (judged as not being formal or structured enough) or to the users' technical incompetence and non-rational behaviour.

As a first move, struggling to get rid of the straightjacket of engineering, Ciborra made a step away from what he saw as an overly deterministic view and in the late 1970s, following his encounter with Enid Mumford's work and the Tavistock Institute studies, started to look at the interaction between information technology and work from a socio-technical perspective. In the years 1980/81 he visited Norway and brought his knowledge and interest in socio-technics to the research community based in Oslo. There he became acquainted with the Scandinavian school of participatory system design in work settings that was already well established at that time. He was actively engaged as a field researcher in the early participatory design experiences in organizations in Norway, Denmark and Sweden and, most importantly, intensely collaborated with a group of dedicated young researchers led by far-sighted scholars and mentors like Kristen Nygaard and Einar Thorsrud.[2] These researchers were actively engaged in searching for new system development methodologies based on workers' participation and more flexible sociotechnical frameworks. In their view, research activity was to be diverted from 'isolated' technical artifacts and focused instead onto the socio-technical system, which comprised *both* computer tools and software programs as technical components *and*, on the social side, the user needs and the social structures of work. Ciborra's recurring questions concerned how IS could be designed so as to meet workers' needs and improve working conditions. His aim was to strike the socio-technical balance between developing good computer systems and obtaining human working conditions for the workers, and that was to be achieved with the help of new system development methods, which allowed users' knowledge and participation as critical design resources.[3]

Ciborra's work within the socio-technical school and his extensive networking activity on both sides of the Atlantic led to the IFIP Working Conference on *Systems Design For, With, and By the Users* held in Riva del Sole, Italy, in September 1982, where he acted as the Conference Chair. Still today, in the memory of those who attended, this Conference is perceived as having been a topical event for the hitherto scattered and amorphous information systems research community. Although the Conference did not have any immediate impact on the field, novel theoretical frameworks and field experiences of participatory systems design were presented and debated, new ideas were aired, and, most importantly, the question of 'participation in design' as a shared concern was put into focus by scholars coming from distant disciplines and distant places. Researchers in computer science, organizational design, management studies, philosophy, sociology, industrial relations and ethnography, coming from Scandinavia and Italy, Germany and Massachusetts, the United Kingdom and California engaged in a collective effort to break disciplinary boundaries and learn new ideas stemming from a variety of backgrounds. This emerging sense of openness was well expressed by Kristen Nygaard in his keynote speech:

> Informatics is the science which has as its subject of study the information aspects of phenomena in nature and society ... and their interaction with other aspects of reality. (Nygaard, 1983: 20)

Overall, the Riva del Sole Conference contributed to make Information Systems Research an interdisciplinary endeavour and a hybrid scientific domain, helping to grow the seed of an emerging multidisciplinary research community.

Yet, as was so typical of him, Ciborra took the Conference as an occasion to displace everyone and move into a different direction. While the view shared by most people justified users' participation on moral and political grounds by taking a strongly prescriptive stance, Claudio advocated a more liberal approach, based on the comparative analytical framework provided by the New Institutional Economics (Coase, 1937; Coase, 1960; Williamson, 1975; Williamson, 1981; Williamson, 1985), which he became familiar with under the guidance of William Ouchi at the University of California – Los Angeles.[4] In his conference paper he argued that workers' participation is necessary for system development essentially for reasons of economic efficiency, as it helps to mitigate the social costs that arise in IS development and technological change.

> An advancement in devising strategies for user participation could benefit from a comparative institutional assessment of governance structures of technological change within organizations. (Ciborra, 1983a: 41)

To deal with the question of how to organize participation in specific sets of circumstances – he contended – one should be able to compare and choose between different alternatives, entailing a whole range of bargains and contractual agreements. Thus, a path to applying transaction costs economics to Information Systems Research was cleared.

Beyond individual decision-making: institutions, information systems and the coordination of exchanges

All throughout the 1980s Ciborra, in a series of articles and book chapters (1981; 1983b; 1984; 1987; 1990), outlined the basic elements of a theory of information systems based on the transaction cost approach. The full results of this research work were presented in a more structured form in his 1993 book *Teams, Markets and Systems*. The IS research programme based on transaction costs economics is expressed in clear words in his 1987 paper 'Reframing the Role of Computers in Organizations: The Transactions Costs Approach' (Chapter 10, in this volume).[5]

> The aim…is to open the MIS disciplines to recent developments in social sciences and economics. The ultimate goal is to define both a new framework and a new language, so that the role of information technology in organizations can be better understood…. A new organizational understanding of information processing must go beyond the individual decision-making paradigm…. The concepts of 'exchange' (transaction) and 'contract' between at least two individuals or organizational units must become the new center of attention. (Ciborra, 1987: 19)

Ciborra's interest in transaction costs theory originated from multiple sources: firstly, from his growing dissatisfaction with the ideological and prescriptive overtones of the sociotechnical approach to participative systems development and organizational design; secondly, from his empirical observations of the theoretical shortcomings and the frequent practical failures of formal systems analysis models; thirdly, and most crucially, from the narrow, control-oriented focus that he perceived in the managerial approaches within the MIS discipline. In his view the transaction costs approach allowed for a more systematic comparative analysis of alternative information systems, and especially for a more integrated treatment of IT and organizational design. Alternative institutional arrangements – markets, bureaucracies and groups – provide different possibilities for economic coordination and collective action, eventually including different forms of participation, and require the design of different kinds of information systems (Ciborra, 1981, Chapter 11 in this volume), which must be tailored to the specific features of the transactions. The basic criterion for analysis and design is transactional efficiency. Therefore MIS, databases and office technologies, by affecting the costs of transacting in organizations and society, should be designed in order to enable organizations and the economy to operate more efficiently. But, by so doing, IT may also affect the relative efficiency and desirability of alternative organizational and institutional arrangements, thus acting as a major force of change, both at the organizational and social level.

A second line of criticism leading to the choice of the transaction costs framework stems from Ciborra's dissatisfaction with the data-oriented and decision-oriented models underlying conventional systems analysis and development methods. Both are judged to be inadequate, although for different reasons. The *data approach* sees an organization as a set of data files and data flows which need to be streamlined and computerized for management purposes, but ignores the economic and social nature of organizations or assumes a non-problematic matching between data processing and organizing processes (Davis & Munro, 1977; DeMarco, 1979; Jackson, 1983; Yourdon, 1982). The *decision-making approach,* initiated by Herbert Simon (1973; 1976), is more organizationally grounded, information being now linked to basic decision-making processes under conditions of uncertainty, but downplayed conflict of interests, opportunistic behaviour, and strategic misrepresentation as critical factors in organizational decision-making. Most critically, it does not consider the possibility that information might be used for different purposes than making decisions, like for instance surveillance, deception, misrepresentation, and power play. The target of Ciborra's criticism is the conventional wisdom supporting EDP-based models, MIS and Decision Support Systems (DSS) (Keen & Scott Morton, 1978). In his view these models of information systems are based on premises about human behaviour that do not convey a correct representation of reality (Ciborra, 1987). Particularly, they assume a much too simplified picture of the organization and do not take into account the real phenomenology of information processes, therefore are bound to fail in practice.[6] As Feldman and March (1981) underline, information processing is a *behaviour,* not just a purely technical or computational activity.

In his effort to build a transaction-costs-based theory of information systems Ciborra was looking for a more realistic view of the role of information in organization and a more effective method of analysis and design of information systems. He found such more realistic view in the hypotheses and in the analytical framework of neo-institutional economics, which he creatively adapted to explore the economic and organizational aspects of the phenomenon of information.[7]

We can summarize the major achievements of Ciborra's work in IS and institutional economics in a number of points:

- Information and information system development are connected to economic and social theory, more specifically to organization theory and organizational design;
- Information systems are redefined as networks of information flows that are necessary to create, set up, control and maintain the organization's (or the society's) constituent transactions and relevant contracts;
- Different contractual arrangements and institutional frameworks need to be supported by information systems showing distinct functional characteristics (Ciborra, 1983b, chapter 11 in this book));
- IT is regarded as a mediating technology, based on standardization and extension of linkages (Thompson, 1967). Computers are then reframed as tools for communicating rather than computing, and information systems are critical for the efficient coordination and governance of the social and economic structures of the society;
- IT affects the type and effectiveness of governance structures in different conditions, and consequently affects economic efficiency and the social costs of coordination (Coase, 1937; Coase, 1960);
- The transaction costs framework can be used to throw light on how IT and EDP can facilitate or hinder the development of new organizational arrangements and processes (Ciborra, 1981);
- Software systems could then be designed explicitly to decrease the costs of transacting and provide search and control routines to facilitate managers' and employees' contracts and commitments within and across organizations (Flores and Ludlow, 1981).

The outcome of Ciborra's research activity in IS and transaction costs is a well-articulated conceptual framework linking information technology and the functioning of economic organization. Most importantly, the framework is enriched and supported by a series of empirical illustrations and cases showing how information technology, when intelligently developed and used, can change the concrete functioning of basic coordinating mechanisms like markets, business hierarchies and teams.

In refining and applying the TC framework Ciborra's inquiry was not limited to questions of economic efficiency, improved performance, or increased transparency, but posed critical questions concerning the dynamic reconfiguration of basic economic and social institutions, thus leading to new insights on the emergence of electronic markets, the diffusion of virtual teams, and the changing nature of the hierarchical form from a tool for local control and supervision to a mechanism for distant coordination in business. This emerging interest in change and innovation, together with the problems and puzzles of the practice of systems development, led Ciborra to initiate a new path of inquiry in the field of organizational learning and change.

Beyond controlled change: learning, drifting, and *bricolage*

Since the mid-eighties the fast pace of change in the field of Information and Communication Technology raised new management problems for business practitioners and opened new spaces for research. Sweeping changes were transforming basic organizational structures and competencies in the firm, the public administration and the government, yielding a remarkable impact on the traditional ways of running corporate business and public affairs. Even though one of the spreading buzzwords in the field was *business innovation through IT,* at the same time repeated failures in the design and implementation of large corporate information systems showed how inadequate were mainstream theories and methods to understand the quality and scale of the ongoing transformations and face the challenges of innovation. Established MIS strategies were proving increasingly ineffective and the growing gap between theory and practice in information systems development became an issue of concern for scholars (Boland and Hirschheim, 1987; Dahlbom and Mathiassen, 1993; Lyytinen and Hirschheim, 1987). A few perceptive researchers were quick enough to perceive that the wind was blowing in a different direction, and Claudio was amongst them. In those years he was involved with Olivetti, Ivrea, studying software production projects and large scale programming. At the same time he was keeping an eye on French and US cases of strategic information systems, such as Minitel, American Hospital Supply, American Airlines' SABRE, and others, which started like bread-and-butter applications but were surprisingly successful, soon granting a competitive advantage to the companies who adopted them (Ciborra, 1993: 175–178). In several writings Ciborra highlighted three major sets of phenomena that characterized the emerging landscape of strategic information systems and leading-edge software technologies:

a. implementation in practice rarely matches the ideal plans and the functional requirements established by developers and engineers; usually the outcomes are perceived as unexpected 'deviations' or 'distortions' from rationality, and are either attributed to methodological inadequacy or to the behavioural whims of 'irrational' users;
b. curiously enough, successful information systems that are developed stem not from formal theories and structured methodologies, or from deliberate designs, but rather from chance events and improvised, serendipitous applications, which are not planned *ex ante,* and are often introduced by the users themselves through reinvention and *bricolage*; indeed, innovation happens

by taking unanticipated paths and timing and assuming a local, apparently unconspicuous character at the outset;[8]

c. both practitioners and researchers seem to have little awareness and understanding of these puzzling phenomena. Consequently, they stubbornly keep designing and enforcing even more structured methods and strategies to harness deviant system and user behaviour, thus failing to exploit the opportunities for innovation hidden in the emergent properties of the systems or in the informal practices of the users. Therefore limited learning comes not only from the failures but also from a misunderstanding of the value of strategic tinkering (Ciborra, 1992, Chapter 9 in this book).

These emerging phenomena raised questions which could not be adequately answered within the neo-institutional framework, nor handled by formal systems developments methods. As a personal memory, I recall some of the problems with Neo-Institutional Economics discussed with Claudio in those years, and his efforts to combine or supplement transaction costs theory with a more dynamic perspective that could account for the manifold phenomenology of systems inertia, learning and change. Ciborra understood that Transaction Costs Theory was a powerful tool to make a static comparative analysis and an efficiency assessment of alternative governance structures (pure or mixed). However, the theory discounted, at least at that stage of development, the problem of learning costs involved in the transition (or transformation) from one type of structure to another. While the theory could deal with static efficiency nicely, it had little to say about dynamic efficiency, which is a critical issue in all projects of IS development and organizational innovation. Effective ICT-based innovation and in general any innovative endeavour require economies of velocity and learning rather than economies of transaction or task execution (Ciborra, 1990). With time and use governance structures, together with their associated resources, routines and human skills, tend to become highly specific and deeply rooted assets, showing high inertia to change. As structures and rules are institutionalized within specific cultural and environmental conditions, or, in the language of economics, become *sunk costs* that cannot be easily recovered, organizations suffer from a loss of flexibility and show limited capability for learning and change when such cap ability is highly needed due to changing environmental conditions. Thus, both the practical problems of information systems development and the theoretical limitations of the neo-institutional framework contributed to Ciborra's shift to search for new forms of theorizing that could account for the dynamics of IT innovation and change.[9]

Exchange and work with other researchers also played a major role in Ciborra's emerging interest in change and innovation, and in this respect the academic year 1986/1987 was full of felicitous encounters. Claudio spent several months at Harvard University as a visiting scholar in the Graduate School of Education and was in close contact with a number of major scholars who had a significant influence on his new orientation. Particularly, he worked with organizational psychologist Chris Argyris, becoming acquainted with organizational learning theories and intervention practices and creatively transplanting them into the ICT field; also, at the Harvard Law School he attended the lectures of social critic and political theorist Roberto Mangabeira Unger on *False Necessity* (Unger, 1987), which was instrumental to the research work on the *formative context* (Ciborra and Lanzara, 1994). In the same months he engaged in intense intellectual conversations with social psychologist Shoshana Zuboff, professor at Harvard Business School, who at that time was writing her book *In the Age of the Smart Machine* (Zuboff, 1988), an in-depth analysis of the implications of the new ICT for work and power in the modern business firm and the society, and a book in which Ciborra found – he later said – *'the kind of interpretive depth I would like to achieve myself.'*[10]

These encounters and the new intellectual experiences led to a significant turn in Ciborra's research interests and work. Although his involvement with the institutional economics of information systems was never put aside as a subject of research and teaching, he became interested in the phenomenology of ICT-based innovation and in the learning processes that may support or hinder an organization's capability to adopt ICT. Particularly, questions concerning the sources of cognitive inertia and limited learning in organizations and, on the other hand, questions concerning the deployment of idiosynchratic capabilities, the smart exploitation of strategic assets leading to rapid restructuring, and the role of *bricolage* in innovation and change became central in his research (Ciborra, 1992).

Three articles, all included in this book, stand out among others as a result of this new line of research. They address distinct problems: the first one addresses the question of innovation in organizations and introduces the notion of *formative context* in information systems research (Ciborra and Lanzara, 1994; Chapter 7); the second one contributes to the field of strategy studies and to the Resource Based View of the Firm, establishing a conceptual link between information systems, organizational learning and knowledge management (Andreu and Ciborra, 1996; Chapter 8); and the third one illustrates the idea of the *platform organization*, a new lens to look at an organization's transformation and strategy in action (Ciborra, 1996; Chapter 6).

In the attempt to account for the puzzling dynamics of ICT-based innovation in organizations, Ciborra and Lanzara (1989; 1994) introduced the distinction between the work routines and the underlying *formative context* (Unger, 1987) into information systems research. A formative context is a social and institutional script embedded in the organization of work and in the cognitive imageries supporting organizational life. Although the idea of the formative context has its antecedents in ethnometodology (Garfinkel, 1967) and in social and political theory (Unger, 1987), it points to features which also belong to the phenomenological perspective, namely the two-layered structure of knowledge and reality, that is, on the one hand the ongoing practical routines which are the focus of attention and, on the other hand, the underlying 'context' that gives shape and meaning to the routines and is tacitly taken for granted. In Ciborra and Lanzara's use of the term, the formative context is an attempt to encapsulate within one concept both a cognitive and an institutional dimension, merging cognition and organization, society and epistemology, the material and the symbolic aspect, thus striving to go beyond the overriding mentalistic and individualistic approaches of cognitive science.

The idea of the formative context was intended to capture the ambiguity of innovation and the tension between inertia and change in organizational transformations. It was a response to puzzling questions such as: Why carefully planned projects and deliberately designed systems fail and people hardly learn from the failures and keep repeating the same mistakes? Why some unplanned innovations turn out, surprisingly, to be undisputed successes, but people fail to perceive the potential and the meaning of the novelties and surprises? In the article with Rafael Andreu (Andreu and Ciborra, 1996), Ciborra used the formative context idea to explore the formation of the firm's core capabilities and show how the routine/formative context distinction could be fruitfully applied to Strategic Information Systems and to the development of IT applications better geared to the dynamics and the varied nature of organizational knowledge processes. Also, in his 1996 solo article (Chapter 6 in this book) he fleshed out the idea of the 'platform organization' to account for Olivetti's rapid technological and organizational change. The 'platform' is conceptualized as a loose and flexible system of schemes, arrangements and resources, that works as a formative context both structurally and cognitively. Ciborra argued that the 'platform' is the only organizational form capable of coping with the frantic pace of technological change and responding to the requirements of dynamic efficiency.

From the articles two major theoretical themes emerge, which go beyond the transactional view:

1. information systems share the character of the underlying texture or 'fabric' of the organization or the society, working indeed as formative contexts, both cognitively and institutionally; therefore they are not just a set of tools, resources and technologies supporting the coordination of economic exchanges, but they also touch a deeper, constitutive layer;
2. ICT-based change and innovation in organizations are much more complex and elusive phenomena than change management strategies assume; due to the combined effects of inertial forces and unpredictable events, systems often elude controlled change, rather they change by shifting and drifting.

However, it should be stressed here that Ciborra did not just formulate and lay out his ideas in academic publications, but actively explored their potential and limitations in practice. For instance, the Theseus Institute in Sophia Antipolis, where he was involved for several years (1989–1996) as the Director of the Department of Information Systems and Organization, was for him a laboratory for testing his ideas in teaching and consulting and in debates with a number of colleagues working in the area of technology management and in business strategy studies, particularly Charles Wisemann (1988) and Tawfik Jelassi (Ciborra and Jelassi, 1994). Among other activities, he was instrumental in promoting a course named 'Organizational Learning-in-Action', which was delivered by a group of associate scholars.[11] The course was organized as a *practicum* (Schön, 1987) for experimenting with concrete practical issues concerning organizational learning, the design of IT, and the management of business innovation. Its major thrust was to convey to participants an understanding of the 'patched up' nature of systems in practice and the 'hands-on' experience of the concrete phenomenology of technological and organizational design based on *bricolage*.

By the time Ciborra quit his management responsibilities at the Theseus Institute in 1996 the times were ripe for another change of direction in his wanderings. Having long elaborated his critiques to conventional management science, information systems development, strategic alignment, and the cognitive, problem-solving approach to organizational design, he was drifting towards a new shore, which was not clearly visible yet, but appeared in the offing.

Embracing phenomenology: *Gestell*, care and the quest for meaning in Information Systems Research

In 1995 Ciborra immersed himself in Martin Heidegger's *Sein und Zeit* (Heidegger, 1927/1962), the work in which the German philosopher raised again[12] the question of the meaning of being,[13] articulating, in a highly idiosyncratic and often obscure philosophical language, his views of how we encounter the world and experience the things and tools of our everyday life. Claudio read Heidegger in German, a language that he was proficient in, immediately took stock of it, and in the Spring semester of 1996 he delivered his first lectures on Phenomenology and Information Systems to a crowd of bewildered and fascinated students at the University of Bologna, within his course 'Information Systems and Organizational Design'.[14]

Undoubtedly Claudio was driven to phenomenological analysis by his former research experiences and his relentless intellectual quest. However, the development of his new style of thinking was also helped by changing external circumstances, like new research projects and academic affiliations. In the years 1996–1999, again in Scandinavia, he was involved in case study research on systems development, which revealed the emergence of Corporate Information Infrastructures and posed new challenges to the understanding of technology.[15] A few years later, in 2001, he resigned from his ten-year long post at the University of Bologna to accept a full professorship at the London School of Economics and Political Science. There he found a rich intellectual *milieu* where he immediately 'tuned in' and could finally pursue and teach his phenomenological analysis of information systems in a more systematic manner and in close interaction with his LSE colleagues.[16]

Many were the reasons that led Ciborra to embrace a phenomenological perspective in Information Systems Research. But whatever they may have been, the turn to phenomenology was announced by many of his previous critical themes and was not unexpected.[17] Similar to his previous shifts in theoretical perspective, Claudio's strategy was one of revisiting his former ideas and research findings by looking at them through a new lens and enriching them rather than replacing or rejecting them. Presumably at one point Ciborra felt that taking a phenomenological gaze on information systems and organizations was a consequential step to make in order to accomplish his research programme of building a new language for studying information and information systems as social phenomena. Phenomenology was then embraced by Claudio not as an additional, more powerful theory that would outperform or obliterate previous theories, but as a style of reflection which may reveal aspects and dimensions of technology, information systems and organizational life, that the scientific method employed in conventional management and business approaches fails to capture.[18] Critical of the over-inflated role of formal methods in ICT development, and especially of their ineffectiveness, Ciborra questioned:

> How come researchers privilege the geometry of the lines connecting abstract concepts in a model, while they remain blind to the blurred reality that any, even 'light', ethnographic study would have revealed? (Ciborra, 1998: 11)

Here is where phenomenology comes to the rescue as a 'revealing' method. What phenomenology brings to the discipline, in Claudio's view, is a concern for human experience and existence which formal methods inevitably keep out of the picture. The phenomenological method, in Ciborra's words, invites us 'to put into brackets' what we know about methods, systems, models, systems development and implementation processes, and to be more in touch with the messiness of the everyday world of the designers, managers and users of IT. Only by 'bracketing' what we tend to take for granted we can see the limitations of 'the prevailing cognitive view of organizations, information systems, problem solving, and knowledge' (Ciborra, 2004: 31), and 'we can start to build a new vocabulary around notions closer to human existence and experience' (Ciborra, 2004: 19).

Claudio set out to build this new vocabulary around a cluster of key concepts and words, a map which helped him find his way in what he called 'the labyrinth of information': *Gestell*, Drift, *Bricolage*, Care, Hospitality, Situation, Time, Improvisation, and Mood.[19] Most interestingly, this new language was not built by Ciborra around objects and issues 'other' than the ones predicated by scientific language; on the contrary, the 'words' were articulated to provide a subtler interpretation and understanding of phenomena in the very same domain in which formal, scientific methods claim to render an'objective', 'true' picture of reality. In this connection, Ciborra claimed that the phenomenological perspective helps us to recognize the strategic value of the everyday practices of current ICT applications, such as hacking, tinkering and drifting, or the generative potential hidden in systems' and agents' 'odd' behaviours, which are regarded as marginal or irrelevant in structured, top-down planning approaches (Ciborra, 2004: 21). A richer, closer to experience image of information systems is therefore delivered by means of the phenomenological lens, which is not necessarily at odds with more formal methods. However, they get a different (re)positioning with respect to one another: human existence and the everyday experience of the lifeworld are the grounds for formal, scientific thinking, while the latter is a particular, selective way of cutting into the complexity of the world, not the other way around.

Information is 'encountered' by human agents as a phenomenon of everyday life and information technologies are 'everyday things' (Norman, 1988), not just geometric entities. Therefore any research endeavour undertaken to understand information-related phenomena should begin with practical human experience, not with *mathesis*. The 'geometric' style of thinking does not grasp the whole picture and cannot presume to tell an exclusive, 'objective' truth about phenomena concerning human existence.[20]

To track the multiple threads and paths of Ciborra's phenomenological reconstruction of the field of information systems, particularly his analysis of technology and information as phenomena deeply intertwined with the lifeworld of human beings, would be a much too long story to tell here. However, three main threads seem to be persistent and recurrent enough in Claudio's phenomenological inquiries to deserve further treatment:

- the search for method
- the meaning of technology
- the definition of situated action.

The search for method

Discontent with the geometric style of thinking typical of the methodologies of formalization, measurement and calculation in good currency within the IS discipline, Ciborra took inspiration from Husserl's criticism of the Galileian paradigm of the sciences (Husserl, 1970/1936) to reflect on the practical inadequacies of structured systems development and business reengineering approaches. More than 70 years ago Edmund Husserl, the founder of transcendental phenomenology, highlighted the foundational role of the practices of everyday life in constituting the scientific method. The 'crisis' of the European sciences – Husserl claimed in one of his major works – arises because their mathematization cannot capture the messiness of the lifeworld of the individual agents and the meaning of their everyday experience. This is the very same problem that Ciborra spotted in most of the management and business methodologies of the ICT field:

Human existence,

> which is an essential ingredient of what information is, how the lifeworld gets encountered, defined, and reshuffled, ... how technology gets used every day. (Ciborra, 2004: 19)

is expunged and excluded from the clean, 'sanitized' procedures routinely applied in the development of ICT systems and applications. Having closely observed how designers, managers and users behave *in practice* in a number of case studies of large scale development projects for over a decade, and taking Husserl's diagnosis seriously, Ciborra argues that no development method or business plan may ever hope to be successful, or even reach an understanding of what goes on in organizations and business processes if it is unable to accept the messiness of the world and productively work with it. The everyday puzzles and riddles of the life of organizational actors, their day by day tinkering and hacking, their frustrations and accomplishments, their encounters with surprises and deviations – in other words, the phenomenology of their real life behaviour – should be placed at the centre stage of the researcher's concerns, and then, starting from them, one can eventually proceed to develop methods of intervention more tuned to the complexity of real life practices (Ciborra, 1998). Therefore a deeper understanding of the place and meaning of information systems in human life, claimed Ciborra, can be reached by marrying people's existential traits with the necessarily objectified characteristics of projects and methods.

The meaning of technology

In his co-authored article with Ole Hanseth (Ciborra and Hanseth, 1998; Chapter 5 in this book) Ciborra borrowed from Heidegger the notion of *Gestell* in order to enrich the analysis of large scale information infrastructures in corporate environments and gain a deeper understanding of technology as a phenomenon. According to Heidegger, the term *Gestell* denotes an ordering, an enframing, and is actually the way technology presents itself to us in the modern world – a set of 'in-order-to', enchained possibilities. But *Gestell* is not only 'structure' or 'architecture'; it is rather a dynamic, unfolding form of ordering, inasmuch as it also 'sets up' an available potential for the enactment of further ordering and 'bringing together'. Ciborra used this notion to describe the nature of information technology and the dynamics of information and communication infrastructures in great detail (Ciborra and Associates, 2001). Technology, particularly as it is deployed in the form of information and communication infrastructures, is not just a set of available tools or devices for doing work and for communication (Ehn, 1989; Winograd, and Flores, 1987), but an 'enframing', a way of ordering and connecting the world which is not immediately visible, as it constitutes the hidden, taken for granted background of our daily life activities; it then needs to be revealed or 'unveiled' through phenomenological analysis. One can see that a subtle thread runs in Claudio's evolving thought from the notion of the formative context, where the focus is on limited learning and cognitive and organizational inertia; to the idea of a 'platform organization', where attention instead is given to fluidity, opportunity and recombination; to large scale information infrastructures, where connecting and supporting functions are emphasized. All these concepts reveal Ciborra's enduring interest and efforts at capturing the underlying dynamics of Information Technology as it interacts with human practices and institutional arrangements. The notion of *Gestell* encapsulates them all. *Gestell*, transposed to the field of information systems, helps to unveil and appreciate essential properties of technology which have little to do with its being a set of tools, but rather have to do with how the world, as we encounter it, is enframed for us.

The idea of *Gestell*, together with the other fundamental Heideggerian notion of care *(Sorge)* leads Ciborra to a radical criticism of the strategic literature in information systems and to a new perspective on systems development and the management of technology. Particularly, the target of his critical concerns is the notion of 'strategic alignment' (Ciborra, 1997b; Broadbent and Weil, 1993;

Henderson and Venkatraman, 1993). Because they share the properties of *Gestell*, technology and large scale information and communication infrastructures, cannot be easily aligned by means of management and control strategies. Indeed, their essence and dynamics elude formalization and control. Eventually, successful *ex post* alignment, when it happens, is due to tinkering and serendipitous occurrences, not to deliberate *ex ante* strategy or method. Close field observation of the practical dealings of organizational agents (designers, managers and users) shows that they relentlessly pursue activities of *bricolage*, adjustment, coping and reinvention driven by their ongoing concerns with people, systems, applications, deadlines, mistakes. In other words, phenomenological analysis reveals that in the concrete situations of action in which humans are 'thrown' they are constantly 'affected' by what's going on and 'take care' of the people and things in the midst of uncertainty. Care denotes our primordial existential involvement with the world, that is, the fact that the world 'affects' our being before any thought or theory can be developed. Care is pre-cognitive and pre-theoretical, it is an ontological structure. Care taking implies familiarity with the surrounding world, intimacy with people, solicitousness in decision and action. As Ciborra says, care is a form of 'pious' management, a style of intervention 'that makes questioning the core activity of management research and practice' (Ciborra, 1997b: 79). Here, again, we can discern a thread linking the Heideggerian notion of care to other ideas entertained by Claudio. For instance, consider his adoption of the metaphor of *cultivation* (Dahlbom and Janlert, 1996). Large scale information systems and infrastructures, rather than being engineered or planned, are grown or nurtured by a careful, day by day activity of cultivation and breeding, which exploits the endogenous forces already at work and the evolutionary processes taking place. Consider also his introduction of the metaphor of *hospitality* in technology management and adoption. Hospitality suggests that technology is not just designed and 'plugged' into the organization, but is 'hosted' as a guest, and, precisely as hosts behave with guests, needs to be treated and related to with ambivalent strategies that at the same time show courtesy to the guest and anxiety raised by the strangeness of the guest (Ciborra, 1999b). Both cultivation and hospitality presuppose a care-structure, but the notion of care, in Ciborra's use of the Heideggerian concept, has a deeper existential connotation and sometimes even assumes an ethical sense.

In his effort to spell out the meaning of technology for human existence, we can appreciate the further step taken by Claudio away from his own previous thinking by comparing the notion of care with John Keats's idea of *Negative Capability*, which was a source of inspiration to Claudio for several years. Both care and *Negative Capability* call for a special concern and ability for understanding situations, both point to human skills that an agent must deploy to be able to understand, reflect and act when thrown into an uncertain situation, when 'facing Mystery'. But a crucial difference should not be missed: while *Negative Capability* is a rare quality in individuals and is essentially a peculiar mode of knowing, care stems from a pre-cognitive state of being and denotes a shared practical concern for the world.[21]

The notions of *Gestell*, Care and Concern (*Besorgen*) are further extended by Ciborra in his latest studies on e-government development projects in Jordan (Ciborra, 2005; Chapter 4 in this book) and on risk and digital technologies (Ciborra, 2006b, Chapter 3 in this book), in which he brings economic and phenomenological concepts together in an interesting way. In each of these studies Ciborra deepens his investigation of the challenges and implications of Information and Communication Technologies when they come to us as *Gestell*. In the Jordan case he shows how ICT, when applied to e-government initiatives for the purpose of economic and democratic development, on the one hand reveals the nature of the 'hosting' institutional framework and political culture and, on the other hand, creates new forms of market regulation and state control at the transnational level, becoming a new way to achieve more security in a world threatened by 'durable disorder'. Although this form of governance is deliberately and explicitly pursued and enforced in the interest of the market and the democracy, in reality it contains itself hidden sources of risk and disorder due to the 'drifting' of complex systems and infrastructures. The point that digital technologies, originally developed with the purpose of curbing risk in a variety of industries, may be themselves inherently exposed to (often incalculable) risks is further articulated in Ciborra's article on the *Imbrication of Representations* (Ciborra, 2006b). Again, drawing on Heidegger, Ciborra provides a phenomenological interpretation of risk which goes beyond economic calculus and managerial representations and stresses instead the existential sources of risk, recommending, in modelling risk,

> the need to stay close to, and to safeguard, some essential traits of human existence, in particular the intrinsic openness of life and its fundamental indeterminacy as the key source of our personal worry about risk. (Ciborra, 2006b: 1343)

In Ciborra's view, risk originates from our existential concern about an unknown, potentially dangerous world and from our care about people and things. Risk then, and our concern about it, can be looked at, phenomenologically, as 'care taking care of itself' (Ciborra, 2006b: 1343). Indeed, the project striving to an increasing 'representability' of the world, which is intrinsic to the deployment of sophisticated ICT infrastructures, generates side-effects, unexpected consequences, drifting, and runaway dynamics that increase our ignorance, therefore both our existential concerns for our lives and our concern for risk. Information Systems Research, Ciborra suggests, has not paid enough attention to ICT as a potential source of risk, and this is a gap that needs to be filled.[22]

The definition of 'situatedness'

Perhaps in no other area of research Ciborra departed from his previous ways of thinking and from the discipline's 'conventional wisdom' as in his phenomenological reconstruction of what a 'situation' and 'situated action' are. This thread of Claudio's critical inquiry concerns the nature of action and cognition rather than the design of information systems and infrastructures. However, it has a direct bearing on central conceptual dichotomies of the domains of information systems and knowledge management, namely planning vs situated action (Suchman, 1987), routine vs emergent, improvised action (Weick, 1993; Crossan and Sorrenti, 1996), explicit vs tacit knowledge (Nonaka and Takeuchi, 1995; Polanyi, 1967). In his revisitation of the nature of improvisation he essentially 'deconstructed' the purely cognitive view and crafted a phenomenological understanding of it (Ciborra, 1999a; Ciborra, 2004; Chapter 2 in this book). Going beyond a cognitive definition of improvisation as a 'mindset' (Weick, 1998) of the improvising agent (that is, a set of mental resources and skills) he regarded it as a 'mood', that is, 'a special disposition or attunement with the situation' (Ciborra, 2004). While in the Artificial Intelligence and the knowledge management literature improvisation is understood as a form of fast problem solving driven by ongoing, instantaneous feedback, Ciborra described improvisation as a form of extemporaneous, situated action – an event that happens 'outside' the normal flow of events and is driven by the mood by which an actor encounters a situation and moves within it, to his 'attunement' to the situation. By the same token, while in the cognitive perspective improvisation is opposed to planned activity (thus in improvisation thinking and doing, planning and execution become simultaneous), Ciborra contrasted it with other moods like panic and boredom, which also affect, in different ways, the manner by which an actor experiences time and 'tunes in' the situation. It is then the mood of the actor and his existential experience of time that ultimately define the meaning of a situation for the actor 'from *his* or *her* point of view', not (just) his cognitive ability at instant problem solving and acting (Ciborra, 2004; Chapter 2 in this book). Rather than (and before) 'states of mind', moods are 'states of being': they characterize the relationship between an actor, his situation, and his situated action in a pre-cognitive, existential fashion. Moods are the expressions of how one 'feels' or 'fares' in a situation, or rather of who one 'is' in the situation. Thus, following Heidegger, Ciborra suggests that there is no cognition without 'affectedness', without being emotionally or existentially affected by the situation. To wit, without affectedness there can not even be the experience of a situation (Ciborra, 2006a). Although Ciborra's contribution to this line of research reaches perhaps its deepest existential connotation, it is altogether of great consequence for a better understanding of situated practices and of the improvisational skills which are being increasingly appreciated in the management literature as important human and organizational assets to face the uncertainty of the contemporary business world. Ciborra's reflections on the notion of situation, together with his ideas about *bricolage* and care, point to new paths of research, bringing original new insights to the field of Information Systems and broadening the scope of the knowledge management disciplines.

Epilogue and legacy: a quest for being

In this short account I have tried to show how Claudio Ciborra's contributions to Information Systems Research have never been disjointed, since the early beginnings of his career, from a genuine concern for the social and human consequences of ICT, to the point that in the latest period of his life his inquiry into the nature of ICT merged more and more with questions about the place and meaning of it in human existence. In Ciborra's intellectual journey phenomenology was a constructive response to the challenges in the field of Information Systems that were revealed in his critical appraisal of IS development methods, strategic management of ICT, and organizational knowledge. But in phenomenology Claudio also found an answer to some of his deepest intellectual and existential concerns, which have been ever present all through his research career, being perhaps the inner engine of his intellectual quest. It is impossible to say in which direction Claudio, had he lived longer, would have pursued his phenomenological inquiries, and whether phenomenology would have been a safe harbour or just a temporary passage to proceed to further inquiries. For sure, all we can say is that with his wanderings across many theories and perspectives Ciborra strongly contributed to shape the profile and the agenda of the information systems discipline, which, beyond different points of view and ongoing controversies, has been enormously enriched by his work.

In my account I have also tried to show that the overall unity and coherence of Ciborra's work are to be found in the very process of research – something that he referred to as 'his method' (Ciborra, 2002), less in the variety of views and positions that he held, which often reveal unsettled tensions and inconsistencies. In other words, the research threads were many, the inquiry was one. This underlying coherence has not been noticed or appreciated enough by scholars, who have often been displaced and disoriented by what they perceived as sudden changes of direction and perspective, or whimsical choices they could not really understand. For example, some of his early colleagues regarded Claudio's switch from socio-technics and participatory system development to transaction cost economics as falling back to a rationalistic-positivistic position, a sort of ideological choice for the views of liberal economics, which were judged to be antithetic to the social and political ideology underlying the socio-technical approach. Later on, he upset the MIS people by denying validity to their deterministic, linear development and strategy frameworks, especially pointing at the theoretical platitude and the practical irrelevance of such frameworks. At a later stage of his research he displaced the Resource Dependency people, with whom he had done some work on learning models of the firm, by moving to phenomenology. And even in the latest years some of his LSE colleagues were puzzled when they saw that he kept working and teaching on Transaction Costs Economics and ICT, while at the same time he had wholly embraced phenomenology and was busy developing his phenomenological analysis of information systems. How could he possibly do that? People were always trying to cope with him, trying to catch up with his latest move, and often they were caught up in confrontations with him. Such puzzlements and misunderstandings can perhaps be cleared up if one considers Ciborra's lifelong dissatisfaction with the conditions of academic life, at least within the mainstream discipline, and his inquisitive spirit in approaching theories and perspectives. On the one hand, playing the role of the outsider and taking distinctive theoretical positions was part of Ciborra's way of practicing research and affirming his own identity in opposition to mainstream research and established academia. Claudio thrived in stirring up established situations, challenging ideas, raising controversies, confronting people, and upsetting the waters of the IS discipline. This was indeed a form of intervention in the field and the community, directed at provoking mutual (re)positioning, divergent thinking and new levels of understanding. One might therefore say that together with the 'inquiring' Claudio there always was a 'fighting' or 'political' Claudio, and they were one and the same.[23] On the other hand, if we consider his 'inquiring' side, Claudio never intended his engagement with a theoretical perspective as a lifelong commitment to it. He was essentially committed to digging out problems and revealing phenomena. Theories were for him lenses to look at and capture different features of the phenomenon of information. They never implied underlying ideological choices, but rather stances which had to do with discovery and understanding. His critical re-visitations of previous theories and methods were never done for the sake of critical destruction, but always undertaken with the goal of going beyond them to generate new insights and questions. Yet, at the same time it is undeniable that his fast-learning capability to absorb new ideas and master new theories provided a powerful resource for his 'political' action within the discipline.

In reading the following chapters one can then understand them both as steps of an ongoing process of questioning – *different kinds* of questioning around ICT – and as ways of taking different stances within a field of unsettled controversies. For sure they are not canned answers and solutions, as is often the case in academic publications. Indeed, the impression one gets by going through the chapters is that the Author invites us to look through different 'windows' opened on a possibly interesting landscape that needs to be explored. But one also gets the feeling that in spite of the shifting viewpoints and the strong articulations of his work the Author always keeps his eyes firmly focused on the very same, privileged target: the meaning of information systems in human life.

Undoubtedly, the main thrust of Ciborra's contribution to Information Systems Research has been in two major endeavours:

a) the development of an integrated theory of information systems and organizations based on transaction costs analysis, and
b) the phenomenological analysis of Information and Communication Technologies both as pervasive infrastructures of society and as mundane artifacts of our everyday life ('everyday things', Norman 1988).

If we take a look at Ciborra's Citation Record on the Harzing's Publish or Perish website on the internet, his influence on the IS community in these areas of research is quite impressive,[24] and still growing. Yet, in spite of these records, I would like to suggest that ultimately Claudio's legacy does not reside in a specific theory or field of applications, but rather in his idiosynchratic style of doing research, in his manner of being inquisitive and restlessly curious about things, asking questions, trying out answers, and moving forward to further questions. His style of inquiry stemmed from the kind of person he was, from his way of being, *beyond* or *before* his actual intellectual capabilities. The mobility of his ideas and positions reflected the mobility of his existence: both were always in a state of ferment and unsettledness. As a LSE colleague once remarked, he was never 'at rest' with himself. In a way, Claudio managed to turn himself into a one-man lab for carrying out intellectual experiments and practical interventions in the field of information systems. By so doing, in his quest he also made an existential use of himself. This was simply his way of being or perhaps the kind of being he wanted to attain.

However, Ciborra's story is not a one-man story. It is closely intertwined with the history of the IS discipline in the past three decades. He left us with a rich agenda that needs to be pursued further. Consider, for instance, the following threads:

- the study of situatedness and situated action in organizational analysis and in the design of interactive systems;
- the empirical analysis of the efficiency implications of ICT in organizations and economic systems, pointing to the appraisal of problems of business innovation, strategy, groupware, networks and outsourcing;
- the study of large scale Information and Communication Infrastructures and their implications for social development and democratic government;
- the still little explored area of the analysis of risk implications of digital technologies for contemporary society;
- the initiation of the social study of ICT and a broad reconceptualization of the essence and meaning of ICT in human affairs.

Most relevantly, Claudio's research achievements, of which his 'method' or style of research is a crucial one, opened up the discipline and made it more interesting by building an inner tension into it. He was a living example of how any research endeavour always thrives in the tension between tradition and projection to the future, between the experiences and things which make our world in the present and the enactment of events that re-set the clock of time and give new meaning to human activity and existence by opening up to future possibilities. This tension generates what phenomenologists call a 'horizon', that is, a limit line in the offing and a temporal boundary which characterize the way we live the situations of our daily life – who we are, what we do, and what we care about. The boundary can be aimed at, but never reached or overcome. Claudio experienced such existential tension in a particularly dramatic way, especially in his latest years, and was able to convert it felicitously into a remarkable scientific achievement. In the end, Claudio's intellectual inquiry and his quest for being were one and the same, and together they make his legacy to us.

A personal note, with acknowledgements

French historian Paul Veyne reminds us that 'writing history' is inevitably a retrospective reconstruction of past events, ordering them in a next–next-next sequence, which may not accurately reproduce the facts 'as they really happened' (Veyne, 1972). My account makes no exception. For sure Claudio's journey was more erratic than I was able to tell; his ride had ups and downs; his searching and finding was more serendipitous and occasional than I was able to convey; there was more tinkering, recombination and thematic overlapping in his work than my interpretation would suggest; and he faced tensions and inconsistencies in his research that perhaps I should have emphasized more. In my remembrances of him, he often had the *allure* of an errant knight wandering in the peripheral regions of the discipline's established kingdom and thriving in opposition and controversy, but at the same time striving for recognition. In writing this account I have made an effort to go back in time and immerse myself in things and events that I have shared with Claudio, and then to distance myself from them so that I could make them into a story. Due to my long research partnership and friendship with Claudio it has not been an easy thing to do, and often I felt caught between the contrasting pressures of biographical involvement and self-effacement. In the end, with all the limitations, this is the story I have been able to write.

In my work I have been helped by many colleagues and friends who have known Claudio Ciborra as a friend, colleague, or teacher, and have provided remembrances, points of view, and many valuable bits of information, sometimes even in short 'glimpses' of conversation, which have completed my collection of memories and enriched my own understanding of his work and personality. Therefore my individual 'authorship' owes much to their intellectual friendship and to our shared memory. It is obviously impossible for me to mention them all, but I am sure they know who they are. Here I wish to especially thank Chrisanthi Avgerou, Antonio Cordella, Ole Hanseth, Jannis Kallinikos, Frank Land, Lars Mathiassen and Andrea Resca for their helpful comments to earlier drafts. Together with Leslie Schneider and Piercarlo Maggiolini, they have also provided valuable information which has been useful in writing this account.

Notes

1. With this perspective in mind, by the mid 1970s an informal network of IS scholars had developed a growing interest in socio-technical ideas. Among them were Enid Mumford and Frank Land in the UK, Louis Davis and James Taylor in the US, Christiane Floyd in Germany, Adriano De Maio in Italy. In the next few years Claudio would become part of the network (personal communication by Frank Land).
2. In this group he met, among others, computer scientists Lars Mathiassen and Finn Kensing from Aarhus University (DK), social researchers Tamar Berman of the Work Research Institute in Oslo, Pelle Ehn of the Swedish Center for Working Life, and Leslie Schneider, an American cultural anthropologist then visiting at the Norwegian Institute of Social Research in Industry. Among other things, Leslie helped Claudio to establish his first connections with the American research community.
3. In particular, within a large national project jointly launched by the Iron and Metal Workers Union (NJMF) and the Norwegian Computing Center, Claudio Ciborra and Leslie Schneider studied the implementation of 'data agreements' betwen management and the unions in a variety of different government and industrial settings. One of the main goals of the project was to build knowledge in the union and the workers about computers and technology so as to reinforce their capacity to actively participate into change processes and to improve their contractual power. (personal communication of Leslie Schneider, e-mail dated 4 June 2008).

4. Ciborra visited UCLA in 1981/82 and its Center for the Quality of Working Life then headed by Louis Davis. Under the stimulus of William Ouchi he became immediately interested in transaction cost economics. This period can be considered a turning point in his career.
5. An earlier version of this paper was first presented at the 1985 ICIS Conference in Minneapolis, to an audience including leading researchers from MIT and other major US universities. This event, together with further contributions to ISR and Transaction Costs Theory, gained Ciborra the recognition and respect of the IS international community.
6. The poverty of the theoretical base of the MIS discipline was authoritatively stigmatized in those years by Aaron Wildawsky (1983). Even Jay Galbraith's celebrated book *Organizational Design* (Galbraith, 1977), which developed a more systematic connection between information technology, task uncertainty, and organizational structures, and was for many years an important reference for IT and OD researchers, including Ciborra, was at one point regarded by Claudio as 'incomplete'. Galbraith's approach did not account for empirically observable phenomena characterizing the behaviour of organizations and the daily life use of information, such as strategic misrepresentation, opportunism, rhetorics, a posteriori rationalization, camouflage, etc. (see Ciborra, 1987).
7. In developing his neo-institutional economics of information systems Claudio had fruitful exchanges with American scholars, among which Tom Malone and Charles Jonscher of the Sloan School of Management, Tora Bikson of RAND, Paul Strassman, and Margrethe Olson of New York University, with whom he published a paper on electronic work groups (Ciborra and Olson 1989),
8. Ciborra's interest and sensibility for the phenomena of noise and disorder in systems are reflected in his early co-authored article, published in *Human Relations*: 'A Methodological Inquiry of Organizational Noise in Sociotechnical Systems,' still written in a sociotechnical perspective. Research on this topic with Milan Politecnico colleagues Migliarese and Romano had started since the late 1970s. The thrust of the article is that out-of-the-norm events may bring unexpected variety into the smooth functioning of the system which, rather than being eliminated, can be exploited for the purpose of change, restructuring and innovation (Ciborra, Migliarese and Romano, 1984).
9. The problem of 'transition costs' generated by friction and inertia in organizational change was targeted by Claudio as early as 1986 in an unpublished manuscript 'Routine vs innovation: a phenomenologicalnote on limited learning', first draft, June 1986.
10. Personal communication to the author, Cambridge, MA, January 1987. Claudio repeatedly acknowledged that Shoshana Zuboff was at that time one of the rare persons to whom he could speak freely about his thoughts, feelings and aims with no fear of being misunderstood or dismissed.
11. The group included Victor Friedman, Shahaf Gal, Giovan Francesco Lanzara, Wim Overmeer, and Claudio Ciborra himself. The role of designing and coordinating the course was assigned to a different member every year. The course was held for five years, from 1991 to 1995. Ciborra resigned from his position as the head of the department in 1996, but taught at Theseus until 2000.
12. 'Again' means after Parmenides, Aristotle, and St. Thomas Aquinas, who were very influential on Heidegger's thought.
13. That is, what it means for something (anything) 'to be' (Dreyfus, 1991).
14. Ciborra taught at the University of Bologna from 1990 to 2001, in the Department of Organizations and Political Systems. Since 2001 he also taught the same course on the phenomenology of IT at IULM in Milan (Istituto Universitario di Lingue Moderne).
15. Researchers were working at the Universities of Gothenburg and Oslo, where Ciborra held part-time positions as a visiting professor. Bo Dahlbom, Ole Hanseth, Eric Monteiro and Kristin Braa, among others, were participating in the project. Claudio became particularly interested in the research work on information infrastructures and the economy of standards carried out by Ole Hanseth for his Phd thesis. Also, the interaction

with Bo Dahlbom, a philosopher working in the field of information systems and the head of the Swedish Viktoria Institute, was reported by Claudio himself to be particularly engaging. Together they talked about establishing the Mediterranean branch of the Viktoria Institute in Naples, which they called the 'Antenna in the South'.

16. At LSE Claudio worked closely with many scholars to a variety of projects and papers, particularly with Jan Angell, Chrisanthi Avgerou, Antonio Cordella, Tony Cornford, Jannis Kallinikos, Lucas Introna, Frank Land, Susan Scott, Carsten Sorensen and Edgar Whitley. Together with these colleagues he was finally able to establish a broad field of research on *The Social Study of ICT* at the Department of Information Systems of LSE at a more institutional level.
17. Claudio had encountered phenomenology as early as 1986, when he read a preliminary draft of Terry Winograd and Fernando Flores' *Understanding Computers and Cognition*, which drew extensively on Heidegger's views of tools and his distinction between 'ready-to-hand' and 'present-at-hand' in the analysis of computers, computation, and cognition (Winograd and Flores, 1987). But even before that, in 1986, he wrote a draft paper 'Routines vs. innovation: a phenomenological note on limited learning', in which he used Alfred Schutz's phenomenological concepts to explore problems of change and limited learning (first draft, unpublished manuscript, June 1986). Reportedly, strong stimuli to read Heidegger's *Being and Time* in 1995 were conversations with Anna Maria Morazzoni, a musicologist of Milan and a close friend of Claudio.
18. Both Heidegger's inquiries into the meaning of being and the essence of technology (Heidegger, 1962; Heidegger, 1978) and Husserl's critique of scientific method and emphasis on the primacy of everyday life provided Ciborra with interpretive tools for a phenomenological re-visitation of theoretical concepts and management issues which he had already dealt with and which were now reconsidered in a fresh new perspective.
19. Ciborra presented the 'vocabulary' in its most complete form in his *Labyrinths of Information* (2002), a collection of highly suggestive short essays, which can be regarded as his phenomenological testament. Half jokingly he called them 'words of wisdom'.
20. In his work Ciborra emphasized the phenomenological critique to formal scientific knowledge and the 'geometrization' of reality, disregarding the critical stance that phenomenology, especially in the works of Heidegger and Merleau-Ponty, also assumed towards culture, which is the background of human practices. If the cultural background is viewed as something that interferes with the immediacy of human experience and hides the true essence of reality, then it becomes difficult to understand why culture-embedded practices should allow a more authentic access to Being. Although Heidegger changed his position on history and culture in his later works, this is a broad ambiguity built in the entire phenomenological framework, of which Ciborra, according to Jannis Kallinikos, was apparently aware. Personal communication (e-mail dated 17 September 2008). I am indebted to Kallinikos for pointing out this problem to me.
21. To be more precise, both *Negative Capability* and *Care* point to a special kind of sensibility and openness to the world 'as it comes to us.' Agents exhibit *Negative Capability* when they don't ask why, what and how, don't reach out for pre-established objectives, but accept the ambiguity of a situation in order to interpret it, becoming 'instruments' for sensing and understanding. Agents 'care' about a situation when they let themselves be affected by the situation in a manner that their 'being' is attuned to the situation. Here the understanding of a situation has its roots in how-we-are-in-the-world, which is a pre-cognitive existential trait.
22. Ciborra's latest studies on social development, e-government and the risk implications of ICT reveal his growing concern for ICT and globalization issues. He pursued further this line of research in a World Bank funded project on ICT and institutional trust in Latin America countries with his LSE colleagues Chrisanthi Avgerou, Antonio Cordella and Jannis Kallinikos, a project that he could not complete due to his premature death. See the LSE working paper (Avgerou, Ciborra, Cordella, Kallinikos and Smith, 2006).

23. I am indebted to Lars Mathiassen for pointing out to me the more political aspects of Ciborra's work and role within the IS community, (personal communication, e-mail of 29 August 2008). I would only add that the inquirying and the fighting Claudio are not necessarily at odds with one another. If we want to stick to the phenomenological jargon, both aspects were part of Claudio's way of being-in-the-world, and certainly they were part of his style of research (his 'method'). In other words, his way of doing research reflected his mode of being.
24. The website and the data have been signalled to me by Lars Mathiassen (e-mail of 22 June 2008). *http://www.harzing.com/resources.htm#/pop.htm* (accessed 22 June 2008). The Author Impact Analysis is based on Google Scholar.

References

Andreu R. and Ciborra, C. (1996). Organizational learning and core capabilities development: The role of IT, *Journal of Strategic Information Systems* **5**: 111–127.

Avgerou C., Ciborra, C. and Land, F. (2004). (eds) *The Social Study of Information and Communication Technology*, Oxford: Oxford University Press.

Avgerou, C., Ciborra, C., Cordella, A., Kallinikos, J. and Smith, M.L. (2006). *E-government and trust in the state: lessons from electronic tax systems in Chile and Brazil*, Working Paper Series 146, Department of Information Systems, London School of Economics and Political Science, London, UK, May, pp. 1–38.

Boland R. and Hirschheim, R.A. (1987). (eds) *Critical Issues in Information Systems Research*, Chichester: Wiley and Sons.

Broadbent M. and Weill, P. (1993). Improving business and information strategy alignment: learning from the banking industry, *IBM Systems Journal* **32**(1): 162–179.

Ciborra C. (1981). Information Systems and Transactions Architecture, *Journal of Policy Analysis and Information Systems* **5**(4): 305–324.

Ciborra C. (1983a). The social costs of information technology and participation in system design, in U. Briefs, C.Ciborra and L. Schneider, (eds) *Systems Design for, with, and by the Users*, Amsterdam: North Holland Publishing Company, pp. 41–50.

Ciborra C. (1983b). Markets, Bureaucracies and Groups in the Information Society: An Institutional Appraisal of the Impacts of Information technology, *Information Economics and Policy* **1**(2): 145–160.

Ciborra C. (1984). Management Information Systems: A Contractual View, in Th.M.A. Bemelmans (ed) *Beyond Productivity: Information Systems Development for Organizational Effectiveness*, Amsterdam: Elsevier Science Publisher, pp. 135–145.

Ciborra C. (1986). *Routine vs innovation: a phenomenological note on limited learning*, first draft, June 1986, unpublished paper.

Ciborra C. (1987). Reframing the role of computers in organizations – the transaction costs approach, *Office Technology and People* **3**: 17–38.

Ciborra, C. (1990). X-Efficiency, Transaction Costs, and Organizational Change, in P. Weiermair (ed.), *Studies in Economic Rationality*, Ann Arbor, MI: University of Michigan Press, pp. 205–222.

Ciborra C. (1992). From thinking to tinkering: the grassroots of strategic information systems, in *The Information Society* **8**: 297–309.

Ciborra C. (1993). *Teams, markets, and systems*, Cambridge, UK: Cambridge University Press.

Ciborra C. (1996). The Platform Organization: Recombining Strategies, Structures, and Surprises, *Organization Science* **7**(2): 103–118.

Ciborra C. (ed.) (1997a). *Groupware and Teamwork*, Chichester: John Wiley.

Ciborra C. (1997b). De profundis? Deconstructing the concept of strategic alignment, *Scandinavian Journal of Information Systems* **9**(1): 67–82.

Ciborra C. (1998). Crisis and foundations: an inquiry into the nature and limits of models and methods in the information systems discipline, *Journal of Strategic Information Systems* **7**: 5–16.

Ciborra C. (1999a). Notes on improvisation and time in organizations, *Accounting, Management and Information Technologies* **9**: 77–94.
Ciborra C. (1999b). Hospitality and IT, *PrimaVera* Working Paper 99–02, University of Amsterdam, Department of Accountancy and Information Management, pp. 1–14.
Ciborra C. and Associates (2001). *From Control to Drift: The Dynamics of Corporate Information Infrastructures*. Oxford: Oxford University Press.
Ciborra C. (2002), *The Labyrinths of Information: Challenging the Wisdom of Systems*. Oxford: Oxford University Press.
Ciborra C. (2004). Encountering information systems as a phenomenon, in C. Avgerou, C. Ciborra, and F. Land (eds), *The Social Study of Information and Communication Technology*, Oxford: Oxford University Press, pp. 17–37.
Ciborra C. (2005). Interpreting e-government and development: efficiency, trasnparency or governing at a distance? *Information Technology and People* **18**(3): 260–279.
Ciborra C. (2006a). The mind or the heart? It depends on the (definition of) situation, Claudio Ciborra, *Journal of Information Technology* **21**(3): 129–139.
Ciborra C. (2006b). Imbrications of representations: Risk and Digital Technologies, *Journal of Management Studies* **43**(6): 1339–1356.
Ciborra C. and Hanseth, O. (1998). From Tool to Gestell: Agendas for Managing the Information Infrastructure, *Information Technology and People* **11**(4): 305–327.
Ciborra C. and Jelassi, T. (eds) (1994). *Strategic Information Systems*, Chichester: John Wiley.
Ciborra C. and Lanzara, G.F. (1989). Change and formative contexts in information systems development, in H.K. Klein and K.Kumar (eds), *System development for human progress*, Amsterdam: North Holland, pp. 21–40.
Ciborra C. and Lanzara, G.F. (1990). Designing Dynamic Artifacts: Computer Systems as Formative Contexts,' in P. Gagliardi (ed.), *Symbols and Artifacts: Views of the Corporate Landscape*, Berlin: Walter De Gruyter Publ. Co., pp. 147–165.
Ciborra C. and Lanzara, G.F. (1994). Formative Contexts and Information Technology: Understanding the Dynamics of Innovation in Organizations, *Accounting, Management, and Information Technology* **4**(2): 61–86.
Ciborra C., Migliarese, P. and Romano, P. (1984) A Methodological Inquiry of Organizational Noise in Sociotechnical Systems, *Human Relations* **37**(8): 565–588.
Ciborra C. and Olson, M.H. (1989). Encountering electronic work groups: a transaction costs perspective, *Office Technology and People* **4**(4): 285–298.
Coase R. H. (1937). The nature of the firm, *Economica* **4**(November): 386–405.
Coase R. H. (1960). The problem of social cost, *The Journal of Law and Economics* **3**: 1–44.
Crossan M. and Sorrenti, M. (1996). Making sense of improvisation, in J.P. Walsh and A.S.Huff (eds), *Advances in Strategic Management*, Greenwich, CT: JAI Press, **14**: 155–180.
Dahlbom B. and Janlert, L.E. (1996). *Computer Future*, Department of Informatics, Goteborg University, unpublished paper.
Dahlbom B. and Mathiassen, L. (1993). *Computers in Context: The Philosophy and Practice of Systems Design*, London: Blackwell.
Davis G.B. and Munro, M.C. (1977). Determining management information needs: a comparison of methods, *MIS Quarterly*, June: 55–66.
DeMarco T. (1978). *Structured analysis and systems specification*, New York: Yourdon Press.
Dijkstra E. F. (1976). *A discipline of programming*, Englewood Cliffs, NJ: Prentice-Hall.
Dreyfus, H. L. (1994). *Being-in-the-World*. Cambridge, MA: The MIT Press.
Ehn P. (1988). *Work-oriented design of computer artifacts*, Stockholm: Arbetslivscentrum.
Feldman, M.S. and March, J.G. (1981). Information in organizations as signal and symbol, *Administrative Science Quarterly* **26**(2): 171–186.
Flores F. and Ludlow, J.J. (1981). Doing and speaking in the office, in G.Fish and R. Sprague (editors) *DSS: Issues and Challenges*, London: Pergamon Press.
Galbraith J. (1977). *Organization design*, Reading, MA: Addison-Wesley
Heidegger M. (1962). *Being and Time*, New York: Harper and Row (original German Edition: 1927).

Heidegger M. (1978). The question about technology, in *Basic Writings*, London: Routledge.
Henderson J.C. and Venkatraman, N. (1993). Strategic alignment: leveraging information technology for transforming organizations, *IBM Systems Journal* **32**(1): 4–16.
Hirschheim R., Klein, H. K. and K. Lyytinen, K. (1996). Exploring the Intellectual Structures of Information Systems Development: A Social Action Theoretic Analysis, *Accounting, Management and Information Technology* **6**(1/2): 1–64.
Husserl E. (1970). *The Crisis of European Sciences and Transcendental Phenomenology*, Evanston, Il: Northwestern University Press (original German edition: 1936).
Jackson M. (1983). *System Development*, Englewood Cliffs, NJ: Prentice-Hall.
Keen P. and Scott Morton, M. (1978). *Decision Support Systems: An Organizational Perspective*, Reading, MA: Addison-Wesley.
Lyytinen K. and Hirschheim, R. (1987). Information systems failures: A survey and classification of the empirical literature, *Oxford Surveys in Information Technology* **4**: 257–309.
Nonaka I. and Takeuchi, H. (1995). *The Knowledge-creating Company*, Oxford: Oxford University Press.
Norman D.A. (1988). *The Design of Everyday Things*, New York, NY: Basic Books.
Nygaard K. (1983). Participation in System Development. The Task Ahead, in U. Briefs, C.Ciborra and L. Schneider (eds), *Systems Design for, with, and by the Users*, Amsterdam: North Holland Publishing Company, pp.19–25.
Polanyi M. (1967). *The Tacit Dimension*, New York: Anchor Books.
Schön D.A. (1987). *Educating the Reflective Practitioner*, San Francisco: Jossey-Bass Publishers.
Simon H.A. (1973). Applying information technology to organization design, *Public Administration Review* **May–June**: 268–278.
Simon H.A. (1976). *Administrative Behavior*, New York: The Free Press.
Suchman L. (1987). *Plans and Situated Actions*, Cambridge, UK: Cambridge University Press.
Thompson J. (1967). *Organizations in Action*, New York: Russell Sage.
Veyne P. (1972). *Comment on ecrit l'histoire*, Paris: Editions du Seuil.
Weick K.E. (1993). The Collapse of Sensemaking in Organizations: The Mann Gulch Disaster, *Administrative Science Quarterly* **38**: 628–652.
Weick K.E. (1998). Improvisation as a mindset for organizational analysis, *Organization Science* **9**(5): 543–555.
Wildavsky, A. (1983). Information as an organizational problem, in *Journal of Management Studies* **20**(1): 29–40.
Williamson O.E. (1975). *Markets and Hierarchies: Analysis and Antitrust Implications*, New York, NY: The Free Press.
Williamson O.E. (1981). The economics of organization: the transaction costs approach, in *American Journal of Sociology* **87**(3): 548–577.
Williamson O.E. (1985). *The Economic Institutions of Capitalism*, New York: McMillan.
Winograd T. and Flores, F. (1987). *Understanding Computers and Cognition*, Norwood, NJ: Ablex Publishing Company.
Wisemann C. (1985). *Strategy and Computers*, Homewood, IL: Dow Jones-Irwin.
Yourdon, E. (1989). *Modern Structured Analysis*, Englewood Cliffs, NJ: Prentice-Hall.
Zuboff, S. (1988). *In the Age of the Smart Machine: The Future of Work and Power*, New York: Basic Books.

Part I

Tracing Ciborra's Thought: From Institutional Economics to Phenomenology

1

The Mind or the Heart? It Depends on the (Definition of) Situation*

Claudio U. Ciborra

> Dorabella: 'Nel petto un Vesuvio d'avere mi par'
> *(In my breast is like having a Vesuvius)*
>
> from Cosi' Fan Tutte – Da Ponte – Mozart

> *The mob within the heart police cannot suppress.*
>
> E. Dickinson

> *Unter jedem Gedanken steckt ein Affekt.*
> *(Under any thought hides an affect)*
>
> F. Nietzsche

> *We must acknowledge drives (emotions)*
> *as the most primitive manifestations of the active principle*
> *by which we grasp knowledge and hold it.*
>
> M. Polanyi

Introduction

These days the adjective 'situated', the noun 'situation', the Latin expression *'in situ'*, and the abstract concept of 'situatedness', are liberally employed by those researchers and scholars who want to take and articulate alternative approaches to the study of organizations, the analysis of knowledge and change, the design of sophisticated technical systems, and in general the understanding of the complex interactions between people and technologies. These alternative perspectives have been developed and deployed against the positivist paradigm in social and organizational inquiry (Burrell and Morgan, 1979) and the normative discourse in organization science aimed at finding law-like relationships among organizational facts, events and behaviours (Deetz, 1996). They support especially the interpretivist paradigm, but are also employed in other radical or critical discourses.

A few examples taken from the recent organization theory and information systems literatures exemplify the 'situated' perspectives. In the theory of organizational change triggered by the introduction of technological innovations, Orlikowski (1996) contrasts 'situated change' to planned, deterministic and radical change. In relation to knowledge management Schultze and Leidner (2002) illustrate an interpretive discourse, which highlights 'the dynamic and situated nature of knowledge' (p. 224). In a more post-modern perspective, Haraway (1991) urges the abandonment of the study of formalized knowledge in favour of 'situated knowledges'. In her seminal research on planning in relation to expert systems and human communication, Suchman (1987) contrasts 'planned vs. situated action', suggesting that designers ought to develop systems and programs apt to take into account the emerging circumstances of action. Orr (1996) uses the situated action perspective to study how repairmen actually fix photocopier breakdowns during their maintenance interventions. Bricolage and improvisation (Brown and Duguid, 1991) are forms of situated action that are important in organizational breakdowns and emergencies, (Weick, 1993) and when operating in those turbulent environments that high tech companies routinely face (Ciborra, 1996). Lave and Wenger (1991) unveil the characteristics of learning as a 'situated process' and the importance of situatedness of experience in communities of practice (Wegner, 1998). The concept also crosses other disciplinary boundaries, from Artificial Intelligence (AI) (Clancey, 1997) to media studies, where scholars write about the 'situated culture' in which we are part through networks of direct and interpersonal communication (O'Sullivan *et al.*, 2003, p. 8).

All these notions are so taken-for-granted within the interpretive approaches in contemporary social and organizational studies, that when Orlikowski (2002) sets out to enlarge and enrich Giddens' (1984) structuration theory framework for analyzing the use of information technology in organizations, she employs the terms situated/situation thirty one times in a single paper, without ever feeling the need to define them.

A common denominator in the discourses that introduce or use the notion of situatedness is their explicit, but more often cursory or implicit, reference to phenomenology (usually via ethnomethodology), as the original source of the concept. Thus, Suchman (1987, p. 39) recalls Dreyfus' (1991) introductory work to Heidegger to highlight the 'transparency' of the situated character of action. When Winograd and Flores want to illustrate the importance of being 'thrown in the situation' for grasping the more abstract notions of decision and information, they refer to Heidegger (1962) and Dreyfus (1991). Wenger (1998, p. 281, note 35) also sees one of the sources for the social theory of learning and communities of practice in the theories of situated experience based on the phenomenological philosophy of Martin Heidegger. In technology design Robertson (2003) notes that phenomenological approaches related to situated action have 'played a major role in the shaping and progress of Computer Supported Collaborative Work' systems. Finally, in a recent monograph on action, systems and their embodiment in social practices, Dourish (2002, p. 121) pays his debt to the importance of the 'situated' perspective, indicating that 'Suchman's work can be related directly to the work of the phenomenologists. In that Suchman's work is in the ethnomethodological tradition established by Harold Garfinkel, who himself drew extensively on the work of Alfred Schutz', who, we may add, drew heavily on the research of Husserl (1970) and Heidegger (1962), the founding fathers of phenomenology.

Unfortunately, if our tribute to the original roots of the concept of situatedness expresses an authentic commitment, and not just a lip service to the founding fathers, we are bound to encounter a crisis caused by a major oblivion. The best way to illustrate the crisis the current liberal use of the notion of situatedness faces is to refer back to Orlikowski's 2002 methodologically influential paper on the 'practice lens'. In sharp contrast with the thirty one quotes of situated/situatedness, other terms are mentioned in the same article, albeit only three times: emotion/ emotional. The latter terms are neither defined nor actually used throughout the paper, and interestingly one of the three mentions can be found in a footnote where the author thanks an unknown reviewer for having reminded her about 'the importance of emotional connections in people's use of technologies'(p. 425, note 8). For a reflective reader who has at heart the phenomenological roots and the wider tradition in which the notion of situatedness was first launched all this should sound at best puzzling. To wit, German is the original language of phenomenology. 'Situated' is the translation of the German 'befindlich'; 'situatedness' is 'Befindlichkeit'. The latter, discussed in Section 29 of Heidegger's *Being and Time*, has been infelicitously translated as 'state of mind'(Heidegger, 1962, p. 172) (see Dreyfus, 1991, p. 168). In any event, 'Wie ist Ihre Befindlichkeit?' is a courtesy form in German for asking: 'How are you?' Hence, the original term befindlich not only refers to the circumstances one finds himself or herself in, but also to his or her 'inner situation', disposition, mood, affectedness and emotion. In particular, Heidegger (1962, p. 182) states that understanding (i.e. cognition) is always situated, meaning that 'it always has its mood'. In other words, situatedness refers in its original meaning to both the ongoing or emerging circumstances of the surrounding world and the inner situation of the actor. Surprisingly, concern for the inner situation, or even the 'state of mind' of the actor, cannot be found in any of the contemporary texts that make liberal use of the idea of situatedness. Hence, understandably, the *de facto* lack of hospitality for the notion of emotion in Orlikowski's leading article on the situatedness of technology use.

The main purpose of this paper is to address such a troubling 'situation' head on and counter the oblivion of the original roots that the notion of situatedness sports in contemporary discourses once one trespasses philosophy disciplinary boundaries. It does so by carrying out a detailed comparison between the original and the more recent treatments of the concept. In order to overcome the superficial cacophony largely due to its ubiquitous use, some tough methodological questions need to be addressed, such as what are the contours of a situated understanding of organizational life and technology use; can a researcher extract himself or herself from the situation being described; how and to what extent can a situation be subject to an objectifying empirical analysis; and last but not least, what is the role of emotions, moods, or dispositions of the heart in (the study of) a situation?

The paper aims at providing new background materials and a first discussion of their implications, so that a fresh questioning around the notion of situatedness can start in the fields of management studies, organization theory and information systems, especially among those interested in seeking and developing alternatives to the positivist perspectives.

The organization of the argument is as follows. First, the meaning of situatedness in the recent literature on information technology and organizations needs to be assessed in greater detail. What is really meant by situated action, learning, change etc.? Second, since such an investigation still leads to fairly vague definitions and statements, one also needs to look at the few controversies in the literature generated by opponents to the situatedness perspectives, in particular in organizational theory and cognitive science (specifically, AI). Third, two case studies will be put forward to spell out similarities and differences between the current renditions of the situated perspective and the original one. The case studies are the empirical investigation of situated action as carried out by Suchman (1987), while the other is extracted from the early lectures on the phenomenology of religious life given by the young Heidegger less than a decade before the publication of his opus *Being and Time* in 1927. The comparative exercise is aimed at eliciting in a systematic fashion aspects related to the background, scope and articulation of the different definitions of situatedness, their methodological implications, how the empirical material is collected and interpreted and the main conclusions drawn. Concluding remarks summarize the new tasks that lie ahead if one wants to take situatedness more seriously and comprehensively, possibly within the scope of a renewed, authentic phenomenological tradition.

A closer examination

Critics may have a point when expressing the impossibility of identifying a well-delineated research position on situatedness, and rather having to deal with a whole congeries of closely related views (Vera and Simon, 1993). Namely, it is difficult to establish the precise contours of the contemporary use of the term situated in social and organizational analysis, in particular when one wants to establish what are its actual links with phenomenology. In the following is our attempt to come to grips with what the most quoted and influential authors had in mind when launching and using the term in the eighties. In AI and management information systems fields, Winograd and Flores (1986) briefly mention the importance of the situation in which understanding takes place and to support their line of argument they quote a passage from Gadamer, a student of Heidegger, which evokes the difficulty of capturing (let alone modelling) the subtleties of a situation: 'To acquire an awareness of a situation is, however, always a task of particular difficulty. The very idea of a situation means that we are not standing outside it and hence are unable to have any objective knowledge of it. We are always within the situation and to throw light on it is a task that is never entirely completed' (Gadamer, 1975, quoted in Winograd and Flores, 1986, p. 29).

In her work of the same period, Suchman (1987) defines situated actions simply as: 'actions taken in the context of particular, concrete circumstances...the circumstances of our actions are never fully anticipated and are continuously changing around us…situated actions are essentially ad hoc' (pp. viii–ix). The notion of situatedness is crucial in order for Suchman to show that the foundation of actions is not plans, but 'local interactions with our environment, more or less informed by reference to abstract representation of situations and of actions' (p. 188).

Soon after, Lave and Wenger (1991) express their dissatisfaction with the vagueness of the definitions of situatedness in the literature, also feeling uneasy about their narrowness: 'On some occasions 'situated' seemed to mean merely that some of people's thoughts and actions were located in space and time. On other occasions, it seemed to mean that thought and action were social…, or that they were immediately dependent for meaning on the social setting that occasioned them' (pp. 32–33). In order to discuss the features of situated learning that takes place within communities of practice, they suggest to go beyond the notion of situatedness as an empirical attribute of everyday activity. Instead, they propose to look at it as an overarching theoretical perspective, that is as 'the basis of claims about the relational character of knowledge and learning, about the negotiated character of meaning and about the concerned…nature of learning activity for the people involved' (p. 33). This more general perspective implies that there is no activity that is not situated and underlies the need for a 'comprehensive understanding involving the whole person' (*ibid.*) Unfortunately, the latter idea is not developed any further, and their association between situated understanding and the whole person remains unexplored both theoretically and empirically. Ten years later, these ideas and concepts are very much in use within the broadly defined interpretivist accounts of learning, knowledge management and technical innovation, but little has been added towards their deepening and clarification: a sort of taken for granted adoption prevails, possibly becoming a new (alternative) management fad. On the same account, references to phenomenology are often made, but never quite fully explored and exploited. Collateral aspects are mentioned such as transparency, ready-at-handiness and so on (see for example Suchman, 1987, p. 39) but nobody actually seems to quote Section 29 of *Being and Time* where Heidegger (1962, pp. 172–182) introduces the notion of situatedness (Befindlichkeit), contrasting it with the privileged role attributed then (and now) to understanding, cognition and the purely mental. Such an account can be found in Dreyfus (1991, Chapter 10 on Affectedeness), but only within the boundaries of a specialized philosophical study of the first Division of *Being and Time*. Winograd, Flores and Suchman have been influenced by Dreyfus' work, hence the interesting cross-fertilization from philosophy into computer science, anthropology and organizational theory taking place on the West Coast at the end of the seventies. Still, the definitions these authors deploy seem to remain on the surface, not exploiting all their ramifications: in particular, factors such as emotions or moods (part of the comprehensive understanding of the 'whole person') are not picked up, neither then nor more recently. Lack of proper references to phenomenology, while using its ascendance, may also induce the reader not versed in philosophy to believe that what these authors say about situatedness is indeed all what phenomenology has had to say on the subject. The consequence is a non-problematic use of the terms situated/situatedness by scholars and practitioners who embrace the interpretivist or radical perspectives in management and organization studies. Those terms end up meaning just 'context' or 'emerging circumstances' of action and knowledge.

Debate and controversies

Another means to spell out the definition of situatedness in the contemporary debate is to examine the unfolding, and the temporary outcomes, of recent controversies around the scope and utilization of the concept in both organization theory and cognitive science/AI.

Within the former, Contu and Willmott (2003) address the situated learning theory critically, especially its scope. They do not examine situatedness *per se*, but the way they look at the dissemination and practice of situated learning elicits some features of the interpretivist and phenomenological approaches as they are being applied today especially in the corporate world. The authors acknowledge first that situated learning is a conceptualization that offers an alternative to cognitive theories of learning. While in the latter learning is portrayed as a cognitive process involving a selective transmission of abstract elements of knowledge from one context (i.e. the classroom) to the site of their application (the workplace), Lave and Wenger (1991) see learning as integral to everyday practices, to the lived-in world. Looking at learning as a situated process means appreciating that it is embodied (lived-in), historically and culturally embedded. Furthermore, Contu and Willmott note that the new perspective does include a due attention to the exercise of power and control in organizations. They point out, however, that the subsequent popularization of the idea of situated learning, carried out for example by Brown and Duguid (1991) and Orr (1996) with the notion of communities of practice, has adopted a more conservative approach, casting situated learning as 'a medium, and even as a technology, of consensus and stability' (Contu and Willmott, 2003, p. 284). This is the outcome of a subtle cleansing process, whereby the organizational context of learning is looked at 'in terms of a transparent background rather than a contested history' (*ibid.*, p. 293) In particular, the situation of learning (typically, the community of practice) is conceived as 'unified and consensual, with minimal attention being paid to how learning practices are conditioned by history, power, and language' (*ibid.*).

Without going further into the detail of this critique, and accepting that the focus on power and historicity has got lost in the popularization of the concept of situated learning (but were these dimensions adequately emphasized by Lave and Wenger, to begin with, or yet again just mentioned in passing, like their quick reference to the 'whole person', subsequently not elaborated any further?), one should not be surprised if most of the 'situatedness studies' end up supporting a consensus and stability framework for organizational analysis and design. This is often the way any interpretive discourse is portrayed lately: as a discourse that 'acknowledges the multi-vocal fragmented, and conflicted nature of society, yet also focuses on the integrative values that allow organizations and communities to function in harmony' (Schultze and Leidner, 2002). Note that the accusation of a consensus and stability bias is then extended to the root disciplines of the interpretive discourse, i.e. ethnomethodology and phenomenology. So that authors ranging from Burrell and Morgan (1979) to Deetz (1996) have felt it necessary to put next to the interpretive perspectives others that highlight radical change and transformation, radical humanism, critical and dialogic discourses, and so on (see also Crotty, 1998).

A more pointed critique has been put forward within the AI/cognitive science fields by Vera and Simon (1993) in a special issue of Cognitive Science dedicated to the situated action paradigm. Recall that researchers like Suchman (1987) take the view that 'plans as such neither determine the actual course of situated action nor adequately reconstruct it' (p. 3). But plans are precisely the main form of symbolic representation on which AI systems designed to interact with the environment are usually grounded: in this way the situated action idea is aimed at undermining those efforts in AI and robotic research based on planning programs. The counterargument put forward by Vera and Simon (1993) states that symbolic systems *are* able to interact with the situation by receiving and processing sensory stimuli from the world. Such systems can deal with the reckoning of local circumstances, perceive and represent social relations if they have an impact on the system and produce appropriate responses even for temporally demanding tasks embedded in complex environments. For example, if Suchman's (1987) concern is the mutual intelligibility between people and machines in a situation of technology use, (see the case study below) then Vera and Simon (1993) indicate that such an understanding, and the correlated situated actions, cannot obtain without internal symbolic representations, learning, planning and problem solving programs which feed upon them. In sum, 'the term situated action can best serve as name for those symbolic systems that are specifically designated to operate adaptively in real time to complex environments... It in no sense implies a repudiation of the hypothesis that intelligence is fundamentally a property of appropriately programmed symbol systems' (p. 47). Situated action is here regarded as an approach homogenous, though in competition, with the ones of cognitive science and AI. It differs only for a matter of degree: can a symbol-based system be so sophisticated to capture emerging circumstances? Can it be so rich to represent embedding networks of social relations? Can it be so fast to perform meaningful action on the fly? In principle yes, reply the cognitive scientists: when reconstructing situated decision making symbolic representations of the ongoing problem space can be drawn, algorithms can be identified, problem solving programs can be written, which include the stuff AI applications are made of: plans; if-then-elses; means-ends chains, etc. In such a view, a physical symbol system interacts with the external environment by receiving sensory stimuli that it converts into symbol structures to be stored in a memory device, and it acts upon the environment in ways determined by the newly acquired symbol structures. The memory is an indexed encyclopaedia, where representations of external situations are stored as they come in. Stimuli coming from the environment invoke the appropriate index entries, and so on. In other words, cognitive scientists argue that one can design and build symbol systems 'that continually revise their description of the problem space and the alternatives available to them' (Vera and Simon, 1993, p. 13). This mimics one of the key ideas of the situated action literature, i. e. the importance of moment by moment capture of the full situation of action. To be sure, the controversy lies in whether highly adaptive symbolic systems can actually be built. Suchman reviews the developments of AI and the various attempts at representing situations, for example, through scripts, (Schank and Abelson, 1977) and sees the task of reconstructing a meaningful knowledge background and context of action as infinitely long, hence unachievable in practice. In the end, Suchman insists, the situation cannot be fully translated into a series of symbols, or a mental state. It is something 'outside our heads that, precisely because it is non-problematically there, we do not think about' (p. 47). It is not just knowledge about the world, it is the world as an inexhaustibly rich resource for action (pp. 43 and 47).

Two case studies

The stage is now set to compare the contemporary perspectives on situated action, and their claim to constitute an alternative to the positivist and cognitive views of learning, knowledge, change and organizations, with the original thinking tried out early on within phenomenology. The recent availability of the teaching notes and lecture transcripts of the courses that Heidegger gave between 1919 and 1926 (before the publication of *Being and Time*), offers fresh material made of discussions, investigations and applications of the emerging phenomenological method to a range of domains, also suitable for utilization for our present purpose, in particular the investigation of what is a situation, why to study it and how to analyze it. In his early courses held at Freiburg and Marburg Universities Heidegger addresses precisely these questions (to be sure, among many other directions of inquiry), and on the basis of his answers we can try to trace in what direction our understanding of situatedness has evolved when jumping from continental philosophy around WWI to the recent, mostly Californian renditions imported into anthropology, organization theory and information systems, and ascertain what went lost, or what was gained along the decades in translating 'befindlich' into the contemporary 'situated'.

To this end we pick two case studies to be compared in a systematic fashion. As representative of the contemporary school of thought we select the research on the limits of planning and the power of situatedness by Suchman (1987). The reason is its comprehensiveness associated with the influence it has had on different domains such as cognitive science, AI, human-computer interaction, organization theory and learning theories (Heath and Luff, 2000). Furthermore, Suchman's research is empirically well grounded and deals more than other works with issues of method, in particular how to study situated action in a real setting. Heidegger's lecture notes on the Phenomenology of Religious Life, a course held in the winter semester 1921 offer the material for the second case study: the analysis of the situation of the early Christian communities, and in particular of what was the situation of being an early Christian as gleaned through the Letters of St. Paul (Heidegger, 2004).

In terms of the amount of detail presented here, the balance is definitely tilted in favour of Heidegger's phenomenological interpretation of the Pauline Letters for a number of reasons. First, Suchman's work is widely available and read in our scientific community. Second, many essential points of her study have already been mentioned and used in the first part of this paper. Third, Heidegger's early lectures have been published in German in the last ten years and begin to be available in an English translation only now: so, it is new material that needs to be reported more extensively. Finally, it is also a matter of restoring a balance. Too many times the contemporary studies of situated action and learning make only a cursory reference to phenomenology: a short quote from *Being and Time* seems to suffice even for the more attentive scholar. And, as noted above, the quote never seems to refer to the section dedicated to situatedness/Befindlichkeit! Instead, we aim at giving to the original notion and its methodological implications the space they deserve within the limits and constraints of the present publication. In any case, the skewed treatment of the cases contains no judgement on their respective grounding, validity or importance. The materials of the two studies are presented in a consistent manner, structuring them into five main subsections: background and motivation; definitions of situatedness; methodology of inquiry; findings and research outcomes.

The first case study – the situation: coping with a complex photocopying job

Background and motivation

The original audience of Suchman's research is constituted by designers of intelligent machines, and colleagues in the cognitive sciences. For them, busy in constructing computational models of action for robots and expert systems interacting with the environment, purposeful action is determined by plans, and plans have a logical form based on symbolic representations of outer states of the world and inner states of the machine. Suchman's perspective on the scope and validity of plans comes from another angle, the one of studying how people make sense of everyday activities, seen as interactions between the acting person and the surrounding social and material circumstances (Suchman, 2000).

Definitions

As already mentioned, the situation is defined as the full range of resources that the actor has available to convey the significance of his or her action and to interpret the actions of others. Concern for the situation denotes the material and social circumstances of every course of action (p. 50). Specifically, when analysing how users deal with photocopiers and their intelligent help systems, it appears that, 'the situation of the user comprises preconceptions about the nature of the machine and the operations required to use it, combined with moment by moment interpretations of evidence found in and through the actual course of its use'(p. 119). Note that the temporality of situated action is the moment by moment. It points to the fleeting circumstances on which the making sense of the action relies, but which these accounts of action routinely ignore. In contrast, plans, while providing sense or meaning to an action through a formalized representation of events, resources and interactions over (clock) time, do not help cope with unexpected breakdowns and more generally emerging circumstances. In the empirical study two interdependent situations are monitored: the one of the user with her preconceptions, puzzles, and interpretations and the one of the machine dictated by a plan encoded in a program written by a designer. The interdependency between the two is determined by the actions of the users, the machine and the communication to each other of the respective actions.

Methodology

The overall empirical thrust of the analysis is to observe 'how people use their circumstances to achieve intelligent action' (p. 50). In general, to study the action *in situ* requires accounts of formal representations and their 'productive interaction with the unique, unrepresented circumstance in which action in every instance and invariably occurs' (p. 189).

Operationally, the problem of studying situated action is described as 'akin to the problem of a detective who is just sent out and told to report back on what going to the grocery store is all about and how it is done' (p. 111). After having tried paper and pencil observations as means to build reports of actions, and having being confused herself about the problematic interactions between the users and the photocopier, Suchman comes to the methodological conclusion that 'to understand the problem would require the use of an adequate, i.e. videotaped, record' (p. 110, footnote 3). Video technology is then deployed in a sort of uncontrolled experimentation. The situation is constructed so as to be visually observable: two users of a photocopying machine interacting with its embedded expert help system. The experimental setting is created artificially by giving the users a complex task to perform with the machine; after that they are left on their own to cope with the task, the machine and the help system. The data thus obtained are a corpus of videotapes of first-time users and the expert help system: 'a record of events which is not pre-judged as to its analytic interest either in advance or in the making' (p. 114). The videotape transcripts are subsequently organized according to an analytic framework that distinguishes the actions of the user not available to the machine, those that are actually available (as gleaned through a key-hole by the machine), the effects of the machine on the user and the embedded design rationale contained in the programs of the expert help system. Users were also asked to read the instructions aloud and their conversations recorded: this constitutes the verbal protocol accompanying the videotapes.

Audiovisual technology, Suchman points out, offers the following advantages: it provides a record of the action and its circumstances that can be replicated, is available for repeated inspection, and is independent of the researcher's analysis (p. 113). It thus conforms to the key tenets of scientific experimentation, after all.

Findings

The help expert system is designed to provide the user with the relevant information on how to operate the photocopier for a given job. Information is released step-by-step so that the user is guided through a complex task. But to offer the appropriate instruction the system must recognize not only the overall goal of the task, but also each action needed to accomplish it, and for which then it is able to convey an instruction to move the job to the next step. Thus, one can identify a recurrent sequence where the machine presents an instruction, the user takes an action, the machine acknowledges the action and sends the next instruction to the screen interface to be read and acted upon by the user. The expert system is based on a plan developed by its designer that matches goals, outcomes, and actions. Among the evidence collected through the videotaped sessions, perhaps the most interesting ones are those featuring the 'communicative breakdowns', where the respective situations of the humans and the machine get out of synch, and the pre-designed plan embedded in the expert system shows its inability to capture all the relevant aspects of the users' situation, thinking and action. Two instances stand out:

False alarm

Here the users do not understand the instructions of the machine, are puzzled and come to the conclusion that they must be mistaken. But this is not the case: the machine sees nothing wrong and communicates the next instruction. The output however is not what the users expect. The help system does not intervene because it detects no error. The users are left wondering: 'What do we do then?' (p. 164), and start ascribing spurious intents to the machine, acting consequently. The machine remains unable to detect the misunderstanding on the part of the users.

Garden path

A misconception of the user produces an error. The machine does not interpret the action as a faulty one, but as performed in the context of a different procedure. Thus the error of the users is not detected, actually is mistaken for some other correct action. Nor the users understand that the machine is now following a different plan towards another goal. The users then get the next instruction, a fact that by itself conveys the message that they are on track. That is obviously not the case. Only the users' action effects keep being available to the machine, not their intentions reflecting the particular situation at the moment of action. The situation of the user and the one of the machine begin to evolve differently, but this divergence is initially masked, so that no counteraction is initiated by either of them.

Outcomes

While research and development in cognitive science are aimed at representing mental constructs, such as goals or plans, and writing programs for their manipulation so that systems guided by these programs can interact intelligently with their environment, the alternative research strategy implemented by Suchman is aimed at exploring the relation of knowledge and action to the particular circumstance in which they occur. The empirical study confirms that the organization of situated action is an emergent property of moment-by-moment interactions between actors and their relevant environments (pp. 178–179).

Expert systems are built on a planning model of human action. 'The model treats a plan as something located in the actor's head' (p. 3). directing his or her behaviour. But the evidence provided for example by the 'false alarm' and the 'garden path' shows that the planning model confuses plans with situated actions, and ignores the fact that intentional action emerges out of the interplay between representations (as featured in plans) and local circumstances that typically lay outside pre-designed plans.

In general, the empirical study highlights the profound asymmetry between people with their capability of *ad hoc* improvisation and machines unable to access the moment-by-moment contingencies stemming from situated interactions. This has important design implications. While the AI specialist tries to embed into expert systems more and more sophisticated plans, never achieving the richness of the situation (the world), Suchman's recommendation is to keep plans vague and open for possibilities. Plans, and more in general representations, should work as signposts or guide people in their interactions with the technologies, leaving ample room for experimentation and serendipity. The local interactions between the actor and the emerging circumstances are bound to remain essentially outside the plan's scope. 'To get at the action *in situ* requires accounts not only of efficient symbolic representations but of their productive interaction with the unique, unrepresented circumstances in which action in every instance and invariably occurs' (p. 189). Finally, countering the pretence of cognitive science and AI to build intelligent artefacts using a theory of the mind based on symbols processing, Suchman envisages an alternative approach aimed at building 'interactive artefacts', rooted on rich accounts of situated human actions and shared understanding.

The second case study – the situation: living as an early Christian

Background and motivation

Leaving aside the multiple philosophical debates which phenomenology was confronting and relating to at the beginning of the 20th century, the attempts by Husserl (1970) and later Heidegger (1962) are of relevance here to place philosophy, and in particular phenomenology, as a foundation of all the other sciences. While the latter are based on a series of presuppositions and assumptions, which are not further discussed within their respective 'regional domains', phenomenology strives to be a style of thinking with the least possible presuppositions, a primal science. But, where to anchor it, then? And how to do it? In his earliest course, the War Emergency seminar during the winter semester of 1919, Heidegger (2001a) puts forward a number of key ideas. First, that one should stay clear of a history of philosophy or a review of philosophical ideas. What matters is 'philosophizing' as part of life. The standpoint, or better the springboard of philosophical inquiring should be then 'factical life' itself, the stream of life taking place in the surrounding world in which we enact philosophy. 'Because factical life experience is more than a cognitive experience, more than even the simple experience of taking cognizance, philosophy in the face of it must undergo a total transformation. What is had, lived, experienced in factical life experience is more than a mere object for a subject and its theory forming activity, it is a world *in* which one can *live* (one cannot live in an object)' (Kisiel, 1995, p. 154). That is the foundation. Heidegger wants to avoid the 'common sense' standpoint immersed in the everyday life, since it is warped by public interpretations, by what people say and by the unreflective absorption in mundane affairs. He also rejects the theoretical standpoint because instead of a dynamic flow of experience and historicity, delivers a brute collection of objects, resources and relations present at hand. The outcome is a 'de-vitalizing' of experience and history (Guignon, 2002, p. 82). Phenomenology 'does not derive from a system of relations, a network of general concepts, that can be stretched to reach everything... Instead it inquires the givenness of concrete life situations, basic situations, in which the totality of life expresses itself. Life is in every situation, it is all there' (Heidegger, 1993, p. 231).

How to access the flow of life in the world and the ensuing historical experience? In discussing how phenomenology can disclose the life-experience Heidegger refers to Husserl's 'principle of all principles': all philosophical pronouncements must be grounded in something immediately accessible to us. For example, 'the logic of the grasp of the object, and the conceptuality of the object... must be drawn out of the mode *in which the object is originally accessible*. Also decisive for the definition of the life situation in which the object comes to be experienced and, further, the basic intention in which the experience from the outsets aims at the object (how the sense of the situation and of the anticipatory intentional grasp (the preconception)) is "given its due"' (Heidegger, 1962, p. 17). Life, thus, must be 'understood in a primal scientific way as leaping out from its source' (Heidegger, 2002, p. 82). The here and now of the situation offers such a primordial insight into life (Guignon, 2002, p. 86). For example, the situation in which philosophizing itself occurs: philosophy, as a knowing comportment must be then understood in the situation where it takes place, where it is enacted, that is the University (see the Appendix to the 1919 lectures titled 'On the Essence of the University and Academic Studies' (Heidegger, 2001a)).

More in general, concern for factical life expresses the re-balancing of activities advocated by Heidegger in Descartes' famous statement '*Cogito, ergo sum*' (I think, therefore I am). The thinking, far from being primal, is just the tip of the iceberg of something that is pre-theoretical and pre-thought: living, being. Thinking is supported by being, and phenomenology is an inquiry into factical life, that is being-in-the-world (*Dasein*). The accent of inquiry is then shifted towards the '*sum*' (Heidegger, 1962, pp. 130–131). To be or to live means for Heidegger essentially to *care*. What we care for is what is meaningful. We live in the world, i.e. we care about the world, and the world is automatically meaningful for us. Objects and circumstances stand out because they are endowed with such meaningfulness: that is how our experience encounters them in life, without them having 'to run around naked' (Heidegger, 1962, p. 69).

Definitions

The situation plays a key role in the phenomenological method as the privileged access point to the foundation, to factical life. A number of characteristics are added by Heidegger in the following courses in years 1920–22, and new terms are tried out and subsequently abandoned. For example, the notion that in philosophizing as part of life, the 'I' of the observer/actor cannot be carved out from the situation. Hence, the adoption in the earlier courses of the term of I-Situation, to remind us that the I-in-the situation should always be at the centre of our reflection. The situation is a situation for someone, the self always 'swims together (with everything else) in the situation' (Heidegger, 2001a, p. 206 – quoted by Guignon, 2002, p. 85). Furthermore, by focusing on the situation, one can avoid the dichotomy between subject and object, which finds its sense only in a perspective that is *already* theoretical, thus depriving the lived experience of any life. Rather, the situation is an event that constitutes the 'I' and the 'world' simultaneously. Second, the situation is not static, as part of life, nor is a process (still prone to be analyzed scientifically as a physical or chemical process), but it is an event. Temporality is a relevant dimension of the situation, and is the temporality of life, not necessarily clock time: 'the situation has a *narrative* structure' (Guignon, 2002, p. 85).

Third, while the other sciences are engaged in a relentless effort of objectification and reification, philosophizing wants to dwell close to life as it is lived, and not objectified. On the contrary, 'the phenomenological method works in its articulation, thanks to a critical destruction of objectifying forces, that are always there ready to stick to the phenomena' (Heidegger, 1993, p. 255).

How then to talk about a situation, without objectifying it, without 'extracting life' out of it in order to analyze it? (Heidegger is well aware of the challenge: 'The problem of a situation without objectification has not been set out so far in the philosophical literature' (Heidegger, 1993, p. 258)). Recall the ubiquity of meaningfulness in the world that surrounds us. We live and encounter the world in a smooth way because most of the things, people and situations we meet are endowed with meaning: since we care things and people in the situation matter and are significant in some ways. The situation is defined typically by a background motivation; shows a tendency that characterizes the course of events in some prevailing direction; has a sense of fulfilment: in short, it is a narrative that makes sense.

Analyzing a situation entails getting to the main sources of its meaning. Heidegger (2001a) identifies three: sense of content, sense of relation and sense of actualization or enactment. Sense of *content* refers to the various entities we recognize in a situation: things, people, physical and temporal circumstances etc. Sense of *relation* illustrates the network of meanings and references, which the various aspects and entities of the situation are embedded into: the semantic dimension of the situation. Just stopping at such descriptions of a situation would entail an objectifying description, where life has been taken out (*entlebt,* in German). 'The situation-character disappears. The unity of the situation explodes. The experiences, no longer possessing a unity of meaning or a unity of content, lose the unity the situation gave them' (Heidegger, 2001, p. 206 – quoted in Guignon, 2002, p. 85). Finally, sense of *actualization* or *enactment* (see also Weick, 1979), linked to the happening, the situation as an event, the situation as an action: this is the key dimension that guarantees a study of the situation as part of the stream of life and not as an objectifying desk exercise. Furthermore, the sense of enactment captures other fundamental dimensions of the situation and its temporality: a sense of history and a sense of embodiment.

In the courses held in 1921–22 dedicated to the commentary of various books by Aristotle, and in particular the Nicomachean Ethics and the Rhetoric, Heidegger uses the term Befindlichkeit to define situatedness for the first time, and he does that when translating creatively Aristotle's concept of *pathos*. In rhetoric one of the aims of the speaker is to affect the situation of the audience, its *pathos*. The translation Befindlichkeit is useful to capture the non-cognitive dimensions of the situation, in particular the situation of the actor in the situation, his or her moods, emotions, disposition. The passions are the 'ground out of which speech grows...the ground possibilities in which human existence (*Dasein*) primarily orients itself concerning itself, finds itself. This primary orientation, the illumination of its being in the world, is not a knowing, but a finding oneself' (Heidegger, 2002, p. 262).

In general, there are many situations, but which one is worth studying? Heidegger's reply is quite clear. Situations are points of access to life. The most promising situations, which can reveal the anchoring of our thinking and understanding to life are those where life comes to the fore in a stark, tumultuous way. These are typically situations of radical transformation, when entire modes of living and understanding give way to radically new ones. Becoming an early Christian, even before the Church were established, is living such a situation. Moreover, according to Heidegger (1993, pp. 61–62), the big breakthrough brought about by the Christian religion, as opposed to the prevailing Greek philosophical thinking at the time, was the importance of the inner life (later on exalted in the writings of St. Augustine and his reference to 'inquietum cor nostrum' (our restless heart)). Studying the situation of the early Christians obliges us to give high importance to the sphere of inner life as an integral part of the situation. Finally, the early Christian texts reveal a non-theoretical way of understanding, which later on will be lost with the establishment of the Church, in particular with the import of the Greek classic philosophy into the foundations of the Christian religion. That is why the study of early Christianity is so attractive for Heidegger: it is a way to access life in a moment of radical transformation and while it is expressing its inner, non cognitive dimensions, in ways that are not yet caged by theoretical thought.

Methodology

In general, phenomenology has the same problem of the scientific method, that is how to escape the 'natural attitude'. But the solution it tries out is the opposite of the theoretical and the objectifying, where the emotions are barred, and the lived experience cleansed. Phenomenology looks for an a-theoretical comportment and interpretation beyond the natural attitude. The religious experience has an extraordinary methodological importance for Heidegger, because it represents an historical instance of such an a- theoretical approach to life.

Regional sciences, say history, or theology, or Neokantian philosophy, each would have its own method to study the life of the early Christians, availing themselves of key early documents such as the Pauline Letters. Thus, one could carry out an historical study of the Roman Empire in the first century of our age and examine the situation of the various religious movements. Theology would offer an exegesis of the dogmas and religious concepts contained in the Letters. Neokantians would investigate the cognitive frames of religious thinking as emerging from the New Testament, of which the Letters are a part.

All these inquires would enrich our knowledge, suggests Heidegger (2004), and would help us in clarifying the sense of content and the sense of reference characterizing the situation of the early Christians. But it is only with the phenomenological method that one can focus on the sense of enactment and thus get to the situatedness of the life of the early Christians, and simultaneously overcome obvious hurdles such as the different language in which the Pauline Letters were written compared to our modern language; the fact that we have to rely only on texts, some of which are apocryphal; the fact that in carrying out this inquiry we do not reflect upon the role of the observer (Heidegger) while he engages in the interpretation. On the other hand, the Pauline Letters constitute the closest document available that captures the life of the early Christians: the first were written twenty years after the Crucifixion. Paul identifies himself resolutely with the members of the communities he addresses the Letters to (the Thessalonians, the Galatians, the Romans etc.): he has helped founding those communities and every letter starts with his spirited acknowledgement that he is one of them. The Letters give us access to Paul's inner world and to the communities of the new religious practice simultaneously.

But how to engage with the phenomenological interpretation? At a turning point of his course, Heidegger invites his students and himself to pay attention 'no longer to the object-historical complex, but rather see the situation such that we write the letter along with Paul. We perform the letter writing, or its dictating, with him.' (Heidegger, 2004, p. 62) This is the closest way available if not to enact, at least to evoke and actualize what was the situation of the early Christian communities and Paul as one of their members and founder.

Findings

We pick two aspects of the situation of the Christian communities among the various exposed to Heidegger's phenomenological interpretation: how the communities lived temporality and how they related to the existing social order.

The second coming (Parousia)

The early Christian communities lived a different temporality, they lived their time in a special way. (Heidegger, 2004) We are just a couple of decades after Christ' death and Resurrection, and the new communities are waiting for the second coming of Christ (or Parousia) that will lead all peoples and the defunct generations to salvation, to the Lord. But it is not only about a future event, also the past matters. In the First Letter to the Thessalonians, Paul refers to the 'having become' that characterizes all the Christians after the Announcement. This event is the beginning of the Christian spirituality and history. It is an experience that colours all the relations of the extant religious situation at that time. To have become, and to know of that event shapes the opening of the situation to the future. Such knowledge becomes integral to the situation of being a Christian. The letter emphasizes the knowledge of the new temporality shared by all members of the community, and deals with the future event of the second coming. The issue is *when* this is going to happen. Heidegger points out that Paul addresses the burning question posed by the Thessalonian community not in terms of content (e.g. indicating a date, a when) or in terms of relations, but with a precise sense of enactment: how should they live the situation of waiting. He provides a knowledge that belongs to the factical life of the Thessalonians in their steadfast faith (Kisiel, 1995, p. 185). Paul again emphasizes the identification with his audience. 'You ask when, but you know it very well, as I do.' And he admits that he himself 'could endure the wait no longer' (First Thessalonians, 3:1,5). It is the very inner world of Paul that is being shared with the members of the community to whom the letter is addressed.

And the first thing they all know is that those who predict peace and security and nothing to fear are doomed, because 'The day of the Lord will come as a thief in the night.' (5:1) Hence, it is useless to prepare oneself, rather the 'when' is a situation of waiting, highly uncertain and characterized by a sombre alertness, endurance, tension and vigilance. The time the early Christians live assumes here a historical character. The 'when' is determined by the awareness of having become and by the actualization of their factical life experience in and through every moment, nothing else (Kisiel, 1995, p. 186). What characterizes the temporality of these communities is a time devoid of any length that can be planned, ordered or organized.

As though not (hos me)

Another community, the Corinthians, ask Paul how to relate to the existing social and institutional order. While waiting for the second coming, how to be a husband, how to be a slave, or how to be a freeman? This was confusing since Paul predicated that there would be no more slaves or patrons, no more Greeks or Jews, no more circumcised or non-circumcised. Still, the members of the communities had all one or more of these positions, roles and identities. Again Paul replies with a text that contributes to enact the situation of those people. 'Let each remain in the same situation in which he was called' (1 Cor. 7:20). Far from revolting against the existing order, or accepting it passively, live each of those roles, positions and identities, but 'as though they were not' valid. A slave should live as a slave, but give no particular value to that status, the same for the husband with the wife, the Greek or the Jew. Accept the existing order and at the same time re-enact it while depriving it of any legitimacy. Thus, the sense of content and the sense of relation of the situation of the early Christians are left untouched. The meaning of the relations with the world derives not from the relative importance of their content or the network of relationships, but from the way they are re-enacted. Thus, something remains the same, and simultaneously is radically transformed. Relations and contents do not determine the situation and the factical life of the early Christians, instead, 'The relation and the sense of lived significance are determined out of the original enactment' (Heidegger, 2004, p. 85).

Outcomes

Heidegger (2002, p. 54) emphasizes that the access to and explication of the genuine situation of understanding present special difficulties. The situation is not something that jumps at us, or we fall into. One needs to work one's way toward the situation. The attitude is not the objectifying one, nor of blissful unconcern and tranquillity. 'The situation...does not correspond to a safe harbour but to a leap into a drifting boat, and it all depends on getting the mainsheet in hand and looking to the wind' (Heidegger, 1962, p. 30). In particular, the phenomenological method is itself embedded into an I-situation. Hence, the rationale of its approach directed eminently towards enacting an attunement between the situation of the interpreter and the one of Paul. By 'dictating' together with Paul the Letters Heidegger is able to evoke the situation of the early Christian, a situation of angst, calculated wait, uncertainty and sombre vigilance. Its salient aspects are the peculiar way to live the time left between the Resurrection and the second coming, and the apparent coexistence with the established order, undermining it by devoiding it of any legitimacy. Temporality is characterized not by clock time but by the *kairos*, the moment of opportunity and surprise of the second coming, and the importance of the inner life, the Befindlichkeit, which overshadows the surrounding institutional and historical circumstances. The life of the Christian is enormously difficult, always re-enacted in need and affliction (Kisiel, 1995, p. 190). The Pauline Letters enact this situation by intensifying the anguish and the gloominess.

Discussion

The two case studies show that there are two distinct agendas in the appreciation of situatedness, and that there is an evident discontinuity in the intellectual trajectory that connects phenomenology (at least in Heidegger's rendition) and the contemporary interpretivist schools. This is not the place to ascertain how the transfer and translations across the decades, the continents and the disciplines have transformed Heidegger's notion of Befindlichkeit into today's notions of situated action, knowledge, learning and change. Still, when contemplating the gap between the initial and the end points, one cannot help but feeling a slight sense of vertigo. Heidegger had the programmatic vision of founding phenomenology by steering clear from the mind, cognition, psychology and in general any regional science, while staying closer to everyday factical life. He puts forward a rich and multiple notion of situation, in which inner life is as important as surrounding circumstances, where the pre-theoretical is preserved by giving space to the moods, emotions and dispositions not linked to thinking, ('One could say at the limit that the factical life is emotional, not theoretical' (Heidegger, 1993, p. 220). In this respect, Befindlichkeit captures the multiplicity of meanings of being in a (inner and outer simultaneously) situation. In comparison, the current renditions of situatedness are much narrower, and deprived of the inner dimension. As mentioned above, authors like Suchman point to the importance of fleeting circumstances or 'the world that stays out of our head'. But also the heart is out of our head, still it remains consistently ignored by those discourses committed to an alternative approach. The difference gets even more apparent at the methodological level. Contemporary studies bend to the dictates of the scientific method: they strive to keep the observer separate from the situation to be studied. They set up experiments; they record them through technical means so as to obtain an evidence that is objective, can be evaluated independently, and can be shared. Things and people in the situation become objects, and events present themselves as processes occurring in objective time. But, when the situation is decomposed in this way, 'the self comes to appear as a detached spectator making observations – one item among others in the space-time coordinate system…The world is "dis-worlded" and the stream of life is robbed of its character as living…it gives us a misleading picture of reality and our own selves' (Guignon, 2002, p. 86). Heidegger, instead, is interested in enacting, re-enacting, or at least evoking situations. The sense of a situation can be grasped by going beyond objectification or a semantic analysis: it needs execution here and now, and full participation in such an execution. One needs to dictate the Pauline Letters again, after 2000 years, to actually 'understand' them.

Then, there are more subtle differences, where the claims of the contemporary scholars are still the same as Heidegger's, but their implementation goes in another (usually scientific and cognitive) direction. Thus, for example, take the notion of time. The study of the temporality of the situation has a far-reaching importance in Heidegger's thinking and will lead in *Being and Time* to the exploration of the time we ourselves are. Getting close to experiencing the temporality of the early Christian communities can be regarded as one of his preparatory works towards introducing a new notion of time. In Suchman's and others' works reference to the importance of fleeting circumstances, moment-by-moment unfolding of action never challenges the ubiquity of clock time. The empirical study of situated action never hints to a different or problematic notion of temporality. The clock regulates the video and audio recorders.

Also, the distancing from cognitive science shared by the two agendas is handled differently. While Heidegger makes all sort of efforts to stay away from epistemology and cognition, and the evidence is successfully provided by the outcome of his interpretation of the Pauline Letters, that leads to evoking a situation coloured by moods, emotions in facing uncertainty and the wake, the objectifying study of situated action reports instead the mismatches between the plans embedded in an expert system and the reasoning of novice users. It identifies sequences of instructions, communication failures, and mis*understandings* between users and the expert system. Note how the latter portrait of situated action may become an easy target for the symbol representationists: preconceptions are symbols stored into 'memory' and interpretations of evidence get translated into perceptions of stimuli and their symbolic processing. Despite repeated denials, the mind and the focus on the cognitive level of *ad hoc* problem solving still prevail. On the other hand, the leaning towards the heart in Heidegger's phenomenological method is quite clear. In the loose sheets for his course in 1919–20 dedicated to the phenomenological intuition, Heidegger notes: 'Understanding – as intuition – goes along with and into the fullness of a situation...The phenomenological understanding is nothing else than an intuitive going along the meaning. It must stay close and present to the total situation of the phenomenon...Capacity to accompany – being intimate, "love." Love as motivating ground of the phenomenological understanding – given necessarily in its sense of enactment' (Heidegger, 1993, pp. 185 and 262). And, more in general, 'The true philosophical attitude is never the one of a logical tyrant, who frightens life through his staring at it. Rather it is Plato's Eros'(*ibid.*, 263). To be sure, Heidegger is aware of the difficulty of carrying out such a task, and espousing such a method: 'The first task is therefore the appropriation of the situation in which understanding is rooted; the full, concrete appropriation is by itself a task that will perhaps exceed the powers of the present generation...Those who attempt something else mistake in principle precisely what should be their aim...the pure cognition of the labyrinthine basic character of human existence' (Heidegger, 1962, pp. 32–42).

Conclusion

Our going back to the roots of phenomenology in order to restore the original notion of situatedness and compare it with the contemporary debate on situated action leaves us with three main research agendas. The first, leaning towards AI and cognitive science, states that situated action can be implemented through computer programs interacting with the environment and processing symbolic representations of what happens in the environment. The second, which claims to be an alternative grounded in the social sciences (phenomenology via ethnomethodology) is based on a social ecology of the mind: goals and plans are a vague guide to action. They must be complemented by the *ad hoc* improvisations of humans exploiting the circumstances and what the world offers at the moment of action. The heart is totally missing from the first agenda. Emotions, moods are sometime referenced in a footnote, but do not seem to fit the second agenda, either, despite Suchman's (2000, p. 9) later claim to have fallen with her original study in 'a classical humanist trap'. Finally, we have Heidegger's research program where the notion of situation includes at all moments the inner life of the actor, his or her mind *and* heart, and where any form of understanding is situated, meaning 'affected'. It is the *pathos* that characterizes the whole person in his or her situatedness in the world. (Heidegger, 2002, p. 192) Empirically, the first agenda seeks the construction of expert systems able to interact with worlds of limited variety. The second is validated by studying routine activities within stable organizations and tasks: micro breakdowns reveal those improvisations members are able to sport and confirming the situated nature of whatever plan or procedure they are supposed to follow. Phenomenology is interested in studying situations of radical transformation, since there what it means to 'find oneself' in a situation, to live, comes to the fore in a sharper way. Overcoming the current state of oblivion and neglect, due consideration of the third, original agenda should remind contemporary scholars and practitioners that articulating situatedness in organizational analysis and interactive systems design is still going to be a challenging task, and indeed a 'touchy' one.

Note

This chapter originally appeared in (2006) *Journal of Information Technology* **21**(3): 129–139.

References

Brown, J.S. and Duguid, P. (1991). Organizational Learning and Communities of Practice: Towards a Unified View of Working, Learning and Innovation, *Organization Science* **2**(1): 40–57.

Burrell, G. and Morgan, G. (1979). *Sociological Paradigms and Organizational Analysis*, London: Heineman.

Ciborra, C. (1996). The Platform Organization: Recombining Strategies, Structures, and Surprises, *Organization Science* **7**(2): 103–118.

Clancey, W. (1977). *Situated Cognition: On Human Knowledge and Computer Representation*, Cambridge: Cambridge University Press.

Contu, A. and Willmott, H. (2003). Re-embedding Situatedness: The Importance of Power Relations in Learning Theory, *Organization Science* **14**(3): 283–296.

Crotty, M. (1998) *The Foundations of Social Research: Meaning and Perspective in the Research Process*, London: Sage.

Deetz, S. (1996). Describing Differences in Approaches in Organization Science: Rethinking Burrell and Morgan and their Legacy, *Organization Science* **7**(2): 191–207.

Dourish, P. (2002). *Where the Action is: The Foundations of Embodied Interaction*, Cambridge, MA: The MIT Press.

Dreyfus, H.L. (1991). *Being-in-the-World: A Commentary on Heidegger's Being and Time, Division 1*, Cambridge, MA: The MIT Press.

Gadamer, H.G. (1975). *Truth and Method*, New York: Seabury Press.

Giddens, A. (1984). *The Constitution of Society: Outline of the Theory of Structure*, Berkley, CA: University of California Press.

Guignon, C. (2002). Philosophy and Authenticity: Heidegger's Search for a Ground for Philosophizing, in M. Wrathall and J. Malpas (eds), *Heidegger, Authenticity and Modernity, Essays in Honor of Hubert L. Dreyfus – Vol. 1*, Cambridge, MA: The MIT Press, pp. 79–101.

Haraway, D.J. (1991). *Situated Knowledges – Simians, Cyborgs, and Women: The Reinvention of Nature*, London: Free Association Books, pp. 183–201.

Heidegger, M. (2004). *The Phenomenology of Religious Life*, Bloomington, IN: Indiana University Press.

Heidegger, M. (2002). *Gesamtausgabe – Band 18 – Grundbegriffe der Aristotelischen Philosophie* (1924), Frankfurt am Main: V. Klostermann.

Heidegger, M. (2001). *Phenomenological Interpretations of Aristotle: Introduction to Phenomenological Research*, Bloomington, IN: Indiana University Press.

Heidegger, M. (2001a). *Towards the Definition of Philosophy*, London: Athlone Press.

Heidegger, M. (1993). *Gesamtausgabe – Band 58 – Grundprobleme der Phanomenologie (1919/20)*, Frankfurt am Main: V. Klostermann.

Heidegger, M. (1962). *Being and Time*, Oxford: Blackwell.

Husserl, E. (1970). *Logical Investigations*, London: Routledge and Kegan Paul.

Kisiel, T. (1995). *The Genesis of Heidegger's Being & Time*, Berkley: University of California Press.

Lave, J. and Wenger, E. (1991). *Situated Learning – Legitimate Peripheral Participation*, Cambridge: Cambridge University Press.

O' Sullivan, T., Dutton, B. and Rayner, P. (2003). *Studying the Media*, London: Arnold.

Orlikowski, W.J. (2000). Using Technology and Constituting Structures: A Practice Lens for Studying Technology in Organizations, *Organization Science* **11**(4): 404–428.

Orlikowski, W.J. (1996). Improvising Organizational Transformation over Time: A Situated Change Perspective, *Information Systems Research* **7**: 63–92.

Orr, J. (1996). *Talking about Machines: An Ethnography of a Modern Job*, Ithaca, NY: Cornell University Press.

Polanyi, M. (1958). *Personal Knowledge: Towards a Post-critical Philosophy*, London: Routledge and Kegan Paul.

Robertson, T. (2003). The Public Availability of Actors and Artefacts, *Computer Supported Collaborative Work* **11**: 299–316.

Schultze, U. and Leidner, D.E. (2002). Studying Knowledge Management in Information Systems Research: Discourses and Theoretical Assumptions, *MIS Quarterly* **26**(3): 213–242.

Schank, R. and Abelson, R. (1977). Scripts, Plans and Knowledge, in P. Johnson – Laird and P. Wason (eds), *Thinking, Readings in Cognitive Science*, Cambridge: Cambridge University Press.

Suchman, L.A. (2000). Human/Machine Reconsidered, Introduction to the 2nd revised edition of *Plans and Situated Actions* – draft – Lancaster University.

Suchman, L.A. (1987). *Plans and Situated Actions: The Problem of Human Machine Communication*, Cambridge: Cambridge University Press.

Vera, A.H. and Simon, H.A. (1993). Situated Action: A Symbolic Interpretation, *Cognitive Science* **17**: 7–48.

Weick, K.E. (1993). The Collapse of Sensemaking in Organizations: The Mann Gulch Disaster, *Administrative Science Quarterly* 38(4): 628–652.

Weick, K.E. (1979). *The Social Psychology of Organizing*, Reading, MA: Addison – Wesley.

Wenger, E. (1998). *Communities of Practice: Learning, Meaning and Identity*, Cambridge: Cambridge University Press.

Winograd, T. and Flores, F. (1986), *Understanding Computers and Cognition*, Norwood, NJ: Ablex.

2
Improvisation as Mood

Claudio U. Ciborra

Abstract

Improvisation is being appreciated by the management literature because of its key role in a variety of contingencies in the current turbulent times. Improvisation can be described as a form of extemporaneous, situated action. To date the study of both phenomena has been mainly cognitive. This exposes them to the critique according to which they would not add value to the symbolic knowledge and representation paradigms developed in Artificial Intelligence and knowledge management systems. The paper suggests a different point of departure: improvisation should be regarded as a mood, and not a mindset. We can learn about improvisation by contrasting it with other moods such as panic and boredom. The new perspective indicates that the cognitive approaches are limited since they disregard the 'situation of the actor'. Moods capture the situatedness of the actor as opposed to the situation of the action only. Also, a phenomenological analysis unveils the fundamental relationships between moods, existence and time, which can lead to a new explanation of the 'extemporaneous' character of improvisation.

Introduction

Despite the multiple definitions of improvisation available today in the management and organization theory literatures (see for example Kamoche *et al.*, 2002), one commonality strikes the eye: the ubiquitous and undisputed cognitive perspective on the phenomenon. At individual level, a problem needs to be solved in the context of emerging circumstances and improvisation is the response sported on the spur of the moment (Weick, 1998; Barrett, 1998; Suchman, 1987), exploiting tacit knowledge, and combining thought and action (Brown and Duguid, 1991; Moorman and Miner, 1998). And collective improvisation gets discussed within the framework of distributed cognition (Hutchins, 1996). Or *et al.* (1996) define improvisation in general terms as 'intuition guiding action in a spontaneous way', but when called to the job of defining further what they mean by intuition and spontaneity they settle for the mental. Thus, they refer to Simon's

(1989, p. 38) idea by which intuition is 'analysis frozen into habit and into capacity for rapid response through recognition'. And the link between the two melds together cognition and action. In a similar vein, Schön (1983, pp. 26–27) wrote about 'on the spot surfacing...and testing of intuitive understanding of experienced phenomena while action is ongoing'. Even within the domain of jazz, the leading setting that has provided much inspiration for the managerial study of improvisation, Berliner (1994, p. 492 – quoted in Weick (1998)) submits that 'improvisation depends, in fact, on *thinkers* having absorbed a broad base of musical *knowledge*, including myriad conventions that contribute to formulating *ideas logically*, cogently and expressively' (my emphases). And Weick (1998) himself looks at the fundamental role of cognition in improvisation as 'retrospective sensemaking', but he worries that the notion of intuition used by many authors to explain the process of improvisation needs to be unpacked in more detail, given its key role in making improvisation possible. Viewing intuition as rapid *processing of experienced information* does not suffice. On the other hand, when addressing spontaneity, the same author uses the following image: '*thinking* on your feet' (Weick, 1998) (again my emphasis).

Moorman and Miner (1998) conclude that, 'any entity that can reasonably be thought of as planning or executing action can also be thought of as improvising'. We regard such prevailing cognitive perspectives on improvisation, especially when they do not deliver anything new or substantial to key (e.g., time related) aspects of the phenomenon, as suspect. Indeed, if improvisation is just quick problem solving that takes into account emerging circumstances by some sort of ongoing feedback on the very design of the action being undertaken, then the critique of cognitive scientists, such as Vera and Simon (1993) to the whole situated action paradigm applies to it too. The latter authors ask, 'what's new, or so special?' In principle, when reconstructing improvised decision making symbolic representations of the ongoing problem space can be drawn, algorithms can be identified, problem solving programmes can be written, which include the stuff of which Artificial Intelligence (AI) is made: plans; if-then-elses; means-ends chains etc. But, once improvisation gets analysed as quick design and simultaneous implementation of plans of action, factoring early feedback from execution, where has its magic gone? Can such an analysis offer anything new or alternative to the prevailing managerial and systems models that put at the centre of their discourse information, knowledge modelling and planning?

To overcome such an impasse we suggest to step back and revisit the intellectual roots of situated action, of which we consider improvisation as special case, in phenomenology (e.g, as we shall see later, Heidegger (1962) uses at least four different words for the term 'situation'). This will allow us to check whether a different tack on the issue can be followed. Indeed, both Husserl (1962) and Heidegger (1962) have put forward a way of understanding how we encounter, know and act upon the world of which only some elements have been retained and used in the existing situated action approaches. Others have got lost, and learning from their misdirection may help us in overcoming the present intellectual deadlock.

Our analysis starts by spelling out the achievements and limitations of the overwhelmingly cognitive approach to improvisation as a form of situated action. Next, we can explore the pivotal notion of situated action in a wider methodological context by referring to the original ideas of phenomenology: in particular, that a situation is defined both by emerging circumstances of the world, and by the ongoing situation of the actor, the latter captured by his or her affections, feelings or moods. This leads the way for a new approach to improvisation that is not purely cognitive but existential. Specifically, improvisation is regarded as a mood. We can then study the characteristics of improvisation, and especially its problematic relationship with time, by contrasting the improvising mood with other which are opposite to it, such as panic and boredom. The conclusions summarize the range of topics that this new study of improvisation illuminates, such as the key role of moods in situations, and situated knowledge as always moody knowledge.

Paradoxes in the study of improvisation

Improvisation is currently treated in the management and organization literatures as a form of situated action where the emphasis is placed on its temporal dimension and its description is largely based on a cognitive perspective. Thus, improvisation is an activity where composition and execution, thinking and doing converge in time (Moorman and Miner, 1998), or occur simultaneously (Weick, 1993). Key aspects of such a form of thinking in the midst of the action are:

- the focus of attention is on emerging circumstances and current conditions (Eisenhardt and Tabrizi, 1995)
- intuition guides action where no script seems to be in control (Hatch, 1997): improvisation has little to do with scripted plans
- on the spot surfacing, restructuring and testing of intuitive understanding (Schön, 1983)
- solving a problem with no preoccupation on how to do it beforehand (Spolin, 1963)
- situational decision making.

This short list shows how definitions may vary in their attempts to grasp selected aspects of the phenomenon. But they share a common approach, the cognitive perspective, and a common understanding of the temporal dimension: quick, simultaneous and on the spur of the moment.

There is a situation, and it is emergent: the trick of improvisation, as opposed to scripting and planning, is to capture in the emergent problem solving all the latest circumstances. Thus, improvisation is about compiling scripts on the fly and problem solving on the spur of the moment, and so on. But, no matter what the specific description, it is, after all, about problem solving, scripting and thinking. This entails at least a couple of paradoxes.

The first regards the temporal dimension of improvisation. Do not be mislead by 'improvised' inquiries into the root of the word, such as the opposite of the Latin word *proviso*, i.e. not stipulated beforehand (Weick, 1998), or *improvisus* meaning not seen ahead of time (Barrett, 1998). The fact is that there was no noun in Latin that means improvisation having its roots in 'improv…'. The word used the Romans was instead: *extemporalis actio* (Quintillian, 1993). This term is still used today and one of the attributes most frequently adopted to describe improvisation both in music (jazz) and managerial literature is indeed 'extemporaneous'. The modern literature seems to be concerned with the simultaneity of different activities, such as thinking and doing, and the speed of knowing and acting. For example, to discover a way to do a 22-second information search in 2 seconds (Weick, 1998). But does extemporaneous mean just fast and simultaneous? It does not. Etymologically it means outside of time, or outside the normal flow of time. Interestingly, most of the literature takes no notice of this, and Weick (1998) rightly points out that if speed is the main characteristic of this activity, then in many circumstances coping with a faster tempo would condemn the agent to using pre-planned, repetitive procedures to keep the performance going. In other words, higher speed may encourage, not improvisation, but a sudden reversion back to old ideas and routines. We are, then, left with the paradox of improvisation being advocated on the one hand for fast product development, prompt market decision making, and successful organizational performances, and on the other the enactment of such activities, which requires simplification, accelerated production, less slack, forcing people back on older ideas and away from adaptive improvisation. In sum, gaining speed may undermine spontaneity and extemporaneity.

The second paradox regards the supposedly radical difference between planning and improvising. The cognitive view of improvisation is rooted into, and echoes very closely, the earlier study of situated action vs. planning carried out by Suchman (1987), based in turn on Mead's (1934) distinction between situated and ad hoc improvisation on the one hand and representation of action (in the form of future plans and retrospective accounts) on the other. In Suchman's study the situation is defined as the full range of resources that the actor has available to convey the significance of his or her action and to interpret the actions of others. Specifically, in analysing how employees deal with photocopiers that break down, Suchman (1987) suggests that, 'the situation of the user comprises preconceptions about the nature of the machine and the operations required to use it, combined with moment by moment interpretations of evidence found in and through the actual course of its use'. Note here many of the ingredients of the theory of improvisation: preconceptions, interpretations, evidence; and the temporal dimension it is the moment by moment. 'Action is contingent on a complex world of objects, artefacts and other actors located in space and time. And this is an essential resource that makes knowledge possible and gives action its sense' (Suchman, 1987). Thus, the situated action paradigm states the importance of fleeting circumstances on which the making sense of the action relies, but which these accounts of action routinely ignore. In contrast, plans, while providing sense or meaning to an action through a formalized representation of events, resources and interactions over (clock) time, do not help cope with unexpected breakdowns and more generally emerging circumstances.

But are the two approaches really different, ask Vera and Simon (1993)? The debate held in a special issue of Cognitive Science (1993) points to the weaknesses of the situated action perspective and to the limitations of a mainly cognitive perspective on it. Vera and Simon (1993) argue that the AI perspective on action, based on physical symbol systems and symbolic processing is far from being an alternative to the situated action perspective, in fact such a planning view is relevant to the latter.

In such a view a physical symbol system interacts with the external environment by receiving sensory stimuli that it converts into symbol structures in memory, and it acts upon the environment in ways determined by symbol structures. The memory is an indexed encyclopaedia, where representations of external situations are stored. Stimuli coming from the environment invoke the appropriate index entries. 'Sequences of actions can be executed with constant interchange among (a) receipt of information about the current state of the environment (perception), (b) internal processing of information (thinking), and (c) response to the environment (motor activity). These sequences may or may not be guided by long-term plans (or strategies that adapt to the feedback of perceptual information)' (Vera and Simon, 1993). In other words, the cognitive scientists argue that one can design and build symbol systems 'that continually revise their description of the problem space and the alternatives available to them' (*ibid.*, 13). This mimics one of the key ideas of the situated action literature (as recounted by Suchman (1987), and Winograd and Flores (1986)), i.e. the importance of moment by moment capture of the full situation of action. Plans can be seen not just as symbolic representations of fixed sequences of actions, but as strategies that determine each successive action as a function of current information about the situation. Here we come full circle to the second paradox: the AI perspective coincides very closely with the definition given above of improvisation as 'situational decision making'. If Suchman's concern is the mutual intelligibility between people and machines, and the underlying shared understanding between people in interaction, then Vera and Simon (1993) submit that such an understanding, and the correlated situated actions, cannot get along without an internal symbolic representations, and learning, planning and problem solving which feed upon them. In sum, 'the term situated action (and its derivative improvisation-the present author would add) can best serve as name for those symbolic systems that are specifically designated to operate adaptively in real time to complex environments…It in no sense implies a repudiation of the hypothesis that intelligence is fundamentally a property of appropriately programmed symbol systems.'

We cannot enter here into the arguments in favour or against such a bold final statement (the reader should consult the special issue of Cognitive Science). In any event, Suchman's (1993) reply in the same issue, and in her later writings (Suchman, 2000) does not put forward significant differences. In her recount, when reporting about the study at Xerox, she was forced by circumstances to enter into the discussion with colleagues in the cognitive sciences, but she would come at it from another angle, the one of studying how people make sense of everyday activities, seen as interactions between the acting person and the surrounding social and material circumstances. Still, the definition she originally offered of situated action remains cognitive/interactionist (Mead, 1934) one, and as such an easy target for the symbol representationists.

We submit that the view of situated action and improvisation as cognitive enterprises is possibly the source of the two paradoxes just examined and that we need to explore other dimensions to find a way out from the conceptual dead end.

Befindlichkeit or the situation of the actor

One way to overcome the block is to go back and revisit the roots of the situated action framework, roots that lie in phenomenology.[1] In his major work, Being and Time, Heidegger (1962) employs at least four different German words for situation: Stelle, meaning position and place; Lage as condition and disposition; Situation as the culminating limit situation of making a choice; and Befindlichkeit. It is precisely the last term that can help us in opening new dimensions. As often happens in Heidegger, it is a word whose meaning and usage are being stretched even in the German language. It is derived from the common expression '*Wie ist Ihr Befindlichkeit?*', a courteous way to ask, 'How are you?' Thus, *Befindlichkeit* is the situation one finds oneself in. But what situation? The loose arrangements of resources in the environment? The emerging physical and social circumstances? Not at all: the expression refers to the existential situation of the actor. 'How do you feel today?' Thus, Heidegger uses the term *Befindlichkeit*, translating from the Greek Arisitotle's notion of dianesis (disposition), to combine the ideas of situatedness ('situated' in German is translated as *befindlich*) and of feeling and faring, of where and how one finds itself existentially (see also Dreyfus, 1991; Inwood, 1999).

Note, somewhat ironically, how *Befindlichkeit* captures the common way of inquiring about the situation of the people we encounter everyday. So routine and ubiquitous an habit, yet still totally absent not only from the symbolic representations of human problem solving as put forward by the AI scientists – that one would expect – but also, and this is fatal, from the alternative, situated action approaches.

We can then appreciate the value of Vera and Simon's critique in suggesting that there is a basic commonality in the two approaches – after all, both consider the actor as a 'cognitive robot'. The discussion between the two camps revolves around how the robot solves the problems, learns about circumstances and plans or reacts to emergent conditions. Later appeals to 'situated and embodied knowledges' (Haraway, 1991) and the urge of feminist theorizing to reconceptualise what objective knowledge can be, (Suchman, 2000) do not help either. Suchman quotes Haraway on feminist objectivity as being about 'limited location and situated knowledge, not about transcendence and splitting of subject and object.'

However, both authors evade a reply to the ordinary question, the how-are-you of the actor, his moods, feelings, affections and fundamental attunement with the situation.[2] What is missing from this situated action literature is precisely an inquiry into and the appreciation of the situation of the actor, specifically his moods.

The thesis of this paper is that only by bringing back into the picture the situation of the actor, those fleeting personal circumstances (captured by the term *mood*), and not only the emerging environmental circumstances, that we may get to a fresh understanding of improvisation. One that the mere cognitive perspective seems to be unable to deliver, except as a dead, ex post reconstruction of problem solving routines designed and acted on the spur of the moment. In organization theory few authors have mentioned the importance of the emotional dimension next to the cognitive one. But still fewer have been able to put the latter dimension to work. Thus, Nonaka (1994) reminds us of the relevance of emotions in the processes of knowledge creation. In particular, tacit knowledge is deeply rooted in an individual's actions, experience, as well as in the ideals, values, or emotions he or she embraces. Still, 'what shapes the way we perceive the world is the cognitive dimension of tacit knowledge' (Nonaka and Konno, 1998). A more successful attempt to give the emotional dimension at least an equal standing to the cognitive one has been carried out by Hatch (1997a) in analysing ironic humor in processes of organizational change and stability.

Any actor enters into the situation with a mood that is elusive and can hardly be controlled, designed or represented in symbols: fear, anxiety, happiness, panic or boredom. Moods are the uncontrollable changing skies of the otherwise flat world of cognition and action, whether planned or situated. Precisely because moods come and go like the weather, Heidegger (1995) suggests they are very close to who we are in the situation. They are so ephemeral, sometimes superficial and unexplained, but they precede, or better ground, any mental representation of the situation and action strategy. But moods are far from being just private states. They disclose the world; they set the stage of our encounter with the world. It is not by surprise that they enjoy within phenomenology the highest prestige, far above everything psychological or cognitive (Blattner, 1999).

When we encounter the world in a situation, certain things, people or circumstances matter. This 'mattering' is grounded in one's *affectedness*. (Heidegger, 1996; Inwood, 1999) Hence affectedness discloses *the world as* a threat, boring or exciting. It sets the stage shaping problem definition, solving, design and action. In other words, our being open and encountering the world, our being amidst people and circumstances, and the related intentional projects of action, be they planned or situated, are constituted within a fundamental attunement, the mood: moods can change, but we are never without one. In this respect, not only is symbolic representation not primary, neither is cognition. Moods provide the ground in which our encountering the world and defining the situation take place. We can seldom choose such a ground: rather, we are thrown from it into the situation. Moods colour indelibly our being in the situation. They are like a fog, or a low cloud, coming from nowhere but giving an opaque tonality to the situation and our being in the situation itself. The most powerful moods attune us with the situation so strongly it almost seems there are no moods at all (and this is the trap in which even those who write about 'embodied knowledge' seem to fall nowadays, by failing to put moods at the centre of attention). Moods are the fundamental ways in which we are disposed in such and such a way, they are not the direct consequence of our thinking, doing and acting: they are rather the presupposition, the medium within which those activities take place.

In sum, phenomenology would indicate that the way we *care* about the world unfolds according to the passing mood that attunes us with the situation. Intentionality, the reading or re-registering of circumstances that we perform either by planned or improvised action, the in-order-tos of projects, the selection of appropriate means ends are all rooted in such a ground, our basic attunement. The study of situated action in general, and the one of improvisation in particular, has focussed so far only upon the later stages of this process, on the encounter between intentions and situations, but has systematically failed to reckon the (moody) situation of the actor.

The study of improvisation as a mood

Looking at improvisation as a special disposition or attunement with the situation, a different way of being amidst the world and being thrown into it opens up a different point of access to the phenomenon. In what follows we will try out a new study of improvisation precisely through the access point of 'improvisation as mood'. When taken seriously, this complicates at first our enquiry.[3] Actions can be studied as the carrying out of projects, plans or intentions, or as emergent responses to circumstances, as the cognitive tack suggests for both ends of the debate, symbolic representation and plans or situated actions. As mentioned above, instead, moods are always there; they cannot be forcibly brought about and are not necessarily linked to a plan or an action: they are the ground or the medium for them, but not the other way round. We slip into them unaware. Hence it is difficult to make an attunement itself into an object of knowledge. In this way, by trying to make it conscious, the attunement is destroyed or irremediably altered. An attunement can only be awakened and ascertained: it is not there just as an object ready at hand to be analysed (Heidegger, 1995). Awakening means letting a mood unfold. We can grasp it only in terms of what confront us in a situation, of what first irrupts then disappears. The phenomenological approach avoids the analysis of consciousness and tries to maintain the immediacy of everyday being-there in a situation. Thus, for example, instead of making the mood of boredom as an object to be contemplated, as some state that arises on its own, Heidegger (1995) suggests we should consider it 'in the way that we move within it, i.e., in the way that we seek to drive it away'. In trying to pass the time we can encounter boredom first hand (see below).

Let us then awake and ascertain improvisation as mood by recounting the vivid episode described and interpreted by Weick (1993) in his study on the Mann

Gulch fire disaster. Improvisation, according to Weick, is what allowed Dodge, the smokejumpers' captain, to rescue himself when most of the members of the team died in a suddenly exploding forest fire in Montana. Dodge was able to invent and implement on the spot a rescue procedure, consisting of burning the high grass in front of him with a match and throwing himself into the burning weeds. When the wall of the main fire, blown by the wind, arrived, it passed over him because he had created a clearing in which the fire could not find dry grass for fuel to continue burning. This is a typical example of highly situated action, since such procedure was not known or learnt (it became part of the standard smoke-jumper training *after* this tragic episode): it comes out of a reading of the situation at that very moment – high grass, matches, incoming firewall; it is quick–Dodge's fast reasoning lead to the solution to the problem – the fire needs fuel, hence let's eliminate the fuel source, 'how do I do it?', surprisingly by creating a new fire, and so on. As usual the ex post analysis of Dodge's skilful improvisation leaves the observer with a bitter aftertaste. Namely, an ex post analysis shows an ingenuous problem solving strategy, artfully and promptly implemented. Such an extemporaneous (when first performed in Mann Gulch) action strategy can be easily represented and reproduced after the fact, so as to becoming a training routine. Once again we encounter the comparison puzzle: what are the differences with planned action?

The time dimension seems not to be problematic either: Dodge was quick in framing the problem, discovering a solution and implementing it 'just in time'. Apparently he was calm throughout, since after the first match he considered using another one. Again, the special characteristics of improvisation and situated action elude us, and we are left with a cognitive interpretation of improvisation, very close to what symbol systems planning and representation supporters claim to be able to reproduce with a sophisticated AI application.

At a closer look, however, what gets lost in a cognitive perspective of situated action or symbolic representation, and which makes Dodge's actions a true case of improvisation, is what happened to his team members. They were running very close to Dodge; they were exposed to the very same situation; thanks to the wind lifting the clouds of smoke a couple of times, they could even see what Dodge was doing. He yelled at them to do the same or join him by jumping in his man made fire, but apparently they couldn't hear him because of the noise of the burning fire. They failed to understand. Even worse, they came to the conclusion that Dodge was out of his mind and committing suicide, so they carefully avoided the area of man-made fire, staying in the high grass just next to it. When eventually the wall of fire reached them, they lacked time to do anything else than run, but they were too slow and they died within few meters of Dodge's burnt out area. This tragic outcome seems to defy the cognitive interpretations: distributed cognition worked against the team members; the rescue routine was misread; the same situation (recall that the whole team was contained in a very small area) did not lead to the same interpretation, design and action.

Let us then interpret the ways people behaved in the Mann Gulch situation, and the design and implementation of action as moody ways. In other words, let us put at the centre stage the existential situation of the actor. We submit that what decided the different outcomes, the opposite understandings, the alternative situated knowledges were not the physical circumstances on the fire scene, but the contrasting moods the actors were in. If the smokejumpers were just cognitive robots, with more or less similar experience, once exposed to the same situation they would have come up with similar answers, or be able to quickly imitate a rescue procedure invoked by one member of the team. On the contrary they were confronting a culminating, supreme situation; they were spatially close but existentially far apart in respect to this supreme situation. Their fundamental attunements with the situation varied greatly and their different moods affected distinctively their understanding and ways of acting. Both Weick (1993) and Maclean (1992), the latter the author of the original novel on the accident, provide us with some evidence in this respect. The team members were victims of panic, and in this fundamental mood they interpreted what Dodge was doing as 'going nuts' and an explicit authorization by their captain for everyone to go mad. Panic determined their experiencing lack of time and being overwhelmed by the world, the forest on fire. Maclean (1992) colourfully describes Dodge's mood in the following way: 'Inside Dodge there was the only cool spot in the total fire scene.' This coolness is the hidden source of his capacity to improvising, to finding all the time necessary to come up with a solution, though paradoxical, and implementing it.

The reinterpretation of this case points to a new way of studying improvisation as mood, by contrasting it with other moods, and let its salient characteristics emerge by comparison. But there are many moods out there, which ones to choose for this comparative exercise? As we have already remarked many times, improvisation strikes us because of its sudden, extemporaneous and full effect. That is the reason why we should contrast it with affections characterized by their negligible or null effect and by their being sticky with clock time. Good candidates are of course panic, as shown above, and boredom. Both have problematic relationships with leading to any form of effective action and with the passing of clock time, though in different ways and for different reasons. We examine them in order.

The mood of panic

Our existence unfolds by our relentless taking care of the world, usually encountered as an intricate web of interdependent tools, of ready at hand artefacts, resources and people. This is how we are most the time amidst the world. In this environment we develop and implement specific projects, made of sequences of in-order-tos, framed into plans, strategies or immediate, almost unconscious reactions to emerging circumstances. When the fundamental attunement of panic sets in, this ordinary way of understanding and acting in the world stops. The world overwhelms us. It ceases to appear as a set of tools ready for use; and we lack the time to implement our in-order-tos. Resources are not at hand; time is not available. We are led to inaction or to engage frantically in whatever action comes to hand. Angst for the lack of time in pursuing further exploration of alternatives may lead to paralysis of decision-making, which may turn into inaction or the haphazard, compulsive pursue of an activity picked by those available in the situation, but with no really adaptable strategy. At the limit, that our being-in-the-world is, from the moment of birth, permanently set towards death, suddenly emerges as the alternative that has always been there, but which gets forgotten through being amidst the daily chores and care. Death sets in as the implicitly preferred choice, the only one that can calm down the highest levels of anxiety determined by panic.

This is the structure of panic as mood. Care is aimless. The world is unusable. Intentionality has nowhere to go except to consider the supreme alternative of death. Time is lacking. As the Mann Gulch accident shows vividly, entering the situation with the mood of panic closes off the sensible choice of alternatives, and especially the invention and implementation of new ones. Imitation, as a strategy of action, is also impeded and falls victim of that mood.

The mood of boredom

If panic implies that things, including time, matter too much (the world overwhelms us), in boredom nothing really matters: the world is indifferent and time never seems to pass. If in panic we fall victim to the world and time, in boredom we try to kill time while being immersed in a fog of indifference. Depending upon the acuteness of the mood, Heidegger (1995) distinguishes three main states of intensifying boredom: becoming bored by something specific (a train does not arrive and we are waiting at the station watching the clock and trying out all sorts of pastimes); being bored with something (a nice evening spent with friends–time flew–still, when we get back home, we feel bored); finally, profound boredom–it is boring for one.

Starting from the superficial ways in which we deal with boredom in the everyday life, we can encounter the intimate relation of this mood with time. At first, it is under the form of whatever pastime we engage in to overcome boredom, we pass the time in order to master it, because time becomes long in waiting for a train that is late. Already our superficial, ordinary way of coping with the first level of boredom, being bored by something specific, highlights a relation to time which is not objective. When we are bored, our attunement, our way of being-amidst, is characterized by being in a time that passes too slowly, amidst a world that does not offer many resources to endure the long time.

The second type of boredom has a less specific object. We recognize retrospectively that we were bored by the evening partying out. Still, when we were passing it we had fun: actually, we never watched the clock. It seems at first a more superficial, fleeting type of boredom, but at a closer look it is more profound. Precisely because no specific pastime was deployed during the evening, it is apparent that the party itself had been all along a clever, 'preventive' pastime used to fight boredom before it even arises. By deciding to allow ourselves an evening out and have fun with friends, we have given ourselves time intentionally dedicated to find ways to pass the time. 'We have found an occupation that diverts our attention away from time as it drags and from its oppressing us' (Heidegger, 1995). This type of mood is not triggered by a specific, apparent cause, nor it is tied to a specific event or situation, rather it seems to stem from our existence. The second form of boredom is less situation-bound than the first. Note how by not experiencing the flow of time through spending out the evening, we make the whole evening a 'single stretched now'.

Finally, the more profound form of boredom, 'it is boring for one'. We are empty, we want nothing from the particular resources available in the situation, we seem to be able to lift ourselves above and beyond the particular circumstances. As a result, the whole situation becomes indifferent. We no longer stand as subjects in front to objects/resources: we 'find ourselves in the midst of beings as a whole, i.e., in the whole of this indifference' (*ibid.*, p. 138). What is peculiar of the last form of boredom is that at first there is no pastime in sight. Time does not drag us, neither we make it stand still. Rather, one feels 'removed from the flow of time', indifferent to time, timeless. Yet, indifference means all beings withdraw in retrospect (the past), in every prospect (future) and in the very respect of the present. Such a profound indifference is linked to the whole time horizon which surrounds. What is striking of this form of boredom is that all dimensions of time (clock time; past, future, the now etc.) do not seem to matter. There is no determinate time-point when boredom arises; we do not worry at all about the clock, as we do not worry about beings and the world; we are not annoyed by any 'stretched now', i.e. the time span during which this boredom holds us. Actually, the profound boredom 'can take hold of us in an instant like a flash of lightning' (*ibid.*, p. 148). Time is there but in an unarticulated unity that 'entrances' us. In sum, it is not only beings (objects, resources, people) that refuse themselves, but time itself.

The ex-temporality of improvisation

Panic and lack of time; boredom in its various forms and passing the time are intertwined. Passing the time creeps into our being bored, as lack of time fuels panic. These moods appear to be far from superficial or contingent upon special events. They are profoundly concentrated on us, our situation and time, which is not clock time, rather our time.

We submit that the opposite of improvisation is not planned action, but boredom or sometimes panic. If in the latter unarticulated time and refusal of beings lead to inaction, we can look anew at improvisation as the 'moment of vision', as the look of resolute decision in which the full situation of action opens itself and keeps itself open to our initiative of re-registering, recombination and intervention. The cognitive perspective focuses on how smart improvisers are able to quickly re-register the world and recombine resources. But this is possible only because suddenly the world, its resources and people matter differently, so that they can be singled out and recombined differently. And quickness is far from implying rigidity and reverse to the already known. Improvisation is that particular mood where the reconfiguration of the ground takes place in which we encounter the world (and devise and carry out those projects and actions objects of the cognitive perspective). Before action and before design there is a being thrown in a range of possibilities. The mood situates you in respect to these possibilities, discloses some and conceal others. The ones revealed, will matter and be object of the simultaneous planning and actions of the improviser. Moods like fear, laughter or boredom involve above all a self-revelation, a disclosure of oneself as caring (or being indifferent to) things in some definite way (Blattner, 1999). Improvisation is that moment of vision and self-revelation where all the possibilities linked to the being-in-the-situation emerge out of the fog of boredom. Improvisation is the antidote to panic and boredom because it is 'extemporaneous', i.e. it ruptures the way time entrances us in both situations, either by being completely missing, or totally undifferentiated. Improvisation is then rupture, or as the conductor Pierre Boulez describes it in music *'Einbruch'*. Only if the temporal entrancement is ruptured do beings no longer refuse themselves, possibilities for action emerge, graspable in the situation and give to the actor the possibility of intervening at the specific moment and in the specific circumstances. The ex-temporaneous moment of vision is not some now – point we simply observe or describe ex post. 'The moment of vision is a look of a unique kind, which we call the look of resolute disclosedness for action in the specific situation' (*ibid*., p. 151) What Dodge did was to have this decisive look at the fire and achieve the paradoxical commitment to *be* fire thrown into fire.

On the basis of or analysis, we can take exception, then, from the cognitive view expressed by Moorman and Miner (1998), according to which any entity capable of planning or executing can improvise. In the new perspective evoked so far, we would rephrase their statement as follows: any entity existing, being able to reflect on its existence and endowed with moods, feelings and emotions is able to improvise.

Concluding remarks

The study of improvisation as situated action carried out within the cognitive perspectives in common currency leaves us somewhat disappointed. We can easily find in it all the ingredients of more routine, planned action: goals, selection of alternatives, implementation, design and problem solving. The temporal dimension of improvisation is explained away. Extemporaneity is reframed as simultaneity and quickness, which it is obviously not. Improvisation was described by the Romans as neither quick nor unplanned: it was called extemporalis actio. This begs for attentive interpretation. Cognitive theories of situated action and knowledge have been of no avail in this respect.

We have submitted that one reason for this lack of assistance may lie in the distorted way in which the cognitive approaches consider situatedeness: they omit due consideration of the 'situation of the actor'. Implicitly, they deal with the situation as a set of emerging circumstances, but consider the actor as a passionless, problem solving robot (with body or without depending upon the latest flavour of the critical or feminist theorizing).

Considering the situation of the actor with the same attention that the situated action paradigm dedicates to the fleeting circumstances of action poses a difficult problem, especially if one wants to avoid any drifting into a mental, symbolic representation of the mind (via frames, scripts, mindsets etc.).

Here, we can find shelter by going back to the origins of phenomenology, the philosophical line of thought that in the last century celebrated the notion of situatedeness. Phenomenology was the first to suggest that moods capture the essence of the fleeting attunement of the actor with the situation. Moods are far from being a marginal, colourful add-on to our cognitive explanations of how the actors behave in situations. They are the ground for our encountering the world, understanding and acting in the situation. There is no situated action without a mood, when we deal with human beings rather than cognitive robots. We have looked then at improvisation as mood. Phenomenology avoids considering moods as yet another mental object to be studied in an objective way, rather it puts forward a different research method, according to which moods are best accessed by evoking, awakening and comparing them. As a consequence, improvisation has not been contrasted with plans and procedure, as it is customary in the cognitive inquiries into this phenomenon, but with other moods, the ones of panic and boredom, dropping the usual counterpoising of improvisation and planning.

Such a comparison exercise and the careful study of how moods are related to time, has allowed us to come closer to the meaning of the original definition of improvisation as an extemporaneous activity. We have not been able to demonstrate ultimately that improvisation is a mood rather than a mindset, but new research directions have been laid out for a pre-cognitive, existential way of understanding this activity. In this respect, we hope to have carried out, in a more radical way, the project of linking the study of improvisation as an activity which has palpable contact with the human condition (Weick, 1998).

To be sure, the existential perspective here outlined has a number of implications. To begin with, improvisation as moment of vision and disclosedness toward decision is much rarer than perhaps appreciated so far. Many forms of improvisation appear as pastimes against boredom. Few are actually antidotes to panic in emergencies. Second, if we accept Heidegger's (1995) statement according to which profound boredom defines the modern condition, a nocturnal light is cast on the last hundred years or so of management and organization science. Emphasis placed on programming, planning and rational choice possibly conceals what goes on most of the time in most organizations for most people: boredom. Emphasis on decision making has entranced us and distracted us from appreciating that important decisions occur very seldom, while what prevails are all sort of pastimes (programmes, methods, models) that punctuate the life of workers and managers within and outside organizations.

Acknowledgements

Many thanks to Mike Cushman for the revision of the manuscript, to Bo Dahlbom for his useful critiques; Susan Scott for having organized the Panel on Time and

Globalization at the American Management Association Conference in Toronto where these ideas were originally presented; and last but not least Mary Jo Hatch who urged me a few years ago to be bolder and more radical in addressing the theme of improvisation.

Notes

1. A first attempt in this direction, but still 'imprisoned' in cognitivism, was carried out in Ciborra (1999).
2. Here, the feminist literature not only trails behind the phenomenological philosophers, such as Heidegger, but also ancient authors like Adam Smith, more usually associated with the deprived notion of economic man as the actor of economic organization, in particular the market. Smith's (1853) most acclaimed oeuvre was in reality The Theory of Moral Sentiment, a monumental effort to link social and economic behaviour to the study of sentiments and passions, such as sympathy. An earlier effort (two centuries earlier) can be found in the proponent of objective method, Descartes with his influential – at the time – The Passions of the Soul (1988). In the same vein, more recently, Simon (1967) submitted a cogntive explanation of emotions. It is ironic that moods, affections and feelings are, instead, absent from the feminist theorizing on knowledge: situated, but acted by a passionless robot, without a body (as in Suchman's (1987) study), or with one (mechanical?) in the later works of Haraway (1991) and Suchman (2000). We also take exception from the recent attempts to amend the prevailing cognitive approach by referring to neurophisology and emotions (Damasio, 1995). Phenomenology as developed by Heidegger in his early courses just after the first World War was already targeting and destructing the central role attributed to the mind (cognition) by putting on the center stage affectiveness and moods, or quoting Saint Augustine,'the heart' (Heidegger, 2004).
3. Some attentive author does mention the emotional or affective side of improvisation (e.g. Crossan and Sorrenti, 1996). But, once again, concern for emotions seems to be just grafted on an overwhelmingly cognitive perspective (Eisenberg, 1990). If anything, the jazz metaphor helps Hatch (1999) to pinpoint the importance of the'groove and feel' factor involved in improvisation.

References

Barrett, F.J.(1998). Creativity and improvisation in jazz and organizations: implications for organizational learning, *Organization Science* **9**(5): 605 622.

Berliner, P.F. (1994). *Thinking in Jazz: The Infinite Art of Improvisation*, University of Chicago, Chicago.

Blattner, W.D. (1999). *Heidegger's Temporal Idealism,* Cambrige: Cambridge University Press.

Brown, J.S. and Duguid, P. (1991). Organizational learning and communities of practice, *Organization Science* **2**(1): 40–57.

Ciborra, C.U. (1999). Notes on improvisation and time in organizations, *Accounting, Management and Information Technologies* **9**: 77–94.

Crossan, M. and Sorrenti, M. (1996). Making sense of improvisation, in J.P. Walsh and A.S. Huff (eds), *Advances in Strategic Management* **14**:155–180, Greenwich, CT: JAI Press.

Damasio, A.R. (1995). *Descartes' Error: Emotion, Reason and the Human Brain,* New York: Avon.

Descartes, R. (1988). *The Passions of the Soul,* Indianapolis: Hackett.

Dreyfus, H.L. (1991). *Being-in-the-World, Cambridge,* MA: MIT Press.

Eisenberg, E. (1990). Jamming! Transcendence through organizing, *Communications Research* **17**(2): 139–164.
Eisenhardt, K.M. and Tabrizi, B.N. (1995). Accelerating adaptive processes: product innovation in the global computer industry, *Administrative Science Quarterly* **40**: 84–110.
Haraway, D. (1991). Situated knowledges: the science question in feminism and the privilege of partial perspective, Chapter 9 in *Simians, Cyborgs and Women,* pp. 183–201, New York: Routledge.
Hatch, M.J. (1997). Jazzing up the theory of organizational improvisation in J.P. Walsh and A.S. Huff (eds), *Advances in Strategic Management* **14**:155–180, Greenwich, CT: JAI Press.
Hatch, M.J. (1997a). Irony and the social construction of contradiction in the humour of a management team, *Organization Science* **8**(3): 275–288.
Hatch, M.J. (1999). Exploring the empty spaces in jazz: how improvisational jazz helps redescribe organizational structure, *Organization Studies* **20**: 75–100.
Heidegger, M. (1962). *Being and Time,* New York: Harper and Row.
Heidegger, M. (1995). *The Basic Problems of Phenomenology,* Bloomington, IN: Indiana University Press.
Heidegger, M. (2004) *The Phenomenology of Religious Life,* Bloomington, IN: Indiana University Press.
Husserl, E. (1962). *Ideas,* New York: Collier Books.
Hutchins, E. (1996). *Cognition in the Wild,* Cambridge, MA: MIT Press.
Inwood, A. (1999). *Heidegger Dictionary,* Oxford: Blackwell.
Kamoche, K.N., Cunha, M.P. and Cunha, J.V. (eds) (2002). *Organizational Improvisation,* London: Routledge.
Maclean, N. 1992). *Young Men and Fire,* Chicago: The University of Chicago Press.
Mead, G.H. (1934). *Mind, Self and Society,* Chicago: The University of Chicago Press.
Moorman, C. and Miner, A.S. (1998). Organizational improvisation and organization memory, *Academy of Management Review* **23**(4): 698–723.
Newell, A. and Simon, H.A. (1972). *Human Problem Solving,* Englewood Cliffs, NJ: Prentice Hall.
Nonaka, I. (1994). A dynamic theory of organizational knowledge, *Organization Science* **5**(1): 14–37.
Nonaka, I. and Konno, N. (1998). The concept of 'Ba'-Building a foundation for knowledge creation, *California Management Review* **40**(3): 40–54.
Quintillian (1993). *The Institutio Oratoria,* Vol. IV (H.E. Butler trans.), Cambridge, MA: Harvard University Press.
Schön, D.A. (1983). *The Reflective Practioner,* New York: Basic Books.
Simon, H.A. (1967). Motivational and emotional controls of cognition, *Psychological Review* **74**: 29–39.
Simon, H.A. (1989). Making management decisions: The role of intuition and emotion, in W. Agor (ed.), *Intuition in Organizations: Leading and Management Productivity,* Newbury Park, CA: Sage, pp. 23–39.
Smith A. (1853). *The Theory of Moral Sentiments*, London: H.C. Bohn.
Spolin, V. (1963). *Improvisation for the Theater: A Handbook of Teaching and Directing Techniques*, Evaston, IL: Northwestern University Press.
Suchman, L. (1987). *Plans and Situated Actions: The problem of human-machine communication,* New York: Cambridge University Press.
Suchman, L. (1993). Response to Vera and Simon's situated action: a symbolic interpretation, *Cognitive Science* **17**: 71–75.
Suchman, L. (2000). *Located accountabilities in technology production*, Draft, Department of Sociology, Lancaster University.
Vera, A.H. and Simon, H.A. (1993). Situated action: a symbolic interpretation, *Cognitive Science* **17**: 7–48.
Weick, K.E. (1993). Organization redesign as improvisation, in G.P. Huber and W.H. Glick, *Organizational Change and Redesign,* New York: Oxford University Press.

Weick, K.E. (1993a). The collapse of sense-making in organizations: the Mann Gulch disaster, *Administrative Science Quarterly* **Dec.**: 628–652.

Weick, K.E. (1998). Improvisation as a mindset for organizational analysis, *Organization Science* **9**(5): 543–555.

Winograd, T. and Flores, F. (1986). *Understanding Computers and Cognition,* Norwood, NJ:Ablex.

3

Imbrication of Representations: Risk and Digital Technologies*

Claudio U. Ciborra

Abstract

Though emerging from different venues and backgrounds, risk management and digital applications are both based on sophisticated techniques of representation. This paper tracks the multiple overlappings and convergence between these two streams of representations. Initially digital technologies play a background role, as a tool to execute the algorithms of risk calculus. Then, they are useful in managing surveys and data analysis for those areas where risk management needs to store data on, for example, accidents. With the extension of markets for trading risk, computers and networks (or Information and Communication Technologies, ICT) become the tools of choice to allow the efficient functioning of industries like insurance. In other industries, like banking, where 'the business' is a vast archipelago of applications running on systems and networks, it is apparent that these integrated systems are inherently exposed to risk. Hence, these humble tools become both the infrastructure of the risk industry, and also the source of new, often incalculable risks; they move from a clear-cut subordinate relationship (as tool) to that of *imbrication*. Risk representations become more calculable and formalized, but this is obtained at the price of an incalculability of the risks of the infrastructure itself. The analysis of the multiple patterns of imbrication of representations between risk and digital technologies is applied to a range of empirical domains: from software engineering and information systems (the subservient infrastructure); to operational risk in banking; and finally to the future scenario of the democratization of finance, whereby Global Risk Information Databases (GRIDs), become gigantic machines to represent, compute, and trade all sorts of individual and social risks.[1] Overall, the paper seeks to characterize the multiple links between risk and digital technologies in organizations and draws in part on the phenomenology of representation and Heidegger's studies of Care and Concern and his later work on the essence of modern technology.

Introduction

Today, the debate inside banks and insurance companies about how to face Basel 2, Solvency 2 and International Auditing Standards recommendations agree on a couple of important points that are going to set the agenda on how these organizations will operate in the future. First, introducing risk and value will change deeply traditional accounting practices. A risk calculus requires to take into account all possible values of accounting variables in the future, attributing to each of them a probability distribution. Also, the accounting principle of summing single values, cannot be applied to risks: the risk of a portfolio of shares or policies is not given by the sum of the single contracts, but also by their correlations. Hence, second, placing risk as the basic principle for enterprise control increases the complexity of its management, adding the dimensions of time (the future) and weight in the reciprocal influences between the control variables. What is needed is a new 'reference model', that is, a new representation of how the firm works and should be managed; the debate is open as to whether this new representation should be the same across organizations, across the functional areas of the same organization, and as to the actual level of detail or approximation required. Third, whatever type of new representation is selected and constructed, it will come alive only through a sophisticated 'data system', consisting of databases, processing engines, algorithms – all the customary ICT tools needed to run a computer-based representation of the firm. Industry consultants and practitioners acknowledge that there is going to be a deep interdependency between risk management and data systems and the designers of one can learn from the designers of the other: 'Technology can realize a virtuous circle: the data system becomes the central tool of the new organizational arrangement that supports its use' (De Felice and Moriconi, 2004).

This is just a specific instance in two important industries – banking and insurance – where representations are based on risk cross paths with representations enabled by computer technology. But the phenomenon is general and not confined to selected industries (Douglas and Wildavsky, 1982). This paper presents an inquiry into the past and future interdependencies between risk and digital technologies, considering both the early days and application areas, where technology was just considered a tool to implement a calculus needed for the quantitative models of risk management, and also future scenarios where digital technology under the form of an ubiquitous GRID (Global Risk Information Database) (Shiller, 2003, chapter 14) may constitute the infrastructure to enable a democratization of risk management at the level of the entire society, affecting the very life-world of each of us. We shall initially track the distinct development paths of risk management techniques and digital technologies, and then their increasing convergence by looking at them as two technologies of representation, one focusing at first on a distinct trait of human existence, the other on key characteristics of computer technology (Ciborra and Hanseth, 1998). However, far from keeping distinct these two representation domains, the human and the non-human, we are going to show the ramifications of an unfolding *imbroglio* (Latour, 1999) for which the word 'network' turns out to be too *Cartesian* and tidy. The concept of *imbrication* better captures the reciprocal, self reinforcing, often non-linear, impacts of one representation upon the other.

To be sure, over the last four decades technical and managerial representations share a basic belief in the power of organizational control. They portray a systematic assessment (as in the scientific study of work by F.W. Taylor) involving an orderly and rigorous study of risk which can make its management more effective (Beniger, 1986). Better control strategies are seen to be the paramount way of mitigating, reducing or annihilating risk. The focus of Basel 2 like recommendations on operational risk is a good example of this approach (Power, 2005).

With the advent of the Internet, network computing and inter-organizational systems, the boundaries of units of analysis – such as a 'software project' or a 'business firm' – become too narrow for capturing all the various ramifications of the dynamics entertained by digital technology and risk. For example, consider recent developments in ideas of 'democratizing finance' (Shiller, 2003) which seek to transfer a sophisticated calculus to the level of individual existence so that life choices, change and innovation are devolved to the level of the individual. This way of looking at, and practicing, finance as a science for managing risk 'democratically' gives digital technologies an overarching importance and a new role. They become 'GRID technologies', i.e. an information infrastructure that allows the calculation of indices and units of accounts, so that risks can be now represented for the purposes of trade, pooling and sharing on global markets by large numbers of individuals. Here, the powerful means of representation provided by GRID technologies at the society level, may dramatically change the effectiveness and detail with which risk is represented at the micro-level.

Building and managing such complex infrastructures is far from being a linear process. Despite tight managerial control, careful planning, appropriate risk management, and so on, ICT infrastructures tend to have a life of their own; they *drift* (Ciborra and Associates, 2000) as a result of improvised usages, unforeseen technical interdependencies between old (legacy) and new platforms, quirky design choices, surprising user resistance, and other unpredictable behaviours of both systems and humans. In short, the infrastructure deployed to compute individual and global risks in minute detail can be a source of low frequency, high risk events if it breaks down or deviates from expected usage. Imbrication is here at work: the powerful digital 'tools' that enable the more sophisticated representation of risks are at the same time the cause of a potential irruption of the 'incalculable', of not easily representable risks due their man-made character arising from insidious, rare, and undetectable side-effects (Beck, 1992; Giddens, 1990).

The argument is structured as follows. Risk and digital technologies as two technologies of representation are introduced within a phenomenological approach. Next, the vicissitudes of these two technologies are examined in domains broadly related to information systems; from software engineering to current approaches to operational risk. However, it is with the deployment of ICT in markets accompanied by economic, rather than just technical or managerial thinking, that the more intimate and potentially further imbricated relationship between the two technologies of risk management and digital technology begins to emerge. In the final two sections we explore the doubleedged outcome of such imbrication: GRID technologies allow both the penetration of quantitative risk calculi into our everyday life world, and also function as potential vehicles for incalculable, man-made risk. The execution of one project of ubiquitous and powerful quantitative representation of risk may trigger the irruption of that which cannot be readily represented. At the same time, it is only through the implementation of powerful representations through GRID technologies, that risk can be represented in an objectified and standardized way in the very core of human existence and the institutions we have created.

The phenomenology of risk and information technology

What are the key components of the notion of risk that can be found within information systems, managerial and economic literatures (Renn, 1998)? Risk is essentially a function of actions, events, imagined outcomes and their values (Scheytt et al., 2006). Its essential dimensions are a time horizon, a notion of subjective judgement (that is likely to be highly socialized in form), and an openness to uncertainty and change (March and Shapira, 1987). If one of these ingredients is missing, we are confronted with problems that cannot be characterized in terms of risk because they involve no uncertainty, change or innovation, concern problems with no impact (no value), or those which have already occurred in the past and so make irrelevant a consideration of their prospect in the future. This notion of risk is very much anchored to the idea of the cognitive self, to an idea of decision making and, more specifically, to the calculation of objectified quantities related to time, value and impact.

Information systems provide an array of tools and applications, data models, and data analysis techniques which support the multiple exigencies of calculating risk in multiple settings and for a variety of purposes. All the literatures examined below agree in the broad definition considered above, but are informed by two complementary schools of thought. The first, behavioural, cognitive and economic literature points to the biases in cognition and decision making that can make the utilization, if not the very calculus of risk problematic or distorted in actual situations of action (e.g. March and Shapira, 1987). The second literature, largely ignored by the previous one concerns the famous 'risk society' argument and focuses on the growing importance of incalculability, especially in highly integrated, globalized systems (Beck, 1992; Giddens, 2003). We could acquiesce in such visions and the somewhat rigid division of labour between the various risk literatures. However, in the light of recent developments, like the new radical change of perspectives introduced by Basel 2, Solvency 2, and especially future scenarios pointing at even higher levels of micro and macro convergence (or, better as we shall see, imbrication) between the technologies of risk and computing, we prefer to build and adopt for our present purposes a more integrated, if ad hoc, framework of analysis centred on a few basic tenets:

- That both risk management and computing be regarded as 'functions' sharing the same properties, i.e. that whatever is their argument (to use a mathematical metaphor) they execute the same type of representational operations: they formalize, objectify and quantify.

- That we need to understand the dynamics of each, and how they have interacted in the past and will interact according to emerging scenarios.
- That we should critically examine taken for granted definitions, such as the idea that technology is just a tool which seems to be accepted by many literatures on risk, and the rigid division between how human decision makers represent and face risk within economic institutions and society, and how computer models can contribute to, or influence, such a human representation of risk.

First, we should honour those dimensions of risk, such as value and man-made change, which point to the importance of human existence, to the question 'Who am I and what do I wish?', or to the general intrinsic motility, openness and unpredictability of life. In other words, in positing the relationship between risk and human agency we do not only need to overcome the narrowness of the neo-Cartesian model of the human agent as calculating machine, but also the more powerful notion of economic man, his differential risk attitudes, limited cognitive capabilities, strategic orientation and proclivity to exchange (March and Shapira, 1987). When modelling risk, we recommend the need to stay close to, and to safeguard, some essential traits of human existence, in particular the intrinsic openness of life and its fundamental indeterminacy as the key sources of our very personal worry about risk. But the argument is not simply about life and the indeterminacy of danger or certainty of death (Heidegger, 1962). Ontological strength understood as existential meaning is given to the mundane notion of risk through our generic disposition in life, through our care and concern about people, things and the world that surrounds us. Risk is imagined both because the world is dangerous and unpredictable, and because we are restlessly concerned about it (*inquietum cor nostrum*, our restless heart, as St Augustine would put it).

To follow Heidegger's formulation, risk can be looked at as a hedged form of care (*Sorge*) or concern: care taking care of itself. Care is concern both about the present as well as having to care about the future; more precisely, care in the present encompasses possible outbursts of care in the future. Care would wish to have a smooth unfolding, wanting to avoid peaks and crises even in its own deployment. Hence, the notion of risk would be expressed as a concern of care about itself (*Besorgnis*, or apprehension; Heidegger, 2001, p. 101). The objectification of this existential concern in the form of various sorts of representations of organizational and economic risk is a consequence of the tendency of such concern to forget about itself and life in general, focusing instead on the things, resources and people it relentlessly deals with, rather than on the open and anxiety-ridden project of human existence that provides its momentum. In naïve forms of risk calculation, care and concern become quantified objects which can be represented, calculated and manipulated.

Now, let us turn to technology as a distinct source of representation. Various organization theory scholars have contributed to a phenomenological perspective. Zuboff's (1988) idea of ICT as 'informatting' technology implies that all the different data models and representations contained in systems provide a powerful set of representations of the key processes of the firm which can be an important means to convey, share and harness knowledge well beyond the standard, automated visions of the firm. Cooper (1992) also emphasized the representational powers of ICT, as well as Kallinikos (1995), recalling Heidegger's (1962) idea of technology providing a world view (see also the applications of Bloomfield and Vurdubakis 1994). However, a more comprehensive view of technology which may be of relevance for the study of the representation of risk and for the representations provided by ICT, needs to include the ideas about the essence of technology as originally put forward by Heidegger (1978). Through the notion of *Gestell*, Heidegger tried to grasp the essence of modern technology as 'enframing' and as converting everything encountered, natural or human, into a standing reserve stock (*Bestand*) of resources to be harnessed for further deployment. The river is a source of hydroelectric power. A forest is the support for enrolling public opinion through newspaper advertising. Nature can be critically represented as a gigantic petrol station! *Gestell* is the process of gathering, reunifying and recycling resources for production and use, and can be translated as 'GRID'. In other words, the representations provided by ICT, should always be seen as a part of a relentless process of creating resources that are objectifiable, representable and thus better stocked and circulated for further use (see also Vattimo, 1992). This dynamic increase in the portions of reality which become representable and reusable is not without any danger, Heidegger suggests. On the contrary, the danger lies precisely in the power of representation of the unfolding *Gestell*, i.e. the incalculability and scale of those domains that cannot be reached by the unfolding powers of representation. We are becoming a 'risk society' (Beck, 1992) at the same time that we are becoming an 'information society' enabled by the diffusion of the GRID/*Gestell*.

We are now in the position to link the idea of *Gestell*, and its relentless power to generate world pictures to the quantitative representation of risks made more and more possible by sophisticated forms of ICT infrastructures. In essence, we encounter how the growth of risks made possible by ICT infrastructures allows a new domain of interest to be created by the power of *Gestell*: care itself (through the need for care to take care of itself – *Besorgnis*). Care becomes, as unveiled by the new representations supplied by the ICT infrastructure, a *Bestand*, a standing stock, reserve of resources and activities ready to be deployed. In this way, care is transformed from an existential characteristic of operating in the world, into a generalized capacity, risk, which must be represented, formalized and computed. But this, as noted by the risk society literature (Beck, 1992; Giddens, 1990) does not come without a price to pay, that is the presence of more and more man-made risks, such as those created by building more and more integrated infrastructures (Ciborra and Associates, 2000).

In what follows we track the intertwining of different representations of risk and the enabling representations supplied by the data systems in a number of instances. Different practices are presented through 'vignettes' informed by relevant literature (occasionally backed by direct empirical research by the author which is not presented here) in a longitudinal perspective (from past practices to new visions) and by a sort of evolutionary line (from low to high convergence).

Each vignette contains a description of the practice of risk calculation as presented in the professional and/or academic literature, and the range of problems that emerge when trying to implement that practice using various applications of information technology. The goal of this analysis is to put flesh on the concept of the phenomenological understanding of care presented above. In addition, the aim is to reflect on ideas of imbrication between the two forms of representation as a dynamic unfolding process.

The software project

According to the positivist definition adopted by Boehm (1991), to launch the discipline of software risk management, risk management deals with risk exposure, where risk exposure is treated as the potential loss multiplied by the probability of loss. Potential loss is described by the components of the unsatisfactory outcome of a project, which leads management to identify lists of the risk factors that are seen as causes of overall negative outcomes. Risk factors have to be addressed, eliminated, mitigated or avoided, depending upon their probability of occurrence and the size of their impacts. Various techniques are used to carry out the analysis. For example, decision trees can provide a framework for analysing the role of risk factors and the sensitivity of final outcomes. Regression analysis allows the development of a model which relies on the data of past software projects (Fairley, 1994), and which aims to elicit those factors which can explain the variation of the effort put into one particular project relative to the main trend identified by the regression curve. Simulation (e.g., Monte Carlo methods) helps in identifying the behaviour of the intervening risk factors. Other approaches are based on disciplines such as statistics, mathematical modelling of decision making and graph theory. Note that most of these techniques presuppose the use of computer applications as essential calculating tools. But the role of this technology is 'invisible' in the literature that focuses on the modelling of risk and the relevant algorithms.

Quantitative representations are not without problems in software engineering as well as in other fields of risk management (Renn, 1998). For example:

- The quantitative combinations of variables, such as magnitude of impact and probability, assume equal weights. Low-probability/high-impact events may get the same weight as high-probability/low impact ones, and this might distort the representation of risk emerging in a given situation. However, attributing differential weights may prove to be an uncertain or impossible task.
  - Probabilities tend to be extracted from the relative frequencies of past events. When this is not an adequate approach to anticipate future events, calculation may have limited predictive power.
  - People perceive the magnitude of impact and its probability differently, which leads to an appreciation of risk that may differ from the formal outcome of the algorithms.
  - The desirability of effects may vary among different decision makers.

- The institutional and organizational contexts may influence the actual risk levels to which human agents are exposed, and may impact on the various risk-mitigating or risk-handling actions indicated by the purely technical calculus of risk outcomes.

In summary, the first set of approaches based on the use of sophisticated formal representations is accompanied by necessarily crude simplifications characterizing the risk situation. In particular, only one decision maker tends to be identified (the management of the firm or the project) as being responsible for assessing and evaluating risk and for formulating remedial policies based on the relevant calculus. Computer systems just 'sit' in the background and are assumed to deliver the computable representations which decision makers and designers order them to run.

The risks of management information systems

The causes and consequences of risks, as well as risk-management actions, are embedded in institutional and organizational structures, and are generally intertwined in social processes and networks of relationships. All the stages of effective risk management take place within the constraints posed by such social and organizational contexts, and are compelled to respect the opportunities offered by those constraints. A few practitioners of software risk management have stressed the importance of organizational processes to complement or support the representations provided by the quantitative techniques (e.g. Charette, 1996).

The broader organizational perspectives on risk identified above address the issue of implementation within the concrete organizational or institutional setting that surrounds any risk-calculating algorithm. Not only do these approaches widen the scope of risk analysis and the range of risk factors taken into consideration, but they also point to the inevitable gap between models and their deployment. This often shows that managerial practice is at odds with the prediction of the formal representations or methods themselves. Leaving aside the results of the important literature focusing on the psychological, and behavioural aspects of risk management (see March and Shapira, 1987, on the actual behaviour of managers facing risks; and Perrow, 1984, on the influence of organizational settings and routines; also Loewenstein et al., 2001; Tversky and Kahneman, 1974), we focus here on the literature dealing specifically with risk management of information systems (IS) development within business organizations.

Lyytinen et al. (1998) address a range of organizational aspects by looking at various IS and software risk approaches. They highlight one important cognitive aspect in risk management: the scope of managerial attention to the factors to be taken into consideration in any calculus or qualitative assessment. They find that various IS approaches to risk management may focus on specific areas, such as business strategy, although risks can be hidden in any of the multiple stages of the development and deployment of a system. In order to introduce structure into this potentially limitless field of interest, the authors propose a socio-technical framework for comparing various approaches, according to key domains defined by Leavitt's (1964) analysis which connects four main variables: strategy, technology, structure and tasks. But such a commendable exercise aimed at reducing conceptual complexity proves to be of dubious use, since it is based on a misrepresentation of the nature of risk calculus, namely the assumption of the equivalence of the sociotechnical notion of variance control to attain system equilibrium, with the goals and scope of risk management in an organization. Within the socio-technical theoretical framework, variances are problems that need to be handled by an appropriate control system based on the coordination and communication of the members of the organization among themselves, usually involving technical infrastructure. Control actions are based on feedback from a disturbance that *has occurred*. Risk, by contrast, is about *future* disturbances: immediate feedback from an occurred variance is not the only issue, nor is equilibrium necessarily a main feature. Risk management concerns uncertainty regarding future events and results in betting on outcomes, using insurance to mitigate their impact, and other strategies. In particular, all risk management contracts must be signed *before*, not after, a breakdown has occurred, and before the information that would create a sense of urgency arises (Shiller, 2003, p. 30). Variance control in a socio-technical system is, instead, about detecting breakdowns *ex post* and taking counteractive, equilibriumrestoring measures (Herbst, 1974). Even the fact that socio-technical systems must engage in equilibrium-seeking when dealing with variances is an idea that has been challenged (Ciborra et al., 1984). Variances (and indeed risks) are sometimes the source of innovation and new order (or self organization) stemming from *disequilibrium*. Hence, reduction to a pre-existing order may constitute a repressive policy that kills innovation.

This is just one instance showing that, unfortunately, IS approaches do not distance themselves enough from the tenets of the engineering and technical representations, or at least do not challenge them. At the limit, they put forward a richer list of risk factors which are often overlooked by the practitioner who focuses on a particular project as opposed to a business perspective (McFarlan, 1981). However, IS approaches rely on the same key fictions of purely technical perspectives, such as that of the 'unbiased' decision maker. For example, the ideal ranking risks on the basis of expected impact has not been empirically supported. March and Shapira (1987) report a vice-president stating, 'You don't quantify the risk, but you have to be able to feel it'. The same authors conclude that, although there is ample evidence that the risk-taking behaviour of managers is often far from optimal, such behaviour may indeed consist of accommodations of individuals and organizations to the 'subtle practical problems of sustaining appropriate risk-taking in an imperfectly comprehended world' (March and Shapira, 1987). Modelling, quantitative representations and planning seem to possess, then, a limited scope; what essentially matters in handling risk is the focal organizational context.

It is not a surprise that, within the IS account, the computer as supplier of representations of risk is still relegated to a marginal role. Despite the enlargement of the menu of risk factors, and the possibility to handle long lists of them through qualitative data analysis applications, such a role is deemed neither influential nor noteworthy. ICT may have strategic relevance for the business policy of the firm and may be the object of a careful analysis of the risks it may have on the functioning of the firm, but it remains a humble tool as far as the risk calculus is concerned.

Representations of operational risk

The notion of operational risk emerged in the banking environment as a residual category for those (mainly internally generated) risks not covered by the more common market and credit-risk management practices. It extends the regulatory principle that banks should hold some capital as a buffer against risks to their loans and credit operations (market-risk exposure). Other things being equal, this buffer should be enlarged if it is to take account of the way banks can incur risks not only from investment portfolios and from lending money to outside customers, but also if their internal ICT systems fail. More precisely, Basel 2 consultative documents originally defined operational risk as 'the risk of direct or indirect loss resulting from inadequate or failed internal processes, people and systems or from external events' (Basel Committee, 2001, par. 6). In this respect operational risk is an organizational concept that subsumes both the technical and managerial models and approaches which emerged in the discussion of IS and risk. However, the concept of operational risk has given rise in a deeper way to analyses and discussions that address the organizational dynamics of managing risks within hierarchies. In order to overcome the limitations of their narrow focus and naïve hypotheses about human behaviour and risk, it would be advisable for the managerial and technical IS literature to take notice of these developments, especially those occurring in critical accounting (Power, 1997).

The problems that emerge during the implementation of operational risk deeply concern the role that computers can play as tools to process data for operational risk management. It is therefore useful to mention here the results of Power's (2005) analysis of the puzzles, dilemmas and contradictions of operational risk that point to the ramifications of lack of knowledge, the role of biased data when assessing risk in organizations and the influence of internal politics. The issues raised all affect the representation of risk that computing is able to deliver to support effective operational risk management:

- What data is relevant to operational risk? Historic losses? Expected or unexpected ones? What about sudden catastrophic events?
- Is this data reliable? Apart from rare events for which data is unavailable, as well as for the most frequent ones, there can be opportunistic massaging to hide errors.
- Effective learning and correction of mistakes since the negative event occurred can also make historic data irrelevant, because operations have been modified in the meantime.
- Collecting data from multiple organizations (a sort of best-practice exercise in reverse) is a possible solution, but requires the sharing of troubling and

embarrassing information: hence one can expect to see pooled databases of this kind remain half empty.

- The 'key under the lamppost' effect. Data that is eventually collected systematically under existing internal auditing and information systems becomes the basis for measurement of operational risk. However, this gets to be defined by the databases available and not by the actual multiplicity of potential risks, which are not all covered by the existing systems when representing and recording historical risks.

Similar dilemmas affect the risk modelling stage, where Power (2005) notes that:

- The use of risk measurement techniques is not immune from organizational politics.
- Rational calculation processes have to be marketed and sold internally, but this is not always accomplished successfully and so its scope is rendered, at best, fragmented and a matter of negotiation.

In general, the main approaches to the management of operational risk are of two different types, similar to those which emerged in the discussion of risk in IS development: a 'soft' calculative approach and a 'hard' approach. The first tends to rely on a variety of ranking and scoring techniques for qualitative variables, with the goal of directing attention to key risk drivers. The hard approach is based on the discipline of market risk management and the relevant quantitative techniques based on calculating costs and utilities. The problem with the latter approach is that it aims at enacting market techniques within a fundamentally non-market organizational setting. Different types of representation emerging from different institutional contexts stir and cause frictions.

Economics and financial practice: new scenarios

The main difference between the economic and technical representations of risk is the possibility envisaged within economics of including a dimension of *intersubjective validity* through the notion of *utility*, which describes the degree of satisfaction or dissatisfaction with an event or an action among a variety of stakeholders (Renn, 1998). Harms and undesired effects can be framed as (social) costs (Coase, 1960) and thus become utilities or disutilities for different parties. Costs can be allocated by various mechanisms, market-like or non-market. Specifically, utilities can be traded; after all, utility can be measured by the amount of money one is willing to pay to avoid a potential harm. Economics thus introduces at least a social dimension in representing risk, albeit in the narrow sense of a system of exchange of utilities/disutilities. Such a dimension is missing from the IS technical and managerial perspectives, which are unable to deal with questions such as: Risk for whom? Who is going to pay to avoid a certain risk? Also, a social dimension includes some of the psychological aspects of risk, by distinguishing risk-taking from risk-neutral or risk-averse attitudes of economic agents.

Psychological and social effects can then find a common denominator to measure the degree of harm or utility: money.

Economic perspectives provide a good introduction to the inquiry into the reflexivity of GRID technologies in relation to risk. By GRID technologies we mean ICTs that increasingly have the characteristics of ubiquitous, mediating (Thompson, 1967) information infrastructures. Their hardware is characterized by the extension of the links (networks) to the individuals and organizations they support. Software guarantees the standardization of the linkages for the seamless transfer of data and to provide access to powerful databases that can track usage and produce profiles of users. By analogy with the electricity grid, ICT-based grid technologies can provide ubiquitous access to content and people, allow fast transfer or exchange of content and communication, and enable more sophisticated processing of data in relation to various patterns of usage of the grid itself. The leading public example of grid technologies is the Internet, in its present and future forms (known as I2); but within narrower corporate boundaries there are also full-scale Enterprise Resource Planning (ERP) systems, web services and intranets that feature many elements of a grid technology. Economic perspectives highlight *contract enabling* as one of the significant potential uses of GRID technologies, because this kind of technology would provide the adequate information flows and databases to 'create, set up, control and maintain the network of exchanges and relevant contracts' (Ciborra, 1981) that build up the fabric of economic institutions, such as markets and firms. The infrastructure character of such technologies can contribute, on the one hand, to the generation of new, surprising risks (see Ciborra and Associates, 2000). On the other hand it can be used to manage a growing variety of risks for which appropriate financial markets can be created. For instance, 'this new technology can do cheaply what once was expensive by systematizing our approach to risk management and by generating vast new repositories of information that make it possible for us to disperse risk and contain hazard' (Shiller, 2003, p. 2).

There are multiple ways in which GRID technologies can act. First, there are overall trends in the formalization of transactions, and the continuing erosion of the boundaries between markets and hierarchies in favour of markets (Ciborra, 1983; Malone et al., 1987). Thanks to ICT, 'buy' has extended its reach in relation to 'make': there will be more externalization or outsourcing of activities, regulated by market contracts. As a consequence, markets will be more efficient because of the decrease in transaction costs and will extend spatially and become closer to the functioning of a perfect market (always with the approximation determined by the initial state of a particular market).

Moreover, powerful GRID technologies can have other effects on the costs of 'transition', or change and innovation, via their enabling of new opportunities for managing risk, as pointed out by Shiller (2003). In particular, GRID technologies can have an impact on the realm of finance and become a powerful tool for the management of risks. Finance can reduce harms on individuals by dispersing negative effects among a large number of people. This already happens on the stock market, through the limited liability company form, through social security and through some forms of individual insurance. But such risk management could take place on a much broader scale and be tailored to the needs of individuals, way beyond their life insurance schemes, precisely thanks to GRID technologies. Whenever people can mitigate their risks through new digital financial instruments, e.g. when changing a career or taking up an innovative course of studies (both high-risk personal choices), personal transition costs can be reduced and more individual and social innovation can be fostered: 'Financial arrangements exist to limit the inhibitions that fear of failure places on our actions and to do this in such a way that little moral hazard is created' (Shiller, 2003, p. 2).

GRID technologies could provide a new risk management infrastructure, by fostering the extension of the market and by enhancing the possibilities for measuring utilities and introducing new units of account and measurement. Huge databases containing information on individuals (collected from tax or credit card transactions) allow for the construction of new powerful indexes against which everyone would be in the position to bet on the risk relating to a particular career, a profession, house prices in a given area or the GDP of a certain country. All this would allow a person or a country to share on a global scale the risks of engaging in new ventures. In the past, complex financial arrangements such as insurance contracts were expensive to design and customize. Now, however, 'computer programs, using information supplied electronically in databases, can make complex financial contracts and instruments. The presentation of these contracts ... can be fashioned by this technology to be user friendly' (Shiller, 2003, p. 10). Well-functioning markets for risk-sharing require data for the effective estimation and pricing of risk. This can also reduce the transaction costs in the continuous negotiation of contracts, claims, adjustments and payments. GRID technologies can help to create 'a new financial order' by providing '... finely detailed, continuously-updated, widely available data on incomes and asset prices as well as aggregated data on these and other values relevant to the risk faced by individuals, organizations, corporations and governments. Properly used, this new universe of information would allow better management of an ever wider spectrum of risks ... ' (Shiller, 2003, pp. 189–190) and would help to devise new risk management contracts across the globe. Risks could be objectified and quantified on an unprecedented scale for trading and pooling, and the activities to which they are attached will be carried out in a much more widespread and reliable way, since the relevant risks can be shared among a broader consumer audience.

The risk of infrastructure deployment

As with any previous major revolutionary technology, ICT has impacts on work, employment, skills and organizations that can be disruptive, if not destructive. Technology is a major force in the capitalist process of creative destruction (Schumpeter, 1976). Change and innovation create new risks at individual and societal level, and ICT is one of the culprits. But, as the last section has shown, ICT in the form of GRID technologies can come to the rescue by allowing a 'democratization' of those financial tools that are today confined to stock, market, derivatives and a restricted number of life insurance schemes: by encompassing a wide array of personal risks stemming from the relentless pace of change of technology-based capitalism. But it is here, perhaps, that Shiller's (2003) vision encounters its limits, creating a need to invoke sociological perspectives on risk and modernity.

Implicit in Shiller's (2003) advanced conception of ICT as GRID technologies is the powerful idea held also by economists, according to which technology is a 'tool' that can contingently be applied as much to good as to bad ends (Ciborra and Hanseth, 1998). Thus, digital technologies represent a powerful tool for enhancing productivity as well as decreasing transaction costs; or, through the sophisticated sharing of risks on financial markets, for fostering change and innovation even at the micro-level of the individual economic agent. Of course, their application needs to be well governed, balancing costs and benefits for the various stakeholders through appropriate trade-offs. However, nowhere in the economist's conception can one trace the doubts observed by others that technology can be autonomous (Winner, 1977); behave as an actor with its own logic (Latour, 1999); or possess a far-reaching influence that affects how humans see reality and deploy technology according to patterns that are not purely instrumental (recall Heidegger's inquiry, 1978).

In this respect, consider the notion of technology 'drift'. The drift of technical infrastructures has been identified as a ubiquitous phenomenon found in a variety of corporate large-scale ICT projects (Ciborra and Associates, 2000). When global companies engage in the launch of new ICT platforms to support new standardized and integrated business processes, they are immediately faced with the problem of deciding how to handle their existing and relatively successful legacy systems. Compromises need to be made with all the main actors on the stage, ranging from the angry orphans created by the substitution of the old standards, to the installed base and its autonomous dynamics. Compromises require time to be devised and implemented: some form of consensus needs to be gathered to align the new resources and processes and there will be a need to make adjustments on a continuous basis. This causes a distinctive phenomenon: technologies and processes drift, so what one obtains at the end of the implementation process is not what the system was designed for originally. The models are not only corrupted, but are in a permanent state of redefinition. Implementation never ends. Time drifts too. The corporate timescale becomes more varied, with processes that are carried out at the speed of light operating alongside others that never really finish, or need to be painstakingly managed to completion. Management scholars, consultants and application vendors urge corporations, especially top management, to take action and their prescriptions are straightforward. In order to overcome the present state of fragmentation, and the widespread number of deals through which infrastructures are built, one needs to increase the standardization and integration of data, processes and businesses. These not-so-new, top-down and control-oriented directives accelerate technology drift.

In order to explain some of the paradoxical outcomes of ICT and the practical impossibility of maintaining a steady course during deployment, we submit that the basic assumptions of management models, old or new, may suffer from the following shortcomings:

- Linear reasoning prevails. Organizations and their management are seen as means – end chains. Goal directed decision-making, leadership and will are expected to enact and fix plans (Weill and Broadbent, 1998).
- Control and planning are regarded as key activities performed by organizations, and hence as essential design principles (Beniger, 1986).
- Evolution and change are seen as processes of improvement based on feedback that should be carefully monitored, and where possible measured and managed (Earl, 1996).
- Learning by mistakes is supposed to take place effortlessly.
- Private hoarding of knowledge and other key assets is both essential to gaining an advantage at the individual and organizational level and a source of potential opportunistic behaviour that requires to be kept in check. Again, control over key, unique resources becomes an increasing concern.

Sociological perspectives (e.g. Beck, 1992; Giddens, 1990) urge us (including the well advised practitioner) to consider other important (and somewhat paradoxical) sources of risk, namely integration and standardization themselves:

- The effort to create through ICT a lean, agile and standardized corporation takes too long a time in itself to be compatible with the rapidly changing requirements of the business and the market. The alignment of resources remains an elusive target precisely because of such efforts.
- Technical integration may bring with it a number of side-effects and unexpected consequences, for example interference between different standards or an infrastructure that is well-tuned but too rigid.
- The control scope of organizations is bound to be limited, even if an enterprise invests heavily in digital technologies. Actually, huge investments in ICT may cause runaway dynamics (Arthur, 1994). Technology itself appears to evolve and diffuse along unexpected trajectories (Latour, 1999).
- Learning is not straightforward. Drift is the outcome of vicious circles where learning from mistakes fails to take place (Argyris and Schön, 1996).
- Unpredictable knowledge-spillovers play a key role both inside and between organizations in triggering innovation and learning (Steinmueller, 1996). Learning is part of the more general phenomenon of reflexivity, by which institutions, organizations and individuals change, usually in unpredictable ways as a consequence of previous innovations and changes.

Digital technologies are contributing to both the generation of new side-effects and to further reflexivity: digital organizations are simultaneously more controlled and more unpredictable. Unpredictability and increased runaway dynamics are also caused by the way the new risk management apparatus tends to show consistently the characteristics of higher levels of formalization, standardization and integration, which is an ideal landscape where side-effects can spread and diffuse at higher speed to provoke disrupting impacts. In particular, GRID technologies, as with any infrastructural technology, may pose unforeseen hazards arising from collateral or systemic risks, which are typically not the ones the technical and engineering perspectives have in mind as risks that they should avoid when developing new computing and communication platforms. These collateral risks stem from the fact that, in order to mitigate individual and social risk, GRID technologies involve a higher degree of interdependency between individual lives, the data they generate and the common databases, for example through the use of new identification and encryption technologies. Higher levels of transparency are required to ensure the trustworthiness of transactions and related claims.

As mentioned above, only the pooling of individual data allows the construction of reliable indices and units of accounts. If better indices can mitigate moral hazard issues in individual or organization risk contracts, their establishment, enabled by GRID technologies, also requires the setting of standards and complex legal devices as an essential first step. Leaving aside the legal devices, standardization comes with a price of higher complexity and hidden new forms of fragmentation (Hanseth and Braa, 2001). Hence, every action, device or rule that sets out to reduce or mitigate risks may create side-effects of uncontrollable origin and manifestation, which can disrupt the newly-established control apparatus. Again, we encounter the phenomena that seem to elude the economic analysis but have been highlighted by the sociologists of risk society and modernity: those of reflexivity and runaway dynamics (Beck et al., 1994). Reflexivity refers to the fact that every new technology or regulative measure aimed at controlling risks, such as the GRID technologies, inevitably creates new risks which originate from regions beyond the control of the new powerful platforms. In other words, the more we are able to extend the frontier of (formalized) knowledge thanks to technology, the more dangerous could be the events emerging out of the regions of our ignorance.

Discussion

While for certain practices the ruling vision concerning the operation of a risk calculus is dominated by low or zero imbrication and a purely instrumental role for technology, the more risk and ICT penetrate economic institutions; not only do they reveal themselves as powerful technologies of representation, but also their interdependencies and essential reflexivity become much more important and cannot be ignored. The phenomenological framework can contribute to the analysis of the full dynamics of imbrication between various processes of representation, as we have seen in the most advanced scenario of a new democratization of finance and risk.

Concern as a human and organizational condition is always in motion: it unfolds by being attracted to the unaccomplished and to the unknown, and tends naturally to objectify its target to make it more knowable and controllable. Thus, when concern looks at itself, it almost immediately sees itself as risk. GRID technologies allow concern to pursue even further its own objectification into quantifiable risk, which can then be managed and marketed on an unprecedented scale. But GRID technologies also create new side-effects and unexpected consequences that, in a way, enlarge the regions of the unknown outside the reach of objectified concern: the incalculable, the 'gigantic'. These regions of ignorance soon become a vacuum of knowledge, the new attractor for further genuine and anxious concern, further objectification and, hence, a further extension of the GRID. But the *Leitmotiv* will remain the same: more knowledge, less control.

Regarding imbrication, the mechanism is more subtle than a mere overlapping or mutual reinforcement of objectifying representations, of risk and information modelling. It is more 'active' than that. Its sense possibly can be best captured by the technical meaning of the term imbrication in the (French version) of the Unix operating system: *imbrication* is the relationship between two lines of code, or instructions, where one has as its argument (on which it acts) not just as the result of the other, but also the ensuing *execution of that result.* In the case discussed above, more sophisticated ways to quantify risks are essentially linked not only to more detailed modelling, but also to the construction of the infrastructure or GRID, to the material enactment and representation of the risk information. The latter enactment process generates in its turn the uncalculable, i.e. the realm of man-made risks or of a risk society.

Faced with such a runaway process, one must advocate the design and diffusion of 'forgiving technologies' (Renn, 1998) or technologies of *Gelassenheit* (Ciborra and Hanseth, 1998; Heidegger, 1959), that is, technologies which can tolerate a large range of human error or technical breakdown, providing sufficient time and room for initiating counteractions as authentic, and not disowned, expressions of concern.

Concluding remarks

Information systems offer an interesting arena within which to study the complex and rapidly evolving relationship between digital technologies and risk. Given its intrinsic interdisciplinarity, such a field has hosted in the past decades both the technical and managerial perspectives on risk management. However, the IS literature on risk has not been particularly innovative or rich in scope. Economic perspectives can help overcome some of its major limitations. They also help to reflect on the emerging ramifications of the convergence between advances in GRID technologies, on the one hand, and the democratization of financial tools on the other. The supposed new financial order and its individualized risk management approach is a technology-based order, in which there is a reshuffling of the boundaries between the processes and activities that can be formally represented and the realm of ignorance. But the more sophisticated, integrated and standardized that technological platforms become, the more they tend to behave autonomously and drift. Sociological perspectives are needed to take into account the implications of emerging systemic risks, side-effects and runaway dynamics. Closer scrutiny is therefore required of the penetration and ubiquity of GRID technologies, and the opportunities they offer to manage a whole array of new risks surrounding the individual agent. A phenomenological perspective, based on the notion of risk as concern for concern itself, has been suggested in order to begin to capture, and reflect upon, the intricacies which relate life, risk and digital technologies.

Notes

This chapter originally appeared in (2006) *Journal of Management Studies* **43**(6)1339–1356. [*Journal of Management Studies*] Editor's note: Claudio Ciborra died on 13 February 2005. This paper is based on the original version submitted, his last piece of academic work, as amended by the editors. Had Claudio been alive he would certainly have made efforts, among other things, to develop and integrate the Heideggerian theme of 'care' in more detail. Notwithstanding this, we believe that this paper enriches this Special Research Symposium, merits publication in its own right and is a testimony to Claudio Ciborra's distinctive contribution to the fields of information systems and risk management.

1. [*Journal of Management Studies*] Editors' note: We draw the reader's attention to the fact that that in the later part of this paper the description of GRID technologies shifts from the original definition (Global Risk Information Databases) to entail all large-scale interconnected infrastructures.

References

Argyris, C., and Schön, D.A. (1996). *Organization Learning II*, Reading, MA: Addison-Wesley.

Arthur, W.B. (1994). *Increasing Returns and Path Dependence in the Economy,* Ann Arbor, MI.: University of Michigan Press.

Basel Committee on Banking Supervision (2001). *Consultative Document: Operational Risk, Bank for International Settlements*, Basel: Bank for International Settlements, January.

Beck, U. (1992). *Risk Society: Towards a New Modernity,* London: Sage.

Beck, U., Giddens, A., and Lash, S. (1994). *Reflexive Modernization: Politics, Traditions and Aesthetics in the Modern social Order,* Cambridge: Polity Press.

Beniger, J.R. (1986). *The Control Revolution: Technological and Economic Origins of the Information Society,* Cambridge, MA: Harvard University Press.

Bloomfield, B.P. and Vurdubakis, T. (1994). Representing Technology: IT consultancy reports as textual reality construction, *Sociology* **28**(2): 455–477.

Boehm, B.W. (1991). Software risk management: Principles and practices, *IEEE Software* **8**: 32–41.

Charette, R.N. (1996). The mechanics of managing IT risk, *Journal of Information Technology* **11**: 373–78.

Ciborra, C. (1981). Information systems and transaction architecture, *International Journal of Policy Analysis and Information Systems* **5**(4): 305–24.

Ciborra, C. (1983). Markets, bureaucracies and groups in the information society, *Information Economics and Policy* **1**: 145–60.

Ciborra, C. and Associates (2000). *From Control to Drift – The Dynamics of Corporate Information Infrastructures,* Oxford: Oxford University Press.

Ciborra, C. and Hanseth, O. (1998). From tool to Gestell, *Information Technology and People* **11**(4): 305–27.

Ciborra, C., Migliarese, P. and Romano, P. (1984). Analysing organizational noise, *Human Relations* **37**(8): 565–88.

Coase, R. (1960). The problem of social cost, *Journal of Law and Economics* **15**(1): 1–44.

Cooper, R. (1992). Formal Organization as a representation: remote control, displacement and abbreviation, in M. Reed and M. Hughes (eds), *Rethinking organizations: new directions in organization theory and analysis,*London: Sage, pp. 254–272.
De Felice, M. and Moriconi, F. (2004). Basel 2, Opening Speech, Scuola Normale di Pisa, October.
Douglas, M. and Wildavsky, A. (1982). *Risk and Culture: The Selection of Technological and Environmental Dangers,* Berkley, CA: University of California Press.
Earl, M.J. (ed.) (1996) *Information Management: The Organizational Dimension,* Oxford: Oxford University Press.
Fairley, R. (1994). Risk management in software projects, *IEEE Software* **11**(3): 57–67.
Giddens, A. (1990). *The Consequences of Modernity,* Cambridge: Polity Press.
Hanseth, O. and Braa, K. (2001). Hunting for the treasure at the end of the rainbow. Standardizing corporate IT infrastructure, *The Journal of Collaborative Computing* **10**(3–4): 261–292.
Hart, O. (1995). *Firms, Contracts, and Financial Structures,* Oxford: Oxford University Press.
Heidegger, M. (1959). *Gelassenheit,* Tuebingen: Neske.
Heidegger, M. (1962). *Being and Time,* London: Routledge.
Heidegger, M. (1978). The question about technology, in *Basic Writings,* London: Routledge.
Heidegger, M. (2001). *Phenomenological interpretations of Aristotle,* Bloomington, IN.: Indiana University Press.
Herbst, P. (1974). *Socio-Technical Systems,* London: Tavistock.
Kallinikos, J. (1995). The architecture of the invisible: technology is representation, *Organization* **2**(1): 117–140.
Latour, B. (1999). *Pandora's Hope: Essays on the Reality of Science Studies,* Cambridge, MA.: Harvard University Press.
Leavitt, H.J. (1964). Applied organization change in industry: Structural, technical and human approaches, in W.W. Cooper, H.J. Leavitt and M.W. Shelly (eds), *New Perspectives in Organization Research,* Chichester: Wiley, 55–71.
Loewenstein, G.F., Hsee, C.K. , Weber, E.U. and Welch, N. (2001). Risk as feelings, *Psychological Bulletin* **127**(2): 267–286.
Lyytinen, K. Mathiassen, L. and Ropponen, J. (1998). Attention shaping and software risk: A categorical analysis of four classical risk management approaches, *Information Systems Research* **9**(3): 233–55.
Malone, T.W., Benjamin, R.I. and Yates J. (1987). *Electronic markets and electronic hierarchies,* Communications of the ACM **30**: 484–97.
March, J. and Shapira, Z. (1987). Managerial perspectives on risk and risk-taking, *Management Science* **33**(11): 1404–1418.
McFarlan, F.W. (1981). Portfolio approach to information systems, *Harvard Business Review* **59**(5): 142–50.
Perrow, C. (1984). *Normal Accidents: Living with High-Risk Technologies,* New York: Basic Books.
Power, M. (1997). *The Audit Society: Rituals of Verification,* Oxford: Oxford University Press.
Power, M. (2005). The Invention of operational risk, *Review of International Political Economy* **12**(4): 577–599.
Renn, O. (1998). Three decades of risk research: Accomplishments and new challenges, *Journal of Risk Research* **1**(1): 49–71.
Scheytt, T., Soin, K. Sahlin-Anderson, K. and Power, M. (2006). Organizations, risk and regulation, *Journal of Management Studies* **43**(6):1331–1337.
Schumpeter, J.A. (1976). *Capitalism, Socialism and Democracy,* London: Routledge.
Shiller, R.J. (2003). *The New Financial Order: Risk in the 21*st *Century,* Princeton, NJ: Princeton University Press.

Steinmueller, W.E. (1996). Technology infrastructure in information technology industries, in M. Teubal, D. Foray, M. Justman and E. Zuscovitch (eds), *Technological Infrastructure Policy: An International Perspective,* Dordrecht: Kluwer, pp. 117–139.

Thompson, J. (1967). *Organizations in Action,* New York: McGraw-Hill.

Tversky, A. and Kahneman, D. (1974). Judgement under uncertainty: Heuristics and biases, *Science* **185**: 1124–31.

Vattimo, G. (1992). The Transparent Society (translated by Devod Webb), Cambridge: Polity.

Weill, P. and Broadbent, M. (1998) *Leveraging the New Infrastructure: How Market Leaders Capitalize on Information,* Boston, MA: Harvard Business School Press.

Winner, L. (1977). *Autonomous Technology: Technics-out-of-control as a Theme for Political Thought,* Cambridge, MA: The MIT Press.

Zuboff, S. (1988). *In the Age of the Smart Machine: The Future of Work and Power,* Oxford: Heinemann.

4

Interpreting E-government and Development: Efficiency, Transparency or Governance at a Distance?*

Claudio U. Ciborra

Abstract

E-government is being promoted by international agencies and G8 nations as a means to obtain efficiency, accountability and transparency in the governance of economically less developed countries. In particular, the model for good governance is the one advocated by new public management: the minimal, service-delivery state. The paper shows, first through the case of Jordan, how e-government is difficult to implement, given the characteristics of the local administration, the socio-economic context and the dynamics of the technological infrastructure. On the basis of such evidence, it asks more generally whether the marketization of the state, embedded in e-government, makes sense as the paramount approach to improve democracy and foster development. It turns out that the transformation of citizens into customers is problematic, and the correlation between good governance and minimal state with development can hardly be demonstrated historically.

If such failures are both pointed out by institutional economics theory and by current practice, the paper explores possible reasons why these projects continue to attract development aid funds. Specifically, the paper puts forward a new interpretation centred on the newly established link between aid and security. In this light, e-government appears to be one of the new tools for the rich metropolitan states to govern 'at a distance' (through sophisticated methodologies and technologies) the potentially dangerous, weak, borderland states. But such an approach, as many ICT fixes for the private sector have shown, may also fail and backfire: new ICT applications can drift away from the set targets and global, durable disorder within and between states may sustain intact. New research approaches leading to new practices are desperately needed.

Introduction

Heidegger (1978), one of the continental philosophers most concerned with the role and essence of technology in our modern world, suggests that trying to figure out whether technology is a bad, good or neutral tool is just a technical, instrumental quest. If one wants to get to the essence of modern technology, one should avoid falling into the trap of a technical, means-ends discourse. If the essence of a tree is not something vegetable, the essence of modern technology may not be something technical or instrumental.

We can retain from Heidegger's investigation two basic ideas on the essence of modern technology. The first is that technology is a way of revealing, a revealing that challenges nature, people, society, and the world we live in. Second, that the challenge posed by modern technology has a very special and consistent form, captured by the German word *Gestell*. In a way, *Gestell* has the characteristics of what we would call, in information systems, an ICT infrastructure–enabling and aligning all the processes in an organization. But the idea of infrastructure has a static connotation (coming from structure), while the German noun has a more dynamic accent, since it contains the root of the verb *stellen*, which means ordering and aligning.

The essence of modern technology is a way of revealing that challenges the world by ordering it, that is by ordering resources, processes, people, and relationships. All are made present, available through order, calculus, and formalization. So that they can be recombined, aligned, aggregated and made ready for ... further ordering.

The interplay between ordering and revealing can guide our investigation into the deployment of information technology in the public administration and can help us in unveiling the complex phenomenon of e-government models, methodologies and policies deployed today by many governments and international agencies, with a special focus on the less developed countries.

E-government is information and communication technology (ICT) applied to ordering at least three kind of processes. First, it attends to the relationship (transaction) between the administration and the citizen (customer) and the related re-engineering of the activities internal to the administration. (Bellamy and Taylor, 1998). A second level regards the way in which the boundaries between the state and the market are redrawn, by the creation of an electronic, minimal state, more transparent, agile and accountable (Heeks, 1999; Stiglitz *et al.*, 2000). A third level deals with the purpose of aid policies aimed at introducing e-government into developing countries. Better accountability and improved transparency are the characteristics of good governance, and the latter becomes the *conditio sine qua non* for the rich states and international agencies to supply aid to the less developed countries (UNDP, 2001). The study of the way in which e-government becomes a technology of ordering at these three different levels unveils at the same time hurdles, risks and inner contradictions. The composite analysis of the ordering and revealing effects of ICT in government can offer a new picture of this phenomenon.

The Kingdom of Jordan, as a case study of an innovative and extensive application of e-government ideas and models, provides a paradigmatic example of how ICT are being introduced in a less developed country and shows what the risks of failure in implementation are. Based on the empirical evidence provided by the case, we examine the more general implications of e-government and new public management in the transformation of the relationship between the state and the citizen. We then deal with the consequent re-orientation of the administration towards the model of the minimal, service delivery, state and point to its inner contradictions. Finally, we offer an interpretation of the new emerging order linking aid policies and the new style of governance 'at a distance' that the rich metropolitan states want to establish by funding e-government projects in less developed countries. Again, attempts at increasing the levels of order and control, for example through e-government applications, may backfire and maintain the present international regimen of durable disorder. Concluding remarks follow including ideas for further research.

A case study: e-government projects in Jordan

As a point of departure let us consider a case study related to the implementation of e-government systems, services and applications in the special context of a developing country, The Kingdom of Jordan.[1] C. Barrett, Intel CEO, has declared during a meeting in the region that:

> Jordan has set a precedent for change in the Middle East region. It has demonstrated the achievements that can result from strong cooperation between the public and private sectors, particularly in the field of information and communications technology. (Reach, 2001)

Indeed, Jordan is a textbook case for its vision to become the Singapore or Bangalore of the Middle East in the adoption of new information and communication technologies. In its attempt to follow some of the best practices indicated by international agencies, from the World Bank to the UN, and the donors of various leading Western and Far East countries, combined with the commitments expressed by the top of the State (the King himself and the newly created Ministry of ICT (MoICT)), Jordan incarnates the new thinking and practice on how to introduce ICT to enable rapid social and economic progress (MoICT, 2000). There is a variety of initiatives that may attract the interest of the observer: they regard the creation of new jobs in the ICT sector and the launch of a software industry (Reach, 2001); second, the diffusion of ICT in rural areas and the promotions of e-learning (projects like 'Connecting Jordanians'; or broadband to the schools), and last but not least the establishment of e-government (MoICT, 2001). The e-government initiative is significant for a number of reasons. First, in Jordan the public sector is still the largest employer, thus representing a very important economic organization. Second, one can find in this domain many of the actors also present in the other projects: donors; public and private partnerships; foreign governments wanting to provide help, and so on. Third, there is the possibility of studying the deployment of a new infrastructure inside a large, complex administration in the context of improving its efficiency but also to support the growth of the nation. This allows us to extend to the government organization in a developing country what we have learned in previous research projects about the strategic deployment and management of ICT infrastructures in the corporate world (Ciborra and Associates, 2001).

The e-government strategy spelt out

Jordan's e-government plans are aimed at using new technologies to facilitate inter and intra-agency communication and cooperation, as well as provide information and services to its citizens more efficiently. The programme relies on four foundations: introduction of e-services, infrastructure development, education and training, and legal change. It focuses on the following broad objectives:

- increasing information accessibility;
- improving government performance and efficiency;
- reducing costs;
- enhancing the competitiveness of government;
- ensuring transparency and visibility;
- promoting the ICT sector;
- e-skilling the public sector; and
- boosting e-commerce activities.

The e-government initiative is being implemented under the direction of a task force, an eight member public/private committee headed by the newly formed MoICT. The new Ministry has been created following the privatisation of the postal services from what was the Ministry of Post and Telecommunications. It is responsible for setting the telecom policy and coordinating the e-government initiative, besides attracting investment in the ICT sectors, and setting the ICT policy and strategy plan for the telecom and postal sector. In particular, the Ministry will issue the technical standards and articulate the policy for the various government agencies to bring their data, services and transactions on-line (MoICT, 2001).

A number of Fast Track projects were launched in 2001. They include motoring services, taxation (income and sales) services, and land registry. Next will be the G2B and G2C portals and a government personnel directory. A new network is envisaged to enable government introduce knowledge management, empower and connect government staff. A Program Management Office will establish standards and protocols for interconnecting government services – together with the system integrators – and for the development of a holistic view of a security strategy.

Four government departments are involved in the main fast track projects: The Department of Land & Survey (DLS); and three under the umbrella of the Ministry of Finance – the Income Tax Department (ITD); the Drivers & Vehicles Licensing Department (DVLD); and the General Sales Tax Department (GSTD).

Deloitte & Touche is the consulting firm awarded the contract for the analysis and design of the various processes and information requirements.

The principles guiding the consulting firm in this particular contract are:

- establishing proper governance structure for coordinating and promoting e-government initiatives in Jordan;

- identifying and implementing e-services which can be deployed rapidly and provide visible benefits to citizens as a 'proof of concept' for e-government;
- implementing a common infrastructure whose services could be leveraged by all governmental entities;
- considering using multiple channels (beside the Internet) for providing services, based on the level of their accessibility in Jordan;
- identifying and applying the changes necessary in Jordan's existing legislation system for enabling e-service delivery;
- using a phased approach for implementation;
- monitoring citizen feedback and continuously evolving e-services based on users requirements;
- raising government employees and citizens awareness about e-government by proper communication and educational programmes; and
- planning for and managing change.

In two cases, ITD and DVLD, all the front office activities were analysed by the consulting firm. In the other two projects only a selection of front office services were studied due to time constraints.

Based on the projects' final recommendations, the MoICT will issue a Request for a Proposal (RFP) to select partners for the purpose of creating the detailed functional and technical design, carrying out the implementation and launching of the relevant e-government services (MoICT, 2001).

Emerging risks

> Beyond the Internet...e-Government requires an unprecedented degree of organizational agility – an agility that really involves enterprise transformation in the fullest sense. On the most basic level, this means that an organization is able not only to optimize the value of relationships with customers, but also to build a culture capable of making sharp turns at a moment's notice – not once, but over and over again...In other words, the outcome will be a true linking of front – and back-offices. (Deloitte Research, 2001)

Since, in general, e-government is about the deployment of a complex ICT infrastructure, it faces a number of risks in relation to implementation, project management and policy, all risks that have to be appropriately managed (Snellen and Van de Donk, 1998; Fountain, 2001; Heeks, 2002).

Though the analysts of the Fast Track projects were still completing the analysis and design work at the time of our study, a few difficulties, some of them unexpected, could be identified. Here is a flavour of the most important ones, similar to those that, in the private sector and corporate world, have often proved to be cause of major disruption or at least significant drift in use (Ciborra and Associates, 2001). For one application, the one concerning the Department of Driving Licences and Motor Vehicles, we narrow down our study in order to show some of the hurdles which also point to some general problems regarding the prevailing style of e-government projects both in developing and advanced countries, to be further discussed in the next section.

Jordanian public administration is not a green-field site as far as IT is concerned. Rather, over the years, each Ministry, department and agency has been implementing a number of applications. All these efforts come to represent the 'installed base' of existing systems and applications which any new e-government initiative has to deal with. There are Ministries or areas more advanced than others and a variety of infrastructures, often incompatible or plainly not integrated or networked. Thus, when considering the Fast Track projects, the one at ITD is relatively more advanced, or ranks higher on the 'technical readiness' scale. In other services (e.g. Sales Tax) new systems have been introduced, but due to lack of involvement and user participation, there is resistance to acceptance; the DLS uses a database that does not support spatial techniques and an upgrade is in order: these, and others, are stand-alone systems. The analysts have found duplications, redundancy and low quality of data. Note that these negative aspects have been observed in connection with the already automated procedures and files, not in relation to manual ones.

In sum, the IT readiness within the government administration is uneven: it is a matter of technology (old and new platforms coexisting and new ones being implemented all the time, often independently from the e-government projects); the *de facto* independence and autonomy of the Ministries; the different practices in systems implementation; sometimes inappropriate user involvement and training; the need for a deep culture change towards the new ways of working, and so on.

The case of DVLD

We can see the interplay between the three dimensions of technology, practices and culture at work in one specific Fast Track project: Drivers & Vehicles Licensing. This is a very much-heralded application in the consulting reports celebrating e-government in the US (implemented as web services in Nevada, Arizona, Pennsylvania and Alaska) (Deloitte Research, 2001). Stiglitz *et al.* (2000) cite it as an instance of how government can improve the efficiency of its services: a case where policy should encourage governments to undertake the redesign of internal activities through the use of ICT.

It is a quintessential application where the idea of e-service comes to the fore: better service to the citizens, decreased transaction costs; and opportunity for streamlining old-fashioned office operations. It is a show case application. Though the analysis was not yet finished at the time of our study, a number of unexpected, potential risks emerged, which seem to indicate that this application will be much more complex to implement than originally planned for. More generally, the DVLD case is, in itself, a 'hologram' which enshrines many of the crucial problems of transferring e-government models and methodologies from advanced private and public organizations in developed countries to organizations operating in less developed countries.

First, the existing platform and software will be hard to convert: we deal with a non-centralized architecture, with non-systematic updating of the local and central databases, and mostly written in antiquated COBOL programs. The databases are not relational, hence it is cumbersome to run queries and give instructions. Overall, there is a low technical readiness; and employees are not very computer literate. If the technical backwardness was expected, it came as a big surprise that the sheer number of 'dependencies' of the services surpassed the planning targets of the analysis phase. What looked like a straightforward application turns out to be decomposed into over 130 services that need to be documented. The list of dependencies is also impressive (about 35) and casts a shadow on the easiness of implementation. In other words, having a driving and other type of transport or vehicle licences involves internal transactions with the Prime Ministry (specifically, the General Intelligence Department), The Public Security Department, the Chamber of Commerce, the Ministry of Exteriors, the Ministry of Industry and Trade, The Ministry of Health, the insurance companies, the local municipalities, and so on. Of course, dependencies vary according to the product or service (public vehicles; trucks; buses; private vehicles etc.).

All this is making the analysis job very complex. Add to this that the analysts need many statistics on the actual state of things: statistics which are unavailable, unreliable and late. Some processes have kept an uncertain description because their unfolding is hard to identify in a reliable manner. Next, consider the 'angry orphans' phenomenon: the IT specialists threatened by the new application which will entail dropping COBOL (the old standard) and responding by creating obstacles that make the analysis work very difficult and incomplete.

Also, the new system must reduce the transaction time between the DVLD and the various dependencies. If this is not achieved, the mere speeding up of the procedures internal to DVLD will not have a significant impact on the overall service delivery time (made of the internal time combined with the dependencies time). Finally, a basic requirement is the possibility of shuffling documents between Departments, electronically. This is difficult until the DVLD adopts the Electronic Transaction Law and its recommendations (MoICT, 2002). Once this problem is solved, then one has to tackle the electronic integration through 35 different organizations, with many of those dependencies not being computerized or having incompatible systems. On top of it, integration will entail interlinked accounting practices, since citizens have to pay for some of the dependencies involved. Currently they pay each Ministry or agency separately, while an integrated procedure would require redistributing separate payments from a global price of delivery of the service in a one-stop-shop fashion.

In such a maze, the ways out chosen by the analysts might further endanger the implementation process:

- the analysts get the information and authority they need by bypassing the Department altogether; typically, they would turn to the Public Security Department; in due time this might worsen the animosity between them and the DVLD Department; and

- missing a reliable standard documentation (the 'raw processes' are hard to access), MoICT design standards and global best practices imported by the consultants are made to replace the missing or unidentified activities.

These moves may solve the problem for the analysts of meeting their deadlines, but may render implementation more risky, in the sense that new processes will be grafted upon unclear, poorly understood activities.

In this respect, the final worries concern change management. The need for huge change management and training efforts is to be expected: to overcome resistance; to educate the computer illiterate; to change the management model. The latter will imply a radical cultural transformation: moving from a rigid, control oriented management style to a process organization servicing the customer (Caldow, 2001). Note that the transition is not from a public bureaucracy to a market organization (the concern of all the new public management literature) but from a military culture to a business/market culture.

The high risks and complexities of such a transition point to what may be the dangers hidden in this apparently banal application. Put in a nutshell: successful implementation and delivery of e-services demands the transformation of some parts of the Jordan state from a security apparatus into a transparent service agency, where a driving licence is not a public security or general intelligence document, but a quasi commercial product.

In sum, even in the analysis phase, a mundane application, chosen because of its low risk and high yield in terms of engaging the citizens into the idea and experience of e-government turns out to be, a hologram in the small of the difficulties of e-government in a developing country: extremely complex; high risk; and calling into question the role of the state in relation to its citizens: a service provider or a public security apparatus?

From this perspective, the Electronic Transaction Law requires among other things that its provisions be interpreted according to the international trade conventions (Article 6) (MoICT, 2002). This may be easily adopted by a Department providing certificates to citizens, and thus transform its administrative acts into market services, but it may be much more difficult to implement by a security or intelligence arm of the State.

Finally, note that the case shows the two effects of modern technologies: ordering and revealing. E-government allows an unprecedented ordering of transactions within the administration and between the administration and outside institutions, firms and individuals (citizens as customers). At the same time, though, its deployment can proceed only by revealing the nature of the administration, and more in general of the Jordan state, and the contradictory requirements for its transformation.

Customer service or development?

> The change is equally enormous for government itself, especially in this new view of citizen as customer…In this sense, the Internet represents more than

> just a new channel for service delivery. On its deepest level, the Internet is a catalyst that challenges age-old assumptions about how governments operate... In fact, in just a few short years, the Internet has started to shift the organizing logic of government from a product or process-centric approach to a customer-centric model. (Deloitte Research, 2001)

The epochal transformation of a government department from a public security/military culture into a market-like service is just one extreme instance of the changes implied by most e-government applications (Cabinet Office, 2000).

This is part of a wider shift whereby citizens become customers, as recommended by the new public management movement (Ferlie *et al.*, 1996; Barzelay, 2001). However, such a move has wide-ranging implications (Fountain, 2001a), which can explain the difficulties today's prevailing style of e-government applications are encountering, especially in less developed countries (Pratchett, 1998).

First, the notion of 'customer' entails a number of market mechanisms, which cannot be completely transferred to a public administration possessing a monopoly of the service. For one thing, in a competitive market the customer has choice, which is not always the case for the citizens/customers (who else can supply driving licences besides the DVLD?) Also, citizens have no real exit option and prices do not reflect the matching of supply and demand for this service.

On a closer look, another difference stands out: firms try, primarily, to satisfy shareholders and not customers. Customer relationship management does not have a value *per se*, but only as an instrument to increase shareholder value. In order to do that, firms proceed to segment the market; and to implement various forms of price discrimination: tactics that can increase the inequality among customers. But equality of service is, in principle, the goal of an administration providing a universal service.

Furthermore, any attempt to govern transactions through market-like mechanisms implies a certain degree of standardization of the service provided. The less such a service can be standardized, the more the bureaucracy, especially the one facing directly the customer/citizen (the so called 'street level bureaucracy'), will be involved in stereotyping, simplifying, and basically serving those clients who are easier to serve – given also that the bureaucracy is subject to internal performance monitoring. This will generate a new form of discrimination based not on price, but on access and relative ease of interaction.

In the private sector service, quality, customer service and handling of complaining customers correlate with socio-economic status. In the public sector the more service provision and customer complaint handling is market-like, the more it will end up reflecting citizens' status inequalities.

More generally, the perfunctory equivalence between citizens and customers places them in a special role, that consumers described by rational choice theory. Whether this fiction works in actual markets or not is of secondary importance, given that the variety of roles played by citizens cannot be reduced to the one of consumers with clear preferences influenced by prices and quality. Public administration operates in areas where goals and preferences are ambiguous, and are difficult to identify and express. This is especially the case for those vulnerable citizens lacking scope for choice, as is often the case in less developed countries.

Customers making choices within a market context tend to be involved in transactions of a narrow scope and instantaneous nature. The market is a wonderful means to aggregate such spot encounters between demand and supply. However, the more a transaction is specific, sticky and long term, the more markets tend to fail and must be governed by long term, integrative arrangements (Williamson, 1975). The citizen, a member of a democracy, a community or even a police state, is in a long-term relationship, which cannot be fully divided down into transaction bits to be aggregated. The expression of political, long lasting obligations and the development of a polity are hard to obtain through purely aggregative relationships. Such processes only become possible in the context of a participatory democracy, where popular sovereignty matters more than consumer sovereignty. State governing bodies and administrative apparatuses are all part of the effort to 'govern' the population (Dunleavy and O'Leary, 1987). They are the arms of politics, seen as the art of conflict resolution, but the latter is at odds with market segmentation and demand aggregation (Fountain, 2001a).

It is then not so obvious that by introducing more efficient electronic transactions, a bureaucratic or military administration will become more transparent, efficient and market-like. First, it will maintain its monopoly. Second, it will be compelled to standardize services so as to be able to offer them electronically. But such a standardization will entail stereotyping, segmenting, and privileging those segments of the population that can access the services more easily. Democracy will not be increased nor competition; favouritisms and bribery might simply be offered to new intermediaries. Is it all about agencies as efficient e-service providers or political institutions as instruments of democracy? As shown in the DVLD case, the irony is that the two cannot be disentangled, and the provision of efficient e-service may require dramatic transformation in the governance of the population (an issue of governmentality, as Foucault would point out (Burchell *et al.*, 1981)).

In the case of the Jordanian public administration the e-government initiatives reveal the incongruence of some aspects of the organization and institutions, which are not conducive to the implicit tenets of the new models. We submit that e-government will further unveil the contradictions, already embedded in new public management, that being how the re-ordering of citizens as customers and the re-shaping of public administration as a firm operating on a market are bound to encounter institutional mismatches.

E-government and the minimal state

> Our goal is an information and technology sector in Jordan in which the free market is given the widest possible scope to contribute to the economic development of the country. (Reach, 2001)

Looking more closely, technology puts into question the wider context and logic within which it is being applied. Does the model of state enabled by e-government really support development (Heeks, 2001)?

However, e-government is supposed to be conducive to development, by sustaining good governance. In the strategies of the international organizations like the World Bank and the IMF (gathered around the so called Washington and Monterey consensuses) good governance is delivered by a specific model of 'minimal' state, or the service delivery model, of which the marketisation aspects analysed above are a major feature (Kahn, 1997). The model is supposed to address state failures due to governance breakdown, corruption, rent seeking, distortions in markets and the absence of democracy. In particular, the service delivery state can provide law and order; enforce property rights; and deliver public goods and services to the customers/citizens. It is minimal, transparent and accountable. The model comes with the idea that development is enabled by a well working market economy, where contracts can be enforced; property rights are clear and stable; corruption is low; there are few restrictions on competition (markets are rent free, with few monopolies; no subsidies; ubiquitous access to information); and investors are confident because property rights are stable (North, 1997).

To be sure, the minimal state model embeds the style of governance present in advanced Western economies. E-government together with other institutional reforms is aimed at helping nations to leapfrog underdevelopment and attain a final governance configuration, which is similar to the one of developed countries.

Still, any e-government initiative should entail a due consideration of the problem of governance and development, especially of their dynamic interaction.

Namely (Kahn, 2002):

- the few states which actually have experienced a high-growth economy do not rank highly on the various dimensions of good governance (corruption; democracy; transparency etc.); and
- the institutional reforms needed to transform the developing country into an advanced one portray only the end 'state', but do not tell us anything on how to actually enact the transition from the initial to the end state.

In particular, it is hard to establish a clear correlation between the service-delivery state and development (Kahn, 2002). Actually, the few high growth economies in Asia show that their earlier decades were characterized by a much more interventionist role of the state (Wade, 1990), for example with states actively manipulating property rights (land reform) and allocating rents to growth enhancing activities and groups (e.g. training entrepreneurs). Also, they had only slightly better governance quality than many poorly performing countries. The same applies for corruption levels: not significantly different and in some cases even worse than average (Thailand).

Furthermore, even if the service-delivery, minimal state is characterized by low transaction costs, the idea of such a state says nothing about the transition towards its attainment, how to manage the process and how to minimise the 'transition' costs.

This is a drawback common to much new institutional economics *à la* Williamson (1975): in order to compete and survive, institutions and organizations need to lower transaction costs, but, unfortunately, this recommendation is not enough to explain why certain institutions or organizations are able to make such moves, while other are unable to implement them. Embedded in the new institutional economics are very naïve ideas about change, political transition costs and learning, since they are assumed to be frictionless processes (Ciborra, 1990).

In the detail of the DVLD case, it is apparent how an efficient model of delivering driving licences through the Internet, as a notion, may clash with the entrenched ways of working of the administration, and in general, with the extant model of the state and the nature of the relationship between state and citizen. In other words, while focussing on good governance, the minimal state and e-government, the consensus policies tend to underestimate what it takes to imitate learn and implement new conducts, procedures and practices.

Looked at in this perspective, the role of ICT is less clear-cut, less significant and, most probably, irrelevant. First, what matters are transformation and learning capabilities, which are not necessarily supported by efficiency-enhancing applications (Fukuda-Parr *et al.*, 2002).

The distinction is subtle but of great importance. E-government for good governance is simply a description of the applications one could get in order for an efficient government to serve its 'customers'. The flaw is that this strategy may work where the state has *already* a typical advanced country configuration. It does not help the transition, or probably might even hinder it.

We can conclude that the present range of applications and systems, usually labelled e-government, is attached to a model of state, the service delivery one, which resembles closely the state form in advanced Western economies. However, there is the suspicion that such a model may be irrelevant to actually triggering development. At the limit, the reverse can be true: once an economy is fully developed, then the service delivery model makes sense and e-government can function, as some, but not all, applications of service delivery in the UK, US and other advanced countries show. (Fountain, 2001; Dunleavy *et al.*, 2001).

As the Jordan case points out, though in a very embryonic form, seeking the implementation of efficient service delivery will lead at best to the point where a radical transformation is required to make the applications function, but ICTs do not enable such changes *per se*: they presuppose them.

What then, about developing countries getting trapped in spending resources to push major reforms like e-government on the basis of models, which may not work in contexts that are significantly different from the advanced ones (Heeks, 2002)? The risks could be of more cynicism and disillusion, and investments in ICT could turn into some form of growth-reducing rents.

More specifically, why do countries like the Kingdom of Jordan get trapped in facing high enforcement costs of policies to renew the state through e-government and other new public management reforms? And why do donors and international agencies seem to be driven into the same tunnel vision, of promoting and supporting designs that are unrealistic, since they tend to ignore the complex problems of transformation, and are linked to an idea of state, the e-service delivery one, that actually may not be conducive to development (Wade, 2002)? In sum, technology introduced to order the state apparatus according to a precise model and organization, which also entails the re-alignment of its functions and relationships with the outside markets, leads us to question whether the models inscribed in the technology of e-government will deliver economic and social development. In trying to address this puzzle, on the one hand we touch the limits of the e-government, good governance and service-delivery state consensus discourse, on the other these experiments with new technologies and make us reflect upon some important, implicit dimensions of the phenomenon, which now we try to interpret in a wider context (Avgerou, 2002).

On drift, aid, and durable disorder

The trajectory of e-government in developing countries cannot be identified and understood by looking at the technological features only, or the dynamics of the local public administration in isolation, or development as a separate issue. Rather, it needs to be 'reconstructed', bottom up, by observing the interplay between the various actors involved in the automation initiative. In the case of the Kingdom of Jordan, they are the various international agencies; foreign governments; consulting firms; software and hardware vendors; and so on. For example, with the assistance of the Amir Program (entirely funded by USAID), the MoICT plans to enable 'build-own-operate' and 'build-own-transfer' relationships between public and private sectors to introduce the new e-services (MoICT, 2001).

We have seen the inner contradictions and the limitations of the models and methodologies the main actors pursue, propose and deploy. To be sure, they invest into, and support on an ongoing basis, the idea of e-government. They are driven by the promises of the technical innovation, the key tenets of the new public management manifesto, and the marketisation of the state as the paramount means to achieve economic growth and social progress (UN, 2001; Kirkman *et al.*, 2002; G8-DOT Force, 2002). But, we have observed, they seem to be blind: their blindness prevents them appreciating the risks and pitfalls of implementing the new models.

Here, we need to turn to the recommendation of those anthropologists who have studied the discrepancy between the development discourse and what happens on the ground (Ferguson, 1990): one needs to refocus the main object of enquiry on those underlying structures which seem to make a significant difference, namely 'global flows of finance and investment, international markets and, of course, national and supra-national politics' (Gardner and Lewis, 2000).

Our analysis of the phenomenon of e-government initiatives for less developed countries needs, then, to place the specific tactics of the various actors into a broader, geopolitical framework able to offer a new interpretation to their projects, initiatives and concrete actions. We find the elements for a contextualized interpretation of the issues that have emerged so far in a document, the National Security Strategy of the USA (White House, 2002), which summarizes the fundamental traits of the present world economic and political order. It is this meta-order, which is set to frame the reforms such as e-government and envisages a common model of national governance centred on the idea of the minimal state and free markets:

> the United States will use this moment of opportunity to extend the benefits of freedom across the globe. We will actively work to bring the hope of democracy, development, free markets, and free trade to every corner of the world. The events of September 11, 2001, taught us that weak states, like Afghanistan, can pose as great a danger to our national interests as strong states. Poverty does not make poor people into terrorists and murderers. Yet poverty, weak institutions, and corruption can make weak states vulnerable to terrorists networks and drug cartels within their borders.

In the National Security Strategy the link is established between the danger posed by 'weak states' and what can happen within their borders, and the need for a countervailing influence, based on the ideas of free markets, trade, democracy and development, to be pushed across the globe, to every corner of the world. Throughout this document aid, reform of the state, and free markets are intimately connected with the issue of security (Duffield, 2001).

Let us, then, take the issue of security seriously, as the source of this White House document warrants, and look at the current efforts of e-government initiatives in developing countries according to this different, more global perspective.

Any successful technical and organizational innovation requires a stable alignment of the actors: the designers, the vendors, the users, the sponsors, etc. (Latour, 1993). The successful implementation of e-government is no exception. In this respect, what is striking for the Jordan case, as well as other cases of e-government in less developed countries (Bhatnagar, 2004), is that the implementation of the projects takes place through multiple interventions of ministries and departments; aid agencies; consulting firms, NGOs; multinational companies; multilateral financial bodies; foreign states; regional entrepreneurial associations, and a variety of alliances between them (Reach, 2001).

Note that many of these actors are private organizations, and a first, superficial reading of the alignment required today by e-government consists of complex and articulated forms of private-public partnerships, where the presence of powerful intermediaries like the computer vendors, or the global consulting firms, indicates that aid in this domain is more and more delivered by non-state entities (Sassen, 2004).

This would be yet another sign of globalisation: the weakening of the traditional influence of the national states, in favour of a more fragmented, overlapping set of private and public intermediaries. One could conclude that states are handing over, if not outright subcontracting, their tasks and resources in relation to aid to more specialised and professional agencies. This would be part of the increasing externalisation of activities traditionally performed by states, now delegated to multinationals and NGOs.

The US Security Strategy document is important in this respect because it suggests a different interpretation. The public-private networks and contractual regimes of aid practice are the new means by which 'metropolitan states' want to achieve security on a global scale (Duffield, 2002). Underdevelopment is now dangerous, not only for the people directly immersed into it but for us as well. Under the rubric of human security the concerns for stability of the metropolitan states have been made to merge with the social agenda of the aid agencies. If poverty and underdevelopment encourage conflict and instability, then sustainable development, of which e-government initiatives are an essential factor, can also play a security role. The networks of aid practice become the ways for the metropolitan states to cross the borders of the marginal, weak states and implement flexibly new forms of governance, both of the economy and the state (Duffield, 2002).

Typically, e-government and its counterpart, the self-regulating market, are technologies of control (Beninger, 1986) able to shape the networks and systems of opportunity within which less developed countries operate. In this way, control by the metropolitan states is not direct or centralized but flows through a network of open circuits that are non hierarchical, but 'rhizomatic' (Rose, 2000).

Note, also, that behind the notion of 'good governance', as supported by e-government, a subtle shift has taken place: underdeveloped, potentially dangerous states are now monitored and regulated as a social body. Through free markets, accountability, transparency, and corruption-curbing policies, it is the very culture and conduct of people that needs to be impacted. In other words, through ICT and new public management visions what one tries to affect is the 'governmentality' (Foucault, 1991) of the weak states, that is the way they think about their own functioning and reform, by providing a very specific approach to regulate the conduct of citizens, e. g. by transforming citizens into rational choice customers. More generally, modern regulatory techniques create the possibility of modulating the behaviour of populations through controlling processes and networks, rather than disciplining individuals, as in the old colonialism. Further, this takes place at a distance or with little territorial presence (of experts and functionaries), rather than through territorial occupation (as it used to happen with colonialism). Like the computer and network-based systems they end up implementing, such techniques involve continuous measurements of conduct, risk and readiness. You 'invest' in aid where you get the fastest and most reliable return, so, you need to measure throughout. The same applies to the management of the projects and the comportment of the experts (Duffield, 2001). Information technology represents a driving force by allowing for the new way of accounting and risk analysis to take place (Power, 1997).

The new flexibility and accountability of the development aid practice are valued because of the changing geopolitical situation. We started with a political landscape made up of strong states facing each other, competing through political alliances, nuclear deterrence and arms superiority, and where aid was a means for strong states to seek alliances with weak, but strategically positioned states in the less developed parts of the world. Now we move to a landscape characterized by low intensity regional conflicts; 'glocal' terrorism, where the old forms of alliance and deterrence are not effective any longer. The present situation has been described as one of 'durable, endemic disorder'.

We submit that e-government initiatives are part of that new portfolio of aid projects, for which 'a new possibility of achieving security has emerged in which non state organisations now provide innovative forms of mobilisation, means of intervention ... in the interest of global liberal governance. But far from solving in this way durable disorder, the latter continues to subsist as a side effect of the very way metropolitan states try to address the new security dilemmas and develop the new public-private systems of influence' (Duffield, 2002).

A number of elements seem to support this interpretation. First, there is the changing nature of war and security in the last few years and the well-known events happening in various parts of the globe. In the borderlands nations, conflict destroys the social fabric; widespread human right abuse and the use of civilians as deliberate targets become organic components of the new style of war; 'ethnic cleansing' provides a strong justification for intervention and a stronger than before 'will to govern'. Except than for extreme cases, like Afghanistan in the most recent past, this will to govern through reform cannot find an expression in a direct intervention. Rather, it becomes the engine animating the new style of governing at a distance through the public-private networks of aid and the reforms programmes such as e-government.

There is a strong parallel between modern technology as understood by Heidegger (see above) and development. Indeed, development has always involved some form of mobilisation for order and security (Escobar, 1995; Cowen and Shenton, 1995). Today, order is achieved by allowing the archetypal self regulating process, the market, to install itself and expand, by creating and enacting those institutions that allow the free market to emerge. The minimal state, accompanied by new public management and e-government ideas, is the typical reform that the public-private network of aid practice seeks to deliver. (Kahn, 2002) Such networks set up originally as short-term remedial interventions tend to become a permanent framework giving coherence and linking aid and political actors. (UNDP, 2002) In Jordan, for example, the public-private network includes such actors as UNDP and USAID, but also Cisco, Microsoft, EDS, besides the key ministries.

On the surface the issues raised by the G8 Digital Opportunity Task Force (G8-DOT Force, 2002) cover the relative e-readiness of a developing country, the digital divide, higher levels of efficiency through marketization, and more transparency. However, the present study of e-government applications suggests that the G8 agenda may be a façade of what the phenomenon of e-government policies for developing countries is not. Below the surface, the driving forces are order and security in a new war context; the market as achieving self-regulating order without direct intervention; aid as a technology of control and ICT as a technology enabling such strategies.

Development, here understood as a technology for governance, a way of ordering the relationship between people and resources to produced desired outcomes, meets the paramount modern technology for control: ICT. The meeting is triggered by the dangers of the new war and the ensuing concerns for security. E-government is linked to the idea of good governance and thus the two projects converge within a framework that wishes to reduce the role of the state, to encourage non-state mechanisms of regulation through privatisation, markets, private enterprise and techniques of new public management. Development and e-government: two technologies for ensuring order and control join forces to face the threats to security posed by the new war. Will this marriage deliver?

As shown in the case of sophisticated information infrastructures in large multinationals (Ciborra and Associates, 2001), the deployment of ICT as a technology for control is never fully effective, and tends to generate a variety of side-effects and out of control dynamics that threaten the very management control strategy that dictated their introduction. We submit that the same may happen at the global, geo-political level (Walsham, 2001). The metropolitan states' wish to control at a distance the borderland states, through reforms and new infrastructures implemented through the flexible network of private-public aid agencies, may fail. Their attempts backfire leading to: more systems unevenly distributed within administrative departments and agencies; knowledge spread unevenly in the population; more autonomy; and scattered resistance. The collateral effects of the new alliance may then contribute to exacerbate the durable world disorder, as well as corporate and administrative disorder; that is reinforcing a system of governance where systemic collapse is avoided through the constant crisis management and relentless introduction of sophisticated technologies, while, at the same time, not addressing root problems and creating new occasions for drifting of institutions, states and technical infrastructures (Duffield, 2002).

Further research and concluding remarks

A whole range of promising research topics related to e-government emerge from the last, more comprehensive, perspective. What follows is an initial selection.

ICT in actual development

Forget the dubious links between ICT in government, free markets and development. A new study of the role that ICT can play in developing countries should focus instead on the link with the 'actual existing development' (Duffield, 2002). New scattered wars generate a variety of businesses: trans-regional supply and service chains transporting arms, people, documents, and so on and thus generate a shadow economy, opaque and non-territorial of impressive proportions, according to some observers. Organized, scattered violence generates an informal economy, labelled 'the actually existing development'. The latter has emerged not because of 'official' development: it has arisen despite of it. There are no statistics about the extent and quality of the use of ICT in this shadow sector of the economy. But this deployment, whatever its extent, would be important evidence illustrating the multiple roles played by technologies for coordination and information in actual existing development.

Risk analysis and other technologies of ordering

The vast deployment of the new technologies of control and governance at a distance is supported by the systematic adoption of the new public management models, whereby professional experts are substituted by managers and administrators, and new extensive accounting systems and performance monitoring techniques are applied. In particular, consider the logic of risk analysis (Power, 1997) through which every aspect of a complex reality is ordered and made calculable so as to be amenable to control and governance, from the degree of danger of a war zone, or the hazard posed by a rogue state, up to the e-readiness of a nation, the chances of success of an aid intervention and the risks of a systems development project (Kirkman *et al.*, 2002). Risk analysis in itself is a technology aimed at ordering reality to set it up for calculation, uncertainty reduction and colonization of the future (Dean, 1999). But this way of proceeding creates new dangers, new ignorance, new uncertainties and thus new risks (Beck, 1987).

The new knowledge frontier

The increased ordering of resources and relationships made possible by such techniques as new public management, project management and quality control may clash with the local, idiosyncratic knowledge which characterizes the scattered territories and communities in the new war (Avgerou, 2002). Frequent knowledge gaps are bound to appear whenever the two logics meet or, most probably, stumble upon each other (Grillo, 1997). These are the new zones of uncertainty, ignorance and hence risk (Hobart, 1993). These are the pockets that keep disorder alive and thriving; and where new knowledge is created, which flows outside the circuits of securitized development aid and e-states. What are the characteristics and dynamics of these knowledge flows? How are they managed? What innovations at the margins does it generate?

If this current analysis captures, at least in part, what is going on in this domain, it is highly likely that, in the world of durable disorder, institutions and organizations, both state and private, end up operating more and more as pasted up assemblages, despite, or rather because of, the relentless action of ordering, calculation, planning and control. They do deliver governance and knowledge; and they plan and influence the allocation of resources and the conduct of people, but with much less overall coherence and consistency. They resemble as Foucault, and lately Rose (2000) remind us, a Tinguely's sculpture machine – full of parts that come from elsewhere, strange couplings, chance relations, cogs and levers that do not work as expected – but nevertheless produce policies, actions and social dynamics. Its precise mechanical components and its disordered assembly create multiple zones of uncertainty, platforms for imagining new combinations and enacting local improvisations. It is towards these interstices that attention should be given to identify those natural experiments, transgressive initiatives, and alternative practices in technology design and use (Ciborra, 2002; Heeks, 2002). These could represent the seeds of models alternative to those, based on the pursuit of order and control, being today deployed uniformly across the globe in private as well as public organizations, in economically developed as well as economically less developed countries.

In a more normative sense, one would need not only to understand how many of the present models, methods and solutions contribute to durable disorder in corporations and states, but also to find out, and actively cultivate, all those instances of alternative designs and approaches – present in the knowledge-intensive business within the metropolitan states and in the communities of the borderlands states – where new practices and models emerge daily.

Again, it was Heidegger (1978) who suggested, in discussing the danger represented by modern technology, that, where the greatest danger lies, the all encompassing ordering effect of Gestell, the same essence of technology, must harbour a 'saving power'.

Along the fragmented knowledge frontier traced by the advancing technologies of ordering and by the resisting idiosyncratic practices – a frontier that cuts across organizations, states and communities in advanced as well as in economically less developed countries – lies today the new laboratory for critical research on the dynamics of e-government, and, more in general, complex ICT infrastructures.[2]

Notes

This chapter originally appeared in (2005) *Information Technology and People* **18**(3): 260–279.

1. This is part of a research project carried out within the Centre for the Analysis of Risk and Regulation at LSE, and funded by PricewaterhouseCoopers. The project investigates the multiple risks of implementing complex ICT infrastructures in a variety of large organizations, both public and private. The case is based on more than 20 interviews carried out at all levels of the Jordan administration; the consulting firms; the systems integrators and the aid agencies. Many project documents were consulted. Data was gathered on the field during June 2001. The help of Diego Navarra is gratefully acknowledged. Further details of this project can be found in Ciborra and Navarra (2005).
2. Claudio Ciborra died before he could make the final revisions to this paper. The Editors wish to thank Mike Cushman of the Department of Information Systems, London School of Economics and Political Science, for preparing this paper for publication.

References

Avgerou, C. (2002). *Information Systems and Global Diversity*, Oxford: Oxford University Press.

Barzelay, M. (2001). *The New Public Management*, Berkley: University of California Press.

Beck, U. (1992). *Risk Society: Towards a New Modernity*, London: Sage Publications.

Bellamy, C. and Taylor, J. (1998). *Governing in the Information Age*, Buckingham: Open University Press.

Beninger, J. (1986). *The Control Revolution: Technological and Economic Origins of the Information Society*, Cambridge, MA: Harvard University Press.

Bhatnagar, S.C. (2004). *E-Government: From Vision to Implementation: A Practical Guide with Case Studies*, New Delhi: Sage Publications.

Burchell, G., Gordon C. and Miller P. (1991). *The Foucault Effect: Studies in Governmentality*, London: Harvester Wheatsheaf.

(The) Cabinet Office. (2000). *E-Goverrnment: A Strategic Framework for Public Services in The Information Age*, Spring. London: The Stationery Office.
Caldow, J. (2001). *Seven E-Government Leadership Milestones*, IBM Institute for Electronic Government: Washington, D.C.
Ciborra, C. (1990). X-Efficiency, Transaction Costs, and Organizational Change, in P. Weiermair (ed.), *Studies in Economic Rationality*, Ann Arbor, MI: University of Michigan Press, pp. 205–222.
Ciborra, C. 2002. *The Labyrinths of Information: Challenging the Wisdom of systems*, Oxford: Oxford University Press.
Ciborra, C. and Associates. (2001). *From Control to Drift: The Dynamics of Corporate Information Infrastructures*, Oxford: Oxford University Press.
Ciborra, C. and Navarra, D.D. (2005). Good governance, development theory, and aid policy: risks and challenges of e-government in Jordan, *Information Technology for Development* **11**(2): 141–159.
Cowen, M. and Shenton, R. (1995). The Invention of Development, in J. Crush (ed.), *The Power of Development*, London: Routldege.
Dean, M. (1999). *Governmentality: Power and Rule in Modern Society*, London: Sage Publications.
Deloitte Research (2001). *E-government's Next Generation: Transforming the Government Enterprise through Customer Service*, New York: Deloitte Consulting (Global).
Duffield, M. (2001). *Global Governance and the New Wars*, London: Zed Books.
Duffield, M. (2002). Reprising Durable Disorder: Network War and Securitisation of Aid, in B. Hettne and B. Oden, (eds) *Global Governance in the 21st Century*, Stockholm: Expert Group on development Initiatives, Ministry of Foreign Affairs, pp. 74–105.
Dunleavy, P. and Leary B.O. (1987). *Theories of the State*, London: Macmillan.
Dunleavy, P., Margetts, H., Bastow, S., Tinker, J. and Yared, H. (2001). Policy Learning and Public Sector Information Technology. *Proceedings American Political Science Association Conference*. **August**, San Francisco.
Escobar, A. (1995). *Encountering Development*, Princeton: Princeton University Press.
Ferguson, J. (1990). *The Anti-politics Machine: 'Development', Depoliticization, and Bureaucratic Power in Lesotho*, Cambridge: Cambridge University Press.
Ferlie, E. Pettigrew, A., Ashburner, L. and Fitzgerald, L. (1996). *The New Public Management in Action*, Oxford: Oxford University Press.
Fountain, J. E. (2001). *Building the Virtual State*, Washington D.C.: Brookings Institution Press.
Fountain, J. E, (2001a). Paradoxes of public sector service, *Governance: An International Journal of Policy and Administration* **14**(1): 55–73.
Fukuda – Parr, S., Lopes, C. and Malik K. (eds) (2002). *Capacity for Development, New Solutions to Old Problems*, London: UNDP /Earthscan.
Gardner, K. and Lewis, D. (2000). Dominant Paradigms Overturned or 'Business as Usual'? Development discourse and the White Paper on International Development, *Critique of Anthropology* **20**(1): 15–29.
G8-DOT Force. (2002). *Digital Opportunities for All*. www.dotforce.org. (accessed July 2002).
Grillo, R.D. (1997). Discourses of development: The view from anthropology, in R.D. Grillo and R. L. Stirrat (eds) *Discourses of Development: Anthropological Perspectives*, Oxford: Berg.
Heeks, R. (1999). *Reinventing Government in the Information Age*, London: Routledge.
Heeks, R. (2001). *Understanding e-Governance for Development*, Manchester: IDPM, University of Machester.
Heeks, R. (2002). Information systems and developing countries: Failure, Success, and Local Improvisations, *The Information Society* **18**(4): 101–112.
Heidegger, M. (1978). The Question Concerning Technology, in *Basic Writings*, London: Routledge, pp. 307–342.
Hobart, M. (ed.) (1993). *An Anthropological Critique of Development: The Growth of Ignorance*, London: Routledge.

Kahn, M.H. (1997). State Failure in Weak States: A critique of new institutionalist explanations, in J. Harris, J. Hunter and C.M. Lewis (eds) *The New Institutional Economics and Third World Development*, London: Routledge.
Kahn, M.H. (2002). State Failure in Developing Countries and Strategies of Institutional Reform, *Proceedings ABCDE Conference*. June, Oslo.
Kirkman, G.S., Cornelius, P.K., Sachs, J.D. and Schwab, K. (2002). *The Global Information Technology Report: Readiness for the Networked World*, New York: Oxford University Press.
Latour, B. (1993). *We Have Never Been Modern*, New York: Harvester Wheatsheaf.
MoICT. (2000). *Launching E-government in Jordan: Readiness and Approach*, http://www.mopc.gov.jo/egovment_n_egoreport.htm (accessed June 2002)
MoICT. (2001). *Implementing Jordan's Information and Communications Technology Strategies: 2002 Work Plan,* Ministry of ICT, Amman.
MoICT. (2002). *Electronic Transactions Draft Law for the Year 2001,* Ministry of ICT, Amman.
North, D. (1997). The New Institutional Economics and Third World Development, in J. Harris, J. Hunter and C.M. Lewis (eds) *The New Institutional Economics and Third World Development*, London: Routledge.
Power, M. (1997). *The Audit Society: Rituals of Verification*, Oxford: Oxford University Press.
Pratchett, L. (1998). Technological Bias in an Information Age: ICT policy making in local government, in I. Th. M Snellen and W.B.H.J. van de Donk (eds) *Public Administration in an Information Age*, Amsterdam: IOS Press.
Reach 2.0. (2001). *Launching Jordan's Software & IT Industry*, Reach, Amman.
Rose, N. (2000). *The Powers of Freedom: Reframing Political Thought*, Cambridge: Cambridge University Press.
Sassen, S. (2004) *De-Nationalization*, Princeton: Princeton University Press.
Snellen, I.Th.M. and Donk van de, W.B.H.J. (1998). (eds) *Public Administration in an Information Age*, Amsterdam: IOS Press.
Stiglitz, J.E., Orszag P.R., and Orszag J.M. (2000). *The Role of Government in a Digital Age*, New York: CCIA.
United Nations (2001). *World Public Sector Report: Globalization and the State*, New York: UN.
UNDP (2001). *Making New Technologies Work for Human Development*, New York: UNDP.
UNDP (2002). *Human Development Report: Deepening Democracy in a Fragmented World*, New York: Oxford University Press.
Wade, R.H. (1990). *Governing the Market: Economic Theory and the Role of Government in East Asian Industrialization*, Princeton: Princeton University Press.
Wade, R.H. (2002). Bridging the Digital Divide: new route to development or new form of dependency? *Global Governance* **8** (4): 443–466.
Walsham, G. (2001). *Making a World of Difference: IT in a Global Context*, West Sussex: Wiley.
(The) White House (2002). *The National Security Strategy of the USA*, Washington, D.C.: The White House.
Williamson, O.E. (1975). *Markets and Hierarchies: Analysis and Antitrust Implications*. New York: The Free Press.

5

From Tool to *Gestell*: Agendas for Managing the Information Infrastructure*

Claudio U. Ciborra and Ole Hanseth

> Actually, Gestell concerns us very directly. Gestell is ... more extant (seiender) than all the atomic energy, all the machines, more extant than the impact of organization, information and automation.
>
> (Heidegger, *Identitaet und Differenz*, 1957)

Abstract

The recent managerial literature on the development of corporate infrastructures to deliver sophisticated and flexible IT capabilities is based on a set of assumptions concerning the role of management in strategy formulation, planning and control; the role of IT as a tool; the linkages between infrastructure and business processes; the implementation process.

This paper deconstructs such assumptions by gradually enriching the conventional management agenda with new priorities stemming from other styles of taking care of infrastructures. A first, enlarged agenda stems from the economics of national infrastructures. Managing such infrastructures consists of enacting tactics of interference with an almost autonomous 'installed base'; aligning multiple stakeholders; fighting battles of standards; coping with irreversibility of investment decisions. Thus, economics shows that the scope for managerial control is severely limited. Various streams of social studies of technology provide an even more challenging agenda in which the infrastructure itself is an actor or an intermediate actant involved into complex games of reciprocal inscription and translations of stakeholders' interests.

The original, straightforward management agenda appears, then, to be lacking: its foundations are irremediably shaken. The paper finally evokes a philosophy-based agenda, the only one valuable in the uncharted territory where the usual foundations do not deliver any longer. Such an agenda speaks a language of weak agency: releasement; dwelling with mystery; capacity to drop the tools; valuing marginal practices. Will the last agenda play a key role in coping with the information infrastructures of the next millennium?

Introduction

Since the second half of the 1990s IBM has been formulating and deploying an extensive new fabric of processes and tools in order to be able to operate efficiently on a worldwide basis as a global company. Consider one of the major components of such global business processes: customer relationship management (CRM).

CRM consists of an array of processes that streamline all the activities between IBM and its customers across markets, product lines and geographies. It affects more than 120,000 employees world-wide and it is based on a variety of existing and new systems and applications that automate and link multiple business processes. The logic of CRM is quite straightforward, despite the myriad of activities it involves and people it affects. CRM is supposed to be the backbone of the successful completion of any business transaction IBM is engaged in: from the early opportunity identification to the order fulfilment and customer satisfaction evaluation. Thus, CRM prescribes what is needed to execute a full negotiation cycle around any customer transaction. In this respect, the ideas and models developed by Winograd and Flores (1987) were explicitly considered by the internal IBM team who originally developed CRM. The complex bundle of the main components of CRM, processes, roles and IT tools can be looked at a part of the corporate infrastructure of the new, global IBM. Indeed, internally CRM is nicknamed the 'new plumbing' of IBM.

CRM shows many features of a corporate infrastructure (Broadbent and Weill, 1997): it is shared by a vast number of IBM members and departments; it includes various sorts of standard ways of operating, embedded in procedures and software; it has required the uniformization of many existing practices and systems; it links systems and people according to a precise sequence of business purposes. Finally, it is managed through a significant set of management units and practices dedicated to its strategic management and operational deployment.

Issues like efficiency, timeliness and flexibility, together with the need for strategic alignment between the redefined processes and IBM's globalization strategy fill the management agenda at the top and middle levels of the organization. In this sense CRM is a typical example, though of a very large size, of what attracts the attention and the efforts of a number of consultants and managers in coping with the building and implementation of vast corporate infrastructures.

Rather than being a point of focus for our study, cases like CRM are a point of departure for a journey around the very notion of infrastructure and its management. Instead of trying to identify critical success factors for developing infrastructures, (Broadbent *et al.*, 1996) we want to investigate what is taken for granted, or left out or at the margins of the typical infrastructure management agenda. The latter is based on a set of assumptions and various forms of obviousness that seem to hide, rather than clarify, what is at stake in managing complex infrastructures. What we aim for is a gradual 'releasement' of the main implicit constraints that characterise the management discourse on infrastructure, to move progressively to formulating a distinct agenda. We will first use the economic perspective on infrastructure to show some crucial limitations of the conventional management approaches. Economists point out that what for managers and consultants appears as an aberration or a limiting case is in reality much more frequent: infrastructure as installed base is more often than not 'out of control', and tactics to govern it are much more subtle and limited than one gets the impression of in consulting the management agenda. The recalcitrance and wide range effects of infrastructure, if not its autonomy, are the subjects of theories such as actor network theory that can further enlarge and make evolve the infrastructure agenda. Finally, tapping Heidegger's questioning about the essence of technology, we will establish an intriguing agenda able to evoke a new 'disposition' ('management' will appear by then too strong a word) *vis a vis* infrastructure, and find through another case of corporate networking the embodiment of such different disposition.

In this way we will come full circle. After all, it was reading Heidegger's *Being and Time* (1977) that triggered Winograd and Flores (1987) to come up with a new vision of management as a network of commitments to cope with the breakdowns of business transactions. And it was this vision that contributed to the original conception of CRM as the new backbone of the IBM way of doing business globally. This paper is an opportunity to revisit one of the intellectual sources that gave rise, though indirectly, to CRM and use it to understand the essence of modern information infrastructures, but also to come up with a deeply reformed agenda for taking care of them.

The plan for our discussion looks as follows. First, we describe what are the key features of a corporate infrastructure according to the management perspectives in good currency. We will point to the internal limitations and dilemmas of the relevant agenda. Second, we show how the economics concerning the development and governance of large infrastructures can contribute to open up the typical managerial agenda, namely, economics points out the severe limitations social institutions may face in trying to govern large infrastructures. The latter aspect is further elaborated by various schools of thought in the area of social studies of technology. They portray infrastructure as a network of humans and non humans having 'a life of its own'; and as an underlying institutional and cognitive context that influences behavior inside and outside organizations. On the basis of this wider understanding we turn to Heidegger's notion of technology as '*Gestell*' (enframing) and try to come up with a Heideggerian understanding about 'how to cope with infrastructure?'. The emerging agenda is at odds with the one we started with: the managerial. The case of corporate Internet/Intranet use at Hoffmann La Roche is an instance where some of the tenets of such an alternative agenda are put in practice. An open question ends the paper: which of these agendas will be the most relevant to take care of the corporate information infrastructures in the new millennium?

The management agenda: alignment and control

Corporate infrastructure as a concept emerged in the 80's in relation to the planning of large corporate information systems. It emphasized the standardization of systems and data throughout the corporation as a way to reconcile the centralized

IS department and resources on the one hand, and the distribution of systems and applications on the other. More recent developments in networking focus on the communication (of data, documents, etc.) aspect of infrastructure. Today, managing an infrastructure to deliver effective IT capability means dealing with problems such as: aligning strategy with IT architecture and key business processes information requirements (Henderson *et al.*, 1996); universal use and access of IT resources; standardization; interoperability of systems and applications through protocols and gateways; flexibility, resilience and security. Ideally, infrastructure reconciles local variety and proliferation of applications and usages of IT with centralized planning and control over IT resources and business processes.

The boundaries and contents of infrastructure are set by defining the value of variables such as *reach* and *scope*. Reach is the number of activities or processes actually touched by the infrastructure, while scope is the type and variety of applications running on it (i.e. the range of processes being partially or totally automated through the infrastructure) (Keen, 1991). Depending upon these two variables, and especially the strategic intent of the firm, infrastructure can play different roles: utility, dependence, and enabling (Weill *et al.*, 1996). In the first role, infrastructure is just a utility aimed at saving costs of processing and communicating information throughout the organization. Its architecture maximizes efficiency in processing and transmission but does not interfere much with the nature of applications or business processes. In the second case the performance of key business processes depends upon the infrastructure, like the use of an ERP package in a specific area of the business. Enabling infrastructures provide architectures and platforms for new applications and new businesses (think of the Internet as a platform for electronic commerce).

Schematically, a typical management (and consulting) agenda concerning the creation and governance of a corporate infrastructure would entail the following activities:

- Analysis of the firm's strategic context so as to elicit the key business drivers.
- A joint consideration for the need to improve or transform existing business processes and infrastructure (various combinations are possible in the sequence and significance of the change in both areas). Formulation and implementation of a relevant BPR and technical change plans.
- Envisioning the related changes in roles, responsibilities, incentives, skills, organizational structures required by BPR and infrastructure reforms.

Empirical studies and insightful thinking related to the actual management of infrastructures point out some problematic aspects of the pretty straightforward agenda just set out. For example, empirical findings suggest that the more firms undergo change, the higher the need for investment in infrastructure. One may ask, however, are there decreasing returns to infrastructure? (Cordella and Simon, 1997). Or, does more investment mean more sophisticated infrastructure or just facing maintenance and adaptation costs of an existing, rigid infrastructure? Relatedly, is it better to have a highly flexible infrastructure that enables the firm to seize a wide range of future, unplanned business redesign options, or a highly consistent (i.e. aligned) infrastructure with the current strategic intent? Thus, should one aim for alignment, as repeatedly suggested by the literature, or for flexibility? Extensive review of top managers' opinions seem to lead to no clear-cut conclusions (Duncan, 1995).

More in general, the models of strategic alignment, the agendas that spell out what to do in order to extract the maximum IT capability from corporate infrastructure and the empirical studies of how corporate infrastructures are developed and used in practice all seem to include the same kind of caveats. Consistently, authors suggest that (Luftman, 1996):

- aligning business and technology strategies is an ongoing executive responsibility: 'strategic alignment is a journey, not an event';
- managers must be ready to learn and adapt, no matter what is the alignment pattern selected at one point in time;
- there are expression barriers that prevent the clear articulation of the strategic intent of the firm, and thus hamper the effort for an explicit strategic alignment; and
- there are barriers that due to political, cultural or economic factors impede the smooth implementation of any strategic plan concerning infrastructure.

While the management agendas are very effective in guiding the *formulation* of an infrastructure plan, they do not give any special advice on the *implementation* and adaptation side. They only provide wise words of caution: the business world out there is complex and varied and changing; any of the models on which the management agenda is based should be used with a grain of salt, and so on. In other words, all the caveats repeat the same message: of course the world out there is complicated and cannot be captured fully by a static model, but that is due to the unavoidable difference between models and real life.

However, these obvious caveats and words of caution make the management agenda largely irrelevant for action, since it does not deal with the key transition between having a nice vision and producing that vision (Argyris and Schön, 1996). Management agendas are obvious, sound and look pragmatic. In reality, they are deceivingly persuasive. They are not actionable, being highly simplified and based on sweeping generalisations and abstractions (such as 'strategy', 'utility', 'infrastructure'). The rest of the paper is dedicated to the getting closer to the 'of course', the obvious dismissal of the intricacies of 'real life' that 'naturally' cannot be captured by a model, to the 'experience' to which the caveats implicitly make reference. It is this long journey towards the sources of obviousness that gradually will change radically the infrastructure agenda.

The economic agenda: the tactics of cultivation

The management agenda is not only deceivingly sound, simple but highly abstract: it is also too narrow. It looks at infrastructure just as a large information system, where systems and applications may be heterogeneous, but control and resource allocation can be centralized. However, the case of large, national infrastructures reminds us that the management of infrastructure goes beyond the boundaries of centralized, hierarchical control of a resource. Economics, and especially the economics of standards and network infrastructures (Hanseth, 1996; Hanseth *et al.*, 1996), can help us in overcoming the narrow MIS mindset that lurks in many managerial discourses about infrastructure. Though not strictly relevant in our context, the problem of pricing can be a good entry point to see how economics broadens the management agenda. The problem, schematically stated, is how to price the service given by a common, collective good such as an infrastructure. The notion of pricing a public good has several facets: how to let people who use more pay more; how to avoid free riding; what is the trade off between universal service type of delivery *versus* a customized service; how to reach a critical mass of infrastructure users? Who should pay for the positive and/or negative externalities generated by infrastructure use? How to cope with the issues of installed base (infrastructure inertia) and flexibility (i.e. the costs of infrastructure change)?

Beyond their economic relevance, a correct and balanced answer to all these questions is a key factor for the take off and long term growth of any infrastructure. But they also point to another issue: the scope for control over an infrastructure can be limited, and management have to live with a resource that they can govern only in part (pending the issue of transaction costs (Coase, 1960)). Relatedly, the governance of infrastructure is a problem, not a given, since there can be multiple stakeholders with conflicting interests. The outcome is that the infrastructure can expand and grow in directions and to an extent that is largely outside the control of any individual stakeholder.

Second, building large infrastructures takes time. All elements are connected. As time passes, new requirements appear which the infrastructure has to adapt to. A whole infrastructure cannot be changed instantly – the new has to be connected to the old. The new version must be designed in a way making the old and the new linked together and 'interoperable' in one way or another. Hence, the old – the installed base – heavily influences how the new can be designed. Infrastructures develop through extending and improving the installed base (Hanseth, 1996).

The focus on infrastructure as 'installed base' implies that infrastructures are considered as always already existing, they are never developed from scratch. When 'designing' a 'new' infrastructure, it will always be integrated into and thereby extending others, or it will replace one part of another infrastructure. This has been the case in the building of all transport infrastructures: Every single road – even the first one if it makes sense to speak about such – has been built in this way; when air traffic infrastructures have been built, they have been tightly interwoven with road and railway networks – one needed these other infrastructures to travel between airports and the end points of the travels. Air traffic infrastructures can only be used for one part of a travel, and without infrastructures supporting the rest, isolated air traffic infrastructures would be useless.

A large information infrastructure is not just hard to change. It might also be a powerful actor influencing its own future life – its extension and size as well as its form. Consider the issue of 'standards' as a part of a more general phenomenon labelled 'self-reinforcing mechanisms' (Arthur, 1988; 1996) and 'network externalities' (Katz and Shapiro, 1986). Self-reinforcing mechanisms appear when the value of a particular product or technology for individual adopters increases as the number of adopters grows. A standard which builds up an installed base ahead of its competitors becomes cumulatively more attractive, making the choice of standards 'path dependent' and highly influenced by a small advantage gained in the early stages. Thus, the development and diffusion of infrastructural technologies are determined by 'the overriding importance of standards and the installed base compared to conventional strategies concentrating on programme quality and other promotional efforts' (Grindley, 1995).

Self-reinforcing mechanisms are, according to Arthur (1996), outside the scope of traditional, neo-classical economy, focusing on diminishing return on investment (utilization of natural resources being the paradigm example). Schematically, there are four sources of self-reinforcing processes Arthur (1988): Large set-up or fixed costs; learning effects (improvement through experience); coordination effects (advantages in going along with others); and adaptive expectations. Key effects of self-reinforcing mechanisms are:

- *Path-dependence;* i.e. past events will have large impacts on future development and in principle irrelevant events may turn out to have tremendous effects.
- *Lock-in;* i.e. when a technology has been adopted it will be impossible to develop competing technologies. 'Once random economic events select a particular path, the choice become locked-in regardless of the advantages of alternatives' (Arthur 1996).
- *Possible inefficiency;* i.e. the best solution may not necessarily win (David 1987).

Information infrastructures are paradigmatic examples of phenomena where 'network externalities' and positive feedback (increasing return on adoption) are crucial, and accordingly technologies easily being 'locked-in' and turning irreversible. All factors mentioned above apply. The positive feedback from new adopters (users) is strong. The usefulness is not only dependent on the number of users, in case of e-mail for instance, the usefulness is to a large extent its number of users. Technology becomes hard to change as successful changes need to be compatible with the installed base. As the number of users grow, reaching agreement about new features as well as coordinating transitions becomes increasingly difficult. Vendors develop products implementing a standard, new technologies are built on top of it. As the installed base grows, institutions like standardization bodies are established, and the interests vested in the technology expand.

It follows that designing and governing an infrastructure differs from designing an MIS, due to the far reaching influence of the installed base and the self-reinforcing mechanisms pointed out by the economists. The very scope of the management agenda should change. Infrastructure is not just a complex, shared tool that management are free to align according to their strategy. The economic perspective highlights a much more limited and opportunistic agenda involving trade offs and dilemmas, and a number of tactics. David (1987) points out three dilemmas and corresponding tactics one usually faces when developing networking technologies:

- *Narrow policy window.* There may be only brief and uncertain 'windows in time,' during which effective interventions can be made at moderate resource costs.
- *Blind giants.* Decision makers are likely to have greatest power to influence the future trajectories of network technologies, just when suitable informational basis on which to make system-wide optimal choices among alternatives is most lacking. These actors, then, resemble 'blind giants' – whose vision we would wish to improve before their power dissipates.
- *Angry orphans.* Some groups of users will be left 'orphaned'; they will have sunk investments in systems whose maintenance and further development are going to be discontinued. Building gateway devices linking otherwise incompatible systems can help to minimize the static economic losses incurred by orphans.

One tactic David (1987) finds worth considering is that of 'counter-action' – i.e. to prevent the 'policy window' from slamming shut, before the policy makers are better able to perceive the shape of their relevant future options. This requires positive action to maintain leverage over the 'systems rivalry', preventing any of the presently available variants from becoming too deeply entrenched as a standard, and so gathering more information about technological opportunities even at the cost of immediate losses in operations efficiency.

Possibly, the most important remedy to help overcome the negative effects of positive feedback and network externalities, i.e. lock-in and inefficiency, is the construction of gateways and adapters (Braa and Sandahl, 1998, David and Bunn, 1988, Hanseth and Monteiro, 1998, Katz and Shapiro, 1986). Gateways may connect heterogeneous networks, being built independently or based on different versions of the same standards. David and Bunn (1988) argue that '...in addition to short-run resource saving effects, the evolution of a network technology can be strongly influenced by the availability of a gateway innovation'.

Relying on all these, and other tactics, changes deeply the scope of the management agenda. While from a technical and strictly managerial perspective the business is to design, build, align and control an infrastructure, the thrust of the economic understanding of the dynamics of infrastructures would point out that 'cultivating' (Dahlbom and Janlert, 1996) an installed base is a wiser and sounder strategy. The concept of cultivation focuses on the limits of rational, human control. Technological systems are regarded as 'organisms with a life of their own' and cultivating means developing tactics of interference with such an organism. 'Cultivation is a conservative belief in the power of natural systems to withstand our effort at design, either by disarming them or by ruining them by breakdown' (Dahlbom and Janlert, 1996).

Social studies of technology: who sets the agenda for whom?

Considering technological systems as organisms 'with a life of their own' implies, possibly to the extreme, that one can look at existing *technology itself as an actor.* Infrastructures are then socio-technical networks where components, usually considered as social or technological, are linked together into networks. The 'development organization' as well as the 'product' being developed are considered unified socio-technical networks (Latour, 1991; Callon, 1991). Acknowledging the importance of the installed base implies that traditional notions of design as performed by humans only have to be rejected. The idea of cultivation as the outcome of design carried out by multiple agents (one of which is for example the installed base or the infrastructure standards) captures quite effectively the role of both humans and technology. The installed base is a powerful actor. Its future cannot be consciously designed, but designers do have influence – they might cultivate it. But what is the actual level of agency one can attribute to infrastructure? The installed base acts in two ways. It can be regarded as an actor involved in each single development activity, but perhaps more importantly, it plays a crucial role as a mediator and coordinator between the independent non-technological actors and development activities. If humans strive for control, i.e. making the world appropriate for engineering tasks, strategies for cultivating infrastructures should be considered strategies for fighting against the power of the installed base (Monteiro and Hanseth, 1995).

To enrich the infrastructure management agenda along this line of reasoning we tap in what follows various streams of research stemming from the area that can be broadly labelled social studies of science and technology.

Actor network theory sees technological, human and social elements as linked together into networks, based on the assumption that technologies are always defined to work in an environment including non-technological elements – without which the technology would be meaningless and would not work. In the same way, humans use non-human objects (technologies and other artifacts) in all their dealings – our existence in the world is based upon the existence of these very objects. Neither humans nor technological artifacts should be considered as pure, isolated elements, but as heterogeneous networks. Elements in such a network are not initially defined as human, social or technological, they are referred to by a common term – 'actant'. These assumptions do not deny any differences – or borders – between what is social or human and what is technological. However, these borders are seen as negotiated, not as given.

Two concepts from actor network theory are of particular relevance for enlarging our infrastructure agenda: *inscription* (Akrich, 1992; Akrich and Latour, 1992) and *translation* (Callon, 1991, 1994; Latour, 1987).

The notion of inscription refers to the way technical artifacts embody patterns of use. During the design, the designer works out a scenario for how the infrastructure will be used. This scenario is inscribed into it. The inscription includes programs of action for the users, and it defines roles to be played by users and the infrastructure. By inscribing programs of action into a piece of technology, for example through BPR, technology becomes an 'actant' imposing its inscribed program of action on its users. To have any effect, programs of action should not only be inscribed into isolated technological components, but rather aligned networks of technologies, humans and social institutions.

The inscribed patterns of use may not succeed because the actual use deviates from it. Rather than following its assigned program of action, a user may use the system in an unanticipated way, she may follow an anti-program (Latour, 1991). When studying the use of technical artifacts one necessarily shifts back and forth 'between the designer's projected user and the real user' in order to describe this dynamic negotiation process of design (Akrich, 1992, p. 209).

The strength of inscriptions, whether they must be followed or can be avoided, depends on the *irreversibility* of the actor-network they are inscribed into. It is never possible to know before hand, but by studying the sequence of attempted inscriptions one can learn more about exactly how and which inscriptions were needed to achieve a given aim.

A different style of managing alignment emerges. Stability and social order, according to actor network theory, are continually negotiated as a social process of aligning interests. As actors from the outset have a diverse set of interests, stability rests crucially on the ability to translate, that is, re-interpret, re-present or appropriate, others' interests to one's own.

Design is translation – 'users' and others' interests may, according to typical ideal models, be translated into specific 'needs,' the specific needs are further translated into more general and unified needs so that these might be translated into one and the same solution.

Designing technology is more than the design of pure, isolated technological artifacts. These are designed together with non-technological elements like documents, work practices, organizational rules and structures, etc. When a solution is working, all these elements constitute an aligned heterogeneous network. When making these aligned networks, existing technology will also be re-interpreted, inventing new ways of using it.

Finally, as in economics, also the social studies of technology indicate that a key feature of infrastructure is the difficulty of changing them as they are growing. Callon's concept of the (possible) irreversibility of an aligned network captures the accumulated resistance against change quite nicely (Callon, 1991, 1994; Hanseth and Monteiro, 1997). It describes how translations between actor-networks are made durable, how they can resist assaults from competing translations. The degree of irreversibility depends on the extent to which it is subsequently impossible to go back to a point where that translation was only one amongst others, and the extent to which it shapes and determines subsequent translations.

The crucial issue in design of infrastructures, as seen by the designers as well as managers, is the settlement of standards.[1] Standards are considered universal in the sense that there is one definition satisfying the needs for all users. This definition is assumed to be complete, ensuring that all correct local implementations will work in the same way.

This view is not acknowledged in the science and technology studies (STS) field. The maybe most basic finding within STS is the local and situated nature of all knowledge – including scientific knowledge. Latour and Woolgar (1986) describe how scientific results are obtained within specific local contexts and how the context is deleted as the results are constructed as universal. Universals (theories, facts, technologies) are constructed as the context is deleted, basically by being taken as given, in the same way as other universals are infrastructure standards in fact 'local' (Bowker and Star, 1994; Timmermans and Berg, 1997). They are not pure technical artifacts, but rather heterogeneous actor-networks (Hanseth and Monteiro, 1997; Star and Ruhleder, 1996). When a classification and coding system like ICD[2] is used, it is embedded into local practices. The meaning of the codes depends on that practice (Bowker and Star, 1994).

All universals are shaped by their history and context of origin. The universals are shaped by the interests of their originators. They are not objectively reflecting some reality (in case of scientific facts of theories) or neutral tools (in case of universal technologies). They embed social and political elements. Based on this perspective, infrastructures should rather be built by establishing working local solutions supporting local practices which subsequently are linked together rather than by defining universal standards and subsequently implementing them.

A very famous study of infrastructure is Thomas P. Hughes' (1983) work on the development of electricity networks. His work can be read as an actor network theory study, and accordingly seen as an actor network theory about infrastructure.[3] Hughes defines a 'technological system' as a heterogeneous collection of technical components, humans and institutions which includes the pure 'technical' system, its designers and support organization, regulating bodies, etc. Such systems are both socially constructed and society shaping. They are actor-networks.

Large technological systems seem to evolve in accordance with a loosely defined pattern. According to Hughes, they tend to acquire what he calls style and momentum as they mature. Technological systems have a mass of technical and organizational components; they possess direction, or goals; and they display a rate of growth suggesting velocity. The large mass of a technological system arises especially from the organizations and people committed by various interests to the system. Manufacturing corporations, public and private utilities, industrial and government research laboratories, investment and banking houses, sections of technical and scientific societies, departments in educational institutions, and regulatory bodies add greatly to the momentum of modern electric light and power systems. Inventors, engineers, scientists, managers, owners, investors, financiers, civil servants, and politicians often have interests in the growth and durability of a system. And as a system grows, it becomes more attractive for others to adapt to it. This makes Hughes' concept of momentum closely related to the self-reinforcing processes at the center of the economics of standards. The development of the Internet, including all its designers, standardization bodies and local network operators, is a good example of a technological system with considerable momentum.

In the development of infrastructures and infrastructure technologies, a phenomenon Hughes (1983, 1987) calls 'reverse salients' (corresponding to the phenomenon Rosenberg (1994) calls 'technical imbalance') plays important roles. Reverse salients denote those elements that are 'lagging behind' and for that reason causing major problems for the further development of the whole technological system. When a reverse salient cannot be corrected within the context of an existing system, the problem becomes a radical one, the solution of which may bring a new and competing system.

In the early 1880s, direct current has turned into such a reverse salient, as the voltage could not be transformed across long distances. A 'battle of the systems' then ensued between alternating and direct current, culminating in the 1890s, not with victor and vanquished, but with the invention of devices, i.e. gateways, making possible the interconnection of the two systems.

Exploiting the momentum of existing installed bases as underlying infrastructures, i.e translating them into allies, will always be important when establishing new infrastructures. To make an infrastructure 'grow', it needs to be planted in 'fertile soil'. The potential success of this strategy is illustrated by the way WorldWideWeb has been designed to build upon the existing Internet. To escape the reverse salients of an installed base that seems unwilling to adopt to new requirements, moving its users to a new one connected through gateways is the maybe most important strategy.

Adaptation is a response to different environments and adaptation to environments culminates in *style*. There are countless examples in this century of variation in technological style. A 1920 map of electricity supply in London, Paris, Berlin, and Chicago reveals, to Hughes, remarkable variation from city to city in the size, number, and location of the power plants. The striking variation is not in the amount of light and power generated, but in the way in which it is generated, transmitted, and distributed. The differences were primarily due to variation in regulatory legislation that expressed fundamental political values. Natural geography and regional and national historical experiences are also factors Hughes found to shape technological styles.

By having style infrastructures embody a representation of the functioning of the organizations they support, especially when they are deployed with joint efforts of BPR (Broadbent *et al.*, 1995). In other words, infrastructures are not just made of networks, data flows and work procedures, but also are embodiments, or 'vehicles', of emerging modes of work organization, of new cognitive imageries and institutional arrangements. More specifically, they interact with both the structural and institutional arrangements associated to a given division of labour, and the assumptions, frames and mental images people hold while routinely enacting and practicing that specific division of labour: infrastructures are immersed and nurture 'cognitive ecologies'.

Infrastructures can be then regarded as 'formative contexts', i.e. sets of the pre-existing institutional arrangements, cognitive frames and imageries that actors bring and routinely enact in a situation of action (Ciborra and Lanzara, 1994). As such, they constitute the background condition for action, enforcing constraints, giving direction and meaning, and setting the range of opportunities for undertaking action. Infrastructure as a formative context can shape both the organization of work and the set of social scripts which govern the invention of alternative forms of work, the future ways of problem-solving and conflict resolution, the revision of the existing institutional arrangements and the plans for their further transformation.

Infrastructures as formative contexts show a pasted up nature, and a makeshift one, where old and new systems, artifacts and practices (automated and manual) are tested, discarded, retrieved, collated and combined over time. Typically infrastructures are subject to 'shift and drift' phenomena (Berg, 1997; Ciborra, 1996). The ways they are implemented and used never fully correspond to the original plans and visions, and design processes more often than not take paths unthought of at the start, almost beyond the actors' will. Thus infrastructures possess an open nature and are subject to continuous reinvention, i.e. to an innovative adoption process carried out by the users themselves. In part, they are characterized by formalized components, such as hardware, software, rules, functions etc., but these do not completely dispose of how infrastructures behave in everyday life. Surrounding these stylized components, usually laid down as a result of *ex ante* design, there are routines and interventions carried out by users who may take unplanned courses of action or by designers who happen to be temporarily with the project, introduce quirky or irreversible design choices, and then leave. All these routines and interventions are continuously developed, tried out, retained or discarded, retrieved and combined, on a local, often tacit basis, outside or at the margins of the master plans and designs, in an endless process of *bricolage* (Ciborra, 1994). In sum, infrastructure as formative context possesses a double nature. On the one hand, it appears to be highly stable and inescapable, given its pervasiveness; on the other it is the culture bed for experiments in organizational restructuring and innovation, within certain economic and technical constraints. A regimen of permanent, ineliminable fluctuations characterizes infrastructures in use.

Infrastructure as *Gestell*

In describing the general features of CRM, IBM's initiative to set up a global new infrastructure made of redesigned processes supported by an array of IT tools, we found two sides of the phenomenon. The apparent one is that CRM has been developed and managed according to the 'classical' tenets of the managerial literature on BPR. The not so explicit, or actually hidden side is that the basic 'philosophy' of CRM was influenced by the vision of management as networks of commitments developed by Flores and Winograd (1987): the task of management is to cope with breakdowns of business transactions by completing all the necessary negotiation and coordination loops needed to executing a transaction. Such vision of what management, information and decision making is all about is based on the attempt to bringing Heidegger's philosophy to bear on to the field of business organizations and information systems. Specifically, notions such as 'being thrown into the world', engagement, breakdowns and ready-to-hand tools are picked up by Winograd and Flores and harnessed to deliver both a new perspective of the management of business processes and the design of IT tools (of which the software coordinator was the concrete implementation). After the broader endeavour by Dreyfus (1982) to bring phenomenology to bear into the field of IT and in particular artificial intelligence, the one of Winograd and Flores has been perhaps the most influential attempt in this direction. They were followed by further contributions. Specifically, Ehn (1989) has focused on the key metaphor of IT as a tool ready to use, in order to develop ideas about the design of user interfaces that can render information systems less conspicuous in the work flow. More recently, Kallinikos (1995) carries out a brilliant study of the '*vorstellen*' (representing) property of technology. Introna (1997) revisits the world of management, information and power in light of Heidegger's work in a comprehensive way, though he does not focus on the specific role of technology. Today the latter seems to be still the domain of interest of the philosophers, who try to go beyond the more strictly exegetical study of Heidegger's writings on technology and see whether a new radicalizing philosophy of technology can be put forward.

In what follows, our focus will be on the question of technology as discussed by Heidegger and the notion of infrastructure and its relevant management agenda, while we leave to another occasion the analysis of the management of business transactions as networks of commitments, how they are implemented in CRM and other instances.

We submit that the works of Winograd and Flores (1987) and Ehn (1988) need to be overcome. Namely, they convey – especially the latter – the idea that Heidegger's conception of technology can be found in the notion of 'tool'. This is misleading. Heidegger in his major work '*Sein und Zeit*' focuses on the notion of tool to describe phenomenologically how we encounter the world. We do not encounter it as an assemblage of objects we can describe geometrically or physically, but as 'in order to' devices endowed with functions. As such we 'use' the objects before describing them. Description is only a very peculiar and selective instance of taking care of the world: the measuring and scientific one. The relevance and modernity of those pages of Heidegger's major work for the field of user-interface design of computer systems could not go unnoticed. However, this is *not* what Heidegger had to say about modern technology, the latter being in its essence anything *but* a tool.

For Heidegger (1978) the essence of modern technology is denoted by the German word '*Gestell*'. *Gestell* means in German 'skeleton', frame or shelf. Note, in passing, that the word '*Untergestell*' means chassis and infrastructure (again meant as a light physical support).

But Heidegger uses the word *Gestell* in a new sense stemming from the two parts composing the word in German: the prefix *Ge* and the word *Stelle* derived from the verb *stellen*. *Ge* in German is the prefix that denotes reunion, gathering, or collecting and reassembling (think of *Ge-sellschaft* = society; or *Ge-meinschaft* = community; or, the example introduced by Heidegger himself, *Gebirge* = mountain

(*Bergen*) chain). *Stelle* and *stellen* have a variety of meanings. The noun means place, spot, location. The verb means generically put, place, stand, set, arrange, regulate, provide, order, etc.

Thus, *Gestell* means literally the reunion of the placing, arranging, regulating, ordering. Of what, and how? And what has such a reunion to do with technology? First, Heidegger suggests that the essence of technology is not something technical, i.e. linked to the more or less fascinating technical aspects of highly sophisticated tools for production, transport, communication, or power generation.

The essence of technology as a phenomenon lies beyond the appearances. Specifically, Heidegger (1977) approaches what lies behind the captivating appearances of modern technology from two slightly different angles.

In his 1949 Bremer lectures Heidegger (1994) starts by remarking that despite the power of modern technology of shortening distances, things remain for us still far. 'All the mastering of farness does not deliver any proximity', rather we experience the world as an undifferentiated 'without distance'. But such a 'without distance' has definitely a place: it constitutes the stock or standing reserve (*Bestand*) of all what is available (present-at-hand). What supplies this stock of undifferentiated resources that represent the world as experienced by the modern man? It is the supplying itself (*bestellen*) that is, the infinite chain of actions of ordering, requiring, demand and supply.

> The forester who measures the felled timber in the woods... is today ordered by the industry that produces commercial woods, whether he knows it or not. He is made subordinate to the orderability of cellulose, which for its part is challenged forth by the need for paper, which is then delivered to newspapers and illustrated magazines. the latter, in their turn, set public opinion to swallowing what is printed, so that a set configuration of opinion becomes available on demand. (Heidegger, 1994)

Man, far from being the master of this enchaining process, is, under various forms, as a worker, a manager, or a citizen who reads the newspapers, 'employed' (i.e. ordered and organized) by this process, thus becoming himself part of that standing-reserve. This circulation process is self-feeding and leads to nothing else than its perpetuation. The process becomes so universal to embrace the world, nature, history and the destiny of mankind.

The gathering of the multiple actions of ordering and their enchainment is called *Gestell*.[4] The Gestell captures all what is extant and makes it available through a stock to be put in circulation. Machines are built and applied, science generates new solutions that get converted into new systems and applications because of the *Gestell*, not the other way around. Nature itself loses the property of being an object (*Gegen-stand*) and becomes *Be-stand*, i.e. standing reserve of available resources to be exploited in the process of circulation.

It is because of this 'distortion' in what we encounter as real, things, people, the world, that 'machines created by the technology can only shorten distances, but at the same time do not bring about any proximity, precisely because the essence of the technology does not give access to proximity and farness', but just undifferentiated, average availability (Heidegger, 1994).

The second approach to the definition of *Gestell* is employed by Heidegger (1978) in his later Munich conference on 'The question concerning technology'. There, Heidegger starts directly from the instrumental definition of technology (a tool, a means to an end) and inquires into the notion of instrumentality, i.e. causality. Causality as a way 'bringing-forth', presenting. The essence of technology lies in its capacity to bring forth, to reveal 'The revealing that rules in modern technology is a challenging', setting upon resources, putting nature and man to demand to yield. It is a way of expediting, of driving on to the maximum yield. 'Such challenging happens in that the energy concealed in nature is unlocked, what is unlocked is transformed, what is transformed is stored up, what is stored up is in turn distributed, and what is distributed is switched about ever anew. Unlocking, transforming, storing distributing, and switching about are ways of revealing...' (Heidegger, 1978). Again, *Gestell* refers to the ways through which the ordering and setting up unveils what is extant as standing reserve of resources (including human) made available for future deployment.

We are now in the position of looking at the links between *Gestell*, or the essence of modern technology as arrived at by Heidegger, and some key aspects of the modern corporate information highways.

First, the emphasis put by Heidegger on the enchained processes of ordering highlights a paramount aspect of how infrastructure is conceived today by the management literature. Networks are not only there to facilitate communication, but to reduce costs of transacting, in supporting the alignment, disintermediation and interlocking of business processes within and between organizations. This is precisely the phenomenon of the intertwining of networks and computers as a layer on which enterprise packages can run to implement the linking of business processes (ERP) and the management of the workflow, for example as prescribed by methodologies like BPR.

Second the self feeding nature of such a process, and its reliance on planning and standards emerged as central themes of the economics literature, are also included in the *Gestell*. Standards, network externalities, imitation are all factors that contribute to the momentum of the self-feeding process of infrastructure development and diffusion.

Furthermore, note how the way in which Heidegger defines *Gestell* as a reunion of ordering process, or even literally as 'a frame that sets up', overcomes in a felicitous way the dichotomy between the 'structural', i.e. static, aspects of infrastructure and their dynamics. In *Gestell* both dimensions are hosted, while the term infrastructure seems to privilege the structural aspects only.

More uncertain remains the role of characteristics such as installed base and irreversibility. They could be linked to the notion of standing reserve, but in our modern vision of infrastructure it is the inertia of the successive accumulation of systems and applications the outstanding feature of such a reserve. Heidegger, instead, seems to pinpoint the process of accumulation of 'resources' made available as future input to the relentless ordering process. Of the dynamics aspects of the technology, *Gestell* seems to give a priority to its accelerating, self feeding aspects, while the study of infrastructures puts at least an equal emphasis on the inertial effects, eventually as the key determining factor of the quasi autonomous nature of sophisticated system technologies in modern organizations. In this respect Feenberg argues that the unilateral way of looking at the implications of *Gestell*, are due to the 'unhistorical understanding of essence (in this case of the technology) to which most philosophers are committed'. In order to capture the phenomena of resistance to and diversion of the *Gestell*, one should focus on the 'socially concrete stages of development that itself has an essential logic we need to uncover'. A first attempt in this direction has been done by studying the unfolding of infrastructures in a number of large corporations (including IBM – see above). This study provides also material to consider a final aspect of our essay: is there scope for a 'Heideggerian agenda' in dealing with information infrastructures?

Towards a Heideggerian agenda? The case of Hoffman la Roche

Heidegger's ideas about 'what to do' are developed in a successive step of his inquiry into the essence of technology, namely around the notion of danger (*Gefahr*) (Heidegger, 1994).

Gestell does not deliver the nearness to things. It does not deliver 'the world' (that is the 'there' where man's existence unfolds). Everything instead is just undifferentiated standing reserve of resources ready to be deployed. *Gestell* becomes the world, but a world of a special kind, that can subsist only thanks to the oblivion of the authentic one. Through oblivion *Gestell* chases away 'the world'. This chasing represents, according to Heidegger, the essence of the *Gestell*: it is the danger. With a play of words, the danger is the essence of the essence of technology. However, Heidegger does not commit himself to a favourable or negative stance towards technology. He states that such stances belong to the technical discourse on technology, and do not deal with its essence. They implicitly assume technology as a set of tools, that can be good or bad, be deployed in a positive or negative way. These stances address only the 'instrumental' dimension of technology, i.e. they adhere to the technical discourse on technology missing that which is non technical (non instrumental) in the essence of technology.

What is the essence of the danger, then? It is that *Gestell* comes to represent what 'is' and what 'is not'. The danger lies in the fact that *Gestell* delivers 'representations' of all what subsists, and these become the 'real world'. If one can talk about the domination of technology, one should speak of 'the domination of the essence of the technology that orders in its appropriating even and precisely the representations man makes about it...The essence of technology, the *Gestell*, carries out its own simulation' (Heidegger, 1994). The outcome of such representing and simulation is the essence of the danger, able to encompass any discourse pro or con the technology and its effects (see on all these aspects the thorough analysis of (Kallinikos, 1995).

More radically, technology works outside the sphere of means and ends. It is *not* an object, or a tool among many. Rather, it is the hidden trait of all what today is 'real'. In sum, 'Heidegger's concern is the human distress caused by the technological understanding of being, rather than the destruction caused by specific technologies...The danger, then, is not the destruction of nature or culture but certain totalizing kinds of practices – a levelling of our understanding of being' (Dreyfus, 1993).

Recall what we discussed in relation to the social studies of technology, i.e. the contextual – at the same time cognitive and institutional – role of infrastructure. We can, then, appreciate the relevance of Heidegger's thought. Information infrastructures can, as formative contexts, shape not only the work routines, but also the ways people look at practices, consider them 'natural' and give them their overarching character of (false – see Unger (1987)) necessity. Infrastructure becomes an essential factor shaping the-taken-for-grantedness of organizational practices. Imagining, world views and reform initiatives, or new designs are moulded by the subtle and hidden influence of infrastructures.

How to deal with 'the danger'? Again, Heidegger avoids to fall into the 'easy' role of being a romantic and reactionary critic of technology (as a mistaken and superficial reading of his works on the subject has lead some to conclude). His argument, as Dreyfus (1993) has aptly noted, is much more open, subtle and complex.

Gestell having the power to enact a world in which everything is a resource available to yield would seem to leave little hope for any change, since any change or even debate about change would be somehow 'supervised' and governed by the *Gestell* itself (precisely as a formative context). Recalling Hölderlin's verses, Heidegger (1978) does not agree with such a conclusion, and submits that where the greatest danger lies, also lies the opportunity for rescue. 'Although a technological understanding of being is our destiny, it is not our fate...Although the technological understanding of being governs the way things have to show up for us, we can be open to a transformation of our current cultural clearing' (Dreyfus, 1993). It is in the nature of destiny that in a sudden, unpredictable moment the destiny of being can lead itself onto other unexpected, and different directions. These other directions will not put aside the technology, the essence of which still delivers the world through the *Gestell*, but such an essence will be able 'to heal itself, by finding its hidden truth' (Heidegger, 1994). This shift of gears cannot have anything to do with a destiny that can be planned in a logical and historical way, nor as 'the outcome of a process of history that can be constructed', or 'managed' we may add. Heidegger indicates a few ways in which such a sudden transformation can concern man:

- *Releasement,* that is a comportment toward technology which expresses a 'yes' and a 'no' simultaneously. 'We let technical devices enter our daily life, and at the same time leave them outside' (Heidegger, 1992).
- *Openness to the mistery,* in order to remain open to the meaning hidden in technology, and the rehabilitation of astonishment at that which is.

- *A new sense of responsibility.* The traditional notion of responsibility means to be in control of what comes from us. Releasement, instead, implies responsibility in accepting what is largely beyond our control, the unforeseen.
- *Shifting fluctuations to the centre stage.* 'Take up practices that are now at the margins of our culture and make them central, while de-emphasising practices now central to our cultural self-understanding' (Dreyfus, 1993).

Surprisingly, in our investigation on the present practices of infrastructure deployment and management, we encountered at least one significant case where the relationship between organization and technology is enacted according to a 'releasement' approach. With this example, that runs against our initial one of a radical, centralized and global process redesign (CRM), we conclude outlining the practical implications of the four main points above, which might denote as steps towards a Heideggerian agenda concerning modern technology, and information infrastructures in particular.

The case in question is the one of the use of Intranet and Internet technology as the backbone of strategic marketing at Hoffmann La Roche (hence Roche), the number six pharmaceutical company in the world. The strategic marketing function at Roche's headquarters in Basel comprises a couple of hundred people. This function was created in the 1980s to centralize and globalize Roche marketing worldwide. At the same time, the headquarters must operate with national companies (affiliates) that still have a strong power and autonomy in the local markets. So far, there is no new process re-engineering aimed at streamlining and unifying marketing worldwide. Adaptation to local markets, and especially national regulations, has still a paramount importance that impedes the enactment of fully global processes (the pharmaceutical industry belongs to the class of heavily regulated industries).

Marketing a pharmaceutical product is 'knowledge intensive' as many other activities in a pharmaceutical company. Knowledge is created in developing a new product; knowledge emerges from the clinical trials and is consolidated in the new drug application; further knowledge is acquired and processed once the product is in use. Knowledge comes from various sources, inside and outside the company, and is continually gathered, processed and communicated throughout the product life cycle. Strategic marketing sifts, filters, accumulates and distributes the knowledge necessary to market a product worldwide. Strategic marketing can only intervene in and influence indirectly the local marketing activities, namely by providing the background knowledge that is essential to carry out marketing in each country. Such knowledge has many forms and supports: training on the product features; clinical tests information, both before the launch of the product and after; prescription strategies etc. Most of the knowledge is a 'template' that has to be locally adapted, enriched and modified.

In the second half of the 1980s strategic marketing championed a major technological innovation: the establishment of the first corporate network, supporting a variety of applications. The purpose of the network and its applications, that went under the name of MedNet, was to further increase the levels of globalization and integration through standardization. MedNet had many of the properties of a *Gestell* (Ciborra, 1996).

But after eight years of development the use of the applications running on the network – consulting literature, accessing clinical trials data, office automation applications, etc. – was very low, with some affiliates developing competing systems of their own, like Roche France adopting an alternative platform: the Minitel (MedTel), or others using Internet.

Despite repeated attempts at 'internal marketing' MedNet, it was eventually discontinued in the mid 1990s. Its negative aspects, especially the costs affiliates had to bear, compared to the low level of use dictated its end. The purely technical infrastructure remained in place, while the application portfolio was phased out. Since a couple of years ago a new array of Intranet and Internet applications have taken the place of MedNet.

Intranet/Internet in Roche do not only represent an infrastructure, but also a new style of networking and IT use. In contrast with the headquarters-based formative context hidden in the MedNet concept, the one of a centralizing bureaucracy wanting to harness IT to standardize local behaviour, Internet/Intranet provide an emerging formative context, the one of decentralization, autonomy and loose coupling. Headquarters use a 'releasing' attitude to accompany, and so far not impede or slow down, the unfolding of this context both in the product areas and in the affiliates.

No big plan is guiding the deployment of the new infrastructure. Actually, the no plan/ no strategy attitude seems to be most favorable to let the directions and issues of Web use emerge: the process is not mature enough to be managed; it is still in a 'discovering' stage; and as such is nurtured and 'cultivated'. The fact that Internet/Intranet cost less, or at least much less than MedNet, favours the hands off, releasing attitude of top management. In the new practice, while possibly a new context for doing business is emerging, terms like alignment or BPR simply have no meaning: they lack a relevant management context. Words like drifting, *bricolage* and cultivation seem to better capture what is going on today, not only in the affiliates, but in the very headquarters among the various product areas.

One can thus find in the Roche case an alternative model of infrastructure development and diffusion from the one of top down, strategic alignment. There is no strong top down direction, but releasement; no alignment *by fiat*, but loosely coupling between local context and technology initiatives. Thus, the infrastructure expands by the decentralized linking of local initiatives that are born as spin offs of headquarters initiatives. The latter constitute a reference model for imitation, and provide the content allowing the local Web sites to be built already with a minimal (critical mass) content. The 'grassroots' initiatives enjoy two key features: they are local (and sometimes expressed in local language -while MedNet was always at fault in this respect), and they retain a link with the headquarters' content. The power of the periphery is harnessed to reinforce the diffusion of the infrastructure, and not as a source of resistance. Affiliates, or product areas can refuse to adopt other products', or countries' or headquarters' templates, when developing their own sites, or, they can simply say no to building a site or accessing an existing one.

What is striking is that all this seems to fit nicely with the way knowledge is managed in Roche marketing activities: key knowledge is centrally created around the development of the product, but a lot of complementary knowledge is generated and resident close to local markets. The Intranet/Internet as a technical infrastructure, and the present management approach, a mixture of releasement and cultivating strategies, seem to fit the loosely coupled nature of knowledge distribution within and across the business. In a managerial perspective, it is a case of a surprising 'alignment and fit' through the decoupling of tools, processes, local and central practices, in the aftermath of the hard and costly lesson learned from the MedNet failure: the impossibility of enforced, top down alignment. From a philosophical perspective, it highlights that even in current business practices of large multinationals, possibly for those which are highly knowledge intensive, an authentic Heideggerian agenda, not the one centered on the notions of tool and breakdown fixing, but the one of releasement in front of the *Gestell*, may be still highly relevant.

Notes

This chapter originally appeared in (1998) *Information Technology and People* **11**(4) 305–327.

1. Standards are found everywhere, and as such they have been much in focus in STS. Standards is indeed the issue addressed in STS. Not primarily technological standards, by rather standards in form of universal scientific facts and theories. These studies also, we believe, have something to tell us about information infrastructure standards.
2. ICD, International Classification of Diseases, has been defined under the authority of WHO, and is used in health care institutions in most of the world.
3. The similarity between Hughes' work and ANT is pointed to both by Hughes (1987, p. 77: 1994, p. 102) and Michel Callon (1987, p. 101). The system concept presupposes usually that a distinction can be made between the system itself and its environment. The actor-network concept has the advantage of avoiding this type of problem and the many difficult questions concerning methodology it raises. According to Callon (1987) Hughes avoid this pitfall by using the systems concept in a pragmatic way. By continuously stressing all the connections linking the 'inside' and the 'outside' of the system, he comes close to the actor-network concept.
4. The most frequent English translation of *Gestell* is 'enframing'. Alternative translations are 'the com-positing' or simply 'com-posite': both suggestions aim at retaining the original meaning of '*stellen*' in English, though they seem, alas!, to lack the 'enframing' effect.

References

Akrich, M. (1992). The de-scription of technical objects, in W.E. Bijker, and J. Law (eds), *Shaping Technology/Building Society*, Cambridge, MA: The MIT Press, pp. 205 –224.

Akrich, M. and Latour, B. (1992). A summary of a convenient vocabulary for the semiotics of human and nonhuman assemblies, in W.E. Bijker, and J. Law (eds), *Shaping Technology/Building Society*, Cambridge, MA: The MIT Press, pp. 259–264.

Argyris, C. and Schön, D. (1996). *Organizational Learning II*, Reading, MA: Addison Wesley.

Arthur, B. (1988). Self-reinforcing mechanisms in economics, in P.W. Anderson *et al.* (eds), *The Economy as an Evolving Complex System*, New York: Perseus Press.

Arthur, B. (1996). Increasing returns and the two worlds of business, *Harvard Business Review*, July–August.

Berg, M. (1997). On forms, containers, and the electronic medical record: some tools for a sociology of the formal, *Science, Technology and Human Values* **22**(4): 403–431.

Bowker, G. and Star, S.L. (1994). Knowledge and infrastructure in international information management. Problems of classification and coding, in L. Bud-Frierman, (ed.) *Information Acumen: The Understanding and Use of Knowledge in Modern Business*, New York: Routledge, pp. 187–213.

Braa, K., and T. Sandahl. (1998). Documents in infrastructures:challenges for design, in W.R.J. Baets (ed.) *Proceedings from 6th European Conference on Information Systems*, pp. 1025–1040. Euro-Arab Management School, Granada, Spain, pp. 1025–1040.

Broadbent, M. and Weill, P. (1997). Management by maxim: how business and IT managers can create IT infrastructures, *Sloan Management Review*, Spring.

Broadbent, M., Weill, P. and St. Clair, D. (1995). The role of IT infrastructure in business process redesign, *CISR WP278*, Sloan School of Management, May.

Broadbent, M., Weill, P., O'Brien, T. and Neo, B.S. (1996). Firm context and patterns of IT infrastructure capability, *International Conference on Information Systems Proceedings, Cleveland, OH.*

Callon, M. (1987). Society in the making: the study of technology as a tool for sociological analysis, in W.E. Bijker, T.P. Hughes and T. Pinch, *The Social Construction of Technological Systems*, Cambridge, MA: The MIT Press, pp. 83–106

Callon, M. (1991). Techno–economic networks and irreversibility, in J. Law (ed.) *A Sociology of Monsters: Essays on Power, Technology and Domination*, New York: Routledge, pp. 132–161.

Callon, M. (1994). Is science a public good? *Science, Technology & Human Values* **19**(4): 395–424.

Ciborra, C.U. (1994). From thinking to tinkering, in C.U. Ciborra and T. Jelassi (eds), *Strategic Information Systems*, Chichester: John Wiley & Sons.

Ciborra, C.U. (1996). Introduction: what does groupware mean for the organizations hosting it?, in C. Ciborra (ed.) *Groupware & Teamwork: Invisible Aid or Technical Hindrance?* Chichester: John Wiley & Sons.

Ciborra, C.U. and Lanzara, G.F. (1994). Formative contexts and information technology, *Journal of Accounting, Management and Information technology* **4**(2): 61–86.

Coase, R. (1960). The problem of social cost, *Journal of Law and Economics* **3**(1): 1–44.

Cordella, A. and Simon, K. (1997). Decreasing returns to infrastructure, *IRIS Proceedings*, Oslo.

Dahlbom, B. and Janlert, S. (1996). *Computer Future*, University of Goteborg.

David, P.A. (1987). Some new standards for the economics in the information age, in P. Dasgupta and P. Stoneman (eds), *Economic policy and technological performance*, Cambridge: Cambridge University Press, pp. 206–239.

David, P.A. and Bunn, J.A. (1988). The economics of gateways technologies, *Information Economics and Policy* **3**(2): 165–202.

H. Dreyfus, H.L. (1982). *What Computers Can't Do: The Limits of Artificial Intelligence*, New York: Harper and Row.

Dreyfus, H.L. (1993). Heidegger in the connection between nihilm, art, technology and politics, in C. Guignon (ed.), *Heidegger*, Cambridge: Cambridge University Press.

Duncan, N.B. (1995). Capturing flexibility of IT infrastructure, *Journal of Management information Systems* **12**(2): 37–57.

Ehn, P. (1989). *Work-Oriented Design of Computer Artifacts*, Stockholm: Arbetslivscentrum.

Grindley, P. (1995). *Standards, Strategy and Policy Costs*, Oxford: Oxford University Press.

Hanseth, O. (1996). *Information Technology as Infrastructure*, Ph.D. Thesis, University of Gøteborg.

Hanseth, O. and Monteiro, E. (1997). Inscribing behavior in information infrastructure standards, *Accounting, Management and Information Technologies* **7**(4): 183–211.

Hanseth, O. and Monteiro. E. (1998). Changing irreversible networks, in W.R.J. Baets (ed.), *Proceedings from 6th European Conference on Information Systems*, Euro-Arab Management School, Granada, Spain, pp. 1123–1139.

Hanseth, O., Monteiro, E. and Hatling, M. (1996). Developing information infrastructure standards: the tension between standardisation and flexibility, *Science Technology and Human Values* **21**(4): 407–426.

Heidegger, M. (1957). *Identitaet und Differenz*, Stuttgart: Neske.
Heidegger, M. (1977). *Sein und Zeit*, Frankfurt: Klostermann.
Heidegger, M. (1978). *Basic Writings*, London: Routledge.
Heidegger, M. (1992). *Gelassenheit*, Stuttgart: Neske.
Heidegger, M. (1994). *Bremer und Freiburger Fortraege* (1949), Frankfurt: Klostermann.
Henderson, J.C., Venkatraman, N. and Oldach, S. (1996). Aligning Business and IT strategies, in J. Luftman (ed.), *Strategic Alignment*, Oxford: Oxford University Press.
Hughes, T.P. (1983). *Networks of Power: Electrification in Western Society, 1880–1930*, Baltimore: John Hopkins University Press.
Hughes, T.P. (1987). The evolution of large technical systems, in W.E. Bijker, T.P. Hughes and T. Pinch (eds), *The Social Construction of Technological Systems*, Cambridge, MA: The MIT Press, pp. 51–82.
Hughes, T.P. (1994). Technological Momentum, in M. R. Smith and L. Marx (eds), *Does Technology Drive History? The Dilemma of Technological Determinism*, Cambridge, MA: The MIT Press, pp. 101–114.
Introna, L. (1997). *Information, Management and Power*, London: Macmillan.
Kallinikos, J. (1995). The architecture of the invisible: Technology as representation, *Organization* 2(1): 117–140.
Katz, M. and Shapiro, C. (1986). Technology adoption in the presence of network externalities, *Journal of Political Economy* **94**(4): 822–841.
Keen, P.W. (1991). *Shaping the Future*, Boston MA: Harvard Business School Press.
Latour, B. (1987). *Science in Action*, Buckingham: Open University Press.
Latour, B. (1991). Technology is society made durable, in J. Law (ed.) *A Sociology of Monsters. Essays on Power, Technology and Domination*, New York: Routledge, pp. 103–131.
Latour, B. and Woolgar, S. (1986). *Laboratory Life: The Construction of Scientific Facts, Princeton*, NJ: Princeton University Press.
Luftman, J. (ed.) (1996). *Strategic Alignment*, Oxford: Oxford University Press.
Monteiro, E. and Hanseth, O. (1995). Social shaping of information infrastructure: on being specific about the technology, in W. Orlikowski, G. Walsham, M.R. Jones and J.I. DeGross (eds), *Information Technology and Changes in Organisational Work*, London: Chapman & Hall, pp. 325–343.
Rosenberg, N. (1994). *Explaining the Black Box*, Cambridge: Cambridge University Press.
Star, S.L. and Ruhleder, K. (1996). Steps towards an ecology of infrastructure: design and access for large information spaces, *Information Systems Research* **7**(1): 111–134.
Timmermans, S. and Berg, M. (1997). Standardization in action: achieving universalism and localization in medical protocols, *Social Studies of Science* **27**: 273–305.
Unger, R.M. (1987). *False Necessity*, Cambridge: Cambridge University Press.
Weill, P., Broadbent, M. and St. Clair, D. (1996). IT value and the role of IT infrastructure, in J. Luftman (ed.), *Strategic Alignment*, Oxford: Oxford University Press.
Winograd, T. and Flores, F. (1987). *Understanding Computers and Cognition*, Reading, MA: Addison Wesley.

6
The Platform Organization: Recombining Strategies, Structures, and Surprises*

Claudio U. Ciborra

> This paper is an attempt to shoot a moving picture of an organization and its strategy in action, which are fluidly changing to cope with chaotic environments and therefore cannot be captured by existing organizational models. The author presents a new conceptual lens that helps us look at the elusive, complex process of organizational transformation.
> (Ikujiro Nonaka)

Abstract

The global technology strategy of Olivetti, a leading European computer firm, is analyzed over the last decade in order to illustrate how high-tech firms undergo transformations which not only tend to destroy their best core competencies, but also affect their very business identity. Task uncertainty is so pronounced that conventional ways of looking at the organizational structures and processes, such as the transaction costs approach or the strategy-structure link, need to be amended in favor of a more dynamic perspective. Such a perspective looks at organizations as platforms, or contexts, out of which specific structures are extracted, tried out and discarded in a pragmatic manner. A platform is a meta-organization, a formative context that molds structures, and routines shaping them into well-known forms, such as the hierarchy, the matrix and even the network, but on a highly volatile basis. Hence, the platform organization may appear to be confused and inefficient but its value lies in its readiness to sport whatever organizational form is required under the circumstances. Platforms are characterized by surprises, and organization members, no matter how they see themselves after the fact, are busy improvising and tinkering. Drawing on similar studies carried out in Silicon Valley, one can draw the conclusion that high-tech firms can survive if they are smart at doing what 'savages do daily', i.e. *bricolage*

> In searching out the truth be ready for the unexpected, for it is difficult to find and puzzling when you find it. (Heraclitus)

> Men and women confronting change are never fully prepared for the demands of the moment, but they are strengthened to meet uncertainty if they can claim a history of improvisation and a habit of reflection... Learning to savor the vertigo of doing without answers or making shift and making do with fragmentary ones opens up the pleasures of recognizing and playing with pattern, finding coherence within complexity, sharing within multiplicity. (Mary C. Bateson)
>
> When the artists and sculptors I know work, there's a sort of free play idea. You try things; you experiment. It's kind of naive and childish, it's like kids in a playpen. Scientists work that way too – for example genetic scientists that I have been involved with seem to work similarly. It's kind of like throwing things out and then following the ideas, rather than predicting where you're going to go. (Frank O, Gehry)

Introduction

At the heart of industrial development, in the new knowledge economy, is our ability to play with a virtually limitless set of possibilities in order to find ever better ways of doing things (Romer, 1986). What generates economic growth are such notions as the interchange ability in product parts, and organizational activities, as well as the capacity to continuously try out new combinations of resources. Indeed, radical shifts in the organization of work from the factory system to mass production to flexible manufacturing have led to quantum leaps in productivity (Smith, 1922). Today, such modern forms of economic organizations as alliances or networked and federated firms, are considered to be at the forefront in terms of combinations of routines and transactions which can deliver higher efficiency in the new economy (Miles and Snow, 1986). However, one should not ignore that uncertainty, as well as speed and frequency at which recombinations take place, are equally important issues to the particular efficient configuration of resources emerging at a given point in time. On the one hand, the birth rate of new organizational forms which populate the industrial landscape can be measured in decades, if not half centuries. On the other, the current pace of competition and technological development requires a much quicker generation (and elimination) of new arrangements, at least in the high-tech industries. To wit, in a rapidly changing environment none of the well-known organizational arrangements may work to optimize resource utilization. We submit that, at best, one can only settle for a shapeless organization that keeps generating new forms through frequent recombination. Using a real case scenario from a high-tech firm, we put forward a model of a chameleonic organization, the platform, conceived as a laboratory for rapid structuring (Giddens, 1984; Weick; 1993a). The platform turns out to be an unrecognized source of productivity in the high-tech industries, because of its intrinsic potential to efficiently generate new combinations of resources, routines and structures which are able to match the present, turbulent circumstances (Kogut, 1991). From a *structural* point of view the platform is the resilient outcome manufactured from the ingenious reconciliation of existing organizational mechanisms and forms, picked by management according to subjective and situated plans and interpretations (*'bricolage'*; see Lévi-Strauss, 1966; Weick, 1993b). Its most distinctive qualities are its flexibility, movement and transformation obtained from intersecting, penetrating and collating different organizational arrangements, such as the network, the matrix, and even the hierarchy. As a result, it looks fragmented and intertwined; still it may be the only form capable of surviving in a high-tech industry where a monolithic, rigid business identity would not seem as able to cope with the frantic pace of technological change. In contrast to any traditional form, we have here the celebration of all the qualities of the random, the apparently incidental, the seemingly oppositional, as well as the surprising, and like the concept of 'building-as-landscape' in deconstructive architecture (Vidler, 1989), the platform emerges as an exciting mixture of ready-made arrangements and interpretations, and of half-realized, not-yet-made solutions and visions. From a *cognitive* point of view the platform works as a collective, cognitive engine enacted by a pool of flexible human resources for exploring and trying out multiple combinations of old and new organizational arrangements. It is a model which turns upside-down our beliefs about what is structural and permanent in the strategy-structure dyad, as well as what is subjective, informal and ephemeral (Lanzara, 1983; Hedlund and Rolander, 1990; Bahrami, 1992). It does so, simply because its job is of a different nature: to meet frequent, sudden and radical changes, not just in products, markets and technologies, but in the very business identity and industries to which it temporarily belongs. Specifically, its purpose is to support managers when facing frequent surprises, that is to say, events which appear to be incomprehensible or inconceivable (Weick, 1993a).

Our empirical case is Olivetti, a leading European computer vendor which has undergone innumerable organizational changes in the last 30 years. As an example of 'network corporation', Olivetti represents an exciting setting for exploring how a strategy-inaction unfolds, as its 'unique management style' gives rise to policies and strategies which are often called into question or criticized. This Italian multinational is regarded as an 'unpredictable giant,' one which does not belong to the same world as the American and Japanese manufacturers who dominate the computer industry, and who, while understanding each other, still find it to difficult to forecast and make sense of Olivetti's strategic moves.

The unveiling of the platform organization has required a different analytical approach from the one common in industrial organization research. In fact, new forms like the network corporation are currently explained by referring to established concepts in organization theory, business policy, industrial organization and economics of information (Teece, 1992). Though different in perspective, all these disciplinary explanations share the same basic assumptions: there are goals which guide the agents' decisions; there is a complex problem to be solved or task to be executed; a corresponding strategy is deployed to achieve the goals and solve the problem; and a new structure is put in place to implement the solution. Hence, unitary, multidivisional, matrix, or networked organizational structures are seen by scholars and practitioners as the rational responses to support such moves. To be sure, decision makers would admit that day-to-day management is run in a more organic, ad hoc fashion, and that textbooks and journal articles seldom capture the actual intertwining of market events and managerial responses. They (especially in their ex post rationalizations), would also willingly concede to using schemes and models, such as the network, derived from studies of business organization and competitive analysis. The gap between what theoretical, ex post explanations and models can deliver and the actual 'garbage-can' style of managerial choice (March and Olsen, 1976) is considered to be a fact of life by practitioners, and as an unavoidable result of the limitations of any modelling approach by scholars. In order to allow the new concept of the platform organization to emerge and to contrast it with kin concepts, we have taken instead an alternate approach. First, the difficulties which appear when one endeavors to reconcile business practices with the actual choices in strategy formulation and structural design are attributed more to the oversimplification of the current conceptual models than to a supposedly natural divide between theory and practice, knowledge and action. Second, using first hand evidence from the deployment of Olivetti's global technology strategy in the last decade,[1] we conclude that current organizational models tend to focus only on snapshots of a complex, evolutionary process. This, then, may be one of the reasons why observers and competitors who rely on those models remain puzzled. Snapshots can be relevant for actors and scholars to make sense of a complex process, and can provide reference for ex post reconstructions of what happened. On the other hand, they represent 'postcards' which can hardly capture, let alone help interpret and explain, the forces behind the constant evolution, revolution, and de-volution of managerial action. And since such postcards are repeatedly relied upon and used by management when recounting events and rationalizing choices, they easily get embedded into the scholarly interpretations and grounded theories. Actions, or better rationalizations of actions, and theories reinforce each other, and become 'natural' explanatory frames, retrieved when facing events or explaining phenomena, but also reproduce a self-sealing blindness to the new, and to the extant (Argyris, 1990). As a consequence, it is only by reading between the lines that usually annotate the stylized explanations, in their 'wrinkles' and especially in the interstices between practice, current interpretations, and what is left out, or explained away by referring to the obvious background that both business practitioners and researchers are supposed to share, that one can find the true limits of current models and interpretations, and the roots for alternative ones.

The paper unfolds as follows. First, background information about Olivetti is outlined and the formulation and implementation of its global technology strategy in the last decade are analyzed, followed by a description of the ways in which Olivetti has struggled to maintain its identity across sudden and radical changes. Then the paper focuses on some major and minor alliances and acquisitions that the company has established in the 1980s and the surprises they have generated, and discusses the origin, nature and main characteristics of the emerging platform organization that has resulted from the more recent Olivetti's strategic moves and restructurings, and compares the platform with other kin concepts drawn from the literature on new organizational forms. Finally, the paper shows the internal functioning of the platform as an engine for organizational improvisation, *bricolage* and recombination. The conclusions indicate relevant directions for further research.

Snapshots from the Recent Olivetti History (1977–1990)

In 1989 Olivetti ranked ninth among the top world computer manufacturers. It was sixth at the beginning of the decade, eighth in 1982, and it managed to survive during a period of great technological change and industry shake up (MeClellan, 1985). In Europe, it has trailed IBM and jockeyed with Siemens and Bull in the first placements. Though strongly, rooted in Italy, – only less than 40% of its turnover is sold on the home market, making Olivetti the most 'international' of the European computer manufacturers. The number of employees has gone from 70,000 in 1976 to 47,000 in 1984, and up to 57,000 in 1989 following the acquisition of Triumph-Adler. Returns on revenue had been increasing up until mid-80s, but are now steadily declining. By the 1980s, turnover per employee had more than doubled. At the beginning of the 1970s Olivetti was *not* a computer manufacturer: 80% of its sales consisted of mechanical and electrical calculators, typewriters, and office supplies, including furniture. But by 1977, computer equipment had come to already represent 43% of sales. By 1982 it had reached 71%. In 1984 Olivetti launched its first personal computer with the MS DOS standard and became, for a couple of years, the world's second-largest producer of PCs. Thus, towards the end of the 1980s, computer products had come to represent a steady 84% of all sales. Today, Olivetti remains a manufacturer of personal computers and workstations, minicomputers, printers, electronic typewriters and word processors, as well as being a provider of software services and system integration. Since the 1970s the Italian company has crossed at least two technological discontinuities: from mechanics to electronics in its traditional products, typewriters and calculators, and from electronics to microprocessor-based personal computers and workstations. Correspondingly, radical changes have taken place in the work organization, from the mechanical assembly lines to work groups, and to the adoption of highly sophisticated factory automation. In the last decade the number of employees in R&D has steadily increased, from 4.8% of the total work force to 7.4% in 1989. In the 1970s researchers were mainly mechanical engineers, while lately they have become, almost exclusively, software specialists. What has become of Olivetti in the early 1990s? An investment research report submits the following, concise description:

> A huge distribution company constantly in search of new products, through both its own R&D and external means. Once found, it then sells these products through the various distribution channels that it has either developed internally or acquired for profit. In some ways, it can be envisioned as a combination

of Tandy (electronic retailer), NCR (financial and retail computer systems and minicomputers), and Epson (personal computers and peripherals). (Goldman Sachs, 1987)

Devising and implementing a global technology strategy

In a systematic comparison aimed at evaluating the correlation of the R&D intensity of firms in various industries (measured in terms of firms' own funded R&D spending as a percentage of sales revenues) to worldwide corporate sales growth and company gains in world market share, Olivetti stands out in the computer industry for spending relatively less than competitors like Digital or Bull, but having an above average growth (as opposed to Bull) (Franko, 1989). Correspondingly, the task for the Italian multinational in defining its global technology strategy can be identified as follows: what is the combination of moves and technology acquisitions needed to bolster what otherwise may be a weakness in product breadth and technology, in order that its aggressive distribution channels may be constantly replenished with competitive end products and services? A boundary condition, not to be underestimated, for the resolution of such a problem is the management of the dramatic changes required to transform and adjust the internal organization (skills, work force size, work organization, R&D, production processes, management and marketing cultures) each time a new technology is internalized (Emery and Trist, 1970). Despite its not stunning economic performance, Olivetti's number of attempts and successes in managing such a technology strategy is judged as one of the highest in the world, and a key to its longer-term survival (Goldmann Sachs, 1987).

To the outside observer, Olivetti's technology strategy-in-action has presented two faces in the last decade. First, in the articulated mix of moves deployed to give substance to an opportunistic technology acquisition strategy one recognizes the wisdom that Olivetti's management presents to the outside world. Its 'darker' side is the idiosyncratic and unique style of management which continues to baffle competitors and allies alike when they deal with the Italian company. One may find it difficult to follow the logic of the continuous changes in structures, the debilitating see saw of hopes, failures and unexpected successes of many strategic moves, (especially the alliances, see below) and the sudden shifts in conduct that seem more the result of a day-to-day myopic search, than the outcome of the grandiose plans evoked whenever a new global move is announced. In what follows a qualitative account is given of how Olivetti has defined its technology strategy, together with the interpretations as put forward by the company's top decision makers.

The Vice President for Strategy concedes that the technology strategy has developed mostly in an *implicit* way during the period that led from typewriters to PCs. Take, for example the latter technology: the PC. Initially, Olivetti was a minor player, not only in terms of volume, but also R&D. For one thing, its location was geographically marginal to the *loci* where crucial innovations in hardware, software and systems were taking place. Also, the overall thrust remained unclear. Initially, when one is only a minor player in the computer industry, there is the temptation to rapidly become a global competitor, and thus to spread R&D resources over many directions. Yet, this tends to dilute efforts considerably, as many European computer manufacturers were made to realize in the 1970s. The implicit, emerging strategy was to focus instead on only some areas of strength, such as distributed or personal data processing, abandoning the whole mainframe business with a much-debated disinvestment. In these areas a series of interventions were thus carried out to support internal R&D. Strategic choice depended upon circumstances. It could have been the acquisition of a company that had a low market value, but which gave access to a niche in an important country, as for Acorn computers in the UK; or, a joint venture with a technologically more advanced competitor in order to revamp a product line and rescue what was left of an internal design team, as in the case of OCI, the successful joint venture with Canon Italy. Looking back at the technology strategy emerging over the years, the Strategy managers have mentioned with confidence two factors that account for its inner logic:

1. The *product life cycle* (from emerging technologies to mature products):
   - global alliances are established in order to secure growth, by having access to markets, capital, new technologies and joint product development;
   - joint R&D with key suppliers (e.g., Intel, Microsoft) is pursued in order to tap the sources of innovation for products yet to come, the development of which falls largely outside the control of Olivetti. This implies placing bets on who the key suppliers will be at the next round of innovation (see below for the ramifications of this point);
   - pre-competitive research (for example through projects funded by the EEC) is aimed at collecting resources for basic research and new applications;
   - venture capital is selected to identify opportunities and access new technological developments in a focused way;
   - joint ventures are built to revamp old businesses or re-enter markets previously abandoned;
   - and finally, acquisitions are pursued to gain market share in established businesses and mature products.
2. The *product complexity* and the company's relative strength:
   - for surviving alongside technology leaders joint ventures are sought;
   - in order to gain access to specific, sophisticated technologies venture capital is deployed;
   - less complex products may simply require to increase market share through acquisitions.

The global technology strategy is enacted through a number of organizational units within the company. The Strategy Department is mainly responsible for the definition and launch of the technology strategy, and coordinates the activities related to their implementation. Within its boundaries separate units deal with each of the strategic directions identified above, from collaborative research projects to venture capital, and acquisitions. The Strategy Department has its own corporate R&D, which has enlarged and shrunk over the period considered. The various lines along which the technology strategy has been developed over time and the shifting definition of the supporting organizational structures point to the complexity of the process. But do not be deceived: the neat systematization and rationalization that Olivetti's top managers provide during seminars and interviews should not conceal the pragmatic nature of the entire process and its inherent uncertainty, nor should the role that surprises have played during implementation be underestimated.

Identity building across discontinuities

In general, then, top management at Olivetti links, at least ex post, their global technology strategy to the product life cycle, or better, to the various generations of products that have been put on the market in the last 30 years. However, as mentioned above, two conflicting accounts must be reconciled. On the one hand management point to an approach whereby a set of strategic responses is deployed to meet a set of technological changes. On the other, they admit that no implementation plan could match the actual sequence of actions: tactics have it over strategy. We submit that a reflection on the role played by management and business identities at each technological turning point can contribute to the linking of such opposing views. To begin with, one should realize that Olivetti is constantly dealing with successive 'technologies' life cycles' rather than mere product generations, to the extent that the company originally assembled mechanical typewriters, then electrical ones, then electromechanical systems, electronic typewriters, PCs and minis, while today it is assembling generic computer platforms. During each period, when a technology was clearly prevailing over the others, management had amore focused product life cycle approach in setting a technology strategy. However, in order to implement such policies, Olivetti management needed an identity, first as a firm operating in the mechanical industry, then as an office equipment vendor which sold a variety of office systems and products ranging from typewriters to photocopiers, then as a computer manufacturer which sold PCs and minis, and lately as a system integrator operating predominantly in the software industry. The key issue during each 'technological stage' has been to build the identity (culture, mission, market position, design skills, relationships with customers and suppliers, etc.) as a major player in that industry. Once such an identity is acquired, the management of the life cycle of specific products follows suit. During each stage, owning an identity or not matters, as lacking one can severely hamper managerial action, even when good knowledge of the market and the technology is available. To wit, entering into a new industry makes you feel marginal, and in lacking self-confidence one may be excessively coy in trying out new policies and products. This becomes less and less the case when the new identity builds up, although other problems may emerge, such as excessive arrogance, sometimes accompanied by bureaucratization, which works to stifle flexibility and effective response capability to new situations. Of course, this has always been the case for firms in industries which have gradually changed their product range or initiated a diversification strategy. The distinctive aspect, however, for Olivetti and other companies which operate in the same industry and share similar histories, for example NCR, is that the technology—as distinct from the product—life cycle is extremely short and is becoming increasingly shorter. Thus, these companies must migrate from one industry to another, and even create new ones, at a pace which would be very fast even for simply implementing product changes within a stable technological horizon. The most frustrating implication of this identity building process is that a new identity must be trashed when one would like to keep it, i.e., when, after a painful learning process one has become not only a pioneer, but a leader. On several occasions, Olivetti had to give up the idea of being a pioneer (as in the case of mainframes, 30 years ago, or the multimedia workstation a decade ago), but this has not exempted the company from the necessity to implement 'strategic exit' (Burgelman, 1994) given the shifts of technological paradigms and their close succession (less than three years, lately). For example, Olivetti reached a very high level of perfection in mechanical 'calculators' (their performance could compete with the early electronic ones), precisely when it was time to abandon that technology to embark in the more uncertain job of assembling electronic 'systems'. Similarly, when it was still proficient in VDUs and minis, it had to try out the PC, and while the M20 was one of the first models to appear on the market, Olivetti had to discontinue it, because IBM was quickly imposing the MS-DOS standard. At each discontinuity the competencies acquired in a given field became in part useless, given the competence-destroying character of many innovations (Anderson and Tushman, 1990).

In such a perspective, the problem of defining the mission and direction of R&D, and in general terms, the global technology strategy, does not consist in choosing an alternative among various product lines or markets, but more radically, in repeatedly asking the question, 'what business are we in', i.e., what is the identity of the product, the market, the production process, and the boundaries between what should be done internally and what has to be procured externally, knowing that many of the core innovations are in the hands of external suppliers. The subjectivity factor also should not be overlooked in this regard. Though the technology strategy could be seen as the outcome of objective forces, such as market pull and technology push during a given technological stage, the subjective, interpretive element represented by management perception is what shapes the ultimate thrust to action. Even for a given product technology, the strategist has difficulties in finding objective features on which to develop a plan for action. For example, at the end of the 1980s one could consider the PC as a product being pulled by the market. And indeed the PC could be looked at just as a commodity, a box, for which vendors should acquiesce for low margins and, if anything, scramble to find new means to increase market share and production volumes. But, another perspective can be envisaged: one of the PC as an engineering workstation in a nutshell. According to the latter perspective, management should turn their attention to the core of workstation technology, i.e., chips and their architecture, present and future. What will be the new standards? The subjective element seems to suggest that in searching for an identity across a technological or business discontinuity requires determination and commitment, quickness and passion, but also wisdom and detachment. Indeed, in such a fluid industry, extreme confidence, caution or attachment may hinder curiosity and openness, while an attitude tolerant of knowledge and ignorance may improve adaptability (see the notions of 'negative capability' in Unger (1987); and 'wisdom' in Weick (1993a) and Bateson (1994)).

The organizational structures which support the technology strategy must be able to cope simultaneously with the management of discontinuities and incremental innovation. This has put, over time, a premium on the firm's ability to develop multiple, often inconsistent competencies, to deal with the emerging, divergent technological and organizational requirements (Burgelman, 1983). As a result, existing structures, procedures, and schemes which influence action are usually under severe strain, and managers end up feeling they are operating in a very fuzzy organizational environment. For instance, even if structures are in place to guide behavior and there is an effort to revise them radically every year, everyone knows that they are only marginally relevant at the moment of action, and what really matters is the possibility one has of relying on a personal network of colleagues located in the various units of the organization. Thus, while functional departments come and go, and may well represent formal changes in authority and communication, still decision making occurs through a set of arrangements (network, hierarchy or clan, or mixture thereof) which evolves according to a logic difficult to capture, for no written record is available and no formal memo sanctions the actual changes. Only crucial events which form the background memory of the organization members can provide insiders with a record of the evolution of such latent structures. As an example, consider the formal shifts in the organization of the corporate R&D unit Dor, to whom it reports, its management and its direction, with the relatively little impact they seem to have on the company's conduct:

- the changes in the assignments, responsibilities and mission of Dor are so radical, but also so temporary.
- some aspects which were fuzzy, like its true mission and its relationship with the rest of the organization, probably continue to stay fuzzy after each change. One mainly relies on individual personalities to make the unit shift (drift) in a direction reputed to be the most suitable; the rest of the organization knows it, and top management know that the rest of the organization knows; hence, who needs to be officially informed?
- actual decision-making involves very much the previous network and everybody seems to be aware of it; this further confirms that formal modifications are marginal, and that true changes will emerge from surprises along the present, inevitable drifting route, or will continue to be enforced by the old boys' network.

To conclude, the degree of complexity required to operate in the computer industry does not only affect the nature of the primary task to be accomplished, but the very identity of the business. Coping with identity uncertainty requires responses which are at least one order of magnitude higher than dealing with 'simple' task uncertainty. Note that such a distinction may blur during action, when events and circumstances present themselves as a melange difficult to disentangle, and actors cope with them by retrieving established models, but at the same time discarding them pragmatically. Though managers picture themselves as busy in decision making (forecasting, planning and selecting alternative courses of action) according to the strategy models in good currency, they would be better described as engaged in 'sensemaking' (Weick, 1979), i.e., in relentlessly picking up the pieces and left-overs of the 'broken cosmologies' (past plans, marketing choices, goals, and outlooks) and trying to paste them together in order to make a new sense of the emerging technologies, markets and industries they are enacting. The rapid succession of identities puts a strain on the strategy-structure link (Chandler, 1962) and, as a result, formal structures appear continuously revised, fragmented and trumped up. However, since an underlying continuity is maintained (e.g., the top management group is relatively homogeneous and stable), there must be then a hidden context which keeps providing sense to managerial action. In order to unveil such an underlying context, it is interesting to analyze how Olivetti copes with major breakdowns, or surprises, when implementing its technology strategy.

Alliances, acquisitions and surprises

The ability to implement a global technology strategy by setting up alliances of various sorts and exploiting them more for their unexpected outcomes than for their original goals has become, over the years, one of Olivetti's core competencies, a capability which other computer companies, such as Apple, DEC, and even IBM (now in a period of dramatic change after years of undisturbed leadership in their own markets), seem eager to imitate. Partnerships have been sought for two main reasons: access to capital and know-how in order to achieve rapid growth. Growth is needed to survive during the ongoing computer industry shakeout, when a rather fragmented industry structure gives way to an oligopoly with only a few major players left. In this scenario, Olivetti has tried to become a global competitor, in terms of sales volume, geographic scope of operations and product range. Internal growth would be the preferred alternative, but the required speed of transformation is so high compared to the resources available that alliances are often sought instead. The economics of growth and change is characterized by many unexpected, paradoxical manifestations (Knight, 1921), and Schumpeter remains unsurpassed in qualifying it as a process of 'creative destruction' (Schumpeter, 1942).

As a first example, take the main strategic alliance Olivetti was involved with during the past decade, the one with AT&T. Established in 1983, it was a very asymmetric partnership given the size of the companies (AT&T was roughly ten times larger than Olivetti), type of core technology (telecom vs. office equipment), type of culture, history, location and markets served. Originally the agreement included an equity participation of AT&T by about 24% of Olivetti capital, but it had a broader scope for which the equity participation was supposed to indicate a formal commitment. In general, it is possible to classify the main goals of that alliance as follows (Ciborra, 1991):

- those aimed at governing competition, by creating a constellation of anti-IBM firms; to impose a new operating system standard (Unix) in Europe and to ease the access of both companies to each other's markets;
- those related to enriching the partners' competencies, such as mastering the convergence between telecom and computer technologies; transferring complementary managerial skills, for AT&T had public monopoly savvy, while Olivetti was strongly marketing oriented; sharing R&D projects and results; and perhaps, most importantly, the need for the two corporations to be global competitors both geographically and technologically. AT&T wanted to become, after the deregulation, an 'information company', rather than a just telecom operator. Olivetti aimed at overcoming once and for all the narrow boundaries of the European market.

The global agreement represented a framework for collaboration in various sectors including R&D; reciprocal sales of each other's products; joint development of new ones; up to the cross-transfer of personnel. Now the alliance is history, for AT&T got out of Olivetti in 1989. Yet, even before reaching the breakdown point, at which time the two companies gave up the systematic development of a common strategy, the alliance had a hilly evolution, one where only a few of its stated goals were attained. On the other hand, there were also some positive surprises obtained. For example, Olivetti, as a supplier to AT&T, became almost immediately a major vendor of PCs to the American market. It also found itself in the best position to jointly develop Unix-based systems with the Bell Labs. AT&T investment was a success because Olivetti stock value almost quadrupled. The transfer of personnel reached its peak when the head of Olivetti of America, Mr. Cassoni, went to manage the troubled AT&T Information Systems division. To be sure, there were disappointments on both sides; joint R&D never went beyond Unix, for which AT&T maintained an undisputed leadership and the delivery of PCs was later discontinued because AT&T did not seem to be able to sell them in large quantities. In general, the management of the US company became gradually wary of wanting to become an 'information company' and retrenched to its core business, to what it knew best, that is telecommunications and networking. Consider what happened during the daily management of the alliance. Most likely, power games, procedures and practices to curb opportunism were the stuff of which continuous renegotiations of the alliance were made (Williamson, 1985). But these were relevant only for mundane aspects of the partnering process. The alliance constituted a general framework, a declaration of common intents: the content of the alliance was given by detailed agreements, for example on the development of new products or the formulation of common projects. In the absence of such detailed agreements, the alliance could still work very smoothly, i.e., be a satisfactory investment when it involved equity acquisitions or a satisfying subcontracting arrangement that might even deliver lower transaction costs compared to the market. Nonetheless it was a failure, since it did not allow one or both partners to reach their stated goal of rapid growth and diversification. In other words, efficient alliances may be ineffective and meaningless. In retrospect, this may in fact be the major flaw in the Olivetti-AT&T strategic partnership. The collapse of the alliance was not due to fears of being robbed by an opportunistic partner, but rather to the lack of appropriate learning skills in exploiting the alliance as a new resource. Thus, organizational inertia rather than patent preoccupation turned out to be a determining failure factor (Argyris, 1982).

In this respect, compare the successful acquisition of Acorn, a small, innovative UK computer firm, with the problematic relationship with AT&T's Bell Laboratories. In the former case, while preserving the autonomy of Acorn, top researchers of the British firm were transferred to Olivetti's R&D department. Dor (Garney and Roberts, 1992), among them Dr. Hauser, who revolutionized that department. New products based on Rise technology introduced by the British company were jointly developed, and a new direction of research in multimedia workstations was established. In accordance with Olivetti's partnering policies Acorn had been originally acquired to gain market share in the UK and a strong foothold in the education market. After the acquisition both of these objectives lost their importance due to the very troubled financial situation of the company. However, it came as a surprise that Acorn's labs contained a wealth of people, skills and ongoing projects which turned out to be of strategic relevance, putting Olivetti on a new track (at least as far as corporate R&D was concerned). More precisely they envisioned for Olivetti the option to be a leader in workstation technology instead of being just a follower of IBM. Under Dr. Hauser, and for a period of five years thereafter, Dor emphasized an autonomous development activity in multimedia workstations, by 'second guessing' through prototypes and exploratory products the features to be included in future portable office systems. Dor was thus restructured as a network of laboratories, each developing Specific functionalities of an advanced workstation: image, speech recognition, multimedia, artificial intelligence, etc. An e-mail network connected the laboratories situated in Ivrea (Italy), California, UK and Germany, and nearby research, university and industrial innovation centers. To be sure, all this did not happen automatically, but was the result of circumstances joined with the capability of Olivetti's Vice President for Strategy, to 'detect' the weak signals that the small, financially troubled British company was sending out. He was able to interpret them and value the invisible assets existing there, by taking the bold move of having a senior scientist of the newly acquired company head corporate R&D. With a further implication: recall that at the time. Dor reported to and advised the Strategy Department, thus the new ideas brought in by Dr. Hauser reached directly to the locus. where global and sectorial technology and partnering strategies were conceived and implemented.

Olivetti, through its different partnering moves towards AT&T and Acorn obtained two important results, though in serendipitous ways: first, to be part of the 'club' to set the standards in the PC and mini market (e.g., the relationship with AT&T greatly simplified the choice to adopt Unix as a new standard); second, to accelerate internal learning and absorption of new knowledge through a marked deprovincialization of management. Almost for any alliance then the elements of surprise and *bricolage* seem to play a role at least as important as the specific contractual arrangement selected. Sometimes, as in the Acorn case, an acquisition is carried out to appropriate certain standardized assets, which turn out to be volatile, or simply not there; invisible assets are discovered subsequently and appropriated. The specific contractual form, far from being selected intentionally, happened to be there to allow the transfer of skills and know-how. In the AT&T case the global agreement paved the way to a pure supply transaction, i.e., the sales of PCs to AT&T. When the US company first decided to sell PCs, Olivetti was not even thought of as a potential supplier; it was the existence of the recent alliance which suggested AT&T should procure the boxes from Olivetti rather than from a low cost manufacturer in the Far East. Nor did Olivetti plan for such a supply contract. The newly designed, automated factory (located in Scarmagno), able to assemble, in a flexible way, varying volumes of different PCs, had to quickly be modified and transformed into a rigid assembly line producing very large volumes of just one model. Surprises, rather than technology strategy, seem to determine structure. Structures happen to be there, or, if not ready at hand, they are the outcome of the artful recombination of what is at hand under the specific circumstances. Again, what are the qualities of an organizational context which lets such recombinations take place without too much stress? We suggest that such qualities can be found in the structure of Olivetti's new products, the computer platforms. Namely, the design of the product has always had some influence on the design of the organization manufacturing it. For example, in Olivetti when the first electronic and modular typewriters were introduced, the job design also shifted towards semi-autonomous production units, or 'modules'. Since the structure of 'hard' products impacts the analysis and design of the tasks and the production process, the influence of the dominant product design on the organization tends to stay within operations. In the case of information technology, and its 'soft' abstract and systemic artifacts, the influence of the dominant design of a system can encompass the organization as a whole.

The organization as a platform: an emerging comparison

Two major findings have emerged so far. First, in a case like Olivetti ex post rationalizations do not do justice to the richness, contingency and unpredictability of managerial action in defining a technology strategy and its implementation. Secondly, one major source of uncertainty in defining a strategy is given by the rapid succession of technological discontinuities, which require not only the dismantling of assembly lines or product teams, but a deeper transformation of the bundle of cognitive frames, cultural views and structural arrangements linked to the very technology that has to be abandoned. In brief, the shift in technology paradigms, especially when they are, as in this case, competence-destroying (Anderson and Tushman, 1990), requires the exit from the extant 'formative context' (Unger, 1987) which generates the prevailing identity, i.e., design approaches, production organization, and marketing strategies, and the rapid establishment of a new one. Note that such a transformation can never be achieved completely. With each new technological generation, management and the organization do not start from scratch: the company which today manufactures PCs cannot be considered a grassroots start-up in relation to the company that until yesterday used to build typewriters. Since the extant, dominant designs are difficult to dislodge, the prevailing organizational arrangement at a given point in time is a pasted-up combination, a sedimentation of successive formative contexts, whereby the people who sell PCs and minis may be still imprisoned in the typewriter salesman, 'mind-set'. Or, specialists who design standardized computer platforms may be subtly entangled with the attitude prevailing when proprietary operating systems were being developed. Within the boundaries of such a trumped-up combination of frames and organizations, where the old can hardly be distinguished from the new, surprises are bound to appear. The managerial competence in strong demand is the ability to quickly respond to and learn from surprises, combined with the artful courage of exposing oneself to situations which may trigger knowledge creation (Nonaka, 1994), as for example, through the various forms of external linkages that Olivetti management has been busily setting up and dismantling in the last couple of decades. A first consequence is that the paramount criterion in evaluating Olivetti's past and current organizational arrangements put in place to support its global technology strategy is flexibility, rather than efficiency of coordination structures, or alignment with the diversification strategy selected. Take, for instance, the sweeping change in organizational structure which took place at the end of the 1980s, whereby the holding was created, and separate companies were set up to sell office products, systems and networks, software and peripherals, splitting functions like R&D, and most importantly, the up-to-the-moment unified sales organization. The reorganization was an attempt to smash internal management bottlenecks and increase the response to vertical market needs. At the same time, however, a due concern for efficiency would have pointed out that there were overlappings and rivalries between similar departments in the separate companies which formed the holding, given the basic homogeneity of the underlying technology, the chips and the boxes. What, then, are the implications of that and other restructurings that preceded and followed it?

As mentioned above, an interesting clue can be found in the emerging technological discontinuity characterized by the computer platform: we submit that, in the period considered, the organization of Olivetti replicates, in some important respects, the design and the functioning of the platform.[2] Consider how organizational structures are designed and redesigned. Management pick existing models prescribed by organization theory and established management practice, or imitate solutions implemented by competitors. This concerns the broad architecture or configuration of the formal organization, the one modified by fiat and thus always in want of legitimation (hence the adoption of prevailing management thinking). As far as the real organization, as opposed to the formal organization, is concerned management proceed in the same way, that is as a magpie (Brown and Duguid, 1991). But this time the relevant perceptions, imaginations and solutions, are much more subjective, local and ad hoc, i.e., carried out under the influence of the extant formative context. In such a culture bed of practices and visions, the impacts of market forces, new approaches and solutions are often mediated by the characteristics and functions of the technologies embedded in the product. In a computer firm the design of the technological systems becomes easily a focal point where problem solvers look to find the most appropriate solutions. 'Archetypal' technological designs will lurk in the back of their minds when trying to cope with a new challenge, or will appear as a self evident, familiar, and, thus reliable concept, to be employed as a 'leading metaphor' in attacking a new problem that needs a 'creative' solution (Greenwood and Hinings, 1988). The platform even found a formal representation in the organizational chart of the main operating company, OS & N, and was understood by management in a first instance as an arrangement able to offer performances that were analogous to the ones of computer platforms. The single *components* of the organizational platform may represent the well-known organizational arrangements: departments, functions, divisions, etc. Each unit so defined increases clarity of mission and facilitates reporting and control at least at a local level. The *integration* of the different components is flexible and cannot be read by the chart alone. Depending upon the technological mission, functions like R&D, which are repositories of generic competencies, can be recombined towards the goal of the moment (market driven applications, firmware, data communications, etc.). Operations are shaped simultaneously to serve the new markets. Integration deals also with the units and organizations outside the boundaries of Olivetti. Thus, venture capital, joint R&D projects and global alliances are set up and dismantled according to circumstances.

The platform concept influences also the product and technology strategies and it appears to be a formidable trigger for recombinations at the firm and industry level. Thanks to the existence of platform standards, technologies are developed independently from products: 'at the last minute' technologies can be bundled into specific products required by the market, or as a response to competitors' moves. Correspondingly, the relationships between R&D and the marketing function become much tighter. Development tends to be more closely geared to marketing: sales forecasts and marketing evaluations for a new product tend to be swiftly transferred and hardwired into platforms. Platforms and their shortened life cycle tend to elicit industry leaders that prevail only temporarily with one product; for example, Compaq had been the early leader for the 386 platform, while Olivetti arrived among the first with the 486 family. The best boards are exchanged by the computer vendors through OEM agreements and other forms of alliances aimed at cutting development time, time to market and volume. To be sure, such agreements and alliances last for the product life cycle, i.e., one chip generation. At an industry level the net result is a growing externalization of the sourcing of many components. The industry itself is becoming a modular platform, in the sense that a vendor can avail itself of many small and large suppliers for the different standardized components. These are then assembled in a unique product: a standardized platform with a certain number of add-ons and pluses.

A second clue which can be useful to make sense of the 'erratic' structural transformations in Olivetti lies in the recombination processes which change the plastic configuration of the platform in response to environmental changes. Bahrami (1992), studying a sample of high-tech firms in the Silicon Valley, suggests that they must cope frequently with 'kaleidoscopic change', where a small, apparently insignificant variation can dramatically alter the entire action set (the task, the market, the business) of the organization. Growth patterns are volatile; it is hard to capitalize on early success, periodic readjustments will not do, and crises cannot be solved once and for all. In such an environment the firm must sport a variety of flexible responses: ability to react quickly; resilience in front of disturbances, and being capable to face the consequences of chaotic change (Stacey, 1991), i.e., radical surprises. The platform organization can be seen as the 'arrangement' suited to cope with chaotic environments, where sudden events can tilt established patterns of identity, organization, culture, routines and capabilities.

After the classic descriptions of structural configurations aimed at generating sophisticated innovation, such as the adhocracy (Mintzberg, 1983) and the self-renewing organizational 'tents' (Hedberg *et al.*, 1976), three organizational forms have been recently discussed in the literature to capture the dynamics of the flexible firm operating in highly turbulent environments. A due consideration of their features allows us to pinpoint the special traits of the platform. Miles and Snow (1986), and Thorelli (1986) were among the first to identify the *network,* as a flexible cluster of firms or specialized units coordinated by market mechanisms instead of a vertical chain of command. Indeed, Olivetti presents itself as an example of network corporation, and can be regarded as a 'dynamic network' like today's IBM and Apple, relentlessly building an 'undecipherable maze of international agreements and alliances to protect market share, enter new arenas, seek technical innovations, and promote the adoption of technical and/or systems standards' (Miles and Snow, 1992). The platform organization differs from the network because it functions at two distinct levels: the structural one of the routines and transactions, (similar to the network corporation) and the one of the higher order context where the re-architecturing of structures is frequently carried out. At this level, the dynamic recombination of bundles of routines and transactions matters, rather than the properties of a specific, albeit new arrangement, such as the network. Boyton and Victor (1991), in their model of 'dynamic stability' envisage a subtle, yet crucial modification in the definition of what a firm is: a 'treasury of process knowledge'. Management is able to apply organizational knowledge to a variety of end products (Teece, 1983; Prahalad and Hamel, 1990; Kogut and Zander, 1992), and this allows to decouple the process know-how capabilities from the generation of a whole array of product innovations. Since the product life-cycles become shorter and more unpredictable, it makes sense to rely on process capabilities which serve a general purpose, and are flexible, generic and relatively stable. Thus, the resulting model of the dynamically stable organization contains two levels: one of the products (frequently changing) and one of the processes (which change more slowly). Boyton's perspective, however, does not seem to deal explicitly with the issue of organizational arrangements and their change. Finally, Bahrami (1992) comes closest to the platform idea in her study of high-tech firms in the Silicon Valley, organizations described as 'structured and yet chaotic'. These firms have developed 'dualistic organizational systems', made up of a 'bedrock' and temporary arrangements. The bedrock is the formal structure which only periodically undergoes major transformations. What is changing frequently are the overlays of temporary project teams and multifunctional groups. Such dualistic arrangements enable high-tech firms to deal with a crucial issue: how to create a relatively stable setting within which people and resources can be flexibly deployed. However, Olivetti seems to be a case which begs for a different explanation: its formal structures change very frequently and abruptly, while, we submit, the informal networks remain relatively stable. Hence, the platform organization cannot be identified with the formal structure: it is a much more elusive bedrock, harder to recognize and analyze as an organizational arrangement.

The platform as a system of schemes, arrangements and resources

Organizational structures can be compared on the basis of their efficiency in dealing with transaction or coordination costs. The multidivisional form, the matrix and also the hybrid arrangements such as the network can be selected on the basis of their relative ability to coordinate businesses at the lowest cost (Williamson, 1975; Teece, 1992). The efficiency perspective, however, assumes implicitly that the technology of products and processes remains relatively stable, so that there is time to set up a new structure, fine-tune it and evaluate its results; that is, if the technology and the task are known and stable, one can engage in exercises of vertical integration versus market externalization, and then compare the results at the margin (Coase, 1937). In the industries where Olivetti operates, however, the rules of the game are quite different. We enter the world of dynamic technologies: (Ciborra and Lanzara, 1990) it is hard to tell what operating system will prevail in two years time, or what chip architecture will be the industry standard. Firms are uncertain about the technology trajectory they are on, (Dosi, 1984) and consequently about their industry and business identity. Whenever perceptions change, the very business mission and primary task can shift abruptly: is Olivetti in PCs or computer platforms; should it become a low cost manufacturer or a system integrator? In such a turbulent environment, plans to vertically integrate or disintegrate in order to lower transaction costs may miss the point. The issue may be not so much whether to integrate or not but with whom, in what industry: with a telecom company, a chip maker, a large software vendor, a media company, a consumer electronics giant, or a mix thereof? Schemes which prescribe how to set up efficient organizational structures around a complex, primary task lose part of their normative relevance, for one cannot know in advance the complexity of the task, nor its precise nature and contours. Specifically, analyzing and evaluating the platform organization at a fixed point in time is of little use: it may look as a matrix, or a functional hierarchy, and one may wonder how well its particular form fits the market for that period and what its level of efficiency really is. What should be appreciated, instead, is the whole sequence of forms adopted over time by the organization, and the speed and friction in shifting from one to the other. A useful way to look at the platform organization may be as a 'string', that is, the sequence of forms it is able to display, and the temporal links between them. The platform can be studied longitudinally, as a bundle of trajectories punctuated by stations. At each station, one may find a familiar organizational structure (the matrix, the network, etc.) that somehow does the job, usually in an inefficient way, for circumstances keep changing and leave little time to fine-tune. And there are tracks: riding on them means for the organization members to change their formative contexts while passing through instabilities, turmoil, experimentation, and doubts about structures, design criteria, technologies, missions and identities. The platform organization retains all that: the static and dynamic mechanisms, the certainties and the doubts, the visions and their smashing, the ready-made junk routines and the not-yet-made ones.

How do top managers take the organization from one station to another along the trajectories which define its evolving business identity? In other words, how do managers go about the job of recombining structures? The Olivetti case shows rather vividly that in the computer industry strategic management mainly consists in placing bets about what will be its next primary task; all the other choices, such as alliances, vertical integration and so on, follow the provisional outcome of such bets. The platform, being easily reconfigurable, is particularly suited to supporting the practice of betting and what it entails, i.e., high flexibility in exiting when one is losing or moving in rapidly to reap the ephemeral benefits, or adapting to the new circumstances that require a commitment to a new risky move (Ghemawat, 1991). Betting can hardly be planned in advance. Something deeper is involved at each turn, especially if the previous bet has been successful: the identity of the business may have changed as an outcome of a particular move, so that past experience or consequentiality are of little use. The platform is a context which supports such opportunistic, semi-blind strategic betting: its identity and mission are allowed to drift in order to keep them, open to networking with the most appropriate constellation of partners dictated by the need of the moment. Because of its fuzziness and intertwined structure, the platform seems also to defy any attempt to make sense of standard approaches to gain a competitive edge, for example by pursuing the competitive strategies identified by Porter (1980). On the one hand, the platform organization upsets such sort of neat prescriptions, because it looks hybrid, blurred, and often 'stuck in the middle'. On the other, it can be swiftly set up to respond to a competitor's move in a given industry according to the rules of competitive advantage. It is chameleonic: thus, for example, if

Olivetti were facing a threat by NCR, rather than Compaq, it could rearrange its internal resources in order to sport the appropriate, competitive attitude, and stage an attack against the specific rival firm or class of firms. Indeed, one of the striking characteristics of the platform consists in being programmed for perpetual transformation, for generating new organizational arrangements and cognitive frames, and for constantly branching out to other, radically different businesses, identities and industries.

How do managers make their daily decisions in such a complex and elusive organizational context? The unpredictability due to the strategic betting, the mimetic behavior and the sedimentation of arrangements due to the ineradicable inertia of pre-existing routines and structures all conjure to picture the platform as a generic context, full of junk organizational routines that can be harnessed depending upon the needs of the moment. Traditional organizations, even the newer forms, come with a bundle of requirements and expectations that create a reference context for managerial action. In the platform organization management have to enact the context while they act, make choices and envision strategies (Daft and Weick, 1984). In conventional organizations the landscape is given, and management are the foreground figures. In the platform, background landscape and foreground actions are painted both simultaneously and disjointedly, each giving meaning to the other in the process. Managers have to adopt multiple standards in order to move around the redundant parts of the platform. They may have to behave according to a hierarchical context (arrangement and mind-set) in some parts of the organization, or as network operators (again organizationally and cognitively) in a network setting. As improvisers and *'bricoleurs'*, they stay creative in the face of surprises, because they are accustomed to operate in chaotic conditions and pull order somehow out of the resources and routines at hand (Weick, 1993a). In this perspective, the platform works as a met organizational context that creates simultaneous dependencies and belongings (Hedlund, 1986). While in a matrix a manager reports to two bosses; in the platform a manager may operate within two or more organizational forms at the same time. Note that such met organizational context is not 'designed', rather it emerges as the result of the managers' situated rationality and actions, while they busily recombine those very arrangements, and artfully operate them, reproducing the conditions for which the betting and recombination processes can be tried out once more.

In sum, the platform is far from being a specific organizational structure, where one can recognize a new configuration of authority and communication lines. Rather it is a virtual organizing scheme, collectively shared and reproduced in action by a pool of human resources, where structure and potential for strategic action tend to coincide in highly circumstantial ways, depending upon the transitory contingencies of the market, the technology and the competitors' moves. Schematically, the platform can be regarded as a pool of schemes, arrangements and human resources. First, it is a virtual and collective cognitive scheme (Weick and Bougon, 1986; Sewell, 1992) which governs actions of recombination. It is an *'habitus'* (an habitual mind-set) (Bourdieu, 1977) unique to Olivetti top management, composed of organizing principles such as 'betting', 'opportunistic deployment of partnerships', 'pragmatism', 'fast learning from emerging technological architectures', and so on. These principles are rerun in the heads of managers and surface in their acts of improvisation: being shared collectively they maintain coherence in an organization where structures are continuously eroded. The Olivetti '*habitus*' allows managers to cope with unpredictability, even if formulation and implementation of plans are carried out in a traditional fashion: the '*habitus*' gets into action when facing surprises and often leads to the unexpected utilization of existing resources. Secondly, the platform is supported by a composite bedrock of practices, that consists of pasted-up routines, transactions and other organizational arrangements. In the platform one is continuously confronted with the coexistence of a multiplicity of organizational structures. Flexibility is achieved in practice by pasting up structures that have a high potential for action in response to chaotic events. Finally, the platform is based on a community, the pool of human resources, which can be described in the Olivetti case as the old boys' network at top management level. Those managers are improvisers in the sense that they are able to reinterpret *ex nouo* given resources in terms of schemes, which may differ significantly from those that led to the acquisition of those very resources.

Concluding remarks

Our study confirms what the trade press and academic scholars suggest: the global technology strategy has been vital for Olivetti and has produced an array of moves and organizational interventions that have made it a 'network firm'. But our attention has been also attracted by the fact that strategy and the resulting organization emerged implicitly rather than being laid out at the outset. Although management and industry observers tend to give a systematic, ex post reconstruction, where each step of the technology strategy finds precise reasons and justifications, our study suggests that behind the charts shown on the official transparencies, what prevails is a pragmatic muddling through. Even when there were precise goals and plans, e.g., in setting up alliances and acquisitions, these have not met the target: surprises appeared instead. Such surprises and the relevant organizational responses have become the main object of our investigation. We have concluded that evaluating success or failure of strategic moves by the attainment of the goal for which they were originally set up misses the point. What does matter is the process, its stations and tracks; often, the sheer engaging in a move has contributed to push Olivetti along new technology trajectories in the making. Furthermore, the study of the consequences of surprises reveals that the organizational outcome of the technology strategy in practice, as opposed to the one in theory, is a pasted-up organization where elements of the old are intertwined with trials of the new. The overall picture is a fuzzy organization, which differs from the formal charts and their modifications, but is sufficiently responsive to the new. In such a context, learning from surprises turns out to be a valuable core capability as much as being able to analyze technologies and competition. In order to capture such emerging organizational features, we cannot rely on traditional models, or even on newer ones such as the network firm. They all suffer from the fact of being too tidy and preplanned, given the high levels of uncertainty management has to face. We have used the notion of computer platform as a metaphor to capture what goes on in an organization that operates in the highly turbulent computer industry. On the surface, the platform organization looks as a stable pool of 'junk' resources, 'badly organized' according to efficiency criteria, but ready to be deployed when the technology or marketing strategy requires it. At a deeper level it is a collective cognitive scheme which allows managers to try out relentlessly new organizational combinations.

Further (action-) research is needed to ascertain the impact on management of such 'revelations' about the way of operating of the platform, whereby what is considered important when reconstructed and communicated in public is looked at as marginal, and what they know members would take for granted as the shared, muddy operating background experienced everyday is brought to the surface and celebrated as 'foundation'. Indeed, the disturbing confusion which permeates Olivetti's internal organization is made the center of the theoretical notion of platform, while the chart in which the company is portrayed as a network firm, is taken just as a 'nice' ex post account. Another research theme regards the extent to which it is possible to systematize the way of operating of the platform, to find a more detailed model, or even the underlying 'laws' of such a happenstance organization. Can strategic tinkering be governed (Mintzberg, 1991)? Once again, the analogy with architecture may suggest here a positive answer (Nadler *et al.*, 1992). Deconstructivist 'buildings-as-landscapes' obtain movement through the artful display of shifting masses, collapsing solids, juxtaposed and twisted volumes (Johnson and Wigley, 1988). They seem to disregard the rules established by modern architecture, still they stand stubbornly solid and make a unitary stylistic statement over their environment, precisely because behind their deceptive disorder lies a deeply thought answer to some of the canonical problems of architecture. For Olivetti, what would be required is to go back to its roots and find such stylistic unity embedded in its present organization. The concept of platform could contribute to let such unity emerge in front of the observer and the practitioner.

Finally, the platform with its emphasis on fragmentation, fuzziness and displacement, should not be discarded, even by those who enact it, as the inevitable outcome due to high environmental uncertainty and imperfections in the formal organization. Rather, it should be appreciated as a necessary culture bed for experimentation and recombination, that provides the decision maker with an almost infinite variety of elements (schemes, visions, mechanisms and arrangements) to compose new temporary solutions faster and more efficiently. Top management in high-tech firms like Olivetti ought to admit that their job in coping with technological discontinuities is not to make decisions at the center of a 'network firm,' rather they should acknowledge that what they do is tinker at the periphery of that pasted-up organizational platform they constantly enact. Being smart *bricoleurs* makes business sense, especially when business itself appears to make very little sense.

Acknowledgements

Many thanks to Olivetti's top management, and especially to Elserino Piol for their time and intelligence without which this study would have been impossible. Thanks to Chris Argyris, Mario Citelli and Tora Bikson for their comments on the previous drafts. Responsibility for the contents stays solely with the author.

Notes

This chapter originally appeared in (1996) *Organization Science* 7(2): 103–118.

1. The field research has been conducted by the author in 1989–1991 and has consisted of 25 in-depth interviews. The research has followed a clustered hierarchical design. This approach is particularly appropriate for examining and interpreting ongoing processes in real-world contexts, especially when the processes to be studied are not sharply separable from their organizational contexts. The highest level of the design has been the Vice-President for Strategy, Elserino Piol. A dozen managers of the Strategy Department and nine divisional managers in the areas of R&D and Integrated Circuit Design have been targeted for one or more interviews. Each interview lasted more than two hours on average. The Vice President for Strategy has been interviewed at various points of the field study, including the final feedback sessions on earlier drafts of this paper.
2. The present trend in CPU technology is given by the possibility of hardwiring more and more functions on a single chip, and devolving part of the extra computing power to managing applications such as large data bases, sophisticated user interfaces, etc. Thanks to downsizing, a PC manufacturer can, in principle, compete with vendors of mainframes and minis, to the point that chips are not simply components, but platforms. Platforms based on a chip can host and reconfigure a whole stream of technologies: they can be used as the core component of a mini, a powerful PC, a server or a workstation, i.e., they are a technology independent from the classes of products of which they are a part. Each use depends upon adding new functions, specializing others and adapting their performance to selected criteria such as robustness or speed.

References

Anderson, P. and Tushman, M.L. (1990). Technological Discontinuities and Dominant Designs; A Cyclical Model of Technological Change, *Administratiue Science Quarterly* **35**: 604–633.

Argyris, C. (1982). *Reasoning, Leaming, and Action,* San Francisco, CA: Jossey-Bass.

Argyris, C. (1990). *Overcoming Organizational Defenses: Facilitating Organizational Leaming,* Needham, MA: Allyn & Bacon.

Bahrami, H. (1992). The Emerging Flexible Organization: Perspectives from Silicon Valley, *California Management Review* **34**(4): 33–52.

Bateson, M.C. (1994). *Peripheral Visions-Leaming along the Way,* New York: Harper Collins.

Bourdieu, P. (1977). *Outline of a Theory of Practice,* Cambridge, UK: Cambridge University Press.

Boyton, A.C. and Victor, B. (1991). Beyond Flexibility: Building and Managing the Dynamically Stable Organization, *California Management Review* **34**(1): 53–66.

Brown, J.S. and Duguid, P. (1991). Organizational Learning and Communities-of-Practice, *Organization Science,* **2**(1): 40–57.

Burgelman, R.A. (1983). A Process Model of Internal Corporate Venturing in the Diversified Major Firm, *Administrative Science Quarterly* **28**: 223–244.

Burgelman, R.A. (1994). Fading Memories: A Process Theory of Strategic Business Exit in Dynamic Environments, *Administrative Science Quarterly* **39**(1): 24–56.
Chandler, A.D. Jr. (1962). *Strategy and Structure,* Cambridge, MA: MIT Press.
Ciborra, C.U. (1991). Alliances as Learning Experiments, in L. Mytelka (ed.), *Oligopolies and Markets,* London: Pinter.
Ciborra, C.U. and Lanzara, G.F. (1990). Designing Dynamic Artifacts: Computer Systems as Formative Contexts, in P. Gagliardi (ed.), *Organizational Culture and Symbolic Artifacts,* Berlin, Germany: De Gruyter.
Coase, R. (1937). The Nature of the Firm, *Economica,* November, 387–405.
Daft, R.L. and Weick, K.E. (1984). Toward a Model of Organizations as Interpretation Systems, *Academy of Management Review* **9**(2): 284–295.
Dosi, G. (1984). *Technical Change and Industrial Transformation,* New York: St. Martin's.
Emery, F.E. and Trist, E.L. (1970). Socio-technical Systems, in F.E. Emery (ed.), *Systems Thinking,* Harmondsworth, UK: Penguin.
Franko, L.G. (1989). Global Corporate Competition: Who's Winning, Who's Losing, and the R&D Factor as One Reason Why, *Strategic Management Journal* **10**: 449–474.
Garney, E. and J. Roberts (1992). Clashes of Technology and Culture: Enterprise Acquisition and the Integration of New Ventures, in J. Merceau (ed.), *Reworking the World,* Berlin, Germany: De Gruyter.
Ghemawat, P. (1991). *Commitment-The Dynamics of Strategy,* New York: The Free Press.
Giddens, A. (1984). *The Constitution of Society: Outline of a Theory of Structuration,* Berkeley, CA: University of California Press.
Goldmann Sachs (1987). *Investors' Report on Olivetti,* New York: Goldman Sachs.
Greenwood, R. and Hinings, C.R. (1988). Organizational Design Types, Tracks and the Dynamics of Strategic Change, *Organization Studies* **9**(3): 293–316.
Hedberg, B.L.T., Nystrom, P.C. and Starbuck, W.H. (1976). Camping on Seesaws: Prescriptions for a Self-Designing Organization, *Administrative Science Quarterly* **2**: 39–52.
Hedlund, G. (1986). The Hypermodern MNC: A Heterarchy? *Human Resource Management* **25**(1): 9–25.
Hedlund, G. and Rolander, D. (1990). Action in Hierarchies: New Approaches to Managing the MNC, in C.A. Bartlett, Y.L. Doz and G. Hedlund (eds), *Managing the Global Firm,* London, UK: Routledge.
Johnson, P. and Wigley, M. (1988). *Deconstructivist Architecture,* Boston, MA: Little, Brown and Company.
Knight, F.H. (1921). *Risk, Uncertainty, and Profit,* Boston, MA: Houghton Mifflin.
Kogut, B. (1991). Joint Ventures and the Option to Expand and Acquire, *Management Science* **37**: 19–33.
Kogut, B. and Zander, U. (1992). Knowledge of the Firm, Combinative Capabilities, and the Replication of Technology, *Organization Science* **3**(3): 383–397.
Lanzara, G.F. (1983). Ephemeral Organizations in Extreme Environments:
Emergence, Strategy, Extinction, *Journal of Management Studies* **20**(1): 73–95.
Lévi-Strauss, C. (1966). *The Savage Mind,* Chicago, IL: University of Chicago Press.
March, J.G. and Olsen, J. (1976). *Ambiguity and Choice in Organizations,*
Bergen, Norway: Universitetsforlaget.
MeClellan, S.T. (1985). *The Coming Computer Industry Shakeout: Winners, Losers and Survivors,* New York: John Wiley & Sons.
Miles, R.E. and Snow, C.C. (1986). Network Organizations: New Concepts for New Forms, *Califomia Management Review,* Spring.
Miles, R. E. and Snow, C.C. (1992). Causes of Failure in Network Organizations, *Califomia Management Review* **34**(4): 53–72.
Mintzberg, H. (1983). *Structure in Fives: Designing Effective Organizations,* Englewood Cliffs, NJ: Prentice Hall.
Mintzberg, H. (1991). The Effective Organization: Forces and Forms, *Sloan Management Review* **32**(2): 54–67.

Nadler, D.A., Gerstein, M.S. and Shaw, R.B. (1992). *Organizational Architecture:Designs for Changing Organizations,* San Francisco, CA: Jossey-Bass.

Nonaka, I. (1994). A Dynamic Theory of Organizational Knowledge Creation, *Organization Science* **5**(1): 14–37.

Porter, M.E. (1980). *Competitive Strategy: Techniques for Analyzing Industries and Competitors,* New York: The Free Press.

Prahalad, C.K. and Hamel, G. (1990). The Core Competence of the Corporation, *Harvard Business Review* **68**(3): 79–91.

Quinn, J.S. (1978). Strategic Change: Logical Incrementalism, *Sloan Management Review* **20**(1), Fall: 7–21.

Romer, P. (1986) Increasing Returns and Long-run Growth, *Journal of Political Economy* **94**: 1002–1037.

Schumpeter, J. (1942) *Capitalism, Socialism and Democracy,* New York: Harper & Brothers.

Sewell, W.H. Jr. (1992) A Theory of Structure: Duality, Agency, and Transformation, *American Journal of Sociology* **98**(1): 1–29.

Smith, A. (1922). *The Wealth of Nations,* London, UK: J. M. Dent.

Stacey, R.D. (1991). *The Chaos Frontier: Creative Strategic Control for Business,* London, UK: Butterworth.

Teece, D.J. (1992). Competition, Cooperation, and Innovation: Organizational Arrangements for Regimes of Rapid *Technological Progress, Joumal of Economic Behaviorand Organization* **18**(1): 1–25.

Thorelli, H.B. (1986). Networks: Between Markets and Hierarchies, *Strategic Management Journal* **7**: 37–51.

Unger, R.M. (1987). *False Necessity,* Cambridge, UK: Cambridge University Press.

Vidler, A. (1989). Frank Gehry's Architectural Movement, *Casabella,* March, 4–21.

Weick, K.E. (1993a). The Collapse of Sensemaking in Organizations: The Mann Gulch Disaster, *Administrative Science Quarterly* **38**(4): 628–652.

Weick, K.E. (1993b). Organization Re-design as Improvisation, in G. Huber and W. Glick (eds), *Organizational Change and Redesign,* New York: Oxford University Press.

Weick, K.E. (1986). Organizations as Cognitive Maps: Charting Ways of Success and Failure, in H.P. Sims and D. Gioia (eds), *The Thinking Organization,* San Francisco, CA: Jossey Bass.

Williamson, O.E. (1975). *Markets and Hierarchies: Analysis and Antitrust Implications,* New York: The Free Press.

Williamson, O.E. (1985). *The Economic Institutions of Capitalism,* New York: The Free Press.

7

Formative Contexts and Information Technology: Understanding the Dynamics of Innovation in Organizations*

Claudio U. Ciborra and Giovan Francesco Lanzara

Abstract

Most accounts of computer-based innovation in organizational settings assume a naïve picture of organizational change, overlooking events, features, and behaviours that, though unexpected and puzzling, may be the sources of inventions, new knowledge, new organizational routines and arrangements. The ambivalent, untidy, and often unpredictable character of IT-based innovation and change is hardly captured, even by more recent theoretical approaches that have nevertheless provided a deeper understanding of the complex interaction between technology and organizations. Based on field observations of the failures and successes during a major systems development effort in a large European computer manufacturer, we tell a different story: We submit that failures at innovation, surprises, and a whole range of related phenomena can be accounted for by introducing the notion of formative context, that is, the set of institutional arrangements and cognitive imageries that inform the actors' limited learning, irrespective of their strategies, interests, espoused theories, and methods. Still, we suggest, plenty of opportunities for innovation lie in the open, pasted-up nature of formative contexts and a new vision of design based on 'context-making' interventions can bring them to light.

Introduction

In the last three decades a whole variety of computer-based information systems have invaded our workplaces in organizations and institutions, in some case radically changing their familiar landscape. These multiple waves of innovation in information technology have yielded remarkable transformations in organizations and aroused new research interest in the dynamics and the complexities of institutional change. Countless studies have looked at the impacts of automated systems on issues such as task allocation and execution, information flows, decision-making, upgrading/downgrading of skills and employment. In such studies the new skills have been regarded either as technical tools supporting a more efficient execution of work routines, or as organizational technologies automating control operations and coordination processes and bringing about a new organization of work.

Successes, failures, conflicts and power games around the design and use of new technologies are also reported in the literature (Boland and Hirschheim, 1987; Lyytinen and Hirschheim, 1987), together with instructions regarding which actions and remedies should be taken to obtain specific organizational outcomes; for example, the application of structured design methods (De Marco, 1979; Jackson, 1983, Yourdon, 1982); or users' participation in systems development (Briefs *et al.*, 1983; Mumford and Henshall, 1979); or, finally, the political skills and strategies required for the effective management of change (Keen, 1981; Markus, 1983).

Despite their different perspectives, these stories of technological and organizational innovation share a sort of deterministic explanation, which assumes a linear, straightforward consequentiality among the actors' choices, actions, and outcomes of the institutional processes, and attributes to systems a 'closed', purely instrumental character: systems are 'designed' ex ante, embed preestablished and non-ambiguous purposes, and provoke 'impacts' accordingly. In other words, it is assumed that designers and implementers have a clear view and stance with respect to what a system should or should not do, and that the system itself will behave to the rule. According to such stories it seems that despite their intrinsic complexity, systems never exhibit unexpected features or behaviours, and hardly influence the premises, the goals, and frames adopted (often unawarely) by the actors engaged in the innovation process.

We regard this genre of storytelling as too coarse. By assuming a simplistic picture of the dynamics of organizational change, these stories miss the deeper, multiple realities of systems' design and computer-based innovation in organizational settings. Further, they overlook the increasing number of novel and puzzling behaviours exhibited by systems when they are in use, and therefore fail to account for events and features that, because they fall outside the scope of the original plans, sometimes happen to be the source of inventions, new knowledge, new organizational routines and arrangements. In many an instance some of the novelties – be they positive or negative – are not even perceived by organizational members and analysts. As a consequence, the understanding of the complexities of systems' design and change may be inadequate and the implementation process may suffer severe limitations.

In the attempt to better understand the implications of information technology and to overcome the deterministic flavour of many previous stories and explanations, a number of different researchers in recent years have carried out more refined empirical studies and developed more theoretically articulate frameworks to account for the complexities of technological and organizational innovation. To name only a few, Miller and Friesen (1980) first, then Greenwood and

Hinings (1988) introduce the notion of 'archetype' and 'change track' to provide a descriptive account of the dynamics of organizational transitions; Barley (1986), Orlikowsky and Robey (1991), Poole and DeSanctis (1990) use Anthony Giddens' theory of structuration (Giddens, 1959, 1984) to capture the 'structuring' role of technology and reconceptualize its complex, 'dual' character (Orlikowsky, 1992); Zuboff on her part, in a broader, neo-Weberian mode, delves deeply into the subtle interactions between knowledge, work, and power brought about by the advent of the 'smart machine' (Zuboff, 1988). These approaches all strive towards the search for new concepts and frameworks better suited to allow for a more satisfactory treatment of the complex interactions between organizations and information technology and have, indeed, produced valuable results. But, perhaps with the notable exception of Zuboff, they overlook some important points that we regard as crucial. First of all, they tend to be too general, and they concepts developed retain a much too abstract character. For instance, as Orlikowsky's recent work shows, what Giddens' structurational approach can offer to our field of interest is a sort of metatheory to systematize a wide range of phenomena in a coherent manner, with an altogether heavy reproductive and ordering bias. The same underlying interest in pattern reproduction and continuity is revealed by Greenwood and Hinings' design archetypes and tracks. As we shall see in the following, concepts like 'structuring' or 'archetypes and tracks' do not seem to us apt enough to capture and convey the fragmented, ambivalent, untidy, and often unpredictable character of change and innovation in organizational settings. More specifically, they seem to be at a loss in accounting for actions and behaviours that may not be necessarily consistent with the reproduction of existing patterns, or even with the structuring of whatever new pattern, but simply 'branch out' of the currently practices repertoire of routines. Second, in these approaches the issue of design practice is much talked about but never tackled seriously: Design is thought about as a method rather than as a practice or intervention. How then do such abstract frameworks come to bear when we come to the question of how a specific structure is actually produced (not simply described) or how a new system of organization is designed in practice? To what extent do they generate and convey usable, practical knowledge, that can be of help to systems designers when they are involved with designing within their unique organizational settings? We feel that the field of information systems needs more practical, action oriented, close-to-experience concepts to deal with the ambiguities, and with the opportunities, of real change and design situations.

Based on evidence from a case of software production in a large computer manufacturing company, this paper explores a different path. We propose an interpretive vocabulary for helping systems' designers and organizational actors better deal with the ambiguous and interactive settings they find themselves in, and we sketch a tentative framework for systems' development based on local, practical experiments, that we call 'designing-in-action'. Our argument is built on distinct, but interconnected parts. First of all, we submit that computer-based information systems are not just technical tools or organizational technologies, but also, as the case will show, embodiments or 'vehicles' of emerging modes of work organization, of new cognitive imageries and institutional arrangements. Not only do they bring about new routines for work or incrementally adapt old ones, but they also enact whole new patterns of behaviour and modes of thought.

Second, and more specifically, we argue that computers – or, for that matter, any other innovative artefact- do interact with both the structural and institutional arrangements associated to a given division of labour and the assumptions, frames, and mental images that people hold while routinely enacting and practicing that specific division of labour. The repertoire of current skills and practical knowledge of people at work and the cognitive ground itself upon which they are built are also deeply affected. Systems are relatively open and plastic, no matter what their initial purposes or designs may be. But once designed and introduced into the organization, they tend to evolve along paths that are often unexpected or irreversible, subtly changing the ways people design and carry out their work practices, experiment with alternative arrangements and routines, or implement alternative visions and designs.

Third, most of these change processes, because of their cognitive and social embeddedness, are largely unnoticed in organizational and design settings. But being unaware of them may cause failure of any effort aimed at steering or redirecting the course of innovation. Indeed, a major obstacle to effective experimentation and adoption, and more generally to flexibility and innovation, is limited learning, that is, the limited human capacity to reflect upon and reframe the institutional and cognitive grounds that support the habitual 'ways of doing things', individual and organizational. Consequently, the capability of implementing new patterns of action is also limited (Argyris *et al.*, 1985; Argyris and Schön, 1974, 1978). Yet, the effective adoption of new systems can only occur through processes of learning where organizations become competent in smoothly turning anomalies and novelties into innovative patterns of behaviour. Failure to do so will predictably yield situations where people and organizations – to recall a verse of T.S. Elliot – 'had the experience but missed the meaning'.

In order to interpret the puzzling evidence shown by the case and to investigate the nested mix of practical, cognitive, and institutional elements influencing routines' execution and change, we must take a theoretical step that we regard as crucial: We must draw a distinction between the work routines as they are carried out daily in organizations and the 'formative context' within which those routines are 'formed' and receive their meaning and scope in an actual situation of action. Originally the distinction comes from phenomenology and ethnomethodology (Garfinkel, 1967; Schutz, 1960) and was later used in anthropology (Bateson, 1972) and social and political theory (Unger, 1987). As Blackler (1992) has recently pointes out, the awareness of such distinction is paramount in reframing many of the technical and management issues emerging around the design and adoption of new technology in organizations. In this paper we explore the idea and the salient characteristics of formative contexts in detail, stressing their subtle and pervasive influence in the design and operation of new routines and systems. The open, pasted-up nature of systems and routines, and the embedded quality of practical knowledge informing human skills are shows to be positive assets to be purposefully exploited rather than handicaps to be removed. The main implications for a new vision of design based on 'context-making' intervention and online practical experiments are finally sketched. The outcome of such 'designing-in-action' should be systems and routines that help organizational actors perform a perpetual activity of reflection and self-questioning.

Our argument is based on data gathered during a 6-month field study of a major effort at technology innovation involving about 400 persons. We have conducted on-site participant observation of the work process, and semi-structured interviews with the major actors – designers, personnel officers, and programmers – at different stages of the system's development project. Also, in the course of our analysis we have given our partners some feedback about the phenomena that we observed, as we made sense of them. Such interaction allowed us to collect further data for testing and refining our understanding and helped the actors to become more aware of their own behaviours and discover features about their work that they hadn't previously perceived or thought about.

Puzzling evidence: the case of the software factory

The R&D department of a large European computer manufacturer was assigned by top management the task of developing the operating system of a new minicomputer line. The challenge of coordinating and controlling hundreds of programmers working simultaneously at the same piece of software caused concern for the already precarious internal organization of the department. Market analyses signalled that the industry needed a competitive solution within two years time, maximum: Beyond that horizon the technology and market trends for operating systems were impossible to forecast. Hence, the imperative of a quick time to market for the new system in the making.

In an initial move to face the complex task under such time pressure, the chief software designers chose to shape the overall department's structure according to the functional organization of the new system. A team of programmers was set up for each function the system was designed to perform. A hierarchical structure was set up to connect the various teams. The overall design choice was based on an analogy, widely supported in the data processing profession, between the work organization's and the software structure: the current belief for successful software development prescribed designers to use the same organizing rules for both the artefact to be built and the people who should perform the job (Daly, 1979). The organizing rules suggested were:

- Keep each software segment small so that it can be easily understood; correspondingly each software team should be small so that it can be effectively controlled;
- Each software segment should be loosely coupled to other segments; each software team should be assigned a unit of work, which allows for minimal coupling among software teams;

- The scope of effect of a software segment should be a subset of scope of control; software teams should report to a manager so that the decisions made within the manager group have minimal effect on the work of other managerial groups;
- As software is decomposed into a hierarchy of segments, higher-level segments perform decision-making and lower-level segments do the actual work; correspondingly, the managerial hierarchy performs decision-making and the lower organization levels perform the actual work;
- Pathological connections, i.e., those communication links not respecting the hierarchical software structure should be avoided; in the same spirit, sideways connections among programmers in the original structure should also be avoided.

As a way of controlling costs in systems building activities, the organization mandated that the system development process be divided into phases and that specific documentation be produced at the end of each phase so that work progress could be monitored and corrections made when necessary. In parallel, the personnel department started out to define tasks, roles, rewards, and career paths for each unit in the functional organization. The hierarchy looked as follows: a chief programmer, responsible for developing one or more subprograms, controlled the interfaces between modules within a subprogram. Interfaces between subprograms within a class were controlled by the first line manager, who was responsible for the development of a software class, and so on.

Unfortunately, cooperation between the software designers and the personnel department proved to be lukewarm. The former thought that there were more urgent deadlines to be met in actually constructing the system; the latter tended to ignore the analysis of the technical details of each task, given their ignorance of software production. When the actual project started, it was apparent that communication from one activity to the succeeding ones was carried out in various, unexpected forms: for example, by having one person carry out a whole sequence of activities, thus centralizing information; by oral communication among members of a subproject; or by notes often discarded after their initial use. As a result, the project proceeded without any effective management review and control, and the everyday work organization of the programmers remained *terra incognita* for both groups.

After some time, the project was plagued by problems that computer manufacturers often face in this type of endeavour: delays, sky-rocketing costs, poor documentation, back-logs. It was evident that the project could not be managed by manual methods, fragmented documentation and loose planning. Continuing time pressures urged the department heads to move swiftly to a more modern project organization, by establishing stricter controls over the development process, and improving software productivity significantly. Specifically, more advanced tools were needed to provide support for the system designers in the collection, control and processing of design specifications and programs, such as:

- Improved organization hierarchy through chief programmers and a thoroughly documented and enforced design methodology;
- Standard techniques to decompose software in functional entities;

- Strict software documentation, usually computer generated, that is, a direct output of the design process. Such documentation is structured and accompanied by a hierarchical chart;
- Design walkthroughs according to pre-established review formats employed at each level of software decomposition;
- Strong management planning and control systems to help plan and control software quality, time and cost.

More in general, all major software interfaces and data structures had to be better defined before the detailed design. They would form a 'contract' to be monitored and controlled throughout design and testing. Standards would represent the way through which interfaces and personnel communicate with each other.

When a major restructuring was decided by top management, two innovations were introduced to increase productivity and improve the organization of work. The first one consisted of a structured methodology for rationalizing software development, that is, a set of guidelines, very much inspired by the principles above, to organize work, divide it into stages, define precise goals and activities for each stage, such as analysis, programming, documentation etc. (DeMarco, 1979). At the espoused level the idea of a structured methodology appealed to everybody in the R&D department, because it supported key values of the software culture: rationality, order, transparency and consistency. In fact, the software engineering methodology was supposed to change the activities of systems analysts and programmers from an art to an engineering task. As for any engineering activity, the aim of the methodology was to provide a framework and tools to allow programmers to complete their job in a prespecified time period and at a minimal cost. Three concepts shaped the methodology: modularity, top-down development, and a structured approach. Modularity isolated the logical parts of the system that belonged together. Each module performed some logical subset of the total system processing. The communication between modules was carefully controlled, and as a result the internal programs needed not be known by other modules. The basic structure of the modules was designed to facilitate a better organization. Since the workload could be parcelled out among programmers according to skill levels, the limited scope of each module made local development an easier task to execute and monitor. Last but not least, the standards developed for interfacing modules formed a basis for the programmer's communication. Each module could be more easily optimized. Explicit schedules for testing could be generated. Changes could be isolated to closed modules: they could be made without widespread changes in the overall system.

This was the theory (Konsynski, 1984). Surprisingly enough, the practicalities in the use of the structured methodology led to a very different outcome: to everybody's astonishment the usual messy organization crept rather quickly in to the rational grid of the methodology, devoiding it of any real and lasting impact. At the espoused level, structure was in, and sloppy development practices were out; at the actual behaviour level, structure was out, and a sort of 'garbage can' (March & Olsen, 1976) organization was in.

On the other hand, the second innovation – the so-called 'software factory' – turned out to be an undisputed success. This concept included a set of development tools that allowed software manufacturers and programmers to perform the innovative aspects of software development and automate most of the structured tasks. Typical functions performed by the software factory are:

- Programs accept rough software documentation and check all data variables, insert a definition of each data element; format documentation according to predefined standards; generate data base maps and flow charts;
- A requirement language processor and a language processor allow for cross correlation between system specification and the design documentation, and check for completeness;
- A software library allows for effective storage and subsequent retrieval of functional software modules, facilitating extensive sharing and reuse of models both within a given development as well for exchange among different developments;
- High-level programming languages are dedicated to automatic code generation.

The software factory selected for the department consisted of a computer network connecting hundreds of workstations, on which the set of software tools ran to support the programmer's job. The network allowed resource-to-resource communication both by monitoring dependencies between software modules and by distributing the builds over the network; many modules were compiled on multiple computers simultaneously, or on one centralized mainframe, rather than one at a time on a single batch machine, as it occurred previously. The factory provided a capability for system-to-user communication via automatic triggers that notified people about changes to specific files. And it supported person-to person communication through its task manager. Thus, for example, there were commands for revision control and for creating file dependencies (Cardwell & Miner, 1991).

The software factory linked each programmer to his/her fellow worker though electronic mail facilities, forming a new programming environment for interactive and simultaneous software development. In the new environment, individuals gained the power to make decisions that would otherwise require discussion, transactions, or hierarchical approval: The software developers discovered that the tools would automatically notify appropriate team members of ongoing changes, and previous version of the software could be retrieved if necessary. The software factory represented the running memory of the project resulting from individual actions and team interactions. Indeed, it became the basic infrastructure for the daily work of the programmer: Everybody took the 'factory' for granted as *the* environment for 'programming-in-the-large'.

However, the success did not help the diffusion of structured methodology. The lesson stemming from its failure was hardly learned: With costly investments, new attempts at developing and enforcing 'more structured' methodologies were again carried out, with no better results. Various explanations were aired for the cyclic failures and the apparent impossibility to put in order the work flow. Some programmers suggested that a messy organization was in the interest of the chief designers: It gave them ample room for maneuvering and politicking. Others claimed that a more formal structure and further automation were necessary. A group of dissatisfied programmers, backed by the union, went so far as to try out a 'democratic' work group. But the majority of programmers were wary of such a grass-root experiment, because they considered it inapplicable to complex programming tasks. Its advocates, too, conceded that the alternative organization would require extra effort and commitment that just were not there.

At a closer look, however, the actual work organization showed some striking features, indicating that programmers operated through the software factory in a way that sharply differed from the various images and theories that they and their managers espoused. Though not officially acknowledged, group work was widely practiced 'below the surface'. Namely, much of the coordination that supported it took place via the electronic mail and software tools. The messaging system provided an informal channel for direct communication between programmers; the tools allowed for the integration of different pieces of code and would keep automatic updating of the parameters of the program, when other interlinked programs were changed. The software factory was then not just a production tool but also an 'organizational technology' able to 'informate' the whole Department (Zuboff, 1988). The network could support enlarged work groups comprising several programmers at a time, crossing both the physical barriers defined by the departments geographical layout and, more importantly, the organizational boundaries between the units of the hierarchy. As a result, the real tasks, roles, and communication patterns were governed neither by the formal structure defined by personnel, nor by the vague functional scheme set up originally by system designers. They were, instead, the product of informal cooperation and bargaining taking place through the computer network.

Note how the software factory and its tools changed the nature of communication and teamwork. In the previous arrangement, horizontal communication between peer groups was considered pathological. It was then hoped that through the structured methodology would enforce a structure of communication. Thanks to the network, instead, a new underlying factor was allowed to emerge as an effective support for better communication: trust. Team members learned to trust each other instead of making decisions on their own or reporting through the organizational hierarchy. Each developer was responsible for fully testing his/her own software modules prior to putting them in the pool of modules that was used by other developers. The trust in each other, coupled with confidence in the tools' ability to reconstruct an earlier development state, increased productivity by maximizing autonomy.

At a closer inspection a number of puzzling questions emerge from the case. Why did carefully planned changes, such as the structured methodology, fail, while other changes of equal scope and applied according to the same logic, turn out to be unquestioned successes? How come there was no learning from mistakes when failures occurred? Why did the various groups involved in the project – personnel, top-management, designers, and programmers – keep oscillating between complaining about the *status quo* and taking initiatives with very little impact? And finally, why did everybody fail to perceive that the programmers were working in a radically different way thanks to the software factory?

Interpreting the case: the idea of a formative context

Approaches in good currency: task complexity, power games, cultural factors

When we tried to clear out what to us was a puzzle, we first turned to the main available perspectives in the literature to account for technical change in organizations, namely: the complexity/uncertainty of the technology and the task (Galbraith, 1977; Herbst, 1974); the power relationships between various interest groups (Crozier and Friedberg, 1977; Keen, 1981; Marcus, 1983); or the analysis of organizational culture (Schein, 1984, 1992; Smircich, 1983; Van Maanen and Barley, 1984).

To be sure, in the case described, the complexity of programming-in-the-large coupled with the actors' bounded rationality may explain why the structured methodology failed. While software engineering manuals suggest that proper planning, management and control, structure, formal rules and regulations, and task discipline are necessary in order to achieve a more reliable and well-understood product, empirical skills, backed by organization theory (Galbraith,1977), consistently show that the development of complex software programs is an 'organic' task, where 50% of the typical programmer's time is spent interacting informally with other team members, and that such a task resembles a R&D activity more than manufacturing (Brooks, 1982; Dijkstra, 1976; Hauptman, 1986). Note, on the other hand, how the software factory was better suited for the new and complex task of the R&D department. It both improved individual productivity and allowed for flexible coordination and bargaining between the work places linked to the network.

If actors, when trying out the structured methodology, may have ignored the limitations of the managerial philosophy dominating the software engineering field, it still remains to be explained why they were not ready to learn from the failures and ignored the work organization that was emerging in the software factory. Unfortunately, even the approach based on political analysis is of little help here. *All* the actors, regardless of their position in the hierarchy, their particular interests, and their influence on the process, seem to be blind to mistakes and novelties. For example, those in favour of a more structured methodology were to be found not only among the systems designers but also in the programmers' group. And the opposition to the union-supported reorganization did not come from management only. Instead, all the actors equally ignore the emergent work organization, which, by the way, would have provided ample opportunity for creating a power basis to influence the technology and the work flow. In sum, each group new how to master its own routines, but did not grasp what went on in the department and was not able to intervene in an effective way, no matter what its goals were.

Why did the actors show, then, such limited capability to learn from the failure and successes of the two innovations? Being dissatisfied with the previous approaches, we tried with cultural analysis. Indeed, the actors' blindness could originate from the dominant software and organizational culture pervading the R&D department. Deeply ingrained, shared images of hierarchical control, specialization of work, decomposition and modularity of task constitute a self contained, coherent universe from which there is no escape for the actors. That is partly the case. But then, how come at one stage they begin working in a new way? Where do the new routines come from? If the culture factor can help us, at a general level, to account for the actors' unawareness of their own behaviour, it fails to account for the 'deviant' emergent practices in the software production work. When the programmers begin to use the software tools, what kind of practical knowledge do they bring to the situation? And in which ways is such knowledge embedded in the context of action, that is, embodied in the tools and in the specific structure of the task, or draped in the organizational structure and in the process of collectively executing the task? Furthermore, how can we explore the implications and the consequences for learning and action of the actors' unawareness of their current practices? Because of their stability and continuity bias cultural analysts have often disregarded issues of technological discontinuity, design and innovation.

The influence of the formative context

If we want to dig more deeply into the case and bring its richness to the surface, we need to bring the culturalist interpretive schema to bear more explicitly on the specific action and design situation. A more operational, action oriented concept must be introduced: The actors, when skilfully executing the routines, when implementing innovations and imagining alternatives to improve their effectiveness, are under the influence of a pervasive and deep-seated texture of relations, or *formative context*, which accounts for their skill, the inertia of their learning, and the unawareness of their actual practices.

The formative context is the set of the pre-existing institutional arrangements, cognitive frames and imageries that actors bring and routinely enact in a situation of action (Unger, 1987). A formative context comprises both an organizational and a cognitive dimension and has far-reaching, subtle differences: It constitutes a background condition for action, enforcing constraints, giving direction and meaning, and setting the range of opportunities for undertaking action. Though a formative context provides the ground for routine execution and influences the creation of new routines, actors are usually not aware of the formative contexts that inform their practical and argumentative routines. They tend to take them for granted, except in the case of major breakdowns (Bateson, 1972; Garfinkel, 1967; Schutz, 1960).

The outcome of a formative context in a work setting is a texture of routines, roles, and tasks that come to possess an 'aura of naturalness' for those who daily execute the routines in that context. The type of context that influences the members of the R&D department can be characterized as *hierarchical*. The hierarchy, the functional decomposition as a strategy for problem-solving, the drive toward structured formalization, to conflict between technical and bureaucratic roles, the informal organization of work seen as opaque and dysfunctional, etc., are some of the institutional arrangements and preconceptions that can be associated to it. The hierarchical formative context is retrieved and enacted by the actors in situations through specific motives and decisions (Pentland, 1992), when they need to make sense of their everyday routines and invent changes to achieve higher effectiveness.

Thus, when we interviewed the programmers and asked them to provide a description of their jobs, they would describe them according to the hierarchical system of roles and tasks, but they would not mention the role of the software factory, first because it is taken for granted, like the telephone, and second because it is not a part of the current, accepted descriptions of tasks and roles in the organization. The software tools and the work routines by which they were actually doing their job did not surface explicitly in their verbal accounts, but stood – so to speak – in the background of their focus of attention and awareness. For instance, the programmers currently used the electronic mail facilities – it came 'natural' to them – but never mentioned that such facilities supported direct all-to-all communication and coordination of work. They 'talked' to each other all day long via the messaging system but apparently did not realize that by such 'moves' (Pentland, 1992) they were enacting a new 'organized' way of building up the software code and programs, which implied working and thinking in a network. Furthermore, when we asked them why they kept rehearsing the application of the structured methodology in the face of its evident failures, they answered that the failures were due to sloppy applications and to capricious human behaviour, that the methodology was basically sound and was the 'obvious' thing to do for such a complex programming task.

When later on in our analysis we made them notice that they were actually achieving group coordination by accomplishing the programming job in ways that strongly differed from what they espoused, initially they seemed puzzled and claimed that electronic mail was only a technical tool, but later on, taking a second thought, they slowly began to realize that in their practical dealings and relations they were in fact following two different logics at the same time: One was draped in (and in a way given by) the software factory and allowed for online, interactive and simultaneous, network-based, informal coordination and mutual adjustment; the other was formally stated in the official organizational design provided by the system designers, and was based on formal procedures, hierarchical control, authority, and formal reporting to the higher level managers.

The hierarchical formative context blocks the learning of the department's members; it makes them blind to the mismatch between structured methodologies and the uncertainties of the development process: To recognize the mismatch and reflect upon it would mean threatening large regions of the context itself. Also, the conflicts generates to support the present organization or to change it in a radical way (like the democratic work groups) hinder the creation of a set of concepts and a language to describe those changes that have occurred but do not lead to higher formalization and standardization. Attention is focused, instead, upon the existing hierarchical arrangement, whether the purpose is to negate or to strengthen it.

In fact, the case shows that the interaction between daily work routines and the underlying formative contexts to which they are linked is a complex one, especially in periods of transformation, when new events bring about sweeping changes. To wit, the introduction of the software factory, though implemented within the hierarchical framework, leads to unexpected outcomes, such as the establishment of the extension of new horizontal links between workplaces, the emergence of routines and behaviours, like working and bargaining in a network, that may point to a formative context of a different kind. Such context, that can be described as networking, is difficult to access because contexts show a pasted-up nature, and a makeshift one, where old and new routines are tested, discarded, retrieved, collated, and combined along a main stream of sense.

Finally, note how the case, and the notion of formative context we have introduced to interpret it, not only show an instance of limited learning during technological and organizational change, but also open up a new field of inquiry and design. Namely, when developing a system like a software factory, the object of design and construction – be it deliberate or unintended – does not only consist of new organizational routines, programs, procedures, databases and flows but, more importantly, of a new formative context. This can shape both the organization of work and the set of social scripts that govern the invention of alternative forms of work, the future ways of problem-solving and conflict resolution, the revision of the existing institutional arrangements and the plans for their further transformation.

Kin concepts: affinities and differences

As we have used it here and elsewhere, (Ciborra and Lanzara, 1989, 1990), the notion of a formative context shares some similarities with a number of kin concepts that recently have come in good currency I the field of organizational studies, such as frames of reference (Shrivastava and Schneider, 1985), organizational culture (Gagliardi, 1986; Schein, 1984, 1992; Smircich, 1983; Van Maanen and Barley, 1984), structuration (Giddens, 1979, 1984; Orlikowsky, 1992), or theory-in-use (Argyris, Putnam and Smith, 1985; Argyris and Schön, 1974, 1978) (see Figure 7.1).

Such similarities might lead one to question the need for introducing a new concept. What does the formative context do that the other concepts don't?

To begin with, a formative context designates what binds, in a loosely connected texture, an individual or a collective (group, organization) to an established world of objects and relations, and to the associated cognitive imageries, presuppositions and meanings of which that world is the embodied vehicle. It comprises what actors take for granted in their daily practical routines and transactions, what somehow they perceive as having an 'institutional' valency for them. The context is 'formative' in that it shapes the ways people perceive,

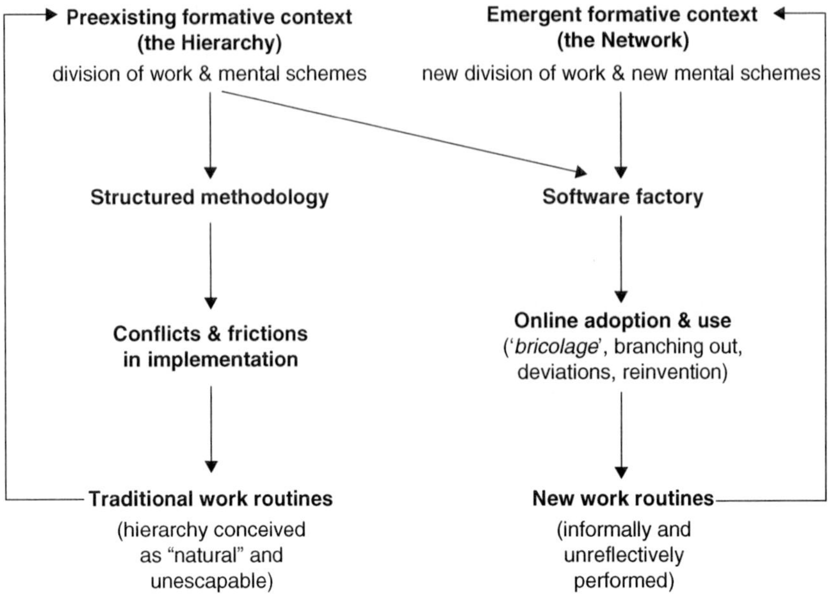

Figure 7.1 The process of innovation: The influence of the preexisting and the emergent formative contexts.

understand, make sense, perform, and get organized in a situation bounded in space and time. It is 'formative' because it may help people see and do things in new ways, or, on the contrary, make them stick stubbornly to old ways. Following Bateson (1972), *context* is used here in its interactional or transactional meaning, rather than psychological. Thus it is directly related to the manner in which individual or collective experience is organized, and to choices and actions that can variously punctuate and modify the flow of experience.

When enacted in a situation of action, formative contexts are expressions of a social cognition that transcends the individual. Such cognition may well be embodied in material or symbolic artifacts, organizational structures and procedures, institutional settings, and, most crucially, in the relationships or 'couplings' binding actors and their work tools in a sort of microecology of stable uses and shared meanings. Thus, by introducing the notion of formative context in organizational analysis, we want to capture both the institutionally embedded quality of social cognition and the cognitive dimension of institutional and organizational arrangements. Also Greenwood and Hinings (1988) with their notion of design archetype point to the need for concepts that capture the *dual* dimension of organizations – cognitive and institutional-and at the same time allow for a more synthetic treatment of the phenomena of organizational change, momentum, and inertia. In this perspective, on the one hand institutions and organizations embody and 'act out' established assumptions and cognitions, and pose different cognitive demands to their members, depending on how roles, ranks, and tasks are defined and assigned; on the other, shared cognitive and learning processes, and the outcomes of them, feed and *crystallize* into established artifacts and repertoires or cognitions that work as 'cognitive institutions' in their own right, and can be modified or updated only through complex social and institutional mechanisms. As Mary Douglas (1986) has nicely pointed out, institutions – social and political-are established systems of premises or programs for action that help people think and act, or prevent them from doing so when they want to do it differently. To borrow Seymour Papert's felicitous expression, they are-like the telephone or the computer- tools people use to think and act with (Papert, 1980).

Even this short account might shed some light on the differences between the idea of a formative context and purely cognitive concepts like frame, script, or schema as they have been developed in the cognitive sciences (Abelson, 1976; Minsky, 1985, 1987; Shank and Abelson, 1977) or in the psychology of choice (Tversky and Kahnemann, 1981). Being based on the pervasive idea of representation as an explicit symbol system, when applied to the analysis of organizational phenomena (Shrivastava and Schneider, 1985; Sims and Gioia, 1986), they lead to an excessive mentalization of organizations reality. Using purely cognitive constructs, like frames or schemata, misses the fact that many important human skills and organizational abilities need not be associated with a capacity for external symbolic expression. In other words, it may happen that individuals and organizations know how to *do* things that they cannot yet *say* or explicitly *represent*. Furthermore, these notions apply more easily to individuals rather than to collectives. Being conceived as structures or schemata that sit in the individual's mind, they are too individualistic. When transposed to the analysis of organizational phenomena, they lead to theorize, by analogy, a sort of organizational mind where all the representations are stored, waiting to be 'acted out' in some behavior or performance. What gets lost is the social dimension of organizational cognition, that is, the fact that all organizational cognition is directly expressed by a situated collective performance and produced within a social interaction (Pentland, 1992).

Secondly, and most importantly, a formative context is to be understood in the perspective of action science (Argyris *et al.*, 1985; Argyris and Schön, 1978; Schön, 1983). The idea that a formative context is an action-oriented concept is not easy to grasp. When actors undertake action, they enact a context in a situation bounded in space and time, and respond to it. In order to have a formative context there should be an action going on. For example, cultural features, organizational arrangements, design archetypes, and even material artifacts can become 'items' of a formative context, when people use them as unquestioned grounds or 'vehicles' for executing or designing routines in a situation of action.

It is precisely the need to focus on action that makes it difficult to use Greenwood and Hinings's concept of a design archetype for our purposes, notwithstanding the similarities. Archetypes assume a basic coherence between various organizational elements and are used mainly for classificatory purposes, but fail to see that in practice, as Burns has remarked, 'working organizations seem to be makeshift assemblies of relationships and activities which operate in accordance with several quite different sets of principles and assumptions' (Burns, 1981). Also, they overlook the possibility that in a situation of action actors may be unaware of the archetypes guiding their routines and behaviours, and that such unawareness may influence *both* their choices and designs *and* the meanings they give to them. Finally, the concept of a design archetype may be useful to the analyst to gain knowledge *about* types of change or inertia, but is of little help to the agent if the question is *how* to produce a specific change or design in the situation in which he or she is engaged.

Similarly, though the notion of formative context is naturally inscribed in the culture oriented approach to organizational analysis, the concept of culture has been used in the literature mainly in a descriptive fashion and has dealt with the domain of action only in a restricted way. Thus, for example, organizational culturalists such as Schein (1984), Van Maanen (1984), or Smircich (1983), who provide very perceptive and valuable insights on a variety of organizational phenomena, do not have an explicit agenda for design and intervention. And even those who have applied cultural analysis to the issue of change in institutional settings (Gagliardi, 1986; Pfeffer, 1981) seem to focus their attention on the conscious mental level, working on explicit representations and symbols, disregarding the taken-for granted routines, institutional arrangements, and artifacts that populate our organizations and deeply affect our behaviours, imageries, and perceptions. But we claim that there might often be an important gap between observable behaviours and routines *and* background culture. The culture of a person or organization may become an item of the formative context if it is somehow relevant to the design or completion of an action, but it does not necessarily coincide with the context. That happens because people tend to design routines in response to a situationally-determined context that has mediating and 'filtering' (formative) properties with respect to their culture, and of which they may not be aware. Consequently, it may happen that people, who hold the same 'cultural' assumptions at a general level, design remarkably different routines and behaviours pointing to different contexts.

One of the key issues of this paper, namely the complex, recursive relation between action and its institutional, or structural, background is being currently explored by authors that use Giddens' structuration theory (Giddens, 1979, 1984) as a general framework for reconceptualizing the role and impact of information technology in organizations (Orlikowsky, 1991, 1992; Poole and De Sanctis, 1990). Though a full appraisal of the differences and similarities to our approach is beyond the scope of this paper, we shall briefly provide some reasons why we would resist interpreting the data of our case in a structurational perspective. Stemming from a theoretical interest in the more general problem of social reproduction (Giddens, 1976), the notion of structuration has an inherited bias for stability and reproductiveness that makes it awkward to deal with change (Sewell, 1992). Interestingly enough, structuration, as it has been applied to the IT field, has proved effective in elucidating the control mechanisms built in the technology or the self-reinforcing processes of preexisting institutional patterns and frameworks in organizational settings, highlighting the continuities and the regularities in those processes (Orlikowsky, 1991). But in our field study, on the contrary, we were exposed all the time to empirical evidence of fractures, inconsistencies, deviations from current routines, emergent properties in the process of change, which called for interpretation: Few things seemed to fall in place. Rather than a rule-based structural 'syntax' of social change and transformation we needed a more pragmatic conceptual vocabulary that would help us better capture the actors' perspectives and situated meanings when they are involved in action, account for their limited learning, and at the same time render the messy, makeshift, pasted-up character of the activities going on in a process of design and change. When performing their work routines or inventing new ones, actors do not directly respond to structures, rather they tacitly enact a context, which is often embedded and implicit and has *formative* rather than *structuring* properties. Indeed, modalities of structuration may come to bear in a situation of action only within (and by means of) an enacted context, *as it* is *perceived by the actors.* Thus, while structurational approaches bend toward the search for general patterns across a wide range of situations, behind the formative context idea is a curiosity for the uniqueness and the *gusto* of specific design and action settings.

The distinction (and the connection) between organizational routines and their background formative context is of paramount importance when we come to the question of how to design and implement innovation, for, when designing a new system, the object of design and construction-be it deliberate or unintended-does not only consist of new routines, programs, and procedures but, more importantly, of a new formative context. Hence, strategies for change and design must be able to unfreeze and restructure cognitions and meanings that are hidden in the practical relations of people to their formative contexts. This is not easy to do, because smooth functioning of organizational routines tends to disconnect individuals and organizations from their underlying contexts. In such conditions, effective change becomes problematic. Argyris and Schön (1978) rightly point to this problem in their analysis of limited learning cycles, based on the distinction between an espoused theory and a theory-in-use. To be sure, what Argyris and Schön call theories-in-use share with formative contexts the same tacit, embedded quality that makes them hard to access and change. But, unlike a theory-in-use, a formative context needs not have a causal structure. Rather, it has *a fabric*, textured with associative relations linking a wide variety of materials. While theories-in-use inform individual or organizational capacity to produce behavior in specific circumstances and tend to stay constant across situations, formative contexts express the engrained, sedimented cognitions, and the enduring, 'institutional' artifacts that those theories-in-use have yielded and stabilized in organizational history.

Formative contexts, systems, and organizational routines

The implications of the formative context idea for understanding the dynamics of innovation in organizations must now be further spelled out. More specifically, the following issues emerging from the case need to be explored: (a) Why do systems and routines designed according to a given logic get implemented and used according to a different logic? (b) What makes formative contexts change or, in any event, drift in spite of their high resilience and pervasiveness? (c) What are the interactions between contexts and actors, both at the cognitive and the organizational level?

The pasted-up nature of information systems

If we now go back to the case, we may take it as an instance of what everyone can experience in the everyday life of an organization: Systems and routines are subject to 'shift and drift' phenomena. The ways they are implemented and used never fully correspond to the original plans and visions, and design processes more often than not take paths unthought of at the start, almost beyond the actors' will.

Systems, and the processes that lead to their construction, possess an open nature and are subject to continuous reinvention, that is, to an innovative adoption process carried out by the users themselves (Rice and Rogers, 1980). In part, they are characterized by formalized components, such as hardware, software, rules, functions, etc., but these do not completely dispose of how systems and processes behave in everyday life. Surrounding these stylized components, usually laid down as a result of ex *ante* design, there are routines and interventions carried out by users who may take unplanned courses of action or by designers who happen to be temporarily with the project, introduce quirky or irreversible design choices, and then leave. All these routines and interventions are continuously developed, tried out, retained or discarded, retrieved and combined, on a local, often tacit basis, outside or at the margins of the master plans and designs, in an endless process of *bricolage*. Yet, though they constitute a 'noncanonical' form of practice (Brown and Duguid, 1991), they are not without implications for implementation. There is no way to avoid their influence on how a system or process will actually be and behave in its real-life operation. They are the outcome of an on-line design activity that we call *designing-in-action*.

But our perspective would be limited if we consider only the formal and informal adjustment routines that punctuate the development of any system (Nelson and Winter, 1982). The routines point to, and are an expression of, a formative context that comes to govern the choices and actions of users and designers (note how the latter distinction tends to blur: Both users and designers fully share the responsibility for developing routines and affecting formative contexts). The context itself, however, has not and cannot have a coherent and orderly structure: It results from a pasted-up combination of everyday practices and tinkering, a sedimentation of local and global arrangements. Thus formative contexts 'shift and drift.' For example, the formative context underlying the routines of a given information system as it is concretely used may not coincide with the one that has governed the design and the development of the same system. It may reflect instead the actual, idiosyncratic division of work that emerges from the actors' daily interactions with the system. Thus, the software factory had impacts that were not planned within the context that formed the background of its implementation. In this loosely connected set of practices, routines, and frameworks, single components are always up for grabs, while the set shows strong resilience as a whole.

In sum, formative contexts posses a double nature. On the one hand, they appear to be highly stable and inescapable, given their wishy-washy, sticky pervasiveness; on the other hand they can be regarded as the culture bed, at the routine level, for experiments in organizational restructuring and innovation, within certain economic and technical constraints, themselves subject to local revision and manipulation. A regimen of permanent, in eliminable fluctuations characterizes such culture bed (Ciborra *et al.*, 1984).

Each fluctuation, as the case of the software factory shows, can 'escalate', be amplified and become the new way of running and conceiving things, thus contributing to shape the emerging formative context. Whether local fluctuations in practices and routines can escape the preexisting formative context, be intentionally tried out and developed by actors in everyday situations, depends heavily upon the degree of cognitive openness and vulnerability the actors, the systems and the formative contexts allow for, or, in the words of the poet Keats, on the degree of *Negative Capability* they are equipped with, that is the capability 'of being in uncertainties, Mysteries, doubts, without any irritable reaching after fact and reason'.

Practical knowledge and the problem of routines' change

Negative Capability is indeed a quality that the actors in the case seem to lack. As soon as mistakes, failures, or novelties destabilize their deeply-engrained way of doing things, the actors, instead of using them to question the status quo and design new courses of action, stick to their old way, showing distinctive limited learning skills (Agryris, 1977).

In general, a preexisting formative context is responsible for molding practical knowledge of people at work, perfecting the learning skills and biasing the imageries of those who engage in design and change. Individual skills and organizational routines supporting everyday practices are grounded on a knowledge-base that is taken for granted when engaging in action. Established repertoires of experiences and frames that have proved successful in similar occasions enable the actors to smoothly and unreflectively perform their routines (Polanyi, 1966). The formative context embeds such a knowledge-base, which represents the hidden, background component of skilled performance, straightforward organizational routines, and quiet functioning of institutional arrangements.

Due to the embedded quality of practical knowledge that informs human skills, one tends to pay attention to the locus of performance, while *at the same time* becoming unaware of the formative contexts. Consequently, people exhibit poor capability at surfacing, questioning, eventually smashing them when they need to do so. A source of limited learning is to be found precisely in how knowledge for action is split in the two levels of ready-at-hand routines and underlying formative contexts: If the focus of attention is on the former and the performance is successful, the latter tend to fade in the shadows of unawareness, becoming prewritten and unquestioned social scripts. Failures and novelties threatening their stability will seldom trigger a learning process leading to their restructuring: formative contexts gain thus a semblance of 'natural necessity' (Bateson, 1972; Garfinkel, 1967).

Knowledge and experience sealed in formative contexts are expressions of what may be called the rationality of the obvious: they are, in a way, ready-at-hand cognitive resources that need not be questioned or tested every time one uses them. But the incapability of questioning the obviousness of contexts generates cognitive inertia in organizations, precisely when a high capability for change and innovation is required, for example when applying a new technology. At the extreme, as in the software factory case, people start out practicing new routines without being fully aware that they are dealing with a new formative context. So, actors are not able to see the new routines and do not talk about them while actually performing them, because the underlying formative context falls out of their cognitive reach.

This also means that whenever a knowledge-based system, or even a bread-and-butter computer application such as a payroll procedure are designed and implemented in an organization, the basis for competence and the relevant formative context are affected in at least three ways. First, the boundary is shifted between what is tacitly held as background knowledge and what we are aware of as foreground 'situational' knowledge (*where* in a specific work situation the focus of attention is explicitly directed to). Second, the basis for the invention, testing, and adoption of new forms of practical knowledge surrounding the use of the system in the work setting is altered. New practices, informal rules and ways of circumventing routines are tried out and set in place within the constraints defined by the new infrastructure and its intrinsic requirements. Third, any invention of alternative practices, any radical departure from existing routines is deeply conditioned by the new mix of background and situational knowledge, the new set of formal and specialized tools required by the system and the local practices, and informal know-how developed by using the new system.

Reframing information systems: Cognitive and institutional implications

Our argument will now be pursued further by taking as an instance the field of information systems, where the question of being able to restructure and invent organizational routines is of crucial importance. According to a view in good currency, information systems consist of routines, procedures, and technologies to process data electronically. Designing an information system means designing and implementing functional requirements and specifications leading to formal and rigorous encodings, software routines, databases, and so on (DeMarco, 1979; Hice *et al.*, 1978; Jackson, 1983). Recently this view has been challenged and more attention has been paid to the work, control, and decision processes served by the information system: The relevant object of system development is the organization and the control of work, not data flows or information as such. Finally, another perspective is based on the notion of transaction costs: An information system consists of the flows of data designed to efficiently support the network of economic transactions taking place within the organization (Ciborra, 1993; Williamson, 1981).

All the three approaches-as others do-rely on the implicit assumption that information systems can be realistically and rigorously described and designed in terms of data flows, work routines, or economic transactions. In this perspective, knowledge necessary for the design and the implementation of the new system can be acquired by interviewing users about their current routines and activities within a given user/analyst interaction. Such interaction may indeed involve conflicting interests and visions *vis-a-vis* the technology or the organization, but is supposed to be *transparent* with respect to the meaning given to the notions of data flows, databases, decisions, tasks, functions, etc. In other words, the three approaches limit their inquiries and methods to the explicitly visible patterns of activities, though segmented and grouped in different ways. They construct pictures of information systems based-each in its own way-on a distinctive kind of obviousness.

Taking a different perspective, we submit that the components of an information system-data flows, work procedures or transactions – retain a more complex quality than what is currently assumed in these naively realistic pictures. These components are *second-order constructs* both from a cognitive and an institutional point of view. They are visible embodiments of ways of organizing reality, cognitively and institutionally, which are deeply entrenched in the formative contexts we bring to projects and organizational situations (Boland, 1979; Suchmann, 1987; Weick, 1985). What is considered the 'natural necessity' of a data flow, a work routine, or a pattern of transactions is *contingent* upon a formative context that may change as institutional arrangements and cognitive images evolve, shift, and break down. When that happens, what is taken to be data, routine, task, or organizational function may lose its habitual meaning, and is seen and 'acted out' in a different way.

We can now formulate a thesis that, as we shall try to show in the last section of the paper, is full of consequences for the design and the use of new technology. That the software factory is an innovation containing, as it is concretely used, the seeds of a new formative context is not, in itself, an exceptional event. Any information system and, more generally, any artifact or tool affecting the division of work and the practical knowledge of people at work, shows the features of a formative context.

Indeed formative contexts mold information systems. They do it cognitively: The use of information systems embodies forms of practical knowledge concerning the gathering, processing, and distribution of information. By introducing new modes and procedures through which individuals and organizations deal with knowledge, an information system may cause a shift and a restructuring of the cognitive frames and assumptions underlying human performances and governing human actions. In other words, the hardware and the software may convey a varied cognitive imagery through which people grasp their world, undertake action, and communicate in a specific situation. They do it institutionally:

An information system can be regarded as supporting a set of contractual and institutional arrangements between individuals and organizations. By bringing about specific ways of organizing social relations and performing economic transactions, an information system embeds a set of rules, norms, and constraints that partially come to govern the processing, the communication and the use of information. *Designing a system means, to a large extent, changing and restructuring the institutional bonds and background conditions upon which, even at the microlevel, people establish and enact their practical dealings and relations.*

Information systems, then, should always be treated and designed at two distinct levels: the one of the formed routines and the one of the formative contexts. It is unlikely that a routine, even a payroll application, can be designed without at the same time affecting its formative context, and it is difficult to restructure organizational practices if the underlying context is not restructured, too. System design cannot escape the issue of how to inquire and design formative contexts.

Systems design as context-making

Are we equipped theoretically and practically to conceive and design systems as formative contexts? If real-life systems are, to a large extent, the outcome of 'pasting-up' and bricolage activities, what criteria should govern their construction? How can we tap relevant knowledge embedded in formative contexts and connect it to effective system design and implementation? These questions lead us to propose a style of design, based on practical on-line experiments, exploiting rather than denying the qualities of systems and practical knowledge described above (Moran & Anderson, 1990).

The challenge: toward a new agenda for design

Current systems design practices, being mainly oriented to designing databases and procedures in a cost-effective way or according to some principle of economic or political equity, tend to overlook the institutional and cognitive frameworks within which routines are formed, and given legitimacy and meaning. To wit, no matter how formally rigorous or participation-oriented they are, these practices seem unable to question and affect the quality of the actors' relations to the institutional and cognitive frameworks that they establish and inhabit in organizations. On the contrary, by not distinguishing clearly between routines and formative contexts, they tend to obscure the knowledge necessary to relate routines' change or persistence to the restructuring of formative contexts, to track the complex feedback loops binding contexts and routines, and to analyze the quality and the fabric of the contexts.

While current design methods capture and emphasize the functional or problem-solving role of a routine, they fall short of understanding how the same routine may reproduce or break powerful imageries and institutional bonds at a deeper level. Conventional methods are based on the assumption that people will 'automatically' start out adopting novel patterns of behavior and new ways of looking at things just because a new machinery has been cast into the organization; or else they claim not to disrupt the present organization, when in fact they do it, again leaving the actors incapable of effectively handling technical change and unaware of the emergence of a new formative context, as in the case of the software factory. Thus system designers keep reproducing the conditions for the recurrent discrepancy between theory and actual system performance.

But can the design of formative contexts be within the actors' institutional and cognitive reach? To begin with, consider those highly successful systems, that have established new standards in business: in general, they do not seem to be the outcome of a carefully planned design and project management. To the contrary, they reveal once again their quasi-accidental quality, the uniqueness of their discovery, their pasted-up, experimental nature. For example, strategic information systems (Wiseman, 1983, such as the renowned one developed in the late seventies by McKesson Chemical and American Hospital Supply (Guild, 1988), seem to derive their quality from the inventive exploitation of the potential of computer systems already in place for other 'more serious,' but hardly imaginative purposes such as accounting.

What seems to matter here, more than a formalized methodology that freezes action and thought, is the *serendipity* of the process, the actors' willingness to explore routines, activities, and events that 'branch out' of a main design, system, practice, or sense, and their capability to take the chances offered by the pasted-up nature of systems and practices, instead of trying to harness them to further standardization (Hedberg and Jonsson, 1978; Weick, 1985).

If we are to face the challenge that the complexity of real-life systems in organizations is calling for, current design practices need to be redirected. We argue that these should amount to more than property determination and requirements specification, to more than exercises in routine problem-solving or interest-accommodation, for they should deal with the structures and frameworks within which such exercises take place, i.e. with shaping and restructuring formative contexts. What is badly needed is competence in context-making rather than new techniques of problem-solving, game-playing or participation. Most importantly, actors need to learn practices that help them question and restructure the formative contexts that influence their cognitions and actions.

The intervention: designing on-line practical experiments

How can people deal with the design of formative contexts? The answer is to be searched for in the very nature of formative contexts. Recall the following:

- Formative contexts are seldom replaceable all at once; rather they change in a piecemeal fashion. The actor's imagery tends not to follow the machinery right away, at least not so rapidly and smoothly or in the direction expected;
- Formative contexts and the processes through which they are formed possess a trumped-up quality: Single components are continuously replaced or combined with new ones in a process of tinkering and practical experimentation that need not be methodical or systematic;

- Consequently, context change and context-making are not governed by law-like constraints or stable developmental tendencies; on the contrary, they proceed by 'branching out' and fluctuation. Full control and centralized standardization of the process are usually impossible;
- Formative contexts are surfaced in situations, actions, behaviors. It depends upon our awareness and learning skills to be able to reflect and intervene upon them.

Thus, one can change formative contexts only by intervening in situations. Intervention, as we propose it, is a strategy of action to come to grabs with the pasted-up nature of contexts, both cognitively and institutionally. Practical intervention in a specific organizational setting challenges the institutional arrangements and the cognitive imageries on which established routines are based. It aims at creating conditions that help people question and gain insight into formative contexts, *while* actually designing or executing routines in situations. The logic of intervention is in many respects different from the logic of analysis. Its epistemology draws-on a theory of action (Argyris *et al.*, 1985; Argyris and Schön, 1978). It is concerned with acting and learning in situations by making practical experiments to test formative contexts, to surface conflicts and inconsistencies, to explore deviations from routines and envisage the alternative contexts that they may lead to. From such online experimental activity analysis is not all excluded, but it cannot be done independently of the situation at hand: It is a sort of analysis-in-action. Being often difficult or impossible for people to conduct an inquiry of this kind while they are engaged in designing, the presence and activity of a 'watcher' or 'reflector' become crucial for intervention and designing-in-action. The reflector-who is a designer in his own right-helps designers and users to carry out evaluative and reflective functions on their own ways of thinking and acting in the design process. As it was conducted in a number of projects (Lanzara, 1991; Lanzara and Mathiassen, 1988), a context-making experiment would involve the following activities:

- Living with the process and closely watching the designers' activities and interactions as they progress in their work;
- Keeping track of the design process and mapping it as it unfolds, recording and memorizing events that designers perceive as relevant;
- Eliciting information from the designers through recurrent questioning, in order to make them explicitly describe and account for what they are doing, why, and how: objects, activities and reasons for action that they often take for granted;
- Helping designers reflect upon design assumptions, institutional constraints, strategies for action, aims and objectives, problems encountered, options for solutions, anomalies and deviations from normal routines;
- Engaging in joint evaluations and self-evaluations, trying to assess the meaning of events and situations that designers perceive as relevant for the process and the outcome of design;
- Designing on-the-spot experiments in self-observation and self-evaluation by which designers can see themselves and their formative contexts mirrored in the others' pictures of shared objects, events and situations;

- Helping the designers to proceed from self-observation to construction and testing of alternative pictures, frameworks and institutional arrangements, working out all the thinkable (although not necessarily feasible) consequences of imagined contexts in terms of routines and activities.

In other words, the reflector's role is that of a mirror where people can look at themselves as they are seen and described by another mind. Actually, a better analogy would be a videotape where one can look at oneself 'in action'. This is what trainers and coaches usually do in sports like skiing or soccer, or what choreographers do with dancers, in order to pinpoint and correct mistakes, and develop new ways of performing. Because of the reflector's presence and inquiry, a domain of discourse is created that gives a kind of objective existence to people, events, actions, and processes. Thus an additional abstract dimension is introduced in the design process by making it 'double back on itself' (Olafson, 1979). This 'doubling back' is what allows people to have access to and intervene in the formative context with the purpose of challenging and changing it. The reflector is an active medium that may facilitate this process by helping designers go beyond their current ways of doing things, by making visible and discussable what is generally held invisible and undiscussable.

Although the primary purpose of the reflector's intervention is to break up consolidated knowledge and institutions, it should not be viewed as a merely destructuring activity: It involves projects, programs, and skills to transform deeply-engrained scripts, to depart from current practices, to respond to surprises in real-time, and to act with the 'materials' of ambiguous and ever-shifting situations. Unfreezing and disrupting previous contexts require the invention of alternative practices, systems and organizational arrangements that possess a certain quality, namely the capability for self-questioning, for being viable means to further rounds of transformation (Weick, 1977).

The role of the designers themselves shifts from problem-solvers to context makers. Their task should be to create a milieu where all participants are given the opportunity to project their own formative context upon one another, and thus, precisely because of this mirroring effect, become able to see it and reflect upon it (Lanzara, 1991). What is involved here is more than instrumental problem-solving or interest accommodation within a given context. Rather, it is the modification of the institutional and cognitive conditions that may constrain or liberate a whole set of problem-solving activities, of norms for conflict resolution, which ultimately determine what a system does in an organization.

The outcome: systems and routines for self-questioning

We believe that our new understanding of the emerging properties of systems, and our new approach to systems development as context-making and designing-in-action have important implications for the functions computer-based systems are designed to perform.

In other words, we submit that the making of formative contexts as one of the basic activities in systems design should influence the very object of design. As a final exercise we indicate, then, the qualities that systems and routines may come to possess in this new perspective:

- Systems should facilitate rather than hinder the process of reinvention that any complex technological artifact undergoes when put to use;
- Application software should be designed in such a way that they do not conceal their relations to formative contexts, but make those relations explicit and questionable;
- Systems should be designed as media for enhancing coordination and communication: problems and solutions shift all the time, and systems, because of their open, pasted up nature, benefit from loosely coupled forms of organizing;
- Systems and applications should provide on-line feedback to users on the organization of work, and on coordination and communication patterns which emerge from their use;
- Systems should be 'expert', though in a quite different way from current conceptions: In addition to supporting or replacing knowledge-based established routines of professionals and managers in specific domains of expertise, they should support their capabilities for reflection and inquiry within the contexts in which they are embedded, helping them to build up, question, and modify practical knowledge according to the emergence and the shift of problematic situations and contexts;

Finally, systems should be designed as proactive, dynamic mirrors of human action, supporting and enhancing perpetual individual and institutional self-questioning: in short, they should play the role of 'reflectors', helping the users connect their practical and argumentative routines to the established or emerging formative contexts, rather than concealing that connection, as they often do.

We claim that such qualities and uses of technologies and systems would give the users a further cognitive and behavioral empowerment and would support a more flexible organization, escaping the rigidity of many conventional applications. Furthermore, we suggest that in systems development higher capabilities for dealing with process phenomena on-line should replace or at least complement the current product-and-performance-oriented attitudes.

Concluding remarks

What we have been claiming so far is that current ways of looking at systems development fall short of understanding it as a phenomenon in the domain of action and change. In our view, they all share a fundamental flaw: They assume a direct consequentiality between conditions, choices, and actions leading to change and innovation.

Participation, consensus and users' know-how are by all means necessary but not sufficient conditions for effective design and implementation: There are other sources of difficulty stemming from cognitive, behavioral, and institutional bonds. Preexisting formative contexts plainly impede actors, regardless of their goals, interests, and espoused theories, to connect imagined alternatives to actions, to detect mistakes and appreciate novelties. On the one hand, the open, pasted-up nature of systems and development processes defies many formalized and participative attempts at mastering and steering a process toward specifically programmed objectives; on the other hand, such nature can be purposefully exploited to design-in-action, to make things change by intervening in situations and experimenting with makeshift artifacts, or to keep going when the situation seems to be hopelessly 'blocked'. This is what makes systems, organizations, and people working with them capable of overcoming inertia and vicious circles when environmental turbulence requires high levels of flexibility (Emery and Trist, 1965; Lanzara, 1983).

The reframing we have proposed leads to a further outcome, which can shed a new light on the role of systems *per se*. Namely, systems share many of the qualities of formative contexts, and designing a system interferes, if not coincides, with enacting a formative context, that is, a cognitive, institutional, and behavioral artifact, and a makeshift one. This artifact influences not only the routines that form the everyday world of people at work, but also, and most importantly, the ways people make sense of their routines and imagine future changes to their lifeworlds (Boland, 1979; Boland and Day, 1982; Weick, 1985). Our approach takes such everyday practice seriously (Moran and Anderson, 1990), instead of exorcizing it in the name of imperatives dictated by a misplaced notion of technical rationality and by an artificial split between knowledge and practice.

Acknowledgements

The core ideas and arguments of this paper were preliminarily presented in May 1987 at the IFIP Conference on Information Systems Development for Human Progress in Organizations held in Atlanta, GA, USA. Since then, revised versions have widely circulated among many colleagues who, with their suggestions and critical comments, have helped us to improve it. We thank Chris Argyris, Richard Boland, Shahaf Gal, David Hickson, Lars Mathiassen, Donald Schön, John Van Maanen, Karl Weick, Shoshana Zuboff, and anonymous reviewers.

Note

This chapter originally appeared in (1994) *Accounting, Management & Information Technology* **4**(2): 61–86.

References

Abelson, R.P. (1976). Script processing in attitude formation and decision making, in R. Carroll and W. Payne (eds) *Cognition and Social Behavior*, Hillsdale, NJ: Erlbaum and Associates.

Argyris, C. (1977). Organizational learning and management information systems, *Accounting, Organizations and Society* 2(2): 113–123.

Argyris, C. and Schön, D.A. (1974). *Theory in Practice: Increasing Professional Effectiveness*, San Francisco: Jossey Bass.

Argyris, C. and Schön, D.A. (1978). *Organizational Learning: A Theory of Action Perspective,* Reading, MA: Addison-Wesley.
Argyris, C., Putnam, R. and McLain Smith, D. (1985). *Action Science,* San Francisco: Jossey Bass.
Barley, S.R. (1986). Technology as an occasion for structuring: evidence from observation from CT scanners and the social order of radiology departments, *Administrative Science Quarterly* **31**(1): 78–108.
Bateson, G. (1972). *Steps to an Ecology of Mind,* New York: Chandler Publishing.
Blackler, F. (1990). Formative contexts and activity systems: Postmodern approaches to the management of change, in M. Reed and M. Hugues (eds), *Rethinking Organization,* London: Sage, pp. 273–294.
Boland, R. (1979). Control, causality and information systems requirements, *Accounting, Organizations and Society* **4**(4): 259–272.
Boland, R. and Day, W. (1982). The process of system design: A phenomenological approach. *Proceedings of the Third International Conference on Information Systems,* Ann Arbor, MI.
Boland, R., and Hirschheim, R. (eds) (1987). *Critical Issues in Information Systems Research, New* York: John Wiley and Sons.
Briefs, U., Ciborra, C. and Schneider, L. (eds) (1983). *System Design for, with, and by the Users,* Amsterdam: North Holland.
Brooks, F.P. (1982). *The Mythical Man-month,* Reading, MA: Addison-Wesley.
Brown, J.S. and Duguid, P. (1991). Organizational learning and communities-of-practice: Towards a unified view of working, learning and innovation, *Organization Science* **2**: 40–57.
Burns, T. (1981). *Rediscovering Organization: Aspects of Collaboration and Managerialism in Hospital Organization,* University of Edinburgh, UK.
Cardwell, S. and Miner, K. (1991). *Distributed Computing and Organizational Change Enable Concurrent Engineering,* Hewlett Packard, Palo Alto.
Ciborra, C.U. (1993). *Teams, Markets and Systems: Business Innovation and Information Technology,* Cambridge, UK: Cambridge University Press.
Ciborra, C.U. and Lanzara, G.F. (1989). Change and formative contexts in information system development, in H.K. Klein and K. Kumar (eds), *System Development for Human Progress,* Amsterdam: North Holland, pp. 21–40.
Ciborra, C.U. and Lanzara, G.F. (1990). Designing dynamic artifacts: Computers systems as formative contexts, in P. Gagliardi (ed.), *Svmbols and Artifacts: Views of the Corporate Landscape,* Berlin: Walter de Gruyter, pp. 147–165.
Ciborra, C.U., Migliarese, P. and Romano, P. (1984). A methodological inquiry into organizational noise in sociotechnical systems, *Human Relations* **37**(8): 565–588.
Crozier, M. and Friedberg, E. (1977). *L'ucteur et le systeme,* Paris: Editions du Seuil.
Daly, E.B. (1979). Organizing for successful software development, *Datamation* (December): 107–1 19.
DeMarco, T. (1979). *Structured analysis and system specification, New* York: Yourdon Press.
Dijkstra, E.F. (1976). A *Discipline of Programming,* Englewood Cliffs, NJ: Prentice Hall.
Douglas, M. (1986). *How Institutions Think.* Syracuse, NY: Syracuse University Press.
Emery, F.E., Trist, E.L. (1965). Socio-technical systems, in C.W. Churchman, and M. Verhulst (eds). *Management Sciences: Models and Techniques,* Oxford, UK: Pergamon Press.
Gagliardi, P. (1986). The creation and change of organizational cultures: A conceptual framework, *Organization Studies* **7**(2): 107–134.
Galbraith, J.R. (1977). *Designing Organizations,* Reading, MA: Addison-Wesley.
Garfinkel, H. (1967). *Studies in Ethnomethodology,* Englewood Cliffs, NJ: Prentice Hall.
Giddens, A. (1976). New *Rules of Sociological Method,* New York: Basic Books.
Giddens, A. (1979). *Central Problems in Social Theory: Action, Structure and Contradiction in Social Analysis,* Berkeley, CA: University of California Press.
Giddens, A. (1984). *The Constitution of Society: Outline of A Theory of Structuration,* Berkeley, CA: University of California Press.

Greenwood, R. and Hinings, C.R. (1988). Organizational design types, tracks and the dynamics of strategic change, *Organization Studies* **9**(3): 293–316.
Guild, D.W. (1988). Two examples of strategic information systems. *Proceedings* of the *Workshop on Information Systems Strategic Planning,* World Trade Center, New York.
Hauptman, O. (1986). Influence of task type on the relation between communication and performance: The case of software development, *R&D Management.*
Hedberg, B. and Jonsson, S. (1978). Designing semi-confusing information systems for organizations in changing environments, *Accounting, Organizations und Society* **3**(l): 47–64.
Herbst, P.G. (1974). *Socio-technical Design: Strategies in Multidisciplinary Research,* London: Tavistock Publishing.
Jackson, M. (1983). System *Development,* Englewood Cliffs, NJ: Prentice-Hall.
Kanter, R.M. (1983). *The Change Masters,* New York: Simon and Schuster.
Keats, J. (1817). Letters to George and Tom Keats, in C. Baker (eds), *Poems and Selected Letters of John Keats,* New York: Bantam Books.
Keen, P.G.W. (1981). Information systems and organizational change, *Communications of the ACM* **24**(l): 24–33.
Konsynski, B.R. (1985). Advances in information system design, *Journal of Management Information Systems* **1**(3): 5–32.
Lanzara, G.F. (1983). Ephemeral organizations in extreme environments: Emergence, strategy, extinction, *Journal of Management Studies* **20**(1): 73–95.
Lanzara, G.F. (1991). Shifting stories: Learning from a reflective experiment in a design process, in D.A. Schön (ed.), *The Reflective Turn: Case Studies in and on Educational Practice,* New York: Teachers College Press, pp. 285–320.
Lanzara, G.F. and Mathiassen, L. (1988). Intervening into system development area projects, in G.C. van der Veer, T.R.G. Green, J.M. Hoc, and D.M. Murray (eds), *Working with Computers: Theory versus Outcome,* London: Academic Press, pp. 177–214.
Lyytinen, K. and Hirschheim, R. (1987). Information systems failures: A survey and classification of the empirical literature, *Oxford Surveys in Information Technology* **4**: 257–309.
March, J.G., and Olsen, J. (1979). *Ambiguity and Choice in Organizations,* Bergen: Universitetsforlaget.
Markus, M.L. (1983). Power, politics and MIS implementation, *Communications of the ACM* **26**: 430–444.
Miller, D. and Friesen, P. (1980). Archetypes of organizational transitions, *Administrative Science Quarterly* **25**: 269–299.
Minsky, M. (1975). A framework for representing knowledge, in P.H. Winston (ed.), *Thepsychology of Computer Vision,* New York: McGraw-Hill.
Minsky, M. (1977). Frame-system theory, in P.N. Johnson-Laird and P.C. Wason (eds), *Thinking: Readings in Cognitive Science,* Cambridge, UK: Cambridge University Press.
Moran, T.P. and Anderson, R.J. (1990). The workaday world as a paradigm for CSCW design, in *Proc. CSCW PO,* Los Angeles: ACM.
Mumford, E., and Henshall, D. (1979). *A Participative Approach to Computer Systems Design,* London: Associated Business Press.
Nelson, R. and Winter, S. (1982). *An Evolutionary Theory of Economic Change,* Cambridge, MA: Harvard University Press.
Olafson, F. (1979). *The Dialectics of Action,* Chicago: The University of Chicago Press.
Orlikowsky, W.J. (1991). Integrated information environment or matrix of control? The contradictory implications of information technology, *Accounting, Management and Information Systems* **l**(l): 9–42.
Orlikowsky, W.J. (1992). The duality of technology: Rethinking the concept of technology in organizations, *Organization Science* **3**(3): 398–427.
Orlikowsky, W.J. and Robey, D. (1991). Information technology and the structuring of organizations, *Information Systems Research* **2**(2): 143–169.
Papert, S. (1980). *Mindstorms, New* York: Basic Books.

Pentland, B.T. (1992). Organizing moves in software support hot lines, *Administrative Science Quarterly* **37**: 527–548.
Pfeffer, J. (1981). Management as symbolic action: The creation and maintenance of organizational paradigms, in B.M. Staw and L.L. Cummings (eds), *Research in Organizational Behavior,* Greenwich, CT: Jai Press, pp. 1–52.
Polanyi, M. (1966). *The Tacit Dimension,* Garden City, NY: Doubleday.
Poole, M.S. and De Sanctis, G. (1990). Understanding the use of group division support systems: The theory of adaptive structuration, in J. Fulk and C. Steinfield (eds), Organizations *and communication technology,* Newbury Park, CA: Sage Publications, pp.173–193.
Rice, R.E. and Rogers, E.M. (1980). Reinvention in the innovation process, *Knowledge* **1**(4): 488–514.
Schein, E.H. (1984). Coming to a new awareness of organizational culture, *Sloan Management Review* **Winter**: 3–16.
Schein, E.H. (1988). *Process consultation. Volume I: Its role in organizational development,* Reading, MA: Addison-Wesley.
Schein, E.H. (1992). *Organizational Culture and Leadership* (2nd edn), San Francisco: Jossey-Bass.
Schön, D.A. (1983). *The Reflective Practitioner: How Professionals Think in Action,* New York: Basic Books.
Schutz, A. (1960). *Collected Papers,* Vol. 1: *The Problem of Social Reality.* The Hague: Martinus Nijhoff.
Sewell, W.H. (1992). A theory of structure: Duality, agency, and transformation, *American Journal of Sociology* **98**(1): 1–29.
Shank, R., Abelson, R.P. (1977). *Scripts, Goals, Plans, and Understanding: an Inquiry into Human Knowledge Structures,* Hillsdale, NJ: Erlbaum Associates.
Shrivastava, P. and Schneider, S. (1985). Organizational frames of reference, *Human Relations* **37**(10): 795–809.
Sims. H.P. and Gioia, D.A. (eds) (1986). *The Thinking Organization: Dynamics of Organizational Social Cognition,* San Francisco: Jossey-Bass.
Smircich, L. (1983). Concepts of culture and organizational analysis, *Administrative Science Quarterly* **28**(3): 339–358.
Suchmann, L. (1987). *Plans and Situated Actions,* Cambridge, UK: Cambridge University Press.
Tversky, A. and Kahnemann, D. (1981). The framing of decisions and the psychology of choice, *Science* **211**: 453–458.
Unger, R.M. (1987). *False Necessity,* Cambridge, UK: Cambridge University Press.
Van Maanen, J. (1984). Doing new things in old ways: The chains of socialization, in J.L. Bess (ed.), *College and University Organization,* New York: New York University Press.
Yourdon, E. (1982). *Managing the System Life Cycle, New* York: Yourdon Press.
Weick, K. (1977). Organization design: Organizations as self-designing systems. *Organizational Dynamics* **6**(2): 30–46.
Weick, K. (1985). Cosmos versus chaos: Sense and nonsense in electronic contexts. *Organizational Dynamics* **14**(2): 50–64.
Williamson, O. (1981). The economics of organization: The transaction costs approach. *American Journal of Sociology* **87**(3): 548–577.
Wiseman, C. (1985). *Strategv and Computers,* Homewood, IL: Dow Jones-Irwin.
Zuboff, S. (1988). *In the Age of /he Smart Machine,* New York: Basic Books.

8

Organizational Learning and Core Capabilities Development: The Role of IT*

Rafael Andreu and Claudio U. Ciborra

Abstract

The resource-based view of the firm (RBVF) focuses on the firm's resources and capabilities to understand business strategy and to provide direction to strategy formulation. This paper emphasizes the learning aspects of capability development and explores how information technology (IT) can contribute to it.

As a standardized resource widely available, IT can participate in the fundamental process that transforms resources into capabilities and eventually into core capabilities. In this way, IT can become – embedded in core capabilities – an active component of the firm's competitive advantages.

The process by which resources end up being components of core capabilities in firms is a learning process that can be described and understood using RBVF concepts. Furthermore, the development of IT strategic applications (also called 'strategic information systems' or SIS) follows patterns that closely parallel the structure of that learning process. For this reason we propose an organizational learning model based on the RBVF, and use it to derive guidelines for management action aimed at improving IT effectiveness in organizations.

The paper is organized as follows: the RBVF framework is summarized, including the concepts of capabilities and core capabilities and the organizational processes that lead to them. Next, an organizational learning model is presented: an interpretation of capability development that emphasizes situated learning and knowledge accumulation. The model is then used to show how IT can contribute to core capability formation in a firm: management action can mould the process to some extent, although it often unfolds 'naturally' embedded in an organizational context that is both determined by and determinant of learning. Finally, guidelines are discussed to come up and build strategic IT applications, based on the previous analysis. Short conclusions follow.

The resource-based view of the firm framework

The resource-based view of the firm (RBVF) conceives a firm as seeking to acquire hard to imitate, valuable resources and capabilities:

> For managers the challenge is to identify, develop, protect and deploy resources and capabilities in a way that provides the firm with a sustainable competitive advantage and, thereby, a superior return on capital. (Amit and Schoemaker, 1993)

The firm's quest for differentiation is a process that develops distinctive capabilities, also called *core capabilities.* Core capabilities are capabilities that differentiate a company strategically, fostering beneficial behaviors not observed in competitive firms (Leonard-Barton, 1992). A capability has *strategic potential,* and thus becomes core, with potential for competitive advantage, when it is (Barney, 1991): (1) *valuable* (i.e. exploits opportunities and/or neutralizes threats in a firm's environment), (2) *rare* (i.e. the number of firms that possess a particular capability is less than the number needed to generate perfect competition in an industry (Hirshleifer, 1980), (3) *imperfectly imitable* (for instance because of unique conditions in its acquisition process, because the link between the capability and sustainable advantage is causally ambiguous (Lippman and Rumelt, 1982), or because it is socially complex), and (4) *with no strategically equivalent substitutes* (i.e. with no alternative ways of achieving the same results).

Core capabilities develop in organizations through a transformation process by which undifferentiated resources, available in open markets (where all firms can acquire them), are used and combined, within the *organizational context* of each firm, with *organizational routines* to produce *capabilities,* which in turn can become core and the source of competitive advantages if the above conditions are met. Since this transformation process takes place within an organizational context and uses specific organizational routines, the resulting (core) capabilities are highly dependent on them. As the process unfolds, the *path- or acquisition-dependency degree* increases, making the results more and more idiosyncratic to the firm in which they develop. Hence, the transformation is a path-dependent learning process. We consider now, in more detail, its major phases.

Although iterative and evolving, the process starts with a set of existing *resources.* A *resource* is any available factor owned [...] by a firm (Amit and Schoemaker, 1993). We may add that resources are assets available in the firm without specific organizational effort. IT is understood as a resource in this sense. *Capabilities* are developed by combining and using resources (and/or other capabilities) with the aid of *organizational routines.* An *organizational routine* is a particular way of doing what an organization has developed and *learned,* and in the utilization of which that organization is very efficient and effective, to the point of becoming almost automatic, a 'natural' reflection of its 'way of being'. These routines embed organizational knowledge acquired through learning (Nelson and Winter, 1982; Dosi *et al.*, 1990; Grant, 1992); consequently they have a strong tacit dimension which makes them difficult to imitate and change.[1]

Capabilities are seen in the RBVF literature from many different perspectives. Teece *et al.* (1990) define them as a set of differentiated skills, complementary assets, and routines that provide the basis for a firm's capacities in a particular business. Amit and Schoemaker (1993) define capabilities *vis-a-vis* resources:

> Capabilities refer to a firm's capacity to deploy Resources, usually in combination, using organizational processes, to effect a desired end. [...] Unlike Resources, Capabilities are based on developing, carrying, and exchanging information through the firm's human capital.

Consequently, developing capabilities involves organizational learning: learning how to combine and use resources, and also the learning already embedded in the organizational routines employed. The interplay among resources, organizational routines and capabilities is very rich: existing capabilities can be made more sophisticated by combining some of them into new ones with the aid of organizational routines; new organizational routines may also develop by combining old ones with available capabilities. At a given point in time an organization is characterized by specific and interrelated sets of 'stocks' of resources, capabilities and organizational routines. Since learning takes place within a firm's organizational context, core capabilities are *path-dependent* – their *specificity degree* is high. This is crucial for making them difficult to imitate and hence resulting in advantages sustainable and durable. *Path-dependency* means that the way a firm owns an asset (a capability) depends on the process through which it acquired it (Dierickx and Cool, 1989; Dosi *et al.*, 1990; Collis, 1991). The concept of *specificity degree* relates to the idea of 'specific purpose': As capabilities develop through a process that uses idiosyncratic routines and takes place in a specific organizational context, the results become less and less 'general purpose' (i.e. less and less efficient/effective if they are taken away from where they originated (Montgomery and Wernerfelt, 1988).

Figure 8.1 summarizes the process. It is complex and not necessarily planned for; many times it 'just happens'. Planning and making it happen, however, are genuine management activities, as discussed below. In general, the degree of specificity and path dependency increases from bottom to top in Figure 8.1, as more learning and selection are involved.

Learning in the capability development process

The transformation process that produces core capabilities from resources involves learning. Learning is important because (1) it implies path-dependency and specificity in the resulting core capabilities, and (2) consequently, it is one of the causes of their inimitability, which is crucial for competitive advantage. By analyzing in detail the learning processes involved we will derive practical suggestions on how to harness IT as a key component of a firm's core capabilities.

The first transformation step develops capabilities from standard resources. Two different types of learning take place at this step: The first aims at *mastering the use of standard resources,* and produces what we call *efficient work practices*. Individuals

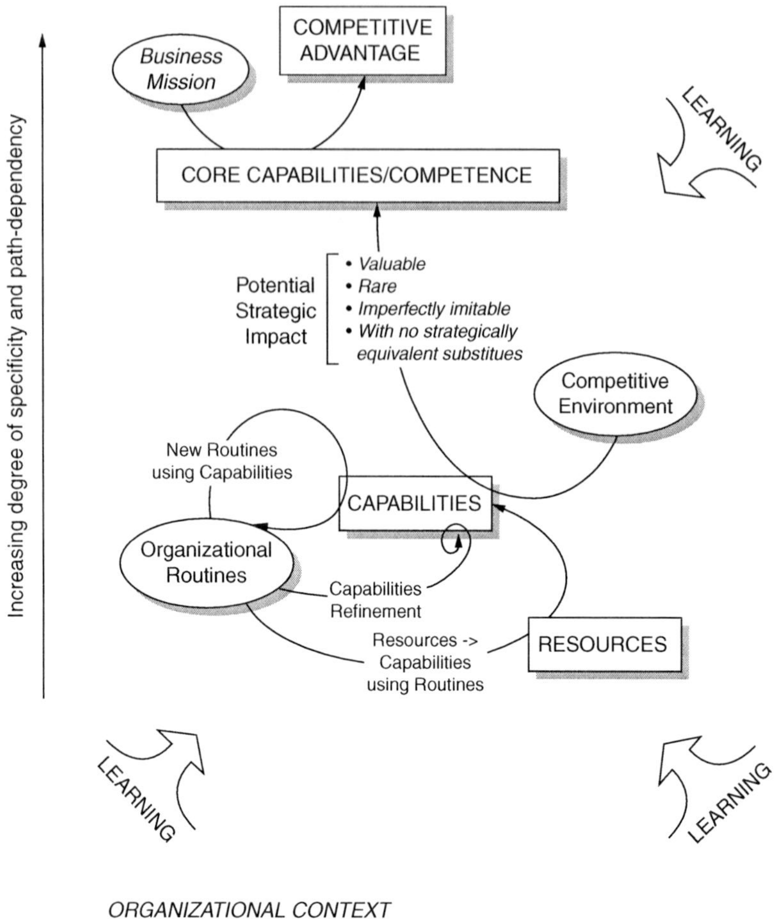

Figure 8.1 The Capability Development Process: from resources to competitive advantage

and groups in the firm learn how to use resources in the context of a given organizational situation. The quest for better work practices may even trigger a search for new resources, more appropriate for the practices under development. Or, the appearance of new resources (say new technologies) may motivate individuals and groups to 'take advantage of them' through new work practices. Thus, there is in fact a *learning loop* between resources and work practices. We call it the *routinization learning loop*. The environment in which learning occurs is an organizational context, which influences the learning process and is in turn influenced by its result (i.e. new working practices become part of the context, thus increasing the knowledge base of the organization (Giddens, 1984; Orlikowski, 1992). Such an organizational context has the characteristics of a *formative context* (Ciborra and Lanzara, 1990; Mufioz-Seca and Riverola, 1994).[2] Work practices are 'formed' within it, and receive their meaning and scope from it. Work practices resulting from this learning loop are concrete, detailed, specific and operative, close to the concept of *skills;* they are instances of what has been called *modus operandi* (Bourdieu, 1977) – in fact, they tend to lose their value when taken away from the specific situation in which they were developed and are afterwards used. From a different perspective, work practices are the first step in the firm's 'internalization' of resources. Mastering the usage of a spreadsheet by an individual or a team in a specific department is an example of this type of learning.

The second type of learning creates capabilities from existing work practices. Several characteristics of this learning are important: (1) it involves combining work practices and organizational routines; (2) the result has a strong *potential* connotation, as capabilities convey what an organization is *capable* of doing if properly triggered – i.e. capabilities involve *generalizing* work practices and putting them in a wider context that defines how they work, so that they are instances of opus operatum (Bourdieu, 1977); (3) the result – capabilities – is easily described in terms of *what* they do and how they do it, but *for what* they do it is taken for granted, not necessarily well defined and rarely challenged; and (4) since needs for new routines for work practices can be detected during the process, it also becomes a learning loop, that we call the *capability learning loop.* The objectives of the learning involved in both these loops are close to the concept of *static efficiency* (Ashby, 1954; Ghemawat and Ricart, 1993).

To summarize, learning at this basic level results in a continuously improving set of capabilities – specialized and idiosyncratic ways of using resources for given purposes. These purposes are functionally well defined and stable over time, although how they are attained may change even drastically, for example with the emergence of a radically new technology (resource) or a revolutionary new use of an old resource (Penrose, 1959). The driving force for continuous capability improvement is static efficiency, and the change agents are individuals and groups in the organization who become the repositories of the resulting capabilities. The learning processes often occur spontaneously, although the organizational climate and context, and the incentives, power and motivational systems are ultimately responsible for differences in the quality of the process from one organization to another. Although efficient, capabilities lack a sense of why they exist, or at least the reasons for their existence are seldom challenged at this level. This sense develops as they evolve into core capabilities through yet another learning loop. See Figure 8.2.

In the next learning process capabilities evolve into core capabilities. Core capabilities are capabilities that differentiate a company strategically, [...] fostering beneficial behaviours not observed in competitors. There are two main reference points against which capabilities can be calibrated to check their potential to become core: *the competitive environment* and *the business mission of the firm.* When faced to its competitive environment, a firm learns why some capabilities have strategic potential (they are rare, valuable, etc.) A converse influence, from core capabilities to capabilities also exists through the competitive environment, as (1) core capabilities of different firms competing in a given environment (industry) define the 'standards of excellence' in that environment, and so they point

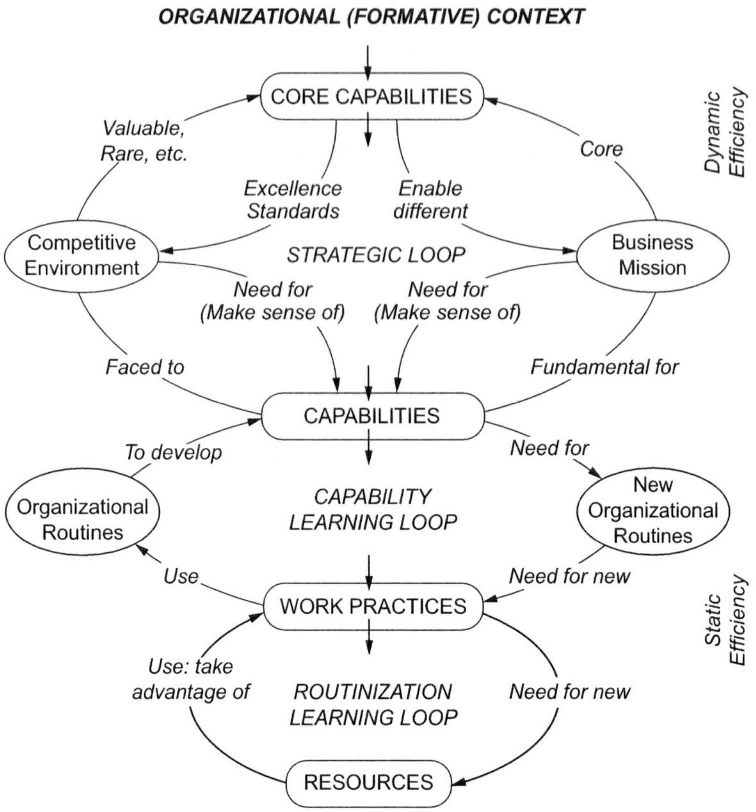

Figure 8.2 Learning in the capabilities and core capabilities development process

out what capabilities each firm should develop in order to compete effectively; and (2) it is when confronted with the competitive environment that capabilities acquire a sense of why they are important, thus clarifying their role and scope. In addition, capabilities are difficult to imitate in part because of the learning involved in the routinization and capability loops: to develop similar capabilities, competitors must go through those learning loops.

A firm's business mission is also relevant for identifying core capabilities. It is in its context that capabilities acquire meaning, as some of them emerge as fundamental for carrying it out. Capabilities fundamental in this sense are candidates to become core. Again, there is a converse influence. Core capabilities can enable new missions which, if accepted as such, trigger new capabilities → core capabilities transformations. All these interrelationships give rise to another learning loop linking capabilities and core capabilities; we call it the *strategic learning loop* (Figure 8.2).

The strategic learning loop also takes place within the firm's organizational (formative) context, and so it is influenced by the context. Furthermore, its outcome – core capabilities – in turn reshape the context itself. At this level

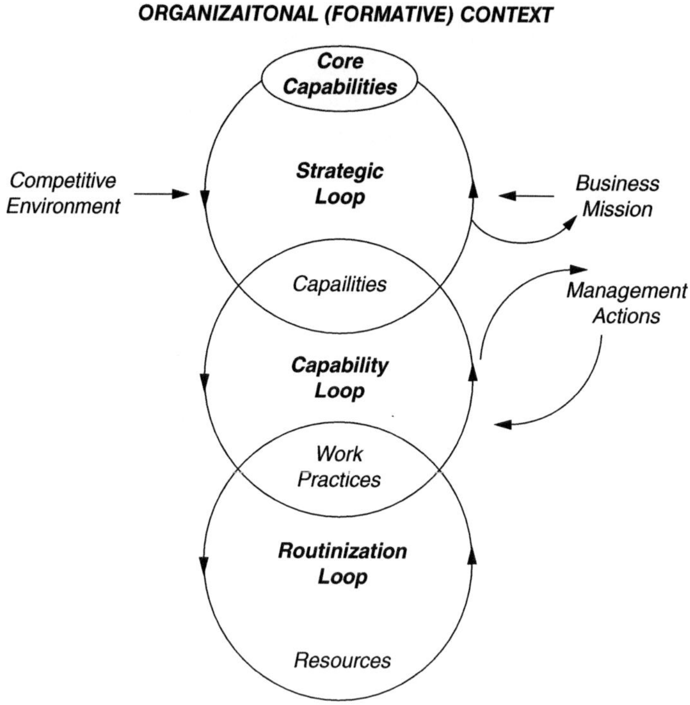

Figure 8.3 Basic learning processes in the core capabilities formation process

capabilities can be described and understood not only in terms of *what* they do and how they do it, but also in terms of when, beyond the static efficiency criterion that dominates the other two learning loops. In a context where is clear which capabilities are core and why, these loops are given added motivation and direction (e.g. in the search for new organizational routines or resources); we are in the realm of dynamic efficiency. For example, competitive environment changes can render a highly efficient (in the static sense) capability worthless because it becomes irrelevant to compete under the new conditions. Continuously checking the interrelationships among capabilities, core capabilities, competitive environment, business mission and organizational context, and responding to the challenges that arise as the firm and its environment evolve over time, is the essence of the strategic learning loop.

Finally, it must be noted that inertia belongs to the very nature of organizational contexts, as a consequence of the learning involved in their continuous development and updating (Kim, 1993). Consequently, *drastically changing* the context is difficult, although sometimes necessary – for example to respond to radical environment or business mission shifts. However, drastic changes in the mission of the firm are not likely to happen, as its evolution also occurs within the organizational context. Hence, revolutionary changes in organizational context or business mission require *radical learning* – becoming aware of what the context is and explicitly stepping out in order to innovate in a radical manner. As core capabilities are components of the organizational context, radical learning means learning how to *do* radically new things (in the bottom learning loop of Figure 8.2), that are *important in radically new ways* (which implies activity in the top learning loops) (Argyris and Schön, 1978).

Figure 8.3 is a summary of Figure 8.2. We conceptualize the RBVF framework as involving three learning loops, which develop firm's capabilities and core capabilities starting with resources, using organizational routines and taking into account the firm's competitive environment and its business mission. One basic loop routinizes work practices using resources; a second one combines work practices and organizational routines to form capabilities; and the third gives meaning to capabilities in the context of the firm's competitive environment and business mission, thus identifying core capabilities. The knowledge of 'which capabilities are distinctive and fundamental to compete' is strategic in nature and becomes part of the organizational (formative) context in which all firm's activities, including learning, occur. Those learning loops tend to unfold spontaneously, and they depend strongly on the individuals' and groups' perceptions of the environment, the business mission, and even their own learning abilities. Management actions aim at giving to the learning processes the appropriate direction at a given point in time (Argyris, 1993).

The case of IT: from a resource to a key component of core capabilities

We now turn to information technology (IT). By IT we mean all computer and telecommunications technologies available in open markets, where firms can acquire them. IT is an enabling technology, although it may also play the role of a constraint, in the sense of not being enabling enough (Scott-Morton, 1991).

In this section we use the learning model just introduced to explain how IT applications can help develop core capabilities in companies. The topic relates to IT applications known as strategic information systems (SIS), since these help to shape core capabilities in the companies that develop them. The goal is twofold: (1) revising a few cases that have led to well known SIS shows that they followed the pattern suggested by the model, and (2) applying the model to the case where IT is one of the resources employed throws light into how the corresponding transformation process could be managed.

One well known SIS is ASAP, launched by AHS Corporation (now Baxter Healthcare). ASAP started as an operational, localized response to a customer need (Short and Venkatraman, 1992). Because of difficulties in serving a hospital effectively, a manager of a local AHS office started to give prepunched cards to the hospital's purchasing department, so that ordering clerks could transfer orders expeditiously through a phone terminal. This local, ad hoc solution gradually led to linking more customer hospitals in the same way, eventually through PCs. AHS management realized the positive impacts on profits of such an electronic link with customers, and allocated resources for its further development (Ciborra, 1992,

1994). The parallel of this process with the basic structure of Figure 8.2 is clear. Initially, IT was a resource used in a new work practice to solve a localized client's problem. It was an unsophisticated response to a specific operative problem. Generalizing the solution and making it available to more clients is a clear example of what in the learning model is the development of capabilities. The *potential* characteristic is present, and organizational routines used in the relationships with clients are not only brought into play, but also refined as the second learning loop of the model would predict. Furthermore, the capability had strategic potential, as it was valuable and difficult to imitate, in particular by some of the AHS's competitors. It was *valuable* because ASAP *effectively contributed to the positioning of AHS as the 'prime vendor'* (Short and Venkatraman, 1992) *for hospitals;* it was *difficult to imitate* because *the important competitors (for example Johnson & Johnson) just couldn't play the same game, at least in the short run, as they were organized in too many decentralized divisions in order to respond quickly enough.* Thus, ASAP actively contributed to the competitive positioning of the firm by exploiting an environmental opportunity: the so called 'incumbent's inertia' (Lieberman and Montgomery, 1988) of the major competitor. A valuable organizational and competitive positioning fit was built in the system, which became a major ingredient in the core capabilities' arsenal of AHS. Furthermore, the system evolution led to a shift in 'distinctive business competence' (Short and Venkatraman, 1992) that helped to *sustain* competitive advantage.

A different illustration of IT impact on core capabilities is Mrs. Fields' Cookies (INC., 1987).[3] Mrs. Fields' business started to commercialize the cookies that Mrs. Fields had prepared at home for years. The first store was under tight personal control of Mrs. Fields herself, who designed not only the cookies' recipes. but also a definite approach to sales, promotion, store style and even personnel recruitment and management. As the number of stores grew, a computerized information system was developed using commodity technology. The system was a bread-and-butter application, that recorded operations data from the stores and reported them to headquarters for centralized control. Although it permitted to run the operation with a remarkably low number of staff workers, it evolved into a system whose main impact was a very different one: it turned into a way to convey to all stores the *Mrs. Fields' way of doing things, independently of the (usually not too well trained and highly mobile) personnel, and also a means by which all personnel could communicate, as often us they liked and in a person to person basis, with Mrs Fields herself.* The case again illustrates how work practices developed with the aid of commodity IT, followed by a period of generalization, as the organizational routines used by Mrs. Fields in the first stores were 'encapsulated' and effectively transmitted to other stores, finally spreading the 'Mrs. Fields' way' throughout more than a thousand of them. It also illustrates an interesting and fundamental characteristic of IT. To the extent that the communications infrastructure and systems put in place were a central ingredient of the company's core capabilities (because of their impact in replicating the Mrs. Fields' way throughout the organization), they *were an important part of the organizational context, that furthermore they contributed to effectively transmit to the whole organization*. Thus, IT-based applications can not only be instrumental in shaping up the firm's core capabilities, but also in *effectively incorporating them to the firm's organizational context, thereby making them apparent to all organizational levels and giving meaning to all learning processes, which otherwise would operate more 'in a limbo'* (Ciborra and Lanzara, 1990).

Another interesting case deals with changing the organizational context. IT applications, consistently with the structure of the above learning model, can effectively contribute to make the shift actually happen in organizations. Consider what a Spanish Savings Bank did recently. In order to make branch managers responsible for all their activities, as dictated by a decentralization move that top management wanted quickly implemented, they used an existing IT application that permitted each branch manager to check, as often as s/he wanted, her/his performance against objectives. Under the application's new use, *any* branch manager can now check, in real time, how *any other brunch* is doing against its objectives. Strong competition among branches developed, thereby contributing to the emergence of a new 'way of doing things' at the branches, consistent with what management wanted to implement. The existing application was a basic one developed for control purposes. Once a fundamental shift in the firm's organizational structure was decided upon, the application became central for a completely different purpose, similar to that in Mrs Fields', but different in a fundamental aspect: the organizational context to be communicated was radically new. Thus, IT applications can also play an active role in the difficult task of making the slow evolving organizational contexts change faster.

All the examples show that the proposed organizational learning model is useful to describe how IT applications can contribute to core capabilities development and thereby become part (even a fundamental one) of the resulting core capabilities. Although more detailed field research is needed to explore this claim in depth, the model helps us understand how IT can contribute effectively to firms' competitiveness. Furthermore, it allows us to consistently think about what kind of management actions are needed to improve the IT transformation process, from a commodity to a strategic asset – i.e. management actions to improve the effectiveness of all learning processes involved. In what follows we suggest how to do so in the context of the learning loops of Figure 8.3.

The *routinization loop* seeks the static efficiency of work practices. Individuals and groups involved should be motivated to experiment and seek alternatives to continuously improve efficiency. Within a concrete organizational context, the work practices formation process should be nurtured and properly organized, and learning reinforced. Such objectives directly suggest basic characteristics for management actions:

- *Nurture the process*. Make sure that individuals and groups are aware of the current organizational context, in which learning occurs.
- *Organize the learning process* for effectiveness. Foster a climate in which sharing of existing work practices and experimentation about new ones can occur, so that

individuals and groups can effectively 'listen to' the accumulated experience of which themselves are depositories (Brown and Duguid, 1991; Kim, 1993).

An intelligent use of IT can also contribute to attaining such actions' objectives, thus reinforcing IT's potential for support to the overall process – not only to the actual learning, but to its management. For example, IT/IS can contribute to the routinization and capability learning loops in several ways, facilitating the learning that takes place and spreading it to all the individuals and groups involved. For example:

- *Support the firm's work practice development process.* One way is through IT applications that facilitate experimentation with new resources, in particular with new sources of information and with IT itself (e.g. encouraging to use new technologies in pilot projects, etc. (see Tyre and Orlikowski, 1993).
- *Share work practices and facilitate communication within groups and among groups.* An 'individual' work practice effectively shared among the individuals of a group is often a new work practice in itself. At the same time, a good communication base facilitates the creation of more efficient work practices, in a way directly relevant to the goal of the routinization learning loop. Groupware is a technology directly relevant for all these purposes, in all its forms. Even straight-forward applications based on simple electronic mail infrastructures may be very effective in facilitating work practices' sharing, and in putting different work practices, 'owned' by different individuals or groups even geographically dispersed, to work effectively together.

The *capability learning loop* generalizes work practices so that their essence is learned and combined with organizational routines to produce capabilities. One basic characteristic of the management actions needed is:

- Put emphasis in *detaching capabilities from the specific and local connotations* that they have as a result of how the routinization learning loop works. *Generalize;* describe capabilities in terms of their essential characteristics, free from unnecessary details. Explicitly try to apply locally generated practices to more general contexts.

IT-based support is also feasible here:

- *Support the firm's capability creation process.* Although few IT applications specifically designed for this purpose seem to exist today, the idea is feasible: data gathered during the ongoing process of capability development can conceivably be stored and made available to future such processes, thus taking future learning more effective. Tools such as knowledge-based (e.g. the so-called *case based reasoning,* or CBR) can be used for this purpose, as can other less sophisticated approaches. Still an additional way may come about through the so called 'electronic brainstorming' processes (Gallupe and Cooper, 1993).

- *Sharing capabilities.* Capability sharing not only contributes to the creation of new ones, but also to the goal of spreading them in the organization, thus effectively helping to communicate and share the organizational context to the extent that those capabilities are part of it.
- *Facilitate reflection, experimentation and training on routines and capabilities.* Routines and basic capabilities must not only be shared and spread in order to become effectively available to the whole organization, but they must also be understood – i.e. be effectively learned, understanding why they work and the fundamentals behind them, thus effectively going beyond the so called operational learning, towards conceptual learning (Kim, 1993). There are many ways in which IT applications can contribute to this goal, for example by facilitating experimentation through simulations or expert systems, or through all kinds of decision support systems (DSS).
- *Support and enable capability diffusion.* Through what has been called 'systems of scope', i.e. systems that help in the 'sharing of global knowledge' in the firm. For example, J.C. Penney, the large department store firm in the USA, has put in place a video link infrastructure that permits store managers (more than 1500 across the USA) to be actively involved in the purchasing decisions *without losing the knowhow of experienced central purchasers.* The result is better purchasing decisions because the system allows the store managers' local market knowledge to be brought effectively into play without renouncing to economies of scale inherent to a centralized purchasing department and to the experience and knowledge of the central purchasing function. Eventually, as store managers learn about purchasing, they actually develop new capabilities that enable decentralization. Other examples include using expert systems to make expertise, knowledge and know-how available throughout the organization, etc.

The *strategic loop,* dealing with core capabilities identification and with the definition of new ones needs to cope with environment changes, involves different management challenges:

- Make sure that *know-how embedded in capabilities is checked against environment conditions and the firm's business mission.* This implies establishing the communication and information channels needed to reach all individuals and groups involved.
- Make *explicit how capabilities contribute to the formation and functioning of core competence.* Make individuals and groups well aware of what the core capabilities are, why, and how they contribute to them.

There is also room for IT-based support in this loop management and actual learning. For example:

- *IT applications that provide information about the competitive environment.* This information is relevant because it conditions core capabilities' identification, organizational context updating and, eventually, business mission reconsideration. Thus, IT applications facilitating access to such information contribute to make management actions more effective – e.g. applications explicitly designed to record information about competitors' actions in the market place.

- *IT applications that disseminate the business mission.* The idea is to help to 'spread the word' about the business mission. Examples include all kinds of quality level information displaying systems used in production plants, or even transactional or procedural applications that effectively 'force' individuals and groups in the organization to behave in a way consistent with the current business mission of the firm.

Embedding IT into core capabilities: some guidelines

The RBVF, coupled with our learning model, allow us to derive practical guidelines for the process that competent managers should foster to come up and build strategic IT applications (Feeny and Ives, 1989).

Apart from IT support in the routinization and capability loops, it is interesting to consider how IT can contribute positively to the strategic learning loop. IT can be instrumental in making capabilities become core (i.e. making them rare, valuable, difficult to imitate, and with no strategically equivalent substitutes). Guidelines to achieve this purpose are:

- *Look out for IT applications that help to make capabilities rare.* At the beginning of the computerized reservation systems in the airline industry, such systems were rare as only a few of the competitors, who took the lead in deciding to develop them, had them. In the Savings Banks industry in Spain, for quite some time only one could offer 24 hours debit card service because its telecommunications and IT base were rare, the result of a bold investment decision made well ahead of its competitors.
- *Concentrate on IT applications that make capabilities valuable.* The ASAP-AHS example is a case in point: the IT application contributed to the competitive positioning of the firm while exploiting an environmental opportunity (the incumbent's inertia of a major competitor). Similar comments can be made of the Federal Express COSMOS system (Smith, 1991). Several procedures have been proposed for precisely the identification of this type of IT applications (Gongla *et al.*, 1989; Andreu *et al.*, 1992).
- *Identify IT contributions that make capabilities difficult to imitate.* Core capabil ities can be difficult to imitate for several reasons (in AHS, for instance, organizational impediments on the competitors' side made their responses slow). The IT-based part of core capabilities can also contribute to their inimitability. Reservation systems pioneers in the airline industry couldn't be easily copied simply because at the time those systems were complex – they required advanced software techniques not available to every player in the industry (and even if they had been, they still would have had to be learned, through

the two bottom loops in Figure 8.2). More recently, a Savings Bank in Spain developed a system that allows to use its debit cards and ATM network to make ticket reservations for theatre or opera shows, sporting events, concerts, etc. For this purpose it developed, in a joint venture with a computer manufacturer, a special purpose ATM that displays complete theatre layouts to choose seats and so on. Owning part of the special purpose ATM design, this bank was able to impose delays in the machine becoming available to competitors, thus making its approach to the entertainment business distribution channel more difficult to imitate than it would had been otherwise. Introducing IT aspects in the classical competitors' analysis during strategy design is a way of identifying IT applications in this area.

- *Concentrate on IT applications with no clear strategically equivalent substitutes.* To the extent that the functionality of applications cannot be achieved by other means, IT contributes to the lack of substitution. One of the competitors of the Bank just mentioned tried to achieve the same functionality and also sell tickets at its branches, using its telecommunications network for seat reservation purposes. However, instead of basing it on automatic teller machines (ATMs), customers have to go to the counter, ask the clerk and wait for a layout of the theater to be printed out before being able to make their choices; they have to then tell it to the clerk, who makes the reservations and the corresponding payment – while other customers wait in line probably to make more mundane banking transactions (and maybe another customer at a different branch just took the tickets in the meantime!). It is unclear whether this Bank is competing effectively; some say that its approach is jeopardizing its banking business. Identifying IT applications in this area is, again, a matter of enriching strategic analysis and design with IT points of view.

All of these guidelines have strong implications for management practices in the IT field. An important one has to do with the background and training of the people involved. They should be aware of and fully understand not only the learning processes, but also the firm's organizational context, its business mission and competitive environment, and how individuals and groups behave when confronted with the different types of learning necessary to develop core capabilities. This is, we think, a direct consequent of IT permeating and affecting all activities in 'organizations (Zuboff, 1988; Scott-Morton, 1991). Appropriate management responses to this challenge can be consistently thought of and designed with the aid of the model presented in this paper.

Concluding remarks

We have drawn upon a stream of different research programs to address in a new way the by-now classic problem of how to make a better use of IT in business organizations. First, the resource-based view of the firm has been invoked to indicate that whatever we do, using a commodity resource such as IT, to increase a firm's competitiveness, must aim at transforming a standard resource into a firm's core capability. Second, a due consideration of the literature on organizational learning has helped us to build a structured model of this strategic transformation process. We have identified three different learning loops, that range from the concreteness of learning-by-doing to the strategic, and at times radical, reflection on the firm's capabilities, mission and environmental opportunities. Third, the recent theories of structuration have helped us in showing the continuous interplay between transformation, learning and context where these processes take place, and exploit their strategic relevance. Finally, the studies and cases of strategic information systems have shown how our learning-based model can actually be used to recount the spontaneous emergence of strategic IT applications and discuss the limits of their sustainability. Furthermore, the model suggests management actions and practical guidelines that can enhance the learning processes taking place in the organization, and hence make the transformation process more effective, by better embedding IT into the core capabilities of the organization.

We are firmly convinced that further research can lead to a new approach to design and develop IT applications geared to the dynamics and varied nature of organizational learning processes that take place within and across the firm's boundaries.

Notes

This chapter originally appeared in (1996) *Journal of Strategic Information Systems* **5**: 111–127.

1. Other definitions of the organizational routine concept have been proposed in the literature. Grant (1992), for example, defines them as regular and predictable patterns of activity which are made up of a sequence- of coordinated actions by individuals. Furthermore, they are conceived as dynamic entities that continuously evolve: Collis (1991), for example refers to dynamic routines as the managerial capability to improve and upgrade firm efficiency and effectiveness. See also Kogut and Zander (1992), and Lado *et al.* (1992).
2. A formative context is defined as the set of preexisting institutional arrangements, cognitive frames and imageries that actors bring and routinely enact in a situation of action (Ciborra and Lanzara, 1990). That groups are influenced by their organizational entourage is widely recognized – the parts of an organization'smemory that are relevant for organizational learning are those that constitute active memory – those that define what an organization pays attention to, how it chooses to act, what it chooses to remember from its experience (Kim, 1993).
3. The fact that this company has had trouble after its first very successful years is irrelevant for the argument that follows.

References

Amit, R. and Schoemaker, P.J.H. (1993). Strategic assets and organizational rent, *Strategic Management Journal* **14**: 33–46.

Andreu, R., Rica J.R. and Valor, J. (1992). *Information Systems Strategic Planning: A Source of Competitive Advantage*, Oxford: NCC Blackwell.

Argyris, C. (1993). *Knowledge for Action*, San Francisco, CA: Jossey-Bass.

Argyris, C. and Schön, D. (1978). *Organizational Learning: A Theory of Action Perspective*, Reading, MA: Addison-Wesley.

Ashby, W.R. (1954). *Design for a Brain: The Origin of Adaptive Behaviour*, London: Chapman and Hall.

Barney, J. (1991). Firm resources and sustained competitive advantage, *Journal of Management* **17**: 1.

Bourdieu, P. (1977). *Outline of a Theory of Practice*, Cambridge: Cambridge University Press.

Brown, J.S. and Duguid, P. (1991). Organizational learning and communities of practice: toward a unified view of working, learning and innovation, *Organization Science* **2**: 40–57.

Ciborra, C. (1992). From thinking to tinkering: the grassroots of strategic information systems, *The Information Society* **8**: 297–309.

Ciborra, C. (1994). The grassroots of IT and strategy, in C. Ciborra and T. Jelassi (eds) *Strategic Information Systems: A European Perspective*, Chichester: John Wiley and Sons.

Ciborra, C. and Lanzara, G.F. (1990). Designing dynamic artifacts: computer systems as formative contexts, in P. Galiardi (ed.) *Symbols and Artifacts*, Berlin: De Gruiter.

Collis, D. (1991). A resource-based analysis of global competition: the case of the bearings industry, *Strategic Management Journal* **12**: 49–68.

Dierickx, I. and Cool, K. (1989). Asset stock accumulation and sustainability of competitive advantage, *Management Science* **35**(12).

Dosi, G., Teece, D.J. and Winter, S. (1990). Towards a theory of corporate coherence: preliminary remarks, Mimeo, March.

Feeny, D. and Ives, B. (1989). In search of sustainability: reaping long term advantage from investments in information technology, *Journal of Management Information Systems* **7**(1): 27–46.

Callupe, R.B. and Cooper, W.H. (1993). Brainstorming electronically, *Sloan Management Review* Fall: 27–36.

Ghemawat, P. and Ricart, J.E. (1993). The organizational tension between static and dynamic efficiency, Research paper no. 255, IESE.

Giddens, A. (1984). *The Constitution of Society*, Berkeley, CA: California University Press.

Gongla, P., Sakamoto, G., Black-Hock, A., Goldweic, P., Ramos, L., Sprowls, R.C. and Kim, C.-K. (1989). SPARK: a knowledge-based system for identifying competitive uses of information technology, *IBM Systems Journal* **28**: 628–645.

Grant, R.M. (1992). *Contemporary Strategic Analysis: Concepts, Techniques, Applications*, Cambridge, MA: Basil Blackwell.

Hirschleifer, J. (1980). *Price Theory and Applications*, 2nd edition, Prentice-Hall: Englewood Cliffs, NJ.

INC. (1987). Mrs. Fields' Secret Ingredient, INC. Magazine, October.

Kim, D.H. (1993). The link between individual and organizational learning, *Sloan Management Review*, Fall.

Kogut, B. and Zander, U. (1992). Knowledge in the firm, combinative capabilities, and the replication of technology, *Organization Science* **13**.

Lado, A., Boyd, N.G. and Wright, P. (1992). A competency-based model of sustainable competitive advantage: towards a conceptual integration, *Journal of Management* **18**(1).

Leonard-Barton, D. (1992). Core capabilities and core rigidities: a paradox in managing new product development, *Strategic Management Journal* **13**: 11 l–125.

Lieberman, M. and Montgomery, D. (1988). First mover advantages, *Strategic Management Journal* **9**: 41–58.

Lippman, S. and Rumelt, R. (1982). Uncertain imitability: an analysis of interfirm difference in efficiency under competition, *Bell Journal of Economics*, pp. 418–438.

Montgomery, C.A. and Wernerfelt, B. (1988). Diversification, Ricardian rents, and Tobin's q, *RAND Journal of Economics* **19**(4).

Muiloz-Seca, B. and Riverola, J. (1994). The improvement dynamics: knowledge and knowledge generation. Technical note 0–694-044, IESE, February.

Nelson, R.R. and Winter, S.G. (1982). *An Evolutionary Theory of Economic Change*, Cambridge, MA: Belknap.

Orlikowski, W.I. (1992). The duality of technology: rethinking the concept of technology in organizations, *Organization Science* **3**(2): 398–427.

Penrose, E. (1959). *The Theory of the Growth of the Firm*, London: Basil Blackwell.

Scott-Morton, M.S. (ed.) (1991). *The Corporation of the 1990s: Information Technology and Organizational Transformation*, Oxford: Oxford University Press.

Short, J.E. and Venkatraman, N. (1992). Beyond business process redesign: redefining Baxter's business network, *Sloan Management Review*, Fall.

Smith, F. (1991). The distribution revolution: time flies at Federal Express, in J. Blackburn (ed.) *Time-Based Competition*, Irwin Business One.

Teece, D., Pisano, G. and Shuen, A. (1990). Firm capabilities, resources and the concept of corporate strategy, *Consortium on Competitiveness and Cooperation* W.P. # 90–9, University of California at Berkeley, Center for Research in Management, Berkeley, CA.

Tyre, A. and Orlikowski, W. (1993). Exploiting opportunities for technological improvement in organization, *Sloan Management Review*, Fall.

Zuboff, S. (1989). *In the Age of the Smart Machine*, New York: Basic Books.

9

From Thinking to Tinkering: The Grassroots of Strategic Information Systems*

Claudio U. Ciborra

Abstract

When building a Strategic Information System (SIS), it may not be economically sound for s firm to be an innovator through the strategic deployment of information technology. The decreasing costs of the technology and the power of imitation may quickly curtail any competitive advantage acquired through an SIS. On the other hand, the iron law of market competition prescribes that those who do not imitate superior solutions are driven out of business. This means that any successful SIS becomes a competitive necessity for every player in the industry. Tapping standard models of strategy analysis and data sources for industry analysis will lead to similar systems and enhance, rather than decrease, imitation. How then should 'true' SISs be developed? In order to avoid easy imitation, they should emerge from the grass roots of the organization, out of end-user hacking, computing, and tinkering. In this way the innovative SIS is going to be highly entrenched with the specific culture of the firm. Top management needs to appreciate local fluctuations in system practices as a repository of unique innovations and commit adequate resources to their development, even if they fly in the face of traditional approaches. Rather than looking for standard models in the business strategy literature, SISs should be looked for in the theory and practice of organizational learning and innovation, both incremental and radical.

Introduction

In order to follow the pioneering examples of American Airlines's SABRE, McKesson's Economost, and American Hospital Supply's ASAP, current prescriptions for designing a Strategic Information System (SIS) include obtaining top management awareness, and identifying and implementing applications that may generate competitive advantage. These systematic approaches are based on two main ingredients: a set of guidelines indicating how Information Technology

(IT) can support the business vis-à-vis the competition; and planning and implementation strategy (Bakos and Treacy 1986; Wiseman 1988; Ives and Learmonth 1984; Cash and Konsynki 1984; Porter and Millar 1985).

After the 1980s generated a wealth of 'how to build an SIS' recipes, the nineties have begun with a period of critical reflection (Hopper 1990). The systematic application of SIS design methodologies did not, in fact, yield a commensurate number of successful cases – at least not when measured against the pioneering technologies cited above. An intensive review of relevant empirical and theoretical literature suggests a number of reasons for these discrepancies.

- On the one hand, the theoretical literature emphasizes rational assessments of the firm and its environment by top management as the means to strategy formulation. It ignores alternative conceptions available in innovation literature that stress learning over thinking and value experimentation at the grass-roots level of an organization as a means to finding new directions.
- Similarly, a careful examination of precedent-setting SISs provides evidence of important roles for serendipity, reinvention, and other factors that are left out of account in the conventional approach to strategy development.

There are both empirical and theoretical grounds, then, for proposing new kinds of guidelines for SIS design. After issues associated with current SIS methodologies have surfaced and the assumptions on which they rest have been reviewed, a quite different approach is proposed and justified.

Consider the following questions raised by current conceptions of SIS design:

- Imitation has always been the driving force behind the diffusion of any technological innovation (Rosenberg, 1982). SIS represents no exception. However, if every major player in the industry adopts the same or similar SIS, any competitive advantage plainly evaporates. Systems that can be copied and built by a large number of firms, where no firms enjoy any distinctive or sustainable advantage in implementation, can only generate normal economic returns. In particular, small firms are at a special disadvantage in applying standard SIS planning approaches and solutions, in that they will find it very difficult to manipulate the industry structure to their advantage through the strategic use of IT.
- Some Inter-Organizational Systems (IOS) require the connection of all major firms in an industry, as is the case for Electronic Data Interchange. This undermines the competitive advantage such systems are supposed to offer the individual firm (Johnston and Vitale, 1988).
- More generally, the competitive analysis of markets and the identification of SIS applications can be purchased as research and consulting services (Barney, 1985a). They are carried out according to current frameworks, use standard data sources, and if performed professionally will reach similar results and systems.

It is not surprising, then, that business organizations should ask themselves:

- Does it really pay to be innovative?
- Are SISs offering true competitive advantage, or do they just represent a competitive necessity?
- How can a firm implement systems that are not easily copied, thus generating returns over a reasonable period of time?

In order to address such issues, researchers and consultants are finding new ways to develop SIS (Clemons, 1986; Feeny and Ives, 1989; Venkatraman and Short, 1990). Those efforts do not typically challenge the current assumptions about business strategy formulation and industry competition. They are likely to be thwarted by the paradox of micro-economics: competition tends to force standardization of solutions and equalization of production and coordination costs among participants. To be sure, all these dynamics unfold *unless* a firm's strategy is hard to copy (Barney, 1985a): the more difficult it is for other firms to imitate a successful SIS, the longer the firm can obtain a performance advantage.

We argue that the construction, or better the invention, of an SIS must be grounded on new foundations, both practically and conceptually. More specifically,

- To avoid easy imitation, the quest for an SIS must be based on unanalyzable, and even opaque, areas such as organizational culture. The investigation and enactment of unique sources of practice and know-how at the firm and industry level can be the source of sustained advantage.
- Developing an SIS is much closer to prototyping and to developing end users' ingenuity than has been realized (Brown and Duguid, 1989). In fact, many SIS have emerged out of plain hacking. The capability of integrating unique ideas and practical design solutions at the end-user level turns out to be more important than the adoption of structured approaches to systems development of industry analysis (Schön, 1979; Ciborra and Lanzara, 1990).

The paper investigates the dilemmas of building an SIS tracing them back to current views of strategic thinking and models of competition. Such theories and models are briefly reviewed in order to show that they represent just one possible approach, and that alternative venues need to be explored for more effective SIS design. A closer look at how some legendary SISs were originally introduced offers clues for a different approach based on organizational learning, both incremental and radical. New principles for SIS development are then set out and justified in more detail. Conclusions follow.

Questionable advantage

The rhetoric of SIS is based on a set of cases ranging from the early adopters such as McKesson (Clemons and Row, 1988), American Hospital Supply [now Baxter]

(Venkatraman and Short, 1990), and American Airlines (Copeland and McKenney, 1988) to companies that went bankrupt because they did not adopt an SIS, such as Frontier Airlines and People's Express. The argument in favor of SISs is backed by frameworks that indicate how to identify SIS applications: strategic thrusts (Wiseman, 1988); the value chain (Porter and Millar, 1985); the customer services life cycle (Ives and Learmonth, 1984); the strategic grid (McFarlan, 1984); electronic integration (Henderson and Venkatraman, 1989); and transaction costs (Ciborra, 1987; Malone *et al.*, 1987).[1]

Much less attention has been given to the problem of how an SIS can provide a significant or *sustainable* competitive advantage, so that a pioneering company can get a valuable performance edge extract from a strategic IT application. In fact, the widely cited SIS success stories often show that such systems provide only an ephemeral advantage, before being readily copied by competitors (Vitale, 1986).[2]

This contention is confirmed by empirical evidence on the patterns of diffusion of SISs.

A recent study of 36 major IOSs in different US industries shows that although the goals set by large corporations differed considerably (e.g., decreasing costs, electronic integration), the driving force for the introduction of such systems was that other firms in the same industry had similar applications (less than 75% of the cases); other systems were developed in collaboration with companies in the same industry (8%), while for another 8% they were individual initiatives soon to be copied by competitors. In sum, 'more than 92% of the systems studied follow industry wide trends. Only three systems are really original, but they will promptly imitated' (Brousseau, 1990).

As a consequence, aiming at sustainable advantage requires continuously generating innovative and competitive applications, and the successfully protecting that unique advantage over some time period. Feeny and Ives (1989) recommend, for example, that in order to reap a long-term advantage from investments in an SIS, a firm should carefully analyze the lead time required for competitors to develop a system similar to the one being considered and it should look for asymmetries in organizational structure, culture, size, etc., that may slow down the integration of the new SIS within competitors' organizations.

Although such suggestions are very valuable, they do not entirely avoid the dilemma faced by SIS design. For example, if it is possible for the innovator to employ a consulting service to identify specific forces that can keep followers and imitators at bay, the latter can always acquire consultants and services to help overcome those impediments. We claim, instead, that more effective tactics for SIS design will come from challenging the approaches to strategy formulation that characterized the SIS field of the 1980s.

Shifts in models of strategic thinking and competition

It is appropriate to begin by considering the rational perspective on *strategy formulation*, applied by authors such as Porter and Millar (1985), from the business strategy to current SIS issues. According to such a perspective, management should first engage in a purely cognitive process: through the appraisal of the environment, its threats and opportunities as well as the strengths and weaknesses of the organization, key success factors and distinctive competencies are identified; next, these are translated into a range of competitive strategy alternatives. There, once the optimal strategy has been selected, and laid out in sufficient detail, the implementation phase follows.

A perspective of this type can be found in most SIS models, such as the critical success factors (Rockart, 1979), the value chain (Porter and Millar, 1985), strategic thrusts (Wiseman, 1988), and sustainability analysis (Feeny and Ives, 1989). However, in everyday practice strategy formulation differs widely from what is implied by such prescriptions and assumptions. Incrementalism, muddling through, myopic, and evolutionary decision-making processes seem to prevail, even when there is a formal adherence to the principles outlined above. Structures tend to influence strategy formulation *before* they can be impacted by the new vision, and the de facto involvement of actors other than the chief executive officer is prevalent. Conflicts and double-bind situations may characterize the stage where strategies are conceived and put to work. Perhaps the most notable counterevidence is provided by the theory and practice of Japanese management, at the same time so successful and so distant from the analytic – even mechanistic – principles set out above (Nonaka, 1988a).

More generally, this school of thought can be questioned on three counts (Mintzberg, 1990):

1. *Making strategy explicit.* The rational bias for full, explicit articulation of strategy assumes, implicitly, that the environment is highly predictable and the unfolding of events is itself sequenced, to allow for an orderly process of formulation, design, and implementation. However, during implementation surprises often occur that call into question carefully developed plans (Bikson *et al.*, 1985). The need for continuous, opportunistic revisions clashes with the inflexibility of the formulation and implementation sequence.
2. *One-way relationship between strategy and structure.* In the conventional perspective, the strategist is regarded as an independent observer who can exercise judgement in a way that is removed from the everyday reality of the organization. For example, when evaluating strengths and weaknesses of the organization, or assessing the critical success factors, it is assumed that strategists can think and make choices outside of the influence of frames of reference, cultural biases, or ingrained, routinized ways of acting. Although a considerable body of research literature shows that such biases are at work in any decision-making process (Tversky and Kahneman, 1981), they are assumed away by the rationalist orientation of most approaches to strategic systems. Everyday life in organizations, on the other hand, shows that organizational structure, culture, inertia, and other endemic phenomena influence the strategy frormulation process, in addition to unexpected implementation outcomes (Weick 1979).
3. *Thinking vs. Learning.* Strategy formation tends to be seen as an intentional design process, rather than as the continuous acquisition of knowledge in

various forms, i.e., learning. We claim, on the other hand, that strategy formulation is often likely to involve elements of surprise or sudden, radical shifts in preference and goals, as well vicious circles that may stifle its development and implementation (Bateson, 1972; Argyris, 1982; Masuch, 1985). Hence, strategic decision making must be based on effective adaptation and learning (Fiol and Lyles, 1985; Levitt and March, 1988) – both incremental, trial-and-error learning, and radical, second-order learning (Argyris and Schön, 1978). Radical learning permits ways of seeing the environment, and commensurate views of the organization's strengths and weaknesses, to be continuously reshaped (Ciborra and Schneider, 1990).

It is appropriate next to consider *the models of competition* that are implicit in today's SIS frameworks. Most rely on theories of business strategy (Porter, 1980) derived from industrial organization economics (Bain, 1968). According to this school of thought, returns to firms are determined by the structure of the industry within which the firms operate. In order to achieve a competitive advantage, firms should manipulate the structural characteristics of the industry through IT – for instance, by creating barriers to entry, product differentiation, links with suppliers, and so on (Porter and Millar, 1985). However, as Barney (1985a) has noted in the field of strategy and Wiseman (1988) in the field of SIS, there are alternative conceptions of competition that may be relevant to SIS development.

One contrasting alternative is the theory of *monopolistic competition* put forward by Chamberlin (1933). In this view, firms are heterogeneous. They compete on the basis of certain resource and asset differences, such as technical know-how, reputation, ability for teamwork, organizational culture and skills, and other 'invisible assets' (Itami, 1987). Differences of these kinds will enable some firms to implement high return strategies. Competition then means cultivating unique strengths and capabilities, and defending them against imitation by other firms.

Another perspective on competition is Schumpeter's (1950), who sees it as a process linked to *innovation* in product, market, or technology. Innovation, in turn, is more the outcome of the capitalist process of creative destruction than the result of a strategic planning process. Ability at guessing, learning, and sheer luck appear in such a perspective to be key competitive factors (Barney, 1985).

It is noteworthy that Chamberlin's and Schumpeter's concepts of competition are consistent with the alternative models of strategy formulation depicted by Mintzberg in his critique of rational analytic approaches. More precisely, we can identify and contrast two different 'themes' in business strategy that can be applied to the SIS field. According to the first, strategy is formulated in advance, on the basis of an industry analysis; it consists of a series of moves that can be planned and subsequently implemented, to gain the second theme, strategy formulation is difficult to plan before the fact, and competitive advantage stems from exploiting the unique characteristics of the firm and unleashing its innovative capabilities.

Looking more closely at some well-known SIS applications suggests that there is a wide gap between the prevailing methodologies, close to the former theme, and business practice, definitely closer to the latter.

Reconsidering the empirical evidence

Four well-known SISs – Baxter's, ASAP, McKesson's Economost, American Airlines's SABRE, and the French Videotex named Télétel (better known by the name of the PTT terminals, Minitel) – will now be reconsidered for the light they can shed on these issues. At a closer look, such cases emphasize the discrepancy between ideal plans for an SIS and the realities of the implementation.

ASAP, the system launched by AHS Corporation and subsequently acquired by Baxter, started as an operational, localised response to a customer need (Venkatraman and Short, 1990). Because of difficulties in serving a hospital effectively, a manager of a local AHS office gave prepunched cards to the hospital's purchasing department; the ordering clerks could then transfer the information on the cards expeditiously through a phone terminal. From this local ad hoc solution to a particular problem, the idea gradually emerged of linking all the customer hospitals in the same way through touch-tone telephones, bar code readers, teletypes, and eventually Pcs. At a later stage, AHS management realized the positive impact such an electronic link with customers ould have on profits and was able to allocate adequate resources for its further development.

McKesson's Economost, another order-entry system, started in a similar way. The former IS manager admits that 'behind the legend' there was simply a local initiative by one of the business units. The system was not developed according to a company-wide strategic plan; rather, it was the outcome of what the French call *bricolage*, i.e., tinkering and serendipity. Interestingly, the conventional MIS unit was responsible not only for initial neglect of the new strategic applications with McKesson, but also, subsequently, for the slow pace of company-wide learning about McKesson's new information systems.

SABRE, the pioneering computerized reservation system built by American Airlines, was not originally conceived as a biased distribution channel to create entry barriers for competitors while tying in travel agents. In fact, it began as a relatively simple, inventory-management system addressing a specific need that had nothing to do with ensuring a competitive advantage. On the contrary, it was supposed to address an internal inefficiency: American's relative inability, compared to other airlines, to monitor the inventory of available seats and to attribute passenger names to booked seats (Hopper, 1990).

A last telling case, at national level, is represented by Minitel. One of the rare – if not the only – successful public Videotex systems in the world, it gives France a still unmatched competitive advantage in the *informatisation de la société* (Nora and Minc, 1978). Today there are 6.6 million terminals in French households and an average of 18 calls a month per owner.

The initial Minitel idea was not unique. Mainframes allow the creation of large centralized data bases, providing information that could be sold and accessed by a large number of customers using dumb terminals. Videotex systems promoted on this basis have failed both for early adopters (e.g., UK Prestel) and latecomers (e.g., the German Bundespost) that could have benefited from better technology, more careful planning, and the experiences of other PTTs. France Télécom (formerly,

Direction Générale des Télécommunications, or DGT) moved into Videotex relatively late. However, there were significant differences in the way the system was promoted to the general public. The vision of the *informatisation de la société* convinced the government to make the Minitel a success story through the diffusion of millions of free terminals. In fact, its free distribution is seen by observers and competitors as the critical success factor for French Videotex. This is only partially true. The free terminals were at the time a necessary condition for success (recall that the launching of Minitel occurred before the diffusion of the personal computer) but not a sufficient one. Nonetheless, at the beginning the use of Minitel was sluggish, probably for the same reason other Videotex systems never took off.

To be successful, the Minitel had to be different from other media; it had to be 'active'. In fact, the system also provided messaging capabilities, but was never promoted as a public email service by the DGT. Only because an act of hacking attracted the interest of the national press was this potential discovered and actualized by millions of users. During an experiment in Strasburg, when a local newspaper put its classified ads section on Videotex, a hacker – probably located at the sp unit of the newspaper itself – started using the Minitel to respond to the ads, establishing a direct, electronic dialogue with their authors. This was the beginning of the Minitel as an electronic mail system (*messagerie*) instead of just a system for accessing a data base (Marchand, 1987). At that point the number of terminals in homes turned out to constitute a critical mass, starting a virtual circle. For instance, the network created a new marketplace where many independent service companies could sell their services. Customers immediately used the 'new medium' – so much so that the national backbone packet switched network, Transpac, broke down due to overload. France Télécom was flexible and pragmatic enough to adapt the infrastructure technically and commercially to the new pattern of usage that had emerged outside the initial vision and plans; it moved 'from the logic of storage to the logic of traffic' (Schneider *et al.*, 1990).

The most frequently cited SIS successes of the 1980's, then, tell the same story. Innovative SISs are not fully designed top-down or introduced in one shot; rather, they are tried out through prototyping and tinkering. In contrast, strategy formulation and design take place in pre-existing cognitive frames and organizational contexts that usually prevent designers and sponsors from seeing and exploiting the potential for innovation.

New foundations for SIS design

The preceding discussion of the models of competition suggested that if an SIS application does not generate significant value, it may not be worth developing. And if it is easily imitated, it can only deliver a short-term, contestable advantage (Wiseman, 1988). The question is then, how to achieve uniqueness in SIS design – or at least a system difficult to emulate – if models of strategic thinking and competitive environments proposed in the 1980's are adequate?

We claim that the development of an SIS that can deliver a sustained competitive advantage must be treated as an innovation process (Takeuchi and Nonaka, 1986; Nonaka and Yamanaouchi, 1989). To innovate means to create new knowledge and resources, goals, tasks, markets, products, and processes. The skills and competencies available in a corporation represent at the same time sources and constraints for innovation (Prahalad and Hamel, 1990).

The creation of new knowledge can take place in two nonexclusive ways. The first is to rely on local information and routine behaviour, extending them gradually when coping with a new task (examples include learning by doing, incremental decision making, and muddling through). Accessing more diverse and distant information, when an adequate level of competence is *not* present, would instead lead to errors and further divergence from optimal performance (Heiner, 1983).

This approach requires allowing, and even encouraging tinkering by people close to the operational level so that they can combine and apply known tools and techniques to solve new problems. No general scheme or model is available; rather, local cues from a situation are trusted and exploited in a somewhat unreflective way, aiming at ad hoc solutions by heuristics rather than high theory. Systems like ASAP or the Minitel were developed in this way. Even when big plans were present, it was *bricolage* that led to the innovation. The value of tinkering lies in the fact that it keeps the development of an SIS close to the competencies of the organization and to the ongoing fluctuations in local practices.

The second route to new knowledge is to attack the competency gap directly, forging new competencies to emerge and consolidate. This is a process of radical learning that entails restructuring the cognitive and organizational backgrounds that give meaning to the practices, routines and skills at hand (Brown, 1991). This approach leads to new systems and arrangements, but not by 'random walks' or tinkering; at the opposite extreme, it intentionally challenges and smashes established routines in particular, it attacks day-to-day assumptions that define competence, learning by doing, and learning by trial and error. From this view point, designing an innovative SIS would involve more than market analysis, systems analysis, requirements specifications, and interest accommodation. Rather, it should deal primarily with the structures and frames within which such exercises take place, i.e., with shaping and restructuring the context of both business policy and systems development. Such a context can be surfaced and changed only by intervening in situations and designing-in-action (Schön, 1979; Ciborra and Lanzara, 1990).

Once a background context has been restructured-in-action, participants in the setting are free to devise new strategies and to look at both the environment and organizational capabilities in radically new ways. New strategic information and supporting systems can then be generated, based on the unique new worldview the designers and users are able to adopt. As an outcome, organizations and SIS should be very different from standard solutions and also very difficult to imitate, because they imply that competitors should abandon not only their old practices and conceptions, but also the contexts in which they routinely solve problems, run existing systems, and build new ones.

This accounts quite well for what has happened in the Minitel case. Even though its success is by now known to everybody, its imitation entails that other PTTs learn effectively, and abandon – or at least discuss – their entrenched beliefs about the function of Videotex, their role as monopolists, their current practices in conceiving and developing systems, and so on. Rather than questioning such beliefs and the host of arrangements that support them, they have reacted in a defensive way. They prefer to find reasons to explain away the Minitel success. For example, they cite the free terminals as the key success factor, forgetting that in most industrialised countries today there is a sufficient installed base of PCs that would make free distribution of terminals almost superfluous. Or they suggest that a crucial role is played by pink email, even though the latest statistics show that the *messagerie rose* has been only a temporary, though important, use of the system.[3] These explanations reflecting old competencies in fact support skilled incompetence (Argyris, 1982) in a way that undermines real commitment to innovation by the various European PTTs and keeps them attached to the status quo.

SIS planning by oxymorons

How can we translate the theoretical reflections just presented into practical guidelines for action? What is required is a novel approach to technological and organizational innovation in a rapidly changing context (Brown, 1991; Bikson and Eveland, 1989; Hedberg and Jonsson, 1978). A way to generate continuously innovative SIS designs is to proceed by moves that may appear to the current wisdom as oxymorons. Along this route, gaining new knowledge does not entail following a procedure or actuating a plan, but fusing opposites in practice and exposed to the mismatches that are bound to occur (Sabel, 1990). We identify seven oxymorons as alternative 'planning' guidelines that can increase organizational skill in developing an SIS. The first four oxymorons are aimed at transforming *bricolage* and learning-by-doing into activities that increase the probability of 'stumbling upon' SIS applications.[4] The other three set the conditions for radical learning and innovation. To bolster incremental learning,

1. *Value* bricolage *strategically*. The more volatile the markets and the technologies, the more likely it is that effective solutions will be embedded in everyday experience and local knowledge. This is the Petri dish for tinkering; here creative applications that have strategic impact will be invented, engineered, and tried out
2. *Design tinkering*. Activities, settings and systems have to be arranged so that invention and prototyping by end-users can flourish, together with open experimentation. It requires setting up organizational arrangements that favour local innovation, such as entrepreneurship or ad hoc project teams (Nonaka, 1988). Ethnographic studies of systems and practices, and design processes that are linked to the local idiosyncrasies of actors, settings and circumstances (Suchman, 1987; Zuboff, 1988) are most likely to succeed.

3. *Establish systematic serendipity.* In open experimentation, designs are largely incomplete, while implementation and refinement intermingle constantly. Conception and execution tend to be concurrent or simultaneous rather than sequential. This is an ideal context for serendipity to emerge and lead to unexpected solutions.
4. *Thrive on gradual breakthroughs.* In such a fluctuating environment, ideas and solutions are bound to emerge that do not square with established organizational routines: deviations, incongruencies, and mismatches will populate the design and development agenda. This is the raw material for innovation; management should appreciate and learn about such emerging practices.

Finally, to establish the preconditions for radical learning and innovation:

1. *Practice unskilled learning.* If incremental learning takes place within existing cognitive and organizational arrangements and does not challenge them, it is condemned to provide solutions that are not innovative. The cognitive and organizational structures that support learning can be challenged by actions, but this may lead to 'incompetent' behaviour, as assessed in relation to old routines. On the other hand, management should value such behaviour as an attempt to unlearn old ways of thinking and doing – one that may lead to new perspectives from which to look at resources, actions and systems (Penrose, 1959).
2. *Strive for failure.* Striving for excellence usually suggests that a firm should do better what it already knows how to do. Such behaviour paves the way for routinized, though efficient, systems (the competency trap). Creative reflection over failures can indicate instead the road to novel ideas, designs and implementations as well as the recognition of discontinuities and flex points.
3. *Achieve collaborative inimitability.* In order to achieve uniqueness or emulation difficulty, do not be afraid to collaborate even with competitors in developing SISs, i.e., to expose the organization to new cultures and ideas, or improve the skills of 'learning by intrusion' (Nonaka, 1988a), and to find clues for new, significant changes in the most obvious routines of another organization.

These seven oxymorons can represent a new 'systematic' approach for the establishment of an organizational environment where new information – and thus new systems – can be generated. Precisely because they are paradoxical, they can unfreeze existing routines, cognitive frames and behaviours; they favour learning over monitoring and innovation over control.

Conclusions

Our inquiry into models and methodologies for SISs supports the hard lesson learned by a practitioner, Max D. Hopper, director of American Airlines' SABRE reservation systems. The era of the conventional SIS is over. Worse, it is dangerous to believe that an information system can provide an enduring business advantage. In brief, it is high time to realize that 'the old models no longer apply' (Hopper, 1990).

In our perspective, the strategic application of IT can be the result of tinkering, or *bricolage*; this is how new ideas from the bottom of the organization bubble up. Or it can be the outcome of an act of radical innovation, where the existing organizational reality, its environment, and IT applications are seen in a new light by the members. In the latter case SISs are intimately associated with business renewal.

The new challenge is to harness IT to tap the core competencies of the corporation, creating new information and knowledge (Nonaka, 1988). If firms can build similar platforms and access the same data, then the competitive advantage related to IT can only come from *cognitive and organizational capabilities* for converting such data into practical knowledge for action. SIS applications are most likely to develop close to –and to serve – the grass roots of the organization, where its core competencies and skills are daily deployed and perfected.

To forestall objections that these approaches may have been too hastily dismissed, I should underscore that my own work on transaction cost analysis is included in this critique. A more detailed version of the paper, with a more thorough view of difficulties inherent in rational approaches in SIS planning, is available from the author on request.

Acknowledgements

Acknowledgements to Tora Bikson, Charles Wiseman, Chris Argyris, Roger Clarke, and the members of the Sisnet group.

Notes

This chapter originally appeared in (1992) *The Information Society* 8: 297–309.

1. It would be beyond the scope of this paper to review in detail these rational frameworks for identifying strategic applications.
2. A 'strategic' system is regarded, for purposes of this paper, as one that confers a unique, sustainable, or otherwise significant performance advantage. Systems that are competitive necessities or that provide only small or short-term improvements are not viewed as 'strategic' developments, however important they may be to a firm's operation. For further discussion of this point, readers are encouraged to consult the collection of articles in Boynton and Zmud (1990).
3. A similar transitional role was played by 'adult films' in the diffusion of VCRs and videocassettes and the growth of related businesses (e.g., video rental services) in the U.S.
4. Such transformations can afford significant potential for innovative SIS development for most organizations since their main prerequisite is only that mission-oriented operations be recognized and given room to move.

References

Argyris, C. (1982). *Reasoning, Learning and Action.* San Francisco: Jossey-Bass.
Argyris, C. and Schön, D.A., (1978). *Organizational Learning: A Theory of Action Perspective,* Reading, MA: Addison-Wesley.

Bain, J.S. and Treacy, M.E. (1986). Information Technology and Corporate Strategy: A research Perspective, *MIS Quarterly,* June: 107–119.

Barney, J.B. (1985). A Framework for Evaluating Strategic Option. Mimeo, *GSM,* UCLA, Winter.

Barney, J.B. (1985a). Types of Competition and the Theory of Strategy: Towards an Integrative Framework. *GSM,* UCLA, Spring.

Bateson, G., (1972). *Steps to an Ecology of Mind,* New York: Ballantine.

Bikson, T.M. and Eveland, J.D. (1989). Technology Transfer as a Framework for Understanding Social Impacts of Computerization, in M.J. Smith and G. Salvendy (eds) *Work with Computers: Organizational Management, Stress, and Health Aspects,* Amsterdam: Elsevier Science Publishers, pp. 28–37.

Bikson, T.K., Stasz, C. and Mankin, D. (1985). Computer Mediated Work: Individual and Organizational Impact in One Corporate Headquarters. The RAND Corporation, R-3308, OTA, Santa Monica, CA.

Brousseau, E. (1990). Information Technologies and Inter-firm Relationships: The Spread of Interorganizational Telematic Systems and its Impacts on Economic Structures. *Proceedings Eighth International Telecommunications Conference,* Venice, March.

Brown, J.S. (1991). Research that Reinvents the Corporation, *Harvard Business Review,* January–February: 102–111.

Brown, J.S. and Duguid, P. (1989). Learning and Improvisation: Local sources of Global Innovation, Mimeo, *Xerox Parc.*

Cash, J.I. and Konsynski, B. (1985). IS Redraws Competitive Boundaries. *Harvard Business Review* **63**(2): 134–142.

Chamberlin, E.N. (1933). *The Theory of Monopolistic Competition,* Cambridge: Harvard University Press.

Ciborra, C.U. (1987). Reframing the Role of Computers in Organizations: The Transactions Costs Approach, *Office Technology and People* **3**: 17–38.

Ciborra, C.U., and Lanzara, G.F. (1990). Designing Dynamic Artifacts: Computer Systems as Formative Contexts, in P. Gagliardi (ed.) *Symbols and Artifacts: Views of the Corporate Landscape,* Berlin: De Gruyter.

Ciborra, C.U. and Schneider, L. (1990). Transforming the Routines and Contexts of Management, Work and Technology, *Proceedings of the Conference on Technology and the Future of Work,* Stanford University School of Engineering, March.

Clemons, E. K. (1986). Information Systems for Sustainable Competitive Advantage, *Information & Management,* November: 131–136.

Clemons, E. K. and Row, M. (1988). McKesson Drug Company: A Case Study of Economost: A Strategic Information System, *Journal of Management Information Systems* **5**(1): 3650.

Copeland, D.G. and McKenney, J.L. (1988). Airline Reservation Systems: Lessons from History, *MIS Quarterly* **12**(3): 353–370.

Feeny, D. and Ives, B. (1989). In Search of Sustainability: Reaping Long Term Advantage from Investments in Information Technology. Mimeo, Oxford Center for Development Studies.

Fiol, C. M. and Lyles, M.A. (1985). Organizational Learning, *Academy of Management Review* **10**(4): 803–813.

Hedberg, B. and Jonsson, S. (1978). Designing Semi-Confusing Information Systems for Organizations in Changing Environments, *Accounting, Organizations and Society* **3**(1): 47–64.

Heiner, R. (1983). The Origin of Predictable Behaviour, *American Economic Review* **73**: 560–595.

Henderson, J.C. and Venkatraman, N. (1989). Strategic Alignment: A Process Model for Integrating Information Technology and Business Strategies, *MIT – Sloan Working Paper,* pp. 3086–3089.

Hopper, M.D. (1990). Rattling SABRE: New Ways to Compete on Information, *Harvard Business Review* **68**(3): 118–125.

Itami, H. (1987). *Mobilizing Invisible Assets,* Cambridge: Harvard University Press.

Ives, B., and Learmonth, G.P. (1984). The Information System as a Competitive Weapon, *Communications of the ACM* **27**(12): 1193–1201.

Johnston, H.R. and Vitale, M.R. (1988). Creating Competitive Advantage with Interorganizational Information Systems, *MIS Quarterly,* June: 153–165.

Levitt, B. and March, J.G. (198). Organizational Learning, *Annual Review of Sociology* 14: 319–340.

Malone, T.W., Yates, J. and Benjamin, R.I. (1987). Electronic Markets and Electronic Hierarchies, *Communications of the ACM* **30**(6): 484–497.

Marchand, M. (1987). *Le Paradis Informationelle,* Paris: Masson.

Masuch, M. (1985). Vicious Circles in Organizations, *Administrative Science Quarterly* **30**: 1433.

McFarlan, W.F. (1984). Information Technology Changes the Way You Compete, *Harvard Business Review* **62**(3): 98–103.

Mintzberg, H. (1990). The Design School: Reconsidering the Basic Premises of Strategic Management, *Strategic Management Journal* **11**: 171–195.

Nonaka, I. (1988). Toward Middle-Up-Down Management: Accelerating Information Creation, *Sloan Management Review* **29**(3): 9–18.

Nonaka, I. (1988a). Creating Organizational Order out of Chaos: Self-Renewal in Japanese Firms, *California Management Review* **30**(3): 57–73.

Nonaka, I. and Yamanouchi, T. (1989). Managing Innovation as a Self-Renewing Process, *Journal of Business Venturing* **4**: 299–315.

Nora, S. and Minc, A. (1978). *L'Informatisation de la societe,* Paris: La Documentation Francaise.

Penrose, E. (1959). *The Theory of Growth of the Firm,* New York: Wiley.

Porter, M. (1980). *Competitive Strategy,* New York: The Free Press.

Porter, M.E. and Millar, V.E. (1985). How Information Gives You Competitive Advantage, *Harvard Business Review* **63**(4): 149–160.

Prahalad, C.K. and Hamel, G. (1990). The Core Competence of the Corporation, *Harvard Business Review* **68**(3): 79–93.

Rockart, J.F. (1979). Chief Executives Define Their Own Data Needs, *Harvard Business Review* **57**(2): 81–93.

Rosenberg, N. (1982). *Inside the Black Box: Technology and Economics,* Cambridge: Cambridge University Press.

Sabel, C. (1990). Studied Trust: Building New Forms of Cooperation in a Volatile Economy, *ILO Conference on Industrial Districts and Local Economic Regeneration,* Geneva, October.

Schön, D.A. (1979). *The Reflective Practitioner,* New York: Basic Books.

Schneider, V., Charon, J.M., Miles, Thomas, G. and Vedel, T. (1990). The Dynamics of Videotex Development in Britain, France, and Germany: A Cross-National Comparison, *Proceedings Eighth International Conference of the International Telecommunications Society,* Venice, March.

Schumpeter, J.A. (1950). *Capitalism, Socialism and Democracy,* 3rd Edition, New York: Harper & Row.

Suchman, L. (1987). *Plans and Situated Actions: The Problem of Human-Machine Communication,* Cambridge: Cambridge University Press.

Takeuchi, H. and Nonaka, I. (1986). The New New Product Development Game, *Harvard Business Review* **64**(1): 137–146.

Tversky, A. and Kahneman, D. (1981). The Framing of Decisions and the Psychology of Choice, *Science* **221**: 453–458.

Venkatraman, N. and Short, J.E. (1990). Strategies for Electronic Integration: From Order-Entry to Value-Added Partnerships at Baxter, *MIT-Sloan School Working Paper,* Mimeo.

Vitale, M. (1986). The Growing Risks of Information Systems Success, *MIS Quarterly* **10**(4): 327–334.
Weick, K.E. (1979). *The Social Psychology of Organizing,* 2nd Edition, New York: Random House.
Wiseman, C. (1988). *Strategic Information Systems,* Homewood, IL: Irwin.
Zuboff, S. (1988). *In the Age of the Smart Machine: The Future of Work and Power,* New York: Basic Books.

10

Reframing the Role of Computers in Organizations: The Transactions Costs Approach*

Claudio U. Ciborra

Summary

The traditional role of computer-based information systems is to provide support for individual decision making. According to this model, information is to be seen as a valuable resource for the decision maker faced with a complex task. Such a view of information systems in organizations does however fail to include such phenomena as the daily use of information for misrepresentation purposes. The conventional systems analysis methods, whether they are data- or decision-oriented, do not help in understanding the nature of organizations and their ways of processing information. The paper proposes what appears to be a more realistic approach to the analysis and design of information systems. Organizations are seen as networks of contracts which govern exchange transactions between members having only partially overlapping goals. Conflict of interests is explicitly admitted to be a factor affecting information and exchange costs. Information technology is seen as a means to streamline exchange transactions, thus enabling economic organizations to operate more efficiently. Examples are given of MIS, data base and office automation systems, where both the organization and its information system were jointly designed. These examples illustrate the power of the approach, which is based on recent research in the new institutional economics.

Introduction

Despite the confidence of many in the relentless advancement of computer-based information systems, as witnessed by such innovations a Decision Support Systems, Distributed Data Bases, Expert Systems, Office Automation and suchlike, critics object that 'Management Information Systems above the level of simple counting and comparing fail because theory is missing to make them work' (Wildavsky, 1983).

This is a recent example of sceptical comments on how computers are misapplied in organizations; the earliest criticisms stem from twenty years ago with scholars such as Ackoff (1967), who stated: 'I believe that these near and far misses in MIS implementation could have been avoided if certain false (and usually implicit) assumptions on which many such systems have been erected had not been made'.

Even among users, i.e. those who actually operate in organizations and deal daily with the small- and large-scale problems arising from the introduction of computers (conflicts, hidden resistance, lack of integration, skyrocketing development costs, education problems, to name a few), there is a growing awareness that theory and practice are still at the mercy of events.

It would however be unfair to suggest that practitioners just muddle through when analysing and designing systems. On the contrary, the current state of the art is dominated by a conventional wisdom, which is composed of a comparatively long-standing set of assumptions and frames which seem to guide the practical theories of actions of designers. It is this conventional wisdom which must be explored: its concepts, views and stereotypes must be critically examined and reframed, in order to improve our understanding of such basic issues as:

- Why and how is information processed and communicated within and between organizations?
- What impact does information technology have on organizational processes and structures?
- What organizational models can guarantee that systems analysis and design are sound and effective?

Present-day designers turn to two theories when addressing the above issues: they either tend to a 'data view' of organizations, or, in the case of those most influenced by business needs, to a decision-making view. These two ways of looking at the problems of computerization are so widely accepted and have been so much taken for granted that they can be said to form the conventional wisdom of today. The origins of the former can be traced directly back to the EDP field, while the latter stem from the influential work of Herbert A. Simon (1976a).

It is somewhat surprising that although information technology has gone through an almost revolutionary process of miniaturization, sophistication and diffusion, the design models and criteria concerning its application in organizations are still based on concepts of the early sixties. This appears still more puzzling when we examine the fields of sociology, political science, organization theory, economics of information and organizations, which have also undergone a sharp innovative process. But none of the new developments in these disciplines seems to have filtered through to the field of data processing, apart from such aspects as the political view of system development (Keen, 1981; Kling, 1980; Markus, 1983).

The aim of this paper is to open the MIS and office automation disciplines to recent developments in social sciences and economics. The ultimate goal is to define both a new framework and a new language, so that the role of information technology in organizations can be better understood. To anticipate, it is argued that a new organizational understanding of information processing must be beyond the individual decision-making paradigm, which at present lies at the core of the conventional wisdom. The concepts of 'exchange' (transaction)[1] and 'contract' between at least two individuals or organizational units must become the new center of attention. This alternative tact enables us to use the results of a new paradigm emerging both in institutional economics and the sociology of organizations. The paradigm, known as the transaction cost approach (Williamson, 1975, 1981), links the notions of information, uncertainly and organization in an original way. Phenomena such as resistance to change, retention of information are not seen anymore as irrational, unexpected flaws in a structured system design, but as factors and behaviours which can be rationally understood and carefully anticipated; and issues such as centralization versus decentralization can be viewed in a different light. The presentation of the argument starts in Section 2 with a critique of the received tradition and its implicit, but widespread assumptions: it is shown that the data- and decision-making views are inadequate and unrealistic, because they are based on a view of organizations as perfectly cooperative systems. The need for an alternative framework based on the new institutional economics is addressed in Section 3: it is shown that by considering organizations as networks of exchanges and contracts between members, both cooperation and conflict can be taken into account together with the various usages of information that individuals employ when cooperating and conflicting. Also, the specific role of information technology is illustrated as a means to lower transaction costs. In Section 4 the new design principles are discussed using examples drawn from the field of data bases, office automation and MIS. The concluding remarks concern the further research paths opened up by the new framework.

A critique of the conventional wisdom

Two current views

In order to reframe our understanding of computer-based information systems in organizations, an essential, preliminary step is to discuss two approaches which are at present in good currency: the data approach and the decision approach. According to the data approach, in applying a computer to an organization it is only necessary to consider (i.e. analyze and design) the data flows and files in that organization. The analyst ascertains management information requirements by examining all reports, files and other information sources currently used by managers. The set of data thus obtained is considered to be the information which management needs to computerize (Davis and Munro, 1977). The data approach ignores the economic and social nature of organizations and is exposed to the hazards of those economic and social processes which characterize the daily life of organizations and which we, as members of organizations, all know (see below).

The second tradition is more sophisticated from an organizational point of view. It can be traced back to Simon (1977) and was further developed by scholars such as

Galbraith (1977) and Keen and Scott Morton (1978). According to this approach, information technology is support to *decision making*. Managers facing complex tasks and environments use information in order to reduce the uncertainty associated with decision making: 'the greater the task uncertainty, the greater the amount of information that must be processed among decision makers during task execution in order to achieve a given level of performance', states Galbraith (1977). Simon writes in a similar vein about programmable and unprogrammable decisions (Simon, 1977) (see also for applications: Ackoff, 1967; Keen and Scott Morton, 1978; Sprague, 1980; Pava, 1982; Huber, 1984).

It could be argued that diffusion of communication and data processing technology poses some limits to the scope of the decision-making view, which emphasizes control and feedback rather than communication processes. But, of greater interest here are some puzzling organizational phenomena which challenge that view and invite the suspicion that it is incomplete. Consider the following evidence by scholars in the field of organizations:

- Information is gathered and taken into account only after the decision has been already made, that is to say, as *a posteriori* rationalization (many computer print-outs are used as high-tech cosmetics to already made resolutions).
- Much of the information gathered in response to requests is not considered in the making of those decisions for which the information is requested (Feldman and March, 1981).
- Most of the information generated and processed in organizations is open to misrepresentation, since it is gathered and communicated in a context where the various interests conflict.
- When, on the other hand, organizations are informationally transparent, as many DP specialists wish, it has been shown that decision makers in two different departments, say Production and Sales, could be playing never-ending information games which lead to overall suboptimality (Ackoff, 1967).
- Information is not only used as an input for the individual decision maker, but is also used to persuade and induce the receiver to action. It could indeed be argued that this use of communication is the essence of authority and management (Flores and Ludlow, 1981).

Thus information is not simply interpreted data, rather it is an argument to convince other decision makers. To be effective it must have attributes other than exactness, clarity, etc.: rather than being purely objective, it must be convincing and adequate to the situation at hand.

Flaws in the decision-making view

We now turn to an analysis of the reasons why the conventional decision-making view cannot explain phenomena such as those just described:

Firstly, the decision-making approach tends to be individualistic. Decision-oriented design strategies focus on the information needs and cognitive styles of the individual decision maker facing a complex and uncertain task. Take, for example, Rockart's design method based on the analysis of the Critical Success Factors, which stresses 'the investigation of current information needs of individual managers' (Rockart, 1979). While it is worth investigating the role that computers play in individual problem solving, a manager in a particular organization cannot be seen as a solo chess player whose only opponents are the 'technology', a 'random environment' or 'nature'. In organizations the key issue is collective, coordinative problem solving (Schelling, 1980; Turoff and Hiltz, 1982). Though this obvious consideration is beginning to make its way in the recent DDS literature, few practical suggestions are provided regarding its implications in systems analysis and design (Sprague, 1980; De Sanctis and Gallupe, 1985).

Secondly, the decision-making control model ignores the fact that organizations are mixtures of cooperation and conflict between participants; its implicit reference is in fact to man-made machine systems (Simon, 1977). When dealing with collective problem solving, the model assumes that all the participants share common goals (i.e. a team, Marschak and Radner, 1972): information problems related to task execution and coordination are once again considered to be caused by environmental or technological uncertainty only. It is, however, more realistic to say that all coordinative problem solving and the relevant information processing take place in a mixed-interest context (Figure 10.1). A minimal respect for the well known conflictual processes existing in organizations would indicate that there are other incentives to gather and use information, apart from task uncertainty: information can be misrepresented; promises and commitments can be false; data incomplete; tracks covered etc., all in order to induce others to make decisions most benefiting us in the first place. Or, another possibility is that information can be selectively disclosed to persuade and bias; what this means is that it can be used as an instrument of power to win or gain a better position in the daily organizational games.

The upshot is that in collective coordination and action there is a distinct form of uncertainty besides that characterizing the task, the technology or the environment:

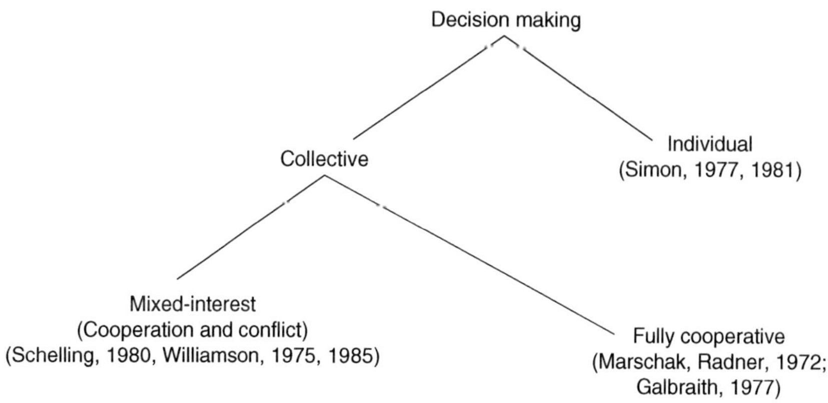

Figure 10.1 Types of decision making models

it is an uncertainty of behavioural, strategic nature, which has its origins in the conflict of interests between organization members. The information which the decision maker receives or gathers both within and outside the organization, may well be 'unreliable' with the result that he/she has to perform a surplus of information processing in order to evaluate its reliability. The fact that it is obtained from human sources means that it cannot be trusted a priori. It can therefore be stated that in an organization at least half of the on-going information processing is dedicated to the solution of tasks and problems by cooperative means, while the other half is concerned with solving problems of cooperation among members who behave opportunistically.

To analyze information requirements and design a system without considering the inevitable opportunistic information processing which takes place in organizations appears to be risky. System implementation can lead to conflict, resistance, and other negative attitudes which, far from being irrational, represent the members' response to the attempt of changing the way of producing and using information in a mixed-interest organizational setting (Markus, 1983).

Thirdly, the conventional wisdom is one-dimensional: it takes hierarchical organizations for granted, thus ignoring many important facets of the economics of organizing. For example, it must be remembered that the boundary and structure of an organization are not indefinitely fixed: they change every time a manager implements a make-or-buy decision, or he/she decides to integrate or disintegrate a stage of the production process, an office or a department. Moreover, it is insufficient to consider large pyramidal corporations only, since regional networks of small firms, which are even more diffuse, operate in a manner more like a peer group, or family, than a formal bureaucracy (Piore and Sabel, 1984). And even within large corporations changes take place at the shop-floor level, where work groups are being introduced at the expense of formal hierarchies. All these developments, which stem from the effort of organizations to respond to the turbulence of the environment, challenge the approach which identifies management and information systems with hierarchies (Simon, 1981; Arrow, 1974). It is in fact time to acknowledge that many systems, including airline reservation, EFT, remote office work, etc. have little to do with the workings of organizations conceived as pyramids of strategic, managerial and operational control systems. They must rather be seen as exchange or market support systems, in that they support market transactions and not procedures of a hierarchy.

Finally, even recent amendments to the conventional wisdom leave contradictions unresolved. Consider the introduction of computers in organizations. At present this process tends to be regarded as a bargaining process between conflicting parties: the decision-making taking place during system implementation is looked at from a political perspective (Keen, 1981; Markus, 1983). However, even these very authors, when considering a specific managerial decision for automation (for example a DSS for budgeting), switch the analysis framework back to the conventional wisdom: the decision maker is seen as a component of a control system, where the system is uncertain and complex, and factual information is needed to keep it under control (Keen and Scott Morton, 1978). How can one agree with such a contradictory treatment of two organizational processes, the implementation of a system and the use of information for managerial decision making? If the former is a bundle of political decisions, why should the latter represent a neutral, purely algorithmic exception? To be sure, the political view of system implementation has had the merit of breaking the ice and showing that, in certain cases at least, organizations cannot be analyzed and changed by using frameworks exclusively derived from systems theory and computer science, but what they in fact require are investigation and design methods which consider political, economic and sociological phenomena.

A transactional view of organizations and their information systems

Economic organizations: markets, hierarchies and groups

It is a tenet of this paper that the processes involved in socioeconomic organizations cannot be analyzed correctly unless formal systems analysis methodologies, such as HIPO, BSP, SADT, or other structured analysis techniques (see Couger *et al.*, 1982), are grounded on an understanding of the nature of organizations and of the way computers can be fitted to support their effectiveness. If we take the field of economic organizations, which is to say firma operating on a market, I argue that the classic answer provided by Coase (1937) to the fundamental question 'Why are there firms and markets?' is of the greatest interest to the whole field of MIS and office automation.

A market is an assemblage of persons desirous of exchanging property, with prices serving both as incentives and coordinating guides to producers in so far as they affect what and how much is produced and demanded. At an equilibrium free-market price the amount produced equals the amount demanded – *with no necessity for a central all-knowing authority.* Individual self interest, an incentive to obtain greater gains together with lower costs, is what permits resources to be efficiently allocated. Note that the market system requires very *little knowledge* of the participants, i.e. their own needs and prices (Alchian and Allen, 1977). The same problems of economic organization, i.e. the control and coordination of diverse, specialized activities, are solved differently in a *hierarch*y or the firm. In a firm, market transactions are eliminated and in their place we find an entrepreneur-coordinator who is *the authority* who directs production (Coase, 1937). Markets and firms are thus substitutes and the replacement of one by the other is a common event. Think again of any make-or-buy decision. A market contract displaces a bureaucratic contract when a travel agency replaces its ticket delivery person with a messenger service. A hierarchy supplants a market when a firm begins photocopying its own circulars rather than paying for the services of a printer (Hess, 1983).

Given the case with which an economic system, with its essential functions of coordination and control, can flow from market to hierarchical organization and back, it should be clear that there is a need for a framework for defining the special role of computer-based information systems in such a diverse organizational context. If systems do in fact support organizational control and coordination mechanisms, what mechanism should they specifically support, the price or the authority relation? In what circumstances should they switch from one to the other, and what criteria are there to tell whether systems are supporting the 'right', i.e. more efficient mechanism? A tentative answer to these questions is the following (Williamson, 1975):

- When transactions are fairly well patterned, the services or products to be exchanged are fairly standardized, and all participants possess the relevant information, i.e. the price, then the perfect *market* is the most efficient resource-saving way of organizing the division of labour with each person producing a service or product and selling it on a market, where he/she can also buy the necessary inputs: the 'invisible hand' (Smith, 1776) coordinates the individual decisions of producing, buying and selling among a large number of independent agents.
- In some contingencies, however, the use of the price mechanism involves costs, prices must be discussed, transactions encounter difficulties due to the complex search for partners; the contract model specifying the terms of exchange is difficult to develop and it is costly to control *ex post facto* the execution of the contract. If the product/service exchange is complex and the transaction uncertain due to a conflict of interests, it can be better, or rather more efficient to avail of organizing agents within the *firm* to mediate economic transactions, rather than to trust entirely to the market mechanism. In this case the 'invisible hand' of the market is replaced by the 'visible hand' of management (Chandler, 1977).[2]
- Finally, there are situations where coordination can neither take place through a market nor through a hierarchically organized form: products and services are so complex, transactions so ambiguous that the parties involved in the exchanges have to trust each other and give up any attempt at a short-sighted calculation of the reciprocal costs and benefits accruing from the exchange. The 'invisible' and 'visible' hands are replaced by the 'invisible handshaking' (Okun, 1981). The organizational arrangement whereby networks of exchanges are governed in a stable manner by informal relationships of trust, has been called a *group* or *clan* (Ouchi, 1980).

Remember that, in general, the obstacles to transacting, justifying the use of the three alternative arrangements, stem from two distinct sources: one is *natural uncertainty* (the product/service is complex and unique, difficult to evaluate and price; there are barriers to communication during the exchange, etc.); the other is *behavioural* or *strategic uncertainty,* which originates out of the joint effect of informational asymmetries and lack of trust between the parties. To sum up, if the world was certain to evolve according to one pattern only, the coordination of activities could easily be streamlined. If people could fully agree, cooperation would be smoothly achieved even in an uncertain and complex world. But when uncertainty, complexity, information, asymmetries and lack of trust cannot be ruled out *a priori,* then the multitude of contingencies which affect work in organizations may require the negotiation of complicated contractual plans to arrange cooperation. Depending upon the degrees of ambiguity in the service or product object of exchange and the goal congruence among the parties, the three arrangements: the market, the hierarchical firm and the clan or group, are the most efficient organizational mechanisms for solving the fundamental problems of organizing.

Information systems

Galbraith's (1977) hypothesis can now be enlarged, if it is to totally comprehend what goes on in organizations. The more complex cooperation and bargaining are, not only because of the uncertainty of the product/service to be produced and exchanged, but also because of the hazards of opportunism, the more difficult it is to achieve a contract to regulate cooperation and exchange, and the more information has to be processed in order to set up and maintain the organizational relationships between contracting members.

Having thus linked the notion of information within organizations to those of uncertainty and opportunism (lack of trust among cooperators), we are now able to reframe the concept of 'information system'. If we look at organizations as networks of exchanges, information systems, whether they be computer-based or not, are made up of networks of information flows and files needed to create, set up, control and maintain the organization's network of exchanges and relevant contracts. Obviously, an information system will prove to be contingent upon the nature of the organization to which it belongs.

In a *perfect market* where coordination and control are achieved through the price mechanism and spot contracting, the information system is highly standardized, formalized, a-procedural, responsive and extremely simple: the *price* is the only input needed to support members of the market make basic decisions, such as buying or selling.

In the *hierarchical firm,* or *bureaucracy,* where open, longer-term contracts regulate the exchange of products and services through the employment relation and the authority relationship (Simon, 1957), the information system is represented by the *rules,* norms and plans which convey, mostly in a procedural fashion (Simon, 1976b), the information concerning what should be done under what circumstances, and how it should be controlled. Finally, in a *clan* business is carried out by parole contract, and partners bind themselves by word or handshake to a complex web of mutual, stable and long-term obligations. Its information system consists of the rituals, stories and ceremonies which convey the values and beliefs of the organization. It is highly informal and idiosyncratic: an outsider cannot gain quick access to the decision rules of a clan; on the other hand its information system, which is anything but transparent, has no need for an army of accountants, computer experts and managers: it is just there as a by-product of well-knit social relations (Ouchi, 1979; Wilkins and Ouchi, 1983; Schein, 1984).

It goes without saying that real organizations include a mixture of the three coordination and control mechanisms outlined thus far, and consequently they avail of a variety of information systems. It is however possible to distinguish the prevailing one locally. For example, in a multi-divisional company, one can identify and overall bureaucratic, hierarchical structure which links through authority relations the various divisions with the central office, and a corresponding information system, say for budgeting, planning and control. Internal markets regulate the exchange of products and services between the divisions: the relevant computer-based information system is a data base containing all the transfer prices. Finally, both within the divisions, departments and in the central office, clans exist among managers, among workers in production work groups, among the employees of an office, with each subculture having its own peculiar jargon, set of symbols, rituals etc. MIS theory has focused on bureaucratic organization to the exclusion of all else. By considering the plurality of organization and information systems we should however realize that there, are *multiple strategies for computerization*, all of which are contingent upon the nature of information processing taking place in a specific organization or part of it. Our framework, then, enables us to overcome the problem of one-dimensionality discussed above.

The role of information technology

If organizations are seen as networks of exchanges, then the organizational use of information technology concerns not only 'data' or 'individual decision making' but also *interdependent* decision making and communication related to exchanging. Information technology belongs to those technologies, like the telephone and money itself, which reduce the cost of organizing by making exchanges more efficient: it is thus a *mediating technology,* i.e. a technology which links several individuals through the standardization and extension of linkages (Thompson, 1967). The costs of organizing, i.e. costs of coordination and control, are decreased by information technology which can streamline all or part of the information processing required in carrying out an exchange: information to search for partners, to develop a contract, to control the behavior of parties during contract execution and so on. The functions of a computer-based information system can thus be reframed as an 'exchange support system'. And in analogy to Simon's typology of decision making (Simon, 1977), a classification of exchanges and the contracts regulating them can be developed:

- *Structured contracts,* i.e. spot contacts which govern transactions such as those occurring in an ideal market.
- *Semistructured contracts,* i.e. longer term, open contracts, such as the employment relation, where adaptation, sequential modifications at low renegotiation costs are permissible.

- *Unstructured contracts*, related to those exchanges which cannot be modelled or 'written down' in an explicit contract form, either because communication between the parties is difficult or because they cannot be satisfactorily spelled out and formalised.

Information technology can support all these types of exchanges and related contracts. Consider first the *structured* contracts. Many of the structured market exchanges have already been automated, from airline reservation systems to EFT banking, to data banks selling pieces of information. Note that the recasting of data processing as a mediating technology indicates that information technology is a means for creating/expanding markets, by lowering search, contracting and control costs. It would be interesting to carry out a census of the running DP applications in the commercial sector today: it is the author's conviction that market transactions rather than bureaucratic firms are at present the main field of application of DP technology, since the structured and standardized nature of those transactions make them more suitable to automation.[3] In what way then can computers support *semistructered* and *unstructured* exchanges? Systems can be dispatchers of heuristic commitments and promises which streamline the negotiation process embedded in any exchange. And this can take place not only on markets. The organization of work, in an office for example, can be seen in terms of coordinative problem solving which is achieved by the exchange, storage, control and retrieval of commitments between the various employees working in that office. In particular, the computer system together with the local network, could enable the parties requires for the execution of a given job to be identified, their mutual interests communicated, their previous/pending commitments recorded and their discretion noted. In this way a personal and collective agenda is built up (Flores and Ludlow, 1981; Fikes and Henderson, 1980) which could support office work conceived as a complex group problem solving (Suchman and Wynn, 1984). Operating systems, such as UNIX, through commands such as 'make', and other OA facilities act as a mediating technology which supports software development performed by various programmers linked to the system. For other applications see Lee (1980), Turoff and Hiltz (1982) and Jarke *et al.* (1985).

Strategies for the joint design of the organization and its information systems

In general, design is concerned with adapting a system to its surrounding environment (Simon, 1981): it is a question of 'fit' between the two (Alexander, 1967). In our case, it deals with adapting a computer-based information system to the existing organization with the latter constituting the environment of the former. But this is true only as a first approximation, when the organization can be held constant and the system varied. According to the framework proposed here, systems can also streamline exchanges by altering the contractual arrangements which build up the organization. Suppose, for example, that a hierarchy, based on the authority relationship is necessary to overcome the information barriers hindering the negotiation of the employment relation through the market. A new information processing utility which eliminates those barriers would make the hierarchy itself both inefficient and superfluous.

There are then many possible interactions between information technology and organization, and the transaction costs framework indicates them in a clearer way than ever before: it also shows specific strategies for the *joint design* of the organization and its information systems, i.e. for the best match between alternative computer systems and organizational forms (Ciborra, 1981). Only market and bureaucracy systems will be considered in the following.

To begin with, consider the information systems models which have been put forward in connection with data bases (Emery, 1969; Chen, 1977). A very attractive alternative offered by these systems is that the hierarchical coordination channels of the firms are superimposed by an information system linking each task to a common information pool. This 'common data base' offers economy in information channels, closer coupling between activities, tighter coordination between decision makers and a common view of the enterprise. In real applications, however, this technical approach does not appear to work. Empirical surveys have shown that in organizations using data bases, data are far from being shared in a common scheme. Political problems impeding the centralized standardization and storage of data are reported by the majority of data administrators interviewed (Davenport, 1979). 'Resistance' to standards, data 'ownershipness' and other such phenomena are usually associated with the psychology of the recalcitrant user and indicate that the implementation of the common data base is at variance with hierarchical organization (Silbey, 1977). Other signals seem to confirm this conclusion. Consider first some technical evidence. The growing interest in distributed data bases having a more complex architecture than the centralized version, can be interpreted as a failure of the later and a need to accommodate data base management systems to the idiosyncrasies of the extent, departmentalized organization.[4] Concepts such as 'site autonomy' of a local data base in respect to the global one, or as heterogeneous, multi-data bases, where different data models coexist, illustrate further the point (Ceri and Pelagatti, 1984).

That such idiosyncrasies play an important role in determining the system architecture is supported by the experience of leading companies who have pushed data base integration quite far: 'Although a homogeneous architecture is attractive at first', writes Beeby (1983), previously at Boeing Commercial Airplane Co.'s Engineering Division, 'it is less attractive over the long run. Factors that argue for a heterogeneous implementation are: diverse applications that impose diverse requirements on data management,[5] need to exchange product data with industry partners and subcontractors who employ different hardware. In the *next* generation systems at Boeing, a homogeneous solution will be pursued whenever practical, but the advantages – and frequently the necessity – of heterogeneous implementation will not be ignored.' And beyond the supposedly technical reasons, experience suggests that important organizational issues are involved.

By using the transaction costs framework, flaws in data base implementation can be understood, and even anticipated. Although the original idea of scholars like Emery, Chen and others, is technically sound, it contains a hidden organizational dilemma. In order to show it, let us assume that their ideal has become reality, i.e., a common data base is available to manage the data of a whole enterprise efficiently. Each departmental manager could then, in principle, access the overall system schema to retrieve the relevant data for his/her decision making. Moreover, the output of each decision taken in any organizational unit would be likewise made generally available through the database. Now, if this were all possible, *the enterprise would not have any reason to exist according to the transaction costs view*: its dissolution would be warranted on efficiency grounds (reduction of overhead costs). The single units or individuals would transact by exchanging services and the intermediate products with each other through market relationships, with the information provided by the common data base becoming the main coordination mechanism. The common data base would be able to standardize the specialized pockets of knowledge scattered throughout the hierarchic organization, thus eliminating both existing information barriers and departmental idiosyncrasies. In this way uncertainty and opportunism play no role, but neither is there a need to use a hierarchy instead of a market as a more efficient control and coordination mechanism. However, it has been shown above that the whole idea of a common database is doomed to failure because it clashes with the nature of managing hierarchical, departmentalized organizations, and the reasons are explained by the transaction costs framework. As a second example, consider the award-winning computer-based information system employed by Benetton, the leading Italian company in fashion knitwear. At a first glance, the system architecture seems to violate the iron law of the layered, pyramidal MIS concept. The network of production plants, design bureaus, subcontractors, warehouses, points of sale (many hundreds scattered all over the world), which build up Benetton's loosely coupled organization (Weick, 1976), is held together by a DP network, whose aim is to decrease transaction costs between the various units, and between them and the market. Data links have been established between the central office in Treviso, Italy and cash registers in the shops: these links enable production and reorder plans to swiftly adapt to market vagaries, by shortening the time lag between customers' needs, as expressed in purchase transactions, and the company's adaptive response. CAD systems decrease the time lag between the design of models and their production. Data bases support the quasi-market relationships between the company's and its subcontractors, and so on. Thus the system seems to fit the nature of Benetton's organization, because it maintains and strengthens its flexibility. It streamlines crucial transaction costs instead of superimposing a rigid, pyramidal system configuration. In this case too, the role of the computer-based information system in supporting Benetton's organizational effectiveness cannot be explained in terms of the misleadingly narrow ideas of the conventional wisdom.

A final example comes from the public administration. Consider the organizational rearrangement, suggested by Strassman (1980), of a large public bureaucracy oriented to providing complex services to customers. Figure 10.2 shows the functional administrative units (1,2,3,...) organized on a specialized basis and integrated by coordinating units (I1,I2,...) to deal with customers (A,B,C,...). The cost of organizing the whole administrative structure depends on the size and complexity of the coordinating and controlling mechanism. The cost of producing a single service is obviously correlated to these factors, because of the services requested by units. Given the size of the whole administration, the central office usually finds it difficult to understand delays or mistakes in the service delivered: costs due to control loss affect both the efficiency of the internal organization and the provision of a service to the client. Again an application of the transaction costs framework enables us to identify an architecture whereby the handling of information is linked to a rearrangement of the organization. Namely, in order to achieve greater organizational effectiveness and higher efficiency, markets can be introduced into the structure to simplify transactions.

Strassman suggests creating *information middlemen* between the customer and the bureaucracy, who can package the information products which they buy from the administration and sell in response to customers' needs (Figure 10.3). This arrangement decreases the information load necessary to centrally coordinate the internal administrative workload. It is the middlemen who selectively access the administrative functions on the basis of customers' requests. Each administrative unit provides the middlemen with a discrete and standardized product, so that it is easier for the central office to monitor the function's

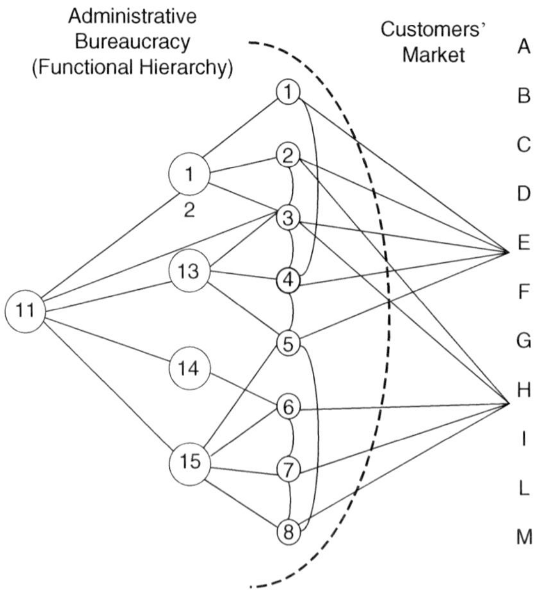

Figure 10.2 Organization of an administrative structure

performance. Information handling is reduced for the customer too: he/she now faces the single middleman and not the complicated and geographically dispersed bureaucracy. Secondly, data processing applied as a mediating technology can further decrease transaction costs. By using personal workstations, the middlemen can access the specialized functions of the bureaucracy via a communication network. The network becomes the means for the customer, via the middleman, to aggregate and coordinate the various tasks required in generating the complex service he/she needs.

By defining the boundaries between the bureaucracy, the middlemen's markets and the customers, data base technology can also immediately find a wider domain of application than in the previous hierarchic-functional arrangement where interventional barriers are difficult to overcome (see above). It could in fact quite easily support market transactions between the bureaucracy and the middlemen. Not only organizational imagination is needed in identifying such changes, as Strassman indicates, but also new intelligence and a new language, so that change is justified according to efficiency criteria and organizational dilemmas are avoided.

Concluding Remarks

An understanding of the nature of economic organizations is an essential prerequisite not only in governing the development of computer-based information

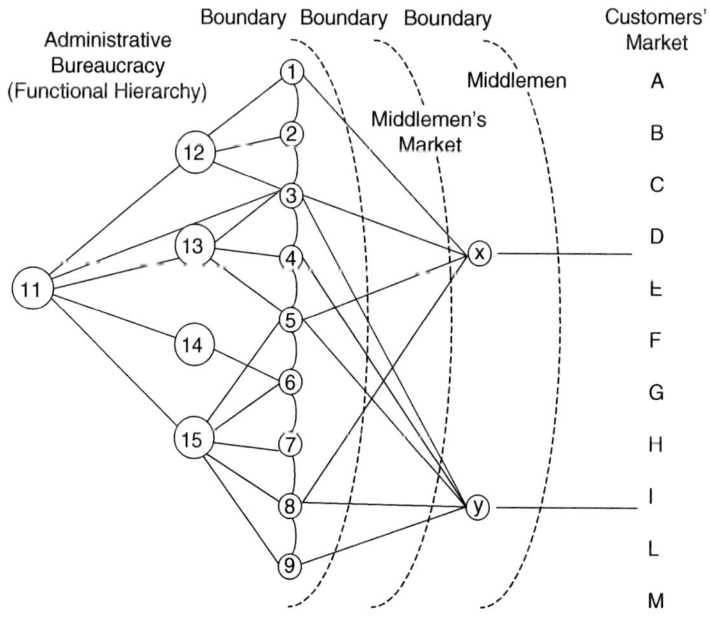

Figure 10.3 The introduction of middlemen

systems, but also in analyzing and designing them in an effective way. The transaction costs perspective can help design information systems appropriate to the functioning of institutions such as markets, bureaucracies and groups. The foregoing analysis can be summarized as follows:

- *Exchange transactions* represent the fundamental organizational relationships between human agents.
- The organization of exchange transactions depends upon contingencies which are both *environmental* (uncertainty and complexity) and *behavioral* (bounded rationality and opportunism).
- Organizations can be regarded as *stable networks of contracts* which govern transactions enabling coordination and control.
- Transacting requires *information* processing to identify partners, define a contract, control its environment, etc.
- Information technology acting as a *mediating technology* can, by lowering transaction costs, improve information handling needed in transacting.
- The application of information technology should not contradict *the nature of the organizational transactions* supported.
- Information technology can, in the interests of efficiency, influence the shift from one organizational form to another. The possibility of lowering transaction costs should be considered in any attempt at *joint design*.

Note that this new framework does not render obsolete the standard systems analysis methods, be they data- or decision-making oriented. On the contrary, it augments them with new organizational and economic background, so that when an analyst goes into an organization with his/her toolbox, he/she has a theory with which to select the relevant organizational phenomena, identify the information requirements and make a forecast of the organizational implications of any redesign put forward.

Obviously, the hypotheses and principles outlined invite further reflection and research *per se*. It might be a good idea to direct *requirements and systems analysis methods* to the structured investigation of key organizational exchanges, the contracts dedicated to their governance, the information processing resources deployed to create, control, change and maintain contracts. Software might be designed to explicitly decrease costs of transacting, i.e. to provide search, contracting and control routines. In formulating an *information technology strategic plan*, the market-hierarchies paradigm (Williamson, 1975, 1985) could provide new insight regarding the dynamic links between business policy, organization structures and information systems.

Finally, empirical research on the *impact of computers in organizations* could be used to test the validity of the framework and the hypotheses generated by its application (Ciborra, 1983). A research project of this kind could also help define more precisely the ways whereby a fit could be obtained between organizational structures and processes, information systems and transaction requirements.

Acknowledgement

Many thanks to P. Boegh Andersen, S. Ceri, M. Colombetti, G.B. Davis, A. Merten, B. Swanson for their useful suggestions.

Notes

This chapter originally appeared in (1987) *Office, Technology and People* **3**: 17–38.

1. The terms transaction and transaction costs are used here in an economic and organizational sense. Traditionally, for the DP profession, transactions refer to the computer operations triggered by a user message and satisfied by the corresponding computer response, i.e. an exchange of data between the machine and user (Bucci and Streeter, 1979). Economic transactions refer instead to the transfer of a good or service between individuals and departments or organizations (Williamson, 1981). It is a social relationship which results where 'parties in the course of their interactions systematically try to assume that the value gained for them is greater or equal to the value lost' (Bart, 1981). However, it should not be excluded that the two concepts might be linked in the case of computer-mediated economics transactions (Ciborra, 1981).
2. More precisely, the firm supersedes the market when the service 'labour' is the object of exchange: spot contracts regarding the use of labour are in face exposed to various hazards, since it is difficult to fully specify in advance the precise services required during the execution of a complex/uncertain task; and to control the real effort provided by the worker, especially in the case of teamwork (Alchian and Demsetz, 1972). Under the contingencies determined by environmental and human factors (uncertainty and opportunism, respectively), market contracts are replaces, for the sake of efficiency, by a longer-term, open contract, the employment relation, whereby the worker accepts, within certain limits (the indifference zone; Barnard, 1938) that someone, the authority, specifies in a procedural way what should be done during the unfolding of events.
3. This conviction is easily justified: in most advanced countries, banks are the main users of data processing. But it is not so much their internal bureaucracy that is automated, it is rather their function as intermediary agents on market transactions (Switzerland had the highest percentage of computers per inhabitant...). Consequently, applications in the credit sector should be looked on as market transactions support systems.
4. A distributed database is a collection of data distributed over different computers in a network. Each node has autonomous processing capability and can perform local applications, besides global ones. 'The organizational and economic motivations are probably the most important reason for developing distributed databases' (Ceri and Pelagatti, 1984). The transaction costs framework justifies this appreciation.
5. For example, in some cases a relational data management may be required, i.e. in an engineering data base, where queries are unpredictable. A hierarchical system is more efficient when the nature of the queries is known in advance, as in a data base for cost accounting (Beeby, 1983).

References

Ackoff, R.L (1967). Management misinformation systems, *Management Science* **14**(4): 145–156.

Alchian, A.A and Allen, W.R. (1977). *Exchange and Production: Competition, Coordination and Control*, Blaton: Wadsworth Publishing Co.

Alchian, A.A. and Demsetz, H. (1972). Production, information costs and organization, *American Economic Review* **62**(5): 777–795.

Alexander, C. (1967). *Notes on the Synthesis of Form*, Cambridge, MA: Harvard University Press.

Arrow, K.L. (1974). *The Limits of Organization*, London: W. W. Norton & Co.

Barnard, C.I. (1983). *The Functions of the Executive,* Cambridge, MA: Harvard University Press.

Barth, F. (1981). *Process and Form in Social Life,* London: Routledge & Kegan Paul.

Beeby, W.D. (1983). The heart of integration: a sound data base, *IEEE Spectrum* **20**(5): 44–48.

Bucci, G. and Streeter, D.N. (1979). A methodology for the design of distributed informative systems, *Communications of the ACM* **22**: 233–245.

Ceri, S. and Pelagatti, G. (1984). *Distributed Databases: Principles & Systems,* New York: McGraw-Hill.

Chandler, D.A., Jr. (1977). *The Visible Hand: The Managerial Revolution in American Business,* Cambridge, MA: Harvard University Press.

Chen, P.P. (1977). The entity relationship model: A basis for the enterprise view of data, *AFIPS Conference Proceedings* **46**:77–84.

Ciborra, C.U. (1981). Information systems and transactions architecture, *International Journal of Policy Analysis & Information Syst*ems **5**(4): 305–324.

Ciborra, C.U. (1983). Markets bureaucracies and groups in the information society, *Information Economics and Policy* **1**(2): 145–160.

Coase, R. (1937). The nature of the firm, *Economica* (November): 387–405.

Couger, J.D., Colter, M.A. and Knapp, R.W. (1982). *Advanced System Development/Feasibility Techniques,* New York: Wiley & Sons.

Davenport, R.A. (1979). Data analysis: Experience with a formal methodology, in P.A.Samet (ed.), EURO IFIP 79 (*Proceedings of European Conference on Applied Information Technology of the International Federation for Information Processing,* London, 25–28 Sept., 1979), Amsterdam: North Holland, pp. 53–64.

Davis, G.B. and Munro, M.C. (1977). Determining management information needs: a comparison of methods, *MIS Quarterly* (June): 55–66.

De Sanctis, G. and Gallupe, B. (1985). Group decision support systems: a new frontier, *Data Base* (Winter): 3–10.

Emery, J.C. (1969). *Organizational Planning and Control Systems: Theory and Technology,* New York: Macmillan.

Feldman, M.S. and March, J.G. (1981). Information in organization as signal and symbol, *Administrative Science Quarterly* **26** (June): 171–186.

Fikes, R.E. and Austin Henderson, D., Jr. (1980). On supporting the use of procedures in office work, Mimeo, Xerox PARC, Palo Alto, CA, December.

Flores, F. and Ludlow, J.J. (1981). Doing and speaking in the office, in G. Fisk and R. Sprague (eds), *Issues and Challenges*, London: Pergamon Press.

Galbraith, J.R. (1977). *Organization Design*, Reading, MA: Addison Wesley.

Grandori, A. (1984). A prescriptive contingency view of organizational decision making, *Administrative Science Quarterly* **29**(June): 192–209.

Hess, J.D. (1983). *The economics of Organization*, Amsterdam: North-Holland.

Huber, G.P. (1984). The nature and design of post-industrial organizations, *Management* Science **30**(8): 928–951.

Jarke, M., Jelassi, M.T. and Shakun, M.F. (1985). Mediator: *Towards a negotiation support system,* Mimeo, Indiana University, June.

Keen, P.G.W. (1981). Information Systems and Organizational Change, *Communications of the ACM* **24**(1): 24–33.

Keen, P.G.W. and Scott Morton, M.S. (1978). *Decision Support Systems: An Organizational Perspective,* Reading, MA: Addison Wesley.

Kling, R. (1980). Social analyses of computing: Theoretical perspectives in recent empirical research, *Computing Surveys* **12**(1): 61–110.

Lee, R.M. (1980). CANDID: A logical calculus for describing financial contracts. Ph.D. Dissertation, Dept. of Decision Studies. The Wharton School, University of Pennsylvania, Philadelphia, PA.
Markus, M.L. (1983). Power, politics and MIS implementation, *Communications of the ACM* **26**(6): 430–444.
Marschak, J. and Radner, R. (1972). *Economic Theory of Teams*, New Haven, CT: Yale University Press.
Okun, A. (1981). *Prices and Quantities*, Oxford: Basil Blackwell.
Olson, M.H. (1983). Remote office work: Changing work patterns in space and time, *Communications of the ACM* **26**(3): 182–187.
Ouchi, W.G. (1979). A conceptual framework for the design of organizational control mechanisms, *Management Science* **25**(9):838–848.
Ouchi, W.G. (1980). Markets, bureaucracies and clans, *Administrative Science Quarterly* **25**(March): 129–141.
Pava, C. (1982). *Microelectronics and the design of organization*, Working Paper, Division of Research, Graduate School of Business Administration, Harvard University, Cambridge, MA, April.
Piore, M.J. and Sabel, C.F. (1984). *The Second Industrial Divide*, New York: Basic Books.
Rockart, J.F. (1979). Chief executives define their own data needs, *Harvard Business Review* **57**(2): 81–93.
Schein, E.H. (1984). Coming to a new awareness of organizational culture, *Sloan Management Review* **26**(5): 3–16.
Schelling, T.C. (1980). *The Strategy of Conflict*, Cambridge, MA: Harvard University Press.
Sibley, E.H. (1977). The impact of database technology on business systems, in B. Gilchrist (ed.), *Information Processing* 77. Amsterdam: North Holland.
Simon, H.A. (1957). A formal theory of the employment relation, in H.A. Simon (ed.), *Models of Man*, New York: Wiley, pp.183–195.
Simon, H.A. (1873). Applying information technology to organizational design, *Public Administration Review* (May–June): 268–278.
Simon, H.A. (1976a). *Administrative Behaviour*, New York: The Free Press.
Simon, H.A. (1976b). From substantive to procedural rationality, in S.J. Latsis (ed.), *Method and Appraisal in Economics*, Cambridge: Cambridge University Press.
Simon, H.A. (1977). *The New Science of Management Decision*, Englewood Cliffs, NJ: Prentice Hall.
Simon, H.A. (1981). *The Sciences of the Artificial*, Cambridge, MA: MIT press.
Smith, A. (1776). *The Wealth of Nations*, Baltimore, MD: Penguin.
Sprague, E.H. (1980). A framework for the development of decision support systems, *MIS Quarterly* **4**(4): 1–24.
Stone, P.J. (1980). Social evolution and a computer science challenge, *Scientia* **25**: 125–146.
Strassman, P.A. (1980). The office of the future, *Technology Review* (January): 56–64.
Strauss, A. 1978. *Negotiations-Varieties, Contexts, Processes and Social Order*, San Francisco, CA: Jossey-Bass.
Suchmann., L.A. and Wynn, E. (1984). Procedures and problems in the office, *Office Technology and People* 2(2): 133–154.
Thompson, J.D. (1967). *Organizations in Action*, New York: Russel Sage.
Toffler, A. (1980). *The Third Wave*, New York: Morrow.
Turoff, M. and Hiltz, S.R. (1982). Computer support for group versus individual decisions, *IEEE Trans. Commun.* **30**(2): 80–91.
Weick, K.E. (1976). Educational organizations as loosely coupled systems, *Administrative Science Quarterly* **21**(March): 1–19.
Wildavski, A. (1983). Information as an organizational problem, *Journal of Management Studies* **20**(1): 29–40.

Wilkins, A.L. and Ouchi, W.G. (1983). Efficient cultures: Exploring the relationship between culture and organizational performance, *Administrative Science Quarterly* **28**(September): 468–481.
Williamson, O.E. (1975). *Markets and Hierarchies: Analysis and Antitrust Implications*, New York: The Free Press.
Williamson, O.E. (1981). The economics of organization: the transaction costs approach, *American Journal of Sociology* **87**(3): 548–577.
Williamson, O.E. (1985). *The Economic Institutions of Capitalism*, New York: McMillan.

11

Markets, Bureaucracies and Groups in the Information Society: An Institutional Appraisal of the Impacts of Information Technology*

Claudio U. Ciborra

Abstract

The issue regarding the impact of information technology on organizations is here reconsidered by applying a new analytical framework. Information technology affects the cost of transactions which take place under alternative institutional arrangements, such as markets, bureaucracies and groups; namely it shifts the boundaries which separate these different types of organizations. Information technology can affect the efficiency of the organizations which apply it and the organizational behavior of their members. Empirical data show how computerization changes organizational patterns according to efficiency considerations. An enlargement of the framework to take into account alternative mechanisms for organizational participation, such as exit, voice and loyalty, allows to examine the impacts of information technology on participation possibilities within organizations.

Introduction

Economic organizations are the means to achieve coordination among individuals and social groupings, which produce, distribute and consume goods and services making up the society wealth.

Coordination, which is essentially an information and communication activity, can be carried out through different institutional arrangements, such as markets, bureaucracies, groups and mixes thereof. These institutional arrangements absorb resources to perform their tasks.

An estimate of the costs of running markets, administrative hierarchies and heterarchical groups can be deduced by looking at the percentage of labour income absorbed by the 'organizers' (i.e., those who direct, coordinate, monitor and record economic activities of production): for the United States this is about

40 percent, roughly equally allocated to those who run markets and those who run administrations.[1]

Information technology, in the various forms of office automation, telecommunications, edp, etc., will have widespread impacts on the quantitative and qualitative dimensions of the employment (e.g., on the subdivision between 'organizers' and 'producers'; the creation/distribution of professional skills, etc.), and on the organizations where work of production and coordination is performed, for the explicit aim of its application is a dramatic increase in productivity and efficiency of organizations.

But efficiency is not everything when economic organizations are considered. They are also social systems characterized by a certain atmosphere and quality of collective life. After all, organizations have the purpose to further (part of) the interests of their members. They are the means to achieve the common goals of groups of individuals.

The consequences of the diffusion of information technology will also regard the new rules for the organization of individuals, their participation and their chances of collective action.

For these reasons I propose here a study on the organizational impacts of information technology which deals primarily with the two issues of efficiency and opportunities for collective action (participation) in economic organizations.

Specifically, this paper sets out the qualitative change in the population of organizations to be expected as a result of the influence of information technology on the efficiency of different organizational forms. It then puts forward a preliminary analysis of the opportunities for individuals to influence the goal seeking behavior of the computer based organizations. In other words, given the diffusion of information technology, what will be the new set of organization constraints for individual participation and what will be the possibilities for members to negotiate their relation with the organization so as to influence its goals?

The two issues are addressed as forecast exercises based on the discussion of qualitative empirical data. Several limitations characterize this type of approach, besides the lack of a robust statistical basis. These are the most important *caveats:*

- The direct link between technology and organization is privileged in the analysis, diregarding other intervening social and economic factors that may change the shape of the organizations of the future. Thus, the analysis should be looked at as a *ceteris paribus* exercise.
- The issue of employment is totally neglected.
- The traditional issue concerning centralization vs. decentralization of power in computer-based organizations is not touched directly. But note that the problem of the most efficient mechanisms to exercise power and control (by setting up markets rather than hierarchies) can be dealt with using the frameworks presented here.

- No cross-effect is considered between different organizations, i.e., how information technology may intervene in the relationships between government vs. firms, or unions vs. firms, etc.
- The impacts of information technology on justice are ignored, i.e., on how institutional arrangements distribute rights and duties and determine the division of advantages from social cooperation (Rawls, 1971).

The latter reminds the reader that a full study of the organizational impacts of information technology would have to deal with at least the three issues of efficiency, collective action and equity.

The paper is structured as follows. After a short review of recent studies and normative considerations dealing more or less directly with the future impacts of new technologies on economic organizations, an analytical framework is put forward to understand organizational forms and information technology as complementary means to achieve efficient coordination. The framework is based on the notions of exchange and transaction costs and points out the role of information technology as a 'mediating technology' which can affect the pattern of contractual relations in different types of organizations. Then the paper presents empirical data regarding the impact of information technologies in a sample of manufacturing and service companies in Italy. A forecast exercise is carried out using the analytical framework to identify what might be the diffusion trends of alternative organizational forms in the information society. Then the paper investigates the 'quality of organizational life', specifically the opportunities for individual participation. For the occasion, the initial framework is integrated with the application of the concepts of organizational exit, voice and loyalty. Concluding remarks including issues of a more normative character follow.

Expected changes in economic organization

Since the classic empirical study by Whisler (1970) on the impact of data processing on the organizational structures of a sample of insurance companies, the development of computer and telecommunication technologies (*telematique* or communication) indicates today the need for a broader approach to the evaluation of the organizational impacts of information technology.

In what follows some of these developments together with their implications are briefly sketched.

Transborder dataflows. The availability of transborder data flows (TBDF) deeply affects multinational organizations.

Specifically, data flows for control functions of headquarters about affiliates tend to increase the degree of centralization of the multinationals. Moreover, within the corporate structure new functional firms are created, such as trading companies, reinvoicing companies, etc., specialized in providing more and more coordination services to the group as a whole. The overall structure of the enterprise becomes a complex mix of product divisions, local affiliates and global functional centers (Antonelli, 1981). The growth of TBDF seems to accelerate the process of international specialization as occurring *within* firms rather than between firms, thus confirming Porat's (1978) hypothesis according to which the information economy is largely bureaucratic in nature.

The cottage industry. Emery (1978) and Trist (1981) see in microelectronics the opportunity for scaling down rather than up, dispersal rather than concentration, and self-management rather than external control of organizations. New forms of social and work organizations, such as 'community workshops', and the reassessment of the household as a socio-technical production system are envisaged. Bureaucracies will give way to self-regulating primary work systems loosely coupled through ephemeral networks. According to Rice (1980) computer conferencing may allow geographic decentralization with the shift of organizational units to rural areas, especially of routine and information transfer activities. Although the issue is a complex one, involving the appreciation of trade offs among telecommunication, transportation and energy solutions, preliminary studies don't exclude the advent of a new 'cottage industry.'

A self-service economy. Considering the structure of the whole economy, Gershuny (1978) identifies two main organizational changes which the diffusion of microelectronics may reinforce:

- Goods substitute services (the privately purchased and owned washing machine substitutes the laundry service), thus creating a different organization of the economy in which production carried out in the household becomes more important.
- Enlargement of the tertiary sector as a consequence of the increased division of labour in the production of capital goods which substitute services. Large bureaucracies needed to provide services will give way to smaller organizations which coordinate, plan and control production and distribution of goods.

Emerging markets. Lemoine (1981) indicates that the 'informatisation' of the tertiary sector will

- lengthen the production cycle of marketable services,
- stimulate the emergence of new jobs such as 'network managers', 'distributors of information', 'suppliers of data banks', etc.,
- transform the quasi-markets through which services are provided within the enterprises into real markets where information goods and services are bought and sold. Functional departments will turn into small, medium sized, highly specialized firms.

Thus informatization would appear as a driving force which reinverses the process whereby in the nineteenth century the 'visible hand' of management has taken over the market functions (Chandler, 1978).

This process is not exempted from risks. For one thing, Lemoine points out that the increased division of labour and the allocation of information service activities to the market may weaken the informal, unofficial exchange and processing of information which take place daily within the firm and which are, for example, of importance for the unions in their bargaining activity.

Will there be then more markets or more bureaucracy as a consequence of the diffusion of information technology?

Will the information society be populated by more transparent or more opaque organizations?

The traditional theory which looks at the impacts of computers as affecting managerial decision making in hierarchies falls short of grasping many of the organizational changes reviewed here. A new understanding is required to evaluate on a common basis the selective impacts of information technology on markets, bureaucracies and other economic institutions and the possible shifts among different institutional arrangements (Ciborra, 1981a and b).

A framework for the analysis of organization and information technology

In this section the preliminaries are put forward for a transactional view of the organization, its information system and information technology itself. This view differs from the traditional way of looking at organizations simply as decision-making hierarchies and considering computers as means to automate decision processes. We will focus successively on the new definition of organization and of information technology.

Organizations

According to the New Institutional Economists (Williamson, 1975), organizations are stable networks of contractual arrangements to govern sets of transactions among individuals. The contractual arrangements define how individuals join together and coordinate their efforts to cope with the complexity of the task environment and the complexity of managing their getting together (exchange uncertainty). Contracts may vary in complexity: spot contracts regulate one-shot market transactions; contingent claims contracts whereby all future contingencies pertaining to the transaction are described and priced; contracts that because of high uncertainty require adaptive, sequential decision making (e.g., the employment relation); contracts that because of their higher duration and: complexity must be based exclusively on mutual trust, shared values and internalized norms. The web of these and other contracts is the texture which builds up, from the micro to the macro level, the economic organization.

In this organizational perspective the information system of an organization can be defined as the network of information flows that are needed to create, set up, control and maintain the organization's constituent transactions and relevant contracts. The information systems to support different types of contracts show distinct characteristics: for example the information system related to spot-contracting is highly formalized, while the one to support 'unwritten contracts' based on trust will be highly informal and idiosyncratic.

Four main types of contractual arrangements (organizational forms) can be identified:

i. *Hypointegrated organizations,* where the network of transactions is full of holes, or failures. Transactions are only loosely coupled and no form of cooperation can be sure to encompass the whole organization, unless severe costs of transacting are incurred. An example is given by the system composed of a local government interacting with the economic and social institutions operating on its territory: bureaucratic institutions are mixed with market elements and for some activities neither government planning nor market forces are effective coordinating factors. The information system of an hypointegrated organization resembles a 'colander'. The gaps represent instances where information flows and transactions cannot go through and memory is dispersed (Ciborra *et al.*, 1978).
ii. *Markets,* where specialization and coordination are achieved through buying and selling of products and services. Costs of transacting are low and the existence of competition assures the transactors about equitability of trade. The market works as a decentralized control system, where the output of each agent is directly metered and rewarded (Alchian and Demsetz, 1972). All the relevant information, i.e., price, quantity and quality, is available all over the market, and no special 'memory' function is required by the individual agent.
iii. *Bureaucracies* are more efficient arrangements of transactions when measurement of individual performance is more difficult due to 'team production' effects (Alchian and Demsetz, 1972), and idiosyncratic performance (Williamson, 1975) and transactions do not occur instantaneously among a large number of agents, so as to elicit rapidly and eliminate opportunistic behaviour stemming from a possible goal incongruence among agents. The hierarchic arrangement of transactions based on legitimate authority is more flexible to face varying circumstances which alter the term of trade and thus increase transaction costs. A body of rules and routines hierarchically structured represents the information system of the bureaucracy: rules convey the information so that decision makers can allocate resources in an adaptative, sequential and coordinated way. Rules represent the 'organizational memory' which embodies the knowledge necessary to maintain the basic pattern of transactions within the organization (Cyert and March, 1963).
iv. *Groups or clans,* where the measurement of performance is more difficult, transactions are highly idiosyncratic and agents are 'locked in' once they initiate to transact so that an arrangement may take place where cooperants can rely on trust, sharing of values and internalized norms, rather than on intensive policing of individual output. The information system of a clan is highly

idiosyncratic and non formalized; information exchange and communication take place through transmission of traditions, internalization of values and norms. Traditions represent the memory of the organization, accessible only after a long apprenticeship (Ouchi, 1980).

Note that real organizations include mixtures of these pure or ideal arrangements. For example, in a multi-divisional company one can identify an overall bureaucratic structure linking through legitimate authority relations the various divisions with the central office. Among the divisions an internal market regulates the exchange of resources (transfer pricing). And both within the departments and in the central office, clan or group forms exist among managers, workers, etc.

Information technology

In the present framework information technology plays the role of a *mediating technology,* i.e., a technology which links several individuals through standardization and extension of linkages. The key feature (and impact) of information technology is the possibility of *lowering the costs of transacting.* Accordingly, data processing can be identified with other devices that lower such costs, for example middlemen and money.

A few examples illustrate how the interaction between information technology and organization is explained in the transactional framework (see Ciborra, 1981a).

Consider first the issue of the organizational change of a functional organization into a multi-divisional. One of the reasons indicated to justify this change is economization on bounded rationality so as to overcome the 'control loss' from the office of the chief executive over the different functions, due to the radial expansion of the functional firm (Williamson, 1975). Investment in vertical information systems may represent here an alternative to such an organizational change, because up to a certain extent it allows to economize on the bounded rationality of decision makers (Galbraith, 1977). Hence, the availability of systems would push upward the size threshold passed which a change from functional to multidivisional organization is indicated.

For the same reason, simple hierarchies become less justifiable below a certain size. Normally, costly decision making is one reason to give a 'peer group' a hierarchical arrangement (Williamson, 1975), but computer-based information systems (compatible with small group idiosyncracies) could support the complex communication network of a large group.

Also, new forms of organizations could be explored. Consider the organizational rearrangement suggested by Strassman (1977) regarding a large functional bureaucracy oriented towards providing complex services to customers. In such an organization, functional administrative units are necessary for the specialization of skills. Costs of organizing the whole structure depend on size and complexity of the coordination and control tasks. The cost of producing the service is also correlated to the coordination costs, because the services requested by the customers must be processed sequentially through pockets of functional expertise scattered in the different administrative units.

A different architecture for information handling allows to achieve greater organizational productivity and higher efficiency in the provision of the service. Namely, through 'information middlemen' who can package information products and responses to administrative needs of the customer, the information load necessary to centrally coordinate the internal work-load decreases. The middlemen are located between the bureaucracy and the customers so that the boundaries between bureaucracy and service market are redrawn. It is the middlemen who selectively access, on the basis of customers' requests, the administrative functions. The performance of the middlemen is easily monitored on the basis of the rate, cost and quality with which the output service is delivered to the customer. The middlemen act as qualified purchasers of services from the various functions; they will then assemble the services according to the customers' requests. The market between the bureaucracy and the middlemen provides an important coordinating function, for each administrative unit supplies the middlemen with a discrete and standardized product so that monitoring the unit's performance is made easier for the central office.

By using personal computers, the middlemen can access, via a communication network, the specialized functions of even a very large, geographically dispersed bureaucracy. The network becomes a means for the local customer, through the middleman, to aggregate and coordinate various tasks to generate the complex service she or he needs.

Empirical data

The data of Table 11.1 regarding a sample of Italian companies that have applied between 1978–1980 technological innovations, ranging from robots to computer-based information systems, show among other things how organizational structures are rather 'turbulent', i.e., undergo changes mainly simultaneously with technological ones (Ciborra and Roveda, 1981).

The same data can be organized differently to show future trends in the organizational population ecology. This is done in Table 11.2, where the impacts of different *technological forms* are shown on the four main *organizational forms* previously examined (for some systems not studied during the empirical survey, such as EFT, office automation, and CAD data derived from the literature have been used). The main findings of Table 11.2 can be summarized as follows:

- the *hypointegrated organizations* undergo an integration process. The information technology fills some of the gaps of the 'colander' structure by providing cheap information goods and services to be sold on new, specialized markets. Data banks support and improve markets connecting previously isolated operators on the territory. Planning information systems integrate the workings of the administrative bureaucracy with the socio-economic processes taking place on the territory. Also, groups, coalitions of interest and more ephemeral social networks could be supported by distributed compunication.

- *market forms* tend to strengthen and expand. Through standardization of transactions and services exchanged, markets are supported by information technology at the expenses of hypointegrated systems and bureaucracies. New markets are created and old markets are improved, for example through EFT in banking, data banks in the information, goods markets, transformation of services to be provided by administrative structures into information products, the design of computer-based internal markets among bureaucratic functions etc. (divisionalization, subcontracting etc.) introduce market elements into hierarchies, which can be supported by distributed systems, local networks and TBDF.
- the *bureaucracy* becomes highly turbulent. On the one hand communication supports the creation of very large multinational organizations. On the other these contain more and more internal market arrangements. In innovative environments, such as those where R&D units of the electronic industry operate, the bureaucratic organization is blended with flexible group or clan features to support matrix patterns. It has been found that information technology affects the bureaucratic form in the following way: – small hierarchies give way to small groups which manage transactions through local networks (this is the case of remote office work, see Olson, 1981).
- the size threshold between functional and divisional organizations is shifted upward: computer-based systems can support larger functional bureaucracies.
- multidivisional forms can grow larger as mentioned above. In summary, the bureaucracy seems to become more and more a mechanism for distant coordination among diversified and scattered units, but it is increasingly mixed with markets elements and loses in efficiency rating as a means of local control.
- *groups* expand their range of diffusion. In highly automated environments the actual work organization is the 'work group'. Subcontracting dissolves small hierarchies and departments of large hierarchies into small groups transacting through markets. Computer-messaging systems facilitate the shift from hierarchical organizations to different ones consisting of constantly changing teams when this is required by the failure of bureaucratic coordination and control mechanisms.

As mentioned above these empirical trends cannot be regarded as a systematic forecast of the organizations mix which will populate the information society. In any case; they do not seem to contradict the scenarios outlined above.

Participation in computer-based organizations

How markets or administrative structures are shaped matters for the quality of life of individuals who operate within or in relation to organizations. The trends presented in the previous section can be further used to address the issue of the

Table 11.1 Qualitative changes in a sample of Italian organizations (no causal link is suggested between the different changes listed).

		Organizational innovation			
Industry	**Organization**	**Macrostructure**	**Work organization**	**Technological innovation**	**Impact on employment**
Textile	Spinning (450 employees)		New maintenance system new shift system informal work groups	New plant	–
	Spinning (500 employees)	–	New maintenance system job enlargement	Improvements of machines	Reduction
	Spinning (200 employees)	New layer of middle managers	Job enlargement	Open-end spinning machines	Reduction
	Spinning (230 employees)	–	Work groups	–	Reduction
	Spinning (650 employees)	Subcontracting	Informal work groups	Automated spinners	Reduction
	Spinning and weaving (200 employees)	Flattening of the hierarchy (reduction of middle managers)	Work groups job enrichment	Automated spinners new plant	–
	weaving (425 employees)	Crisis of the supervisory roles	Crisis of the tasks specialization	–	Reduction
	Clothing (1000 employees)	From functional to multidivisional structure with some matrix features	Changes in the managerial roles	On-line computer-base MIS	Reduction (white collar)
Auto	Large plant (assembly operations) (600 employees)	–	Work groups job enrichment job enlargement	Robocarriers production control system automation	Reduction
	Large plant (assembly operations) (400 employees)		Job enlargement	Industrial robots (assembly)	

	Large plant (manufacturing operations) (600 employees)	–	Job enlargement intensification of pace of work	Industrial robots (welding, coating, painting)	Reduction
Steel	Continuous casting (plant with 12,000 employees)	Flattening of the hierarchy	Work groups job enlargement	Process control	Reduction
	Rolling mill (plant with 30,000 employees)	–	Informal, temporary work groups during breakdowns	Process control	Reduction
Chemical	Ammonia-urea plant (97 employees)	New functional structure	Increased specialization	Open-loop process control (centralized systems)	Reduction
	Petrochemical plant (4600 employees)	Multidivisional structure	New maintenance system	New automated plants	Reduction
Electronics	Computer manufacturer (R&D department 1300 employees)	Matrix organization	Teams job enrichment	New products (from electro-mechanical to electronic)	Increase
Banking	Commercial bank (10,000 employees)	–	Work groups	Management Information System	Reduction
Public administration	Regional government (authority for industry and commerce)	New decision processes	–	Economic data banks	–

Table 11.2 Impacts of Information Technology on the four main organizational forms.

Components	LSI/VLSI (integrated circuits)								
Systems	Large computers			Distributed systems		Microprocessors			
Applications / Organisational forms	Mts	Data banks	EFT	CAD/CAM	Process central	Small business systems	Office automation – Local networks	Industrial robots – N/C	Micro–electronic in the products
Hypointegrated systems	Improved planning of economic activities on the territory	Higher integration (more efficient markets)	–	–	–	Improved decision making of agents	Improved communications	–	–
Markets	Internationalism of markets in bureaucracies	New information markets	More efficient markets	–	–	Improved decision making of agents	New internal markets homework	–	New markets for electronic services
Bureaucracies	Enlargement, reinforcement of hierarchies	New internal markets	Shrinks the Bureaucracy	May increase bureaucratic control on professional work	May increase hierarchial control	Favors decentralized autonomous structures (shrinks the bureaucracy)	Shrinks the bureaucracy homework	May increase central on the work force	May simplify the bureaucracy in the production process
Groups	May leave local autonomy to groups while retaining central control	Faster better coordination between groups	–	Informal groups emerge during breakdowns	Informal groups emerge during breakdowns	Faster the creation of groups	Faster the creation of groups	Informal groups emerge during breakdowns	May faster work groups

opportunities for participation in the new population of organizations, namely what will be the consequence for the role of individuals in organizations, if the forecast just outlined holds true?

To provide a preliminary answer our analytical framework must be enlarged to take into account the organizational mechanisms of participation (Williamson, 1976).

Patterns and costs of organizational participation

According to Hirschman (1970), exit, voice, and loyalty are the basic mechanisms through which economic, social and political systems, individuals, business firms and organizations can recover and learn to recover from unsatisfactory behaviour due to low quality characteristics of the organization outputs.

Exit and voice are the two main means of expressing participation, while loyalty is an intervening factor affecting the balance of the previous two in each specific situation.

Exit is the typical participatory behavior of a customer who, unsatisfied with the product provided by an organization, 'punishes' that organization by not buying its products anymore. The individual with his or her decision strikes back at the unsatisfactory company and the invisible hand of the market acts so that the company loses its revenue if it does not restore the price or quality of its products.

Exit can be easily carried out when transaction costs are low (transactors are not locked into the exchange). Exit is thus a 'clean', 'alienated' form of participation in the self-service economy.

In contrast *voice* is the category of political action. It is exercised by members who are relatively locked into transacting with the organization and want to change it 'from within'. Voice is 'messy' because one has to make himself 'heard' and because there is always a graduation of alternatives for articulating interests.

Exit and voice can be both complementary and substitute strategies. The voice option, for example, is the residual way in which dissatisfied customers may react if the exit option is unavailable or proven to be ineffective. Exit can be the only move left when protest in bureaucracies does not affect the organization goals. Most frequently the two options are combined and *loyalty* alters the mix of the two strategies. If one is loyal to the organization and its outputs, he or she will rather exercise the voice option to a greater extent than exit.

To link the transactional framework with the analysis of participation modes, it is now necessary to analyze the costs of implementation of each participatory mechanism.

Exit is typical of spot transactions occurring on the market. In this case it is a cheap alternative with

- costs of search for other substitute products and organizations,
- opportunity costs due to loss of loyalty, if loyalty guarantees the rapid completion of transactions, higher flexibility in bargaining etc.

Voice is characteristic of transactions where parties have made specific (idiosyncratic) investments. Its costs are:

- the opportunity cost of foregoing the exit option,
- the direct cost of organizing and exercising voice, finding the appropriate means, time, resources, communication channels etc.,
- the costs of collective action, i.e., to set up a sufficient 'volume' to make voice be heard.

Voice is likely to be more effective in 'small numbers' situations (i.e., in small bureaucracies and groups). For one thing, the expected effect of voice is a public good to the members of the organization and following Olson's (1965) analysis of the logic of collective action, only small organizations can hope to provide themselves with a public good. Secondly, small groups are more conducive to highly idiosyncratic investments by members. The cost of voice will get consequently higher as the number of transactors, goods and services in which to invest increases and the individual has to spend more resources in identifying faults of anyone of such elements.

The costs of loyalty are related to the organizational and individual resources invested to establish sharing of values, common traditions, informal communication and internalization of norms.

Finally, note how the costs of exit, voice and loyalty boil down once more to information processing costs related to communication, control and exchange.

A forecast of participation possibilities

We are now able to make a forecast of the future organizations to discuss the opportunities for organizational participation in the information society. If the forecast outlined in section 4 holds true, it is suggested that:

- The integration of *hypointegrated systems* will affect positively the possibility of exercising more fully both exit and voice. This is a consequence of the general increase of the 'degree of organization' allowed by the diffusion of information technology.
- The spreading of *markets,* both among and within firms and groups will make the (individualistic) exit option less costly, more widespread and attractive.
- The enlargement of *bureaucracies* will affect the possibility of making voice coming from the bottom be heard at the top. The increased distance requires greater volume and organizational articulation of interests: (heads of) large departments or divisions can voice, but individuals and groups will have difficulty in getting their say through, if *ad hoc* communication structures are not provided for. The increased pervasiveness of bureaucracy will also make exit more difficult.
- The splitting of small bureaucracies and the diffusion of *small groups* transacting through markets should enhance the efficacy of voice at local (group) level, decrease the attractiveness of exiting from self-managed units, and let loyalty

play a relevant role in contrast with the trends regarding loyalty in markets and bureaucracies.

The emerging picture is thus rather complex. In the information society, individuals seem to have to participate more explicitly as 'exchangers' rather than bureaucrats or politicians. Loyalty will be still important for small organizations, while there will be less incentives to be loyal to gigantic bureaucracies or to impersonal market forces.

The advocates of decentralization should take into account such side effects: namely, it is often not appreciated that decentralization in an economy can mean extending markets thus fostering alienated participation forms such as exit.

Of course, these conclusions have to be largely modified if information technology will be *purposefully* applied not only to the design of efficient economic organizations but also to design efficient participatory mechanisms, i.e., to improve chances of collective action. (Stone, 1980).

Concluding remarks

Economic organizations form the building blocks of the institutions through which any economic policy and program can be implemented.

The impacts of information technology on the economy must be studied not only around the issues of employment, production or power relationships but also for the widespread changes in the institutional arrangements through which the economic processes take place.

Though with severe limitations, the paper puts forward a framework for analyzing the institutional impacts of the new technology (thought of as a *mediating* technology) on the efficiency of economic organizations, as coordination and collective action mechanisms.

The explorative forecasts regarding the future population of organizations stimulated by the diffusion of the new technology and the chances for individual participation should be integrated also by more normative preoccupations for the purposeful, institutional design of the future computer-based organizations. On the one hand, efficiency, as criterion of organizational design, prescribes the drawing of boundaries assigning transactions to markets, bureaucracies or groups or mixtures thereof, so as to minimize the overhead necessary to run alternative contractual arrangements. Information technology affects the costs of specific sets of transactions and can be considered as a support for the optimal, least cost organizational alternative.

On the other, the participation criterion would indicate the design of organizations in which there would be an appropriate balance of exit, voice and loyalty, so as channels are provided to communicate dissatisfaction and exert influence from below in the cheapest and most effective way.

Note how the participation criterion is related to dimensions which are absent from the efficiency framework, namely the definition of goals (effectiveness).

Even in a normative perspective the two criteria are not independent: it is the nature of transactions and related costs of search, contracting, control and the information and communication systems available that determine the most efficient contractual arrangement and the mix of participation possibilities available to the transactors.

Notes

This chapter originally appeared in (1983) Information Economics and Policy **1**(2): 145–160.

1. The estimates are due to Jonscher (1980), who has re-analyzed the matrix of employee compensation compiled by Porat (1977) for the year 1967 in the U.S.

References

Alchian, A.A. and Demsetz, H. (1972). Production, information costs and economic organization, *American Economic Review* **62**(5): 777–795.

Antonelli, C. (1981) Transborder data flows and international business-A pilot study, OECD report DST1/ICCP/81.16, June (OECD, Paris).

Chandler, A.D. (1978). *The visible hand,* Cambridge, MA: Harvard University Press.

Ciborra, C. (1981a). Information systems and transactions architecture, *Policy Analysis and Information Systems* **5**, December.

Ciborra, C. (1981b). A contractual view of information systems, *Proceedings of the EEC Conference on information technology and the representation of power,* Technical University Copenhagen, November.

Ciborra, C. and Roveda, C. (1981). *Impact of information technology upon organizational structures, in microelectronics, productivity and employment,* Paris: OECD-ICCP.

Ciborra, C., Gasbarri, G. and Maggiolini, P. (1978). A participative approach to information systems design of hypointegrated systems, in G. Bracchi (ed.) *Information systems methodologies,* Berlin: Springer.

Cyert, R.M. and March, J.G. (1963). *A behavioural theory of the firm,* Englewood Cliffs, NJ: Prentice Hall.

Emery, F.E. (1978). *The fifth Kondradrieff wave,* Canberra: Centre for Continuing Education, ANU.

Galbraith, J.R. (1977). *Organizational design,* Reading, MA: Addison-Wesley.

Gershuny, J. (1978). *After industrial society? The emerging self-service economy,* London: McMillan.

Hirschman, A.O. (1970). *Exit, voice and loyalty,* Cambridge, MA: Harvard University Press.

Jonscher, C. (1980). A theory of economic organization, PhD thesis, Cambridge, MA: Department of Economics, Harvard University.

Lemoine, P. (1980). *Informatisation and economic development,* OECD report, DSTI/ICCP/80.17, Paris: OECD.

Olson, M.H. (1981) Remote office work: Implications for individuals and organization, CRIS working paper no. 25, New York: Graduate School of Business Administration, New York University.

Olson, P. (1965). *The logic of collective action,* Cambridge, MA: Harvard University Press.

Ouchi, W.G. (1980). Markets, bureaucracies and clans, *Administrative Science Quarterly* **25**(March): 129–141.

Porat, M. (1977). *The information economy: Definition and measurement,* OT special publication 77–12(1), Washington, DC: US Department of Commerce.

Porat, M. (1978). Communication policy in an information society, in: G.O. Robinson (ed.) *Communications for tomorrow-policy perspectives for the 80s,* New York: Praeger.

Rawls, J. (1971). *A theory of justice* Cambridge. MA: Harvard University Press.

Rice, R.E. (1980). The impacts of computer-mediated organizational and interpersonal communication, in M.E. Williams (ed.) *Annual Review of Information Science and Technology* **15**: 221–249.

Stone, P. (1980). A new challenge to computer science, *Scientia* 1–5.

Strassman, P.A. (1977). Organizational productivity: The role of information technology, in B. Gilchrist (ed.) *Information processing 77,* Amsterdam: North-Holland, pp. 503–508.

Trist, E. (1981). The evolution of socio-technical systems, Occasional paper 2, Ontario Quality of Working Life Center, June.

Whisler, T.L. (1970). *The impacts of computers on organizations,* New York: Praeger.

Williamson, O.E. (1975). *Markets and hierarchies-Analysis and antitrust implications,* New York: The Free Press.

Williamson, O.E. (1976). The economics of internal organization: Exit and voice in relation to markets and hierarchies, *American Economic Review* **66**(2): 369–377.

Part II

Building on Ciborra's Legacy

12
Knowledge: Climbing the Learning Ladder to a 'Phenomenological' View*

Andrea Resca

Abstract

Attempts to summarize Claudio Ciborra's work through a single theme cannot succeed due to its breadth and the ease in which he moved between subjects. This paper is a tentative attempt to discover a common theme in his work, with the notion of knowledge identified as an appropriate starting point. Encompassing *learning* and *rationality*, the theme of knowledge has been persistent and evolving in Ciborra's work, with three knowledge combinations reflecting its development: *knowledge-rationality, knowledge-learning* and *everyday-knowledge*. The first combination depicts rationality as a catalyst in the pursuit of specific objectives that determine knowledge. Ciborra continued his exploration of knowledge by theorizing that background knowledge structure objectives were the basis of sense-making and organizational action, while short term knowledge structure was required to address developing situations. This introduced and provided the foundation for the knowledge-learning combination. Ciborra's final knowledge combination was predicated on the interpretation of reality as created by the experiences of the individual, including participation in organizational life where *feelings, moods* and the totality of existence is expressed, delineating the everyday-knowledge combination in the process. Ciborra utilized these and other approaches like the learning ladder in his investigation of complex multilayered subjects like information systems, undertaken from amongst others, a phenomenological vantage point that shaped many of his key contributions.

Introduction

This paper reviews Claudio Ciborra's work since the 1980s, in an attempt to identify a common theme. The first tentative steps towards this aim included a grouping of Ciborra's work according to *subject titles,* yielding *production automation; automobile industry; labour market and working conditions; informatics and speech acts; languages, artificial intelligence and expert systems; software engineering; economics; information systems* and *information society.* These are not exhaustive, but reflect Ciborra's varied interests, while highlighting the difficulty inherent in characterizing his work through any *one subject*. In his seminar at the LSE in June 2004 titled, 'The Mind of the Heart? It depends on the (definition of the) situation', Ciborra adopted a Heideggerian view to critique current interpretations of situated action, knowledge, and learning and change, including an assessment on how phenomenologists and contemporary interpretivists address these issues. In addition to displaying his wide interests and flexibility, the seminar reinforced why Ciborra's research cannot be 'boxed' within a single heading.

Ciborra's work yields one recurring theme: *knowledge*. Although concepts related to this evolved over time, the notion of knowledge consistently appears in much of Ciborra's writing. He posits that knowledge and rationality are related, with rationality facilitating the pursuit of specific ends that determine knowledge, yielding a knowledge-rationality combination. Ultimately, knowledge is the result of logic that defines reality, with four perspectives arising from the knowledge-rationality relationship: unlimited rationality and fully accessible knowledge; limited rationality and tacit knowledge; strategic rationality and opportunistic knowledge, and adaptive rationality and knowledge for change. Technology, and in particular information and communication technology (ICT) is an integral element of this knowledge.

The earlier period of Ciborra's research (in the 1980s), embraces the perspective of strategic rationality and opportunistic knowledge with a focus on *transaction costs* (Williamson, 1975; Ouchi, 1980). Although significant to Ciborra's latter work – when the notions of formative context (Ciborra and Lanzara, 1989) and organizational learning (Argyris, 1982) emerged – this earlier period did not embrace adaptive rationality and knowledge for change. Then, it may be appropriate to consider a further perspective on the notion of knowledge that can be superimposed on Ciborra's work during this period: Piaget's (1974) distinction between background knowledge structure (the basis of sense making and organizational action) and short term knowledge structure (required in order to react to emerging situations). Learning, within a knowledge-learning concept, can be depicted as the facilitator precipitating an alignment between these two knowledge structures. This combination was explored by Ciborra and Andreu (1996, 2001) who interpreted knowledge-learning as possessing *malleability*. The extent of this malleability is dictated by the organizational context including whether knowledge-learning is assessed within a single organization, an alliance between two or more organizations, or a community of organizations (ibid). Each of these propagates knowledge of a different nature.

Everyday-knowledge is the third knowledge combination that Ciborra addresses. Using a phenomenological perspective, he posited that knowledge emerges as a result of the everyday experiences of human beings in their organizational life. The concept of *Care* is important in this perspective. Ciborra portrayed a person's everyday life as a continuous process in which he or she not only looks after themselves, but also others and 'things'. Moreover, the notion of care is treated as a springboard from which related elements are explored including Gestell, hospitality, technological drift and, according to this view, ICT and technology in general, are not only depicted as an instrument for increasing cognitive activity and reducing transaction costs but also as an inner element of people's lives.

Ciborra's studies of improvisation and situated action (Ciborra, 1999; 2001; 2002; 2006) embody this view, with the lens of existentialism utilized to interpret cognitive and institutional themes. His flexibility in adopting various 'lenses' within which to view his subjects is evident in his work on information infrastructure (Ciborra 1998a, 2000: Ciborra and Hanset, 1998), for which he adopted both knowledge-learning and everyday-knowledge perspectives to assess multiple points of analysis.

The final section of this paper explores Ciborra's epistemological approach to his work highlighting his shifting focus between the use of everyday knowledge in examining subjects whose existence is determinant (e.g. through bricolage, improvisation, situated action), and the use of knowledge-learning where structural and institutional elements are present (e.g. organizational alliances, communities of organizations, information infrastructures).

Knowledge and rationality

Up until Ciborra published *Teams, Markets and Systems* (1993), he used the term *knowledge* in relation to the concept of *rationality.* In this publication, and in the first chapter of *Tecnologie di Coordinamento* (1989) this association is utilized to establish a theoretical model for analysing individuals, organizations and ICT. Following Thompson's work (1967), Ciborra states that 'in organisations knowledge is applied according to the principles of rationality; that is, an organisational action relies on knowledge to select appropriate means to reach designated ends' (1993: 20). Commencing with this viewpoint, Ciborra's various theoretical approaches will be elaborated upon.

When comparing the introductory chapters of *Tecnologie di Coordinamento* with *Teams, Markets and Systems,* it is evident that they have several points in common, including four types of rationality and related knowledge: unlimited rationality and fully accessible knowledge; limited rationality and tacit knowledge; strategic rationality and opportunistic knowledge, and adaptive rationality and knowledge for change (Ciborra, 1988). Ciborra depicts knowledge as *fully accessible* with both individuals and organizations possessing access to knowledge required to undertake an activity which results in the optimisation of a subsequent action or decision. The concept of knowledge as explicit, transparent and manageable is a fundamental tenet in scientific management (Taylor, 1911), formal administrative theory (Gulick and Urwick, 1937) and in computer systems capable of processing information and replacing operators in certain scenarios.

A further perspective on rationality is provided by Simon (1976), who defines limited rationality as a state in which knowledge is not fully accessible. Polany's (1966) concept of tacit knowledge exemplifies this notion, depicting the limits that are inherent in both individuals and organizations in creating and transmitting knowledge. Such limits may be due to the shortcomings of a subject to act upon the knowledge he or she possesses, or they could be imposed by the external milieu in which the organization operates. In spite of such limitations, organizations have the potential to significantly increase an individual's elaborative capabilities due to functional decomposition (i.e. through the division of labour, a complex task can be subdivided into simpler and more manageable tasks). In this context, routines and the coordination of activities become the repositories of organizational knowledge, with ICT no longer a substitute for tacit knowledge. Nevertheless, ICT contributes considerably to diffusing information and reducing limited rationality.

A third perspective introduces the concept that knowledge can be used *strategically*. The previously depicted forms of knowledge require the cooperation of organizational participants, and largely ignore opportunistic behaviour arising from conflicting interests. Strategic rationality is posited as the justification for regulating knowledge acquisition and transference where asymmetries in power exist. The transaction cost approach (Williamson, 1975) is applicable in this scenario, with organizations acting as a stable network of relationships and contracts, and where ICT acts as 'the network of information flows that are needed to create, set up, control and maintain the organisation's constituent contracts' (Ciborra, 1993: 116). This stable network of relationships can take different forms. Williamson (1975) includes markets and hierarchies, whilst Ouchi (1980) includes markets, hierarchies and clans. All of these forms, which Weber (1964) defined as 'ideal-types', manifest themselves through their unique ability to manage strategic rationality and opportunistic knowledge.

Opportunism in markets is mediated by price, with perfectly competitive markets ultimately expelling actors that are unable to accommodate competition. The market form of transactions risks failing in some circumstances, such as where high transaction uncertainty exists. In such scenarios, organizational hierarchies can be of benefit due to the open nature of subordinate employment. Under such conditions, during working hours, employees are subject to an authority in exchange for a salary. This relationship produces consent for control over the employees' activities, resulting in a reduced capacity to behave opportunistically. Where task uncertainty is very high however, making the ability to detect self-interest actions by an employee difficult or impossible, clan forms is a possible solution. The level of trust present amongst actors involved in this kind of scenario renders controls superfluous and reduces opportunistic behaviour in favour of common values and beliefs. These are at the core of trust generation, and establish an environment in which community interests becomes the actor's interests. In this context ICT becomes a constituent element of transactions interacting with knowledge; a position that Ciborra posits in *Teams, Markets and Systems*. He formulates the position that ICT can not only support hierarchies, but markets and teams (clans) as well. This is a key message in his book, with ICT influencing transaction costs and promoting organizational forms more capable in governing such transactions.

For an organization facing a turbulent environment, the ability to harness knowledge in order to promulgate organizational transformation could be crucial. In such a scenario of tumultuous change, what is the role of knowledge?

Piaget's (1974) concept of what constitutes knowledge is useful in addressing this question. Piaget depicts background knowledge as a structure that forms the basis for the interpretation of any event or the execution of a task in conjunction with a short term knowledge structure required to deal with emerging situations. These two structures may not always mesh harmoniously, resulting in a resistance to new information, or in cognitive dissonance (Festinger, 1957). The harmonious fusion of background knowledge structure and short term knowledge structure is driven by adaptive rationality and knowledge for change, and includes double-loop learning (Argyris, 1982) and formative context change (Unger, 1987; Ciborra and Lanzara, 1989).

In the perspectives outlined in this paper, the focus has been on cognitive elements. These fall within a subjective epistemological view where knowledge of the world is intrinsically affected by the subject's direct involvement in 'knowing'. Defining a formative context as 'the set of institutional arrangements, cognitive frames and imageries that actors bring and routinely enact in a situation' (1993: 29), Ciborra accommodates an objective epistemological view as well. The assessment of institutional arrangements presented here is congruent with this perspective, for it is possible to know something only if it is analysed as an independent phenomenon. This perspective assists in overcoming the dichotomy between subject-object and agent-environment (Ciborra and Lanzara, 1999).

Does the concept of formative context allow for unity between background knowledge and short term knowledge? It appears that the concept falls only within the category of background knowledge, encompassing institutional arrangements and cognitive frames. If hierarchy is deemed to be the formative context in an institutional setting, the division of organizational labour can be seen in a typical organizational chart in which individuals hold a role (institutional arrangements). This hierarchy also facilitates a mode of reasoning, solving problems and executing tasks, (cognitive frames). Within this context, a key question is what prevents organizational inertia? The establishment of a formative context is derived from the sedimentation of practices and reflections but this sedimentation does not always occur with regularity. The introduction of a technological innovation or a redesign of an organizational structure can give rise to unexpected consequences due to these interventions inevitably not fitting with the existing formative context originating from the acquisition of new knowledge. In some cases this knowledge can lead to the emergence of new ways of acting and interpreting reality which can result in the creation of a new formative context.

The development of the notion of a formative context represents an evolution in the understanding of ICT. Ciborra's work contributed to this, with ICT depicted both as *support* for institutional arrangements and related dynamics (transactions), as well as a *catalyst* for ushering alternative perspectives on the division of labour and of problem solving (cognitive frames). The relationship between ICT and a formative context has led to an assessment of both *routines* and formative contexts themselves. Whilst the former encompasses activities, procedures and transactions, the latter encompasses an examination of the basis for such actions. These two elements are interconnected, with the intervention at one level affecting the other. *In Tecnologie di Coordinamento* and *Teams, Markets and Systems*, Ciborra, focusing on the notions of strategic rationality and opportunistic knowledge, examines mainly *routines*. The introduction of *formative context* represents the first stage by Ciborra to advance an analysis of the concept of knowledge.

Knowledge and learning

Learning is a significant concept in Ciborra's work. In *Teams, Markets and Systems* Ciborra changed the title of the paragraph labelled *Adaptive Rationality* and *Limited Learning* from *Adaptive Rationality and Knowledge for Change*, despite these two expressions appearing to convey the same concept. Two articles epitomize Ciborra's focus on learning: 'Organisational learning and core capabilities development: the role of ICT' (Ciborra and Andreu, 1996), and 'Sharing Knowledge across boundaries' (Ciborra and Andreu, 2001). The latter is an extension of work undertaken in the former, separated by a short period of time.

In the first of these two articles, Ciborra adopts a resource-based view of the firm to assess background knowledge and short term knowledge. Any factor owned by a firm, even without specific organizational effort, is considered a resource (Amit and Schoemaker, 1993). Resources become capabilities due to organizational routines, with knowledge embedded into routines and facilitating the transformation of resources into capabilities. According to the resource based view of the firm, at any given point in time, an organization is comprised of a specific stock of resources, capabilities and organizational routines, with a set of core capabilities rendering the organization inimitable and competitive.

What process leads to the development of an organization's core capabilities? Dosi et al. (1992) define this as a *path-dependent learning process* that is the result of idiosyncratic routines and the specific organizational context in which this process takes place. In the transformation from simple resources to organizational core capabilities, different levels of learning occur. The first level encompasses work practices in which two types of learning take place: learning for transforming resources in an efficient way and, learning through the adaptation of new resources (technological innovation, for example) that leads to the emergence of new work practices. The *routinization learning loop* defines this transformation of resources into work practices as occurring due to organizational constraints that are shaped by a formative context. A second level of learning is depicted by the *capability learning loop* in which this transformation does not account for work practices but rather, *drives them*. The focus is on organizational routines: on programmes and actions in particular that govern an organization achieving a static efficiency in which well defined routines become legitimized as the established way of doing things.

The nature of learning can alter when two additional factors are introduced into this discourse: the competitive environment and the organization's directive. The milieu in which the firm operates contributes to which of its capabilities attain their strategic potential, whilst organizational directives define the criteria required to be competitive and establish priorities. The *strategic learning loop* defines this knowledge as 'necessary to extract core capabilities', reflecting operation within dynamic efficiency, and not static efficiency.

These loops constitute the learning ladder model. A further loop for consideration is that of *radical learning*. This is imposed upon a firm when significant changes occur in the environment or in the business mission. This type of learning is difficult to achieve, as it can conflict with the formative context of the organization. Namely, that background knowledge has to be abandoned in favour of short-term knowledge.

Ciborra's work, 'Sharing Knowledge Across Boundaries' (2001) introduces the concept of *knowledge management*. A number of fundamental questions that can be asked at this time are: Does the nature of knowledge alter if the organizational context under investigation is comprised of two or more organizations engaged in some form of alliance (joint venture and merger, for example)? Does this alter if a large number of interdependent organizations are examined instead? Can the concept of formative context and the learning ladder model be of value in understanding the nature of knowledge?

The formative context is organization-centric and as such is not applicable to the assessment of alliances. The learning ladder provides greater flexibility, but requires a number of caveats. The overarching objective is to construct a new ladder based on the recombination of resources and capabilities of organizations involved in an alliance. Deyer and Singh (1998) define relational quasi-rents as unique inter-organizational linkages able to confer competitive advantage. This negates a reliance on core capabilities and instead draws upon relational rents that emerge from synergies achieved outside of the domain of a single organization. These include synergies resulting from investments in common assets and the development of distinctive know how. Both require a degree of learning in order to reach an effective governance of these processes, with three elements required for success: (1) the complementarity of the organizations' core competence, routines, systems and resources; (2) the ability to transfer the core competence between organizations, and, (3) the ability to generate different practices and learning based on a mix of existing and new resources and routines. Even with an effective governance of the learning ladder, questions remain on whether these requirements are possible and feasible.

If ICT is assessed within this context, the problem of incompatibility and data transfer is a pertinent one. This is often cited as a reason for the failure of ERP systems, with insurmountable problems often blocking or hampering cooperation between organizations. Alternatively, if such issues can be resolved, the acquisition of new competences due to the formation of an alliance may lead to the successful adoption of ICT. Adoption difficulties may emerge even in cases where this technology characterizes itself because of an unfit formative context.

In industrial sectors characterized by an intensive use of sophisticated technology and a reliance on knowledge, diverse forms of organizational cooperation often emerge. Alliances comprised of a small number of organizations are often supplanted by organizational networks involving a large number of organizations. In industries such as telecommunications, software or pharmaceuticals it is common practice for research labs, universities, government agencies and foundations to collaborate. It is often difficult to single out a new learning ladder from the result of such collaboration, or the resources, practices, and capabilities that emerge, for knowledge and learning are diffused across a fluid community of different organizations.

ICT supports an efficient exchange and recombination of new knowledge amongst participating organizations in such a context. In 'Sharing Knowledge Across Boundaries' Ciborra (2001) provides the example of the development of the Linux operating system in order to depict how practices, routines and capabilities cannot be constrained within specific organizational borders, and are instead often widely dispersed. The notion of formative context appears to more aptly capture the nature of this community of organizations, whilst the concept of knowledge provides flexibility in the study of varying organizational contexts including singular organizations, alliances between a number of organizations and communities of organizations.

Everyday knowledge

The term 'everyday knowledge' appears in the introductory chapter of *Tecnologie di Coordinamento* (Ciborra, 1989) as a research perspective to go over limits of the 'strategic rationality and opportunistic knowledge' that has been at the basis both of *Tecnologie di Coordinamento* (ibid) and *Teams, Markets and Systems* (1993). However, phenomenology becomes prevalent throughout Ciborra's work from the mid 1990s in particular, reflecting his belief that it provided a more adequate theoretical backdrop for him than that offered by other methodologies in management science. 'Crisis and Foundations: An Inquiry into the Nature and Limits of Models and Methods in the Information Systems Discipline' (Ciborra, 1998b) epitomizes Ciborra's embrace of phenomenology.

In general, management science displays an inclination towards the natural science paradigm. Husserl (1970) posits that this is the result of three factors: the separation between people and science and the ensuing forgetting of the subjective origin of science; the founding role of every day life in the creation and development of any methodology, and the oblivion of the nature of the authentic human person in the management of organizations and technologies (Ciborra, 1998b: p. 7). Ciborra believed that 'phenomena such as: plans keep being diverted, surprises arise constantly, opportunistic adjustments must be carried out on the spur of the moment, so that planning is espoused while circumstances compel managers to improvise' (Ciborra, 1998b: p. 13).

Ciborra's objective was to reduce the gap between what he perceived was an excessively abstract and sanitized interpretation of reality inherent in current research methodology, and what he observed in an organizational context. If human existence is the primary element required to comprehend, interpret and define reality, Ciborra sought a better reconciliation between this perspective and what management science espoused. This resulted in the notion of care emerging as a means of addressing this issue.

'Care' is used by Ciborra to illustrate how technology is appropriated by users. In the introduction of *Groupware and Teamwork* (Ciborra, 1996), the learning ladder is re-interpreted according to the notion of care. Both the learning ladder and formative context are not distinct from, but rather, set within, a phenomenological perspective. The routinization learning loop, capability learning loop, strategic learning loop and radical learning (formative context substitution) are utilized to depict *taking care* of a technology, as opposed to the use of the resource based view of the firm. Ciborra illustrates the notion of care with respect to the appropriation of technology with the example of groupware.[1]

Ciborra does not present ICT as an instrument for increasing cognitive activity (encompassing an unlimited rationality and fully accessible knowledge perspective, and a limited rationality and tacit knowledge perspective); for supporting transactions and affecting related costs (strategic rationality and opportunistic knowledge perspective), or for constituting a formative context (knowledge-learning combination). None of these focus on the role of ICT as a constitutive element of everyday life, with Ciborra citing Heidegger (1962) and Dreyfus (1994) to present three elements that accomplish this: *perception, circumspection* and *understanding*.

Perception represents technology from a scientific perspective, and can be defined as the sum of everyday characteristics and structures, but which do not become part of a wider context of meaning: technology is not affected by its surrounding environment and may be considered an abstraction due to its ability to overcome the impact of practical uses. *Circumspection* represents technology as an object that faces implementation obstacles with 'breakdowns' improving the implementation of technology. *Understanding* represents technology as 'a thing' which becomes embedded within a context of meaning, and is the sum of instruments that are 'taken for granted'.

The phenomenon of technology drift was also believed by Ciborra (1996) to be the result of 'taking care'. Ciborra defined the notion of drift as the shift of technology adoption in comparison to what was initially defined, with two principal reasons cited: the 'openness' of technology and its 're-invention' property, as embodied by improvisation and bricolage. Bricolage and improvisation have been the subject of two works by Ciborra, 'From thinking to tinkering: the grassroots of strategic information systems' (1992), and 'Notes on improvisation and time in organisations' (1999). The latter was subsequently revised and became incorporated as two chapters within *The Labyrinths of Information* (2002). This work ('Notes on improvisation and time in organisations') focused on the concept of 'taking care', and offered an insight into the relationship between background knowledge and short term knowledge, disputing limited rationality and the tacit knowledge perspective that characterizes current studies on improvisation.

Improvisation is a crucial element in organizational life required to overcome sudden unpredictable situations. It can occur as the result of a 'sequence of actions (that) can be executed with constant interchange among: (a) receipt of information about the current state of the environment (perception), (b) internal processing information (thinking), and (c) response to the environment (motor activity)'

(Vera and Simon, 1993: p. 13, cited in Ciborra, 2002). The depiction of human beings in such a manner differs little from a robot however. Improvisation protagonists are actors whose emotional composition is in the foreground and affects the situation in which the actors are involved. The actor's mood will affect his or her actions.

Ciborra's (2001) work, 'In the mood for knowledge' published as working paper, elaborates on this theme, stressing that 'moods, are far from being a marginal, colourful add-on to our mentalistic explanations of how the actors behave in a situation. They are the ground for our encountering the world; understanding and acting in the situation' (Ciborra, 2001: p. 13). In comparison to the limited rationality and tacit knowledge perspective, knowledge is not only related to individual and organizational limits inherent in its creating and transmission, but also to *moods*. Heidegger (1995) depicted that thinking, doing and acting are immersed in these elements, that ultimately determine what matters and what does not (Heidegger, 1995).

In a seminar delivered in June 2004 at the London School of Economics and Political Science 'The Mind of the Heart? It depends on the (definition of) situation', Ciborra depicted how we understand the world in which we are placed in using the concept of *situation*. Ciborra utilized Heidegger (2004) to define how our understanding of a given situation based on three senses: a sense of *content*; a sense of *relation*, and a sense of *enactment* or actualization. The sense of content represents the entities present in a given situation, such as objects, people and other physical and temporal elements. The sense of relation defines the links between the entities in the situation that lead to its eventual comprehension, whilst the sense of enactment or actualization reinforces these.

Heidegger (op cit) illustrates the sense of enactment with reference to the early Christians' 'Parousia', as well as the notion of 'as though not'. In the case of 'the second coming', he depicts a new dimension of time as Christians wait for Christ to return, reflecting a temporality in which the declination of time is planned and organized with difficulties. In the case of 'as though not', Heidegger reflected on how we can relate to the established institutional order, citing that in front of God there are no slaves, patron, Greeks or Jews and that instead of revolt, we should consider accepting different roles passively, living them 'as though they were not' valid (1 Cor. 7:20). Inner life and disposition overshadow the surrounding institutional and historical circumstances.

By considering moods, enactment or actualization, and the cognitive frames typical of the formative context approach, Ciborra contributed to a redefinition of the relationship between background knowledge and short term knowledge, providing a richer understanding of both personal and organizational life.

The theme of technology drift and corporate information infrastructure was explored by Ciborra during the late 1990s (Ciborra, 1998a; 1998b; 2000). He defined this type of infrastructure as an 'integrated set of equipment, systems, applications, processes, and people dedicated to the processing and communications of information' (Ciborra and Hanseth, 2000: p. 1). This type of infrastructure is typically possessed by larger firms and multinationals, with such networks differing to the single-firm ICT presented earlier in this paper. Ciborra once more utilizes a phenomenological perspective to explore the nature of this infrastructure, while drawing on organizational learning when portraying its implementation and adoption.

Ciborra's exploration of technology drift is diversified. Here, a knowledge-learning perspective is proposed in which a milieu conducive to learning occurs when top-down management intervention takes place within a closed and controllable infrastructure. A learning-centric environment can also be generated with bottom-up management intervention where this occurs within an open and embedded network. At this point, a restraint on control allows the emergence of ad hoc strategies that encourage the development of infrastructure that does not exist within a more rigid framework. It is often difficult to create an environment conducive to learning in other than one of these types of environments.

Weill and Broadbent (1998) highlight the prevalence of top-down studies of organizational learning in the literature, with a hierarchical approach most often encompassing the separation of strategy formulation from implementation. This more formalized process possesses the principal drawback that ad hoc deviations from a 'rigid' plan are often difficult to address successfully. The literature also identifies the ramifications when one set of organizational parameters is adopted, but another set is followed by organizational participants. Single-loop learning is also contrasted with double-loop learning within the implementation of information infrastructure (Argyris and Schön, 1996).

Where organizational parameters followed by participants within a firm diverge from those outlined in its strategy, those shared and legitimized will be the ones adopted and eventually institutionalized. Within this milieu, extant circumstances, including background knowledge, are able to intermittently steer actions in a diverse direction.

Ciborra's work in the late 1990s shifts focus from the concept of *learning* to the concept of *knowledge*. He draws upon both the resource based value of the firm and the model of the knowledge creating company (Nonaka and Takeuchi, 1995) to define an enterprise as a totality of processes and resources that contain the knowledge required to produce and deliver its goods and services. This knowledge is inherent in organizational actors, and in the in procedures, products and technology of the firm (Ciborra, 1998a). Infrastructure is comprised of those elements that connect, accumulate and distribute both tacit and explicit knowledge. Ciborra posited that it was possible to formulate a relationship between the nature of the infrastructure to be implemented and the intensity of knowledge that characterized the adopting enterprise. In particular, the higher the knowledge content (in processes and products), the higher the investment required in infrastructure (Ciborra and Hanset, 1998).

A review of Ciborra's work on technology drift and corporate information infrastructure reveals that the processes of implementation can be classified into 'top down', 'fragmented' (where the organizational context contributes to the introduction of adaptive and ad hoc ways), and 'grass roots' (where no plan or centralized control appears to exist). Ideal knowledge acquisition and propagation characteristics are defined as embodying *routine* (with established knowledge facilitating the transformation of inputs into outputs); *recombination* (where established knowledge is re-used for new processes and products), and are *emergent* (where processes and products continuously require new knowledge). The two dimensions of *implementation processes* and *knowledge types* allow the construction of a knowledge matrix where the factors of 'routine', 'recombination' and 'emergent' are placed across the top, while the factors of 'top down', 'fragmented' and 'grass roots' are positioned on the vertical axis. The use of such a matrix provides a view of the congruency between infrastructure implementation and other characteristics of the organization.

Epistemology

Ciborra's interpretation of knowledge depicts an evolving view over time. From an epistemological perspective, both *objective* and *subjective epistemology* are appropriate in their application to Ciborra's work. The former is based on the assumption that it is possible to know something only if it is analysed as an independent phenomenon. Namely, the world exists independently from a subject's knowledge of it. In contrast, in subjective epistemology, knowledge of the world is intrinsically affected by direct involvement in knowing, with knowledge inseparable from the subject.

Subjective epistemology encompasses the concepts of unlimited rationality and fully accessible knowledge, with knowledge directly accessible and available without the need for a mediator. Limited rationality and tacit knowledge are addressable from a subjective epistemological position as well, with the subject viewed as a repository for knowledge. In the case of strategic rationality and opportunistically acquired knowledge, a subject's self-interest position emerges within a subjective epistemological vantage point, despite events taking place in a social context in which knowledge is outside an individual's sphere. In the case of the knowledge-learning combination, Ciborra and Lanzara (1999) depict that actors routinely enact situations characterized by both cognitive aspects (subjective epistemology) and institutional ones (objective epistemology) which they assess when attempting to overcome the dichotomy between subject-object and agent-environment.

Ciborra depicts the potential for ICT to act as a substitute for an individual, defining it within the perspective of unlimited rationality and fully accessible knowledge. He also cites the potential for ICT to support human endeavour in processing information, reflecting a limited rationality and tacit knowledge perspective as espoused within a subjective epistemological view. When applied to ICT, the learning ladders loops provide a framework for refining the design and implementation of technology. Ciborra's epistemological position is not always evident however, and at times lends itself to a number of interpretations. This is also displayed in his exploration of learning, which raises the question, which epistemology is relevant: objective or subjective? Both the resource based view of the firm and the learning ladder yield an understanding of organizational reality.

In the case of the learning ladder, which encompasses the concept of formative context, relational quasi-rents (Deyer and Singh, 1998) and social knowledge capital, an ontological shift in focus from the singular organization to alliances or communities of organizations is accommodated.

The adoption of phenomenological philosophy represents a significant point of transition in Ciborra's work, despite its parallel evolution with the knowledge-learning combination perspective. Although sharing many points of difference, these two streams often intertwine, as reflected in Ciborra's work on information infrastructure. His latter phenomenological stance reflects an epistemological position that seeks to overcome the dichotomy countering objectivity and subjectivity with existence and being inseparable from the world in which subjects inhabit. This embodies Heidegger's (1962) view that existence is contextual and related to the world as a source of inputs.

In concluding a discussion on Ciborra's epistemological position, it is evident that his latter phenomenological orientation displays an inclination towards subjective epistemology, in contrast to a focus on structural and institutional elements. Ciborra defined technology appropriation through perception, circumspection and understanding on the one hand, and information infrastructure implementation, as viewed through the lenses of learning and knowledge, on the other. The former defines how humans experience ICT use, while the latter illustrates the role of structural factors framing such use, including infrastructures and organizations.

Ciborra adopted a variety of approaches when investigating a complex multi-layered subject such as information systems, including a phenomenological vantage point. Regardless of the breadth of Ciborra's approach, the coherence and applicability of his epistemology yielded a rich cadre of work that continues to be of relevance. This has paved the way for other researchers to pick up the threads of investigation that Ciborra has left the research community with, and continue promulgating the original and insightful legacy that he has left behind.

Notes

This paper originally appeared as Resca, A. (2006) Knowledge: climbing the learning ladder to a 'phenomenological' view, *Journal of Information Technology* **21**(3): 203–210.

1. Although the terminology used by Ciborra varies with terminology used in the learning ladder, it is believed to espouse the same meaning.

References

Amit, R. and Shoemaker, P.J.H. (1993). Strategic Assets and Organisational Rent, *Strategic Management Journal* **14**: 33–46.

Argyris, C. (1982). *Reasoning, Learning, and Action*, San Francisco: Jossey-Bass.

Argyris, C. and Schön, D.A. (1996). *Organisational Learning*, Reading MA: Addison-Wesley.

Ciborra, C.U. (1988). Knowledge and Systems in Organisations: a Typology and a Proposal, in R.M. Lee, A.M. Mc.Cosh and Migliarese, P. (eds.) *Organisational Decision Support Systems*, Amsterdam: North Holland, Elsevier Science Publisher B. V., pp. 229–245.

Ciborra, C.U. (1989). *Tecnologie di Coordinamento*, Milano: Franco Angeli.

Ciborra, C.U. (1992). From Thinking to Tinkering: the Grassroots of Strategic Information Systems, *Information Society* **8**: 297–309.

Ciborra, C.U. (1993). *Teams, Markets and Systems*, Cambridge: Cambridge University Press.

Ciborra, C.U. (1996). Introduction, in C. Ciborra (ed.) *Groupware and Teamwork*, Chichester: Wiley, pp. 1–19.

Ciborra. C.U. (1998a). Introduction, in C. Ciborra (ed.) *Infraglobe*, Milan: EtasLibri, pp. 1–27.

Ciborra, C.U. (1998b). Crisis and Foundations: an Inquiry into the Nature and Limits of Models and Methods in the Information Systems Discipline, *The Journal of Strategic Information Systems* **7**: 5–16.

Ciborra, C.U. (1999). Notes on Improvisation and Time in Organisations, *Accounting, Management and Information Technology* **9**: 77–94.

Ciborra, C.U. (2000). A Critical Review of the Literature on the Management of Corporate Information Infrastructure, in C.U. Ciborra (ed.) *From Control to Drift*, Oxford: Oxford University Press, pp. 15–40.

Ciborra, C.U. (2001). *In the Mood for Knowledge. A New Study of Improvisation*, Working Paper Series, London, London School of Economics and Political Science.

Ciborra, C.U. (2002). *The Labyrinths of Information*, Oxford: Oxford University Press.

Ciborra, C.U. (2006). The Mind of the Heart? It depends on the (definition of) situation, *Journal of Information Technology* **21**(3): 129–139.

Ciborra, C.U. and Andreu, R. (1996). Organisational Learning and Core Capabilities Development: the Role of ICT, *Strategic Information systems* **5**: 111–127.

Ciborra, C.U. and Andreu, R. (2001). Sharing Knowledge Across Boundaries, *Journal of Information Technology* **16**(2): 73–81.

Ciborra, C.U. and Hanseth, O. (1998). Toward a Contingency View of Infrastructure and Knowledge, ICIS Conference Proceedings, Helsinki, December.

Ciborra, C.U. and Hanseth, O. (2000). Introduction, in C. Ciborra and Associates (eds.) *From Control to Drift*, Oxford: Oxford University Press, pp. 1–11.

Ciborra, C.U. and Lanzara, G.F. (1989). Change and Formative Contexts and Information Systems Development, in H.K. Klein, et al. (eds.) *Systems Development for Human Progress*, Amsterdam: North Holland, pp. 21–40.

Ciborra, C.U. and Lanzara, G.F. (1999). Introduction, in C. Ciborra, et al. (eds.) *Labirinti dell'Innovazione*, Milano: EtasLibri, pp. 1–22.

Deyer, J.H. and Singh, H. (1998). The Relational View: Cooperative Strategy and Sources of Interorganisational Competitive Advantage, *Academy of Management Review* **23**(4): 660–679.

Dosi, G. Teece, D.J. and Winter, S.G. (1992). Toward a theory of corporate coherence: Preliminary remarks, in G. Dosi, R. Giannetti, and P.A. Toninelli (eds) *Technology and Enterprise in a Historical Perspective*, Oxford: Clarendon Press, pp. 185–211.

Dreyfus, H.L. (1994). *Being-in-the-World*, Cambridge, MA: MIT Press.

Festinger, L. (1957). *A Theory of Cognitive Dissonance*, New York: Harper and Row.

Gulick, L. and Urwick, L. (eds.) (1937). *Papers on the Science of Administration*, New York: Institute of Public Administration.

Heidegger, M. (1962). *Being and Time*, New York: Harper and Row.

Heidegger, M. (1995). *The Basic Problems of Phenomenology*, Bloomington, Indiana University Press.

Heidegger, M. (2004). *The Phenomenology of Religious Life*, Bloomington: Indiana University Press.

Husserl, E. (1970). *The Crisis of European Sciences and Transcendental Phenomenology*, Evanston, IL: Northwestern University Press.

Nonaka, I. and Takeuchi, H. (1995). *The Knowledge-Creating Company*, Oxford: Oxford University Press.

Ouchi, W.G. (1980). Markets, Bureaucracy and Clans, *Administrative Science Quarterly* **25**: 129–141.

Piaget, J. (1974). *Understanding Causality,* New York: Norton.
Polany, M. (1966). *The Tacit Dimension,* Garden City, NY: Doubleday.
Simon, H.A. (1976). *Administrative Behavior,* New York: The Free Press.
Taylor, F.W. (1911). *The Principles of Scientific Management,* New York: Harper.
Thompson, J.D. (1967). *Organisation in Action,* New York: McGraw Hill.
Unger, R.M. (1987). *The False Necessity,* Cambridge: Cambridge University Press.
Vera, A.H. and Simon, H.A. (1993). Situated Action: a Symbolic Interpretation, *Cognitive Science* **17**: 7–48.
Weber, M. (1964). *The Theory of Social and Economic Organisation,* New York: The Free Press.
Weill, P. and Broadbent, M. (1998). *Leveraging the New Infrastructure: How Markets Leaders Capitalize on Information,* Oxford: Oxford University Press.
Williamson, O.E. (1975). *Markets and Hierarchies: Analysis and Antitrust Implications,* New York: The Free Press.

13
Organizing Technology: Of Hospitality*

Martin Brigham and Lucas D. Introna

Introduction

'In a world populated by mobile, nomadic 'hordes'...there will hardly be a hotter issue than the one of *hospitality*', so said Claudio Ciborra a decade ago (1999: 193, emphasis added). But what does or might hospitality denote now? And more specifically for our purposes, what kind of insights does the concept of hospitality offer to those studying the deployment and use of information technology? Ciborra suggests that an interest in hospitality is part of a fresh vocabulary and emerging landscape of inquiry for thinking differently about our relation to information technology. The implications of this preoccupation with hospitality for the field of information system research, with its long-held concerns for alignment, control and planning and related aspirations that privilege integration, coherence and complementary practices, is the focus of this chapter.

Ciborra's writing (1998b, 1999a, b; 2000, 2001, 2004, to name a few) challenges us, we suggest, to rethink our relationship to information technology in the most general terms. Ciborra's legacy is not one that simply offers us a new set of normative models, guidelines or suggestions of how to develop and use information technology. Nor is he suggesting that we 'go out there' and study in more detail the seemingly endless 'failure' of IT (see Sauer, 1993). Rather, the proposition is that we rethink our very way of approaching the phenomenon of information systems more generally – to take more careful note of our assumed or explicitly chosen ontology. In his view our starting point was wrong from the start.

In building and using tools we tend to think of these as 'objective' material things (separate from us) that we can simply use (or not) to do whatever we want to do. This view is rooted in our everyday intuitions in which the subject/object dualism is taken for granted, that is to say, in a form of naïve realism (or the 'natural attitude' in Husserl's terminology). This relationship between us and our tools is often expressed as a means/ends relationship where technology is designed as a means (or tool) to achieve a particular end (defined by the designers and users). According to this view, we need to understand and manage the 'impact' that IT has on organizations, or social practices more generally, as it is taken up and used in everyday situations. To do this it is proposed that we study many different examples and then inductively build general models that are supposed to 'tell us' how to best manage IT. However when we go into organizations these 'idealised' abstractions never seem to fit the messy specificity of everyday life (Ciborra, 1998b) – every example seems to be an exception to the model that is supposed to describe it. The route out of this is not more models, or more detailed descriptions, but rather a radically different approach, from the start. Ciborra proposes an entirely different ontology to the realist 'tool' paradigm or even the constructivist paradigm.

Ciborra suggests that we ground ourselves in phenomenology – mostly the work of Husserl and Heidegger – and also their successors in the work of Derrida and Levinas. His suggestion is that we do not need to simply proceed to design and use our tools differently, but, critically, that we reconsider radically our very way of approaching or making sense of the phenomena of IT as it reveals itself to us in everyday practice. To facilitate this new approach he puts forward a new vocabulary (quite unfamiliar to our Cartesian ear) – a language of hospitality, care, bricolage/improvisation, *Gestell*, cultivation and drift.

This chapter elaborates the significance of the concept of hospitality for our understanding of information technology and extends this to the related concepts of bricolage and *Gestell*. In doing this, the first task is to provide an account of a phenomenological understanding of technology. We then introduce three inter-connected concepts from Ciborra's work – hospitality, bricolage and *Gestell*. Our concern here is to situate the interest in hospitality and information technology in the wider modern continental European tradition of social and ethical theorizing and to connect hospitality to bricolage and *Gestell*. Following this, we present research findings from a longitudinal study of Vehicle Mounted Data System (VMDS) or, more generically, a Mobile Data Terminal (MDT) at a fire brigade in the UK. We then provide a discussion of the research evidence in terms of a phenomenologically based ontology of hospitality, highlighting how Ciborra's distinctive vocabulary allows us to see mobile data terminals and IT more generally in ways not possible through a traditional Cartesian ontology. The final part of the chapter suggests implications for future research.

On a phenomenological understanding of technology

The problem with the 'tool' view of technology – where technology is seen as objective tools (or mere means) for us to use in order to achieve our objectives (or ends) – is that it suggests these tools are simply of our making and at our behest. More precisely, such a view believes that we can make and use these tools without them immediately and simultaneously (re)making and 'using' us. Phenomenologists (Heidegger, 1977a, b; Borgmann, 1984, 1999; Ihde, 1990, 2002; Dreyfus, 1992, 1993, 2001; Introna and Ilharco, 2004) would argue that technology and humans are each other's condition of possibility for being – i.e. they always and already co-constitute each other. Let us consider an example to see what this means.

When a consultant takes up a mobile phone the consultant acquires a certain capability (to contact and be contacted) but that is not all that happens. We need to look at this seemingly obvious statement of 'consultant,' 'mobile phone' and 'taking up' more closely. The mobile phone only becomes 'a mobile phone' when taken up by the consultant. When it lies on the table it is a potential to be 'a mobile phone', but it only becomes an actual 'possibility for contacting' when it is picked up and one dials the number, and, of course, there is sufficient credit on the account, and it is possible to get a signal, and so forth. In taking up the mobile phone both the mobile phone and the consultant becomes transformed. The mobile phone is no longer 'merely' an object and the consultant becomes a human that embodies the possibility to contact and be contacted at a distance. With the mobile phone in hand the world, now and in the future, becomes revealed in new ways (for example, a person 'far off' is suddenly 'near'); previous possibilities not visible or evident at all suddenly emerge as possible possibilities – some intended, some unintended.

What this example shows is that the mobile phone and the consultant are each other's constitutive condition for being what they are as 'mobile phones' and as 'consultants.' Obviously the mobile phone is just one of a multiplicity of constitutive relations that constitutes the horizon of possibilities for a person to 'be a consultant'. Phenomenologists argue that the realist or constructivist account of technology (and/or organizations) posit these phenomena (consultant and mobile) as if speaking about the one (organization or technology) does not already and immediately draw upon the other for its ongoing sense or meaning – for its way of being what it is already taken as. In other words they are each other's ongoing transcendental condition or possibility for being what they are taken as – 'transcendental' is here understood as 'that which constitutes, and thereby renders the empirical possible' (Mohanty, 1997: 52). Thus, we and our technology are an indivisible unity from the start. Heidegger (1962: 297) argues in *Being and Time* that we humans (which he calls *Dasein*) exist in an ongoing structural openness 'towards' the world in which the self and the world is always and already a unity, a being-in-the-world in his terminology.

In our example thus far we have limited our discussion to the relationship between the person and mobile phone. As such we have not yet revealed the full transcendental or constitutive horizon at work in our example. Recognizing the possibilities or affordances (i.e. the perceived properties of an artefact that suggests how it should be used (Norman, 1988)) of the mobile phone draws on a prior familiarity with a world where things like mobile phones and the act of phoning by using a device already makes sense – we can imagine many where it would not make sense. If we were to locate the mobile phone in a culture where such practices do not exist at all the mobile phone will not even show up as 'a mobile phone'. It might just show up as an odd and strange object lying there. Thus, for our example to make sense at all – also for us as readers – it draws on an already present familiarity of a world in which such things and a practices already makes sense (Heidegger, 1962: 97–98).

Moreover, we do not simply take up a mobile phone for its own sake. We take up technology with an already present reference to our ongoing projects or our concerns. As human beings we are always already projected, we are always already ahead of ourselves – anticipating and actively shaping our future possibilities to be. By this we mean that we, in our everyday going about, are always already immersed in a nexus of concerns that constitute us as that which we are, as, for example, 'managers', 'consultants', 'academics'. The mobile phone will only show up or stand out as something potentially relevant and useful in a nexus of concerns where the possibility of contacting 'at a distance' might be a necessary condition to realize the concerns that constitute the 'who' that such a mobile phone assumes. Heidegger (1962) argues that we are always and already immersed in a whole nexus of concerns. This is why Heidegger (1962: 236) claims that our human way of being is care (care as in things already 'mattering' to us) – we always already care to be somebody in particular rather than just some body. We do not simply bang on keys, we use the laptop to type, in order , for example, to write this chapter, to send e-mails, and to surf the web. Moreover, the writing of this chapter refers to the possibility of a publication. This publication refers to an audience, which refers to a discipline, which refer to future audiences, which refer to other research, which refer to promotion, and so on. It is this prior and already understood nexus of references that makes this activity of typing on this keyboard, here and now, already obvious and meaningful. Heidegger (1962: 118) calls this recursively defining and necessary nexus of projects and tools 'the world' – as in the 'the world of acting', the 'world of business,' the 'world of the academy'. For phenomenologists, technology makes sense and has its being only as something always and already in-the-world. Let us now consider how Claudio Ciborra uses these insights of phenomenology to talk about our relationship with information technology.

Hospitality, bricolage and *gestell*

Hospitality

Ciborra (1999a), drawing on the insights of phenomenology outlined above, suggests that technology is not a 'passive' actor, just there, but is rather an actor which already actively draws upon and remakes the world it inhabits. This 'remaking' is, we will argue, central to problematizing approaches that have emphasized the aligning of information systems with business strategy and practice (for a review see Galliers, 2007). As users draw upon technology much of this 'remaking' will surpass the intentions that the designers attempted to 'build into it.' It would therefore be more appropriate to treat this non-human actor in our midst as a sort of a 'stranger' rather than as a familiar servant. This important insight leads Ciborra to adopt the concept of *hospitality* suggested by Derrida (1999, 2000) as a way to make sense of our ongoing co-constitutive relationship with IT. Ciborra (1998b: 196) suggests that hospitality 'describes the phenomenon of dealing with new technology as an ambiguous stranger'. The adoption of this word seems relatively innocent but it has very important implications for how we conduct ourselves towards IT.

According to Derrida (1997: 110), hospitality is the 'welcoming of the other; the invitation to the stranger'. However, in its Latin root hospitality also suggests something else:

> hospitality derives from the Latin hospes, which is formed from hostis, which originally meant a 'stranger' and came to take on the meaning of the enemy or 'hostile stranger' (hostilis) + pets (polis, poles, potentia) to have power. (Derrida, 1997: 110–111)

Hospitality, to be hospitality, also contains its opposite within itself: without the potential for hostility, hospitality does not make sense. Ciborra suggests, with Derrida, that hospitality is about crossing the boundary between us and the 'stranger' without abolishing this boundary. For Derrida, it is the very threshold of hospitality where questions of justice arise. Hosting technology is about 'establishing a paramount symmetry between humans [the host] and non humans [the guest]' (Ciborra, 1999a: 198). Nevertheless, it is a symmetry based on a fundamentally asymmetrical hosting relationship – asymmetrical since 'we want to honour the guest *and* keep him/her at a distance *at the same time*' (Dikeç, 2002: 229, emphasis added). Yet symmetrical because there is the ongoing possibility of a reversal in which the host becomes guest: host and guest accepts that they may need to reconsider their practices, rituals and customs – not to simply abolish them or to appropriate wholesale those of the other (this would be imposition or assimilation). How does this hosting relationship manifest itself? Ciborra (2004: 114) explains:

> technology, as a guest, presents itself to the host endowed with affordances. Affordances trigger a network of commitments by the host.... But that is just the beginning of an open-ended process: the guest also possesses its own dynamics and will begin to align the host according to certain needs and constraints...

Ciborra argues that in this reciprocal hosting relationship a number of phenomena emerge that are important to attend to if we are to understand the subtlety of this relationship. He suggests that through hosting technology becomes 'humanized'. Affordances become constituted (or reconstituted) and situated in ongoing practices (see also Gibson, 1979). They emerge to those approaching the technology as obvious 'possibilities-to-do' this or that. Note, however, that affordances may seem strange (why would you want to do that?) or may not even show up at all. Indeed they often show up as annoying features of the guest. This is because the guest brings with it its 'own world'. The host must also take heed of these 'needs and constraints' of the guest and not simply try and 'abolish this boundary' by trying to impose its world onto the guest – this would not be hosting, hosting requires that we accommodate the guest, as a guest. Ciborra proposes that in practice we find this accommodation of the guest manifesting itself through practices such as bricolage. Ciborra (1998b: 116) suggests that '[t]hese highly situated human activities are far from being the result of the practitioner as an artist, or a snob. They belong to the core of the human institution of hospitality. They express the thousands of subtle ways in which humans ingeniously discover, discern, interpret and act upon the shades of the encounter with technology as an ambiguous stranger'. Let us consider these in more detail.

Bricolage, improvisation and tinkering

Bricolage is not simply a surplus or incidental activitiy 'added on' by incompetent users that ought to be targeted so as to bring the system 'back under control.' They are essential practices of hospitality. Obviously, they may not always be efficient and they may even look 'wasteful'. However, on closer inspection they may indeed be examples of skilful coping by actors that have a subtle understanding of what it means to host a guest. How does this skilful hosting happen? Can we give a more sophisticated account of them that goes beyond describing them merely as good or bad 'patches' or 'workarounds?' (see Robey et al., 2002).

Ciborra (1999b, 2001) argues that improvisation happens as part of our *Befindlichkeit* (a term he takes from Heidegger). *Befindlichkeit* 'combines the idea of situatedness and of feeling and faring, of where and how one finds itself' (Ciborra, 2001: 6). It reflects a certain mood in which we find ourselves. Mood is understood as a certain attunement with the situation – such as the 'sensing of the mood of the meeting'. Importantly, the 'mood of the meeting' is not something we choose, it is rather something we already find ourselves in when we become aware of it. Heidegger (1962: 172–79) argues that mood is not merely 'feelings' that accompany the 'higher-order' faculties of cognition, will and reason. It is rather the reverse. The so-called 'higher order' faculties have as their necessary condition the already disclosedness of the (im)possibilities of the world that mood as attunement already provides. As Heidegger (1962: 137, emphasis added) suggests: '[t]he mood has already disclosed, in every case, Being-in-the-world *as a whole*, and makes it possible first of all to direct oneself towards something'. Skilled actors, who are in tune with the disclosure of the mood, grasp 'in the moment,' as it were, the world as a whole with all its (im)possibilities.

Ciborra (2001) discusses the well-known Mann Gulch fire disaster first analysed by Weick (1993). He contrasts the behaviour of Dodge (the leader and a survivor of the disaster) with the smokejumpers who died. Dodge survived because he improvised in the moment – what Weick terms a 'cosmology episode'. As a skilled and experienced fire fighter Dodge realized immediately that he had to remove from his surroundings the resources (i.e. grass) that the approaching fire needed to burn. So he lit a fire and jumped into his own smouldering fire. Being attuned to the mood the 'world of fire and fire fighting' *as a whole* the right thing to do was disclosed as evident. He did not need to think and work it out. In the moment he just 'knew' what to do, as Ciborra (2001: 9) describes:

> The team members were victims of panic, and in this fundamental mood they interpreted what Dodge was doing [lighting a fire] as 'going nuts' and an

> explicit authorization by their captain for everyone to go mad. Panic determined their experiencing lack of time and being overwhelmed by the world, the forest on fire.

This is a rather dramatic example of improvisation (see also Lanzara, 1983). Ciborra suggests that the disclosure of the world, in mood, can overwhelm us and shift to a mood of panic or we can respond to it with resoluteness (see Heidegger, 1962: 296). Most bricolage happens, however, as an integral part of 'simply getting the job done' – as we document in our study below. Nevertheless, they are all based on a certain attunement (Dreyfus, 1992).

Hosting technology and accommodating it does not reveal the full horizon of the meaning of technology in the world where it functions as such. There is another horizon that is relevant. This is the way the technology 'sets up' a world in which certain possibilities emerge as possible and others not. We now need to turn to Ciborra and Hanseth's (1998a) use of the Heideggarian notion of *Gestell.*

Gestell as the enframing of technology

Heidegger (1977a: 4) famously claimed that 'the essence of technology is nothing technological'. Technology is not a particular technical artefact of our relationship with this or that artefact. Rather, artefacts, devices, infrastructures – and our relationship with them – are *already* an outcome of, or revealed, as a particular 'technological' mode of seeing and form of conduct that apprehends the world as something to be ordered and shaped in line with our projects, intentions and desires. Technology reveals itself, then, from a prior orientation of being, an involvement whole that is an already present being-in-the-world (see Introna, 2007: 324).

In this 'technological mood' or 'enframing' (*Gestell* in German) problems show up as *requiring* technical solutions: 'Enframing means the gathering together of that setting-upon that sets upon man, i.e. challenges him forth to reveal the real, in the mode of ordering, as standing-reserve' (Heidegger, 1977a: 305). Thus in a technological age the world is already 'framed' as a world available 'to be ordered' – the modern mood, a 'will to power' that is a 'will to technology' (Introna, 2007). Technology makes sense because we already live in the technological mood that discloses or reveals 'our world' as already enframed in this way – as available resources for the ongoing ordering. As Ciborra (2004: 73) explains:

> The Gestell captures all that is extant and makes it available through a stock to be put in circulation. Machines are built and applied, science generates new solutions that get converted into new systems and applications because of the Gestell, not the other way around. Nature itself loses the property of being an object (Gegen-stand) and becomes Be-stand, i.e. standing reserve of available resources to be exploited in the process of circulation.

Ciborra and Hanseth (1998a: 321–322) suggest that IT is a good example of the manifestation of *Gestell.* IT infrastructures act as 'formative contexts, [that] shape not only the work routines, but also the ways people look at practices, consider them 'natural' and give them their overarching character of necessity. Infrastructure becomes an essential factor shaping the taken-for-grantedness of organizational practices. Imagining, world views and reform initiatives, or new designs are moulded by the subtle and hidden influence of infrastructures'. As many organisations become increasingly dependent on IT more and more of our world becomes enframed as available resources. In the end humans also become framed as available resources. How could we respond?

Heidegger suggests that we cannot 'get rid of technology' because it is the modern mood in which we already find ourselves. It is through and beyond this mood that we must find a way to affirm technology. Once we grasp *Gestell* a possibility opens up for things to be otherwise. Ciborra suggests (2004: 77–78; see also Ciborra and Hanseth, 1998: 322), summarizing Heidegger and Dreyfus, that this can take different forms. For our purpose here we highlight the following:

- *The ability to jump, or switch Gestalt*: The jump is needed to get out of the calculative and instrumental thought [of *Gestell*], and approach domains where man [humans] can 'start asking questions of being anew'.
- *Shifting fluctuations to the centre stage*: Taking up practices that are now at the margins of our culture and make them central, while de-emphasizing practices now central to our cultural self-understanding.

We will show what this might mean though a case study below. Now that we have a different language to think about our relationship with IT, let us look at a particular case and see if these concepts will enable us to give a new and innovative way to make sense of the actors in the case.

Contextualizing the research

Studying mobile data terminals at Hereford and Worcester fire brigade

The research took the form of an in-depth, long-term and ethnographically-inspired study of a Mobile Data Terminal (MDT) or Vehicle Mounted Data System (the VMDS as it was known at the brigade). In-vehicle mobile data terminals are increasingly used by emergency services, but also in a wide range of contexts where access to information and the ability to communicate on the move is considered important (for medicine and military purposes, for example, but also for maritime and transportation activities).

Hereford and Worcester Fire Brigade was chosen as a research site because it had implemented a MDT and offered high quality research access. The brigade's MDT was also the first of its kind in the UK fire service and was considered to have important best practice implications for the provision of information to fire crews across the UK. Researching the MDT also provided the opportunity to research generic themes of IT and organizational change in an under-researched part of the public sector (see also Meehan, 1998).

The research was conducted in four overlapping stages that began in 1997 and has continued to date. The first stage comprised 24 semi-structured and taped interviews conducted with all levels of the brigade's hierarchy during 1997–98: the deputy chief fire officer, divisional, assistant divisional, station and sub-officers, watch commanders and firefighters. Interviews focused on the implementation, use and the trajectory of the MDT. Interviews, which were recorded and transcribed, lasted between 45 minutes and a number of hours. Informal group interviews, which were usually not recorded, were conducted with nine crews plus individual firefighters. These usually took place during the 'stand down' time after 9pm in the evening when fire crews could be interviewed at length. Initial ordering of research data followed interview themes but over time data was re-examined in a recursive relationship with theoretical interests.

The purpose of the second stage was to understand how fire crews used the MDT. Observations were conducted for intensive week-long periods plus occasional ongoing visits at six of the largest stations. Observation included demonstrations of the MDT and more typical ethnographic observation of crews' watch routine. The brigade's command and control centre and the brigade's Operational Intelligence Unit were also observed over an intensive two-week period. Written notes were made in a research diary and written up with comments and reflections. The third stage involved the collection of documents about the brigade. This took place primarily at the brigade's head office and Operational Intelligence Unit and included: internal communications and newsletters; brigade policy documents and performance plans; training manuals; minutes from meetings; MDT records and pre-MDT records. The final stage involved archival research on the fire service and comprised of visits to the National Fire Service library. This provided access to Home Office, Office of the Deputy Prime Minister (ODPM) and Her Majesty's Fire Service Inspectorate (HMFSI) reviews and reports, White Papers, parliamentary debates and statutes, specialist fire service publications, and publications from the union and the Chief Fire Officers' Association.

Contextualizing UK fire service provision

Fire services respond to emergency fire calls and have a statutory duty to attend fire-related incidents and undertake fire safety work. The UK Fire Service is publicly funded, but brigades are directly accountable to local fire authorities, which receive funding, policy guidance and instructions from central government. Apart from a seven-year period of nationalised fire services from 1941–48, local fire authorities have controlled the provision of fire services. De-nationalization in 1948 led to local control by 141 city and county boroughs. In 1974, 62 large county brigades replaced city and county boroughs, and in the mid-1980s many county brigades were reorganized. As part of local government reorganization during the 1990s, a number of brigades, including Hereford and Worcester, have become local and independent fire authorities.

In parallel to the local provision of fire services, there are national standards and performance criteria placed on fire brigades. The 1947 *Fire Services Act* specified national criteria for crews attending incidents (e.g. time to get to an incident and minimum number of firefighters), standards for building risk classification (classification depending upon type of density of buildings) and collectively negotiated working practices. De-nationalization also established a corporatist practice of multi-stakeholder national-level decision making. Rhodes (1985) characterized such practices as the embodiment of the post-war assumption of the public sector as a model employer and negotiated change:

> [W]e all know that the Fire Service is very standardised throughout the country.... in spite of the model standards of fire cover recommending a one appliance [fire engine] response everywhere except A and B risk areas, most brigades still send two fire engines to all property fires.... The make-up of appliance fleets is more varied than at first appears to be the case. For example, some brigades have provided all first line appliances with very comprehensive rescue equipment, while others meet the requirement by having a small number of specialised rescue units. (Bassett, 1991: 17)

Throughout the 1980s and 1990s, challenges to national standards, corporatist decision-making and national and local practices have taken the form of central government reviews such as the Audit Commission's 1995 report 'In the Line of Fire'. This report concluded that although the fire service was generally well managed, significant efficiency gains were possible by regionalizing local control centres, restructuring overprovision through flexible working practices and reducing absenteeism. Despite national reviews, there has been, according to Bain et al. (2002), a disconnection between the recommendations contained within reviews and the level of implementation of change from the 1970s onwards. Bain et al. (2002) explain this by the 'weak managerialism' and 'lack of strategic leadership' by senior officers and central government. Bain et al. (2002) recommended 'top to bottom' modernization comprising of a strategic shift from incident management to fire prevention, devolved conditions and working practices, the allocation of resources based upon changing levels of risk throughout the day, regionalized fire provision and greater collaboration between emergency services.

The Hereford and Worcester Fire Brigade

Hereford and Worcester Fire Brigade is one of the 50 brigades in England and Wales, and is responsible for a large geographical area of mostly semi-rural countryside but also busy motorways. Unlike the neighbouring West Midlands Fire Brigade, the brigade is comparatively small, non-metropolitan and not known for being a leader of fire service reform (see Cox, 1994: 27). The brigade is currently comprised of three districts and 27 stations. Five stations are crewed full time (i.e. day and night), three day-crewed and 19 retained/voluntary. The brigade has over 700 firefighters, plus over 100 control room and non-uniformed staff. Fire crews' shifts comprise of operational incidents, training, community fire safety, equipment maintenance and risk assessments. Stations have designated 'turn out' areas that set out the geographical boundary of station responsibility, but crews move outside these boundaries for major or concurrent incidents. In 1974 the fire brigades of Herefordshire and Worcestershire were restructured into the Fire Authority for Hereford and Worcester. This organizational structure remained in place until 1998 when Hereford and Worcester County Council was split into two counties, with the management of fire service provision replaced by a Combined Fire Authority covering both counties.

Information technology and the fire service

Policy statements and reviews of the public sector, such as the White Paper on 'Modernising Government' foreground 'joined up' working and collaboration through IT as a key driver of efficiency and public sector modernization (Cabinet Office, 1999). In contrast, the role of IT has been remarkable by its insignificance in national reports and reviews of the fire service during the 1980s and 1990s. IT is mentioned in the Management Report that accompanies the Audit Commission's (1995a) report, for example, but only in terms of speeding up 'back-office' activities and upgrading mobilizing systems at command and control centres. Front-line IT to support fire crews at incidents or the deployment of IT to foster efficiency is not evaluated. Similarly, Bain et al. (2002) only briefly mentions IT. A lack of strategic direction, tightening budgets throughout the 1980s and 1990s, year-on-year increases in brigades' funding gaps, and expanding demands for safety activities point to a lack of emphasis on IT. In the 1990s context of doubtful government funding for IT projects across the fire service, IT initiatives have been focused on individual brigades with little focus on standardization between brigades or interoperability between emergency services.

Hosting mobile data terminals

The brigade installed the MDT on 36 fire appliances in March 1996. The MDT is located in each of the brigade's fire appliances/engines and mounted on the front dashboard. Screens provide access to risk information on buildings; first response tactical plans for large-scale risks; standard incident officer procedures; chemical information, and Ordnance Survey (OS) maps detailing water hydrants. Risk information, for example, comprises of 'address, station area, map reference, predetermined attendance, directions from the nearest main road, information regarding the structure and location of the premises, significant hazards, site location plans, building construction, water supplies, and any special features' (Goodwin, 1997: 39).

The MDT integrates a wide range of operational information that was previously held on paper, was based at stations, communicated by radio or kept by watches into a standardized and real-time IT infrastructure. Real-time access to the information was often described as 'universal access'. The brigade's Chief Fire Officer describes the functional requirements as comprising of the storage capacity for 2,000 risk records; easy, quick and secure access to information by fire crews; the availability of multiple copies; ease of updating; and the ability to audit information placed on the MDT (O'Dwyer, 1996: 33–34). In addition to real-time access, the management of information was moved from stations to the newly formed 'Operational Intelligence Unit', which is responsible for maintaining risk records, allocating safety inspections and amending operational procedures.

An invitation to the stranger or welcoming of the MDT?

Hospitality cannot begin with hostility. The guest needs to be welcomed and the guest must present itself as something worth inviting in, even as something needing inviting in; and when it came to the inviting in of the MDT nothing was as compelling as the death of colleagues. On 6 September 1993 two of the brigade's firefighters died at a major fire incident at a large poultry processing factory called Sun Valley. This incident was a major event at the brigade with over 20 fire appliances attending the incident. In response to the fire, and after an investigation into the deaths of two firefighters, two Health and Safety Improvement Notices were served on the brigade in May 1994 – one for breathing apparatus procedures and the other for inadequate provision of information. The latter Notice, which led to the implementation of the MDT, stated that the brigade was in contravention of the Health and Safety at Work Act (1992) because:

> the **information held** by the Brigade **and available to fire crews and officers** on particular hazards associated with the design and materials of construction of buildings is **insufficient** to ensure as far as reasonably practicable the health and safety of firefighters. ('The Grapevine', Hereford and Worcester Fire Brigade, 1997: 8, emphasis added)

The basis for the Improvement Notice was the statutory requirement that obliges all brigades to provide information and instructions to firefighters about significant risks they may encounter. At the time of the Sun Valley fire, the brigade's practice, which was common to all UK fire brigades, was to hold a series of paper-based risk cards held in A4 folders (known as 1.(1).D risk cards or '084s' – written, typed and diagrammatic risk information) which were kept in fire appliances. The Improvement Notice served on the brigade set out a two-fold failure of these practices. The first failure was not to have taken advantage of the benefits of IT: fire services lagged behind other emergency services which had introduced IT. The second, and related, information failure was that paper-based records did not afford quick access to information to all fire crews.

In response to the Improvement Notice, the brigade's newly formed Operational Intelligence Unit concluded that there were considerable constraints with the existing paper-based system and recommended the replacement of paper with electronic records. Problems with the system of A4 folders included the spatial dislocation of folders, the problem of storing paper records and the temporal problems of accessing risk information before arriving at an incident, especially for crews attending incidents outside of turn out boundaries (see 'The Grapevine', 1997: 8).

In a fire news magazine the brigade's Chief Fire Officer quotes the Improvement Notice in order to assert that coordination post-Sun Valley necessitates the provision of better information. The Health and Safety Inspector:

> was surprised that a fifth and subsequent appliances which arrived at the scene did not have information that was required to ensure crews' safety and that because of this the Officer in Charge was 'fighting the fire with one hand tied behind his back'.... **the Officer in Charge cannot issue instructions or supervise employees without information.** (O'Dwyer, 1996: 33, emphasis added)

Fire crews often acknowledged that before the MDT there was a flexible but somewhat arbitrary practice of station-based A4 folders, but the above quote directly connects the loss of life with flawed information management practices. Framing the implementation in terms of managing information constitutes the MDT as a tool to improve record keeping and access to information. This is why the Chief Fire Officer states that:

> The system has met all of the criteria set by the brigade and the reaction by firefighters to the introduction of the computer into appliance cabs has been one of cooperation. The system is seen by all ranks...as a valuable tool which will assist them in their difficult task and provide them with immediate on the spot information both on screen and in hard copy. (O'Dwyer, 1996: 37)

There were few voices of dissent from the association of the MDT as a useful device for front-line fire service work. In addition to the framing of the MDT as a tool for managing information, the failure of the previous paper-based folders and maps is an important pre-condition for constituting the MDT as a welcome guest. By this we mean that the framing of the previous practices 'as faulty and inadequate' constituted a technological mood that was important for inviting the MDT in as the obvious and right thing to do.

Welcoming the stranger and forgetting the distance

Ciborra (2004: 114) has suggested that the acts of welcoming often 'trigger a network of commitments by the host...But that is just the beginning of an open-ended process: the guest also possesses its own dynamics and will begin to align the host according to certain needs and constraints'. In constituting the MDT as the solution for the inadequacy and failure of the paper based system it became possible to forget the potential hostility of the MDT – to forget its limits. As Dikeç (2002: 229) reminded us, hospitality requires that we 'honour the guest *and* keep him/her at a distance *at the same time*' as if there is a safe boundary between host and guest and exchanges do not reconfigure the identities of host or guest. The deaths of two other firefighters in the mid-1970s illustrate how information failure depends on practices through which information was maintained, shared and consulted before the MDT. However, it also provides a reminder of the limits within which choices about future information practices can be considered. Framing of the VDMS as the solution for providing 'the right information at the right time' has its limits that need to be remembered if the MDT is also to be kept 'at a distance at the same time.'

Firefighters were sometimes reluctant to talk about the death of colleagues. One reason for this was that there were few practices apart from formalized records which sustained collective remembering (see also Orr, 1996). Nonetheless one sub-officer, who had been with the brigade for over 25 years, recounted the death of two firefighters in the mid-1970s, five days after several risk assessment inspections and widespread communication of the risks of the site. His account emphasized the situated realities of fire incidents that cannot be known completely in advance and that demand improvisation, but also that information failure is marked out by absences. In a passage from the interview, being able to account for the loss of lives in terms of the failure of the management of information is challenged:

> *Firefighter:* [We] lost two firefighters in 1974 [at Hurcott Mills].... they died on a Friday.
> *Researcher:* So they had actually been there almost that week;...it was that week.
> *Firefighter:* ...a crew from another watch went there the previous week, looked at it – shock horror – better let the other watches know...because of the concern expressed by the crew who had visited the place the previous week on the Monday.

He continues that subsequent to the risk assessment there was a fire with two firefighter fatalities caused by a massive flashover:

> that fellow that died in the incident, went [with two others] off on Monday morning to go and have a look at it...they went along and said there's definitely a need here to get risk visits on it so luckily we did have a fair bit of knowledge about the building before we went in...we also found out they had disconnected the sprinkler system.... No matter what information – sometimes you could provide people with every scrap of information that is available on a particular risk, but there is the occasion when no matter how much knowledge you've got tragedies will still occur...[fire] places people in situations that you can't always train either physically or mentally for.

The firefighter's account of an incident over 25 years ago evokes a failure of information in two senses. The first is the impossibility of complete and *a priori* knowledge of the future. The second is that the absence of this firefighter's account of this tragic incident is also an instantiation of information failure that demonstrates that what counts as information failure is evaluated against existing practices and how this delimits what is considered thinkable, speakable and doable in the future. Narratives from long-serving firefighters, the exchanging of 'war stories' between fire crews, for example, are absent from records comprised of formalized, single sentence bullet points. The adoption of the MDT presupposes a comparison with existing paper-based practices because this is the technological mood through which pre-MDT practices are evaluated.

Boundaries, autonomy and the forgetting of hostility

Even if fire crews remembered the limits of the technological framing of front-line information, it still seems odd that they were so totally welcoming of the MDT – senior officers often found this hard to understand too! Did crews not see or anticipate the affordances that the MDT might suggest in terms of the standardization of their work practices and the potential for subsequent rationalization once the MDT was in place? Maybe this welcoming attitude was to do with their understanding of autonomy and of boundaries – the boundaries of where the MDT will be hosted and who it was a guest for. Furthermore, the MDT might also have become framed as the very means to consolidate important boundaries. It is this ambiguous boundary crossing and boundary making that might have contributed to the forgetting of the potential hostility of the guest.

The implementation of the MDT was framed, from the start, to coincide with existing organizational boundaries, particularly in terms of access, control and manageability of information vis-à-vis other brigades (see Bowker and Star, 1999; Monteiro and Hanseth, 1996). The MDT provides information that is available to all fire crews across the brigade, but access and control of information remains centred within the brigade and is compatible with the established brigade boundary for incident responsibility. Domesticating the MDT (see Mansell and Silverstone, 1996) to the brigade – that is, appropriated, objectified and incorporated into the brigade as a local matter – means that a range of actors within the brigade can be aligned with the scope of the MDT because it does not pose a significant challenge to long standing bases of brigade level authority and autonomy. Even the formation of an Operational Intelligence Unit which constituted new forms of control did not significantly undermine the social organization of watches. Fire crews were expected to submit to new forms of surveillance, but risk assessments are still undertaken by fire crews and managed within the brigade.

Neighbouring brigades do not have the MDT nor does the brigade provide IT management services for other brigades (throughout the 1990s West Midlands Fire Brigade was interested in standardization *qua* inter-operability between brigades and providing IT services for other brigades). Standardization of access, control and manageability is best conceptualized not only as a technical matter, but it also presupposes particular organizational practices that are inscribed into a technological infrastructure – in this case, standardization is not associated with challenging watch practices or with inter-operability of IT between brigades.

Attempting to maintain control over the boundaries of the brigade through the MDT, in the context of national reviews that emphasize regional fire services, can also be understood as an attempt to enrol the MDT as an agent of organizational power. The MDT marks out a means of catching up with other brigades particularly the neighbouring 'high-tech' brigade, and denotes an attempt to integrate the brigade into the select group of IT–led brigades. To the extent that the MDT and the Operational Intelligence Unit becomes an institutionalized 'centre of calculation' (Latour, 1988), the brigade is in an enhanced position to shape the boundaries, timing and content of future modernization.

Bricolage and mobile responses: spatial and temporal (dis)connections

Welcoming a guest, in our house as it were, also means adjusting to its modes of being – in some way accommodating it. This might mean developing improvised workarounds in order to live with this ambiguous stranger, rather than just talking to it at the door. Often this means improvising 'around' the visitor in the flow of everyday activity. This is not necessarily 'deviant' or resistant behaviour, rather, as Ciborra (2004: 116) suggests, it belongs to 'the core of the human institution of hospitality. They express the thousands, subtle ways in which humans ingeniously discover, discern, interpret and act upon the shades of the encounter with technology as an ambiguous stranger'.

The brigade was often involved in demonstrating the MDT to other fire services. The brigade's stand, which was part of the first 'IT village' at the 1997 Fire Service exhibition illustrated how carefully planned presentations construct access to information as disembodied. Demonstrations were popular and comprised of presentations with delegates standing round a mock-up MDT. The brigade's officer described the 'full availability for the first time' of previously dispersed paper records, maps and chemical information. Demonstrations centred upon interaction with the MDT with the emphasis upon showing the speed and simplicity of accessing information. At a particular point in the demonstration the officer would press the print button on the keyboard, point to the screen and the printer would begin to print.

Contra formal demonstrations the situated and collective character (see Suchman, 1987) of fire crews' work was made visible through informal demonstrations undertaken as part of observation of firefighters' work. Usage of the MDT gave rise to a number of spatial and temporal effects that crews described as compromising their readiness on the way to incidents. Before the MDT was implemented, each fire crew had a formal and informal division of labour (i.e. one firefighter reading risk records, another locating water hydrants, another navigating, and so on) on the way to incidents. The MDT made this collective structure of interaction much more difficult if not impossible. Bolted to the dashboard, only the Officer in Charge could access risk, map and tactical information on the move. Inside fire appliances this centralized activity to the officer and restricted access to information to interaction between the Officer in Charge and the MDT.

A further practical problem related to temporal pressures on the Officer in Charge whilst on the move and the collective ability of fire crews to check with each other 'how things are going' on the way to an incident. Temporal pressures on the officer intensified because of the compression of interaction within fire appliances around the MDT. Officers described the not insignificant difficulty of putting on fire clothing, boots, accessing the MDT, helping the driver to navigate, watching out for other vehicles, deciding upon an initial 'incident plan' and attending to radio communication to the control centre. The addition of 'pressing buttons' on the screen to initiate prints of MDT records, map directions and hydrant locations was not a simple matter of retrieving information 'ready to hand' for officers under these temporal pressures. As a result of the spatial and temporal configuration associated with the MDT, and the new mobile division of labour, fire crews described how the MDT led to communication problems within crews. For many crews the spatial and temporal effects meant that MDT would not be accessed until the fire appliance reached the incident and was stationary.

The Operational Intelligence Unit undertook the task of transferring paper risk records to the MDT. Stations sent their paper 1.(1).D records to the Unit for transferring onto the MDT. It was quickly noticed by fire crews, however, that a significant proportion of records had not been transferred onto the MDT. 'Nor would these paper files be put onto the [MDT] in the future', said a sub-officer at the Operational Intelligence Unit, and 'they're now in the process of being thrown away'. Although stations were told to throw out their spare paper records maps a number of stations were reluctant to do this and many crews kept copies of records and maps. Fire crews held these 'in reserve' in fire appliances as 'back-ups' (see Faia-Correia et al., 1999). Not only had an attempt to remove paper records not occurred, but crews also consulted concealed 'out of date' records and accessed the MDT screens as they attempted to maintain the collective practice characteristic of pre-MDT fire appliance collaboration.

Rationalizing the number of risk records meant that although fire crews had 'universal access' to records for the entirety of the brigade's area of responsibility, and the overall number of risk records fire crews could access increased, the number of risk records for a particular station's turn-out boundary was often reduced. The problems of arbitrary, unsystematic and often out of date station-based records were replaced with absent records. For fire crews, the small number of records for a particular station was not, however, related to a lack of computer memory, but associated with the brigade's difficulty of recruiting a CAD/CAM specialist and a lack of resources at the Operational Intelligence Unit.

Informal demonstrations problematize the spatial reach and real-time temporality with which the MDT was associated. Crew usage also foregrounded how the 'joined up' access to information on the move also created spaces and times of disconnection. Situated activities (Brown and Duguid, 1991) illustrate how ongoing ambiguities associated with IT infrastructures have to be resolved – acceptance of the MDT by fire crews is possible because 'full functionality' is deferred to the future. In this way fire crews can remain committed to the MDT even while they continued to use 'out-of-date' paper records and maps. The ambiguities associated with use of the MDT, and the consequent enrolment of other actors by fire crews, foreground two points. First, whilst paper back-ups underpin the functionality of the MDT, fire crews simultaneously demonstrate how their work is important. Through the enrolment of an array of materials in support of the MDT fire crews attempt to construct their identity as a 'centre of discretion' (see Munro, 1999) through which they can shape the future trajectory of practices for managing incident information. Second, within their particular structural location, backing-up the MDT with paper records and maps is what fire crews can do to maintain the workability of this leading-edge IT infrastructure, this is a requirement of hosting it.

Gestell and the technological mood that (re)constitutes the MDT

On 17 October 2002 the brigade's budget Working Party set out the initial cost for the 'second generation' MDT, allocating a budget for 2003/04 of £250,000 (Hereford and Worcester Fire Brigade, 2002: 13). Upgrading the MDT demonstrates how the procurement of mobile data infrastructures is an ongoing rather than one-off initiative – technology begets technology. The remit of the MDT has also now expanded to be a central feature in the brigade's strategic response to local e-government initiatives. The brigade fire authority's 'Implementing Electronic Government' Return (Hereford and Worcester Combined Fire Authority, 2003/4: 1–2) remarks on the second generation MDT, but also connects the MDT to 'improved outcomes for citizen' and the brigade's own 'e-strategy':

> Hereford and Worcester Fire Brigade's e-government strategy is already demonstrating its ability to deliver improved services and outcomes for citizens in the community. In 1996 it was the first brigade in the country to introduce a fully e-enabled mobilising and mobile data…. The brigade is currently replacing its [MDT], learning from its significant experience as one of the pioneers in this area of new technology…. In summary, the brigade sees e-government not only as the e-government initiatives but part of a complementary and natural evolution of its own internal e-strategy.

From this statement it can be suggested that, on an empirical level, the MDT can be characterized by expanding local mobilization. Many other fire brigades have also now implemented mobile data terminals: from the late 1990s onwards, brigades in Cumbria, Devon, East Sussex, Lancashire, Norfolk, Nottinghamshire, Northamptonshire, South Wales, Strathclyde and Surrey, to name a few. Significantly, some brigades, such as Nottingham and East Sussex, have started to collaborate to procure and develop inter-brigade MDT.

Recent investment in the electronic provision of local authority services through central e-government initiatives also demonstrates a shift away from a brigade approach to IT implementation. In November 2001 the Chief Fire Officers' Association submitted a bid to the ODPM for a national e-government project (CACFOA, 2001; see also Department for Transport, Local Government and the Regions, 2002). The subsequent national project, termed 'e-fire', was 'made up of five streams of work to develop 'products' designed to help the

Fire Service meet the government's 2005 e-government target' (LFEPA, 2005: 2). Significantly, one of the streams, 'Risk Knowledge Management and Data Sharing' draws upon brigades' MDT initiatives. The ideal of information provision has been reworked from brigade level to 'joined up' inter-brigade and inter-agency collaboration at a national level. In January 2005, the ODPM announced that the data sharing stream of e-fire would be dropped due to the timetable of other e-government initiatives (LFEPA, 2005). Nonetheless, such initiatives demonstrate a pervasive technological mood of inter-operability and standardization between brigades.

In 2003 the government's White Paper 'Our Fire and Rescue Service' (ODPM, 2003) was published. This set out the government's commitment to the modernisation of fire services based on many of the recommendations made by the Audit Commission (1995; 1995a) and Bain et al. (2002). For instance, one of the central provisions of the 2004 *Fire and Rescue Services Act* is a shift toward regional fire services plus central government power to merge fire and rescue authorities 'where authorities fail to work together through voluntary regional management arrangements' (ODPM, 2004: 2). As part of this move to regional fire services, and in the interest of public safety and 'national resilence', the act also provides powers for the central government to direct authorities on the procurement of equipment in order to ensure a standardized approach: 'Generally, it is considered that the maximum gain can be achieved by procuring at a national level and to a common output-based specification those items that are service specific' (ODPM, 2004: 16).

The Draft National Procurement Strategy document (ODPM, 2004) categorizes 'command and control, mobilising and e-fire' information infrastructures as of strategic importance and high cost. This document, together with the 2003 White Paper, sets out a significant shift from a local brigade level to a national and regional approach to IT procurement. One of the first instances of the national drive toward regionalization is the announcement in 2005 of the closing of 46 local command and control centres and their replacement by nine regional and 'state of the art' centres. In late 2005 the ODPM also announced that a new nationwide digital radio system, to include both voice and data communication (including information held on mobile data terminals), would be implemented by 2009. This national radio, information and communication system, called Firelink, will enable interoperability across 46 fire and rescue services in England, eight in Scotland and three in Wales, as well as other emergency services. It will consist of MDTs in over 7,000 fire and rescue appliances across the UK (East Midlands Fire Control Project, 2007: 2).

We cannot predict the future of mobile data terminals as the 'fate of technology', to paraphrase Latour's aphorism, 'lies in the hands of a future community'. However, as the boundaries between information and communication infrastructures and organizational practices are renegotiated, and mobile data terminals are constructed out of local, regional and national practices, these outcomes will not be determined by IT. Rather it is the mood that requires technological solutions that will shape and constitute the development of IT.

The UK fire service is currently reorganizing around national inter-brigade mobile data terminals, regional command and control centres, national e-government initiatives and national/regional practices for IT procurement such as central government's 'Firebuy' scheme. Although the practices of electronic information sharing across brigade's remains underdeveloped and for some unwarranted, over the last decade mobile data terminals, implemented at first at a brigade level, have become an institutionalized and important context for the future trajectory of fire service provision. Mobile data terminals now represent the future of the fire service, but we would suggest that the deployment of the MDT as part of local, regional and national e-government initiatives, and the possible alignment with the nationwide radio system, signifies that mobile data terminals are best understood as constituted by a 'technological mood'; a mood through which information and communication increasingly becomes enframed by IT and which in turn shapes the UK fire service's conception of the future reality of fire service provision.

Hospitality and interruption

Ciborra's (1999a, 2000) emphasis on hospitality foregrounds the possibility of the guest becoming the host. We suggested a guest can be usefully conceived as a stranger rather than a familiar servant, but how might this apply to our study? The MDT was implemented to rectify a lack of information 'at the right place at the right time,' but it also simultaneously reaffirmed access to information at the brigade level, top-down implementation of change, the existing crew/watch structure, and was mostly considered to be distinct from government reforms and senior officer interests. From this perspective it might be concluded that IT infrastructures are often appraised by users against existing preoccupations and information management practices. Should we therefore conclude that this is an example of the incorporation of IT infrastructure within a highly institutionalized context?

The MDT was assimilated into an existing formative context; we would suggest that identities at the brigade cannot be taken as fixed *a priori* or unchanging. With the implementation of the MDT and the formation of the Operational Intelligence Unit, the management of records, maps, chemical information, etc., and the criteria for information held on the MDT, is altered in significant ways from previous practices. MDT records are similar to paper records, but with the introduction of brigade-wide management of information we need to ask anew what counts as brigade 'hierarchy'; 'standardized' practice; 'communication' between stations; 'risks' to firefighters; and the 'boundaries' of the brigade. We suggest that within the horizon of intelligibility of the MDT these very categories become reconstituted. For example, that which is understood as 'hierarchy' becomes connected to the bureaucratic practices set up by the Operational Intelligence Unit not just the organizational hierarchy of officer rank. Similarly, 'standardization' becomes associated with the management of information and not only with collectively negotiated employment standards for workplace practices. Once it is understood that standardization can become associated with information, we can begin to evaluate how the MDT might expand and/or contract connections to local and national e-government initiatives, regional management and access to mobile data. Even though fire crews made considerable efforts to keep the MDT workable – some might consider it a technological failure. The MDT can be apprehended quite differently when it is associated with an emerging constitution of activities centred on new differentiations relating to standards, hierarchy, boundaries and risk that expand the exercise of particular practices of power. Given this new horizon of intelligibility how might we change perspective from a taken for granted approach, in information systems literature, that foregrounds alignment and assimilation?

Derrida (2000) suggests that hospitality is premised on a double-bind: to welcome a stranger requires the host to have the power to host, but unless the host surrenders their own power, there cannot be hospitality because the guest is subservient to the host's wishes – it is more like assimilation than hospitality. By contrast, hospitality can only begin to occur when host and guest begin to unravel their understanding of one another – only by going *beyond* hospitality would the guest really experience hospitality. For our purposes, although fire crews may consider their willing adoption of the MDT in the 1990s as a form of 'hospitality,' it is only when the MDT shifts from its taken for granted functionality and surprises fire crews that hospitality becomes an issue to be responded to.

In our research, the future trajectory of the MDT was constituted by conceptions of the IT infrastructure as an information resource. Ciborra (2000: 30) suggests, however, that IT can never be completely domesticated (see Mansell and Silverstone, 1996; Haddon, 2004) because practices of 'coping, use or reinvention occurs simultaneously': there is an irreducible tension and unending instability within hospitality because hospitality can turn into hostility. Ciborra's definition of hospitality follows Derrida in proposing the two-fold etymology of hospitality as incorporating the possibility of hostility. Hospitality is then better conceptualized in terms of interruptions (see Westmoreland, 2008) reversals and substitutions, where the host-becomes-the-guest and the guest-becomes-the-host. This does not mean the end of practices associated with conditional hospitality because hospitality becomes possible only in so far as it is impossible.

> To think the unconditionality of such concepts [such as hospitality] is not at all to remove thought from the practical experience we wish to call hospitality, gift, forgiveness, or justice. On the contrary, this thinking registers the very desire to go on calling to these names for that which remains impossible as present experience. (Kamuf, 2006: 207, emphasis added)

Without the aporia of hospitality – the ongoing, inherent and impossible tension that is hospitality/hostility – the implementation of IT would, Ciborra (2000: 30) writes, become 'totally "disambiguated," univocal in producing its effects and impacts, hosting would consist of straightforward adaptation and alignment ... systems are objects ... the world of business reengineering models'. *Contra* the assumption that hospitality is completed when the guest 'feels at home', we suggest, following Ciborra, that hospitality can never be finally accomplished – it is our ontological relation with technology as such. A decade after the MDT was implemented the 'problem of hospitality' remains prescient at the brigade.

Ambiguities and surprises also feature in Ciborra's sense of improvisation. Our research has demonstrated the considerable degree of work fire crews undertake to underpin the functionality of the MDT – to make it 'work' as that which it is supposed to be. However, Ciborra's (1999b: 87–89) sense of improvisation goes beyond workarounds to suggest that:

> The world constituted by procedures, methods and systems is suddenly 'up for grabs'. Conventional meanings attributed to 'things', 'actions' and 'events' are re-defined, re-registered and bent to acquire new ones ... during the 'kairos', or 'Augenblick', the moment of vision, that is the moment in which our Being is conscious of itself and the possibilities vis-à-vis the world, rather than being dispersed in the ordinary chores and interests of everyday life.

Our research demonstrates little evidence of this sense of improvisation, so how might we account for Ciborra's *Augenblick* and understand fire crews' response to the MDT? Kamoche et al. (2001) provide a distinction between conditions for improvisation. They differentiate between improvisation that is considered as a 'solution to a problem' and improvisation that is considered an 'opportunity to learn, change or develop' – the latter a closer sentiment to Ciborra's 'moment of vision'. Our research suggests that fire crews embody the former condition – in their minds and practices the MDT is not working as it should so some bricolage and improvisation is needed to rectify this until current problems are resolved – but why should crews have this reaction? Why not simply reject the MDT?

For Ciborra (1999b, 2000, 2001) improvisation problematizes assumptions about the possibilities and limits of rational decision-making, disembodied information, equivocal communication and managerial competency. In terms of our study, it would also challenge the hopes attached to the institutionalization of what many considered a positively transformative IT infrastructure. We have argued that across organizational levels, and across the UK fire services more generally, the MDT is considered 'a success'. For the MDT to be evaluated as successful, improvisations must be conceived as temporary workarounds within the longer-term trajectory of the MDT as the way to be a modernized fire service.

Improvisation also foregrounds a taken for granted way of being, the way we are supposed to be. Unlike the Mann Gulch fire described by Weick (1993), the work that crews do to underpin the functionality of the MDT has not, as far as we know, been a matter of life or death. But of course it could become a matter of existence at any moment – some might argue the work backing-up the MDT makes crews' work less safe! Questioning the veracity of the MDT would presage questions such as: what does the MDT tell us about the (un)certainties of technological innovation, who or what makes decisions at incidents or how are risks evaluated. For Ciborra and Hanseth (1998a: 322) quoting Dreyfus (1993), inducing such 'moments of vision' expresses something akin to Derrida's sense of hospitality. In this aporia the 'take up of practices that are now at the margins of our culture' and 'de-emphasising practices now central to our cultural self-understanding' become possible courses of action. For the brigade this might include the recovery of practices for remembering not associated with paper risk cards or the MDT, understanding the deployment of MDT at other brigades and evaluating how over the last decade the MDT has become connected to the future of fire service provision and not just with the better recording of the past. From the perspective of hosting we might conclude that fire crews' attempt to adapt and 'feel at home' with the MDT has made them 'blind' to the hostility of the MDT – indeed one might say they have been bad hosts. This has created the condition in which alternatives ways of thinking and doing are rendered illegitimate as well as making it impossible for them to understand a future that 'could be otherwise.'

In order to further understand the conditions for the various improvisational acts associated with the MDT we need to reintroduce our third term from Ciborra – *Gestell* or technological mood. Our study of the MDT has demonstrated how people, organization and technology shape each other and hold each other in place: the MDT illustrates how brigade actors are concerned with framing understanding of reality and imposing these understandings on each other. The MDT is not simply a medium for access to information 'anywhere and anytime' but is implicated in the constitution of reality and identities – IT does have power, most importantly the power to transform what counts as important (see also Brigham and Corbett, 1997). From this we suggested that the MDT enframes information and communication by defining it as technological and as such improvisation itself is set within a calculative and instrumental form of thought.

During the 1990s and early 2000s the MDT was considered to be a closed and controllable system that functions at the level of the brigade. The MDT was, we have argued, not associated with a radical break from previous technological, organizational and social practices and was judged as successful in these terms (see also Dahlbom et al., 2000). The top-down implementation, and centralized management of information by the Operational Intelligence Unit, similarly assumes that the development of the MDT can be planned and controlled by the brigade's senior officers and delimited to change driven by the brigade. Additionally, the deployment of the MDT is connected to front-line fire crews' understanding of what is important in firefighting – supporting crews' work at incidents, even though it has been known for over three decades that emergency calls to fires is around 10 per cent of firefighters' work (Home Office, 1971). Some might suggest that in the context of innovation in networked and open IT systems, the IS and management literature on the temporal and spatial flexibilities afforded by IT, and the discourse of disjunctive change, that the MDT is a rather 'old fashioned' infrastructure deployed narrowly to help fire crews. From this perspective, the MDT might be seen as a missed opportunity rather than a success. On an empirical level, we might ask, then, how long the stabilities associated with highly institutionalized boundaries, long-standing national practices, and a demarcation of the MDT with front-line incidents be sustained? We might ask what this 'local controllable' approach to the MDT tells us about the *Gestell* of the brigade in the context of broader debates such as modernization and its relationship to information technology?

Despite reform initiatives throughout the 1990s, it was not until the early 2000s that brigades have become subject to the modernization agenda and central government intervention that has been a feature of the UK public sector for the last two decades. Although the role of mobile data terminals in modernizing fire services cannot be predicted in advance, our longitudinal research has shown how the MDT has been strongly associated with the provision of relevant and accurate information to crews en route or at incidents. Demarcating the MDT as a device for enhancing the provision of information and communication between fire crews has particular consequences, however. It neglects, for example, how universal IT-mediated access to risk records can mean that local knowledge is considered less embodied in fire crews. Fire crews have access to the same information and in principle they can be located anywhere or mobilized to any incident.

To the extent that debate and reflection about the future of mobile data terminals is delimited to framing the role of IT as bringing forth a world to be ordered more comprehensively and efficiently, then modernization of fire services is likely to be premised upon the continuation of an ontology marked out by a Cartesian approach to IT. This is not to say that the MDT has determined the current emphasis on technologically-driven modernization or that there is some kind of inexorable logic that connects the MDT to e-government initiatives. It demonstrates, rather, how the boundaries between organisational practices and IT infrastructures are renegotiated on a terrain defined by a technological mood. Problematizing this mood was one of the central preoccupations of Ciborra's scholarly work. The 'ability to jump, or switch Gestalt' that Ciborra (2004: 77–78) discussed in his last full length book, demands taking the particularities of IT seriously because, as Ihde (1990: 200) suggests, 'any larger Gestalt switch in sensibilities will have to occur from *within* technological cultures'. It also requires of us that the culture of technology that enframes organizational, professional and social issues as technological be questioned anew through a 'releasement' or 'comportment' toward IT that willingly takes up innovations in IT, but is simultaneously not enframed by a technological mood.

This chapter has demonstrated a pervasive technological mood in the provision of fire services at one UK fire brigade. Our analysis should, however, be taken as illuminating the general cultural trajectory of information and communication technologies and, as such, has implications for recasting the study of IT. The presentation and discussion of the MDT concerns, of course, a particular technological artefact in a part of the public sector, but our ambition, echoing Ciborra, is to contribute to how we might rethink our contemporary disposition to IT in the broadest terms.

The analysis of the MDT set out in this chapter is inspired by a phenomenology – an approach that is significant because it argues that IT is constitutive of the human condition. IT is an 'original supplement' in Derrida's terms. Information technologies have, of course, long been associated with bringing about discontinuity in organizational practices, but the phenomenological approach set out in this chapter provides an important and subtle twist on such truisms. We have argued that the essence of IT is not the technological rationalization of tasks, its assimilation into formative contexts or the disjunctive change brought about IT as it reorganizes existing practices. More radically, for phenomenologists, the 'figure' of IT dynamically alters and remakes the 'ground' on which the demarcations and distributions of rationalization, assimilation and disjuncture are made. On this point Levin (1999: 126) writes that the 'enframing that is typical of *Gestell* interrupts the figure-ground interplay.... Instead of a dynamic, spontaneously flowing interaction between figure and ground, a loser, freer, softer differentiation between the periphery and the centre of focus, there is a 'freezing of the flow', interrupting the work of time'. Recovering Levin's 'work of time' is Ciborra's ability to switch Gestalt – the recovery of the ongoing emergence and dissolution of relational configurations that challenges and works through and beyond the ontological primacy and reified effects so often associated with information and communication technologies.

Conclusion

The concept of hospitality set out in this chapter encourages, we think, a new understanding of the problematic of information technology as a contemporary mode of organizing. Ciborra's legacy will, however, be lost if we do not pay careful attention to what he is saying. If we merely assimilate his vocabulary (care, bricolage, *Gestell*, kairos and drift) we will not be hosting him. Ciborra is not just suggesting that we replace our old vocabulary (strategy, alignment, implementation, use and impact) with a new one, although learning to speak a new language is important in order to engage with the world in new ways. This, though, would be only a reversal, an inversion of a particular hierarchy, but nothing more. Ciborra is suggesting that we take a careful look at our ontology – that horizon of intelligibility that conditions our 'taking up' of particular forms of enunciation. If we do not understand, or take seriously, the co-constitutive relationship that phenomenology proposes, we will not be able to understand the radical shift that his vocabulary makes possible. It is this possibility to be truly disturbed or interrupted that is most important if we are to host Ciborra's scholarly legacy. We need to stay open to the hostile possibilities in our guest as we take up these ideas.

Through this new phenomenological ontology of hospitality we see that we can never become comfortable with our technologies because of the paradoxes, ironies and ambiguities they afford (see also Arnold, 2003). An 'original technicity' problematizes information technology as a tool – as a guest at the table of human intentionality – but also interrupts the sovereignty of the host. Technologies do not just 'support' activities, they take us, one could say frame us, in unexpected ways as we draw upon them because technological change is not reducible to a calculating and cordial framework of reciprocity and repayment between host and guest. For Ciborra (1999) this demands a negative capability that remains open to ambiguity, uncertainty and doubt. It denotes, also, a labour of division

(Cooper, 1993) between guest and host that becomes the basis for a deconstructive inquiry into the 'information technology to come'.

We have argued that one of Ciborra's long-lasting legacies should be a phenomenological ontology for the study of IT, an argument we have pursued in this chapter by demonstrating how the horizon of effects associated with the MDT cannot be planned and controlled over time and space. From this unplotted strategy we can conclude that the 'normal science of IT' research is the ongoing (re)co-constitutive relationship through which we are destined to always be the hosts/guests of our technology – we are always already enframed. The MDT, a seemingly innocent replacement of paper records, has shown us that technology's (re)framing cannot simply be located and controlled as often suggested. Through the MDT a new way of seeing, thinking and doing became possible. As these new possibilities emerged they became incorporated into discourses and practices of modernization in ways unanticipated by those that originally conceived them. Finding ways to live with this guest/host is the impossible challenge – the aporia – and Ciborra has helped us on our way. If hospitality is an impossibility that must be continually renegotiated, it is because the guest and the host shift their mutual horizons of intelligibility. We cannot be hospitable, we must be hospitable: it is this internal tension through which life goes on. This is the memory of the future, beyond the limits of thought of the modern technological mood, to which Claudio Ciborra contributed.

Acknowledgements

The empirical research was supported by the UK Economic and Social Research Council (ESRC number: R00429534042). Hereford and Worcester Fire Brigade provided generous access to research the deployment and use of the brigade's mobile data terminal.

Note

This chapter is an extended version of the article: Brigham, M. and Introna, L.D. (2006) Hospitality, improvisation and *Gestell*: a phenomenology of mobile information, *Journal of Information Technology* **21**(3): 140–153.

References

Arnold, M. (2003). On the Phenomenology of Technology: The 'Janus-faces' of Mobile Phones, *Information and Organization* **13**: 231–256.

Audit Commission. (1995). *In the Line of Fire: Value for Money in the Fire Service. The National Picture,* London: HMSO.

Audit Commission. (1995a). *In the Line of Fire: Management Handbook on Value for Money in the Fire Service,* London: HMSO.

Bain, G., Lyons, M. and Young, A. (2002). *The Future of the Fire Service: Reducing Risk, Saving Lives. The Independent Review of the Fire Service,* London: ODPM.

Bassett, T. (1991). Would Larger Fire Controls Covering More Than One Brigade be More Efficient?, *Fire* **84**: 15–17.

Brigham, M. and Corbett, J.M. (1997). Email, Power and the Constitution of Organisational Reality, *New Technology, Work and Employment* **12**(1): 25–35.
Borgmann, A. (1984). *Technology and the Character of Contemporary Life: A Philosophical Inquiry,* Chicago/London: University of Chicago Press.
Borgmann, A. (1999). *Holding on to Reality: The Nature of Information at the Turn of the Millennium*, Chicago/London: University of Chicago Press.
Bowker, G.C. and Star, S.L. (1999). *Sorting Things Out: Classification and its Consequences,* Cambridge, MA: MIT Press.
Brown, J.S. and Duguid, P. (1991). Organizational Learning and Communities of Practice: Toward a Unified View of Working, Learning and Innovation, *Organization Science* **2**: 40–57.
Cabinet Office. (1999). *Modernising Government White Paper,* Command Paper No: 4310, March, London: HMSO.
Chief and Assistant Chief Fire Officers Association [CACFOA]. (2001). *e-Fire: The Fire Service and e-Government: Guidance for Electronic Service Delivery,* November, Tamworth: CACFOA.
Ciborra, C.U. (1998b). Crisis and Foundations: An Inquiry into the Nature and Limits of Models and Methods in the Information Systems Discipline, *Journal of Strategic Information Systems* **7**: 5–16.
Ciborra, C.U. (1999a). Hospitality and IT, in T. Käkölä (ed.) *Proceedings from the Twenty-Second Information Systems Research Seminar in Scandinavia (IRIS 22),* Keuruu, Finland, August, pp. 195–202.
Ciborra, C.U. (1999b). Notes on Improvisation and Time in Organizations, *Accounting, Management and Technologies* **9**(2): 77–94.
Ciborra, C.U. (2001). In the Mood for Knowledge: A New Study of Improvisation, Working Paper 94, *Working Paper Series, London School of Economics and Political Science*, London [WWW document] http://is2.lse.ac.uk/wp/pdf/WP94.PDF (Accessed 1 December 2005).
Ciborra, C.U. (2004). *The Labyrinths of Information: Challenging the Wisdom of Systems,* Oxford: Oxford University Press.
Ciborra, C.U. and Associates. (2000). *From Control to Drift: The Dynamics of Corporate Information Infrastructures,* Oxford: Oxford University Press.
Ciborra, C.U. and Hanseth, O. (1998a). From Tool to *Gestell*: Agendas for Managing Information Infrastructure, *Information Technology and People* **11**(4): 305–327.
Cooper, R. (1993). The Visibility of Social Systems, in K. Hetherington and R. Munro (eds) *Ideas of Difference,* Oxford: Blackwell, pp. 32–41.
Cox, J. (1994). How Wiltshire Set About Selecting New Command and Control 'Kit', *Fire* **97**: 23–27.
Dahblom, B., Hanseth, O. and Ljungberg, J. (2000). Conservative Success: Organization and Infrastructure Evolution at SKF, in C.U. Ciborra and Associates (eds) *From Control to Drift: The Dynamics of Corporate Information Infrastructure,* Oxford: Oxford University Press, pp. 87–104.
Department for Transport, Local Government and the Regions. (2002). *e-Gov@Local: Towards a National Strategy for Local e-Government. A Consultation Paper,* Great Britain: Department for Transport, Local Government and the Regions.
Derrida, J. (1997). Community without Community: Hospitality, in J.D. Caputo (ed.) *Deconstruction in a Nutshell: A Conversation with Jacques Derrida*, New York: Fordham University Press, pp. 106–112.
Derrida, J. (1999). *Adieu to Emmanuel Levinas,* trans. Pascale-Anne Brault and Michael Nass, Stanford, CA: Stanford University Press.
Derrida, J. (2000). *Of Hospitality,* trans. Rachel Bowlby, Stanford, CA: Stanford University Press.
Dikeç, M. (2002). Pera, Peras, Poros: Longings for Spaces of Hospitality, *Theory, Culture and Society* **19**(1/2): 227–247.

Dreyfus, H.L. (1992). *What Computers Still Can't Do: A Critique of Artificial Reason*, Cambridge, MA: MIT Press.

Dreyfus, H.L. (1993). Heidegger in the Connection Between Nihilism, Art, Technology and Politics, in C. Guignon (ed.) *The Cambridge Companion to Heidegger*, Cambridge: Cambridge University Press, pp. 289–316.

Dreyfus, H.L. (2001). *On the Internet*, London: Routledge.

East Midlands Fire Control Project. (2007) Fire Control and Fire link Project Update, *East Midlands Fire Control Project*, Issue 2, January, 1–3.

Faia-Correia, M., Patriotta, G., Brigham, M. and Corbett, J.M. (1999). Making Sense of Telebanking Information Systems: The Role of Organizational Back Ups, *Journal of Strategic Information System* **8**(2): 143–56.

Galliers, R.D. (2007). On Confronting Some Common Myths of IS Strategy Discourse, in R. Mansell, C. Avgerou, D. Quah and R. Silverstone (eds) *The Oxford Handbook of Information and Communication Technologies*, Oxford: Oxford University Press, pp. 225–243.

Gibson, J.J. (1979). *The Ecological Approach to Visual Perception*, Dallas/London: Houghton Mifflin.

Goodwin, P. (1997). Vehicle Mounted Data System: Building on Success, *Fire Engineers Journal*, September, 57/190: 39–40.

Haddon, L. (2004). *Information and Communication Technologies in Everyday Life: A Concise Guide and Research Guide*, Oxford: Berg.

Heidegger, M. (1927/1962). *Being and Time*, trans. John Macquarrie and Edward Robinson, New York: Harper and Row.

Heidegger, M. (1977a). *The Question Concerning Technology and Other Essays*, trans. William Lovitt, New York/London: Harper and Row.

Heidegger, M. (1977b). On the Essence of Truth, in D.F. Krell (ed.) *Martin Heidegger: Basic Writings*, San Francisco: HarperCollins, pp. 113–141.

Hereford and Worcester Fire Brigade. (1997). Vehicle Mounted Data System, *The Grapevine: The Official Journal of Hereford and Worcester Fire Brigade*, **September**: 8–9.

Hereford and Worcester Fire Brigade. (2002). *Budget Working Party Agenda*, October. Hereford and Worcester Combined Fire Authority.

Hereford and Worcester Combined Fire Authority. (2003/4) *Implementing Electronic Government*, IEG3 Return.

Home Office and Scottish Home and Health Department. (1971). *Report of the Cunningham Inquiry into the Work of the Fire Service*, Great Britain: Home Office.

Ihde, D. (1990). *Technology and the Lifeworld: From Garden to Earth*. Bloomington and Indianapolis: Indiana University Press.

Ihde, D. (2002). *Bodies in Technology*, Minneapolis: University of Minnesota Press.

Introna, L. D. (2007). Making Sense of ICTs, New Media and Ethics, in R. Mansell, C. Avgerou, D. Quah and R. Silverstone (eds) *The Oxford Handbook of Information and Communication Technologies*, Oxford: Oxford University Press, pp. 225–243.

Introna, L.D. and Ilharco, F.M. (2004). Phenomenology, Screens and the World: A Journey with Husserl and Heidegger into Phenomenology, in J. Mingers and L. Willcocks (eds) *Philosophy and Social Theory for Information Systems*, Chichester: Wiley, pp. 56–102.

Kamoche, K., Cunha, M.P.E. and Cunha, J.V.D (2001). *Organizational Improvisation*, London: Routledge.

Kamuf, P. (2006). From Now On. *Epoche* **10**(2): 203–220.

Lanzara, G.F. (1983). Ephemeral Organizations in Extreme Environments: Emergence, Strategy and Extinction, *Journal of Management Studies* **20**: 71–95.

Latour, B. (1988). *The Pasteurization of France*, trans. A. Sheridan and J. Law, Cambridge, MA: Harvard University Press.

Levin, D.M. (1999). *The Philosopher's Gaze: Modernity in the Shadow of Enlightenment*, Berkeley: University of California Press.

London Fire and Emergency Planning Authority [LFEPA]. (2005). Progress Report on the National Fire Service e-Government Project ('e-Fire') and Implementing e-Government, *LFEPA Authority Meeting Minutes,* Document No: FEP 657, 13 January.

Mansell, R. and Silverston, R. (1996). (eds) *Communication by Design: The Politics of Information and Communication Technology,* Oxford: Oxford University Press.

Meehan, A.J. (1998). The Impact of Mobile Data Terminal (MDT) Information Technology on Communication and Record Keeping in Patrol Work, *Qualitative Sociology,* **21/3**: 225–254.

Mohanty, J. (1997). *Phenomenology: Between Essentialism and Transcendental Philosophy,* Evanston, IL: Northwestern University Press.

Monteiro, E. and Hanseth, O. (1996). Social Shaping of Information Infrastructure: On Being Specific About the Technology, in W.J. Orlikowski, G. Walsham, M.R. Jones and J.I. DeGross (eds) *Information Technology and Changes in Organizational Work,* London: Chapman and Hall, pp. 325–343.

Munro, R. (1999). Power and Discretion: Membership Work in the Time of Technology, *Organization* **6**(3): 429–450.

Norman, D.A. (1988). *The Psychology of Everyday Things,* New York: Basic Books.

ODPM (2003). *Our Fire and Rescue Service,* Command Paper No: 5808, June, London: ODPM.

ODPM (2004). *Draft National Procurement Strategy for the Fire and Rescue Service: A Consultation Document,* London: ODPM.

O'Dwyer, D. (1996). The Design and Implementation of a Vehicle Mounted Data System, *Fire Engineers Journal* September: 33–37.

Orr, J.E. (1996). *Talking about Machines: An Ethnography of a Modern Job,* Ithaca, New York: ILR Press.

Rhodes, R.A.W. (1985). Corporatism, Pay Negotiations and Local Government, *Public Administration* **63**: 287–307.

Robey, D., Ross, J.W. and Boudreau, M.C. (2002). Learning to Implement Enterprise Systems: An Exploratory Study of the Dialectics of Change, *Journal of Management Information Systems* **19**(1): 17–46.

Sauer, C. (1993). *Why Information Systems Fail: A Case Study Approach,* Henley-on-Thames: Alfred Waller.

Suchman, L.A. (1987). *Plans and Situated Actions: The Problem of Human-Machine Communication,* Cambridge: Cambridge University Press.

Weick, K.E. (1993). The Collapse of Sensemaking in Organizations: The Mann Gulch Disaster, *Administrative Science Quarterly* **38**: 628–652.

Westmoreland, M.W. (2008). Interruptions: Derrida and Hospitality, *Kritike* **2/1**: 1–10.

14

The Hospitality Metaphor as a Theoretical Lens for Understanding the ICT Adoption Process*

Amarolinda Zanela Saccol and Nicolau Reinhard

Abstract

The Hospitality Metaphor proposed by Ciborra represents an alternative view to the traditional models that describe the process of adopting information and communication technologies (ICT).

This Metaphor helps us in considering social, behavioural and existential elements related to the adoption process, offering a critical and dialectical view of it. In this paper, we review the philosophical and methodological basis of this Metaphor and its main statements. We also apply it in analysing a case of mobile ICT adoption. The application of the Hospitality Metaphor enables a clear understanding of this process as an incremental and open one in which social, existential and 'mundane' issues play a major role, and where technology reveals its dubious character, leading to unplanned results.

Introduction

This article aims at contributing to the discussion and application of the Hospitality Metaphor proposed by Ciborra (1996, 1999a, 2002), a concept first put forth by him (1996). Based on the research he conducted in Ciborra and Patriotta (1996), he analyses the corporate adoption of a Groupware system, using the Hospitality Metaphor to describe the process which involves the appropriation, sensemaking and even rejection by users of a new technology, seen as a stranger hosted by the organization.

The hospitality concept focuses on the social, existential and mundane elements related to the adoption of information and communication technologies (ICT), seen as an incremental and open process in which the consequences of an encounter between the organization and the new technology cannot be totally foreseen, planned or controlled.

This is an alternative to positivist models such as the Theory of Diffusion of Innovation (TDI) (Rogers, 1995), as well as to technology acceptance models such as the TAM and its related models (Davis, 1989; Venkatesh et al., 2003). We start by revisiting the references used by Ciborra to understand the philosophical and methodological basis of his Metaphor, attempting to 'bring together' and organize its main elements. We then use the Hospitality Metaphor as the main theoretical lens to study a case of mobile ICT adoption. Based on this analysis we discuss the main distinct contributions of the Metaphor and propose directions for future research.

The philosophical and methodological background of the Hospitality Metaphor

The Hospitality Metaphor focuses on existential and social approaches to help in understanding the process of ICT adoption. It does not follow a rationalistic approach (as defined by Winograd and Flores, 1987), being instead concerned with the process of ICT innovation in ordinary everyday life and how sense-making regarding a new technology is created. This view is based on a philosophical background that increases our sensibility to the issue and therefore causes us to look at the relationship between humans and technology in a distinctive way.

Heidegger (1962) is a core author of this approach. His notion of Being-in-the-world reveals that we are totally interconnected with other things and beings and that the understanding of the world and our existence is constructed with others, through socialization. We are always being-in-the-world-with-others: this means that most of the time we work, interact, communicate and deal with others in a skilful and detached way. There is no total separation between objects and subjects as assumed by Cartesian rationality. Heidegger thus proposes an anti-cognitivist approach, in the sense that he challenges the assumption that we are totally aware of the rules and norms on how to live and proceed; in fact, most of the practices we adopt in our lives are taken for granted.

In the same way, we have no neutral viewpoint from which to observe our beliefs, since we always live and act within the context that they have provided us with (Winograd and Flores, 1987). Most of the time we are circumspect about our environment (Dreyfus, 1991). People simply get absorbed in what they are doing; this is the idea of 'thrownness': the way that we find ourselves being-in-the-world, acting in a very dynamic and immersed way. We do not have time to constantly step back and reflect on our actions; we cannot count on careful and rational planning most of the time (as discussed by Winograd and Flores, 1987).

With his approach, Heidegger brings to the scene a new way of reflecting about our existence, the world we live in and our understanding of it in a very integrated, interrelated way, highlighting the importance of observing ordinary everyday life. It leads to his methodological approach: the hermeneutic phenomenology.[1] To Heidegger, there are no such things as bare, uninterpreted facts or 'wrong' or 'right' interpretations: life is always interpretation. Phenomenology, thus, is hermeneutic; in other words, it is interpretative (Dreyfus, 1991; Gadamer, 1992). Heidegger proposes a 'hermeneutics of everydayness' that involves the understanding of everyday practices and discourse, but in a deeper sense (Dreyfus, 1991). To Heidegger, the hermeneutic circle means that we must begin our analysis from within the practices we seek to interpret, but this choice of the phenomena to interpret is already influenced by our traditional understanding of being. He also claims that theoretical knowledge depends on practical skills – knowledge is created in practice and the world is discovered in the everyday activity of *being-in-the-world* (Dreyfus, 1991).

Thus, Ciborra finds in Heidegger a philosophical and methodological basis that highlights the necessity of approaching organizational phenomena by questioning the models and concepts taken for granted about them, paying attention to the unexpressed aspects of organizational life and interpreting the meaning that people assign to events and things in their everyday lives.

Heidegger's anti-cognitivist approach is taken by Ciborra to contest the models that describe the process of development and adoption of ICT as a process that can be strictly planned, anticipated and controlled. On the contrary, it is only through real, everyday interaction between people and technology that it is possible to see how deeply technology can be integrated into everyday life and the practices of its users. By following this philosophical and methodological basis, Ciborra attempts to understand the phenomenon that underlies the process of ICT adoption, finding it in the idea of hospitality.

Ciborra begins his construction of the concept of hospitality related to the process of ICT adoption by analysing the origins of the phenomenon of hospitality in a general sense, trying to capture its essence as a millenary and universal human institution. Ciborra (1999a) analyses the word hospitality, showing that this term has multiple and even contradictory meanings, such as host, guest, owner and even enemy.

According to Centlivres (1997), in certain ancient cultures such as those of Pakistan and Afghanistan, hospitality is extremely ritualized: it is about honour, the obligation to protect and to serve whoever is inside our 'walls', inside our house. It is about giving the best that one possesses without asking anything in return, almost becoming a 'slave' to the guest. At the same time, the guest is almost a prisoner of the host's hospitality, depending totally on him. There is an implicit contract indicating the host's superiority over the guest. Thus, rituals of hospitality are related with setting the frontiers between the space and the roles of both the host and the guest. Following this view, Raffestin (1997) indicates that hospitality defines the threshold between the exterior and the interior of our territory. Hospitality presupposes an authorization or an invitation regulated by a ritual, which allows the transgression of limits without the use of violence.

Derrida (2000) makes a fundamental claim that there can be no hospitality without our sovereignty over our own home. But there is also a dubious sense: if hospitality implies filtering, choosing whom we want to welcome into our space, it also implies exclusion and even a violent reaction against whoever is not welcome. The foreigner has rights but he also has obligations. Derrida (2000) reminds us that 'foreigner' or, in Greek, *xenos*, is related to the word *xenia*,[2] which means 'a pact'. The foreigner is attached to this collective pact through the rituals of hospitality (for instance, the rituals of guests and hosts exchanging gifts).

However, Derrida (2000: 16–17) also reminds us that hospitality presupposes tolerance, since the foreigner *'does not speak our language'* and is ignorant of our culture or our practices. Raffestin (1997) points out that the host interprets the foreigner according to his own 'language', system of values and codes, that is, his 'semiosphere' (semiotic space). Considering this, Derrida (2000) argues that the imperative of hospitality requires that we transgress certain laws of hospitality, meaning that we need to transgress the conditions, norms, definitions of rights and duties imposed by hosts and hostesses. The full acceptance of the foreigner without any questioning at all seems to be more of an absolute hospitality. We will always face a dilemma between, on the one hand, the rituals of hospitality, its rules, norms, laws and duties and, on the other hand, the unconditional hospitality that requires us to dispense them, and to simply accept the other person, no matter who he is. Therefore, hospitality is a situation fraught with tension.

Thus, to understand the idea of hospitality associated with the process of ICT adoption, it is also necessary to understand how this approach views the role of technology in human life. Ciborra (1996, 1999a, 2002) follows the ideas of Heidegger (1977), who describes the essence of modern technology as highly ambiguous. To Heidegger (1977: 4) *'the essence of technology is by no means anything technological'*. He says that we usually consider technology as an instrument, the means to an end, but *'this instrumental definition of technology still does not show us technology's essence'* (p. 6). According to Heidegger, technology is no mere means; it is a way of *revealing*, in the sense that, when we apply technology:

> The energy concealed in nature is unlocked, what is unlocked is transformed, what is transformed is stored up, what is stored up is, in turn, distributed, and what is distributed is switched about ever anew. Unlocking, transforming, storing, distributing and switching about are ways of revealing. (Heidegger, 1977: 16)

The role of modern technology is to be a *Ge-stell* (enframing). This word derives from the German and means skeleton, frame or shelf. The term *Untergestell* means chassis and infrastructure (Ciborra and Hanseth, 1998; Ciborra, 2002). However, Heidegger uses this term in a different way: *Gestell* meaning a combination of activities such as placing, arranging, regulating and ordering (Heidegger, 1977). Nature is 'challenged' to deliver its wealth for the purposes of men, the *'technological revealing structures a world in terms of exigencies of planning and control'* (Feenberg, 2005: 24).

In this 'framing process' man and nature become exploitable resources (Ciborra and Hanseth, 1998; Ciborra, 2002; Feenberg, 2005). This danger is the essence of technology, since enframing describes a narrow understanding of ourselves and of all things as resources to be organized and exploited efficiently. In this sense, ICT infrastructures can shape the way people do their work and how people see their practices and even redefine their identities (Ciborra and Hanseth, 1998;

Ciborra, 2002). Therefore, we cannot understand things as pure objects; rather, things enter a world through their interpretation in terms of meaning and use. The significance of a new technology lies in how it fits into and changes social networks and institutions. It cannot be taken as an isolated object or event. Ciborra also considers the Actor Network Theory (ANT) (Law, 1992; Latour, 1993, 1999) to discuss the role of ICT infrastructures and how it can be difficult to modify them, as they frequently get out of control.

The ANT sees technology as an actor, connected into a heterogeneous network with humans, institutions and other social elements. In this network, neither humans nor technological elements are pure or isolated, but all are considered actants. The border between the technological and the human is not given, but negotiated instead. Technological artefacts are not simply tools to be applied; they also embody patterns of use, programmes of action to be followed by the users (inscriptions). In this sense, technologies can impose rules and constraints upon the way humans apply them in their actions and decisions.

Although humans can use the technology in alternative and unanticipated ways, certain technologies have a high level of irreversibility, that is, their inscriptions become durable. Ciborra (1999b, 2002) also uses the concept of technological infrastructures as formative contexts, meaning that they are not simply a set of hardware and software but also sets of pre-existing institutional arrangements and cognitive frames that actors routinely enact and bring into a situation of action. Only by revealing our implicit understanding about the technology and making these assumptions explicit, can we open ourselves to different alternatives and possibilities of design and technology use, which enables us to say either 'yes' or 'no' to the technology, letting it enter our world but also to shutting it out (Ciborra, 2002). This is the essence of the process of 'hosting' a new technology.

The main statements of the Hospitality Metaphor as a lens for understanding the process of ICT adoption.

What exactly does it mean to host a new technology within an organization? For Ciborra (1996: 6) hospitality involves

> a good match between the human organization, the artefact and the context. The innovation is used in a way that these three elements turn out to be so interwoven, that they disappear into the fabric of daily work situations

Hospitality thus connects and integrates the world of the host (organization) and the world of the guest (technology) and manages the boundaries and identities between them. By following the 'rituals of hospitality', the organization will attempt to impose its needs, culture and identity upon the technology and the technology in turn will try to impose its standards, languages, infrastructures and interfaces on the organization. Systems development methodologies, for instance, are merely the external side of a ritual imposed by humans upon technology. But no matter how planned and structured they may be, they cannot control the unpredictability and ambiguity of the guest and the results of this encounter (Ciborra, 1999a).

The idea of hospitality diverges from the view of command and control prescribed by structured methodologies of development and implementation of new ICTs: '*in order to remain the master of the house the host must release control and serve the guest*' (Ciborra, 1999a: 10). But what exactly does it mean? Exploring the work of Ciborra (1996, 1999a, 2002) we have attempted to bring together the main elements and features involved in the Hospitality Metaphor. We have identified seven main statements related to it:

- By hosting a new technology, we reinterpret our identities.
- Hosting the new technology will involve learning by doing and improvisation.
- During the hosting process, technology can drift.
- Hospitality involves moods and emotions.
- Hospitality is about appropriation and care.
- Hospitality involves cultivation.
- We cannot forget the dubious character of technology: technology can become an enemy.

By hosting a new technology, we reinterpret our identities

First, Ciborra (1999a) proposes that when we adopt a new technology we somehow redefine our identities, also creating new duties and expectations. By redefining these social arrangements and commitments, we will have to rethink, strengthen or even change our identities. Identity is especially related to one's reputation, which is recognized as important to a person's life, being constantly reinterpreted according to our commitments, regardless of whether they are related to an organization, a job, a way of doing things or any other person or cause we care about – whatever is meaningful in our lives (Flores and Spinosa, 1998).

Along this line of thought, following the ANT view, we are always involved in a heterogeneous network with other people, technologies and things defining who we are in the network (Law, 1992). We must also consider that this is not a one-way relationship: the identity of the guest (the new technology) can also be changed or strengthened in the encounter with the host. Frequently a technology designed for a given purpose is changed, adapted and reshaped by its users, thereby acquiring a new meaning, application and identity (Hanseth and Braa, 1998; Ciborra, 2002).

Hosting the new technology will involve learning by doing and improvisation

Dealing with a new technology means facing the unknown, since, as mentioned before, '*the foreigner does not speak our language*' (Derrida, 2000: 15). People who host it will have to learn about and understand what it is and what it means in practice. Interacting with the new technology will demand an intensive process of learning by doing, trial and error (Ciborra, 1994). Even a formalized training programme and description of how to use it is, in general, too abstract if compared to the intricacies and unexpected unfolding of events that punctuate real practice.

Brown and Duguid (1991) show us that learning how to deal with an unexpected situation frequently occurs, in practice, through the interaction of people who belong to *'communities of practice'*. Within these communities people share their experience and learn in an informal way by narrating their previous experiences and tales of work, collaborating in problem solving processes and socially constructing an understanding of a problem and of possible solutions. That is how people engage in the process of making sense of a new technology or situation (Weick, 1993). This view is compatible with the Heideggerian notion of understanding: knowledge is created in practice; it is by acting in the world that we start giving meaning to objects.

Another important element related to the interaction with a new technology in real settings is improvisation. Improvisation is related to the need to solve problems and act in the face of emergent and unexpected situations, at the very moment they occur (Weick, 1998; Ciborra, 1999b, 2002). At the same time, one cannot 'improvise on nothing': we rely on our previous experiences and knowledge as well as on the recognition of the current setting to be able to improvise (Weick, 1998). Thus, improvisation is about figuring out how to use what we already know (our 'pattern languages' and tacit knowledge), in order to build or act in a different way. This is a form of coping with the challenge of learning how to master a new tool, knowledge or practice. We need to adapt, to play with it in order to make it more familiar and better adjusted to our own reality (Ciborra, 1999a, 2002).

During the hosting process, technology can drift

As the process of hosting a new technology is unpredictable and very full of learning by doing and even improvisation, we have to consider that technology can drift constantly:

> by drifting I mean a slight or significant shift of the role and function in concrete situations of usage, that the technology is called to play, compared to the planned, pre-defined and assigned objectives and requirements. (Ciborra, 1996: 8)

This *drifting* results from two distinct but intertwined processes: one is the openness of technology, its flexibility for being reinvented; the other is related to changes that occur when people get used to the process of *'being-in-the-workflow'*, developing and applying the technology. This includes continuous waves of intervention, bricolage and improvisation. Drifting can happen both in cases of successful and unsuccessful applications of technology.

Hospitality involves moods and emotions

Ciborra (2002) indicates one essential element that lies beyond all the concepts discussed above – our moods. People enter situations – including processes of innovation adoption – with a specific mood that is elusive, cannot be controlled or even represented by symbols. We are always in a certain kind of mood that can change instantaneously or persist unpredictably. Mood is where our cognition encounters the world and it shapes the way in which we interact with others (Dreyfus, 1991). This concept can also be found in the work of Heidegger (1962), for whom mood can refer to the sensibility of an age (such as the romantic age), the culture of a company, the temper of a time (revolutionary) as well as a specific mood in a certain situation, and the mood of an individual (Dreyfus, 1991).

It is important to highlight that according to Heidegger mood refers to a collective, cultural stance; it is not merely an intra-individual predisposition or feelings projected upon the world, but is related to situations and contexts. Moods are pervasive and even go unnoticed; the most remarkable moods sometimes attune us as if there were no moods around at all (Dreyfus, 1991). It is like the weather that lies in the background of a setting.

Moods and emotions play an essential role in the way we interact, accept or reject a new technology and all the changes of practices, roles and commitments that can ensue from it. The way we care about the world unfolds according to our current mood. '*Unless I am in a mood I will not be affected, touched or interested in anything*' (Ciborra, 2002: 161). The consideration of moods brings to light the need to connect the process of ICT adoption with existential concerns, considering the practical issues of the designer and the users in their everyday interaction with the technology.

If the projects of ICT development and/or adoption do not make sense to those who will implement it, they will enter the process in a superficial and uncommitted way. They will not really care about it. We have to consider the balance between the biographical, historical and ethical conditions of the people involved in the projects and the reasons why the project has been deployed at all (Ciborra, 1999a). This '*existential balance*' is frequently precarious and contradictory. People often have to deal with situations where they are 'thrown' into projects and have to cope with events out of their control. All their past experience, cognitive structures and scripts can serve as barriers to learning in the new situation. The success of a hosting process depends on the consideration and 'alignment' between these existential concerns and objective issues (Ciborra, 1999a).

Hospitality is about appropriation and care

Appropriation is a way of integrating the new technology into the everyday life of an organization; it is about becoming an 'owner' of the new technology. Appropriation is related to the sense of care, to our concern for our own lives, to the way in which we devote ourselves to something that is around us in our being-in-the-world (Heidegger, 1962). Ciborra (1996) points out three ways of care whereby our existence unfolds: *perception*, *circumspection* and *understanding* (Heidegger, 1962; Dreyfus, 1991).

Perception refers to how we deal with the new technology as a 'thing', with a very naturalistic, objectified view, resulting from '*a process of abstraction and rationalization, guided by intentional visions and plans*' (Ciborra, 1996: 11). Perception deals with 'unworlded' entities that have not yet become immersed and integrated into our everyday life. We treat the new technology as an object that is separate from us.

Circumspection, in its turn, is the realm of 'use and implementation in situ' (Ciborra, 1996: 11). The technology becomes involved in practical applications and activities. This process, as mentioned before, involves learning-by-doing and working incrementally with the technology. The new technology is inserted and tested within the workflow of organizational activities. It is no longer an abstract and sanitized model, but something that is applied in practice.

Finally, *Understanding* is the highest level of appropriation, when the technology merges with the organizational context, but without completely losing its individual character: understanding a system means becoming so intimately familiar with the innovation nested in our daily workflow that the system itself disappears from the cone of our alert attention, being taken for granted or becoming self evident (fully appropriated) since it gets encapsulated into the routines of our absorbed daily coping (Ciborra, 1996: 11).

We conclude that the process of effectively hosting a new ICT involves these different levels of appropriation. From the first contact with the 'un-worlded' foreign technology, it goes through the process of circumspection (applying and dealing with the new technology in a practical and interactive way) and, eventually, understanding and incorporating the technology into our everyday life, using it skillfully and almost without noticing it. Therefore, successful hosting of the new technology by an organization can be interpreted as having the actors reach an understanding of this technology or, in other words, a deep level of appropriation.

Hospitality involves cultivation

Cultivation (Dahlbom and Janlert, 1997) is related to perceiving the process of systems development as a natural one, in opposition to the traditional view of IS development as a process of construction, which involves selecting, bringing together and organizing a number of objects to form a system. The idea of cultivation considers that it is impossible to have total control over the development process, since it cannot be totally created and controlled by technicians and managers; instead, it is a natural process demanding support and monitoring, protection and care. It is necessary to respect the characteristics of each situation and context of development.

According to the cultivation approach, a new technology (hardware or software) is not merely a material artefact but also has a cultural dimension, which is shaped by the culture of the context in which it is developed. Dahlbom and Janlert (1997) claim that the idea of construction has been imposed upon the notion of cultivation in the process of systems development, although the construction approach would be really valid only if it were possible to construct, in addition to the new system or technology, the organization into which it is placed as well. To the extent that the organization has a life of its own and that it evolves, grows and learns at its own pace, both organization and technology have to be cultivated instead of pretentiously created.

Dahlbom and Mathiassen (1993) indicate that the idea of cultivation presupposes that we do not change or disturb an organization more than absolutely necessary to accomplish a task or goal. It implies believing that the process of development and implementation of a new technology is similar to cultivating a tree: there is no total control over its future shape and size, but it is possible to water it, fertilize it, prune the branches to adapt it to certain dimensions, or train it to grow in the right direction. The one who cultivates has the role of a guide or instructor, more than of a controller, since the tree has a life of its own. The process of cultivation requires guiding this evolutionary process and reducing any disturbance to the organization, working on the elements that are not according to plan and reinforcing those which are moving in the right direction.

We cannot forget the dubious character of technology: technology can become an enemy

The Hospitality Metaphor emphasizes the dubious character of technology, with its own dangers (Heidegger, 1977). It is only by acting, applying and interacting with it that people will discover the technology to be either a very pleasant guest or an enemy, as shown, for instance, by Hanseth and Braa (1998) in their analysis of how an ERP system became an enemy to the organization.

Derrida (2000) presents an interesting example, pointing out that communication technologies, such as the telephone, are used to delimit what is our 'house', who we include or exclude from our network of relationships, who we wish to welcome, to host or not in our private space. The right to the privacy of preserving these spaces and choices has to be inviolable. If the technology causes an 'invasion' of our private space, we have no discretion on our hospitality. It is important to remember that a new technology, like a guest, *'has the right to visit, but not necessarily the right to stay'* (Ciborra, 1999a; Derrida, 2000). Therefore, nobody can anticipate *ex ante* the results of hospitality.

Unexpected consequences indicate that any attempt to fully control the technology is doomed to failure.

In the next section, we will present a Case Study involving the process of adoption of a mobile ICT in a Brazilian Bank. We are going to consider the Hospitality Metaphor as the main theoretical lens for understanding this case and for discussing its main distinct contributions.

The Hospitality Metaphor as a means of understanding the process of mobile ICT adoption

This case study analyses the process of hosting a mobile ICT in a privately owned Brazilian Bank, adopting an interpretative stance, as proposed by Klein and Myers (1999).

Data for this case were collected between May 2004 and September 2004, including interviews with the main actors involved in the hosting process: key users of the technology, business managers, IT technicians and IT managers. We interviewed 14 people in total, working at the Bank's headquarters in São Paulo and at one of the Bank's branches in a capital in the south of Brazil. An additional interview was conducted with an expert from the market who was familiar with the Brazilian banking sector and who provided an external view of the case and its various contextual properties. The researchers paid four visits to the Bank's headquarters in São Paulo and three visits to the southern branch, interviewing, observing the use of the technology and collecting secondary information: documents about the Bank, its business, markets and products, and about the mobile ICT project and its users.

The Bank and this project have also received wide media coverage (the researchers collected around 30 articles and reports published in the Brazilian press, as well as a video reporting the case).

The Bank studied was a medium size company (around 500 employees). It has operated in corporate banking since the beginning of the 1990s, with headquarters in the City of São Paulo and branches in the country's main State Capitals. Most clients were medium or large companies, and its main products were investment funds and loans.

The Bank has used IT innovation as a strategy. The owner (and president) of the Bank was considered an 'IT enthusiast' and the IT sector was very powerful within the organization. The Bank pioneered the use of mobile ICT in the banking industry in Brazil, having started to adopt mobile technology at the end of 2002. The mobile technology was based on a smartphone (combining PDA and mobile phone in a single device) supporting a mobile version of the Bank's Information System.[3]

The application was proposed by the IT Director and was chosen to support the work of the Bank's Account Managers, Business Supervisors and Regional Branch Managers during their visits to corporate clients at their sites. Each manager usually served around 20–25 corporate clients and paid frequent visits to them. Account Managers were driven by results (business goals) and their field visits were an essential part of their task of doing business and prospecting new clients.

The 'official' reason for adopting this technology (according to the external communication of the project to the media and the market, as shown in magazines and business publications in the Brazilian media) was an attempt to reduce the internal costs of communication and to help the convergence of different tools (the project had even been intended to replace Account Managers' PCs with mobile devices), increasing their time in the field and providing them with more information for negotiations. One main argument was that Account Managers would not have to go back to the office to access or to record the transaction data, thus saving time and processing transactions more quickly. But there were other reasons besides these 'official reasons' for adopting the mobile technology, as we discovered interviewing the actors involved in the project in the organization.

First, the Bank used the aesthetic potential of the mobile device to reinforce its image as a very sophisticated and advanced technology user: according to the Bank's IS development manager, *'the moment he* [the owner of the Bank] *saw it* [the smartphone], *he said: 'I want this!''* The smartphone was, at that time (2002), a very innovative device in Brazil. Wherever the users carried the device it became highly visible and therefore reinforced the Bank's identity.

Another 'unofficial' reason, as revealed during the interviews, was that the technology would help to collect and keep information on clients. The first functionality developed in the mobile IS was to record the visit reports. According to the IS development manager:

> The Account Manager deals with golden stuff, which is the information on his relationship with the client. It's very common for an Account Manager to take his clients with him when leaving the Bank.

There used to be a high turnover of Account Managers due to the very ambitious performance goals they had to achieve. Therefore, any tool to keep data about their relationship with clients would be important for the Bank. The smartphone was seen as such a tool, making it possible to control the work of Account Managers, where they were, with which client, etc.

According to the interviewees from the IT Department and some key users that participated in the process, the mobile IS was developed incrementally. As mentioned before, the first functionality developed was the visit report, giving the Bank the valuable information on clients. But, after this, users started to ask for functionalities that would help them in their fieldwork. However, there was no clear idea about all the possible uses of the new technology: *'At that time it was seen as a work instrument that was getting better; we didn't know where it was going, really'* (Business Supervisor who participated in the project). There was no formal planning of the use of the technology and the functionalities were added gradually. The goals of the technology's new uses were discovered in practice.

The rituals of hospitality

According to the IT Director and his main assistant in the mobile ICT implementation project, the smartphones were distributed first to a selected group of 22 Account Managers in March of 2003, as a prize for their discipline in recording visit reports into the existing Bank IS. The second group received the devices as a prize for their high business performance. After that, the devices were distributed to the remainder of the business team (around 170 users in total).

However, although the devices were officially distributed as prizes, they were actually a planned purchase, under contract with a mobile phone company, with 30 devices being received and distributed every month. Thus, after some time, according to the IT Director, *'it wasn't fun anymore; people are not stupid (...). They realized that it was a 'Greek present'* [meaning a 'Trojan horse']. The Assistant to the IT Director involved in the dissemination of the technology and training explained that

> in the beginning everybody wanted it, but after a while when they started getting to know it, using it, they realized it was not as they'd thought (...). Not

> everybody sympathizes with the computer. You can imagine: if sometimes technology is difficult for us from the IT area, imagine [how it is] to the final user! (...) This technology scares people.

This was so because, during everyday use, people were faced with the technical limitations of the mobile technology, such as cell phone network instability, narrow data transmission bandwidth and the mobile device's ergonomic limitations, especially interface problems due to the small screen and keyboard. '*Some people don't feel comfortable, you know, using that little pen, that little screen, people don't know how to use it, how to hold it* (...)'.

They also felt the limitations related to the usage context. Users, for example, feared being mugged in open and public spaces because these expensive electronic devices, like notebooks, were a frequent target of robbers, unfortunately. The smartphone device was also considered very fragile.

Regarding the process of learning how to use the new technology, we verified that, according to users, due to insufficient formal training, people engaged in learning-by-doing in their community of practice. Especially in the regional branch researched by the authors, the users basically had to learn by trial-and-error, '*playing with it, reading the manual, turning it on, looking at each others' devices. Nobody has come to explain how the device works*'. (Regional Branch Manager). More experienced PC users were better able to learn how to use the technology but, in general, users had great difficulty with the new device, especially the mobile computing features.

An essential element in understanding this case is the fact that the use of the new technology was not mandatory. Although its use had been encouraged, there was no penalty for not using the device as expected. This allowed each user to host the new technology in a different and individualized way. Thus, the mobile device had a different personal character for each user. Some of them hosted the new technology intensively, while others rejected it almost completely.

We noticed at least three different reactions: the intensive users ('my life depends on it, I am completely dependent' – a Business Supervisor), resistant users ('If they take it away from me I will not be upset. Nowadays we have too many things to carry' – an Account Manager) and indifferent users ('No, I don't use [the other functions besides the cell phone]; I think it's because of my lack of interest, really' – an Account Manager). Even violent reactions against the new device occurred among certain users, according to the IT Director: 'I've already seen a user wanting to throw the device against the wall'.

In fact, managers used the functionalities they were more familiar with: cell phone and e-mail. The mobile IS had a very low level of use. One could see that people were very familiar with the cell phone and keen to use it, but it was different with the mobile computing features. They were far from being easily integrated into peoples' routine.

Thus, the project of adoption had drifted: the intention of using the mobile device to replace the PCs was frustrated and the level of adoption, in general, was below expectations.

The consequences of the mobile ICT use

Even with the limited use of the mobile IS, the new technology had some advantages according to interviewees' perceptions, such as the possibility of spending more time in the field visiting clients and doing business, getting better personal time management (working during 'dead times'), and less commuting time between clients and the Bank's office. According to some users, it was easier to stay well informed in the field, which provided them with more input for negotiations with clients, especially when travelling. Similarly, they also said that it became easier to anticipate actions or to solve problems due to quick access to information and several means of communication (cell phone, internet, e-mail, SMS), as well as to reach and to be reached by other people during negotiations or decision-making processes. It also became easier to formalize decisions and transaction authorizations via e-mail messages. Considering this type of consequence, the quest for productivity gains was achieved to a certain extent, although these gains were never measured, only guessed at.

However, on the other hand, people faced the undesirable consequences of the new technology. The information overload and permanent reachability, especially for managers, caused stress and feelings of loss of privacy. The mobile ICT had invaded territories, including the users' private life, as well as interrupting face-to-face interactions, with calls or e-mail messages being received during meetings or visits to clients. The users had difficulty in maintaining the boundaries between work and private life. According to an Account Manager,

> At night the e-mails start coming in.. trimm.. trimmm... People here make jokes, but I leave the device recharging by my bedside, so that sometimes it's 3 or 4 o'clock in the morning and I'm already answering an e-mail; people here say: hey, you're going nuts!

This type of consequence has influenced users' moods and emotions according to their own narratives. A Business Supervisor stated that

> We're available 24 h a day. From the point of view of our family life it can become an invasion. I've already caught myself in a restaurant with a friend on the weekend synchronizing and answering e-mails. This frustrates the people you're with and it can even change your mood. You read an e-mail and find out about something that's unpleasant and it ruins your mood, when you could have left it to read on Monday.

Emotions such as a feeling of impotence in avoiding the constant calls, or the frustration of having one's personal time and life invaded, or being overloaded, were voiced by the users. Even the constant interruptions by calls during meetings were considered disrespectful. According to one manager,

> If you're in a meeting it is really nasty, all the time that little noise – ding-a-ling – an e-mail arrives, the person stops talking, what a nasty thing! Even the

> cell phone is invasive; if it rings, maybe you won't pick it up, but at least you'll stop and look at the screen to see who called.

It is important to remember that the technology had been implemented by the Bank also as a tool for controlling information about clients and Account Managers' work. Thus, the technology allows it to reach users more frequently and intensively, but they can find ways to escape control by using their personal cell phones, for instance, as the main client contact channel. According to their own comments, the more intensive users even used the new technology to save the data about their clients in their private computers or PDAs, exchanging data between these devices and the smartphone through infrared communication.

Similarly, some users were using the technology as a thing 'for the English to see' (this is a Brazilian derogatory expression meaning to just simulate to be doing something and keeping only the appearances). For instance, most users continued to make their visit reports the same way as before. According to one Account Manager,

> I know that the life of those who use it a lot becomes an open book. There are people who only call from their personal phone to escape control. And there are also those who pretend to use it but actually don't. I know that they [the Bank] have records of everything, they monitor everything, they know who uses it, what information somebody has accessed, which pages, but then there are people that use it just for 'the English to see', so what is it for?

Thus, due to a lower than expected usage level, the Mobile ICT development project was put on hold since the Bank decided not to invest in improvements and further development of the mobile IS, nor to try to overcome the technical limitations of the technology as a whole. The Bank managers claimed that: *'they don't use it enough to justify new investments'.*

However, all the interviewees agreed that the goal of reinforcing the Bank's identity as a sophisticated IT user had been achieved: clients noticed the devices and were impressed by the technology. The Bank received considerable attention in the Brazilian media due to this innovative use of mobile ICT. But some dubious reactions did also appear: some clients saw the new device as a negative thing, as *'technology to show off'*, or something *'posh'*. Account Managers observed that, depending on the client's profile (for instance, with a client from a company in the inner-state area), they had to be careful about *'showing off'* the new device so as not to cause a bad impression.

Discussion

By using the Hospitality Metaphor as a theoretical lens for analysing the case study, it becomes easier to see that the process of adoption and development of the mobile ICT was incremental and not rigidly planned. There was no formal business case or even a preceding ROI analysis. This finding exemplifies the anti-control view of the IS/IT planning and development process (Ciborra, 1997; Hackney and Little, 1999).

The technology development did not follow linear and pre-planned steps, but unfolded similarly to a natural process that has to be cultivated. This is consistent with the Hospitality Metaphor's anti-cognitivistic view, whose basis lies in the concept of being-in-the-world and being-in-the-flow of events in a very practical way. Owing to organizational dynamics and lack of time, problem solving applications and opportunities for using the technology were discovered in everyday life and work, in a process involving trial-and-error, improvisation and bricolage (Ciborra, 1999a, 2002).

Analysing the distribution of mobile devices among users, the Hospitality Metaphor also helps to perceive the 'rituals of hospitality': the technology as a 'Greek present' (a Trojan horse) revealing its dubious character when applied to everyday activities and real settings. The users' initial enthusiasm was reduced when they found out, in practice, that the technology had many limitations and pitfalls, leading to different individual forms of hospitality. This evidence highlights that any attempt to foresee entirely the level of usage of technology based on forecasting attitudes towards the technology, as in the acceptance models such as the TAM (Davis, 1989) – would have failed in this case.

Thus, the Hospitality Metaphor helps us to understand the drifting process of new technology: as the intention of replacing Account Managers' PCs by smartphones was not achieved and the levels of usage were lower than expected, with each user making sense of the technology in a different way. Similarly, as the Hospitality Metaphor highlights, the learning process involving the new technology included trial and error and learning in communities-of-practice, either to overcome lack of formal training or to complement it.

Other issues that the Hospitality Metaphor clarified in our analysis are the constraints imposed by the new 'guest' upon his 'hosts'. In this case, the mobile ICT imposed technical limitations upon its users, such as poor interfaces and ergonomic limitations. The case indicates that the idea of ubiquitous computing was far from being a reality: the mobile ICT adopted did not 'disappear' from the cone of our alert attention as proposed by ubiquity advocates (Weiser, 1991). Full understanding (the deepest level of hospitality)was, therefore, not achieved, indicating a remaining challenge for mobile ICT designers, developers and researchers.

Another issue that demands further research is related to the contextual limitations of mobile ICT use, discussed in the literature by authors such as Sherry and Salvador (2002) and Kakihara and Sorensen (2002). For instance, users may face the danger of being robbed due to the possession of such an expensive device. The Hospitality Metaphor sensitizes us to pay attention to this kind of intricacy of technology use.

In the same token, each user reacts in different ways to the same 'individual' technology with different levels of hospitality running from dependence to rejection. Users attempt to understand and make their own sense of the new technology considering their own context, roles, identity and daily routine.

In keeping with the emerging social construction of the technology, users also performed their own functional cost-benefit analysis, evaluating the new technology and their work processes in relation to other alternatives, such as their PCs, ordinary mobile phones and PDAs. Considerations of ease of use, complexity and relative advantage emerged from users' narratives and remind us of Technology Acceptance Models, like the TAM (Davis, 1989) or the TDI (Rogers, 1995). These considerations complement the view provided by the Hospitality Metaphor by reinforcing the (traditionally prevalent) business logic view of the system. As this dimension was not the main scope of the research, it will not be developed further in this paper.

Nevertheless, the Hospitality Metaphor was useful for understanding how people integrated the mobile ICT into their everyday lives (or not), highlighting emotional elements involved in the adoption process. Enthusiasm, resentment, frustration and mood changes due to the new technology's invasion of their private life are some of the evidences of user reactions against the new 'guest'. In fact, Lasen (2004) had already claimed that devices such as the mobile phone are 'affective technologies', since some users tend to become attached to this type of tool by carrying it close to their bodies, by customizing and using them to deal with very personal and emotional interactions.

However, the Hospitality Metaphor, by indicating the dubious character of technology, helps us to realize that emotions related to this type of technology are not only of the 'positive' kind, such as attachment, but can also be 'negative': instead of 'becoming an extension of the body' this type of technology can also become a 'dead weight' if it does not make sense to the user.

The fact that a mobile device is a personal tool carried by the user on his body, to be used at different times and in different arenas not only during work hours but also in private life, while it also belongs to an organization, presents new challenges to understanding its process of adoption if compared, for instance, to the adoption of an IS used collectively only inside the organizational setting.

In this sense, the Hospitality Metaphor is very appropriate for analysing the process of mobile ICT adoption, through its emphasis on the emotional aspects of people dealing with technology in everyday life. The 'biographical' elements of the users, such as professional roles, previous perceptions and experiences with technology and current activities, have influenced the mobile ICT adoption process in the organization.

By considering these existential issues, moods and emotions, the Hospitality Metaphor offers an alternative view to the 'traditional' and widely publicized models of technology adoption and acceptance. Moods and emotions are absent from most theories and models that discuss the process of ICT adoption, from the more positivistic ones, such as the TDI model (Rogers, 1995) and the TAM-related models (Davis, 1989; Venkatesh et al., 2003), to the more recent and interpretative ones, such as the Theory of Domestication (Silverstone and Haddon, 1996), or the models of emergent, situated change in the process of ICT adoption (Orlikowski, 1996).

This contribution of the Hospitality Metaphor deserves further research. Emotions and moods are subjects that involve biological, psychological, cultural and sociological elements (Toda, 2001). Considering them in the process of adoption of a new technology would require an interdisciplinary research approach.

The Hospitality Metaphor has also helped us to understand that the motivations for adopting mobile technology were not only technical, rationalistic and economic, although the quest for productivity had been communicated as the main reason for adoption. The mobile ICT was chosen as a tool for strengthening the Bank's identity and also to satisfy hidden agendas such as improving the organizational control of strategic information on clients and work.

Thus, due to the way the mobile ICT was introduced in the Bank – partly justified on a technical/rational basis, partly on the expectation of intangible benefits and hidden agendas, it has provided plenty of room for different levels of hospitality and drifting.

The Bank's managers were very clever in realizing the potential applications of mobile ICT. However, although the technology aided achievement of the strategic goals, internally the project had, in fact, drifted: some goals were not achieved (for instance, greater control over the relationship between clients and Account Managers) and unexpected and undesirable consequences appeared, such as the low actual level of mobile IS use.

A dilemma for managers suggested by this case is how to deal with such drifting innovation. In fact, this dilemma has led the Bank's management to put the project on a 'stand by' status. However, one might suggest that the opposite should have been done: since the level of use was lower than expected, the IT team and managers should care about the project, continue listening to the users after its initial development, and be proactive in order to understand the differences in individual reactions and the reasons why each user had accepted or rejected the new technology.

The managers were able to realize the opportunities for strategic use of the new technology but they were short sighted in understanding the adoption process with an attitude of cultivation, realizing that the interaction between people and technology had developed a 'life on its own'. The Hospitality Metaphor reveals that it is necessary to listen, to adapt, to be flexible, and to improve the technology through its lifecycle within the organization and not only in the initial development phase.

For the consideration of the 'external success' of the mobile ICT (reinforcement of the Bank's image as a very sophisticated IT user) the Hospitality Metaphor analysis can be complemented with other theoretical tools such as the Institutional Theory (Di Maggio and Powell, 1982), which can be helpful for understanding the external actors in the organizational field surrounding the organization and the quest for legitimating the adoption of a new technology. Domestication Theory (Silverstone and Haddon, 1996) also discusses the process of design and dissemination of an innovation from a broad perspective, which considers the different actors involved outside the organization, such as technology creators, customers, suppliers, competitors and the macro organizational environment as a whole (economics, government, etc.).

Nevertheless, by attempting to understand the process of adoption by focusing on the concrete, practical and mundane experience of people's interaction with a new technology in everyday life, the Hospitality Metaphor helps to reveal the actual intricacies of the adoption process, its advantages, limitations and pitfalls in a very original way.

Understanding the dubious character of the new technology, discovered only in practical and everyday use, is one of the main contributions of the Hospitality Metaphor to the case analysis. By highlighting this ambiguous character of technology and its role as an actant, the Hospitality Metaphor can be distinguished from other approaches to emergent/situated change, such as Orlikowski's (1996). The level of human agency over the technology has its limits. We can become hostages to a new technology since it is not merely an artefact but can also shape work, social roles and scripts, as well as institutional arrangements.

Conclusions

The case study presented aimed at identifying the main elements involved in the mobile ICT adoption process at the organizational level, using the Hospitality Metaphor as its main theoretical lens. This Metaphor helps one to understand the difficulties and challenges faced during the process of adopting a new technology, as well as some of its main (positive and negative) consequences.

The Hospitality Metaphor was very helpful in understanding that the adoption of a new ICT is an incremental and open process in which social, existential and mundane issues play a major role. As a result, it offered distinct insights into the process of mobile ICT adoption that can be useful not only for the adopting organization, but also for solution providers, as well as for consultants and other researchers in the Information Systems area.

We believe that this paper can also contribute to the clarification and dissemination of the Hospitality Metaphor, by organizing and presenting Ciborra's concepts didactically.

One should resist the temptation to reduce the approach to a recipe of steps to be followed or to propose a structured normative model, which would contradict the basic tenets of Ciborra's work. In particular, the philosophical and methodological basis that underlies the Hospitality Metaphor provides us with this new form of understanding, affecting the way we see the relationship between technology and people.

Coherently to this approach, we believe that one way of helping to consolidate the Hospitality Metaphor was to apply it to the understanding of a real process of new ICT adoption. Or, as Ciborra's might have said, by *'getting our hands dirty'*.

Acknowledgements

We would like to thank the anonymous reviewers for their very helpful comments. Amarolinda Zanela Saccol would also like to acknowledge CAPES (from the Brazilian Ministry of Education) for the scholarship received during her Visiting Research Student Program at the London School of Economics (2004–2005).

Notes

This paper originally appeared as Saccol, A.Z. and Reinhard, N. (2006) The hospitality metaphor as a theoretical lens for understanding the ICT adoption process, *Journal of Information Technology* **21**(3): 154–164.

1. Both phenomenology and hermeneutics by themselves have different streams, according to different authors. We will not discuss all this background due to its complexity and length. To better understand these philosophical/methodological approaches and their use in Information Systems research, see Introna and Ilharco (2004) about phenomenology and Myers (2004) about hermeneutics. Both works provide a list of the main references on these subjects.
2. This is the name of the chapter in 'Labyrinths of Information' where Ciborra discusses the hospitality concept.
3. The main functions of the mobile IS were: recording visit reports, access to data on corporate clients (bank account statements, products under contract, payments due, assets); money transfers between banks and guaranteed loans (limited liability). Besides these functionalities, the smartphones offered all the functions of a PDA and a cell phone (to make and receive phone calls, send and receive SMS and e-mails, access the internet via a 'mini browser', search contacts' databases using 'pocket versions' of basic applications such as text editors and spreadsheets, etc.).

References

Brown, J.S. and Duguid, P. (1991). Organizational Learning and Communities-of-Practice: Toward a Unified View of Working, Learning and Innovation, *Organization Science* **2**(1): 40–56.

Centlivres, P. (1997). *Hospitalité, État et naturalization*: l'exemple Suisse, *Communications* **65**: 99–108.

Ciborra, C. (1994). The Grassroots of IT and Strategy, in C. Ciborra and T. Jelassi (eds) *Strategic Information Systems: A European Perspective*. 1st ed. London: John Willey and Sons, pp. 3–24.

Ciborra, C. (1996). What Does Groupware Mean for the Organizations Hosting It?, in C. Ciborra (ed.) *Groupware and Teamwork – Invisible Aid or Technical Hidrance?*, Chichester: Wiley, pp. 1–19.

Ciborra, C. (1997). De Profundis? Deconstructing the Concept of Strategic Alignment, *Scandinavian Journal of Information Systems* **9**(1): 67–82.

Ciborra, C. (1999a). Hospitality and IT, *PrimaVera Working Paper* 99–02, University of Amsterdam, pp. 1–15.

Ciborra, C. (1999b). Notes on Improvisation and Time in Organizations, *Accounting, Management and Information Technologies* **9**(2): 77–94.

Ciborra, C. (2002). *The Labyrinths of Information: Challenging the Wisdom of Systems*, New York: Oxford Press, 195 pp.

Ciborra, C. and Hanseth, O. (1998). From Tool to Gestell: Agendas for managing the informational infrastructure, *Information Technology and People* **11**(4): 305–327.

Ciborra, C. and Patriotta, G. (1996). Groupware and Teamwork in New Product Development, in C. Ciborra (ed.) *Groupware and Teamwork – Invisible Aid or Technical Hidrance?*, Chichester: Wiley, pp. 121–142.

Dahlbom, B. and Janlert, L.E. (1997). *Computer Future*. Manuscript received directly from the first author via e-mail.

Dahlbom, B. and Mathiassen, L. (1993). *Computers in Context: The Philosophy and Practice of Systems Design*. 1st. ed. Oxford: NCC Blackwell.

Davis, F.D. (1989). Perceived Usefulness, Perceived Ease of Use, and User Acceptance of Information Technology, *MIS Quarterly* **13**(3): 319–340.

Derrida, J. (2000). *Of Hospitality – Anne Dufourmantelle Invites Jacques Derrida to Respond*. 1st. ed. Stanford: Stanford University Press.
Di Maggio, P. and Powell, W. (1982). The iron cage revisited: conformity and diversity in organizational fields, *PONPO Working Paper-52*, Yale University, pp. 1–43.
Dreyfus, H.L. (1991). *Being-in-the-world – A Commentary on Heidegger's Being and Time, Division I*, 5th edn, Boston: MIT Press.
Feenberg, A. (2005). *Heidegger and Marcuse: The Catastrophe and Redemption of History*, London: Routledge.
Flores, F. and Spinosa, C. (1998). Information Technology and the Institution of Identity: Reflections since 'Understanding Computers and Cognition', *Information Technology and People* **11**(4): 351–372.
Gadamer, H. (1992). *Philosophical Hermeneutics*, Berkeley: University of California Press.
Hackney, R. and Little, S. (1999). Opportunistic Strategy Formulation for IS/IT Planning, *European Journal of Information Systems* **8**: 119–126.
Hanseth, O. and Braa, K. (1998). Technology as a Traitor: Emergent SAP Infrastructure in a Global Organization, in *International Conference on Information Systems* (Helsinki, Finland, 1998) Association for Information Systems, pp. 188–196.
Heidegger, M. (1962). *Being and Time*, San Francisco: Harper San Francisco.
Heidegger, M. (1977). *The Question Concerning Technology and Other Essays*, 1st edn, New York: Harper & Row.
Introna, L.D. and Ilharco, F. (2004). Phenomenology, Screens, and the World: a Journey with Husserl and Heidegger into Phenomenology, in J. Mingers and L. Willcocks (eds) *Social Theory and Philosophy for Information Systems*, West Sussex: John Wiley & Sons, pp. 56–101.
Kakihara, M. and Sorensen, C. (2002). Mobility: an extended perspective, In *Proceedings of the Hawaii International Conference on System Sciences* (IEEE), Hawaii, USA.
Klein, H.K. and Myers, M.D. (1999). A Set of Principles for Conducting and Evaluating Interpretive Field Studies in Information Systems, *MIS Quarterly* **23**(1): 67–94.
Lasen, A. (2004). Affective Technologies – emotions and mobile phones [WWW document] http://www.receiver.vodafone.com/11/articles/pdf/11_03.pdf (Accessed on October 20, 2004).
Latour, B. (1993). *We have Never been Modern*, 1st edn, Trans.: Catherine Porter. Hemel Hempstead: Harvester Wheatsheaf.
Latour, B. (1999). *Pandora's Hope*, 1st edn, London: Harvard University Press.
Law, J. (1992). Notes on the Theory of the Actor-Network: Ordering, Strategy and Heterogeneity, *Systems Practice* **5**(4): 379–393.
Myers, M. (2004). Hermeneutics in Information Systems Research, in J. Mingers and L. Willcocks (eds) *Social Theory and Philosophy for Information Systems*, West Sussex: John Wiley & Sons, pp. 103–128.
Orlikowski, W. (1996). Improvising Organizational Transformation Over Time: A situated change perspective, *Information Systems Research* **7**(1): 63–92.
Raffestin, C. (1997). Re´inventer l'hospitalite, *Communications* **65**: 165–177.
Rogers, E.M. (1995). *Diffusion of Innovations*, 4th Edn, New York: Free Press.
Sherry, J. and Salvador, T. (2002). Running and grimacing: the struggle for balance in mobile work, in B. Brown, N. Green and R. Harper (eds) *Wireless World: Social and Interactional Aspects of Mobile Age*, 1st edn, London: Springer-Verlag, pp. 108–120.
Silverstone, R. and Haddon, L. (1996). Design and the Domestication of Information and Communications Technologies: technical change and everyday life, in R. Mansell and R. Silverstone (eds) *Communications by Design: The Politics of Information and Communications Technologies*, Oxford: Oxford University Press, pp. 44–74.
Toda, M. (2001). The History of Human Society as Molded by Emotion: Past, present and future, *Social Science Information* **40**(1): 153–176.
Venkatesh, V., Morris, M., Davis, G. and Davis, F. (2003). User Acceptance of Information Technology: Toward a Unified View, *MIS Quarterly* **27**(3): 425–478.

Weick, K.E. (1993). The Collapse of Sensemaking in Organizations: The Mann Gulch Disaster, *Administrative Science Quarterly* **38**(5): 628–652.
Weick, K.E. (1998). Improvisation as a Mindset for Organizational Analysis, *Organization Science* **9**(5): 543–555.
Weiser, M. (1991). The Computer for the 21st Century, *Scientific American* **265**(3): 94–104.
Winograd, T. and Flores, F. (1987). *Understanding Computers and Cognition: A New Foundation for Design,* 1st edn, Norwood: Addison Wesley.

15

Rigid Technology and Improvised Implementation: The case of ERP Systems*

Amany R. Elbanna

Abstract

Claudio Ciborra's improvisation argument provides a realistic dynamic account of how organizational practices address technology. This was developed from the study of malleable open-ended technology, but little research has occurred to investigate the theory's validity within different settings. This paper seeks to address this gap, by examining improvisation in the context of a rigid highly structured technology. It presents findings from the successful implementation of an Enterprise Resource Planning (ERP) system within a large international organization, which was subsequently defined by the ERP vendor as being an 'exemplary site'. Through the theoretical lens of Actor Network Theory, the paper reveals the improvisation, enactments and constant work around the plan that took place in dealing with the high contingencies of ERP implementation. The study extends the discussion on improvisation and contributes to an already illuminating argument. It invites practitioners to reflect on ERP implementation practice and review their evaluation methods.

Introduction

One of Claudio Ciborra's most notable contributions to the study of information systems (IS) was his critical readings of the underlying assumptions of the linear, sequential and causational perspective of strategy formulation that has been imported from rational business strategy literature to strategic information systems (SIS). He deconstructed this managerial perspective to highlight both theoretically and empirically its inadequacy in explaining the practice of everyday life within organizations (Ciborra, 1991, 1994, 2002; Ciborra and Hanseth, 1998). His work asserts that the rational management model is highly simplified and based on sweeping generalizations and abstractions (Ciborra and Hanseth, 1998). It emphasizes that the social context of an IS development extends beyond prescriptive management frameworks and the functional design of the technical systems (Ciborra and Associates, 2000; Waema and Walsham, 1990). Ciborra strongly advocated that the static language of planning, controlling and methods need to be replaced by a new language based on improvisation, bricolage, and drift that reflects the dynamic nature of the 'real world', which presents a more realistic account of organizational practices in dealing with technology (Ciborra, 1999a).

The improvisation argument provided a breath of fresh air to the IS research field. Its strong explanatory capability reveals the 'messiness of everyday practices' and affirmed the existence of bricolage and doing with whatever available resources. Improvisation illustrates that this open-ended, subtle, and recurring action in dealing with technology could lead to major unplanned changes such as the redesigning of work practice (Orlikowski, 1996; Ciborra, 1996a).

The improvisation argument developed by Ciborra and Orlikowski is based on empirical studies of open ended and highly tailored technologies such as groupware, intranets and the internet. These studies focused on the use and ongoing accommodation of such customizable technologies that are so general at the user front (Orlikowski, 1996). The implementation project, even in the case of such malleable technology, has however received little attention. Where this has occurred, it is often referred to as a 'deliberate' planned endeavour to deliver the technology to end-users (Orlikowski, 1996).

This paper investigates whether the implementation of a rigid technology represented by Enterprise Resource Planning (ERP) accommodates improvisation argument, contrasting Ciborra's research on malleable open-ended technology. It focuses on investigating the improvisation phenomenon in the rigid and highly structured technology of ERP systems and during its perceived highly structured implementation project. ERP was selected as a contemporary example of a 'recalcitrant technology' with a rigidly defined hierarchy of components and operations that bear upon one another according to a set of rules determining both their functional dependence and temporal sequence (Kallinikos, 2002). ERP implementation occurs in an organizational setting different to that of groupware and other flexible technology, with a project structure and implementation methodology often specific to the system being implemented[1] in contrast to malleable technology. Also ERP – in contrast to the malleable technology – is very costly and often represents the largest single IS investment in the history of many organizations (Sumner, 2000). By focusing on ERP during its implementation, this paper aims to extend the current discussion on improvisation.

This paper draws on Actor Network Theory (ANT) to investigate ERP implementation within a large international organization. The project was deemed a success by both the organization and the ERP vendor, with the latter defining it an 'exemplary site' and acknowledging that it had learnt 'key techniques from the implementation' that 'contributed to future software implementation methodology'.

The paper is organized into six sections. The first provides a brief introduction and presentation of the research question. The second reviews the literature in improvisation, identifying perceived gaps that this research addresses. The third presents the research methodology including data collection and analysis. The fourth section presents the findings and data analysis followed by a discussion. The paper concludes by extending the discussion, in addition to presenting its contribution to theory and practice.

Improvisation

Improvisation argument generally regards technology as intrinsically ambiguous and something that people in the field can appropriate and make sense of as they go along (Weick, 1990, 2001). It views systems design and implementation as being subject to different localities and multiple interpretations (see for example: Orlikowski and Gash, 1994; Doolin, 1999; Avgerou, 2002; Cadili and Whitley, 2005). This approach draws largely on Weick's research on improvisation and sense-making, Mintzberg's studies on emergent strategies, and Suchman's work on planned and situated actions.

Weick's contribution to organization science included new concepts such as 'improvisation', 'bricolage', 'sense-making', and 'enactment', used to express his action oriented view of the organization. He proposes that 'solid facts' are actually ongoing accomplishments that are sustained as much by intense action as by accurate diagnosis, in order to stress that emergent organizational action becomes visible only after the fact. As a result, organizational plans are perceived as pieces of history and not pieces of architecture (Weick, 1993). Weick (1993, 1989) posited that people attempt to make sense of their surrounding by being both proactive and reactive. Whatever they do provides a pretext to future interpretation and actions. This suggests that sense-making occurs amidst a continuous flow of movement that surrounds the actors as they attempt to coordinate their continuous flow of inputs (Weick, 1989). Such action-oriented behaviour resembles the composition and performance of jazz music, in which composition and performance occur simultaneously (Zack, 2000).

Weick adopts a balanced view of improvisation as a blend of both the pre-composed and the spontaneous, following Berliner's (1994) definition that 'improvisation involves reworking pre-composed material and designs in relation to unanticipated ideas conceived, shaped, and transformed under the special conditions of performance, thereby adding unique features to every creation' (Berliner, 1994). From this perspective, improvisation is centred around processes and designs that are continuously being reconstructed (Weick, 1993). This continuous action and reconstruction by surrounding actors produces new versions of the situation to act upon, defined as 'enactment'.

Weick (1993) states that 'plans are based on assumptions of ideal conditions and envision stable solutions to a set of current assumed stable problems', and proposes that the plan acts as a map that creates and labels the territory in which action takes place within a socially constructed world (Weick, 1989). Improvisation views action as a process of sense-making that makes do with whatever materials at hand, which builds on the notion of 'bricolage'[2] from Levi-Strauss' (Weick, 1993, 2001; Levi-Strauss, 1966). The term acknowledges the consistent misfit between the resources and the exact project to be accomplished, emphasising that these ill resources are all what is available and it is up to the organizational 'bricoleur' to make do with these resources. To illustrate this, Weick (1987) presents an interesting example of a military unit that became lost in the Alps during manoeuvres but which subsequently found its way after discovering a map to follow. Later, the unit's lieutenant discovered to his surprise that the map his unit had been following was of the Pyrenees, and not the Alps. Weick theorizes that it was only their continuous action, and not the map itself, that saved the unit (Weick, 1987).

Mintzberg (1994) describes the 'fallacy' of the prescriptive planning approach. He theorizes that this provides an idealized view of how strategies are supposed to be made, in contrast to the reality of how they are actually made. He introduces the notion that strategies emerge through a 'fluid process of learning' (Mintzberg, 1987), which appears without clear intentions as people undertake actions one by one, then respond to them so that patterns eventually form. Mintzberg (1987) suggests that strategy formulation and implementation 'walk on two feet': one deliberate and the other emergent. The decision maker typically starts on one foot and waits until the move of the other foot takes place, then starts to move the first one again, and so on. This implies that a purely deliberate or emergent strategy does not exist, but rather, a mix of both is most likely.

In contrast to structured strategic approach, emergent strategy 'enables management to act before everything is fully understood – to respond to an evolving reality rather than having to focus on a stable fantasy' (Mintzberg and Waters, 1985). In this way, objectives may not be defined at the beginning of the process, but may emerge gradually through a process of formation and learning (Mintzberg, 1994). In this context, strategy formation is an ongoing process that combines 'seeing and doing' with a more conventional approach of 'thinking and planning' (Mintzberg and Westley, 2001), and emergent strategy incorporates the notions of enactment and improvisational action.

Suchman (1987) defines improvisation as action that takes place in order to fill in the gap between routine organizational procedures and actual events occurring in the course of the daily flow of work (Suchman, 1987). Ciborra adopts a similar perspective on improvisation to Weick's, viewing it as a simultaneous mixture of intuition, competence, design and chance, contending that action intermingles the contours of the problematic situation with plans for problem solving and the deployment of resources (Ciborra, 1999b). Ciborra posits that in an after-the-fact analysis, the unfolding improvisation can be backtracked and connected to rational decision-making encompassing goal definition, information gathering, planning, and choice. He explains that this foregrounding of rational decision-making is what appears in many of the managerial presentations on IS development (Ciborra, 2002). Ciborra also recognises the existence and relevance of plans and acknowledges that improvisation contains elements of planning and design: 'the plans, the means-ends chain are there and they are relevant, but they are just the tip of the iceberg' (Ciborra, 1999c). Through a theoretical and philosophical analysis, Ciborra argues strongly that improvisation is grounded in real practices and that planning, decision models, and methods are in contrast 'de-rooted' (Ciborra, 1999b).

Ciborra conducted a number of empirical case studies on IS in organizations. These primarily, if not exclusively, focused on technologies such as the internet, intranets, and groupware applications, where the contingencies of improvisation, bricolage, and sense-making could be clearly expressed. His illuminating study of groupware applications in a number of international organizations reveals improvisation activities and the 'drifting' nature of technology in use (Ciborra, 1996b). For Ciborra (2002), this drift 'is about technology *in use*, as experienced and seen from the swamp of contingent situations and practices [emphasis added]', with the eventual use of an 'open' technology often varying from the initial plans. Having identified drift as being made of bricolage and improvisation and about open technology in use, Ciborra left an open question of what happens to a highly structured technology during implementation?

In another study, he presents the story of diffusion and use of the internet and intranet in a pharmaceutical company. He discovered that this did not conform to a plan or a strategic approach, but reflected improvisation, mushrooming, cultivation and bricolage (Ciborra, 2000b). He compares this with highly structured ERP projects, citing the example of an SAP implementation, and proposes that low-cost and low-risk projects enjoy a relaxed managerial approach that encompassed 'releasement', 'nurturing', and 'cultivation', versus a formalized strategic planning regime. He stated, 'if nobody seems to have a clue where all this will lead to, nobody seems to be panicking about it either' (Ciborra, 2000b). Ciborra however offers little on what the implementation of costly, high risk, less flexible and highly structured technology entails.

In their ERP studies, Ciborra and others seem to shift concepts from the improvisation perspective to a more deterministic one as they seek to account for unintended consequences and unplanned side effects.[3] They depict this as a *counter position* to the management agenda of control and planning (see for example: Ciborra and Failla, 2000; Hanseth and Braa, 2000; Hanseth et al., 2001). In his study with Hanseth for example (Ciborra and Hanseth, 1998), Ciborra challenges the management thinking of planning and control through a theoretical framework that draws on ANT and Heidegger. This framework 'embraces weak agency, encourages dwelling with mystery and values marginal practices'. Although Ciborra and Hanseth in this study critically review the management thinking of planning and control through the presentation of a case study of CRM system implementation, they shift to present another case study of intranet and internet implementation to apply their framework that reveals the practice of bricolage and improvisation. In assessing large integrated systems from an infrastructure point of view that puts organization in the 'mood' for control, Ciborra emphasises that these systems are themselves out of control and prone to drift, resulting in unintended consequences that are divorced from the perceived control. Ciborra, however, did not extend his research to study the bricolage and improvisation during the implementation of such systems.

Research methodology

Research site

Drinko is a global food and beverages company ranked within the top ten in its industrial sector. Drinko owns numerous production, packaging, and sales sites around the world. Each of these is comprised of a company or group of companies that operate locally. This case study focuses on Drinko's business units (BUs) within the UK and 'EUB' (a disguised name for another country). Approximately 25 BUs are encompassed by these two regions.

In 1998, Drinko launched an organisation-wide three years' project in order to implement SAP to replace the existing 225 systems around the company. Drinko identified five business processes as being 'in scope': *sales and operations planning, product supply, procurement, customer order fulfilment,* and *finance*. The project was divided into six phases: mobilization, analysis and conceptual design, detailed design, build and test, transition and in service. This case focuses on the first three phases of implementation, and the role of the SAP project team. The project team was sourced from internal business staff and four consulting firms, disguised and presented according to their functional contribution: Initial Consultants, Business Consulting, Technical Consulting, and Training Consulting.

Although the implementation took four years (1997–2001), Drinko's senior management formally announced that the project had successfully been completed in three years, as planned not taking account of slippage that occurred during the first three phases. The cost of the project reached over £40 million, which was nearly £3 million over the initial budget.

Data collection and analysis

The research follows an interpretive approach of inquiry, which seeks to understand the phenomena from the viewpoint of the participants and their social and cultural context (Kaplan and Maxwell, 1994; Schwandt, 1994; Myers, 1997). It aims to explore the nature of organizational action during the implementation of the ERP system and to provide 'deep insight' into the investigated phenomena (Walsham, 1995; Klein and Myers, 1999: 67).

Data were collected through semi-structured interviews with 13 members of staff working on the project between August 2000 and March 2001. In addition, data were collected informally from two other members of the project team in 1999 and early 2000, prior to the commencement of the formal interviews. Interviews lasted between one and three hours, and were not tape-recorded at the request of Drinko, due to the sensitivity of the information being discussed. Transcripts of the interviews were subsequently produced, with additional observations and notes made after the conclusion of each interview. Where required, participants were re-interviewed at a later date, or contacted via e-mail or telephone to seek further clarification. This methodology provided multiple perspectives on topical issues, in addition to the development of an understanding of the relevant controversies, negotiations and resolutions. Documents were reviewed including company newsletters; versions of the project's business case; internal project reports; two consultancy reports; the business consultants' implementation methodology and a final project report.

Data were analysed utilizing various approaches. Interview data were divided according to criteria that included; actors, events, organisational level and issues resolutions, which was useful in focusing on different themes and the details involved. In addition, interview notes, related material and documents were re-read systematically in chronological order, which provided a useful way to understand the context, develop a sense of the situation and the whole stream of actions involved, and the project progress over time (Vaughan, 1996). This hermeneutic circle (Gadamer, 1976; Klein and Myers, 1999) aided in the construction of a clear picture of the project, its events, incidents, people and artefacts involved.

All names and locations have been disguised at the request of the organization. Quotes that express many informants' point of view are reported by presenting one indicative quote without a reference to the source.

ANT and improvisation

The case study analysis is guided by the conceptual framework of 'ANT' (Latour, 1987, 1988a, 1996, 2004, 2005). The dynamics and empirical orientation of this theoretical perspective provide a relevant account of emergent action, due in particular to its premise that the development of any project is contingent. Law and Callon remark that the sociotechnical process of a project is '*interactive and emergent* [and] their course and fate are not easily predicted [emphasis is added]' (Law and Callon, 1988). This interactive and emergent nature is depicted by Callon and Law (1982) as follows: 'all actors are constructing interest maps all the time.... These then are *working maps* and they are *not static* but they are *reflexively* related to actors' conceptions of their own interests. As more data about the social world are produced and made relevant so their conceptions of the interests of both themselves and others are liable to change' [emphasis added].

A central theme in ANT is the assimilation of alliances by an actor in order to facilitate the pursuit of a specific goal. These alliances are comprised of other actors (human and non-human) gathered and aligned to support the network builder and achieve his goals (Latour, 1987). This process of displacement is called translation and could be achieved through different strategies (Latour, 1987). Callon (1986) clearly defines the anatomy of translation in terms of 'four moments of translation': 'problematisation', 'interessement', 'enrolment', and 'mobilization'. He asserts that these moments are interrelated and could be inseparable in reality (Callon, 1986).

The initial moment of translation, problematization, as the term implies, deals with finding a problem for the presented solution to which other entities could subscribe to. In order to do this, the 'enunciators' need to define the other actors' identities, what they might possibly want and make themselves or other entities as an obligatory passage point. By becoming the obligatory point of passage, the network builders define the way for the actors to proceed if they are to realize their goals. Interessement is the action of interest building. During interessement, interest building occurs by the enunciator, as it attempts to impose and stabilize the identity of the other actors it defines through its problematization (Callon, 1986: 207–208). This process carries the risk that actors may refuse the identification of their identities and define their identity, goals, projects, motivations, or interests in another manner (Latour, 1987, 1988b).

If successful, problematization and interessement lead to enrolment. During this moment, actors accept the roles that have been defined for them during interessement, but which do not imply or exclude, pre-established roles. This moment often entails conflict and struggle, as attempts are made to convince other actors to play the roles they have been ascribed (ibid.). Enrolment may occur through seduction, transaction and consent without discussion (Latour, 1987, 1988a), with efforts made to pull entities toward the enunciator's proposal. The last moment of translation is mobilization. This occurs as wider acceptance of the proposal eventuates. In order to communicate with other actors outside of the network, the network builder creates immutable mobiles. These are mobile objects such as a text, which are capable of reaching and convincing entities to join the network without affecting its relationships or equilibrium (Latour, 1990).

Translation does not necessarily occur in well-defined, linear steps. In reality, moments (tactics) and strategies overlap (Callon, 1986: 203) and 'are never as distinct as they are [presented]' (*ibid.*, 224). Callon (*ibid.*) theorizes that during the process of translation the identity of actors, the possibility of interaction, and the margins of manoeuvre are negotiated and delimited. He depicts these as items of interest for researchers, contrasting this with an approach that identifies and separates the tactics of translation (*ibid.*). He warns that an approach that adopts this more 'literal' examination of the moments of translation could lead to a linear analysis that is devoid of the complexity and essence of the very situation it seeks to assess. In adhering to the approach advocated by Callon and other actor network theorists (Law and Callon, 1988, 1992; Callon and Law, 1989), the moments of translation have been 'loosely' applied in the analysis of the case study data and assessment of the research questions at Drinko.

Findings from the case study: an ANT reading

The initial claim and associations

The SAP project started with a claim articulated by the IT director of SmCo, one of Drinko's small European companies, that SAP had brought significant benefits for SmCo that exceeded expectations. In a Drinko IT conference, he succeeded in convincing the attendees, including Drinko's CEO, that this SAP success in SmCo could be repeated within Drinko. He also convinced the CEO that he would be capable of delivering this success across the organization through an integrated organization-wide SAP system. The CEO believed that 'as he [SmCo's IT director] succeeded there [in SmCo's SAP implementation], he would here [at Drinko] as well'. For this reason, the CEO selected the IT Director of SmCo to become the IT director of Drinko, forming a core alliance for the SAP project network. They decided to extend the network of alliances to pursue their idea.

The Board played the role of money provider and the highest approval authority in Drinko requiring all significant investments to be referred to it for review. Hence, large investments and big projects could be pursued only with the Board's approval and budget allocation. To interest the Board, the aligned IT director and CEO needed – following the business tradition – to prepare a business case document through which they could translate the Board's interests and channel it towards an organization-wide SAP implementation. To do so, they had first to mobilize the single system into their network finding a credible speaker on its behalf to spell out what it can offer for Drinko. They therefore hired a consultant company, the Initial Consultants, to speak on behalf of the system and to work alongside an IT manager from Drinko to prepare the required document.

This document presented the single system as the only favourable scenario, while appearing to explore all possible options, including the 'do nothing' option that is traditionally identified in such a business case. The business case proposal served its purpose as a translation tool by successfully recruiting the Board to join the implementation network of SAP. It was then sent to the BUs involved as an immutable mobile object that would be taken for granted and hence move around to interest and enrol others without being altered. It was supposed to reach out for the BUs' internal networks, interest and unproblematically recruit them guaranteeing their commitment to the project and hold itself stable and unchanged during this process.

Trials to translate the BUs involved

The joining of the SAP project was taken for granted as a black box that BUs would undoubtedly subscribe to by nominating their best managers to join the project team. However, this effortless subscription to the project proved to be unrealistic, as the following two examples indicate.

Counter-translation in America BUs

In moving from its constructed network towards the BUs, the project's immutable mobile was surprisingly challenged. The America BU did not welcome the 'close connections' to the UK[4] that this system would bring. It had another objective at that time, which was to increase its physical distribution capabilities, and hence it was occupied in exploring the idea of merging with another company in that market. So the America BU was not willing to change its agenda for what they saw as an internal UK matter that came 'out of the blue' and about which it had not been consulted beforehand (a Manager from America BU on a visit to the UK office).

Drinko America refused to follow the project network's determined path and started to negotiate with the project team. During this negotiation, the America BU tried to refute all the operational reasons given by the SAP project team to join. In this way, the UK's interests in implementing the integrated system were challenged and interrupted by the America BU interest in a merger. The America BU redefined the UK and displaced its goal of implementing the SAP system and translated it to be primarily seeking efficiency and reducing operational cost.

They then convinced the UK team that the proposed merger would be the only right detour to achieve the aim (the new translated aim) in this market.

This line of argument was also supported by a counter-document that threatened the UK project team that if the merger did not take place 'no one would benefit from that' and 'all of [them] would suffer' (Internal report). This counter translation succeeded to convince the UK to exclude America BU from joining the project network and therefore the project scope was reduced and a new document was produced to reflect this new reality.

Bringing in a powerful actor in EUB translation

According to the initial business case and plan, the organization-wide SAP project intended to cover several BUs. As the America BU succeeded in translating the UK interests and convinced them to adopt its goals, EUB was left as the only BU outside the UK's borders to be convinced to join the SAP project.

The historical relations between the UK and Drinko EUB kept each network isolated in a clustered regional relationship. Revenues were the only flow between them and the only intermediary from EUB to the UK. From the UK point of view, EUB would expect to do 'just the opposite of whatever [they] say, just because it comes from [UK]'. Being aware of the sensitivity between the UK and EUB and the need to avoid repeating the slippage that occurred in the America case, the project network realized that it needed to adopt a careful translation strategy for EUB (see Elbanna 2007 for more details).

When the project management from UK approached Drinko EUB executives to discuss the new SAP system, it found that interesting them, and encouraging them to interest others in their network, required the enrolling of a strong actor who could convince them and pull their whole network towards the UK. Thus, project management enrolled the EUB location and appointed it to be the official project location. In doing so, they followed EUB interest in gaining an explicit organization-wide recognition that assures its identity. Angering the UK's project members by flying them all to EUB would be a strong statement of recognition of EUB role. A statement by the CEO – that the project chose a location within EUB's territory because it had the required expertise – displaced Drinko EUB and channelled it towards joining the project network and pursuing the network's goals. It was through this un-pre-planned in-formalized move during the project that the UK succeeded in mobilising EUB to join the SAP project network. This appeared on-the-fly move reflects deep experience and skilful translation of EUB that had a large effect on the project in line with Ciborra's theorization on malleable technology (Ciborra, 2002).

Clash of problematizations and efforts to re-align

The first phase of the project, 'mobilization', ended up with documents specifying the reduced new scope of the project after the America withdrawal, as well as the teams involved, members' names, and responsibilities. These were prepared at the project's top management level and were supposed to stabilize the constructed network and carry it through the following project phases. The teams continued to work on the next phase, namely the 'analysis and conceptual design', that was a more exploratory exercise, with teams mainly occupied by mapping the processes in different BUs to help understand the general requirements of each unit, in addition to understanding the capability of the system.

The initial objectives of the SAP project were to enable Drinko to meet increased worldwide demand profitably; to give people access to accurate information quickly so that they can make decisions fast; and to simplify core processes and systems across what have been traditionally regarded as separate regional operations. However, according to their initial translation different teams and different BUs identified the objectives in a different way. In EUB, the project was seen to be primarily about a system that needed to be put in place according to a certain schedule. For the UK, it was a way of making transparent and changing the long hidden EUB processes and data. Each process team also translated the project into something different. For the operations planning team, for example, it was aimed at establishing one sales plan for all Drinko but this was abandoned by the sales team, who saw it as a project to create end-to-end sales ordering and accounting processes.

By the end of the second phase of the project, analysis and conceptual design, the deliverables of each team varied according to their understanding of the project. This difference in deliverables has been largely affected by the initial problematization that the project team tailored for each party involved in order to interest and ensure their commitment to the project. It became obvious to top management that they needed to retranslate the parties involved and reset the objectives of the project, as the above scattered aims did lead to 'confused' and 'different' deliverables. Drinko top managers were aware that having 'solid objectives' would help in establishing a well performing network, and the business consultants advised them to refine and simplify the objectives of the system to one that people would remember and focus on.

During brainstorming meetings to simplify the objectives and reduce them to only one, the top management found that keeping the historically distanced EUB enrolled in this project network alongside their UK counterparts was the main challenge facing the project. They realized that obtaining such an enrolment and stabilizing it through inscribing it in the implemented system would be the most favourable achievement this system could reach, something that had not been achieved before. This resulted in the launching of a new project's objective: 'to unify the business' combined with a new two-coloured jigsaw logo.

The previous ad hoc re problematization, although not in the project plan, was an important quick plan and action to meet an emerging problem of having different orientation and understanding of the project deliverables. The improvised re-problematization of the project was engaging for the parties involved. It was particularly appealing to EUB, which felt that this large project was a good chance to gain equality with the UK, especially after UK staff had been 'dragged all the way' to run the project from their new location in EUB. For the reluctant UK staff, who were 'not very happy of course' with their 'displacement' to the

EUB, 'integrating the business' was accepted as 'a challenging mission to deliver' a system of unprecedented control over EUB. The project therefore became the only way to absorb EUB in their network 'once and forever'.

The reversing of the project network

Many controversies and negotiations appeared in the subsequent third phase, 'detailed design', which threatened what was hoped to be a stabilized network. For example, controversies were opened surrounding the team construction, the Business Consultants, the SAP capability, and the construction of a shared service centre as follows.

Back to primary networks

The project team consisted of five separate teams implementing the five chosen modules of SAP. The teams were assigned to two buildings in EUB. Some teams had more EUB members than their UK counterpart and some consisted purely of UK staff. Teams tended to be polarized according to their original primary networks that existed before the construction of the project, into the UK and EUB ignoring the newly constructed project network. Teams from the UK preferred to keep their perceived superior network bounded in a separate building following their tradition of organizing, scheduling, work style and using their favourite project software that is widely used in the UK network. EUB teams also pursued their objectives through creating their own work style, schedules and milestones, and used other 'outdated' and 'old packages' (from the UK point of view) for diagrams and charts.

In their dismay of being part of the same network with EUB and their desire to return to regional polarized relationship, the UK teams found the delay of some teams schedule by the end of phase three a good opportunity to complain about EUB counterparts. They tried to translate top management interest in project success and channelled it towards excluding EUB from the project teams by claiming that EUB involvement affected their delivery, causing delays and uncertainties about the quality and direction of the project. They also juxtaposed with SAP to claim that this integrated system required some processes to be integrated, such as finance and procurement, and that EUB lack of communication would jeopardize the system's configurations and integration (Elbanna, 2003).

Top management had to deal with the emergent delay in teams' delivery and the UK teams' warning regarding the integration of the system's configuration, they decided that better cooperation and streamlining between teams required some enforcement. Therefore, they accepted the UK teams' proposal to restructure and amalgamate some teams to 'force them to work together', which effectively marginalized EUB for the rest of the project. The management response however favoured one party over the other and followed a certain translation of the teams' delay (UK translation) represents an immediate and improvised action to solve a rising problem. They had to re-work the project structure and composition disregarding the plan in order to achieve harmony and ensure delivery.

Counter-enrolment of other systems

Until the start of the third phase of the implementation, 'detailed design', the system was envisaged as a single integrated SAP. The SAP project teams and their collaborating consultants followed that claim and tried to stick to a standard 'vanilla implementation' of SAP. In approaching their potential network actors, the project sub-teams were faced by different problematization and counter-enrolment of different technologies. For example, when the operation planning process team conducted seminars to discuss with users the new processes and how the new system would handle them, they found users were unconvinced that the new SAP system could support the operation's planning process. They were already using another packaged software, Manugistics, to manage production planning and therefore opened the black box of SAP functionalities and compared it to their Manugistics system doubting the SAP capability.

The project team tried to enrol the users in their vanilla implementation project, yet users did not subscribe to that and at the same time realized that the project team involved would not accept anything but a vanilla implementation and that any attempt to convince them to amend SAP would be hopeless. Accordingly, users made it explicit that 'this SAP won't work' and set the continued use of Manugistics as a little deviation from the project plan that would still lead to the main goal of a vanilla implementation of SAP. They translated the project team's interest in such a vanilla implementation by keeping SAP unchanged and offered interfacing it with Manugistics. They supported their argument by bringing in different actors who already used the package, including another recently merged company and some competitors. In that way, UK users succeeded in convincing the project team to work out of their initial plan of having one single integrated system that spanned the whole organization and retain Manugistics to handle production planning in all BUs.

Users in different departments continued to offer similar detours to the project teams, compelling the latter to work out different solutions in order to ensure the membership of different users into the project networks. For example, the product supply team was pushed to accept interfacing SAP with another package for statistics and graphics in order to keep the product supply staff enrolled and committed to the implementation of the system. They also had to please Drinko management who was not satisfied with the reporting functionality of SAP, by complementing it with a packaged decision support system and data warehouse that they felt had better reporting capabilities. Recruiting and ensuring the alignment of different actors in that way meant working out different translations and accepting some detours that were partially out of what was planned for (Elbanna, 2008).

Polarizing the system's network

The project team followed the organization inscription of SAP that requires gathering all the organization services into one centre. They adopted this goal as it presents one of the major advantages of having an integrated system such as SAP that reduces the operational costs and improves efficiency. In Drinko context, this worked against the primary networks of Drinko that were deeply rooted and difficult to dissolve in favour of the project goal. Therefore, controversies were raised regarding the location of the project management suggested single service centre.

UK staff argued that it had to be in the UK and problematized the issue to top management that the only experienced staff that can operate a single service centre efficiently were in the UK and EUB did not have the operational sophistication and competences to operate it. They also made it clear that they could not accept it if it went to EUB and would even perceive it as a 'humiliation' to their capability. EUB also expressed their dismay at sending their services to the UK for processing as if they could not do it themselves. The top management found the issue a potential wrecker for the project network that threatened the project implementation at a crucial time. Therefore, they decided to find an immediate solution to the problem that kept the primary networks happy, enrolled and committed to the project network even if it meant compromising the systems and losing out some of its planned cost cuts and efficiency. Hence, they decided to configure the system awkwardly to have two shared services, one in EUB and the other in the UK to ensure the continuation of the primary networks' alignment into the project network and the implementation of the system.

Discussion

The previous section reveals that the implementation efforts of integrated packaged software such as ERP could be conceptualized as a practice of network building and alignment of different actors to pursue the network builders' goals. The study demonstrates through the case of Drinko that improvisation takes place in trials to render the ERP constructed network sufficient stability and channel different actors to perform their required roles in order for the implementation network to achieve its objectives.

The study reveals that the application of different translation strategies in order to recruit and align various actors could result in creating multiple perceptions of the project and its goals, which affects the coherence of actors' perception of the project and understanding of the required deliverables. Improvisation is then required to find a convergence point for the actors involved that keeps them interested and enrolled in the project, yet at the same time working and delivering coherent parts of the system.

Project management had to redefine the project for all the parties involved and find an objective that could funnel the interests of the actors and realign them to accomplish the implementation project. They had to find a central theme that all actors could relate and subscribe to. Through brainstorming sessions, they realised that unifying the business is what they want from this system and hence launched it as the new solo objective of the project and created a visual two-coloured logo for the project to convey the message. The shift of the project objectives and the creation of a representative logo came about as tinkering of the project direction upon management realization that different BUs and teams perceive the system in a different way.

The case also highlighted the contribution of the actors' background and origin on the instability of the network, which required bricolage in discovering ways to stabilize the network. The descending of main organizational actors from two primary networks was a constant source of improvisation in Drinko. Although successfully recruited and enrolled into the project network, these actors maintained membership with their primary networks. On two occasions, this relationship resulted in the polarization of the implementation project, requiring the development of alternative plans and responses from the project management team.

On one occasion, the UK teams negotiated and advocated new terms to continue their alignment and support for the project based on dismissing most of the EUB members. Having provided a convincing case for the management, the latter responded in approval of a restructuring exercise of the project teams involved resulted in reducing them to three instead of the previous five and hence get rid of marginalized EUB teams' members in this process. The change of teams' structure was an improvised action that emerged out of controversy and dissatisfaction of the UK teams and their success to enrol the top management and convince them that EUB team members hinder the proper development of the system.

On a subsequent occasion, controversy arose regarding the decision on where to locate the shared service centre. UK negotiated to own the shared service centre and Drinko management were aware that if they went with this request they would lose EUB crucial support of the project, and if they did not they would lose the efficiency of the shared service centre that UK staff are capable of achieving. The alternative action satisfied both the UK and EUB BUs by locating a service centre in each country. This unplanned course of action ensured their continued participation in the project and the stability of the network. It emerged as a solution to the organisational othering of the EUB BU (Elbanna, 2007). Although appealing to the actors in the network, the outcome of a dual service centre compromised Dirnko's system capability and delivered a costly and awkward structure for an integrated system that was not originally planned for or budgeted.

Drinko's SAP implementation highlighted how negotiation and action occurring at one stage of the network building affects the future direction of the project. An example of this is the negotiation that resulted in the withdrawal of the American BU from the project. Drinko management recognized that a similar risk existed with EUB, which resulted in the subsequent strategy to 'embrace' it in order to ensure its translation and participation in the project. The occurrence and enactment of the first event created a new reality for future organizational action and also a new way of thinking amongst senior management. Aligning the powerful actor of EUB location allowed the project team to obtain critical support for the subsequent negotiations with EUB, and ensured its participation in the project.

In contrast to the management thinking, the SAP project followed an improvisation pattern from the beginning. Senior management's decision to embark on the project was based on the idea that SAP would benefit Drinko and the success of SmCo could be replicated in Drinko. This was despite the existence of a struggling SAP solution in the UK BU at the time. The decision to embark on the investment in SAP was not a pure rational decision based on information gathering, comparing alternatives including different strategies and other types of ERP, and choosing the most viable one as is usually portrayed in the literature (Parr and Shanks, 2000). Nor did such a process commence by defining clear business objectives for the ERP investment (Markus et al., 2000). This finding is congruent with Avgerou's (2000) position that IS tends to be taken for granted and institutionalized, despite the vagueness of its actual benefits.

The several changes that the project business case document went through during the implementation reveals that the management thinking largely based on taken for granted assumption that the initial business case document represented an immutable mobile that other actors would subscribe to without distorting or changing it is essentially unfounded. This assumption is based on having a clear view and understanding of different organizational actors upfront and the ability to draw an organizational panopticon for the actors involved (Latour, 1990). In the implementation of a large-scale system such as ERP, characterized by the involvement of numerous human and non-human actors, it is complicated to construct such a panopticon that unravels the roles of the actors in advance.

Conclusion

This study responds to the invitation extended by many improvisation researchers to apply the improvisation approach to studies of technologies other than open-ended systems (Orlikowski, 1996; Yates et al., 1999). A detailed depiction has been made of how the implementation of ERP within Drinko followed an improvisation pattern. Implementation was characterized by high contingencies and adherence to work around the plan to obtain solutions to emerging issues. None of these were envisaged beforehand or were incorporated in the ERPs implementation plan. The 'after the fact' presentation of the project followed a managerial agenda that depicted it as a well planned endeavour that delivered planned 'outcome'. This is in line with Ciborra's observation that formal managerial presentation slides represent a glossy surface superficially extracted and removed from practice (Ciborra, 2002).

The negotiation that took place in the process of interesting and enrolling different actors into the project network and the constant trials to achieve sufficient stability of the network present occasions for different actors to open the project black box and negotiate new terms for the alignment. This provides an understanding of the actors' need for improvisation and acting out of plans, which results in an ability to negotiate, find common ground and new terms that guarantee the alignment of the actors. The unfolding course of events following the opening of the project black box could not have been predicted at the beginning, and hence could not have been addressed through a structured approach of methods and plans.

Different actors not only can bring about different terms for joining the project or for the continuation of their recruitment, which invites improvisation and ability to negotiate, but they could also bring different perception of the project itself that could confuse its objectives. These unfolding perceptions require monitoring and confrontation as they surface, which no plans could foresee, and no a priori action could tackle.

Analysis of the case study results in reflection on the general assumption that an IS development methodology is a way of documenting the system to facilitate the joining in of new staff and the upgrading of the system (Hirschheim et al., 1995). This case study suggests that such a notion might be applicable to the technical side of the project, but not to the organizational side. The project documentation portrayed a 'tidy story' of procedures, steps, and approvals. None of the 'messy' stories or explanations of why the system took the form it did were documented apart from a few hints in the confidential and highly restricted minutes of the ERP programme board. New staff would not obtain an explanation on some organizational aspects of the system, such as having two data centres existing in Drinko UK and the EUB, or excluding a significant BU from the organization-wide SAP implementation system scope, or interfacing what is supposed to be an integrated single system with many others that offer similar functions.

This case shows that what was previously reported a highly structured implementation of ERP systems (Brown and Vessey, 1999; Krumbholz et al., 2000; Rebstock and Selig, 2000; Al-Mudimigh et al., 2001) is in practice an ongoing process that mixed seeing and doing. This is in line with Minztberg and Westley's (2001) and Minzberg's (1987) notion that people take actions one-by-one, then respond to them so that patterns eventually form. Evidence from the case demonstrates that improvisation and drift took place on both the technology and organizational side at Drinko. This extends the drift argument, from considering only drift on the technology side (Ciborra, 2000a; Ciborra and Associates, 2000) and seeing only technology 'running away' (Hanseth et al., 2001) towards incorporating the organization acts of improvisation, bricolage and drift.

This study illustrates that even highly structured projects encompassing rigid technology such as ERP enjoy a similar approach of improvisation that was previously attributed to low-cost, low-risk projects of malleable technology such as groupware, intranet and internet (Ciborra, 2000b). The findings invite practitioners to reflect on ERP implementation practices and review their evaluation methods with a view to embracing improvisation and bricolage. The application of ANT in the study of improvisation provides an insightful interactive framework that assists in detecting the inner dynamics of the process of implementing ERP. This extends beyond the appearances of plans, methodology, and measurements to reveal the improvisation and bricolage activities that take place during the organizational efforts to implement the large and complex packaged software.

Analysis of the case study results applying ANT reveals that improvisation is inherent in the process of network building as actors actively interpret their interests in relation to others, and act accordingly. This provides a new insight into the sources and processes of improvisation. The study also contributes to an understanding of the role of the plan in improvisation, by revealing that the plan draws upon the invisible organization that only renders itself visible during implementation. Hence, business plans will change as more actors 'surface' and would only get stabilized at the end of the project as the organization renders itself visible. This study extends Ciborra's notion of improvisation, which he spent over a decade researching, by illustrating its validity in other technological and organizational settings.

Notes

This paper originally appeared as Elbanna, A.R. (2006) The validity of the improvisation argument in the implementation of rigid technology: the case of ERP systems. *Journal of Information Technology* **21**(3): 165–175.

1. ERP systems often come with their own implementation methodologies. The implementation methodology for SAP R/3 for example is called ASAP.
2. *Bricolage* is a French word that means to use whatever resources and repertoire one has to perform whatever task one faces.
3. For more information about this argument and whether it follows a technologically deterministic paradigm, see: Winner (1977) and Bimber (1994).
4. 'UK' here incorporates both BUs in the UK and the corporate headquarters as referred to by organizational members.

References

Al-Mudimigh, A., Zairi, M. and Al-Mashari, M. (2001). ERP Software Implementation: An Integrative Framework, *European Journal of Information Systems* **10**: 216–226.

Avgerou, C. (2000). IT and Organizational Change: An Institutionalist Perspective, *Information Technology & People* **13**(4): 234–262.

Avgerou, C. (2002). *Information Systems and Global Diversity*, Oxford: Oxford University Press.

Berliner, P.F. (1994). *Thinking in Jazz: The Infinite Art of Improvisation*, Chicago, IL: University of Chicago.

Brown, C.V. and Vessey, I. (1999). ERP Implementation Approaches: Toward a Contingency Framework, in Twentieth International Conference on Information Systems (ICIS), North Carolina: Charlotte, pp. 411–416.

Cadili, S. and Whitley, E.A. (2005). On the interpretive flexibility of hosted ERP systems, London: Working Paper Series No. 131, Department of Information Systems, The London School of Economics and Political Science.

Callon, M. (1986). Some Elements of a Sociology of Translation: Domestication of the Scallops and the Fishermen of St Brieuc Bay, in J. Law (ed.) *Power, Action and Belief: A New Sociology of Knowledge*, London: Routledge and Kegan Paul, pp. 196–233.

Callon, M. and Law, J. (1989). On the Construction of Sociotechnical Networks: Content and Context Revisited, *Knowledge and Society: Studies in the Sociology of Science Past and Present* **8**: 57–83.

Ciborra, C. (1994). The Grassroots of IT and Strategy, in C. Ciborra and T. Jelassi (eds.) *Strategic Information Systems: A European Perspective*, New York: John Wiley & Sons Ltd.

Ciborra, C.U. (1991). The Limits of Strategic Information Systems, *International Journal of Information Resource Management* **2**(3): 11–17.

Ciborra, C.U. (ed.) (1996a). *Groupware and Team Work: Invisible Aid or Technical Hindrance*, Chichester: John Wiley & Sons Ltd.

Ciborra, C.U. (1996b). What Does Groupware Mean for the Organizations Hosting It? in CU Ciborra (ed.) *Groupware and Team Work: Invisible Aid or Technical Hindrance*, Chichester: John Wiey.

Ciborra, C.U. (1999a). *Hospitality and IT*, Universiteit van Amsterdam.

Ciborra, C.U. (1999b). Notes on Improvisation and Time in Organizations, *Accounting, Management and Information Technology* 9(2): 77–94.

Ciborra, C.U. (1999c). A Theory of Information Systems Based on Improvisation, in W. Currie and B. Galliers (eds.) *Rethinking Management Information Systems: An Interdisciplinary Perspective*, Oxford: Oxford University Press.

Ciborra, C.U. (2000a). Drifting: From Control to Drift, in K. Braa, C. Sorensen and B. Dahlbom (eds.) *Planet Internet*, Sweden: Studentlitteratur, Lund.

Ciborra, C.U. (2000b). From Alignment to Loose Coupling: From MedNet to www.Roche.Com, in C.U. Ciborra and Associates (eds.) *From Control to Drift: The Dynamics of Corporate Information Infrastructure*, Oxford: Oxford University Press.

Ciborra, C.U. (2002). *The Labyrinth of Information*, Oxford: Oxford University Press.

Ciborra, C.U. and Associates (eds.) (2000). *From Control to Drift: The Dynamics of Corporate Information Infrastructure*, Oxford: Oxford University Press.

Ciborra, C.U. and Failla, A. (2000). Infrastructure as a Process: The Case of CRM in IBM, in C.U. Ciborra and associates (eds.) *From Control to Drift: The Dynamics of Corporate Information Infrastructure*, Oxford: Oxford University Press.

Ciborra, C.U. and Hanseth, O. (1998). From Tool to Gestell Agendas for Managing the Information Infrastructure, *Information Technology & People* **11**(4): 305–327.

Doolin, B. (1999). Sociotechnical Networks and Information Management in Health Care, *Accounting, Management and Information Technology* 9(2): 95–114.

Elbanna, A.R. (2003). Achieving Social Integration to Implement ERP systems, The 11th European Conference of Information Systems, Naples, Italy.

Elbanna, A.R. (2007). Implementing an Integrated System in a Socially Dis-integrated Enterprise: A Critical View of ERP Enabled Integration, *Information Technology & People*, 20(2): 121–139

Elbanna, A.R. (2008). Strategic Systems Implementation: Diffusion through Drift, *Journal of Information Technology* **23**(2): 89–96.

Gadamer, HG. (1976). The Historicity of Understanding, in P. Connerton (ed.) *Critical Sociology: Selected Readings*, Harmondsworth: Benguin Books Ltd, pp. 117–133.

Hanseth, O. and Braa, K. (2000). Who's in Control: Designers, Managers – or Technology? Infrastructure at Norsk Hydro, in Cuao Ciborra (ed.) *From Control to Drift: The Dynamics of Corporate Information Infrastructure*, Oxford: Oxford University Press, pp. 125–147.

Hanseth, O., Ciborra, C.U. and Braa, K. (2001). The Control Devolution: ERP and the Side Effects of Globalization, *The Data Base for Advances in Information Systems* **32**(4): 34–46.

Hirschheim, R., Klien, H.K. and Lyytinen, K. (1995). *Information Systems Development and Data Modeling: Conceptual and Philosophical Foundations*, Cambridge: Cambridge University Press.

Kallinikos, J. (2002). Re-Opening the Black Box of Technology: Artifacts and Human Agency, in Twenty Third International Conference on Information Systems, Barcelona, 14–16 December 2002, pp. 287–294.

Kaplan, B. and Maxwell, J.A. (1994). Qualitative Research Methods for Evaluating Computer Information Systems, in S.J. Jay (ed.) *Evaluating Health Care Information Systems: Methods and Applications*, Thousand Oaks, CA: Sage, pp. 45–68.

Klein, H.K. and Myers, M.D. (1999). A Set of Principles for Conducting and Evaluating Interpretive Field Studies in Information Systems, *MIS Quarterly* **23**(1): 67–94.

Krumbholz, M., Galliers, J., Coulianos, N. and Maiden, N.A.M. (2000). Implementing Enterprise Resource Planning Packages in Different Corporate and National Cultures, *Journal of Information Technology* **15**: 267–279.

Latour, B. (1987). *Science in Action: How to Follow Scientists and Engineers Through Society*, Cambridge, MA: Harvard University Press.

Latour, B. (1988a). Mixing Humans and Nonhumans Together: The sociology of a door-closer, *Social Problems* **35**(3): 298–310.

Latour, B. (1988b). *The Pasteurization of France*, Cambridge: Harvard University Press.

Latour, B. (1990). Drawing Things Together, in M. Lynch and S. Woolgar (eds.) *Representation in Scientific Practice*, Cambridge, MA: MIT Press, pp. 19–68.

Latour, B. (1996). *Aramis or the Love of Technology*, Cambridge, MA: Harvard University Press.

Latour, B. (2004). On Using ANT for Studying Information Systems: A (Somewhat) Socratic Dialogue, in C. Avgerou, C.U. Ciborra and F. Land (eds.) *The Social Study of Information and Communication Technology*, Oxford: Oxford University Press.

Latour, B. (ed.) (2005). *Reassembling the Social: An Introduction to Actor-Network-Theory*, Oxford: Oxford University Press.

Law, J. and Callon, M. (1988). Engineering and Sociology in a Military Aircraft Project: A Network Analysis of Technological Change, *Social Problems* **35**(3): 284–297.

Law, J. and Callon, M. (1992). The Life and Death of An Aircraft: A Network Analysis of Technical Change, in W.E. Bijker and J. Law (eds.) *Shaping Technology/Building Society: Studies in Sociotechnical Change*, Cambridge, MA: MIT Press.

Levi-Strauss, C. (1966). *The Savage Mind*, Chicago: University of Chicago Press.

Markus, L.M., Axline, S., Petrie, D. and Tanis, C. (2000). Learning from Adopters' Experiences with ERP: Problems encountered and success achieved, *Journal of Information Technology* **15**(4): 245–265.

Mintzberg, H. (1987). Crafting Strategy, *Harvard Business Review* **87**(4): 66–75.

Mintzberg, H. (1994). *The Rise and Fall of Strategic Planning*, New York: Prentice-Hall.

Mintzberg, H. and Waters, J.A. (1985). Of Strategies, Deliberate and Emergent, *Strategic Management Journal* **6**: 257–272.

Mintzberg, H. and Westley, F. (2001). Decision Making: It's not what you think, *Sloan Management Review Spring* **42**(3): 89–93.

Myers, M.D. (1997). Interpretive Research in Information Systems, in F. Stowell (ed.) *Information Systems: An Emerging Discipline*, London: McGraw-Hill, pp. 239–266.

Orlikowski, W.J. (1996). Improvising Organisational Transformation Over Time: A situated change perspective, *Information Systems Research* **7**(1): 63–92.

Orlikowski, W.J. and Gash, B.C. (1994). Technological Frames: Making sense of information technology in organizations, *ACM Transactions on Information Systems* **12**(2): 174–207.

Parr, A. and Shanks, G. (2000). A Model of ERP Project Implementation, *Journal of Information Technology* **15**: 289–303.

Rebstock, M. and Selig, J.G. (2000). Development and Implementation Strategies for International ERP Software Projects, The 8th European Conference of Information Systems, Austria: Vienna.

Schwandt, T.A. (1994). Constructivist, Interpretivist Approaches to Human Inquiry, in N.K. Denzin and Y.S. Lincoln (eds.) *Handbook of Qualitative Research*, Thousand Oaks, CA: Sage.

Suchman, L.A. (1987). *Plans and Situated Actions*, Cambridge: Cambridge University Press.

Sumner, M. (2000). Risk Factors in Enterprise-Wide/ERP Projects, *Journal of Information Technology* **15**: 317–327.

Vaughan, D. (1996). *The Challenger Launch Decision: Risky Technology, Culture, and Deviance at Nasa*, Chicago: University of Chicago Press.

Waema, T.M. and Walsham, G. (1990). Information Systems Strategy Formulation, *Information & Management* **18**: 29–39.

Walsham, G. (1995). Interpretive Case Studies in IS Research: Nature and Method, *European Journal of Information Systems* **4**: 74–81.

Weick, K.E. (1987). Substitutes for Strategy, in D.J. Teece (ed.) *The Competitive Challenge*, Cambridge, MA: Ballinger.

Weick, K.E. (1989). Organized Improvisation: 20 Years of Organizing, *Communication Studies* **40**(4): 241–248.

Weick, K.E. (1990). Technology as Equivoque: Sensemaking in New Technologies, in P.S. Goodman and L.S. Sproull (eds.) *Technology and Organisations*, San Francisco: Jossey-Bass.
Weick, K.E. (1993). Organizational Redesign as Improvisation, in G.P. Huber and W.H. Glick (eds.) *Organizational Change and Redesign*, New York: Oxford University Press, pp. 346–379.
Weick, K.E. (2001). *Making Sense of the Organization*, Oxford, UK: Blackwell Publishers.
Yates, J., Orlikowski, W.J. and Okamura, K. (1999). Explicit and Implicit Structuring of Genres: Electronic Communication in a Japanese R&D Organization, *Organization Science* **10**(1): 83–103.
Zack, M.H. (2000). Jazz Improvisation and Organizing: Once more from the Top, *Organization Science* **11**(2): 227–234.

16
Object Lessons and Invisible Technologies*

Edgar A. Whitley and Mary Darking

Abstract

In this paper, we explore Claudio Ciborra's ideas about the technological object. We do so by contrasting these ideas with analysis by Law and Singleton (2005) who advocate a 'methodological radicalism' that moves beyond epistemological uncertainties about the technological object to ontological concerns. Law and Singleton's analysis is comprised of a series of stages that includes fluid objects, which change relatively gently and fire objects, which have more radical discontinuities. This approach is applied to empirical work studying the engagement practices of a large, sophisticated information infrastructure research project, the Digital Business Ecosystem (DBE). At the start of the DBE engagement process, the DBE was an 'invisible technology' in the sense that it did not yet exist. Whilst this circumstance is typical at the beginning of innovative technology projects it nonetheless made the process of engagement particularly challenging, presenting the researchers concerned with questions concerning 'what' it was that participants should engage with. Drawing on the theoretical insights presented by Law and Singleton the ambiguity of the DBE as an object is brought to the foreground. According to their analysis the DBE appears to have the ontological characteristics of both the fluid and the fire object. In order to address this dilemma we draw upon Ciborra's thinking, particularly around the information infrastructure and *Gestell*, as a means of reconciling how technologies like the DBE can be both fluid and fire objects. The paper ends with a discussion of the implications of this work on Claudio Ciborra's legacy for the study of information and communications technologies.

Introduction

In lieu of conversation, there are many ways in which one can reconstruct an academic path that leads back to the richness of Claudio's[1] research interests and contributions. One such path draws on his empirical work on large scale information infrastructures, technological innovations and IT strategies and combines it with his multi-disciplinary perspectives on the social study of information and communications technologies. On this path, one of Ciborra's many academic achievements can be seen in terms of his contributions to our understanding the information technology 'artefact'[2] (Ciborra and Hanseth, 1998).

Of course, being Claudio, he could never be content with an analysis that simply ended up with suggestions that technology is best seen as a tool / ensemble / computational device or a proxy for other human attributes. Indeed, in his later writings, Claudio was heavily influenced by the work of Martin Heidegger who argued that technology's essence was as anything but a tool.

As a research method, Claudio seemed to deliberately focus on difficult cases, those technological *objects* that weren't easily classified and that couldn't be reduced to simply being one thing or another.

In this paper, we use a line of argument presented by Law and Singleton (2005) in their discussion of alcoholic liver disease to explore and develop some of Claudio Ciborra's ideas about the nature of information technology.

The topic of alcoholic liver disease is not an obvious one to apply to questions of information systems (although see Angell (2005)), nor is this paper chosen because of some striking relationships to themes that Ciborra also drew on (especially notions of cultivation and gardening (Ciborra, 1996b; Law and Singleton, p. 341), domestication (Ciborra, 1999; Ciborra, 2002; Law and Singleton, 2005, p. 347; Silverstone and Haddon, 1996) and Karl Weick's inspirational analysis of the Mann Gulch incident (Ciborra, 2002, Chapter 8; Law and Singleton, 2005, p. 347; Lawrence, 2005; Stahl, 2005; Weick, 1993).

Rather, the paper is chosen because it presents a particular analysis of complex, messy objects that challenges us to think about Ciborra's ideas about the nature of the technological *object*. We will argue that there are some interesting similarities between Claudio's thinking and that of Law and Singleton, 2005, but that their paths also separate in important areas and arrive at the technology *object* from different perspectives. We will use these to continue our ongoing, internal dialogues with Claudio and his ideas.

The argument of the paper is presented as follows. In the next sections, we present the key stages of the argument presented by Law and Singleton, 2005 and consider this in relation to examples of Claudio's own thinking in this area. We seek to integrate these two perspectives in the context of fieldwork undertaken around the engagement practices associated with a new technological infrastructure project, the Digital Business Ecosystem (DBE). A particular characteristic of the DBE at the time of the study was that it did not exist as a technological *object* and thus shares many characteristics with the problems being addressed by Law and Singleton, 2005. The technological character of the DBE, however, also relates to Ciborra's development of Heidegger's notion of *Gestell* (Ciborra and Hanseth, 1998). The paper ends with a discussion of the implications of this work on Claudio Ciborra's legacy for the study of information and communications technologies.

Object problems

In their paper, Law and Singleton outline the problems they faced whilst undertaking an academic study of alcoholic liver disease for a UK Acute Hospital Trust.

Their study was to focus on the management and organization of the treatment in the trust and beyond. They soon found, however, that it was more difficult to map the 'trajectories' of typical patients than they had expected. They were, however, unclear as to why this was the case.

Law and Singleton, 2005 therefore consider four ways of responding to the difficulties they were facing. The first is a technological response that suggests that the problems they were facing were simply due to the fact that they might simply not be doing good research. Whilst plausible, their sense was that perhaps there was something else going on in the case and they consider that the problems they were facing implied the need for a managerial response to deal with the messy situation. As they point out, however, messy objects by their very nature defy knowing and, as a result, managerialism becomes an executive tool for creating apparent clarity when it might not exist (Ciborra, 2002; Strand, 2005).

Just because managerialism tries to hide the messiness of organizational life (Whitley, 2005) it does not mean that researchers should give up at that point and so Law and Singleton, 2005 propose two strategies for progression. Their epistemological strategy suggests that messiness arises because of differing perspectives on the situation (Dreyfus and Dreyfus, 1986) in a manner similar to notions of interpretative flexibility (Pinch and Bijker, 1987) that have been applied in both strong and weak forms to technological *objects* (Orlikowski, 1992; Pozzebon, 2001) but see (Cadili and Whitley, 2005; Kallinikos, 2002).

Their final alternative is to question the ontological status of the thing they are studying: what exactly is the nature of the *object*. From this position, the *object* is not simply the same and subject to multiple interpretations, it is in fact different, according to the multiple realities that are enacted into being. Through the use of the word 'enacted' the question of performativity, familiar to ANT influenced studies, comes to light.

In Table 16.1 below, we characterize these four stages of the argument by Law and Singleton highlighting the questions that arise at each stage.

As an aside, it is interesting to note that the first three stages raise interesting parallels with the internal debates that have occurred within information systems, particularly as we reflect upon the nature and location of information

Table 16.1 The first four stages presented by Law and Singleton (2005)

Stage from Law and Singleton, 2005	Nature of 'problem'	Law and Singleton, 2005's case of alcoholic liver disease
1	Technical competence	Are we doing poorly implemented research?
2	Managerialism	Are we attempting to impose a tidy managerial solution onto a fundamentally messy problem?
3	Epistemological	Does the messiness arise because of different perspectives on the problem?
4	Ontological	Have we misconceived the very nature of the object?

systems faculty within academia, although few in information systems have taken the debate to the fourth stage proposed by Law and Singleton (2005).

[Of course, Claudio contributed to these debates himself. Stage one simply never applied to his work and he never had any doubts about the 'rigorous playfulness'[3] of his work. Stage two has direct parallels with his work on strategy and improvisation (Ciborra, 1991; Ciborra, 1996a) and on the role of formal methods (Ciborra, 1998). Stage three is more interesting. Claudio finally 'settled down' in a Department of Information Systems that has a strong history of interpretive research and while he was clearly comfortable with this epistemological position of his colleagues, he was rarely explicit about this aspect of his own work].

Object solutions

Law and Singleton (2005) suggest that one way forward is to question the ontological status of the object. They propose moving from a construct where multiple perspectives of the same object can be said to exist, to an acknowledgement that the object itself may be multiple, drawing to the foreground questions concerning 'when' and 'how' some*thing* counts as an object.

Again, their argument passes through a number of stages. Law and Singleton (2005) begin by drawing on recent, post-ANT studies that develop Latour's original notion of *immutable* mobiles. Immutable mobiles are often mechanisms of long-distance control that are able to maintain their shape despite being part of many (network) relationships. For example, Latour uses the example of scientific instruments such as a pedocomparator for comparing the colour of the soil in a Brazilian rain forest as a means of relating detailed empirical work to high level theories, in this case about about soil erosion (Latour, 1999, chapter 2). The role that these artefacts play in maintaining a network of relations is wholly dependent upon their unchanging nature. However, this maintenance of the network is only achieved and sustained through constant work (i.e. worknet rather than network), building and re-building associations around them (Latour, 2005).

Even this characterization, argue Law and Singleton (2005), may also be too restrictive as in many cases these instruments, objects or things might actually be *mutable* mobiles (Moser and Law, 2006). They present de Laet and Mol's (2000) description of a water pump in Zimbabwe, that changes constantly both in form and function as it is moved between locations and repaired with ready-to-hand materials as parts of it break down. To them, this suggests that there is not a core of stability, there is no essence to the technology (Grint and Woolgar, 1997); 'Oxymoronically, it is something that *both changes and stays the same*' (Law and Singleton, 2005, p. 338).

It is important to recognize that the fluidity of the Zimbabwean water pump extends far beyond the ability to replace bolts with steel bars, or the leather seals with a bit of an old tyre (de Laet and Mol, 2000, pp. 238–242), the pump is also fluid in terms of what it produces (exactly how pure must the water be for the pump to 'work' (de Laet and Mol, 2000, pp. 242–245)) and how closely the local community must be involved in the creation and maintenance of the pump (de Laet and

Mol, 2000, pp. 245–247). The fluidity is therefore enabled by the extensive network that the pump is a part of (Law and Singleton, 2005, p. 338).

Objects that correspond to the idea of mutable mobiles and the Zimbabwean water pump are described by Law and Singleton (2005) as 'fluid objects'. Fluid objects are those that exhibit gradual, incremental change. This change is often gentle, but can occasionally push the 'boundaries of instability' when change is less gentle and may appear discontinuous.

The final stage of their analysis is a post-ANT consideration of how to address issues of invisible work and the colonization of the other. There is a sense of safety in ANT where networks are built around resilient actors, immutable mobiles or perhaps mutable mobiles that nonetheless change gently, fluidly. The unknown, the other or the unexpected are not the focus of these networks which tend to centre themselves on powerful, influential actors. For Law and Singleton, as for other critics of ANT (Lee and Brown, 1994; Star, 1991) this is unsatisfactory, not only from a socio-political point of view but also because the unknown or 'not present' can have a huge impact on the course of innovation or the shaping of networks. Law and Singleton use the example of a British aircraft company that engineered features of an aircraft wing specifically to cope with flying situations that would occur in a European war against the Russians. 'The war' and 'the Russians' were never present but they were still influential in the design of the aircraft. Thus, 'we cannot understand objects unless we also think of them as sets of present dynamics generated in, and generative of, realities that are necessarily absent' (Law and Singleton, 2005, p. 343) and in doing so, we cannot rely on gentle flows from one to another but rather jumps and discontinuities. Such objects they label fire objects: objects that depend upon otherness and that otherness is generative (Law and Singleton, 2005, p. 344). They use the fire metaphor because 'fires are energetic and transformative, and depend on difference – for instance between (absent) fuel or cinders and (present) flame. Fire objects, then, depend upon otherness, and that otherness is generative' (Law and Singleton, 2005, p. 344). They exhibit sudden, discontinuous change that is directly related to the consideration of an absent other, a potentiality. Table 16.2 describes the three parts of the analysis described above.

Table 16.2 The next three stages presented by Law and Singleton

Stage from (Law and Singleton, 2005)	Nature of the object	Example
5	Immutable mobile 'able to maintain its shape despite being part of many (network) relationships'	Pedocomparator
6	Mutable mobile / fluid object: 'something that *both changes and stays the same*'	Zimbabwean water pump
7	Fire objects: 'sets of present dynamics generated in, and generative of, realities that are necessarily absent'	Design of aircraft wing

At this point, we present our empirical work on the Digital Business Ecosystem (DBE). We will then consider the DBE both in terms of the stages from Law and Singleton (2005) and Ciborra's own later writings on the nature of the technological *object*. We argue that our case study exhibits features of both fire and fluid objects that focus attention on questions of the materiality of technology; or more specifically, the materiality of software.

The digital business ecosystem

The digital business ecosystem (DBE) is a concept, a European project and a technology (DBE, 2008). It aims to provide a flexible, distributed infrastructure to tie economic development to the region, supporting local trade and industry through the development of software. The intention is that local ecosystems will gradually federate creating in –regional cooperation by fostering nodes of innovation and integration pan-European, national and local initiatives (Nachira, 2002). The project has drawn inspiration from physical and biological concepts of self-organization and evolution to produce a technological platform that will facilitate the flexible composition of software services. The evolutionary aspects of the DBE set it apart from similar proprietary models such as Microsoft's .Net or SAP's forthcoming business process 'appli-structure', as does the fact that it has been designed as a non-proprietary public infrastructure.

Although the DBE is funded as a European research project, the innovation ecosystems cluster in the EU is equally concerned to ensure that projects like the DBE combine useful scientific advances with major contributions to practice. In the case of the DBE, this meant ensuring that SMEs became actively engaged with the technology. To achieve this, a number of 'regional catalysts' were responsible for coordinating the engagement activities and involving local SMEs. Our involvement in the project was to be actively involved in and study, the process by which small and medium sized enterprises in three regions of Europe (Tampere, Finland; Aragon, Spain; West Midlands, UK) became engaged with the DBE. The field work reported in this paper associated with the engagement activities was undertaken by one of the authors, who was a full time research officer on the project. The research involved attending the DBE engagement events that took place between February and July 2005. In addition, for the engagement study, we carried out interviews in each of the three DBE regions. From 'first contact' to formal engagement, the aim was to describe how the interest of driver SMEs was captured and then sustained.

Studies that focus on SMEs and IT adoption in a generalized sense invariably run into problems of specificity. The varied and distinctive situations facing SMEs together with the range of technologies that form part of their business practices are far ranging. SME classification schema can provide a helpful way of contending with this diversity, as can tools for measuring IT adoption. However, at the stage this research was carried out, narrowing the field was not an issue. Having identified three target groups as part of its engagement strategy (Drivers, Users and Implementers), a significant shift in DBE engagement priorities was agreed by the project. Instead of focusing on recruiting user SMEs (those companies who would use services running on the DBE infrastructure) engagement efforts were focused on driver SMEs (those companies who would provide services) and on influential regional actors such as policy makers. Therefore the SMEs referred to in this paper are small European software houses involved in the development of business systems and services. The targets set for regional catalysts were to recruitthreeto five driver SMEs by the end of the first 18 months of the project. All three regional catalysts achieved this target so, in this sense, engagement in this phase of the DBE was deemed to have been successful.

The process of engaging the SMEs with the DBE project raised many and varied issues from a rich and wide ranging set of perspectives. These are detailed elsewhere (Darking and Whitley, 2005). For this paper, we wish to focus on one particular set of concerns that arose with regard to engagement with the DBE, concerns that mirror those of Law and Singleton and Ciborra, namely why the DBE engagement process was so problematic. This relates directly to the question of what exactly is the object that these SMEs were supposed to be engaging with.

Data collection

The process through which data was collected for this research involved being a participant/observer at engagement workshops and meetings across the three DBE regions. This fieldwork activity was supported by a programme of interviews with regional catalysts and both actual and potential SME drivers. This last point helped us to understand why some SMEs lost interest as well as the motivations for others to become involved with the project.

The beginning of fieldwork was timed to coincide with the first in a programme of training/engagement events which took place in Finland in February 2005. Whilst there were still no technological components of the DBE to show SMEs, this workshop was designed to focus specifically on the technological concepts and architecture of the DBE. Following this event, the researcher attended every training or recruitment event that took place from this point until mid-June 2005.

In addition to the attendance of engagement events, a programme of interviews was scheduled on behalf of the researcher by regional catalysts. Whilst in the West Midlands interviews took place with driver SMEs only, in Tampere regional catalysts felt it was important that the researcher also speak to companies who had opted not to become involved with the project at that stage and in Aragon a local politician and an academic were included. An important aspect of the practice approach taken was to retain the emphases that emerged in each region, rather than seeking identical sets of empirical data. Details of the interviews undertaken are given in Table 16.3 below.

The SME engagement experience

The period in time that this research refers to is a distinctive one because it depicts a period of transition where engagement in the DBE as a technological entity went

Table 16.3 SME engagement interviews

Date	Interview
17.03.05	Interviews: West Midlands Regional Catalysts 1. SME Business Consultant 2. Interview West Midlands Regional Catalysts
02.05.05	Interviews: Tampere 3. Driver SME Tampere 1 4. Meeting with Regional Catalysts 5. Driver SME Tampere 2 6. Driver SME Tampere 3
03.05.05	7. Driver SME Tampere 4 8. Driver SME Tampere 5 9. Driver SME Tampere 6
11.05.05	Interviews: Aragon 10. Professor of Economics – University of Zaragoza
12.05.05	11. Local Politician 12. Interview Aragon Regional Catalysts 13. Driver SME Aragon 1 14. Driver SME Aragon 2
23.07.05	Interviews: West Midlands 15. SME West Midlands 1 16. SME West Midlands 2 17. SME West Midlands 3

from being purely conceptual to something tangible. Following actor–network theory, it is not simply status or weight of numbers that governs why a particular preference or point of view is significant (Latour, 2005). It can be the part that point of view plays in achieving a stable network of associations. For example, the first contact any SME had with a DBE technological component was a significant test of credibility and therefore the opinions and feedback offered at that moment were important, even though they concerned just one SME.

According to actor–network theory, likely sites of engagement between users and new technologies are not as difficult to pinpoint as one might imagine. The work that goes into processes of group formation and enrolment is almost always conspicuous, as it not only involves people but also material and symbolic resources (Latour, 2005). Developing interests and associations together with amassing resources lends substance to the process of enrolment and creates opportunities for the values and objectives of the group to be inscribed. In the case of the DBE, an important form of this kind of opportunity was created through the programming of engagement and training events. These events marked important moments in time when project machinery, technological components and SMEs were brought together for the first time. Through the support of dedicated regional catalysts, consequent events helped to construct a sense of group as familiar faces were seen again.

Throughout the period of study, an important element was missing from the picture: the DBE technology. This means that interest in the DBE often had to be generated before technological components were physically available for inspection. This is not an uncommon situation when it comes to the dissemination of new technologies. Potential users are commonly asked to engage with a concept, an idea of what a new technology is capable of before they can see it for themselves (Borup et al., 2006). By definition, it is almost always too late to start engagement activities at the point when technological components are finalized and so pre-emptive engagement action is invariably required. However, the reality of this situation was that early recruitment events lacked any applied examples or technological demonstrations. This was a 'pre-prototype stage' where even communicating the basic concept of the DBE presented difficulty due to the advanced nature of the technology.

Another of the distinctive features of the original DBE proposal was that it brought together contributions from many different disciplines. In particular, the project was organized into three distinct domains: science, which was concerned with developing the underlying theoretical foundations of the ecosystem element of the project, drawing heavily on theories of autopoiesis and evolutionary development; computing, that was seeking to implement the service architecture, based around open source software development methodologies and peer-to-peer networks; and business, that was working with regional development agencies and the SMEs who would populate and use the DBE system when it was up and running.

Inevitably, at the early stages of the project there were many examples of CP Snow's two-cultures problem (Labinger and Collins, 2001; Snow, 1959) with each of these different domains finding it very difficult to understand and relate to what researchers in the other domains were doing. When members of, for example, the computing team came to speak at early SME engagement events, finding the right level at which to present the key features of the architecture was a serious challenge.

Additionally, higher level 'scientific' or 'business' overviews were often met with a 'so what?' attitude from SMEs. There was also criticism at engagement events and in SME interviews that project partners were indulging in marketing speak. For example, the idea that the DBE was a 'unique technology' that would 'revolutionise European software development' quickly drew criticism. Presentations that focused on higher order concepts rather than what the technology would 'do', coupled with the fact that the technology in question did not exist in any appreciable, tangible form, led to accusations that the project was attempting to sell 'vapourware'. In this way, the very materiality of the technology the project aimed to produce was called into question.

Thus, at one level, it would appear that the difficulties faced by the DBE during the engagement process were not that dissimilar to those experienced by innovative projects, especially when the innovation was driven by researchers from a wide variety of differing epistemological backgrounds.

Interestingly, when faced with such problems the SMEs made repeated and forceful requests for tangibles – documentation, release dates, components to test, code to compile; they wanted to be able to see something of the technological *object.* The absence of these elements hindered the process of gaining the trust of SMEs but it did not altogether quash their interest. When asked why they had remained involved in the DBE given these criticisms, some SMEs would talk about the architectural principles of the DBE. With its 'meta-approach' to standards, languages and ontologies, the potential this architecture suggested for 'levelling the playing field' with respect to small and large software companies was something that carried wide appeal. For others, this was a question of software design methodology. Those familiar with open source methods were happy to proceed with technological components that were works-in-progress whilst others wanted to see the finished product.

Difficulties associated with communicating the exact nature of the DBE technology coupled with the lack of prototypes and demonstrations created serious challenges for early engagement activities. Regional catalysts were placed in the position of having to reassert the fact that the DBE was a research project and that SMEs were being asked to engage in a process of innovation rather than test an existing technology.

Fortunately, the technological architecture of the DBE was one of the most widely cited reasons for why SMEs had remained engaged with the DBE, despite initial doubts they may have had about the project and despite the absence of technological components for them to assess. The 'meta-level' aspects of the DBE technology and their implications for the development of business services were difficult to convey, but once they had been successfully communicated, generally after a prolonged group discussion, SMEs could see an intrinsic value in what the project sought to achieve. Some SMEs were also drawn to the explicitly open source design of the DBE, although questions were raised about whether the project was sincerely open.

Over time, it became clearer what the DBE was meant to be and as a result the nature of the concerns from the engagement process changed. Whereas at the start, they were concerned with how to understand what the DBE might be and what it might deliver, over time the driver SMEs became increasingly concerned with other aspects of the DBE. In particular, they were concerned with its scalability, its longevity and its ability to deliver on all the innovative features that the DBE offered.

Understanding the DBE

In order to understand the technological *object*, Law and Singleton argue that we must be prepared to accept 'that a fluid, shape–shifting and name–changing object is indeed a conceivable possibility' that is 'not ruled out by prior methodological commitments to particular and limited versions of clarity' (Law and Singleton, 2005, p. 34). However, even if we are prepared to accept this possibility their distinct stages are perhaps less helpful for understanding the problems that the DBE faced throughout the engagement process.

Thus, in stage 6 (mutable mobiles), they propose the ontological category of the fluid object, so called because it 'flows and *gently* changes shape, bit by bit', i.e. the changes 'cannot be abrupt' (p. 338). Indeed, the process of staying the same might even *depend* on such changes (p. 339). However, in stage 7, the *fire object*, these changes are not the gentle flows of fluid objects but instead 'take the form of jumps and discontinuities' (p. 343).

These qualitative differences between the two stages strongly suggest that particular objects can *either* be fluid objects *or* fire objects. However, the DBE appears to fit into both and this dual character of the DBE might form the basis for some of the problems with the engagement process. This duality also helps explain why the project attracted the EU funding. The project was initially driven and funded by an EU vision for how SMEs could develop a new environment for competitive collaboration. This public good, however, relied on both the fluid and fire characteristics of the project. The project was funded, in part, because of its fire potential, but had to be developed and implemented using the known fluid practices of FLOSS. It could be argued that Law and Singleton are referring to a single object as opposed to an infrastructure and that therefore the either/or is likely to be more empirically relevant. However, the complex, composite character of objects and technologies appear to be precisely their focus and so another option is required.

In terms of gently changing shape, many aspects of the DBE clearly satisfy the criteria for a fluid object. Perhaps the most straightforward illustration of this can be seen in the open source nature of the software development process. In common with most open source projects, many parts of the DBE software infrastructure are continuously changing and it is this change that will remain central to the sustainability of the infrastructure.

For example, Table 16.4 below shows the various releases of the DBE Studio (one small part of the DBE infrastructure). As the table shows, the software changed ('gently') approximately every two weeks shifting from being more 'concept than technology' to more 'technology than concept'.

Table 16.4 Version information for DBE studio, taken from (DBE Studio, 2008)

Version	Date of Release	Days since last version
Version 0.2.0	2006-02-28 06:54	34
Version 0.1.11	2006-01-25 03:15	16
Version 0.1.10	2006-01-09 15:43	19
Version 0.1.9	2005-12-21 09:10	16
Version 0.1.8	2005-12-05 08:26	14
Version 0.1.7	2005-11-21 09:17	5
Version 0.1.6	2005-11-16 03:54	20
Version 0.1.5	2005-10-27 15:21	2
Version 0.1.4	2005-10-25 15:27	14
Version 0.1.2	2005-10-11 15:47	0
Version 0.1.1	2005-10-11 15:41	6
Version 0.1.0	2005-10-05 19:35	

Commonly, software objects are able to retain their identity even though they go through multiple changes. Open source software in particular is characterized by versioning and frequent releases. In the case of the DBE, Version 0.1.4 is announced with the message 'Big thanks to all that made the *fast turn about* on both reporting and fixing bugs!! :-)'. Version 0.1.7 is announced with 'This release mainly contains bug fixes and *minor* changes' with a similar announcement for Version 0.1.8, whereas the release of Version 1.0.0 (February 2007) talks of 'An *all-in-one* release of the DBE Studio 1.0.0 is available for download from our Sourceforge site. This includes an Eclipse SDK (Windows) distribution with the required GEF, EMF, JEM and WTP feature dependencies' (all extracts taken from DBE Studio, 2008 emphases added). Whilst the release of version 1.0.0 represents a larger jump than the earlier versions, the jump is not a fire-like jump as it does not incorporate the absent other.

However, if we use this gentle change as a basis for understanding the DBE and argue that the DBE is best characterized as a fluid object, then this doesn't explain the problematic engagement process. There is now extensive experience of developing open source projects and if the DBE was *simply* an open source project, then questions of SME engagement with the DBE would simply have been those that any open source project would encounter. Over time, even open source projects have some jumps and discontinuities between versions and this is normally indicated in a change in the major version rather than minor version number (e.g. from version 0.1.0 to version 1.0.0 rather than, as in Table 16.4, from version 0.1.0 to version 0.1.1). Moreover, the empirical evidence from the SME engagement strategies indicates that for many of the SMEs, the open source aspect of the DBE engagement process was relatively unproblematic although some SMEs asked interesting questions regarding the practice of open source development in the DBE project, for example, when the 'first' public release of one element of the DBE was found to be version 16, see (Darking and Whitley, 2005).

At one level, software objects themselves can be seen as something without material properties, although they can be represented in a variety of formats including as electronic pulses in memory, as textual markings on a print-out of source code, as physical marks on for example a CD.

Software does, however, have material effects that, as Latour (2003) suggests, 'cannot be defined impartially in front of judges without generating fistfights in the courtroom' (p. 37). It is something that people work on, it can be exchanged (at least its representation, for example, as source code). Indeed, open source software explicitly uses this ambiguity of materiality/immateriality in its processes. Open source licenses, arguably a defining feature (Chengalur-Smith and Sidorova, 2003), freely permit others to make copies of the expression of ideas (i.e. the software) and develop them for their own purposes (GPL, 2006). The digital nature of software, especially if it is available in source code form, as open source requires, means that use by one person does not deprive others of it. Digital goods do not suffer from the traditional tragedy of the Commons (Gordon, 1954; Hardin, 1968).

At one level, FLOSS is 'just' software, however FLOSS differs from traditional software development in terms of its entanglement with the user and developer communities which shape the software that is developed. Being responsive to the needs of the developer base, supporting and facilitating their business use of software components is a high priority in FLOSS communities. This is often reflected in processes of strategy formation in FLOSS communities which are frequently modelled explicitly on democratic ideals concerning inclusion and transparency.

The vision for the DBE project was much more than simply the development of non-proprietary service architectures for SMEs to use. Thus the engagement strategies could not simply rest upon the provision of a series of smoothly developing set of software tools that mimicked existing commercially available alternatives. They could not, therefore, put-in-stone too many of the distinctive elements of the DBE that had not yet, at that time, been developed into fully fledged aspects of the ecosystem.

The process of engagement with the DBE also had to incorporate the 'realities that are necessarily absent' (Law and Singleton, 2005, p. 342) as 'not everything can be brought to presence' (p. 342) and the DBE is performed by the 'enactment of *different objects* in the different sets of relations and contexts of practice' (p. 342).

In the context of engagement, one of the most conspicuous examples of absence was the ecosystem element of the project. Drawing on the work of the science domain, a key element of the project is the ability of the infrastructure to flexibly combine and recombine software services available on the DBE. Whilst many such trial combinations may not necessarily be viable, a distinctive element of the DBE is this ability to make connections between available services to provide new opportunities for user SMEs to interact.

Any engagement activities with SMEs must therefore account for this aspect of the DBE, as this is one of the long term strategic benefits of integrating services with the DBE. This innovative element could not be present in the earliest stages of the DBE engagement process as it both depended on the practical development and implementation of the evolutionary environment (EvE) and the population of the DBE infrastructure with sufficient services for this element to begin to make realistic experiments in combining services.

A key element of the engagement process, therefore, had to include this other side to the DBE which was absent, discontinuous from the existing software services provided and, unlike some key technologies for the DBE, could not draw upon pre-existing software tools. Therefore, the DBE engaged people and thus came into actual being, by possessing two important characteristics or aspects: It was a potential *idea* of a yet to come – but still absent – 'evolutionary' and open source infrastructure; and it was an iterative and visibly changing open source *project*, existing as a steady stream of releases. That is, the thing itself, the DBE, did not exist as a clear cut 'object', but rather we see it in terms of its productive potentiality and see its iterative changes as something that software objects 'possess' (Latour, 2002).

Getting out the dilemma

At this stage, possible limitations of the analysis presented by Law and Singleton become apparent. The process of engaging SMEst with the DBE had to deal with a technological object that had, at the same time, characteristics of what Law and Singleton, 2005 label in their stage 6 a 'fluid object' which underwent only minor changes over time and their stage 7 'fire object' that was defined, in part, by what was not present and was discontinuous from the existing versions of the technology.

Although their paper suggests that objects could either be fluid objects *or* fire objects, our study of the process of engaging with the DBE suggest that many FLOSS projects might actually have characteristics of both. There is thus a tension: is it possible to not reify fire and fluid objects and yet still be able to highlight and draw on their distinctive characteristics? We turn to Ciborra's work to help us address the paradox that has arisen:

The pre-prototype character of the technology is one way in which this complexity can be seen. The tension between absence and near-presence was a tangible reality for those involved in DBE engagement work. However, in trying to organize training and engagement events, the absence of the technology was instinctively countered by participants through brainstorming activities through which they developed their own sense of how the technology could be integrated with specific business ideas and capabilities both now and in the future. In this way, the DBE was drawn into multiple realities, regardless of its physical absence.

Despite their call for ontological radicalism, we find that Law and Singleton (2005) don't consider the situation where an object can have characteristics of both fluids and fire, perhaps because the empirical base they draw upon doesn't highlight these diverse characteristics. In this section, therefore, we draw on the DBE case study to draw out themes that we feel are implicit in Ciborra's writing about technology. In so doing, we are able to develop Claudio's intellectual legacy by using his, sometimes implicit, ideas about ontology to contribute to both theory and practice in information systems and science studies.

To begin, we note that too much emphasis on the fluid nature of the DBE during the DBE engagement process, could create a formative context (Ciborra and Lanzara, 1994) which could stifle the ability of the SMEs to engage with and incorporate many of the advanced, distinctive features of the DBE that would become available when the project ended. As Ciborra and Lanzara state: 'once designed and introduced into the organization, they [i.e. systems] tend to evolve along paths that are often unexpected and irreversible, subtly changing the ways people design and carry out their work practices, experiment with alternative arrangements and routines, or implement alternative visions and designs' (Ciborra and Lanzara, 1994, p. 63). In the same way, too much emphasis on the not-yet-available future capabilities of the DBE would make it unattractive for SMEs to become involved with the DBE, especially the driver SMEs, as they have a particular desire to work with running code and implementable services.

In his later work, however, Ciborra was able to combine the gentle aspects of technology development such as tinkering and bricolage (Ciborra, 1996a) with the more violent language of 'creative destruction', as found in his discussion of the platform organization (Ciborra, 1996c) where 'schemes which prescribe how to set up efficient organizational structures around a complex, primary task lose part of their normative relevance, for one cannot know in advance the complexity of the task, nor its precise nature and contours' (Ciborra, 1996c, p. 114). In both instances, there is a desire to challenge the ontological security inherent in disciplines that reduce the technological *object* to a simple tool as is inherent in the work of Law and Singleton.

The fusion of what Law and Singleton, 2005 would call fire properties with the gentle properties of fluid objects is implicit in Ciborra's account of information infrastructure. The idea that an object or infrastructure can 'enact a reality' is common to both, as is the idea that realities can shift and change in sometimes gentle, sometimes violent and unpredictable ways. Absence, or a sense of what lies beyond, are recognized and valued by both Law and Singleton and Ciborra.

Ciborra's concept of *Gestell*, taken from Heideggerian phenomenology, emphasized a 'light' understanding of infrastructure as something that triggers reflexivity and remains inherently flexible (Ciborra and Hanseth, 1998). As Heidegger states: 'What is decisive about technē does not lie at all in asking and manipulating nor in using the means, but rather in the aforementioned revealing. It is as revealing, not as manufacturing, that technē is a bringing forth' (Heidegger, 1993, p. 13). Ciborra challenged management perspectives on infrastructure as something fixed and controlled by suggesting that the infrastructure has the power to 'enact a reality' but which cannot be mastered (Ciborra and associates, 2000). However, whilst calling for a re-orientation of ideas on infrastructure around these concepts, Ciborra simultaneously encouraged focus on what lay beyond *Gestell*. For example, he emphasized the 'moment of vision' where insight from beyond the pervasive influence of the *Gestell* could be experienced. He talked about the need for infrastructural engagement where the ability to 'jump or switch' was valued along with marginal practices and an openness to the unknown. In so doing, Ciborra was implicitly pointing at the need to address *both* the fluid object and the fire object advocated by Law and Singleton.

Ambiguity about the materiality of software has led some to suggest that software systems should be seen as 'configurational technologies' (Fleck, 1999) made up of both technical and non-technical components as opposed to some form of object. Viewed in this way software systems themselves can be seen as *Gestell* (Ciborra and Hanseth, 1998) i.e., 'the ways through which the ordering and setting up unveils what is extant as standing reserve of resources (including human) made available for future deployment' (p. 320), as narrative networks (Pentland and Feldman, 2007) or even as expectations that can shape future action (Brown and Michael, 2003; Swanson and Ramiller, 1997).

Claudio often emphasized the role of software in practice and this echoes the insight of Ratto (2005) who suggests that the implicit differentiation between the expressive and functional aspects of software is unhelpful, as software often expresses normative positions about users, programmers and tasks in its 'functional' elements. In so doing he is echoing the views of Orlikowski (2000) who follows Jean Lave's distinction between 'cognition in practice' and 'cognition in the head' to differentiate between the *technological artefact* and *technology-in-practice* (Orlikowski, 2000, p. 408). Thus the same technological artefact might be used by different users in different ways (including non-use).

This emphasis on technology-in-practice highlights the role that software plays in the life-worlds of its users, it is something that people engage with, or not, need to be inspired by, or not. As such it implies a 'mutual entailment' or 'constitutive entanglement' between the material and the social (Barad, 2003, p. 820; see also Latour, 2007; Orlikowski, 2007, p. 1437), something very close to Claudio's ideals.

Ciborra's work emphasizes the need to release infrastructure, allowing new relations to be formed and new organizational visions to emerge. Instead of trying to control or govern innovation, he spoke of tinkering and bricolage as approaches to infrastructure and technology design that were, in fact, commonplace among engineers and developers. Likewise, Ciborra (1996c) speaks about 'broken cosmologies' and 'creative destruction' as new realities are brought about during the course of an organization's life span.

Conclusion

In this paper we have drawn a parallel between Claudio Ciborra's seminal works on information infrastructures and technologies with the work of Law and Singleton on object lessons. Through the case of engagement and the DBE project, we have identified a paradox where an 'invisible technology' *object* can contain properties that are at once fluid and fire based. We draw upon Ciborra's work to help us address this paradox and argue that through his work on information infrastructures and his use of phenomenology, the fluid and fire properties of an *object* can be held within the same frame or *Gestell*. Throughout this paper we draw similarities between the work of Law and Singleton and the work of Ciborra based upon their common aim to study complex, messy objects and show how their distinctive paths achieve complementary but compatible perspectives on the technology *object*. Ciborra's thinking on this issue was rarely directly articulated but the analysis presented by Law and Singleton allows us to develop his ideas in ways that are of direct relevance to information systems researchers.

If we accept the challenge of ontological radicalism Ciborra's ideas highlight the risks of creating formative contexts that present too much emphasis on either the fluid or the fire aspects of the *objects*. Information systems researchers, therefore, need to be able to balance the fire with the fluid and see the *object* as a *Gestell* that has the power to 'enact a reality' but which cannot be mastered. We should not be content with this but should always also focus on what lies beyond *Gestell*.

As can be seen in the case of the DBE, the questions being raised are not simply about stakeholder 'perspectives' or 'balancing interests'. They are complex questions that are to some extent intractable. These are not very palatable observations to make during a time of tension and uncertainty but they are a useful place to start from. The differences between management work and policy work are not always easy to elicit but the need to challenge assumptions and provide a corrective to the power of these professions and institutions is clear. We hope to continue our internal dialogues with Claudio and carry his work forward where it will continue to serve us and benefit this field of research.

Notes

Part of this work was funded by the Digital Business Ecosystem-DBE FP6 Integrated Project (DG-INFSO), Contract Number 507953. This paper originally appeared as Whitley Edgar A. and Mary L. Darking (2006) Object lessons and invisible technologies. *Journal of Information Technology* **21**(3): 176–184. The argument was developed further in Darking Mary L. and Edgar A. Whitley (2007) Towards an Understanding of FLOSS: Infrastructures, Materiality and the Digital Business Ecosystem. Science Studies **20**(2): 13–33. (Also available at http://opensource.mit.edu/papers/Darking_Whitley.pdf). We are grateful to editors and reviewers of both journals for their insights in developing the arguments presented here.

1. Both of the authors worked closely with Claudio Ciborra, especially teaching the MSc specialist option *Interpretations of Information*, where Mary was the class teacher and Edgar shared the lecturing duties. Much of our understanding of Claudio's thinking comes from this invaluable experience. In this paper we use 'Claudio' to refer to the particular insights we gained from working with the person, whilst using 'Ciborra' for the author of the texts.
2. he notion of the technology artefact has recently received prominence in the information systems literature following its use by Orlikowski and Iacono (2001) In this paper, we will refer to the technology *object* to maintain consistency with L&S. We do so, however, fully accepting that neither Claudio (nor, we believe L&S) use the term technology *object* in the sense of subject/object dualism.
3. This expression was used by his friend and mentor Chris Argyris when he spoke at LSE in a seminar organized by Claudio in 2001.

References

Angell, I. (2005). *No more leaning on lampposts: Management the Nick Charles way,* London: Villa Publishing.

Barad, K. (2003). Posthumanist Performativity: Toward an understanding of how matter comes to matter, *Signs* **28**(3): 801–832.

Borup, M., Brown, N., Konrad, K. and Van Lente, H. (2006). The sociology of expectations in science and technology, *Technology Analysis and Strategic Management* **18**(3/4): 285–298.

Brown, N. and Michael, M. (2003). A sociology of expectations: retrospecting prospects and prospecting retrospects, *Technology Analysis and Strategic Management* **15**(1): 3–18.

Cadili, S. and Whitley, E.A. (2005). On the interpretative flexibility of hosted ERP systems, *Journal of Strategic Information Systems* **14**(2): 167–195.

Chengalur-Smith, S. and Sidorova, A. (2003). *Survival of open-source projects: a population ecology perspective.* Paper presented at the International Conference on Information Systems, Seattle.

Ciborra, C.U. (1991). *From thinking to tinkering: the grassroots of strategic information systems.* Paper presented at the International Conference on Information Systems, New York.

Ciborra, C.U. (1996a). *Improvisation and information technology in organisations.* Paper presented at the International Conference on Information Systems, Cleveland.

Ciborra, C.U. (1996b). Introduction: What does groupware mean for the organization hosting it? in C.U. Ciborra (ed.) *Groupware and Teamwork: Invisible Aid or Technical Hindrance*, Chichester: Wiley, pp. 1–22.

Ciborra, C.U. (1996c). The platform organization: Recombining strategies, structures and surprises, *Organization Science* **7**(2): 103–118.

Ciborra, C.U. (1998). Crisis and foundations: An inquiry into the nature and limits of models and methods in the information systems discipline, *Journal of Strategic Information Systems* **7**(1): 5–16.

Ciborra, C.U. (1999). Hospitality and information technology, *A birthday offering for Bo Dahlbom.*

Ciborra, C.U. (2002). *The Labyrinths of Information: Challenging the Wisdom of Systems*, Oxford: Oxford University Press.

Ciborra, C.U. and associates. (2000). *From Control to Drift: The Dynamics of Corporate Information Infrastructures*, Oxford: Oxford University Press.

Ciborra, C.U. and Hanseth, O. (1998). From tool to *Gestell* agendas for managing the information infrastructure, *Information Technology and People* **11**(4): 305–327.

Ciborra, C.U. and Lanzara, G.F. (1994). Formative contexts and information technology: Understanding the dynamics of innovation in organizations, *Accounting, Management and Information Technologies* **4**(2): 61–86.

Darking, M. and Whitley, E.A. (2005). *Project report 27.2 – Studying SME Engagement Practices.* Archived at http://www.digital-ecosystem.org/

DBE. (2008). *DBE project website*, from http://www.digital-ecosystem.org/

DBE Studio. (2008). *DBE Studio*, from http://sourceforge.net/projects/dbestudio

de Laet, M. and Mol, A. (2000). The Zimbabwe bush pump: Mechanics of a fluid technology, *Social Studies of Science* **30**(2): 225–263.

Dreyfus, H.L. and Dreyfus, S.E. (1986). *Mind over Machine: The Power of Human Intuition and Expertise in The Era of the Computer*, New York: The Free Press.

Fleck, J. (1999). Learning by trying: the implementation of configurational technology, in D. Mackenzie and J. Wajcman (eds.) *The Social Shaping of Technology* (Second edition), Buckingham: Open University Press, pp. 244–257.

Gordon, H.S. (1954). The economic theory of a common property resource: The fishery, *Journal of Political Economy* **62**(2): 124–142.

GPL. (2006). *GNU Public Licence*: Free Software Foundation. Archived at http://www.gnu.org/copyleft/gpl.html

Grint, K. and Woolgar, S. (1997). *The Machine at Work: Technology, Work and Organization*, Cambridge: Polity Press.

Hardin, G. (1968). The tragedy of the commons, *Science* **162**: 1243–1248.

Heidegger, M. (1993). The question concerning technology, in D. F. Krell (ed.) *Basic Writings*. London: Routledge.

Kallinikos, J. (2002). *Reopening the black box of technology artefacts and human agency* in the proceedings of the *XXIII International Conference on Information Systems*, Barcelona, pp. 287–293

Labinger, J.A. and Collins, H. (eds.) (2001). *The One Culture? a Conversation about Science*, Chicago: University of Chicago Press.

Latour, B. (1999). *Pandora's Hope: Essays on the Reality of Science Studies*. Cambridge, MA: Harvard University Press.

Latour, B. (2002). Gabriel Tarde and the end of the social, in P. Joyce (ed.) *The Social in Question: New Bearings in History and the Social Sciences*, London: Routledge, pp. 117–132.

Latour, B. (2003). Is *re*-modernization occurring-and if so, how to prove it, *Theory, Culture and Society* **20**(2): 35–48.

Latour, B. (2005). *Reassembling the Social: An Introduction to Actor-Network-Theory*, Oxford: Oxford University Press.

Latour, B. (2007). Can we get our materialism back, please? *Isis* **98**: 138–142.

Law, J. and Singleton, V. (2005). Object lessons, *Organization* **12**(3): 331–355.

Lawrence, C. (2005). From Milan to Mann Gulch: reflections on the intellectual contributions of Professor Claudio Ciborra, *European Journal of Information Systems* **14**(5): 484–486.

Lee, N. and Brown, S. (1994). Otherness and the actor network: The undiscovered Continent, *American Behavioural Scientist* **37**(6): 772–790.

Moser, I. and Law, J. (2006). Fluids or flows? information and qualculation in medical practice, *Information Technology and People* **19**(1): 55–73.

Nachira, F. (2002). *Towards a Network of Digital Business Ecosystems*: European Research Framework 7 Discussion Paper. Archived at http://ec.europa.eu/information_society/topics/ebusiness/godigital/sme_research/doc/dbe_discussionpaper.pdf

Orlikowski, W.J. (1992). The duality of technology: rethinking the concept of technology in organizations, *Organizational Science* **3**(3): 398–427.

Orlikowski, W.J. (2000). Using technology and constituting structures: a practice lens for studying technology in organizations, *Organizational Science* **11**(4): 404–428.

Orlikowski, W.J. (2007). Sociomaterial practices: exploring technology at work, *Organization Studies* **28**(9): 1435–1448.

Orlikowski, W.J. and Iacono, C.S. (2001). Research commentary: desperately seeking the 'IT' in IT research: a call to theorizing the IT artifact, *Information Systems Research* **12**(2): 121–134.

Pentland, B.T. and Feldman, M.S. (2007). Narrative networks: patterns of technology and organization, *Organization Science* **18**(5): 781–795.

Pinch, T.J. and Bijker, W.E. (1987). The social construction of facts and artifacts: Or how the sociology of science and the sociology of technology might benefit each other, in W.E. Bijker, T.P. Hughes and T.J. Pinch (eds.) *The Social Construction of Technological Systems: New Directions in The Sociology and History of Technology*, Cambridge, MA: The MIT Press, pp. 17–50.

Pozzebon, M. (2001). *Demystifying the rhetorical closure of ERP packages*. Paper presented at the International Conference on Information Systems, New Orleans.

Ratto, M. (2005). Embedded technical expression: code and the leveraging of functionality, *The Information Society* **21**(3): 205–213.

Silverstone, R. and Haddon, L. (1996). Design and domestication of information and communication technologies: technical change and everyday life, in R. Mansell and R. Silverstone (eds.) *Communication by Design: The Politics of Information and Communication Technologies*, Oxford: Oxford University Press, pp. 44–74.

Snow, C.P. (1959). *The Two Cultures and the Scientific Revolution*, Cambridge: Cambridge University Press.

Stahl, B.C. (2005). The obituary as bricolage: the Mann Gulch disaster and the problem of heroic rationality, *European Journal of Information Systems* **14**(5): 487–491.

Star, S.L. (1991). Power, technologies and the phenomenology of standards: On being allergic to onions, in J. Law (ed.) *A Sociology of Monsters*, Oxford: Basil Blackwell, pp. 27–57.

Strand, D.L. (2005). Let's be baroque, *European Journal of Information Systems* **14**(5): 500–503.

Swanson, E.B. and Ramiller, N. (1997). The organizing vision in information systems innovation, *Organization science* **8**(5): 458–474.

Weick, K.E. (1993). The collapse of sensemaking in organizations: the Mann Gulch disaster, *Administrative Science Quarterly* **38**(4): 628–652.

Whitley, E.A. (2005). Visiting the red-light zones with Claudio, *European Journal of Information Systems* **14**(5): 477–479.

17

Control Devolution as Information Infrastructure Design Strategy: A Case Study of a Content Service Platform for Mobile Phones in Norway*

Petter Nielsen and Margunn Aanestad

Abstract

This paper depicts the results of an empirical case study on how two Norwegian telecommunications operators developed a business sector information infrastructure for the provision of mobile content services. Focusing on the context of this technology's development, and the strategic reflections behind its design, implementation and operation, control devolution as a design strategy is explored. This analysis draws on insights presented by Claudio Ciborra in his study of the change from alignment to loose coupling in the Swiss multinational *Hoffmann-La Roche*. The paper illustrates how control is played out on different levels, and balanced against autonomy. The theoretical implications of this paper highlight how the differences and transformations between information systems and information infrastructures are conceptualized, with the development of the latter better understood in light of a balance between control and autonomy. Consequently, it is suggested that control devolution as a design approach should be based on a deep understanding of the existing control/autonomy balance as well as the distribution of resources, risks and abilities and willingness to innovate.

Introduction

Claudio Ciborra viewed the implementation and operation of corporate wide information infrastructures as intricate puzzles: as *collages* that emerged through improvisation that were torn by centrifugal forces (Ciborra, 2000a). In his critique of the conventional management literature, Ciborra illustrated how these collages undermine control oriented approaches to the implementation of infrastructure, and demonstrates how conventional management literature have responded by deeming the collages as 'dysfunctional'. In his work, *From Alignment to Loose*

Coupling. From MedNet to www.roche.com, Ciborra describes the emergence of an infrastructure to facilitate external (internet) and internal (intranet) communication in the Swiss multinational *Hoffmann-La Roche* (Ciborra, 2000b). Here he offers key insights by illustrating a direction that diverges from the ubiquitous 'strategic alignment' model. In particular, the use of a strategy that nurtures and cultivates in order to harness the power of the periphery.

The internet/intranet approach in Roche succeeded a previous attempt by the Company to support its continued globalization. During the 1980s, driven by a push for standardization, Roche's Strategic Marketing team implemented the corporate network *MedNet*. This was developed in order to support a new centralized marketing function, and to connect Roche's affiliates. After eight years of development, both the uptake and usage of the network were low. Following changes in the management strategy that Ciborra describes as 'loose coupling' and 'releasement', the Company pursued a different path. Responsibility for this infrastructure was transferred to the internationally dispersed *Therapeutic Units*. Corporate management relinquished centralized control, and internet use to develop without significant support. Without centralized coordination, and based on peripheral grass-roots developments, the internet/intranet approach was now aligned with user needs as opposed to internal strategy.

This paper examines the process of innovation within mobile telecommunications, where formal standardization processes have most often driven development activities. This implies less emphasis and awareness of the significance of improvisation, collage and processes, and reflects where this paper aims to make its contribution; to demonstrate how control and development are intertwined. Previous attempts to account for the difficulty and complexity in developing platforms for mobile content services have not focused on how their process of emergence is related to control, how different control approaches may evolve, or which results are generated. This paper describes how information infrastructures are designed and operated in order to meet specific needs, which are mainly related to control. The notion of information infrastructure will be discussed in the subsequent section, where we will argue that information infrastructure research needs to discuss aspects of control more specifically. The existing literature on corporate information infrastructures has primarily investigated and depicted control as something management pursues in order to manage its business, with control often becoming an aim in itself as it becomes synonymous with management. Inspired by Ciborra's work, and based on an empirical case study, it is demonstrated that this is not always the case. In particular, it will be shown that intentionally relinquishing control can be a prerequisite, as opposed to an impediment, for successful design and operation of information infrastructures, with a more appropriate and nuanced control/autonomy balance perspective (Walsham, 1993). Based on the findings from our case study, the discussion becomes focused on how control is purposefully devolved through this strategy of relinquishing control.

Results from a case study of the design and operation of an information infrastructure are used to illustrate this point, with companies providing commercial content services for mobile phones in Norway. While generally m-commerce in Norway is still recovering in the aftermath of the dot com 'boom and bust' cycle, the Content Provider Access (CPA) platform has created sustainable business since 2000. The CPA platform was implemented by the mobile telecommunication network operators and provides a set of services that give content providers access to the network operators' GSM infrastructure and billing services. This enables these companies to provide and charge consumers for low-cost services in a cost-effective manner. While other m-commerce initiatives have had more limited success, in economical terms, the CPA platform distinguishes itself by being an open and market wide platform. This has required the network operators to coordinate with each other and draw upon their combined resources, as well as that of the various actors in the content industry such as content aggregators, application houses and others. It is argued that the successful design and operation of the CPA platform by the network operators was founded on their ability to relinquish control over the CPA platform and harness the power of the periphery, that is, the initiative and efforts of potential actors. The design strategy was influenced by factors such as the experience of the actors with similar platforms they controlled, the type of services provided, and existing regulations.

The empirical case study reveals that the concept of control itself as under-researched with respect to information infrastructure. The aim of this paper is to contribute to a deeper understanding of not only how the control/autonomy balance relates to business sector information infrastructure but also to information infrastructure in general. Strategies of control, including the lack of it, are observed as operating on various levels, with equilibrium with autonomy often reached, but which alters over time. In pursuing this course of enquiry, novel insights into the emergence of information infrastructures are provided. Further, control devolution may be the only feasible option going forward, which concurrently results in outcomes that are likely to vary from those of control-oriented approaches.

In the next section, a brief introduction to information infrastructure is provided, as well as related conceptualizations of control. This is followed by a discussion on the need for a different concept of control as it relates to the design of business sector information infrastructure. A case study is recounted and analysed to illustrate an alternative strategy which we term *control devolution*. Following our analysis, a discussion occurs of the relevance of the case for conceptualizations of information infrastructures and issues of control. In the final section we provide some concluding remarks.

Information infrastructures and control

Information infrastructure is composed of interdependent and interconnected collections of socio-technical components (e.g. Hanseth, 2000; Hanseth and Monteiro, 1997; Hanseth et al., 1996; McGarty, 1992; Star and Ruhleder, 1996). Collectively, these components provide an underlying platform upon which other actors can provide services and applications, such as an intranet in a global organization or access to the internet. Information infrastructures are not simple, standalone and self-contained information systems, but rather, represent large and open socio-technical networks comprised of heterogeneous actors. The various actors possess varying perspectives on, and only partially control over, the information infrastructure (Neumann and Star, 1996; Star and Ruhleder, 1996). Moreover, an information infrastructure develops over time, through both gradual expansion and the improvement and replacement of its parts. Controlling an information infrastructure is not clearly delineated either in scope (range and users) or time (Ciborra and Associates, 2000; Lyytinen and Yoo, 2002). As a consequence, conventional approaches to design of information systems may not necessarily be applicable for information infrastructure as no single actor is in control and the infrastructure is not constructed 'from scratch' within one project. Emerging design challenges are of relevance, including those related to overcoming start-up problems (Hanseth and Aanestad, 2003) and those required in order to avoid lock-ins (Hanseth and Lyytinen, 2004).

Despite their status as large, heterogeneous networks, information infrastructures still embody a high degree of design activities and choices. Emerging from existing installed bases of technologies, and reflecting many of their design practices and usage patterns, the nature of information infrastructures results in the design process becoming a distributed activity. Even where this is not the case, certain actors are often in a better position to shape its trajectory of evolution (Strauss, 1993). While total control over the information infrastructure is generally not possible, a number of components can be controlled by individual actors. This control challenge for information infrastructure design is reflected in the literature (Ciborra and Associates, 2000; Lyytinen and Yoo, 2002) with different aspects of control evident, including how users will be enticed to use a new information infrastructure through cultivation and bootstrapping (Hanseth and Aanestad, 2003; Rolland and Monteiro, 2002) and how lock-ins can be avoided through flexible standards (Hanseth et al., 1996).

Hanseth and Lyytinen (2004) suggest an analytical distinction between different types of information infrastructures due to their significant variation in scale and functionality. They suggest delineating between three different types of vertical information infrastructures: *universal, business sector and corporate* information infrastructure. While universal information infrastructure has a global scope and corporate information infrastructure is used primarily within a single corporation, business sector information infrastructure involves several different (and heterogeneous) companies within a business sector.

While the early information infrastructure literature discussed universal information infrastructure, in particular the internet (Monteiro, 1998), much of the current information infrastructure literature concerns corporate information infrastructure. Here the theme of control is often discussed, and these studies have emphasized the complexity of controlling information infrastructure and control-through-information infrastructure (see e.g. Ciborra and Associates, 2000 for a collection of studies). These studies demonstrate the distributed nature of technology in dispersed organizations, and in particular how it generates tensions between the global (or central) and the local (e.g. Ciborra and Associates, 2000; Rolland and Monteiro, 2002). A finding from these studies is that since technology itself is difficult to control, it may curb control as much as it enhances it:

> Making larger infrastructures – to obtain enhanced control – means making larger and more interconnected network. Larger networks are harder to change and the role of side effects increases – which leads, paradoxically, to less control. (Ciborra and Associates, 2000, p. 126)

Implementing information infrastructure can therefore appear to be 'striking back on management' in the sense that 'side-effects' become more prominent than 'intended' effects.

The literature reveals a perspective on control that is relatively narrow, with control depicted as something management pursues in order to successfully run its business, to the extent that control becomes an aim in itself – control is management *per se*. Control or rather a *lack-of-control* is seen as a crucial challenge in respect to information infrastructure. The aims and tasks of both managers and designers are to cope with the uncontrollable nature of ii, providing the required 'corporate glue' or, on the other hand, breaking lock-ins to suboptimal practices. A common theme present throughout the literature is that control over information infrastructures in design and operation is *always* pursued. It is argued that such a perspective fails to account for important aspects of the very nature of information infrastructure and that the need for control over technology should not always pursued, be absolute, or an all-or-nothing proposal. Mulgan (1991) opened this 'black box' of control in his account of communication systems as control systems, depicting how control can be exercised in varying forms, while on one hand, control can be horizontally distributed in an endogenous and organic fashion. Each of these types of control is strongly shaped by the means of communication required. Exogenous control depends on a centralized capacity to process information and knowledge, so that the most appropriate commands are given and the most effective strategies followed. It requires reciprocal communication with the target being controlled, with endogenous systems distributing such capacity. Mulgan (1991) depicts the limits to our capacity to exert control, theorizing that control strategies are dependent upon the costs of control, and the requirements of an investment in time, materials and energy. Increasing complexity results in an increasing need for communication in order to maintain exogenous control. In such situations, control becomes costly and is not always feasible. Relinquishing control in an endogenous fashion is often the most favoured approach.

Business sector information infrastructures and design

In this paper we primarily discuss business sector information infrastructure involving complementary as well as competing actors, standards, services and technology providers within a business sector. Some interest already exists in this kind of information infrastructure, as evident from the studies of exchange of structured information such as electronic data interchange (EDI) across various sectors and industries (Damsgaard and Lyytinen, 2001; Forster and King, 1995; Nikas, 2003), telemedicine (Aanestad and Hanseth, 2000) and geographical information systems (Georgiadou et al., 2005). This literature is, however, not primarily focused on managerial control through information infrastructure, but rather the design challenges information infrastructure poses, and how the ensuing complexities can be managed.

Infrastructure is commonly understood as something underlying, beneath and below. Being underlying, infrastructures can also be understood as being below a certain surface in the sense that it is transparent and invisible to its users. Only upon breakdowns does what is underlying become visible, such as when a water pipe ruptures or a mobile telephone network fails. The current literature on information infrastructure lends itself to this metaphor of infrastructure when the strength of their installed base and the mechanisms by which this evolves is considered. As with all metaphors, this analogy also has its limitations. In particular, when discussing business sector information infrastructure design, two issues emerge. First, business sector information infrastructure can be flexible in design, with some actors able to exert strong influence on the installed base and to alter it more radically (Nielsen, 2006). This can result in changes from a limited information system or platform into a business sector information infrastructure. Second, the sunk cost argument for business sector information infrastructure is not necessarily literal. The way in which the information infrastructure appears and is recognized as sunk may be equally important in addressing this question.

A substantial volume of management literature exists defining IT infrastructure is a strategic asset for the firm, and how management can pursue and achieve strategic agility based on infrastructure investments (Broadbent et al., 1999; Ross 2003; Weill and Vitale, 2002; Ross, 2003). The IT portfolio of a firm is founded on information infrastructure, as a set of reliable services based on IT components, human IT infrastructure, shared IT services and applications (Weill and Vitale, 2002). This infrastructure is usually coordinated by the IS group and used to connect different parts of the firm. It can also be utilized to establish links with suppliers, customers and partners. As a long-time investment and common denominator across the organization, the information infrastructure adds stability over time. Having an information infrastructure with appropriate services significantly reduces time and cost of addressing change, and constructing new systems as required. In order to avoid the information infrastructure becoming a liability, IS managers must ensure that their group is made aware of upcoming information infrastructure needs.

With a focus on corporate information infrastructures, the literature provides valuable insights into how information infrastructure can be utilized as a strategic asset and as a means of both meeting change and creating new business opportunities. At the same time, the literature reflects a portfolio approach, whereby information infrastructure is seen as a capability which senior management can invest in, choose where to locate, outsource, or apply a Service Level Agreement (SLA) to and market test. As argued by Ciborra (2000a), however, the context of information infrastructure s is not 'Legoland'. The components and assets of information infrastructures are not so easy to acquire, transfer and to dispose of, and it is a fallacy that management can plan and decide on how to 'pick or drop' components for information infrastructure. Ciborra's emphasis on the inertia dimension of the installed base illustrates how modifying, replacing or splitting parts of an information infrastructure involves high switching costs and sticky assets.

While the critique Ciborra offers is highly appropriate, the management perspective is still useful in highlighting the malleability and strategic opportunities inherent in deploying and changing information infrastructures. Even if information infrastructures are based on sticky components, the components, how they are arranged and the information infrastructure are not immutable. It can also be argued that technology should be organized in relation to people's capacities of exercising control, either by imposing strict authoritarian control or by control devolution (Mulgan, 1991). Information infrastructure can also be strategically designed to create certain control structures. One approach to the design and implementation of business sector information infrastructure is to link together components that were standalone information systems into one information infrastructure. Central actors must take the decision not to pursue an individual, closed or controlled solution, but rather, to connect to and become a part of an underlying infrastructure providing support for a range of activities. The design choice in such settings is not only applicable to start-up or lock-in challenges, as has been depicted for networked technologies. Additional decisions include those related to distribution and allocation of control, autonomy and responsibilities. This paper seeks to add to the existing research on information infrastructures by addressing this area in particular.

A case study of the CPA platform

This section introduces the architecture of the CPA platform and how it is utilized. This is followed by a more detailed description of its origins, design and development.

Change, or design, is not only dictated by technical artefacts and their trajectories, but it also occurs through a negotiation process involving a heterogeneous network of human and technological actors (Law, 1999). The research design applied here traces the technical components involved, the intentions of designers, and is reflected in how the technology is used (Faraj et al., 2004), focusing on '...recognising the depths of interdependence of technical networks and standards, on the one hand, and the real work of politics and knowledge production on the other,' (Bowker and Star, 1999: 34). The case study reported here is based on 39 informal and in-depth interviews with managers and system developers in 23 different organizations related to the development and operation of the CPA platform. The interviews were focused on how the different actors valued the CPA platform and how they had contributed to its design and operation. While the entire set of interviews offered the required background knowledge, this paper draws upon nine of these with employees who work for one of the network operators designing and operating the CPA platform and its predecessors. An additional four interviews occurred with the content providers who directly played a part in influencing these developments.

The CPA platform

The CPA platform has been designed and implemented by the two Norwegian mobile telephone network operators, NorCom and MobiNor, as two independent software platforms. Together, these platforms provide an open and public infrastructure for the provisioning of content services for mobile phones, including yellow pages, ringtones, interactive TV, news, weather information and others.

The architecture of the platform enables a mobile phone subscriber to acquire services through a number of simple steps. For example, if a subscriber wishes to obtain a phone number, he or she first locates the required information for ordering this service from a variety of sources such as the internet, in a magazine or on a banner. This is presented in a short-code form (a phone number with only four digits) and identifies the content provider and the name or code of the item. In order to request the content, the subscriber is required to sends an SMS message from his or her mobile phone to a designated number that contains the message 'phone X' to, for example, number 1905 (step 1 in Figure 17.1).

The SMS is processed as a text message by the message centre (SMSC) of the subscriber's mobile phone network. This recognizes the short-code number 1905, with the request and the subscriber's phone number forwarded to the CPA platform (step 2). The CPA platform will forward the content of the SMS over a TCP/IP connection (step 3) to the content provider associated with the number 1905, without undertaking any further processing. Upon receipt of the request, 'phone' and 'X' are recognized as the service requested with the content provider

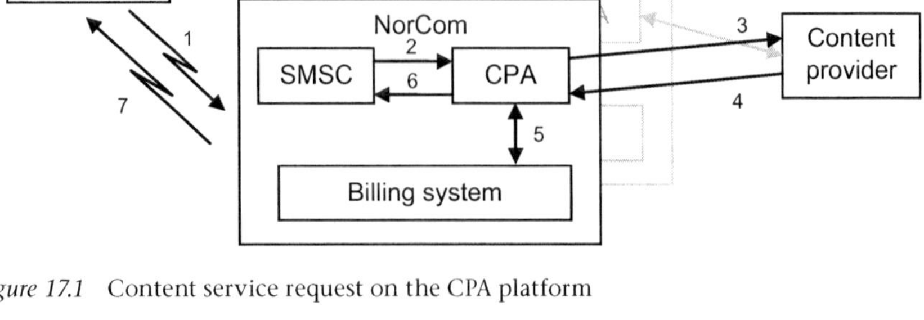

Figure 17.1 Content service request on the CPA platform

subsequently including the content and returning it to the network operator via the TCP/IP connection (step 4). The content provider is required to rate the service according to predefined rating classes ranging from NOK 1 to NOK 60. On receipt of the content, the network operator generates a Call Data Record ('CDR'), which is provided to the billing system in order for it to process the request according to the rating class (step 5). If successful, the content is delivered to the customer by the SMSC (steps 6 and 7). As the subscriber is an existing customer with the network operator, there is no requirement for any further registration or to provide any personal data such as address or credit card details. The charge for the service is added to the subscriber's regular phone bill. When the subscriber pays this, revenue from the service is shared between the network operator and the content provider.

Early content services for fixed line phones in Norway

Content services have been available in the Norwegian telecommunication networks since the introduction of Teletorg. In 1991, content providers were granted access to the existing network in order to provide voice-based information services to fixed line phones. This model was based on the incumbent monopoly operator making available specific number ranges for premium rate calls (e.g. 820 and 829) and charging customers for these through their phone billing. The network operator was only permitted to make a nominal charge for the provision of this billing capability, due to its monopolistic position. The services offered ranged from chat, horoscopes and jokes, to more explicit content.

Based on a combined initiative between the network operator and *IL-forum*, the association which representing content providers, the Norwegian regulatory authorities established *Teletorgrådet* in 1991 to monitor the provision of content services, which also subsequently enforced regulations as well. *MobiNor*, at that time the only telecommunications operator in Norway, was not permitted to offer these types of services Teletorg was promoted as a commercial interface that third parties could utilize in order to provide services to the network.

Proprietary mobile phone platforms as an interlude

With the arrival of NorCom in 1993, MobiNor experienced competition in the mobile phone network for the first time, with the operator eventually capturing over 30 per cent of the Norwegian mobile market. In 1997, both operators launched platforms that facilitated offering exclusive content and utility-based SMS services for their respective mobile subscribers. With the exception of this closed approach to access, service acquisition almost mirrored its successor, the CPA platform. A significant difference was that content services were charged for on a per transaction basis as standard SMS messages, regardless of any included content (NOK 3). Some content providers defined this 'a tragedy', particularly those with previous experiences with premium calling from Teletorg. This resulted in a limited number of content providers, as the production of content necessitated incurring some production costs and experiencing high transaction volumes in order to recoup this. Neither of these eventuated.

Both of these initiatives developed on an ad hoc basis, and were largely based on the initiatives by a small number of enthusiastic employees. These unstructured approaches did not require a sound business case, but as a consequence, they also suffered from a lack of funding. This was partly addressed through joint development activities with content providers.

A further difference with the earlier CPA platform was the provision of exclusive services controlled by the network operators, as noted by the founder of the platform implemented by MobiNor:

> We were talking directly with the content providers, it was us that fixed the codes, so, the point was that the content providers had a relationship with us, and we fixed the rest. We were, so to say, an editor which defined which services to provide.

The services offered by the content providers were utility driven and included national news, stock quotes, weather forecasts and phone directories, and assisted the operators to develop their brand accordingly.

In implementing their platforms, the primary challenge faced by the operators was to amend their billing systems. These were relatively unsophisticated at the time, reflecting the infancy of the mobile telephony sector and the priority on undertaking billing for voice services. Changes required to accommodate content driven services received a lower priority even if they were minor. In response, platforms operating outside the billing system began to emerge, as reported by the founders of the platforms implemented by MobiNor and NorCom, respectively

> When we made a new product with a new price in minutes, they used months to do the same in the old billing system…So it was just not possible to be dependent on the billing system to have the flexibility we needed. So we managed to do that by defining us out on the outside. And you can say that at that time the most flexible billing system was running on a PC in the corner of one of the developers' office.
>
> It was not very easy to change things. We had our first version of our billing system…with flat files and everything, it was a real threshing machine…and when the new billing system came, we were tied on hands and feet's both by technology and possibilities. So, everything was premature deluxe…I remember we hacked everything, because we had no resources for developing.

While these *ad hoc* efforts made the platforms operational, they did not create a successful content service market. Similarly, the network operators failed to experience economic success with their exclusive service offerings. This was caused in part by the marketing costs incurred and because the services were primarily utility-based. The content providers developing services expressed frustration that the full potential of their content was not being realized, due to the pricing policy by the operators and a lacklustre service portfolio.

In the autumn of 1999, a former employee of MobiNor returned to the Company after an interim period working with NTV, one of the more dynamic content providers and TV broadcasters. Aware of the issues with the platform, he began to alter MobiNor's approach to its content. At the same time, a current NTV employee who had experience working with the previous platforms was engaging in discussions with both the network operators. These centred on charging for content at more than the basic SMS price, which would result in a premium rating. The network operators did not approve of this approach to charge 5–10 NOK for content, openly ridiculing such a suggestion:

> So, we felt for a long time like banging our heads to the door there, and this was not because technical issues, because that was the next thing, then one had to build that in addition. The problem was that they simply did not believe that it was possible to create revenues of from it.

The emergence of the CPA platform

As a result of external pressure and internal discussion, MobiNor initiated the development of a new and different content platform. This approach was mirrored at NorCom, and recognized that content providers were more experienced in dealing with the development of new services, marketing them, and pricing them 'correctly'. It was also recognized that content providers could associate their brands with a wider number of services than network operators, and that content providers had wider market access. Based on these factors, the decision to move away from the previous platform gained momentum, but was still hampered at managerial level. This resulted in limited investment in the implementation of the new CPA platform. As a consequence, the initial technical implementation of the CPA platform by both operators was primarily based on specifications from the previous platform. Access was granted to external content providers, but due to a lack of support and internal resources, only a limited number of individuals were made available on a day-to-day basis. Despite this, the required software was developed by the operators, complemented by the cultivation of closer relationships with content providers, as noted by one of these 'pioneers' in MobiNor:

> It was a bit of entrepreneurship spirited, the project, because we had no resources assigned like you are used to in a big company. So we had to make everything ourselves, and find the resources ourselves, in a form of a project. And this resulted in, that the atmosphere, both market wise and business wise and the technical development was entrepreneur directed.

The first content provider to sign an agreement with MobiNor knew little about mobile telephony, but had experience with providing non-utility services using the Teletorg platform. This followed months of rumours that the operator had developed a new platform, and repeated effort to gain access to this by content providers. Once these providers gained access, however, many discovered that the platform was at an early stage in its evolution, and that it was still perceived as 'controversial' by some staff within MobiNor. One of the first providers to gain access iterated the haphazard manner in which MobiNor approached the platform and his company's involvement:

> And then they had something running...and suddenly I showed up, but they had not planned to launch at this early stage. And they had to sort out, what do we do now? And that is difficult in this kind of an organisation. So, finally by being persistent, I could plug into the platform, but it was made clear that the billing could fail to function at any time and without any rights for me to claim compensation.
>
> This project meant a lot to this particular staff member, and he did a lot that he was not allowed to by his manager. He stressed this through internally in MobiNor, in a way that he possibly would not if he were a devoted and nervous guy. So he was scolded a lot in the beginning.

The developers involved with the development of the CPA platform were also amongst its strongest promoters, and did not necessarily possess a telecommunications ethos, as observed by their peers. As the platform continued to evolve and content was added, it became evident to the network operators that the cost of its implementation and operation was marginal, while traffic continued to increase rapidly. This was a key tenet in MobiNor's strategy, as cited by one of it's the middle managers:

> We have not used many resources on marketing the content providers' services, which was a part of our strategy, that we initiate variety and minimise risk. Because there is many that give it a try, those who succeed we make money on, those who fail are not our problem.

When launched in the spring of 2000, the CPA platform enabled content providers to deliver a wide range of services to mobile phone subscribers, and to charge them premium rates for these. Responsibility as to which services to provide and how to market and price these was now undertaken by the content providers. In contrast to previous platforms which were network-provider specific, the CPA platform established a transparent market serving the interests of both the content providers and subscribers. From providing relatively simple services such as ringtones, logos and stock quote subscriptions, the CPA platform has evolved and now provides more advanced services including as an interactive return channel for voting and discussions in TV-shows. To coordinate these events, the TV-broadcasters, content providers and network operators continue their close coordination to develop additional services. The CPA platform also provides billing for content services delivered by MMS, WAP, Web, and positioning services. In 2004, this sector in Norway had a turnover of approximately €120 million, and participation from around 50 firms employing 250 people.

Analysis: relinquishing control

Before content providers were permitted to connect their own equipment to telecommunication networks, the distinction between users and vendors was clear (Branscomb and Kahin, 1996), with the incentives and the responsibility for service innovation and operation assigned to the vendors, that is the network operators. The responsibility and primary control for these still resides with the network operators, even in the case when multiple actors are connecting their equipment to the network operators' infrastructure. Within this study, this control/autonomy balance was observed in two levels. The first involved employees engaged in the development of the CPA platform within both network operators, who were granted the autonomy to pursue their personal initiatives in an entrepreneurial milieu. This autonomy emerged in part as a response to a lack of managerial interest in services which were defined as economically *marginal* and appeared to be 'odd practices' and serendipitous applications of systems (Ciborra, 1994).

A second level in which this balance was observed was in the development of the platform by the network operators. Recognition occurred by a number of individuals that they were not equipped with the resources, risk aversion, or the ability to innovate and create the range of services which the market required. Through the design of the CPA platform, the network operators transferred these elements to the content providers. These companies could now exercise the flexibility they had been seeking earlier. By relinquishing control, the network operators transferred responsibility for these types of services to external participants, including services that were not congruent with their cultivated 'public image'.

The CPA platform was designed, implemented and launched in an unstructured manner that was at the periphery of strategic and managerial control. At the same time, the lack of adequate funding and resources at the outset of the project influenced the evolution of the platform's architecture. While stronger managerial control and the existence of a sound business case would not necessarily have led to a rejection of the platform, these would have impeded the process and resulted in a platform that was different to the one developed and which most likely would have been proprietary. In this particular case, the lack of managerial control was not an organizational challenge for those involved. Rather, its absence was a prerequisite for the appropriate evolution of the CPA platform that resulted in an approach of *control devolution*, with the CPA platform 'pushed out' of the domain of the network operators.

Relinquishing control to external content providers has provided the network operators with the ability to create distance from any unfavourable, explicit or illegal content. In addition to content providers possessing a better understanding of the market, they are also less concerned with the nature of the content they provide. This can result in expedient and often unpredictable activities, as noted by one of the founders of CPA in MobiNor:

> It was primarily colourful advertising, jokes and really just nonsense. But, it appeared as what the subscribers wanted...What these guys knew was that the willingness to pay for services was high...so they began at an early stage to charge NOK 10 for services...So, during a very short period of time, the turnover went far beyond the previous platform, without any investments in service development or marketing by us.

Actors in a sector will pursue strategies that confer control over their assets while strengthening their position in the value chain. Making a fundamental shift in the organizational approach to the control and exclusivity of content service offerings could be perceived as risky. In the case of the CPA platform, the operators were able to protect the core elements of their value chain, including their relationship with and ownership of their subscribers. Recently, MobiNor rejected the proposal by a company that sought to implement its own CPA platform within the operator's network. This reinforced MobiNor's position of strength, with the rejection upheld by the Ministry of Transport and Communication, in part because MobiNor would have limited control over the services provided on this alternative platform. While the CPA platform's architecture resulted in reduced service provisioning control being held by the network operators, it reinforced the control they possessed over their technology and the wider value chain.

The CPA platform architecture was largely shaped by the early decisions to relinquish control and delegate marketing, pricing, innovation and risk. This delegation was driven in part by investment and operational cost considerations. At the same time, these delegations have the effect of making this platform appear as a business sector information infrastructure. While delegation in some instances has been imposed by the network operators, in others, the content providers have proactively pursued the attainment of autonomy since this confers the control required to innovate with confidence and stability. This architecture, along with a balance between control and autonomy, has developed over time, and has occurred perhaps more as a result of the network operators' technical limitations and lack of interest rather than their explicit strategies.

The efforts of the network operators to provide the CPA platform as an open and public business sector information infrastructure depict how information infrastructure can be designed and developed with limited effort. It also depicts the sunken nature of information infrastructure. By a strategy of *control devolution*, the previous standalone platforms were redesigned as one element within shared infrastructure. The concept of sinking depicts how this platform currently appears as a transparent infrastructure through which content providers can deliver their services. At the same time, while network operators have *withdrawn* in contrast to their previous platforms, content providers have *been brought forward* and into focus by innovating, taking initiatives, and providing desired services: a typical example of collage that is continuously extending.

Discussion: control and control devolution

It can be argued that control over technology provides significant benefits by enabling one set of actors to exclude other actors and solutions in the creation of favourable revenue streams (Shapiro and Varian, 1999). The concept of control should however be elaborated along several dimensions in order to depict its multifaceted nature. First, control is not necessarily determinate and can be conceptualized along a continuum ranging from *absolute* to *influential* (Beniger, 1986). Second, an understanding of the concept of control in relation to information infrastructure will vary depending on the perspective of the observer, as has been depicted in the local–global discussion of corporate information infrastructure (e.g. Rolland and Monteiro, 2002). Third, real and perceived control may play equally significant roles. Fourth, the distinction between controlling business sector information infrastructure and controlling the use of business sector information infrastructure is crucial. Fifth, control and autonomy are inseparable aspects of management (Walsham, 1993).

Human actors may be autonomous to a certain extent, but their choices will be restricted within the political context of organizations and business sectors. At the same time, 'control must be balanced in a sensible way in order to gain the benefits of the creativity and energy which rises from autonomous activity on the parts of individuals and groups' (Walsham, 1993: 45). The approach to the control/autonomy balance can be linked to certain *responsibilities* that are synonymous with the provision of technology. When these responsibilities become too problematic for those in control of technology, one possible strategy is to relinquish control over the technology, through *control devolution*. Technology becomes 'autonomous' to a certain degree and is placed in the hands of other actors. In this context, information infrastructure are important means by which control can be exercised and autonomy facilitated. A key challenge is to balance control and autonomy in design as well as in the operation of information infrastructure.

As this case study illustrates, providing the CPA platform publicly yielded some benefits as well as creating new responsibilities. While centralized control over a technology platform can confer benefits to one actor, control will also be attached to responsibilities related to the use of the technology. How the relationship between technological control and usage control are structured is of crucial importance as to how responsibility is distributed. If the responsibility for usage of the CPA platform resides with those in control of the technology, they are required to address how the technology is to be used. This may result in the implementation of mechanisms that strictly hinder unacceptable use, or alternatively, they can relinquish control over elements of the technology. The first approach will most likely involve greater cost, in addition to acting in a limiting manner for the users. This approach is however generally congruent with the common control perspective and approach prevalent in the information infrastructure literature. The second approach will limit the expense of introducing and operating control mechanisms, in addition to 'opening up' the platform for the market to use.

Even if promoters of 'open' technology inevitably sacrifice some control over the future evolution of the technology (Tassey, 1995), the concept of giving away full control over their technology represents that extreme scenario, and represents a radical approach. A more likely strategy is to make the technology *visible* to the market creating the perception that it is not under the operator's central control. This implies retaining control over parts of the infrastructure while at the same time providing open use over others, an acceptable control/autonomy balance.

This case study depicts how two companies engaged in the provision of a business sector information infrastructure relinquished control over a technology platform. This occurred in order to spur innovation, abide by regulatory changes, and to minimize risk to their corporate reputation. In providing the core components of the business sector information infrastructure, these companies controlled the architecture on the one hand, while on the other, the users of the information infrastructure controlled its use. Through minor adjustment to the technical platform for service provisioning, operational control was transferred to external partners in content provision by the network operators. Instead of continuing to be an independent and self-contained information system under the respective control of the two actors, the content platform was redefined to become a *component* of an information infrastructure.

Concluding remarks

Ciborra's work depicts infrastructures as tools that are used to link, structure and control organizations. Concomitantly, both infrastructures and organizations are replete with surprises, blockages, diversions and side effects. Claims about how information infrastructures should be developed are inevitably claims about how organizations, human beings and infrastructure itself should be controlled.

Control, as it relates to technology, is a complex issue and not an 'all-or-nothing' proposition. The control/autonomy balance occurs on various levels related to the design, implementation and operation of information infrastructures. While control over technology is a critical success factor in some circumstances, ignoring attempts to discard old ways of thinking and 'doing' (Ciborra, 1994), as well as relinquishing control over elements of technology, can be equally essential in others. At this point, the proposed theoretical contribution of this paper differs from, but extends, the work of Ciborra.

The pursuit of control is not a necessity. Strategically, developing business sector information infrastructure can result in a polar result: the relinquishing of control. In the case of the CPA platform, the risks inherent in the control of this technology were perceived as hampering implementation and operation. Through a strategy of control devolution, control and responsibilities were transferred by the network operators to the content providers. While real control over the technology still primarily resided with the network operators, its infrastructure attributes enabled them to withdraw from responsibilities in so far as this was externally *perceived* as being out of their control. The technology is not itself autonomous, with the content providers controlling its usage to a large degree.

While control devolution as a strategy provides the opportunity for the network operators to engage with technological architectures which would not have been possible if they retained responsibility of its usage, control devolution also has important implications for the autonomy, openness and possibilities for technology use. Borrowing from Ciborra's description of information infrastructure, it can be stated that while certain *side effects* no longer have repercussions on the infrastructure providers, the infrastructure at the same time allows for creativity as well as eccentric usages and innovations. In these circumstances, the control/autonomy balance is favourable with the network operators, content providers and the process of innovation in general. At a practical level, this paper suggests that information infrastructure management practices should be based on a deep understanding of the existing control/autonomy balance as well as the distribution of resources, risks and abilities and willingness to innovate.

Note

This paper originally appeared as Nielsen, P. and Aanestad, M. (2006) Control devolution as information infrastructure design strategy: a case study of a content service platform for mobile phones in Norway, *Journal of Information Technology* **21**(3): 185–194.

References

Aanestad, M. and Hanseth, O. (2000). Implementing Open Network Technologies in Complex Work Practices: A Case from Telemedicine, in Proceedings from IFIP 8.2. (Aalborg, Denmark, 2000); Dordrecht: Kluwer Academic Publishers.

Beniger, J.R. (1986). *The Control Revolution: Technological and Economic Origins of the Information Society*, Cambridge, MA: Harvard University Press.

Bowker, G.C. and Star, S.L. (1999). *Sorting Things Out: Classification and Its Consequences*, Cambridge, MA: The MIT Press.

Branscomb, L.M. and Kahin, B. (1996). Standards Processes and Objectives for the National Information Infrastructure, in L. Branscomb and J. Keller (eds) *Converging Infrastructures: Intelligent Transportation Systems and the National Information Infrastructure*, Cambridge, MA: MIT Press.

Broadbent, M., Weill, P. and St. Clair, D. (1999). The Implications of Information Technology Infrastructure for Business Process Redesign, *MIS Quarterly* **23**: 159–182.

Ciborra, C.U. (1994). The Grassroots of IT and Strategy, in C. Ciborra and T. Jellasi (eds) *Strategic Information Systems: A European Perspective*, Chichester: John Wiley & Sons Ltd.

Ciborra, C.U. (2000a). A Critical Review of the Literature on the Management of Corporate Information Infrastructures, in C. Ciborra and Associates (eds) *From Control to Drift: The Dynamics of Corporate Information Infrastructures*, Oxford: Oxford University Press, pp. 15–40.

Ciborra, C.U. (2000b). From Alignment to Loose Coupling: From MedNet to, www.roche.com. in C. Ciborra and Associates (eds) *From Control to Drift: The Dynamics of Corporate Information Infrastructures*, Oxford: Oxford University Press, pp. 193–212.

Ciborra, C.U. and Associates (2000). *From Control to Drift: The Dynamics of Corporate Information Infrastructures,* Oxford: Oxford University Press, pp. 193–212.
Damsgaard, J. and Lyytinen, K. (2001). The Role of Intermediating Institutions in the Diffusion of Electronic Data Interchange (EDI): How Industry Associations Intervened in Denmark, Finland and Hong Kong, *The Information Society* **17**: 195–210.
Faraj, S., Kwon, D. and Watts, S. (2004). Contested Artifact: Technology Sensemaking, Actor Networks, and the Shaping for the Web Browser, *Information Technology & People* **17**: 186–209.
Forster, P.W. and King, J.L. (1995). Information Infrastructure Standards in Heterogeneous Sectors; Lessons from The Worldwide Air Cargo Community, in B. Kahin and J. Abbate (eds) *Standards Policy for Information Infrastructure,* Cambridge, MA: MIT Press, pp. 148–177.
Georgiadou, Y., Puri, S. and Sahay, S. (2005). Towards a Potential Research Agenda to Guide the Implementation of Spatial Data Infrastructures: A Case Study from India, *International Journal of Geographic Information Science* **19**: 1113–1130.
Hanseth, O. (2000). The Economics of Standards, in C. Ciborra and Associates (eds) *From Control to Drift: The Dynamics of Corporate Information Infrastructures,* Oxford: Oxford University Press, pp. 56–70.
Hanseth, O. and Aanestad, M. (2003). Bootstrapping Networks, Communities and Infrastructure: On the Evolution of ICT solutions in Health Care, *Methods of Information in Medicine* **42**(4): 385–391.
Hanseth, O. and Lyytinen, K. (2004). Theorizing about the Design of Information Infrastructures: Design kernel theories and principles, Sprouts: Working Papers on Information, Environments Systems and Organizations, vol. 4, number 12 [WWW document]http://weatherhead.cwru.edu/sprouts/ 2004/040412.pdf.
Hanseth, O. and Monteiro, E. (1997). Understanding Information Infrastructures. Manuscript. [WWW document], http://www.ifi.uio.no/~oleha/Publications/bok.pdf, consulted 1 June 2005.
Hanseth, O., Monteiro, E. and Hatling, M. (1996). Developing Information Infrastructure: The Tension between Standardisation and Flexibility, *Science, Technology and Human Values* **11**: 407–426.
Law, J. (1999). After ANT: Complexity, Naming and Topology, in J. Law and J. Hassard (eds) *Actor Network Theory and After,* Oxford, UK: Blackwell Publishers.
Lyytinen, K. and Yoo, Y. (2002). Research Commentary: The Next Wave of Nomadic Computing, *Information Systems Research* **13**: 377–388.
McGarty, T.P. (1992). Alternative Networking Architectures: Pricing, Policy, and Competition, in B. Kahin (ed.) *Building Information Infrastructure,* New York: McGraw-Hill Primis.
Monteiro, E. (1998). Scaling Information Infrastructures: The Case of Next-generation IP in the Internet, *The Information Society* **14**: 229–245.
Mulgan, G. (1991). *Communication and Control: Networks and the New Economies of Communication,* Cambridge: Polity Press.
Neumann, L.J. and Star, S.L. (1996). Making Infrastructure: The Dream of a Common Language, in J. Blomberg, F. Kensig and E. Dykstra-Erickson (eds) *PDC'96,* Cambridge, MA, Palo Alto, CA: Computer Professionals for Social Responsibility/ACM.
Nielsen, P. (2006). A Conceptual Framework of Information Infrastructure Building, Ph.D. thesis, Faculty of Mathematics and Natural Sciences, University of Oslo, Norway.
Nikas, A. (2003). Network Information Infrastructures in the Construction Industry: Emergence and Impact on Work and Management Arrangements, ELTRUN Working Paper Series, Athens.
Rolland, K.H. and Monteiro, E. (2002). Balancing the Local and the Global in Infrastructural Information Systems, *The Information Society* **18**: 87–100.
Ross, J.W. (2003). Creating a Strategic IT Architecture Competency: Learning in Stages, *MIS Quarterly Executive* **2**: 31–43.

Shapiro, C. and Varian, H.R. (1999). *Information Rules: A strategic Guide to the Network Economy*, Boston, MA: Harvard Business School Press.
Star, S.L. and Ruhleder, K. (1996). Steps Toward an Ecology of Infrastructure: Design and Access for Large Information Spaces, *Information Systems Research* **7**: 111–134.
Strauss, A.L. (1993). *Continual Permutations of Action*, New York: Aldine de Gruyter.
Tassey, G. (1995). The Roles of Standards as Technology Infrastructure, in R. Hawkins, R. Mansell and J. Skea (eds) *Standards, Innovation and Competitiveness*, Aldershot, UK: Edward Elgar.
Walsham, G. (1993). *Interpreting Information Systems in Organizations*, Chichester: Wiley.
Weill, P. and Vitale, M. (2002). What IT Infrastructure Capabilities are Needed to Implement E-Business Models? *MIS Quarterly Executive* **1**: 17–34.

18
Transaction Costs and Information Systems: Does IT Add Up?*

Antonio Cordella

Abstract

Transaction cost theory has often been used to support the idea that information and communication technology (ICT) can reduce imperfection in the economic system. Electronic markets and hierarchies have repeatedly been described as solutions to inefficiencies in the organization of transactions in complex and uncertain settings. Far from criticizing this assumption, this paper highlights the limits associated with this application of transaction cost theory that has been prevalent in IS research. Building on the concepts first proposed by Ciborra, the paper argues that information-related problems represent only some of the elements contributing to transaction costs. These costs also emerge due to the interdependencies among the various factors contributing to their growth. The study of the consequences associated with ICT design and implementation, grounded in transaction cost theory, should therefore consider the overall implication ICT has on these interdependences and not only the direct effect it has on information flow, distribution and management.

Introduction

The diffusion of information and communication technology (ICT) in society is always associated with an increased amount of information becoming available. Moreover, 'information society' is not only defined by the greater amount of information required in an ever increasing range of human activities, but also by the expanded number of sources from which information emanates. A significant volume of unwanted unsolicited information is received via traditional physical channels of communication such as post, but increasingly, more is being sent via ICT such as e-mail and the internet. In an era of ever shortening product life cycles and lead times, it has become essential for companies to improve their internal and external information flows. More information is necessary to deal with emergent complexity, dictating a requirement for faster information processing. A key resource for survival in this new environment is the ability to obtain access to more information and to be able to manage this information flow. As Lewis (1996) states: 'professional and personal survival in modern society clearly depends on our ability to take on board vast amounts of new information. Yet that information is growing at an exponential rate.'

ICT has become the major enabler of the efficient exchange and retrieval of information in organizations. However, conflicting approaches indicate that ICT is either a powerful tool to support the economic system managing information or, conversely, one that creates a more complex environment that is difficult to manage. A clear indication of the first perspective is found in ICT studies based on the transaction cost approach (Malone et al., 1987; Ciborra, 1993; Wigand et al., 1997). Such studies argue that ICT supports the economic system, providing a more efficient information flow that facilitates the interaction among economic agents under complex and uncertain circumstances, and reducing transaction costs. On the other hand, the literature addressing the problem of 'information overload' underlines the negative effects of ICT due to a greater level of complexity being faced as a consequence of the increased quantity of information made available by the technology (Palme, 1984; Schultze and Vandenbosch, 1998).

While being cognizant of these different approaches to the effects of ICT on organizational settings, this paper will focus only on the transaction costs approach, depicting that it is possible to identify situations where rather than reducing transaction costs, ICT will increase them. Building on Ciborra's (1993) work on transaction costs theory (TCT) and ICT, the paper will present the main elements of the theory to discuss the effects of ICT on the different dimensions of the transaction cost model. The paper highlights the importance of considering the interdependency among the factors contributing to transaction costs when ICT is designed and implemented to reduce the effects of these factors on transaction costs.

The paper is organized in a number of sections: Section two reviews transaction costs theory; Section three presents a summary of Ciborra's contribution to information system research and TCT; Section four summarizes the debate on TCT and ICT; Section five reviews how this literature has often underestimated the importance of the interdependencies between the various factors contributing to transaction costs to explain the overall effect of ICT on transaction costs; Section six reflects on any possible strategic implications from the ideas proposed in the paper.

Transaction costs

The need for a better understanding of the impact of ICT on organizational structures, such as markets and hierarchies, has increased the attention received by transaction costs theory in the study of information systems. Transaction costs theory represents one of the first attempts to develop a comprehensive theory that considers the structure of the firm as a source of explanation for outcomes, in contrast to viewing the firm as a 'black box' that has little influence in explaining such outcomes.

Presenting a minimalist version of the theory, Williamson (1975, 1985) and Coase (1937) considered the cost of organizing and managing the firm as analogous to the cost of constructing and working in an ideal organizational structure. In contrast, transaction costs were depicted as analogous to the costs associated with the management of the imperfections of this structure. In economic terms, the ideal structure (i.e. the one without imperfections), would be a perfectly informed and efficient market where prices were sufficient to communicate to dispersed buyers all the knowledge required to make a purchase decision (Hayek, 1945). Through the price mechanism, the market efficiently collects and transfers a large amount of information between economic agents; information that would be prohibitively costly to capture and distribute by other means.

Defining the elementary unit of analysis as the economic exchange between at least two individuals, the transaction costs model depicts the exchange process with reference to the resources that are required in order to execute this exchange. While in the optimal case these costs approach zero, when imperfections occur, these costs increase. Inefficiencies and imperfections in the organization of the transactions, called 'market failures', are the result of information and behavioural-related problems, with these imperfections defining the complexity of the transaction (Ciborra, 1993). Economic agents invest in resources to mitigate the effects of these imperfections in the execution of the exchange. These investments are the costs associated with the transactions, and defined as transactions costs. Transactions costs are the consequence of the asymmetrical and incomplete distribution of information among the economic agents involved in the transaction. More specifically, every transaction life cycle is characterized by different cost phases, with each incurring specific information-related costs:

- *Search costs*: the costs of locating information on the opportunities for exchange
- *Negotiation costs*: the costs of negotiating the terms of the exchange
- *Enforcement costs*: the costs of enforcing the contract.

Transactions will conclude successfully only when all the participating agents possess the necessary information to rationally assess the equity of the exchange.

When costs reach a particular level, it can be more convenient to 're-organize' the exchange processes within a structure that more adequately addresses uncertainty and information asymmetry. This shift in the organization of transactions occurs in order for the effects of transaction costs not to jeopardize the opportunity to conclude an exchange that is advantageous to all the involved parties. The model proposes a theoretical apparatus that assists in explaining why alternative forms in the organization of transactions exist.

Markets and hierarchies are proposed as alternative forms in the governance of transactions. Adhering to the underlying assumptions of the theoretical model, transactions that take place once, such as those on the 'spot markets', will incur relatively little transaction costs because they are associated with a low level of uncertainty (both environmental and strategic). In these cases it is straightforward to collect all the required information and to manage this information using the price mechanism. On the other hand, transactions that involve a commitment over time have a certain level of endogenous uncertainty related to the future behaviour of agents and of resource dependencies established within the transactional process (Barney and Ouchi, 1986).

To manage these contingences, investment in resources and strategies designed to address emerging challenges is required. These solutions are maintained by the development and enforcement of rules and regulations that produce a new coordination mechanism to replace the price mechanism. TCT argues that the alternative to the market found in organizational forms and hierarchies, are responses to the need to minimize the transaction costs associated with the management of transactions (Coase, 1937; Alchian and Demsetz, 1972; Williamson, 1975). This both explains and justifies the decision to reorganize the transaction process. The hierarchy organizes exchanges on the basis of rules and procedures within a regulatory framework that is a substitute for prices. Long-term commitment and contractual arrangements are developed to reduce the uncertainty facing agents, while enforcing alternative ways to organize the exchange process (Varian, 1992). The cost associated with the transaction will be lower than the one that, *ceteris paribus*, would be supported if the exchange was managed through a market mechanism. The same uncertainty is managed by a more efficient mechanism, the hierarchy, based on adherence to predefined norms and rules.

Transaction costs theory explains the existence of alternative forms of organization on the basis of their relative efficiencies in response to the combined effects of environmental factors (uncertainty and small numbers) and human factors (opportunism and bounded rationality) (Williamson, 1975; Moe, 1984). Transaction costs for a specific exchange can be captured by the function:

$$Tc = f(U;C;Br;Ia;As;Ob;Cc)$$

where Tc is transaction costs, U is uncertainty, C is complexity, Br is bounded rationality, Ia is information asymmetry, As is asset specificity, Ob is opportunistic behaviour and Cc is coordination costs. Information technologies have also been discussed within the transaction costs model, with their impact on the factors in this equation often questioned.

A number of authors have criticized the assumptions underpinning TCT. Opponents to the Theory have previously criticized its failure to consider the power of stakeholders within organizations (Francis, 1983; Perrow, 1986; Braddach and Eccles, 1989; Collin and Larsson, 1993). Others have criticized what they deem to be unrealistic assumptions, including that market based resources are always available (Bauer and Cohen, 1983; Dugger, 1983; Etzioni, 1988; Dietrich, 1994). Finally, several researchers claim that TCT is an inadequate unit of analysis because it ignores broader contextual issues that influence sourcing decisions, such as organizational learning (Collin, 1993; Elg and Johansson, 1993; Dietrich, 1994).

Some criticism of TCT (Lacity and Willcocks, 1995) focuses on the ambiguity of the definition of the factors contributing to transaction costs. These include asset specificity and uncertainty, which are posited as making the operationalization of the theory extremely difficult. Similarly, some authors question the possibility of clearly defining the micro level unit of analysis of transactions, particularly where ICT outsourcing occurs (ibid).

Ciborra, ICT and TCT

Ciborra (1981) was the first author to propose TCT as an approach to explain the design of computer based information systems. He argues that TCT brings together many of the concepts that had been traditionally used to analyse the effects of ICT on organizations, and that TCT illuminates the transactional dimension of economic exchanges. This includes the problem of the rational action of the organizational agents; the economic view of organizational forms such as teams and hierarchies; the notion of mediating technologies and the use of ICT to support markets, hierarchies and teams. In depicting the transactional dimension of economic exchanges, TCT discusses varying organizational forms as alternative responses that are enacted to overcome problems in the efficient allocation of economic resources. As a result, ICT is proposed as a solution that can reduce transaction costs. Following these ideas, Ciborra views the problem of designing information systems as something connected to the problem of designing an efficient economic system. He states that 'the key feature of…. (ICT) is in the framework proposed here, the possibility of lowering the costs of transacting. Accordingly, data processing can be identified with other devices that lower such costs as mediators and money,' (Ciborra, 1993).

ICT designed to lower transaction costs must take into consideration that the introduction of this technology 'reduces the costs of exchange and increases gains for both parties, if the resources it consumes are less that the transaction costs incurred,'[1] (Ciborra, 1993). It follows that the evaluation of the effects of ICT on the economic system must be considered in the context within which transactions occur. Markets, hierarchies, and teams are alternative solutions enforced to mitigate the effects of the complex set of factors that contribute to the emergence of transaction costs. Alternative frameworks need to be considered when studying the design of ICT in order to reduce transaction costs. Ciborra's (1993) book Teams, Market and Systems is a significant contribution to this debate. Following TCT, this work discusses how it is possible to formulate alternative ICT solutions to enforce the different transactional mechanisms of teams, markets and hierarchies. What characterizes the originality of this contribution is its depth and extensive analysis of alternative transactional mechanisms, in addition to depicting the proposed solutions in terms of ICT development driven by TCT. Additionally, a framework is proposed that guides the decision steps to be followed when assessing the cost-benefits associated with these alternative choices. Building upon the ideas proposed by socio-technical studies, Ciborra (1993) suggests that ICT solutions designed to lower transaction costs should follow the efficiency criterion when designed: cost-benefit analysis is proposed as the optimal approach to aid such design.

Following this paradigm, Ciborra (1993) discusses alternative architectures 'by adapting the analytical model proposed by Williamson (1985) to appreciate how technology and organizational forms jointly can make more efficient certain ways of coordinating the task of producing goods'. A model is proposed that compares alternative organizational forms and the subsequent impact of ICT on these forms. This comparison considers the possible combination of factors contributing to transaction costs and the effect of ICT on these factors. Utilizing empirical data, Ciborra (1993) suggests that the impact of ICT on transaction costs should be appraised not only in quantitative terms but also by taking into account qualitative changes that can be induced by ICT when it fosters a shift in the paradigm of the organization that hosts it: from 'hierarchies to the market', or from 'clans to hierarchies'. If this occurs, Ciborra (1993) suggests that the costs or benefits associated with such a shift must be taken into consideration when assessing the effects of ICT on the economic system. Drawing upon the ideas underpinning socio-technical analysis, Ciborra (1993) concludes that,

> appraising the costs and benefits of information technology is more than accounting or auditing tangible and intangible consequences of computer applications. Apart from the easiest cases, each time we carry out an economic analysis of the actual or expected impacts of information technology, we need a point of view and a conceptual framework on which to ground our evaluation. The point of view has been spelled out by adopting a dichotomy: work tool *versus* organizational technology. The first perspective allows us to look for the automating effects of information technology; the second for the more subtle, but not less relevant, information effect.

Ciborra suggests that care should be exercised in evaluating the costs and benefits ICT can have on transaction costs, because this assessment is not always as clear as it first appears. The problem of assessing the information effects associated with the adoption of ICT, has not been neglected by the author in his latest research. The information effect of ICT, produced by what Zuboff (1988) defines as informating technologies, coupled with Ciborra's depiction of mediating technologies, were starting points for the development of his more recent research on phenomenology and IS. Ciborra (2006) posits that as 'informating' technology, ICT embodies the notion that all types of data models and representations embedded in information systems provide a powerful set of representation of the processes of the firm that is an important means of conveying, sharing and harnessing knowledge well beyond the information stored in systems. ICTs not only represent tools that support information flows, but they possess an enframing force that converts everything they encounter 'into a reserve stock of resources to be harnessed and deployed for further development,' (Ciborra and Hanseth, 1998). ICTs are not tools but are a Gestell (ibid). The phenomenological argument underpinning the vision of ICTs as enframing forces (Gestell) does not allow for claims in favour of the managerial approaches to the study of ICT. These tend to examine the implementation of ICT as a process that can be completely designed and controlled ex ante (Ciborra and Associates, 2000), and hence easily measured ex post. This conclusion had already been reached when Ciborra made his claim that the effect of ICT on transaction costs cannot be assessed ex ante by only examining the results of technologies as automation tools. This paper explores these ideas, including a discussion on the effects of ICT on transaction costs.

Transaction costs and ICT

Following Ciborra's (1981) initial proposal that transaction cost theory is a potential framework for undertaking research in the design and impact of ICT, this model has been used extensively in the field. Typically, studies in information systems based on the transaction costs approach depict ICT as a tool that sustains information needs, providing additional information and information management power. ICT is perceived as a powerful tool to foster the efficiency of the transactional process within which economic exchanges take place. There is little disagreement that the effects of ICT on the economic organization of exchanges continue to be positive.

Malone et al. (1987) discussed the impact of ICT on the market and hierarchies, arguing that ICT facilitates the transactional process, supporting information flow and management during the various phases of transactions. It was theorized that the use of ICT supports market structures where without the presence of ICT, a hierarchical solution would be required. Similarly, Ciborra (1993) argued that the use of ICT reduces information asymmetry and resultantly increases the conditions under which the market mechanism is an efficient allocative structure. Analogous conclusions are also supported by Brynjolfsson et al. (1994) and Wigand et al. (1997). Other authors discuss ICT as a factor behind the increased interest on network and virtual organizations. Ciborra (1993), Malone et al. (1987), and Bakos and Brynjolfsson (1997) highlight that ICT can reduce the effect of opportunistic conduct increasing the possibility of monitoring agents' behaviour in partnerships. None of these works, however, discussed the impact of ICT on transaction costs in light of the interdependency existing among the various factors, both human and environmental, that ultimately generate transaction costs.

In their research, Malone et al. (1987) argue that ICT lowers transaction costs because technology allows information to be communicated in real-time and at much lower costs, thereby reducing the costs that are required in order to find a particular good that is focus of the transaction. These authors also suggest that ICT enables an easier matching between buyers and sellers once goods have been located, and lowers the cost of brokerage. Wigand (1997) posits technology and ICT as enabling the design and deliberate strategic deployment of linkages and networks among cooperating firms intending to achieve joint strategic goals to gain competitive advantage.

Benjamin and Wigand (1995a) discuss how ICT can reduce transaction costs by decreasing coordination costs within the value chain, resulting in benefits for consumers through lower prices. Additionally, producers/retailers can reduce their intermediation and coordination costs. Bakos (1991, 1998) depicts the effect of ICT on electronic markets through its impact on search costs in particular, with a resulting reduction in transaction costs occurring when subsequent exchanges take place in electronic markets.

These various approaches addressing the impact of ICT on transaction costs underestimate the effects of the interdependence among contributory factors. By considering these interdependencies and their combined effects on transaction costs, an assessment can occur of the real effects of ICT on the reduction of these costs.

TCT is grounded in the assumption that the relationship between human and environmental factors is the reason transaction costs increase in the economic system. This is, however, not the only reason why these costs exist. The interdependence of factors contributing to transaction costs can contribute to their increase. Attempts to reduce transaction costs should not aim to reduce the effect of a single factor, but the effects of the interdependencies between factors. Transactions costs are not only the sum of the costs generated by the different factors, but are influenced by the imbricate, interdependent relationship between them. The effect of ICT on transaction costs must be studied by assessing this imbrication. Research in information systems has mainly focused on the first approach. Illustrations of the second can be found in principal agent theory (Grossman and Hart, 1983; Laffont and Martimort, 2002).

The following section extends Ciborra's (1993) notions on TCT and ICT, discussing the effects of ICT on transaction costs by not only considering the factors contributing to transaction costs, but also their interdependencies. This will provide a richer theory in order to understand if ICT is, ceteris paribus, always lowering transaction costs.

Re-thinking ICT's effects on transaction costs

When scholars state that ICT reduces transaction costs by affecting constitutive elements of a transaction such as search, negotiation and enforcement, they usually assess the effect of ICT on one specific transactional problem. For example, ICT can reduce search costs by increasing the amount of information available and the speed at which it is collected and processed (Bakos, 1991, 1998; Ciborra, 1993). However, IS studies that consider the interdependencies among the factors contributing to transaction costs and the effect of ICT on these interdependencies are rare. Ciborra (1993) highlights this problem when pointing out that positive and negative externalities are associated with the use and adoption of ICT in organizations. He does not discuss this issue in detail, however. This paper discusses the implication this concept can have for the further development of research on TCT and ICT. To accomplish this, externalities are explored that are generated by the interdependence of the factors contributing to transaction costs and the effects ICT can have on these externalities are discussed.

This approach embodies the notion that transaction costs are not the sum of the costs generated by the single factors, but rather, are the result of the interlinked relationships between them: they do not sum each other and are functionally interdependent. A simple example is presented that reflects how ICT can reduce uncertainty and increase the amount of information available while augmenting complexity. Transactions take place in settings where human and environmental uncertainties are not isolated but intertwined. Ciborra (1993) posited that ICT reduces transaction costs if the resources it consumes are less than the transaction costs it generates. The reduction of transaction costs occurs only if certain conditions are met, with these unlikely to occur through chance.

When assessing the impact of ICT, an understanding of the interdependencies and imbrication of the factors contributing to transaction costs produces a clearer picture of the problems inherent in the evaluation of the economic consequences of ICT adoption. When the aim is, for example, to understand the effects of ICT on transaction costs, the impact of environmental complexity on transactions needs to occur, due to bounded rationality. If economic agents have infinite computational capabilities, then complexity and coordination costs should not affect the transaction costs. At the same time, environmental uncertainty, information asymmetry and asset specificity affect the transaction because of the risk derived through opportunistic behaviour. The factors are deeply interdependent and when one increases or decreases, this variation requires analysis in relation to the effects reflected in the interdependencies among all of the various factors.

Adopting an analytical perspective congruent with the one proposed by Ciborra (1993), namely that TCT is applicable in depicting the process of designing information technologies, an exploration can occur on what conditions are required to successfully design ICT that reduce transaction costs. The effect of ICT in reducing the impact of any of the factors contributing to transaction cost has to occur in light of the overall consequences that a solution has on the set of interdependencies that generate transaction costs. The impact of the adoption of ICT can be negative as a result of unplanned consequences produced by these interdependencies. The nature and direction of these effects cannot always be considered positive and unidirectional. As already outlined (Cordella, 2001), ICT does not always positively impact transaction costs. The interdependencies between human and environmental factors have to be made explicit in order to assess if the impact of ICT will produce an overall positive or negative effect.

Following the depiction of the three major phases of transactions and the associated costs proposed by Ciborra (1993), a more relevant description of the possible cross-effects of ICT can occur. This facilitates better positioning while designing ICT that aims to reduce these costs. The following presents an overview of the three phases of search costs, negotiation costs and enforcement costs:

Search costs

ICT can lower search costs only if the increased amount of information and/or speed in its exchange is balanced by an equal increase in its ability to manage, process and evaluate that information[2] (Malone et al., 1987). Greater information results in lower uncertainty but greater complexity. The effect of ICT on this phase of the transaction is positive only if the increased information flow is equally balanced by an improvement in the ability to manage it. When this does not occur the costs required to manage the increased information flow provided by ICT will be greater than the advantage supplied by this new information. This will result in a negative effect of ICT, leading to higher transaction costs. The positive effects of ICT on search costs have often been discussed in terms of disintermediation of the exchange processes. Traditionally, intermediaries are considered a necessary transaction costs that has to be incurred in order to reduce the search costs for sourcing and retrieving information. To complete an exchange, the collection of information regarding available options is required, in addition to the location of the goods and their characteristics. Malone et al. (1987) highlight that ICT can lower these costs by making the retrieval process easier and cheaper while providing additional information on the characteristics of the goods. Once acquired, ICT does for free what intermediaries do for a fee. One of the most visible consequences of the diffusion of ICT in electronic markets is the disintermediation of these markets (Malone et al., 1987; Benjamin and Wigand, 1995b; Chircu and Kauffman, 1999).

The above conclusion is predicated on the assumption that ICT reduces the transaction costs of electronic markets by making more information available at a lower cost while making the task of processing the information easier and cheaper. The literature does not in general consider cross-effects in cost benefit analyses, with different conclusions reached that discuss the case of re-intermediation as it occurs in electronic markets (Bakos, 1991; Sarkar et al., 1995). Bailey and Bakos (1997), studying 13 different firms participating in electronic markets, find evidence for the emerging roles of new intermediaries. This implies that disintermediation does not occur and new transaction costs emerge as consequence of the digitalization of the marketplace. The most direct effect of this digitalization on search costs is the problem of matching buyers and sellers. Electronic marketplaces are bigger and more dispersed, making it more difficult to retrieve information about the available goods and their characteristics.

As a result of ICT, customers have access to a greater number of goods and considerable information about these goods. Empirical work by Bailey and Bakos (1997) reveals that this can lead to ambiguous results: 'on one hand lower search costs will reduce the importance of intermediaries by allowing buyers to search directly for appropriate suppliers, while on the other hand the overwhelming abundance of information offered by internet-based market infrastructure my increase the need for intermediaries that can help to match customers and suppliers by filtering information,' (Bailey and Bakos, 1997). This scenario leads to greater transaction costs. What Bailey and Bakos (1997) discover through empirical evidence is presented theoretically in this paper. Namely, once ICT is implemented in order to lower transaction costs, the externalities of the cross-effects of the interdependencies among the factors contributing to transaction costs may be negative, resulting in the overall effect of the adoption of ICT being negative: under this scenario, transaction costs increase rather than decrease.

Negotiation costs

These are the costs of executing the transaction and may include commission costs, the costs of physically negotiating the terms of an exchange, the costs of formally drawing up contracts, and others. Within this stage, better control over the transaction can occur through the use of ad hoc ICT applications, in term of quality evaluation and service provisioning[3] (Malone et al., 1987). A more sophisticated inventory system can reduce the costs associated with the management of transactions when goods require delivery according to specific contractual requirements. Ad hoc systems can be designed to facilitate the evaluation of the services purchased. However, the evaluation of this effect of ICT on the transaction cannot be fully assessed without considering the costs associated with new coordination requirements that emerge as a consequence of the adoption of the ICT application. Moreover, in changing the distribution of information among economic actors, ICT can alter the information symmetry between them, increasing or decreasing it, and offering new opportunities for opportunistic behaviour; what Williamson (1975) defines as conditions of information impactedness. The effects of ICT on this phase of the transaction have to be considered within the associated effects on the interdependent factors. A positive balance is reached if all of the factors are counterbalanced and aligned. It cannot be taken for granted that this always occurs.

Bakos (1998) argues that electronic marketplaces, as physical markets, need to fix prices in order to process transactions, manage inventories, guarantee quality and to monitor the process of transacting. These needs provide a fertile platform for the proliferation of new intermediaries that facilitate these activities in global, bounded-less electronic marketplaces. Sarkar et al. (1995) presents extensive analysis of the process that redesigns the organization of intermediaries in electronic marketplaces. Criticizing the conclusion reached by Benjamin and Wigand (1995a) on the effect of disintermediation in digital markets, they show that the number of intermediaries and their role can increase, potentially leading to higher negotiation costs for the agents that exchange in those markets. The assessment of the effects of the introduction of ICT on transaction costs is once again complex and not unidirectional. Any analysis of this impact must consider the cross-effects and externalities associated with attempts to overcome the limits of the analyses that assume that a change in the exchange channel structure does not have effects on the redistribution of the welfare among the agents that use this structure (Sen and King, 2003).

Enforcement costs

The costs in this phase encompasses those incurred by the buyers and sellers in order to ensure that the virtual goods and services they transact, and the terms under which the transaction is made, are translated into physical goods and services. This encompasses any negotiations that address inadequate delivery, payment disputes, and any investment undertaken to ensure unsatisfied buyers and sellers have their issues remedied through the enforcement of their initial contract. As was evident in the previous two phases, ICT can provide a more efficient environment for the enforcement of the exchange process by facilitating a match between contractual agreements. ICTs can also assist in the process and subsequent monitoring of quality certification. In this scenario, radio tags facilitate the monitoring of production and distribution, making it easier to control the quality of goods. Moreover, ICT can make the information exchange between the parties more expedient, efficient and extensive, increasing the links between them and the resulting quality of the information flaw underpinning the exchange process[4] (Malone et al., 1987). In this scenario, a positive result occurs only if solutions exist to manage the enriched information setting provided by ICT. The enhanced communication flow with additional information increases the requirement for coordination. This scenario can alter the information symmetry and the prospects and risks associated with opportunistic behaviour. The effect of ICT can be positive if specific conditions are matched.

The globalization of the digital economy increases the complexity and the uncertainty in the enforcement of contractual agreements (Milosevic et al., 2003). From the transaction costs perspective this more complex and uncertain environment also makes the definition of contractual agreements more difficult and expensive. Angelov and Grefen (2003) depict that the increased complexity and uncertainty faced by companies in digital markets are the reasons for the increased number of contracts established by companies trading in these markets. In extreme cases, these authors argue that a situation of 'contract overload' has occurred. Daskalopulu and Sergot (1997) provide evidence highlighting the increased complexity of the content of these contracts, which supports the argument presented in this paper: higher costs will be incurred in order to stipulate the use of contracts under these conditions. A greater number of contracts coupled with increased complexity leads to higher transaction costs. An increased number of contracts create the need for a company to invest in contract management systems. The increased complexity of contractual agreements has therefore necessitated investment in technological solutions that facilitate the establishment and execution of electronic contracts (Allen and Widdison, 1996; Merz et al., 1998). Once again, the cross-effects of the adoption of ICT are difficult to assess.

As argued by Ciborra (1993) the evaluation of the effects of ICT on the economic system must take into consideration the socio-technical context within which the transactions occur. Similarly, Lacity and Willcocks (1995) argue that transactions occur in dynamic environments that change over time, rendering it difficult to take decisions that minimize transaction costs without considering the context within which these transactions occurs.

Conclusions and implications for ICT strategies

The transaction costs approach is a powerful theory that describes the potential of information technology to improve information flow and to reduce transaction costs, thereby improving the efficiency of the economic system. This paper has, however, shown that in order to achieve this goal, a more informed approach to the study of the effects of ICT is required. Transaction costs in fact often increase as a consequence of the adoption of ICT. Lower transaction costs can be achieved when the costs associated with ICT adoption do not exceed the cost of the externalities that are affected by this adoption. When this occurs, the usefulness of the strategy producing such a result has expired.

This paper has shown that the externalities linked to ICT can alter from being positive, to becoming negative. The adoption of ICT in this setting will result in significantly increased transaction costs because of the associated extra costs required to accommodate the more complex environment that emerges as a consequence of the effects of externalities. The use of information technology will subsequently be unable to establish the conditions for a more efficient economic system, but will contribute to the creation of electronic disorder and sub-optimal economic results. Accordingly, the use of ICT may present diseconomies of scale when the externalities associated with its diffusion reach a particular level (Cordella, 2001).

The traditional strategy of ICT adoption, based on transaction cost theory utilizing ICT to increase information availability, is undoubtedly efficient when accelerating and increasing the amount of information available and its exchange. ICT makes economic exchanges easier and more efficient, reducing search, negotiation and enforcement costs.

In order to account for the consequences of ICT, externalities, and the associated effects on the coordination of exchanges, an approach other than the traditional one has to be identified. This is required in order to avoid the failure of the economic system as a consequence of high search, negotiation and enforcement costs. By reducing the amount of information, filtering it appropriately, and reducing coordination needs, it is possible to decrease costs while maintaining an efficient economic system when these conditions are met.

The ideas proposed in this paper offer a theoretical explanation for the proliferation of alternative, sometimes opposite strategies, in the design and adoption of ICT to reduce transaction costs. These strategies either conceive ICT as a powerful instrument that increases the amount of information managed in support of transacting on economic exchanges, or see ICT as a powerful tool to reduce the complexity and the amount of information to be considered while transacting.

Notes

This paper originally appeared as Cordella, C. (2006) Transaction costs and information systems: does IT add up? *Journal of Information Technology* **21**(3): 195–202.

1. This is a significant point that will be iterated later in this paper when a discussion occurs of the development of the ideas first produced by Ciborra, in relation to the introduction of ICT as possible instruments in lowering transaction costs.
2. What Malone et al. (1987) call 'electronic communication effect'.
3. What Malone et al. describe as brokerage effect (op cit).
4. What Malone et al. define as electronic integration effect (op cit).

References

Alchian, A. and Demsetz, H. (1972). Production, Information Costs, and Economic Organization, *American Economic Review* **62**: 777–792.

Allen, T. and Widdison, R. (1996). Can Computers Make Contracts, *Harvard Journal of Law and Technology* **9**: 25–52.

Angelov, S. and Grefen, P. (2003). The 4W Framework for B2B E-Contracting, *International Journal of Networking and Virtual Organization* **1**: 78–97.
Bailey, J. and Bakos, J.Y. (1997). An Exploratory Study of the Emerging Role of Electronic Intermediaries, *International Journal of Electronic Commerce* **1**: 7–20.
Bakos, J.Y. (1991). A Strategic Analysis of Electronic Marketplaces, *MIS Quarterly* **15**: 295–310.
Bakos, J.Y. (1998). Towards Friction-Free Markets: The Emerging Role of Electronic Marketplaces on the Internet, *Communications of the ACM* **41**(8): 35–42.
Bakos, J.Y. and Brynjolfsson, E. (1997). Organisational Partnerships and the Virtual Corporation, in C. Kramer (ed.) *Information Technology and Industrial Competitiveness: How Information Technology Shapes Competition*, Dordrecht, Boston MA: Kluwer Academic Publishers.
Barney, J. and Ouchi, W.G. (eds) (1986). *Organisational Economics: Toward A New Paradigm for Understanding and Studying Organizations*, San Francisco, CA: Jossey-Bass.
Bauer, M. and Cohen, D. (1983). The Invisibility of Power in Economics: Beyond market and Hierarchies, in A. Francis, J. Turk and P. William (eds) *Power, Efficiency, and Institutions*, London: Hienemann.
Benjamin, R. and Wigand, R. (1995a). Electronic Markets and Virtual Value Chains on the Information Superhighway, *Sloan Management Review* **36**: 62–72.
Benjamin, R.I. and Wigand, R. (1995b). Electronic Market and Virtual Value Chains on the Information Superhighway, *Sloan Management Review* **36**: 62–72.
Braddach, J. and Eccles, R. (1989). Price, Authority and Trust: From Ideal Types to Plural Forms, *Annual Review of Sociology* **15**: 97–118.
Brynjolfsson, E., Malone, T., Gurbaxani, V. and Kambil, A. (1994). Does Information Technology Lead to Smaller Firms? *Management Science* **40**(12): 1628–1645.
Chircu, A. and Kauffman, R. (1999). Analyzing Firm-Level Strategy for Internet-Focused, 32nd Hawaii International Conference on System Science.
Ciborra, C.U. (1981). Markets, Bureaucracies and Groups in the Information Society, *Information Economics and Policy* **1**: 145–160.
Ciborra, C.U. (1993). *Teams Markets and Systems*, Cambridge: Cambridge University Press.
Ciborra, C.U. and Associates (2000). *From Control to Drift*, Oxford: Oxford University Press.
Ciborra, C.U. (2006). Imbrication of Representations: Risk and Digital Technologies, *Journal of Management Studies* 43(6): 1339–1356.
Ciborra, C.U. and Hanseth, O. (1998). From Tool to Gestell, *Information Technology and People* **11**: 305–327.
Coase, R.H. (1937). The Nature of the Firm, *Economica* **4**: 386–405.
Collin, S.V. (1993). The Brotherhood of the Swedish Sphere: A Third Institutional form for Economic Exchange, *International Studies of Management and Organization* **23**(1): 69–86.
Collin, S.V. and Larsson, R. (1993). Beyond Markets and Hierarchies: A Swedish Quest for a Tripolar Institutional Framework, *International Studies of Management and Organization* **23**(1): 3–12.
Cordella, A. (2001). Does Information Technology Always Lead to Lower Transaction Costs? European Conference in Information Systems, Bled.
Daskalopulu, A. and Sergot, M.J. (1997). The Representation of Legal Contracts, *AI and Society* **11**(1/2): 6–17.
Dietrich, M. (1994). *Transaction Costs Economies and Beyond*, London: Routledge.
Dugger, W. (1983). The Transaction Costs Analysis of Oliver E. Williamson: A New Synthesis? *Journal of Economic Issues* **17**: 95–114.
Elg, U. and Johansson, U. (1993). The Institutions of Industrial Governance, *International Studies of Management and Organization* **23**: 29–46.
Etzioni, A. (1988). *The Moral Dimension: Towards a New Economies*, New York: Free Press.
Francis, A. (1983). Market and Hierarchies: Efficiency or domination?, in A. Francis, J. Turk and P. William (eds) *Power, Efficiency, an Institutions*, London: Hienemann.

Grossman, S. and Hart, O. (1983). An Analysis of the Principal-Agent Problem, *Econometrica* **51**: 7–46.
Hayek, F. (1945). The Use of Knowledge in Society, *American Economic Review* **35**: 519–530.
Lacity, M. and Willcocks, L. (1995). Interpreting Information Technology Sourcing Decisions from a Transaction Cost Perspective: Findings and Critique, *Accounting Management and Information Technology* **5**: 203–244.
Laffont, J.-J. and Martimort, D. (2002). *The Theory of Incentives: The Principal-Agent Model,* Princeton, NJ: Princeton University Press.
Lewis, D. (1996). *Dying for Information,* Reuters Business Information.
Malone, T.W., Yates, J. and Benjamin, R.I. (1987). Electronic Markets and Electronic Hierarchies: Effects of Information Technology on Market Structure and Corporate Strategies, *Communications of the ACM* **30**: 484–497.
Merz, M., Griffel, F., Tu, T., Muller-Wilken, S., Weinreich, H., Boger, M. and Lamersdorf, W. (1998). Supporting Electronic Commerce Transactions with Contracting Services, *International Journal on Cooperative Information Systems* **7**: 249–274.
Milosevic, Z., Jøsang, A., Dimitrakos, T. and Patton, M. (2003). Discretionary Enforcement of Electronic Contracts, in Proceedings of the Sixth International Enterprise Distributed Object Computing Conference (Lausanne, Switzerland, 2002), pp. 39–50.
Moe, T.M. (1984). The New Economics of Organization, *American Journal of Political Science* **28**(4): 739–777.
Palme, J. (1984). You Have 134 Unread mail! Do You Want to Read Them Now? IFIP WG 6.5 Working conference on computer-based document services, Nottingham.
Perrow, C. (1986). *Complex Organizations,* New Your: Random House.
Sarkar, M.B., Butler, B. and Steinfield, C. (1995). Intermediaries and Cybermediaries: A Continuing Role for Mediating Players in the Electronic Marketplace, *Journal of Computer-Mediated Communication*: http://www.ascusc.org/jcmc/vol1/issue3/vol1no3.html.
Schultze, U. and Vandenbosch, B. (1998). Information Overload in a Groupware Environment: Now You See It, Now You Don't, *Journal of Organizational Computing and Electronic Commerce* **8**(2): 127–148.
Sen, R. and King, R.C. (2003). Revisit the Debate on Intermediation, Disintermediation and Reintermediation due to E-commerce, *Electronic Markets* **13**(2): 153–163.
Varian, H.R. (1992). *Microeconomic Analysis,* Norton: London.
Wigand, R. (1997). Electronic Commerce: Definitions, Theory, and Context, *The Information Society* **13**: 1–16.
Wigand, R.T., Picot, A. and Reichwald, R. (1997). *Information, Organisation, and Management: Expanding Markets and Corporate Boundaries,* New York: Wiley, Chichester.
Williamson, O.E. (1975). Market *and Hierarchies: Analysis and Antitrust Implications,* New York: Free Press.
Williamson, O.E. (1985). *The Economic Institutions of Capitalism: Firms, Markets, Relational Contracting,* Collier Macmillan, New York, London: Free Press.
Zuboff, S. (1988). *In the Age of the Smart Machine,* New York: Basic Books, Inc.

19

Dispositioning IT All: Towards a Theory for Thriving without Models

Ian O. Angell and Fernando M. Ilharco†*

Abstract

Against the background of Heidegger's *Being and Time*, we take the ancient Chinese philosophy of chance, together with some core insights from Clausewitz's *On War*, in order to claim that it is the way in which a company is *already* disposed that opens up opportunities for a competitive edge over its rivals. We remind that any specific organization *already* exists, and as such it already has a disposition towards its environment; it is already committed in a self-meaningful manner towards its own survival and prosperity. We contend that plans, intentions, or technologies do not drive action, but rather the disposition in which the company, as a whole, grasps the environment, and from which it assesses its possibilities for profit. We submit that the central notion of *disposition*, introduced in this paper, best serves us in coping and profiting in a world now entangled in information and communication technologies.

Preamble

Much has been written about Claudio Ciborra's ability to inspire both colleagues and students. That inspiration stemmed from his personality, his radical thinking, his iconoclasm, and his drive to 'overturn the tables' (Nietzsche, 1968). His rejection of control, in *From Control to Drift* (Ciborra and Associates, 2000), and his emphasis on bricolage, did much to stimulate the present authors to produce two papers to date, of which this is the second.

Introduction

Many tenets of current mainstream techno-functionalist thinking about organizations, in particular when related to information technology and information systems (IT/IS) do not stand up to rigorous scrutiny (Angell and Ilharco, 2004). Ciborra's contribution in contemporary research is an important mark on this aspect; his work *The Labyrinths of Information* (Ciborra, 2002) is a seminal reference in the subject. On balance, after more than three centuries of positivism, we are left with a world marked not by solutions, but by problems. Indeed, we go as far as to claim that the search for 'solutions' is the real problem of our times! For in this paper we argue that the very concept of solution is unhelpful...we reject the approach that a world so complex, turbulent and novel as ours can be 'solved.' This problem/solution dichotomy is an inheritance of the industrial age, now gone; a dichotomy that, in its turn, relies on a Cartesian dualist approach to being.

In this paper, following a previous work (Angell and Ilharco, 2004), we challenge the state of affairs referred to above, both in terms of its appearances and assumptions. Much in the way Ciborra (1997a, 1998b, 2002) asked researchers and practitioners to address organizational issues, we call for a *krisis*, 'a pulling apart, a separating' from current exact science-based approaches to human action, towards an acceptance of the foundational role of everyday life in creation, development and management of systems and organizations (Ciborra, 2002: 15). We aim to point out a world we already know, where people, notions, feelings, involvements, events happen, change, surprise us, disappear, and come again into being. We intend to present a narrative, not typified by problems and solutions, but instead relying on an intuitive, open-minded and enlightened grasping of transitions and chance, learning and change, action and opportunities. We call this approach *dispositioning* – a theory for thriving without solutions: a theory in which there are no solutions, only decisions, which are circumscribed by a particular entity's disposition.

Theoretically we support our position with an ontological approach based on Martin Heidegger's (1889–1976) phenomenology of being human (Heidegger, 1962) – very briefly reviewed below – and on Nietzsche's post-nihilist thought. From here, within this fundamental context, referring to key pieces of Ciborra's work, we aim at presenting a narrative that makes sense to you, the reader, as you already are in-the-world. We maintain with this paper that the urge of managers to search for solutions is inappropriate in the current ambiguous, complex and chaotic world. That is not to say that we should just give up at the futility of it all. On the contrary, in this present paper we propose *dispositioning*, an approach that we assert will lead on to new opportunities, and help managers thrive and profit in contemporary business, political and social environments.

In-the-worldness

Individually, we, the beings we ourselves are, are already acting in the world. Our own way of *be-ing* in the world is that which is essential about the being we are. Man is a being-in-the-world – this grounding claim, introduced and detailed by Heidegger in his seminal work *Being and Time* (ibid.), is the key ontological foundation of this paper. From this base we will then take the ancient Chinese notion of *shi*, and some insights from Clausewitz (1976) *On War*, to develop our position on strategy and tactics, via the introduction of our notion of disposition.

According to these foundations, we assume that our need to act is the ground for our actions, thoughts, intentions and interpretations, as well as the usefulness thereof, much in the way Heidegger (1962), Nietzsche (1968), Wittgenstein (1967), and others have claimed, suggested and implied. We are always and already in action, using usefulness or appropriateness as a criterion, and so this paper proposes a new overall approach to the way in which organizations might thrive in a world that is immersed in information and communication technologies, and characterized by ambiguity and risk. Always and already in-the-world (Heidegger, 1962), we are experts in acting. Immersed in-the-world we always and already understand (that is, are disposed towards) the world and ourselves (Heidegger, 1962). Intuitively, dealing with beings as ready-to-hand entities, we tend to repeat what has worked previously (Maturana and Varela, 1980, 1992) – 'in warfare [or in economic competition], if a certain means turns out to be highly effective, it will be used again' (Clausewitz, 1976: 171). This tendency shapes our structures, moulds our disposition, affects our mood, and as such it opens specific possibilities for us to act in the future. 'The socially transmitted attitudes, beliefs, and preferred modes of action that collectively constitute culture are neither casual nor random choices. Cultural attributes usually point to ideas and activities that have worked well for a society' (Gray, 1994: 579).

We recall that a human is a 'who', not a thing or an object (Heidegger, 1962). What most distinguishes we humans from other beings, is precisely the 'who' that we are. Each human lives his or her life in its being-ness, bringing forth a world that matters to him or to her. A person is a performer of acts, which are something non-physical – 'a person exists only in the performance of intentional acts, and is therefore essentially *not* an object' (Heidegger, 1962: 73). Each of us is unique, with his own past, intentions, aims, objectives and experiences, his own biological, physical and mental structures. Each of us is a private and personal perspective of it all.

We, as individuals, develop numerous schemas corresponding to different perspectives, different resolutions, different metaphors, and different purposes, each limited from its very creation by the appropriateness of its application. They are all superimposed onto a totality from which we can each choose appropriately to deal with any particular situation. We are *thrown throwers* (Heidegger, 1999) – we must choose. That is, as a *who* I find myself *thrown* into the world, always and already with a past I cannot leave, *throwing* projections, ambitions, and my will into my own future. In action I choose already, transparently, intuitively, and instinctively, most of the time. 'One responds on the basis of a vast past experience of what has happened in previous situations, or more exactly, one's comportment manifests dispositions that have been shaped by a vast amount of previous dealings, so that in most cases when we exercise these dispositions everything works the way it should' (Dreyfus, 1991: 68). Hence, it is impossible to separate the observer from the observed. As observers of ourselves we cannot get it all: no system can totally describe itself (Gödel, 1992). We are each our own issue, and that is what is most essential for us (Heidegger, 1962).

Disposition

Let us now clarify our use of the word disposition, as it relates to an organization-in-the-world. A disposition to act is an implicit systemic property of every organization, perhaps even the very essence of being an organization, and the clue to the identity of its reference state by which an observer chooses to identify and classify it as an organization (Angell and Smithson, 1991). It is the faculty of setting the organization in an order, or the condition of being set in order – namely the situation and position of the elements of the whole, relative to itself and to its environment. It is the due arrangement of the several parts of an organization in reference to its general systemic structure, and especially for the accomplishment of a purpose. This arrangement can be predisposed for tactical action. Disposition can be the distribution of systemic components, their allocation, destination, preparations or measures taken, the arrangement of systemic duties, or the condition or complexion of affairs. It relates to the ordering, control, management, direction, appointment, administration and dispensation of the components. It is the way or manner in which an organization has been disposed, or is situated or constituted, as some kind of situation that comes from the unplanned *shift and drift* (Ciborra, 2000) of the organization, that determines whether the nature or the course of events is perceived either as possible or impossible, and subsequently either as an opportunity or as a threat. Those natures, tendencies, qualities or constitutions of an organization are considered in relation to its apparent or observed influence. Disposition is an inclination, intention, aptitude, capacity or purpose; it is the condition of the organization *being,* that is, it is an organization's essence in Heidegger's (1962) sense, disposed (favourably or unfavourably) towards its environment. A disposition is thus a permanent, normal, natural, and a decisive condition that is always and already there. Different from a mood, disposition is a permanent and structural ability, talent, or genius (or the opposite: disability, lack of talent, idiocy) that a person or an organization might or not have, might or not develop.

We want to stress that the organization does not disposition itself as if towards some concrete situation as it happens. On the contrary, it is already (pre-)disposed to whatever situation comes into play. An account of the etymology of the word disposition confirms our claim. Disposition, as a noun, means the act or the power of disposing, or the state of being disposed, or a final or an orderly arrangement (MW, 2002). It means also a prevailing tendency, mood, sentiment, or inclination, or a temperamental makeup, or the tendency of something to act in a certain manner under given circumstances (MW, 2002). In the human individual, temperament, temper, character, personality are synonymous with disposition (MW, 2002), and we choose to extend these personal traits to a collective of individuals: the organization. By our use of the infinitive 'to dispose', we mean to give a tendency to, to place, to distribute, to put in place, to set in readiness, or to arrange, especially in an orderly way, e.g. *disposing* troops for withdrawal (MW, 2002).[1]

Disposition and to dispose have been English words since the fourteenth century, coming from Middle English, Middle French, and from the Latin *disposition-, dispositio,* which in turn came from *disponere,* which meant to arrange. That latter Latin word joined the prefix *dis-* with the word *ponere.* The contemporary English prefix dis- originated from the Old French prefix *des-/dis-*, meaning not, do the opposite of, opposite or absence of, deprive of, exclude or expel from. This Old French prefix in its turn came from the Latin *dis-*, which literally meant apart (MW, 2002). *Ponere* meant to put, to lay down, to place (MW, 2002), and is assumed to have its origins in the Old Latin *posinere,* which in its turn joined the prefix *po-*, meaning away, akin to the ancient Greek *apo*, to the Latin verb *sinere,* which meant to leave (MW, 2002). Thus, the actual English word position, which comes from the Latin *ponere* (MW, 2002), has a root meaning of *away from leaving,* that is, something that did not leave or is made not to leave, something that is already there. Therefore the meaning of disposition has grounding in something apart from being positioned, that is, in something that is not positioned. Yet, as we saw above, it is also something that is made not to leave, or did not leave. Thus, disposition as something present and not positioned, is something that is already present, already there, disposed in its togetherness; in fact, this latter signification is supported in that the Latin prefix *dis-* is akin to the Latin word *duo* and to the ancient Greek word *dyo* (MW, 2002), which meant two, both or together (Crane, 2002). These ideas link well with the use we make, in line with the way Ciborra (1996, 2002) worked it out, of the Chinese notion of *shi*, which we discuss below.

To summarize, disposition is an *always already there*, which matters, and on which we rely, or more precisely on which we are already relying as the beings we ourselves are, and are becoming. It is the way in which we are disposed that shows up each situation either as a threat or an opportunity, either as a possibility or not – such is the deeper meaning that we want to recover in our usage of the word disposition. Disposition is a permanent, natural and decisive condition, in that it reveals, shapes and conditions not only our actions, but also whatever we might distinguish, either calling it data or information, or just relying instinctively and intuitively while focusing our attention on something else.

Propensity

From this fundamental position we now explain our approach to the contemporary question of competition by taking advantage of ancient Chinese philosophy and focusing on the insights of Sun Tzu (1994), as well as bringing in ideas on strategy from Clausewitz (1976). Of course neither Sun Tzu nor Clausewitz's ideas can be literally translated, either into our language or our era, without losing much of their value, but nevertheless we have much to learn from their essence.

The particular Chinese word *shi* might serve us well as a clue into an appropriate perspective from which to make sense of Sun Tzu's account of strategy. This word *shi*, much used in his works, has no direct and clear translation (Julien, 1999), although most often it is translated as the 'strategic configuration of power'. Julien (1999: 267) recalls that the term *shi* is believed literally to represent a hand holding something, as a symbol of power. He suggests it might symbolize something put into a position, or positioning. *Shi* has both a spatial and a temporal connotation, and should, in many cases, be understood as something like opportunity or chance. *Shi* is not a philosophical or technical concept in the sense of the Western sciences (ibid.: 12). 'It is a simple, practical term, forged initially for the purposes of strategy .and politics' (ibid.). Ciborra first brought this notion to our attention, when he wrote that an organization is powerful when 'it embeds the potential for action. It seeks out the intrinsic dispositions of resources so that they can be recombined when needed more quickly and effectively' (Ciborra, 2002: 122).

The perspective underlying the word *shi* lies in stark contrast to the dominant relevance of causality, the grounding presupposition of much of current mainstream thinking in both IT/IS as well as in management in general. *Shi* implies a different kind of ontology, one that is entirely consistent with the theoretical foundations on which we base this paper. *Shi* assumes that reality is perceived as a closed system, in which each situation has its own propensity and tendencies (ibid.: 221). '[T]he sequence of changes taking place stems entirely from the power relations inherent in the initial situations' (ibid.). Yet the causal relationship is not totally ignored; it is relegated to a 'framework of experience taking place in front of us, where its impact is immediate' (ibid.: 220). *Shi* obliges us to deny an 'imagined series of causes and effects extending all the way back to the hidden reason for things or even to the principle underlying reality as a whole' (ibid.), and to stick to the fundamental, not 'the methodologies or the models, past and future, [but] the trying out itself, the relentless experimenting and not the specific, contingent approach being implemented at a given moment in time' (Ciborra, 2002: 119). A Nietzsche's (1974, n.112) comment clarifies this aspect:

> Cause and effect: such a duality probably never occurs – in reality there stands before us a continuum of which we isolate a couple of pieces; just as we always perceive a moment only as isolated points, therefore do not really see it but infer it. The suddenness with which many events rise up leads us astray: but it happens suddenly only for us. There is an infinite host of occurrences in this sudden second which eludes us.

In trying to grasp the possibilities of the word *shi*, Julien (ibid.) recalls that Chinese thought typically implies an indifference to any notion of a final ending for things. It seeks to interpret reality 'solely on the basis of itself, from the perspective of a single logic inherent in the actual processes in motion'. He analyses the word *shi*, and its self-evident nature to the Chinese (ibid.: 17) in several domains of human activity, namely the political, the military, the aesthetics of calligraphy, painting, literature, history and philosophy. We will concentrate on Julien's analysis in the military domain, where he addresses the phenomenon of strategy.

This approach challenges the traditional Western assumption of the relevance between means and ends in explaining human action. Western philosophical and scientific thought is mainly based on Cartesian epistemologies, which, in turn, rely on Aristotle's notion of the *animal rational*, and on the conception of Being as actuality. This conception holds causality as an evident principle of understanding. Such epistemologies consider that in order to have fundamental knowledge of anything we must acknowledge that there is a cause to every event; and it is that cause that makes the event necessary and therefore – hopefully – predictable. According to Aristotle (1963: 194b) '[w]e never reckon that we understand a thing till we can give an account of its "how and why," that is, of its first cause'.

Shi implies a different ontology from that of causality. The key conjecture that shapes the ancient Chinese strategic thought is that what is worth questioning is not the world as such, in its presupposed objectivity, but rather 'the source of efficacy that is at work everywhere in reality and the best way to profit from it' (Julien, 1999: 262). Therefore, the primary question for us, and the key question we approach in this paper, is not how we plan and implement our options, but how we maintain or develop a useful disposition so that we retain our capacity to function. This approach was illuminated by the notions of bricolage and improvisation set out in Ciborra (2002).

The Chinese ontological assumptions that ground the notion of *shi* lead to the strategic notion that the *potential* of armies, governments, organizations and all powers in general, is *born of their disposition* when engaging each particular situation. The commander must aim at exploiting, 'to his own advantage and to maximum effect, whatever conditions he encounters' (Julien, 1999: 27). Among other factors, as each situation is unique and unrepeatable, a disposition is born out of the conditions of the land, the morale of the troops, the climate, the degrees of organization, and so forth. 'Mere numerical advantage gives way before these superior, more decisive conditions' (ibid.: 28). As part of a situation the commander must stretch his forces to a maximum in order to take advantage of it: '*shi* is like a crossbow stretched to its maximum' (ibid.: 28); 'Their [of those that excel in warfare] strategic configuration of power (*shih*) is like a fully drawn crossbow, their constraints like the release of the trigger' (Sun Tzu, 1994: 187).

Chinese thought on war stands in stark contrast to the ancient Greek vision of the hero, which has confrontation at its heart (ibid.). From the Chinese perspective, the concrete situation in all its configurations, tendencies and surprises, is what counts most in strategic thought. 'Chinese strategy aimed to use every possible means to influence the potential inherent in the forces at play to its own advantage, even *before* the actual engagement, so that the engagement would never constitute the decisive moment, which always involves risk' (ibid.: 35; emphasis added).

Every situation in which one finds oneself may be perceived as a particular deployment or arrangement of things to be relied on, and worked to one's advantage. Art or wisdom lies in an individual cleverly exploiting the *propensity* emanating from a particular perceived configuration of reality, to the maximum possible effect. Such a propensity designates both the particular circumstances characterizing the various stages of the processes in which the world is engaged, and the particular tendency produced in each case (Julien, 1999: 222). Every configuration of things, that is, of power, people, technologies, resources, emotions, ambitions, competitive contexts, possesses an inherent potential that is fulfilled by the manner in which those things are disposed. This manner is thus a specific tendency, a feeling of a good timing, a general atmosphere of the situation that favours particular courses of action and disfavours other options. For example, the growing uneasiness that many managers feel towards mainstream dualistic matrix models, who so readily received the contribution of Ciborra's research, contributes to a disposition of the business audience that makes room for the radical ideas expressed in this paper to get an airing.

Each situation, in its contours and possibilities, forms a *dispositif* that can be used to produce an effect. Thus, '*dispositif* refers to the efficacy of a disposition, its capacity to function spontaneously and inexhaustibly' (Julien, 1999: 9). A strategic *dispositif* is how things – people, IT, notions, products, services, and so forth – are disposed strategically so as to be effective (ibid.). 'On the one hand there is the disposition of things – their condition, configuration and structure. On the other there is force and movement' (ibid.: 11). Yet we should note that this dichotomy is abstract; it just represents reality, it is not reality.

The notion of *shi* sheds a whole new light on Sun Tzu's (1994) classic, *The Art of War*, which, contrasting with Clausewitz's (1976) theory of war, claims that armed engagements should be avoided, and that the excellence in strategy is to win without fighting (Sun Tzu, 1994). Those bound to be victorious would only combat after they are already guaranteed to triumph, while those bound to be defeated seek to win only when battle commences (Sun Tzu, 1994: 177–179; Julien, 1999: 26). This tendency towards non-confrontation in the Chinese strategic thought of the times of the Warring States (403–221BC) is not prompted by any moral concerns, but only by the resolute and pragmatic attitude of being victorious. '[E]very thing should be played out at an earlier stage in the determination of events, when dispositions and manoeuvres, at this point still solely dependent on our own initiatives, can be adjusted at will' (Julien, 1999: 26–27). Strategy was thus the art of making victories pre-determined by adapting to the circumstances and profiting from chance. One must try in advance to arrange the kind of circumstances that might lead to favourable situations. Only fight the battles you already have won (Sun Tz, 1994). How does one do that? We do not advocate recipes or formal methods. What we can and do suggest – and what we develop in this paper – is a general disposition, or more rigorously, a certain way of dispositioning that better adapts to circumstances and chance.

In such ancient Chinese strategic thought the focus was on the situation at each moment, and on its propensity. The relation between means and ends is never made explicit; it is replaced by notions of a setup and its efficacy (ibid.: 37). What counts in strategy 'is not so much the large number of troops or pure brute force but rather exploiting the potential born of disposition' (ibid.: 41). This resonates with Clausewitz's (1976) concept of friction that accounts for much of the gap between the plan drawn up in advance, which is of an ideal nature, and its practical implementation, which renders it subject to chance and surprise.

Hence the organization's strategy would be indelibly linked to its disposition towards a natural process of change, which would evolve to its advantage should it make opportune use of the propensity of the situation (ibid.: 34). A proposed strategy will only be accepted when the receiving organization is well disposed towards it, and even then it seems reasonable that more radical strategies should be introduced incrementally; evolution rather than revolution is needed to avoid the ill effects of a 'shock to the system'. Design only works if it is not contentious to the present disposition of the organization. Inappropriate strategies may result in tension and disruption within an organization. The disposition of an organization can be ill-disposed towards and resist the expansionist intentions of a new strategy; this is well documented, for example, in the case of Roche, analysed in Ciborra (2000), in which a typical strategic alignment approach to the development of an organization IT network completely failed, whereas a hands-off, *ad hoc* and bottom up approach actually achieved results that formed a successful strategy.

The *shi*-based approach is not so much focused on exact outcomes, but rather on whatever the outcomes might be, as long as they are to our advantage. Thus, it is advisable, in going with the flow, to adopt the line of least resistance so that we might more easily achieve a favourable outcome. This adaptability of ours to the outcomes indeed seems to be the proper meaning of the usage of the word 'outcomes' in Clausewitz's theory of war, as well as in the derivative strategic management theories that his book spawned. In Clausewitz's (1976) theory, the notion of friction is used to enable commanders to shift their focus from specific to more general outcomes that would be to their advantage, and that in many cases are impossible to anticipate – 'the strategist must go on campaign himself' (ibid.: 177). In the management field, the emergence of a strand of thought that favours strategy formation over strategy formulation (Mintzberg et al., 1998), that is, the emergence of strategy instead of its planning, is an example of this same shifting focus.

We recall that the challenge, according to the notion of *shi* we are introducing, is not how we plan and implement our options, but how we retain our capacity to function. We are not in control; the situation, shifting and drifting (Ciborra 2000, 2002), always leads. Outcomes cannot be foreseen. We ought not to try and change the situation, but instead profit from its own propensity and the disposition of things. This view is not strange to military strategists. On the contrary, Clausewitz (1976: 89) considers this uncertain and unpredictable character of war as the most basic and comprehensive strategic question of all. Julien (ibid.: 31–32) comments that warfare is the domain of unpredictability and chance par excellence, and thus it remains beyond the scope of theoretical predictions.

Strategic

Where does this all theorizing lead us? We suggest that by revisiting some widely used notions of management from this perspective, specifically strategy and tactics, we can constructively address a way that makes much more sense for companies to cope and thrive in today's complex, ambiguous and challenging world. It is wrong to think of strategies as merely the conscious attempts of strategists to change, to influence and to graft preconceived notions of 'generic' strategies onto the apparently blank sheet of an organization. For organizations have complex dispositions even before the strategists start, and these dispositions will evolve and emerge from human actions, with or without, even contrary to, the considered attentions of these strategists. The emergent disposition of the organization might finesse and even diametrically oppose the original intentions of the strategists, designers and planners.

We are now in a position to outline our views on these concepts, both descriptive (what we understand is happening) and normative (how things ought to be according to that understanding). Putting it simply we will be treating tactics as patterns, on the basis of which an organization acts, whereas strategy is a disposition towards pattern making. Let us go into more detail.

One thing is abundantly clear from the business literature: despite its popularity among business writers, there is no consistent use of the word strategy. This vagueness in the meaning has led to numerous observations and taxonomies, frameworks and voluminous lists of guidelines, as has been identified by leading researchers in this field (Mintzberg et al., 1998). Such approaches basically fail to provide any consistent account of the systemic nature of management.

According to the Oxford English Dictionary (1933), and very much in line with Clausewitz (1976), strategy is: 'the art of the commander-in-chief; the art of projecting and directing the larger military movements and operations in a campaign. Usually distinguished from tactics, which is the art of handling forces in a battle or in the immediate presence of the enemy'. Military strategy has been the source of numerous books from time immemorial, and the business world has zealously taken up the military metaphor. Most business writers agree with Clausewitz's (1976) observation that strategists do not achieve certainty, they only have an edge on the opposition. They concur with Napoleon's notion of strategy as 'planned flexibility', although they may shy away from his policy of selecting only the 'lucky' generals.

Tactics on the other hand are considered not nearly as important. They are 'the arrangement of procedure, the action to be taken, in order to fulfil an end or objective' (Oxford English Dictionary, 1933; entry: 'strategy'). Tactics are what lieutenants do, but strategy is the work of generals. This self-important reality may go some way towards explaining why there are so many business books on strategy, and so few on explicit tactics: a most peculiar situation, since it is the appropriateness of tactical schemas that separate success from failure in the short-term.

A tactically advantageous approach, of concentrating on previously successful procedures, can reduce internal variety and so restrict the capacity to innovate. Thus, all tactics lead to crisis if they are not abandoned in time. Tactics are meant to exploit confidence in the circumstances by prescribing potentially successful moves. They falter as soon as doubt springs from a change of circumstance. If tactics are continued despite the changing environment, they effectively prevent the manager from being innovative, as for example, when information systems change from being a competitive resource to a competitive burden. Support for this statement can be found in the careers of the champions of tactical manoeuvring, whose UK businesses performed exceptionally well during the late 1980s, but whose management skills proved strategically inept as they led their companies to bankruptcy in the 1990s, unable to find new tactics suitable for the changing business conditions. The bursting of the dot.com bubble at the beginning of the new millennium is another well-documented example of initially successful business tactics leading to disaster.

Apart from their inertial influence on decision taking, tactics may allow emergent problems to arise. Even over a short period of time, they can acquire such prominence that managers, rather than focus on the business problems at hand, are compelled to concentrate their energies on their business systems, which were originally designed to support them in dealing with those problems. Of course tactics, plans and methods have their place in day-to-day management and administration. However, action under conditions of uncertainty is essentially where the tried and tested methods do not inspire enough confidence in the application of tactics: a strategy is needed.

In this paper we primarily concentrate on the adjective 'strategic' (we believe the noun 'strategy' is of secondary importance), which describes any influence that has a lasting effect on the disposition of an organization. This influence will have emerged from human actions, but not necessarily from human designs; Ciborra (1992, 1998a, 1998b, 2000, 2002) introduced notions such as drift, bricolage, improvisation, hospitality towards technology, which help us better to describe the way that information and communication technologies are intertwined with the organization. Organizational actors do not have plans, strategies, or goals in their heads that they then implement in action. Rather, as skilled actors they draw on events, reports and communications as 'possibilities for' (Heidegger, 1962; Dreyfus, 1991; Polt, 1999), without having to conceptualize explicitly the strategy, the information, and relationship between them. This is demonstrated clearly in the work of Ciborra (2000, 2002). It is also clear to see that if we take the work of Heidegger seriously, we would tend to think very differently about the role methodology plays in the design process (Winograd and Flores, 1986; Rathswohl, 1991; Introna and Whitley, 1997). Human action will be perceived as a benefit if it increases the organization's ability to generate variety (in line with Ashby's Law of Requisite Variety (Ashby, 1956): 'only variety can destroy variety'), but a loss otherwise. By increasing variety, the organization's disposition is better able to adapt and react, that is, to seize upon changes as opportunities, and thus to profit from the evolving environment. The effective optimization of short-term or even long-term results is not strategic, but the ability to optimize within the organization under varied and variable conditions is. Thus, strategy is never a body of principles, a set of rules, or a plan to be followed, but instead it is merely purposeful human decision and action that is intended to be strategic. Strategy is about trying to create a disposition in the organization so that it might act strategically and profit from its environment. Strategy is about acting strategically, from the inside, culturally and uniquely; it is about the development of actions and pattern of actions that can only be copied with high levels of difficulty (Ciborra, 1992, 2002). However, strategies may increase or they may decrease internal variety, they may or may not achieve success for the organization. Strategy is merely the intention of being strategic, and the road to hell is paved with good intentions.

Strategy is a guiding and essential intention that dominates in every battle and in every war, because it emanates and decisively relies on the way in which the organization is already is disposed. It is the degree to which strategy is embodied, to which it serves the commander's intuitive or analytical judgement on the more adverse, dangerous and surprising conditions, that enables him in '"being clear" about what one intends to achieve with a war, so as to make the right decision at every pulsebeat of war' (Clausewitz, 1976: 120). Because strategy deals with conflict, and therefore with unpredictability and chance, it has not only to enter the field of battle 'emphasising the essential and general, leaving scope for the accidental and individual' (ibid.: 177), but also to do this within a variety of resources, perspectives, ambitions and schemas.

Our position contradicts fundamentally the over-stretched modern-day search for organizational efficiency. The prevalent distortion of Taylor's 'scientific management' portrays all inefficiencies as human faults, to be corrected in the world of the virtuous machine. Cartesian managers believe that efficiency is necessary for a well-run organization, and they forget that efficiency is measured in terms of yesterday. In Darwinian terms, efficiency optimizes a species to a niche, and when that niche changes, as it must, the species becomes extinct. Northcote Parkinson (Parkinson, 1986) anticipated this view of efficiency, when he warned: 'perfection in planning is a symptom of decay'. A motto for dispositioning must be: efficiency is bad for business!

That things do not turn out as expected is an opportunity for enlightened managers to innovate, in so far as they have dispositioned their companies in ways that might profit from complexity, change, and uncertainty. Dealing with the unknown requires a strategic approach – an approach not based on some mythical pro-active mechanistic rulebook, adherence to which most often results in a bureaucratic shambles, but on trusting the best knowledge workers to make decisions, to improvise and enable bricolage. Some researchers even point to redundancy in information as being the very basis of organizational knowledge and a source of competitive advantage (Nonaka and Takeushi, 1995). For redundancy is not waste. It has its uses. Redundancy enables cultural and knowledge sharing, and it should be taken as a necessary condition for the development of new knowledge, which might come to support a competitive edge over rivals. Redundancy can help reinforce or reject values, allow for human forgetfulness and for social checks and balances, allow for error tolerance, and give time to reflect and reconsider. It creates the flexibility/variety needed by the organization to cope with whatever the business environment throws its way.

Strategy should emerge, aiming at improving the structural variation of the organization, because the actions of an organization are always dependent on its structure in the autopoietic sense (Maturana and Varela, 1980, 1992). That is, its resources, culture, experience, visions and ambitions determine an organization's actions. The autopoietic closure (ibid.) of the organization, that is, what the organization is and should become for itself, precisely in the manner in which it grasps its own being, imposes limits on the degree of structural variation it might accommodate. This is readily apparent in the many organizations that revert to a default 'no change strategy', despite all the plans, meetings, and consultants' exercises.

On account of the essential preservation of its 'mineness' (Heidegger, 1962; Ilharco, 2008), the organizational entity that engages in strategy should aim at improving its intuitive possibilities when dealing with whatever situation it finds itself in. The improvement of structural variation, in autopoietic terms, enhances the possibilities for an entity to preserve its mineness, that is, its way of thriving in the world as it is for itself. Thus we should say that strategy should develop a reasonable degree of non-adjustment, of friction, and of unfitness so that the structure of the company would be prepared to maintain itself in whatever situation or surprise that might eventually come about. Only in this way can innovation be absorbed as novelty and not as annihilation (McLuhan, 1994: 69).

The more variety there is in the business environment, the less control the organization has over the course of events. Unfortunately a resilient environment has a potentially unlimited variety of moves in store. This only goes to demonstrate the paramount importance of strategic management (as we mean it) over short-term tactical manoeuvring.

However, as generally accepted by the business world, strategies and tactics often turn out to be no more than recipe lists, agendas or grids. Apparent and self-fulfilling initial successes of such approaches ensure that their validity goes unquestioned in the community, and serve to reinforce the authority of such 'frameworks' and 'methodologies'. However, they will reflect only the palest shadow of organizational complexity. The dynamic and ambiguous complexity of the future just cannot be reduced to simplistic data structures that imply a tidy and convenient homogeneity in organizations that is simply not there. Yet the 'framework' concept is all consuming in the business literature, carrying with it the weight of meaning and authority that is derived from the dominating position of 'hard' science and technology in the mind-set of Western society. It is easy to be seduced into believing in an equivalence between the functionality of framework models and the behaviour of 'real problems', between the 'map' and the 'terrain', where control over the framework becomes control over the underlying problem (Angell and Ilharco, 2004). What we can know about a problem situation is replaced by what we can describe (in our descriptions we are deluded into believing that we are explaining) within the limitation of the framework.

Ciborra and Jelassi (1994) reconsidered some of what are usually referred to as successful cases of IT strategic alignment. They concluded that such cases emphasize the discrepancy between ideal plans and the realities of implementation, actually pointing out the relevance of local practices in absorbing and exploring the potentialities of IT. At the point of action, information systems 'tend to reward concrete thinking, intuition, private verifiable rationality, closeness of the individual case, and inferring personal responsibility from concrete specific process' (Argyris, 1987: 103). The phenomenon of alignment is emerging from practice, and not from the models (Ciborra, 1998a).

'IT can not be *known* as such, as if it were a given and readily understandable object' (Coombs, 1997: 231–255). Rather it is made known through the deployment of initiatives, reports, consultants, vendors, 'how to' guides, system development methodologies, academic texts, new hardware and software, and so forth – namely, what IT is, is grasped in the process of being absorbed by the professionals of the organization, and by its suppliers, partners and clients, in their practices, routines, and particular involvement. All these aspects, within the continuous balance of power, shape IT and are shaped by it. The phenomenon of IT does not have to do primarily with hardware and software, 'but with the way the organization is portrayed to the users through the terms and concepts that the system employs as everyday language. These terms and portrayals of reality actually create the reality' (Coombs, 1997: 254). Coombs suggests that IT requires the 'user to accept a certain picture of the organization, and this is a critical feature in the process of organizational' absorption of IT. That picture affects compliance, resistance, and creativity. Ciborra (1997b) adds that, as IT becomes more and more integrated with the organization, its role seems to be that of a 'collective cognitive scheme'. It is the sharing at a background level of this cognitive scheme, by the people of the organization and of its suppliers, partners and clients, 'that allows managers to improvise effectively' (Ciborra, 1997b: 274). Frameworks focus on specific, unambiguous features of systems, and so they are necessarily restricted and restrictive. In many cases they are just 'pedantic formalities' (Nietzsche, 1968: 91, n.141), losing all sense of the true complexity, of wholeness and endemic uncertainty. Ultimately all of these approaches are merely guidelines. If frameworks are used sensibly, that is to help focus on consequences and not just on intentions, then they can help formulate tactics that will be appropriate within strategic and organizational constraints. For an approach does not have to be valid (logical, tenable, sound, verifiable or based in 'truth') to be useful. However, an approach, valid or otherwise, will come to nothing without the input of a quality individual, the 'thinking manager', who fully embodies the disposition of the organization and can relate to the compromises being made within the system around him.

Dispositioning IT all

Environments are continuously changing, and to be effective a company must generate a variety of responses to match changes in the environment. Hence the company must evolve a disposition in line with Ashby's law of Requisite Variety. It must have the facility, by sufficient internal variety, to respond to perpetual changes in its environment in an appropriate manner, enabling it to function and to contend in a preferred way with, not only the commercial competition, but also the uncertainty, complexity and ambiguity inherent in an unknowable future. Such a disposition is in no way fixed and inflexible. It is inherently ambiguous and constantly being refined and redefined via feedback from its interaction with the risks and opportunities within its perpetually changing environment.

The organization should forget the urge to control the environment, for it is not controllable. By its disposition, an organization attempts to profit from its environment. To do this it senses, interprets and reacts to events observed in the environment. The greater the variety it embodies, the greater the likelihood that the organization will take advantage of the environment. Variety grounds the potential to innovate; innovation affords a greater store of tactics. The immediate survival and expansion of an organization will depend directly and essentially on tactical success, on bricolaging, on profiting from the drift, on improvisation. However, tactics used to achieve competitive advantage may turn out to be of lasting effect on the organization's disposition. Whether this unwitting strategic influence is beneficial is, however, by no means certain. Typically, organizational systems, either human, technological or an entanglement of both, are subject to the 'shift and drift' phenomena (Ciborra, 1998a: 316). The completion of IT projects tends to be delayed, which leads to their costs not only tending to grow significantly, but also ending up with a quite different distribution from the way they were originally planned (Peppard, 1993; Farbey et al., 1993). IT implementations completed according to plan seem to be the exception to the rule. Engineering-based projects in general do not go according to plan. After all that is the most apparent reason for the rise of modern management in a technological world. No big, overarching plan is guiding the deployment of IT (Ciborra, 1998a). 'Actually the no plan/no strategy attitude seems to be most favourable to let the directions and issues of Web use emerge: the process is not mature enough to be managed; it is still a "discovering" stage' (Ciborra, 1998a: 324).

Our position means that not all strategies are effectively strategic; not all strategies achieve their intended strategic aims. Just as importantly, not all strategic effects are the result of strategies – they can be the consequence of unintended actions. There can be no guarantees. With its disposition, an organization may prosper in its environment to a greater or lesser extent – failure may eventually mean extinction. Time constraints cannot be imposed on a strategy – the time factor only refers to the duration of the effect on the disposition. Thus, strategies are not long-term plans. They should not be identified with beneficial change, but only with intended change, and that may not be achieved. Besides, strategy and tactics can be mutually contradictory. Strategies are aimed inwardly at the essence of the organization itself, whereas tactics are aimed out at the environment; competition is tactical, the ability to compete is strategic. Changing trends will require changing tactics, but of course any tactical gain will be transitory. IT applications can be used for both tactical and strategic applications. Whatever! We, however, can never know for sure where an action might lead.

The task of the manager is to develop in advance a grasp of the kind of situation about to evolve, and to work with it. Instead of wishing to impose our own preferences on the situation, we should let ourselves 'go with the flow of things, adopting the line of least resistance' (Julien, 1999: 40). As a setup, *shi* 'consists in organizing circumstances in such a way as to derive profit from them' (ibid.: 32). The crucial point is not to try and create a new situation, but to take advantage of the actual situation in which one engages.

What matters most is the situation as it happens and the kind of advantages we take from it. Success or failure in business will be determined by unique social, political, organizational, and particularly personal factors, which as a whole always and already dispose us in particular ways. Successful managers know that a good technology platform, although necessary, is not sufficient for success. What makes the real strategic difference is the quality and integrity of a firm's workers and their network of contacts; that is, the degree of variety that organization is exposed to, and can handle.

Facing uncertainty is a matter of accepting that the unimaginable can and will happen; and being prepared to deal with it at the level of personal choice. We must deal with this uncertainty by steering the firm with appropriate tactical responses. This must entail a disposition to act, which is free of the organizational guidelines and of preconceptions of problem solving and planning. Ultimately it will be the quality of management, and that of their staff, to observe, interpret and innovate, that will be the major factor in taking decisions appropriate to the commercial environment.

An organization must be steered through the turbulence all around, taking tactical advantage of the environment while avoiding hazards, but only within the constraints of strategies that will enable it to deal with the unknown and the unknowable. Consequently it is a mistake to rely solely on models and mechanisms. For the construction of a model of any organization's context places an artificial boundary around it, and freezes it with a restricted interpretation based on a mechanistic classification that is at best a good analogy of past performance.

There are, of course, countless benefits from using IT, however, those advantages do not come free. We may know the price of IT, but the costs accrue from here to eternity – and we have no way of calculating total costs, because we simply cannot comprehend all the consequences of using this new technology. That technology is a tool is a little relevant aspect of technology (Ciborr, 1998a). It may have just never occurred to some thinkers on IT that technology is not 'a variable' (Lucas, 1990: vii), rather an environment, a language, and as such, managers can never manipulate it to their own will. We shape our tools, and our tools shape us (McLuhan, 1995). Technology is as much a tools as our organizations are tools of technology itself. Hence, we face the challenge with a singular lack of understanding. We just do not know the implications of applying the tools of new technology in organizations. It is only with hindsight that we can recognize the phenomena that emerge when IT is placed in each unique environment.

Instead of attempting to control the oncoming tide of change and innovation, the company should surf the waves by continuously sensing their surroundings, and responding with a barrage of questions. Should we launch a new product? Hire new people? Change our processes? Enter into a partnership? Force a crisis so as to change the culture? Launch a new tactic? Allow lateral thinking to interrogate the organization's assumptions? Whenever there is change, there is opportunity; and this world of ours is nothing but full of change. Thus, the limitations of management, if grasped from the perspective of *shi* are not a disadvantage, but an advantage. So our advice for the enlightened manager is to focus on environmental changes. Do not attempt to alter tendencies in the situation, but instead try to profit from them. Then, from this perspective, even a recession can bring opportunities and growth for the organization.

The efficacy of a disposition, of people and IT, depends on its own renewability (Julien, 1999: 33). *Shi* as a strategic tool must be fluid 'as a flowing water'. Behind this approach is the most central idea of Chinese culture on which *shi* is based: the perpetual change and renewed efficacy, the homeostasis that is the course of nature (Julien, 1999: 34). Victory is gained by originality, by variety, by not repeating strategies or tactics from the past, by transformation and adaptation both to the situation and to the enemy (ibid.: 33; Sun Tzu, 1994: 191–193). We agree with Churchill (in Murray et al., 1994: 43):

> Nearly all the battles which are regarded as masterpieces of the military art, from which have been derived the foundation of states and the fame of commanders, have been battles of manoeuvre in which very often the enemy has found himself defeated by some novel expedient or device, some queer, swift, unexpected thrust or stratagem. In many such battles the losses of the victors have been small. There is required for the composition of a great commander not only massive common sense and reasoning power, not only imagination, but also an element of legerdemain, an original and sinister touch, which leaves the enemy puzzled as well as beaten.

The key tenet of an effective organizational strategy in a complex, turbulent and ambiguous world is constantly to force the organization into being prepared for it all, to urge the organization to reinvent itself, to imagine newer and newer products, services, processes, modes, to make it embody a culture that assumes success to be transitory, and as such to get itself disposed in such a way that it might profit from any emergent situation. The issue is not only of being able to respond promptly, but also of seeing profit where there is danger, of taking initiative where the competition is charging, of being pragmatic while acknowledging that no situation endures. This disposition may be achieved by moulding a culture of challenge, by expanding the network of contacts, by competing through alliances, by hiring different and the best people, by focusing on opportunity rather then on specific outcomes.

Perhaps the most relevant action we might suggest is the most obvious one. Napoleon chose the lucky generals. Companies must do the same: hire lucky managers, plan to be flexible, act and see what happens and then act again, change options, take the initiative, emphasize the essential, and, above all, embody strategy. This latter suggestion is no more than stressing the need to make things clear for the management team, letting and forcing it to be composed of 'lucky generals', always aiming at winning the war, taking no victory for granted, and preparing to abandon any tactic as soon as it has passed its usefulness. An army that fights the previous war is doomed.

Professionals should try to grasp the essence of phenomena, and master it. It is not a question of measuring, but an attitude of relating. By relating notions to actions, one can grasp fuller and deeper meanings of the issues under analysis. Managers should deliberately change perspectives, face phenomena from new and newer perspectives, and get away from the delusion of urgency that immerses the organization in software, hardware, bubbleware, *anyware*, as suggested by the current 'common sense discourse'. This general and common discourse, and we would say this general and common practice, does indeed make managers feel good – they have company, they are with company, they are all doing much the same things. But what does that matter if the whole company is headed for the abyss? The comfort of the common sense and generalized discourse is just an appearance of what Heidegger (1962) calls the *they-self*, the general human tendency to do what others are doing, to think what others are thinking, to be what others are. Managers should look for discontinuities, for new practices, new players, unexpected behaviours, and complex and ambiguous data and performances. If the management team has the ability to change perspectives and contexts, all of these actions might be the very sources of innovation and competitive advantage it is looking for.

Competitive advantage must be understood as transitory. The organization must be ready to abandon an advantage the moment it starts exploiting that advantage. The company must always be looking for alternatives in the markets, products and processes. Ideas of certainty should be avoided; uncertainty should be embraced. Within uncertainty, and by focusing on discontinuities, an organization will see several alternatives for its future. Even past experience would reveal different aspects and details of its competencies and capabilities, enlarging the organization's possibilities to cope and thrive. Uncertainty forces the company continuously to re-evaluate its strengths and weaknesses, to keep the focus on the situation, spotting emergent trends early on.

To achieve this disposition, the company must welcome both variety and redundancy of process into its culture. This means that it must shed its Taylorist inheritance and have more than one department, or one professional, for each function, process, or task. Of course for some minor works there is no point in such duplication, but for a great many organizational functions and processes some overlapping might turn out to be a good thing. Variety can also be achieved by hiring different and 'varied' people. People make organizations. An organization needs to attract and develop its talent workers. In the process, aiming at improving variety, it also should hire professionals with different backgrounds: managers, engineers, social scientists, biologists, psychologists, technicians, economists, journalists etc. For instance, it is our contention that for many companies the function of developing new products might be better achieved with a team that brings together people with very different academic and professional backgrounds, than with a team consisting only of (say) marketing people. Even if in the short-term these marketing people experience a higher output, we submit that in the medium and long run a more varied team has much better chances of achieving more successful products, or of even hitting a jackpot.

Variety is also improved by shaking up the business culture. An organization should allow time to question the assumptions on which its own activity is based. Furthermore, it must change its practices and traditional behaviours, entering a culture of change, and striving to sustain its new patterns of behaviour. The models and frameworks that guide the actions of an organization should be continually questioned, and forced to deliver successful tactics. The company must have the courage to reflect on its tactics whenever its tendency to repeat what has worked in the past prevents it from adopting more successful practices in the present and towards the future. All repetition, all orthodoxy, all inertia must be continuously and continually justified. Originality not repetition will be the motto of the successful contemporary business organization. Table 19.1 synthesises our approach, contrasting it with managers' dominant urge to control the organization and its environment.

This is all very well, but how does one rely on this proposition of dispositioning? How does one put this approach into practice? We retort by saying this type of questioning, is mainly asking for ready-made, one size fits all, solutions; it is part of the problem (Angell and Ilharco, 2004). Is the dispositioning approach realistic? Of course our answer is 'yes', as you must have figured out after reading the paper up to this point. Yet, it is a completely different kind of 'yes' from that of the traditional recipe-based-approaches. We refuse to embark on recipes or step-by-step models that claim to fit all situations of innovation or change. Our overall argument goes deeper than that. It is an ontological and cultural setting that we are offering here. Within it, it is up to you to choose or to design the method or the actions that will leverage your performance through each specific situation. Do not rely overly on any given method that just might have been useful in one previous situation. It is your dispositioning, the way in which, through insight, you get into the situation that is your key advantage. We argue that understanding this way of thinking is very much in line with the present paper.

In this article we often quote Clausewitz and Sun Tzu; you too should be a warrior – the higher being is a warrior in pursuit of knowledge (Nietzsche, 1974: 241–242, # 301) – and as such rely on your own knowledge and experience of action, change and conflict. In a fight you do not look for recipes or two by two matrix models, you just fight your best. What you understood, your past experiences, projections and ambitions (and what you become to understand) are your only and best tools. Don't mistake this for a motivational argument; it is a

Table 19.1 Controlling vs. Dispositioning

Controlling IT all	Dispositioning IT all
Organization leads, and so management will:	*Environment leads, and so management will:*
seek outcomes	take opportunities
aim for cultural cohesion	aim for organizational variety
follow plans	follow the situation
repeat what has worked	be original
seek stability	welcome change
hire what 'they' are hiring	hire 'lucky' people
go into details	stick to essentials
build position	abandon exploitation
defend leadership	enter new realities
seek efficiency	seek redundancy
explore long-term trends	look for emergent trends
That is, change is a problem.	*That is, change is an opportunity.*

practical recognition of how you are in-the-world, it is an ontological argument (Heidegger, 1962).

Only the manager, on the basis of personal criteria, balancing advice from everyone else in the extended organization (suppliers, employees, customers, consultants, even competitors), can access that originality, by deciding which course of action is most appropriate. But do they? More often than not, they do not! The authority of our 'scientific society' forces them to formulate every new solution in terms of a too strict view of technology. They even sense the situation as being a problem, specifically because of the potential offered by technology. 'Give a boy a hammer, and he will look for nails'.

In accordance with the ontology on which this paper is based, we claim that the most important impact on the empirical world of our bid for dispositioning is the potential of its own very readiness-to-hand (Heidegger, 1962), that is, its intuitiveness, and on its becoming instinctive. This empirical relevance is centred on the kind of effects dispositioning might bring to action. Having been understood and apprehended by us (OPDT: 32), it might intuitively and instinctively unfold within our ongoing action in-the-world – this is after all how one fights!

The way in which action and thinking relate to one another, which is the relevant theme for addressing the empirical relevance of this paper, can be found in the essence of being human. Humans are always already acting in-the-world (Heidegger, 1962). Action is our knowing how (Heidegger, 1962, Dreyfus, 1991, Polt, 1999, Polanyi, 1973, Introna, 1997), our constant living and changing, that is, our structural apprehending of possibilities on account of who we are as a *having been* (Heidegger, 1962). What is apprehended becomes part of the totality of past experience that is what we have become (Nietzsche, 1968; 1974). So, describing, thinking and reflecting influence action to the degree they transform the ongoing activity of living beings. This is why 'thinking changes the world' (Heidegger, 1984: 78). Our proposal on 'dispositioning IT all' is devised, as it makes sense for those who access it, to become part of their structures as human beings, and in that way to enter the realms of action.

Notes

*The research of Angell described here was undertaken as part of an EPSRC project GR/R37753 at the LSE: *Enabling the Integration of Diverse Socio-cultural and Technical Systems within a Turbulent Social Ecosystem,* and funded under the Systems Integration Initiative.

†The research of Ilharco presented in this paper is part of the research project *The In-the-Worldness of New Technologies: an Investigation into the Fundamental Meanings of Contemporary Information and Communication Technologies*, started in 2003 and to be concluded in 2010. The author thanks the support received in various phases of the project from the Fundação para a Ciência e Tecnologia (FCT) and from the Fundação Calouste Gulbenkian (FCG), both from Portugal.

1. Dispose also means 'to get rid of', which on the surface seems contradictory to the core meanings. This particular meaning, which we will not take into account explicitly in this paper, is nonetheless full of potential. Possibly, it originated from the consequences of a particular disposition, prevailing tendency, an inclination, a temperamental makeup

to act in a certain manner under given circumstances – all of these meanings imply to a certain extent to have got rid of something or to be in a disposition as to get rid of something else; that is, to act, to choose, which can means to get rid of the course of actions we do not take, choose, or pursue. We hope to expand on this particular meaning in a future article.

References

Angell, I. and Ilharco, F. (2004). Solution is the Problem: A Story of Transitions and Opportunities, in Avgerou, C., Ciborra, C. & Land. F. (eds) *The Social Study of Information and Communication Technology*, Oxford: Oxford University Press.

Angell, I. and Smithson S. (1991). *Information Systems Management*, Basingstoke: Macmillan.

Argyris, C. (1987). Inner Contradictions in Management Information Systems, in R. Galliers (ed.) *Information Analysis, Selected Readings*, Boston: Addison-Wesley.

Aristotle (1963). *Physics*, London and Cambridge: The Loeb Classic Library.

Ashby, W.R. (1956). *An Introduction to Cybernetics: Part Two: Variety*, London: Methuen.

Ciborra, C. (1992). From thinking to tinkering: the grassroots of strategic information systems, *Information Society* **8**: 297–309.

Ciborra, C. (1996). The platform organization: recombining strategies, structures and surprises, *Organization Science* **7**(2): 103–118.

Ciborra, C. (1997a). De profundis? Deconstructing the concept of strategic alignment, working paper, Department of Informatics, University of Oslo, Oslo, Norway.

Ciborra, C. (1997b). Improvising in the Shapeless Organization, in C. Sauer and P.W. Yetton (eds) *Steps to the Future: The Management of IT-based Organizational Transformation*, San Francisco: Jossey-Bass.

Ciborra, C. (1998a). From tool to *Gestell*, *Information Technology and People* **11**(4): 305–327.

Ciborra, C. (1998b). Crisis and foundations; an inquiry into the nature and limits of models and methods in the information systems discipline, *Journal of Strategic Information Systems* **7**: 5–16.

Ciborra, C. (1999). Notes on improvisation and time in organizations, *Accounting, Management and Information Technologies* **9**: 77–94.

Ciborra, C. (2000). *From Control to Drift: The Dynamics of Corporate Information Infrastructure*, Oxford: Oxford University Press.

Ciborra, C. (2002) *The Labyrinths of Information: Challenging the Wisdom of Systems*, Oxford: Oxford University Press.

Clausewitz, C. von (1976). *On War*, Edited and translated by M. Howard and P. Paret, Princeton: Princeton University Press.

Coombs, R. (1997). Joint Outcomes: The Coproduction of IT and Organizational Change, in C. Sauer and P.W. Yetton (eds) *Steps to the Future: The Management of IT-based Organizational Transformation*, San Francisco: Jossey-Bass.

Coyne, R. (1995). *Designing Information Technology in the Postmodern Age: From Method to Metaphor*, Cambridge, MA: MIT Press.

Crane, G.R. (ed.) (2002). *The Perseus Project*, http://www.perseus.tufts.edu, April 10, 2002.

Dreyfus, H. (1991). *Being-in-the-World: A Commentary on Heidegger's* Being and Time, *Division I*, Cambridge, MA: MIT Press.

Farbey, B., Land, F. and Targett, D. (1993). *IT Investment: A Study of Methods and Practice*, London: Butterworth-Heinemann.

Gray, C.S. (1994). Strategy in the Nuclear Age: The United States, 1945–1991, in W. Murray, M. Knox and A. Bernstein, *The Making of Strategy: Rulers, States, and War*, Cambridge: Cambridge University Press.

Heidegger, M. (1962). *Being and Time*, trans. Macquarrie, J. and Robinson, E. Oxford UK, and Cambridge, MA: Blackwell.

Heidegger, M. (1977). *The Question Concerning Technology and Other Essays*, New York: Harper Torchbooks.
Heidegger, M. (1984). *Early Greek Thinking: The Dawn of Western Philosophy*, San Francisco: Harper & Row Publishers.
Ilharco, F. (2008). Authenticity in Organization: Towards Overcoming the Strategy/Structure Cartesian Split in Organizations, in L. Introna, F. Ilharco and Faÿ (eds) *Phenomenology, Organization and Technology*, Lisbon: UC Editora.
Introna, L. (1997). *Management, Information and Power*, London: Macmillan.
Introna, L.D. and Whitley, E.A. (1997). Against method-ism, *Information Technology and People* **10**(1): 31–45.
Julien, F. (1999). *The Propensity of Things: Towards a History of Efficacy in China*, New York: Zone Books.
Lucas, H.C. Jr. (1990). *Information Systems Concepts for Management*, 4th edn, New York: McGraw-Hill.
Maturana, H. and Varela, F. (1980). *Autopoiesis and Cognition: The Realization of the Living*, Boston Studies in the Philosophy of Science. Dordrecht: D. Reidel Publishing Company.
Maturana, H. and Varela, F. (1992). *The Tree of Knowledge: The Biological Roots of Human Understanding*, Boston and London: Shambala.
McLuhan, M. (1994). *Understanding Media*, Cambridge, MA: MIT Press.
McLuhan, M. (1995). *Essential McLuhan*, Ed. Eric McLuhan and Frank Zigorne, London and New York: Routledge.
Merleau-Ponty, M. (1962). *Phenomenology of Perception*, London: Routledge.
Mintzberg, H., Ahlstrand, B. and Lampel, J. (1998). *Strategy Safari*, Hemel Hempstead: Prentice Hall.
Murray, W., Knox, M. and Bernstein, A. (1994). *The Making of Strategy: Rulers, States, and War*, Cambridge: Cambridge University Press.
MW (2002). *Merriam-Webster Dictionary*, http://www.m-w.com.
Nietzsche, F. (1968). *The Will to Power*, trans. Kaufmann, W., and Hollingdale, R.J., New York: Vintage Books.
Nietzsche, F. (1974). *The Gay Science*, New York: Vintage Books.
Nonaka, I. and Takeushi, H. (1995). *The Knowledge Creating Company*, Oxford: Oxford University Press.
OED (1933). *Oxford English Dictionary*, Volume X, Sole-Sz, Oxford: Clarendon Press.
OPDT (1997). *Oxford Paperback Dictionary & Thesaurus*, Julia Elliot (ed.), Oxford and New York: Oxford University Press.
Parkinson, C.N. (1986). *Parkinson's Law*, London: Penguin.
Peppard, J. (ed.) (1993) *IT Strategy for Business*, London: Pitman Publishing.
Polanyi, M. (1973). *Personal Knowledge: Towards a Post-Critical Philosophy*, London: Routledge & Keegan Paul.
Polt, R. (1999). *Heidegger: An Introduction*, London: UCL Press.
Rathswohl, E.J. (1991). Applying Don Idhe's Phenomenology of Instrumentation as a Framework for Designing Research in Information Science, in H.-E. Nissen, H.K. Klein, and R.A. Hirschheim (eds) *Information Systems Research: Contemporary Approaches and Emergent Traditions*, Amsterdam: North Holland, pp. 421–438.
Sun Tzu (1994). *The Art of War*, trans. and Ed. Ralph D. Sawyer, New York: Westview.
Winograd, T. and Flores, F. (1986). *Understanding Computers and Cognition: A New Foundation for Design*, Reading, UK: Addison Wesley.
Wittgenstein, L. (1967). *Philosophical Investigations*, Oxford: Blackwell.

Index